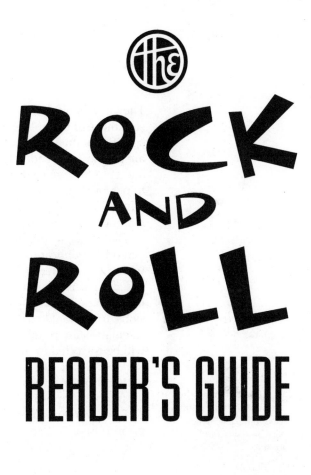

THE ROCK AND ROLL READER'S GUIDE

GARY M. KREBS

BILLBOARD BOOKS
An imprint of Watson-Guptill Publications/New York

To Liz with love...
and to our lifetime of happiness together.

The views included in this book only represent those of the author, unless otherwise specified with a cited source. The reviews are primarily intended to inform, educate, and entertain; since these matters are subject to personal taste and opinion, readers are advised to examine titles firsthand prior to making any purchase decisions.

The books, magazines, fan magazines, and other publications mentioned in this work were neither included nor excluded based on artistic merit or on paid advertising from publishers or authors. Any omissions, unavoidable dating, errors, or misrepresentation are purely unintentional and will be corrected in future editions of *The Rock and Roll Reader's Guide*, subject to the author's criteria, the work's availability, and irrefutable supportive evidence.

Titles were only reviewed if available prior to June 1, 1996.

Senior Editor: Bob Nirkind
Editor: Stacey Guttman
Production Manager: Hector Campbell
Designer: Bob Fillie, Graphiti Graphics

First published in 1997 by Billboard Books,
an imprint of Watson-Guptill Publications,
a division of BPI Communications, Inc.,
1515 Broadway, New York, NY 10036

Library of Congress Cataloging-in-Publication Data
Krebs, Gary M.
    The rock and roll reader's guide / Gary M. Krebs.
             p.   cm.
    Includes index.
    ISBN 0-8230-7602-4
    1. Rock music-History and criticism-Bibliography.
      I. Title.
    ML128.R6K74 1997
    016.78166-dc20   96-32141
                         CIP
                         MN

Manufactured in the United States

1 2 3 4 5 6 7 8 9 0/05 04 03 02 01 00 99 98 97

CONTENTS

ACKNOWLEDGMENTS

Suffice it to say, many people were invaluable to me both personally and professionally as I sweated through the research, writing, and editorial process of preparing this book. Since my family, friends, and colleagues had to suffer the most—being on the receiving end of more than a few of my tantrums and experiencing some shameful neglect—they deserve top acknowledgment and high praise.

Elisabeth C. Alter, who will officially become Liz Krebs as this book is in production, deserves more than my undying love and faithful servitude. Although she is not an editor, her feedback on my queries was objective and authoritative. She was immensely helpful proofreading, digging up rare books, performing various clerical tasks, and, most importantly, providing inspiration, affection, and reassurance when I needed these qualities most. As John Lennon wrote, "God bless our love."

My wonderful family was a great comfort to me from the very beginning. I humbly devote this volume to Mom, Pops, Michele, Evan, Steve, Susan, and Grandma Rose. My new family—Sy, Sandra, Anne-Renée, Tracey, Valerie, Steve, and Jeffrey—are a very special group of people, and I appreciate the warmth and support they have lavished on me. I'm certain that my cats, Cushie and Clint, pranced on my keyboard when I wasn't looking and typed a few offensive keystrokes, but they are forgiven and acknowledged here.

Amidst the downsizing and commercialization of the publishing industry, two individuals stand out for not only having earned my deepest professional and personal respect, but for representing all that is humane about this business: my agent, Bert Holtje of James Peter Associates, whom I prefer to call "an editor's agent," and my mentor, Gerry Helferich, who opened up the world of publishing to me and taught me virtually everything I know about being an editor.

P.J. Dempsey at John Wiley & Sons is another unique figure in book publishing. Rather than dictate the usual form reject for this project when it was in its infancy as a proposal, she had the eye to recognize its potential and pass it on to greener pastures at Billboard Books. My original editor at Watson-Guptill, Paul Lukas, saw to it that the book was acquired. Bob Nirkind, who took over the project, was a tremendous source of inspiration in the final stages, and I greatly appreciate his patience and professionalism. Stacey Guttman, the book's editor, was a pleasure to work with and made the usual editorial back-and-forth a lot of fun.

Many other people were vital to the creation of this work. Oliver Trager was a veritable warehouse of information and materials, particularly in relation to The Grateful Dead and Bob Dylan. Randy Ladenheim-Gil, Lynda Denker, Deirdre Mullane, Stephen Francoeur, Alice Schluger, Mark Lieberfreund, and Phil Saltz were always available to me when I needed editorial consultation, technical support, advice, or just to borrow a book.

Extra special thanks to Philip Lief, Susan Osborn, and everyone from The Philip Lief Group for their general support and enthusiasm.

● 4

From magazines and fanzine publications, I'd like to thank the following individuals: Timothy White and Kara DioGuardi at *Billboard*; Sandy Choron and Dave Marsh at *Rock & Roll Confidential*; Paul Williams at *Crawdaddy!*; Ann Leighton at *Hit Parader*; Greg Loescher and Jeff Tamarkin at *Goldmine*; Sarah Jacombs at *Select*; Yvette Noel-Schure at *Black Beat*; Barbara Seerman at *Guitar*; Ronald Spagnardi at *Modern Drummer*; Robert K. Haber and Amy Tesch at *CMJ*; Eric Wielander at *Village Noize*; Marc Bristol at *Blue Suede News*; Lanette M. Jones and Darryl James at *Rap Sheet*; Katherine Speilmann at *Puncture*; Glenn Sabin at *Jazz Times*; Nan Knott at *Plazm*; and Steven Bush at *Seconds*. Many other publications were equally as generous: *Spin, Sing-Out!, A.P., Q, CD Review, Teen Machine, Tiger Beat, The Village Voice, Ray Gun, Bikini, Warp, Reggae Report, Urb, Soma, Drum Core, Option*, and *Bass*. Please forgive me if I have inadvertently overlooked any names or publications.

I would also like to thank the scores of artist fan clubs and fanzines who showed so much enthusiasm for my project and, usually at their postal expense, mailed me their immensely enjoyable materials. Space does not allow me to name those parties here, but I sincerely hope that their inclusion in this guide spreads their messages far and wide, and that their memberships and subscriptions multiply fourfold as a result of our combined efforts.

Also thanks to the Virgin, Barnes & Noble, and Tower Books superstores for their assistance, as well as to See Hear bookstore in New York City.

These Acknowledgments would be grossly incomplete if I didn't thank the diligent reference librarians at the New York Public Library for the Performing Arts at Lincoln Center (the Music Division, Special Collections, the Archives of Recorded Sound, the Dance Collection, and the Circulating Collections), and at the Performing Arts Reading Room at the Library of Congress. In the New York Public Library, the following branches provided tremendous courtesy and assistance: the Central Research Library on Fifth Avenue (Main Reading Room, the Arents Collection, Rare Books & Manuscripts, Prints & Photographs, and the Oriental Division); the Schomburg Center for Research in Black Culture; the Donnell Library Center; and the Mid-Manhattan Library.

In particular, the "pages" at the Lincoln Center Music Division—Mary Ann Waldron, Kizeeta Williams, Laurie-Lee Roberts, Gloria Sanchez, and Tiffany Folks—cheerfully brought me hundreds (if not thousands) of books, many of which were buried in that distant, eerie-sounding place called the "basement." It was fun watching them guess what project I was working as they reserved books for me on artists ranging from Abba to ZZ Top!

While all of the people listed above contributed immeasurably to this work, none should be held accountable for any mistakes introduced in this volume, for which I must receive full blame. Despite the pains taken to ensure factual correctness and accurate spelling, it is inevitable that in a work of this magnitude things will slip through the cracks. For those affected by inadvertent blunders, please forgive me and be assured that any errors will be corrected in future editions, subject to my criteria, the respective work's availability, and irrefutable supportive evidence. Please send comments to: Gary M. Krebs, The Rock and Roll Reader's Guide, c/o Billboard Books, Watson-Guptill Publications, 1515 Broadway, New York, N.Y. 10036.

Lastly, thank you rock readers and rock fans, who proudly wave their bound tributes to their idols—whether it be Madonna, The Kinks, The Who, Chuck Berry, Jimi Hendrix, Hole, The Doors, M.C. Hammer, The Sex Pistols, Janis Joplin, T.Rex, Pearl Jam, Pat Benatar, Marvin Gaye, David Bowie, or the King of Kings: Elvis. Long may they all rock.

—GARY M. KREBS, *New York City*

iNTRODUCTiON

"Occasionally you get cheesed off
with people writing rubbish about you..."

—Paul McCartney, from *The Beatles Live at the BBC* CD

Several years and a few job titles ago, when I was in the process of editing a book on The Beatles (I won't mention which one), the author of that work alerted me that he had an appointment to interview Ringo Starr for *Goldmine* magazine. Excited that the author was to have such good fortune in meeting a real live Beatle—and moreover at the possibility of his obtaining a blurb for the dust jacket of the book—I passed on the news to a copy editor, who had the office next door. He put his red pen down, slowly looked up from his stack of manuscripts and dryly asked, "Can Ringo read?"

We never did get the quote from Ringo (not for the reason suggested by the copy editor), but that brief exchange planted an idea in my mind. Naturally assuming my sarcastic colleague was incorrect (after all, Ringo was captured on film reading a book in *A Hard Day's Night*), I wondered: Had Ringo actually read any of the books written about him and The Beatles? Or were they all merely passed off as tabloid rubbish and not worth the bother?

Then I had an observation. It's common knowledge pop stars often express hostility about what is written about them in books, occasionally to the point of legal action. (Paul McCartney and Mick Jagger, for example, have both been in such situations.) But why do they get in such a tizzy when worse filth or grander stories of fiction are reported about them on a weekly, if not daily, basis in magazines and newspapers? And, as we head into the next millennium, why worry about a book when false information zips across electronic wires every second of the day on the Internet?

Not quite sure where I was headed with all of this, I went on a mission to track down books about rock stars—especially those written by them. Soon I was busily scribbling down titles and organizing them by artist. Some weeks later, these notes had branched out to three notebooks organized alphabetically by rock stars and groups.

Perhaps I was out to prove to rock stars that there were *some* good books out there about them. Or maybe I was trying to show the critics (both actual reviewers and anyone who has ever had an opinion) that rock stars weren't dumb, lazy prima donnas. After all, hadn't many rock stars—John Lennon, Carly Simon, Jim Morrison, Lou Reed, and Leonard Cohen, to name a few of the most prominent—actually published their literary works to a fair share of critical and commercial success?

At the time these thoughts crossed my mind, little did I know the full extent to which rock stars had published. Of course, a large proportion of books attributed to artists are autobiographies ghostwritten "with" a professional (one would hope) writer, who sometimes receives credit (but often doesn't). Many of these life stories, such as those by David Crosby and John Phillips, tell of lives torn apart by drug addiction and of the high price of fame and excess. Others, such as by legendary promoter Bill Graham, are oral biographies that contain the author's voice integrated with quotes by friends, relatives, and associates. And then there are autobiographical books that incontrovertibly come directly from the writer's pen, such as Joan Baez's early diary, *Daybreak*.

Very often rock stars discover that writing a book isn't nearly as easy as it seems. Perhaps this is simply the difference between the immediacy and spontaneity of performing and recording versus the arduous, often boring chore of facing a computer keyboard alone and producing words that fit together for more than a stanza. Bob Dylan, a figure of incomparable literary stature in both the worlds of folk and rock, struggled for years to meet his contractual obligation for *Tarantula* and refused to publish it when he read the galleys. (Of course, it was eventually released.) By contrast, talented performers as diverse as Nick Cave, Pete Townshend, Kinky Friedman, Ice-T, Ian Hunter, Iggy Pop, Henry Rollins, Linda McCartney, Jimmy Buffett, Curtis Mayfield, Bob Weir, and Marky Mark (God save us!) have all regaled us with their autobiographical works, plays, cookbooks, novels, children's stories, poetry, photographic collections, or other types of authorship. Yet who would think that Charlie Watts, Ron Wood, and Bill Wyman all have published books—in quite different formats—but that the Stones' creative leaders, Mick Jagger and Keith Richards, thus far haven't written anything expressly for print? Of course, many books have been written specifically *about* Jagger and Richards as individual personalities, while the other aforementioned members—Brian Jones aside, whose death seems to be the main thing that interests biographers—have not been so honored.

The Rock and Roll Reader's Guide documents the good, the bad, and the ugly of in-print and out-of-print rock books —with a few priceless gems hidden in the crowd. From biographies and autobiographies to fanzines, chronologies, dictionaries, encyclopedias, pictorials, related works, young adult books, and titles in various formats written by rock stars, this annotated bibliography is intended as a starting point for those researching rock artists and for those fans who simply want to know what's out there related to their heroes.

The guide is intended to be as user-friendly and as accessible as possible. Before you get started, however, it is advisable that you take a quick look through the "How to Use the Guide," so you can get a complete overview of the book's rationale and organization.

Before closing, let's give three cheers for the rock writers who, though greatly unappreciated and often flayed by readers and rock stars alike, continue to prophesize with their pens. From the highest rock authorities such as Dave Marsh, Paul Williams, Greil Marcus, Mark Lewisohn, Peter Guralnick, and Timothy White, to prodigious book-churners such as Mark Bego, Philip Kamin, Peter Goddard, Geoffrey Giuliano, Miles, Malcolm Dome, and Mark Putterford—they're all here, side by side. Who knows? You may look through the guide, see a gap in the literature on one of these stars, and decide to write a pop biography yourself, thereby joining this proud group. Go on, give it a try. It's easy. It's just a rock book.

HOW TO USE THE GUIDE

CRITERIA FOR INCLUSION

Although a wide net was cast, and every effort was made to track down titles for both famous and obscure artists, it is impossible to include every book by and about every artist. Rock books by their very nature have a brief shelf life—some seem to be tossed on street vendor stacks one week after publication—and often this is further dictated by the increasing or decreasing popularity of the artist in question. A good case in point is that while twelve books are included for Culture Club, eleven of these were published by 1986 at the height of the group's popularity. When Culture Club split and Boy George's outrageousness became somewhat passé, the books stopped; Boy George himself ended the Culture Club book drought with his autobiography in 1995.

Titles were reviewed simply based on whether they were available, bound in something resembling book form, and contain print and/or photos. The only exceptions to the first two are magazines (in the Selected General Reference section) and fanzines/fan clubs (in the Publications on Artists A to Z section).

If crucial publication data — author, title, publisher, and year of publication — was available, yet a review copy was not to be found by press time, that particular title would be incorporated under the heading "Other Titles of Interest." If there was any doubt about the authenticity of the data or relevance to the artist in question, the work was not included.

Other items *not* to be found in the guide: books published exclusively in a language other than English (Canadian and British titles, when obtainable, are included); separate newspaper and magazine articles; dissertations (unless issued in book form and available in a public library collection); posters; calendars; booklets accompanying records, tours, and CDs, unless available for resale separately; rock writings not published; technical manuals on learning to play an instrument (unless written by a rock star); songbooks with musical chords (unless accompanied by personal writings or illustrations from the composer); vanity press (self-published) books (unless issued in book form and readily available in a library collection or book store); and books on audio (unless of some additional interest to fans of the artist).

THE UNANSWERABLE QUESTION: *WHO* IS ROCK?

Rock and roll means something different to every fan. In 1980, a room full of hardcore Led Zeppelin fans would have laughed out loud at the prospect of Michael Jackson being considered "rock." Today, however, exclusion of him—or any modern "pop" star from Mariah Carey to Boyz II Men to Michael Bolton—in a rock compendium would completely upset the status quo. Thus, this book represents the most influential names in all pop/rock genres for whom there are books: 1950's–90's classic (or "album-oriented") rock, Motown, pop, rap, disco, folk, hip-hop, heavy metal, alternative (punk, grunge, techno-pop, indie, etc.), and so on. Legendary blues, country, and soul artists who have influenced rock—e.g., B.B. King, Johnny Cash, James Brown, etc.—are, of course, included, as are the most prominent contemporary "crossover" artists: Dolly Parton, Garth Brooks, and Kenny Rogers, to name a few.

Those looking for entries on singers such as Bing Crosby, Frank Sinatra, Judy Garland, Barry Manilow, Barbra Streisand, and Dean Martin will, I'm afraid, be disappointed. While they are wonderful entertainers and certainly have had enormous pop chart successes, no one with a straight face can successfully argue that these performers cross the line from "show performer" status to rock stars. If you dare disagree, answer one question: Where are the guitars, man?

READIN' AND ROCKIN'
ON THE SUPERHIGHWAY

And what about the wonderful world of electronics? The Internet and various CD-ROMs were integral parts of researching this project, but few of these sites or products are mentioned in this guide. The reason for this is twofold: the intention of *The Rock and Roll Reader's Guide* is to celebrate books and writing available in *print*, not electronics; and secondly, because the Superhighway is still in its infancy and thus far has not proven reliability—a fact which may change by the end of this millennium.

While researching this book, I had the opportunity to examine rock fan clubs on the Internet. My findings might surprise those people who have been bitten by the technology bug. While one can access many wonderful things, there are also myriad disadvantages: several Web sites vanished only a few days after being entered; the information in many sites claimed to be up-to-date, but very often wasn't; some of the sites simply borrowed directly from books without citing sources; some created ghastly gossip and errors of fact; even with a high-powered modem, accessing a site can take several agonizing minutes, only to find there's nothing there worth looking at except a poorly reproduced photo; and many were overloaded with conversational interplay that had little relation to the artist at hand.

This is not in any way to discourage people from going online or from using these extensive and fun sources for secondary research; it's simply to provide a word of caution and to explain why they have not been included in this volume.

As for CD-ROMs, already there is serious concern in the industry that yet another product will soon come along to replace them and make them as old-hat as eight-tracks. While CD-ROM products on artists such as The Beatles and Peter Gabriel are valuable research tools and excellent sources of entertainment, they do not have permanent value on the literary shelf. On the other hand, I would gladly give my blessing to a well-prepared guide exclusively devoted to rock CD-ROMs.

ORGANIZATION

The guide is divided into two parts: Part One, Selected General Reference, includes those titles not specifically connected to any one artist; Part Two, Publications on Artists A to Z, concerns works directly related to specific artists and bands.

SELECTED GENERAL REFERENCE

Selected General Reference is further divided into three broad categories: General Reference, Special Subjects, and Magazines. All titles within these categories are alphabetized by author name. I will briefly address these one-by-one, so you know exactly what type of headings and works are included under each.

General Reference
Artist Profiles Books that include lengthy essays on a selected group of artists, e.g. "great drummers," as opposed to a full encyclopedia on hundreds of performers.

Chart Data Works that list chart information from a variety of sources. In many cases, the books contain essays or features on a specific area, such as number one hits, top forty albums, etc.

Chronologies Books that tell the story of rock in some type of day-by-day format.

Critical/Analytical Commentary Collections of critical essays about rock and roll, whether by one or various writers. Also includes works that assemble writings by a number of rock stars.

Dictionaries and Encyclopedias Reference works that contain biographical data on performers in an A to Z format.

Discographies and Collectibles Works that contain release data of interest to collectors or to those who want to build their collections. Price guides for merchandising are included under this heading.

Miscellaneous Reference Reference works that have formats overlapping with one or more categories. Bibliographies, rock lists, etc. are included here.

Pictorials Generally speaking, coffee table books that were published exclusively for illustrative content. Some examples: books from a specific photographer (e.g., Gered Mankowitz); works on rock album/poster art; and broad collections of photographs.

Quizbooks and Quotebooks Books that consist largely of quotes from rock stars or of trivia questions designed to stump fans.

Record Guides Critical works that review specific singles, albums, or artists.

Special Subjects

Concert Events/Festivals Books about major festivals, such as Woodstock and Live Aid.

Film Titles concerning rock on celluloid.

Women and Rock Works relevant to the role of women in rock and roll.

Magazines

This heading is divided into sections on rock and roll (general), blues, country, folk, jazz, rap/hip-hop, and reggae. Magazines on alternative music, heavy metal, etc. are all incorporated under the rock and roll (general) heading. Note: The descriptions of magazines are non-critical and include subscription address only.

PUBLICATIONS ON ARTISTS A TO Z

All entries for solo performers are alphabetized by the artist's last name (e.g., Harrison, George), unless there doesn't happen to be one (e.g., Ice-T is under "I"). Group names are alphabetized by the first name of the band (e.g., Led Zeppelin is under "L"). A solo artist (e.g., Bruce Springsteen) who had a well known back-up band (e.g., The E Street Band) is still included under the artist's name, but the band is written beside it in parentheses (most especially if a book exists concerning a member of the group).

The alphabetization throughout this book is strictly letter-by-letter—for artists, authors, and book titles—ignoring any punctuation within the words and arranging numbers as if they were spelled out as letters. Thus The B-52s come before Big Country.

A tricky decision was determining which solo performers deserved their own entries, even though they were already covered in an entry on a band. The rationale is simple: Solo artists who had significant careers on their own—yet also have several books on or about them *as soloists*—have their own entry. Mick Jagger, and Keith Richards, for example, have their own entries because they have had independent solo careers *and* because there are several books that treat them as separate performers. While Billy Wyman, Charlie Watts, and Ron Wood all have tried solo careers, they only registered one book apiece (all, coincidentally, written works), which does not warrant a solo entry. In any event, the superb books by Wyman, Watts, and Wood are all under The Rolling Stones—where most fans would expect to find them anyway.

A cross-referencing system has been implemented to make researching as simple as possible. For stars who were in several bands (e.g., Eric Clapton), "see also" references have been provided. For stars whose solo careers have equaled their band activities, a "see" reference has been provided in case readers check either name (e.g., Ian Hunter: See Mott the Hoople).

Headings

The books included for each artist are categorized either by format or by editorial focus. Thus, subheadings will vary, depending on what types of books have been published for that respective artist:

Autobiography Memoirs, journals, oral stories, etc. as told by a rock star (and perhaps a ghostwriter).

Biographies The complete rendering of an artist's story, with or without the artist's cooperation. A clear distinction has been made between a "Pictorial" (see below) and a "Biography"; the former may include a great deal of biographical data, but it doesn't qualify as biography because the space emphasis is on illustrative matter. (Of course, many titles included under biographies still have photo inserts or some illustrations throughout.)

Chronologies An artist's story told in a day-by-day or year-by-year format.

Critical/Analytical Commentary Titles that seek to define the artist's significance or critique his or her music. This section also includes compendiums of essays.

Dictionaries and Encyclopedias Works that tackle various topics related to the artist—people, recordings, places, etc.—all in an A to Z format.

Discographies, Recording Guides, and Collectibles Works that chart a group's recording history or serve as pricing guides to merchandising.

Fanzines and Fan Clubs Active organizations and publications that deal primarily with one artist. Fanzines published by fan clubs are listed within the description of the club itself. Note: Only those fanzines and fan clubs who responded to my query letters—or whose publications were available to me on newsstands—have been included. The descriptions of magazines are non-critical and include subscription address only. Subscription and membership costs are provided, but be aware that these are subject to change. Readers are also cautioned to make payments as instructed by the fanzine; while some fanzines accept (and even encourage) cash payments, do so at your own risk.

Film Books focusing on that artist's connection with celluloid.

General Reference A catch-all for works in a variety of formats: bibliographies, compendiums of lists, etc.

Interviews Books devoted to question-and-answer with an artist or individuals in his or her inner circle.

Pictorials Books with higher emphasis on photographs than any specific format or focus. Thus, many books included herein contain some biographical and discographical content.

Quizbooks and Quotebooks These works consist of quotes by rock stars or contain trivia questions designed to stump fans.

Related Works A catch-all heading for books inspired by the lives or legends of rock stars. Many of the books included here are satires and spoofs (e.g., Mark Shipper's *Paperback Writer*).

Tourbooks Chronicles of an artist's life on the road. These works might be straight text or photo documents.

Written Works Works by the artists themselves. These might include poetry, lyric books, plays, stories, novels, cookbooks, collections of art rendered by the artist, etc.

Young Adult Books specifically created for fans 12 and younger. Children's books written by artists fall under the "Written Works" heading (see above), but are cross-referenced here.

Other Titles of Interest Books of note that could not be found and reviewed prior to going to press. Occasionally, notes are provided for those books that have some tidbit of interest.

There are also some headings that reflect the idiosyncrasies of the literature on a particular artist. For example:

Spiritual, Cult, and Fan Mania These headings, which concern the religious or obsessive relationship between fans and artists, have been titled according to the name of the artist: Beatlemania for The Beatles; Dylaneutics for Bob Dylan; Starchild for Jimi Hendrix; etc.

Books by or About Artist Friends, Relatives, Spouses, Colleagues, Etc. These are grouped under a heading "_____ Friends and Family." For example, a book about Brian Epstein, The Beatles manager, would be under "Beatles Friends and Family."

Books About a Group After They Split Written as "Post-_____." For example, "Post-Beatles."

Places Various books deal with the inseparable relationship between the artist and his or her home town or country. Examples include: "Liverpool and London" (The Beatles); "Ireland" (U2); and "Athens, GA" (R.E.M.).

Books Solely About an Artist's Death These titles might deal with causes of death, hoaxes, fan reactions (letters, Internet comments, etc.), and others. For example, "Death of Cobain."

Publication Data

All publication data has been transcribed directly from the jackets, titles, and copyright pages of the books themselves. All titles and review material reflects information on the edition of the book being reviewed only. Readers should be aware that books are perpetually revised and reprinted by publishers, and that paperback and foreign rights to works frequently change

hands. In those instances, everything from a title to editorial content may change radically from one edition to the next.

The bibliographic data is as follows: author(s) last name; full title and subtitle; city of publisher; publisher; date of publication; number of pages; approximate number of photos; back matter (appendixes, bibliography, glossary, etc.); and index. If it is known that a book was first published in the U.K., that fact is noted in parentheses.

Reviews

The reviews themselves are primarily intended to inform, educate, and entertain. The main desire of this author is to answer some or all of the following questions for each book: (a) what is it about? (b) what does it contain? (c) how is it organized? (d) who would be interested in it? (e) what is the tone and flavor? and (f) how does it compare with other books on that artist? If a work may offend the reader's prurient or politically correct interests, I have pointed that out to the best of my ability, but not to overlook the fact that fans of that artist might want the book for those very reasons. Lastly, many (but certainly not all) reviews end with a few words excerpted from another review, with the publication duly credited. These are only for the benefit of expressing an outside point of view; some agree with points I've made, some disagree, and others bring up other issues readers might be interested to know.

Indexes

If you can't find a title looking through the artist entries, it doesn't hurt to check the author name in the Author Index and the title name in the Title Index. As was stated earlier, book titles (and occasionally even authors) can change throughout the years as a book goes in and out of print.

In any case, if it's out there, chances are it's somewhere in this volume; if not, hopefully one of the titles mentioned in here will lead you further along in your journey.

PART ONE:

SELECTED

GENERAL

REFERENCE

GENERAL REFERENCE

ARTIST PROFILES

Cianci, Bob. *Great Rock Drummers of the Sixties*. Milwaukee: Hal Leonard Corporation, 1989. 207 pages. Two hundred black-and-white photographs throughout.

Completely illiterate study of 14 of rock's elite drummers from the 1960's. The book is divided into "profiles," "very special mentions," and "honorable mentions." There is no rhyme or reason as to why certain drummers were selected (or not, as the case may be) and how they were arranged. For example, why was Kenney Jones placed in "profiles" and Ginger Baker shoved into the "special mentions"? Alas, there are several errors on the first page of the book. Go directly to Max Weinberg's work (see Part Two: Publications on Artists A to Z, Springsteen, Bruce: Written Works).

Dalton, David and Kaye, Lenny. *Rock 100*. New York: Grosset & Dunlap, 1977. 280 pages. Approximately 150 black-and-white photographs throughout. Index.

A lively history of the first three decades of rock and roll, as compiled by rock critic David Dalton and guitarist Lenny Kaye. Subjects are arranged chronologically, and then grouped into thematic categories (with Elvis Presley first), such as: "The Originators" (Haley, Berry, Richard), "Beach Blanket Bop" (Avalon, Anka, Darin), "The Big Three" (Beatles, Stones, Dylan), "Psychedelia" (Dead, Floyd, Airplane), etc. A creative concept that just doesn't work: The selection of musicians ends up excluding the leading lights of "big band rock"—The Turtles, Blood, Sweat and Tears, and Chicago—

and a few other major rock movements. Contains some high points, but four and one half pages on The Beatles just won't cut it.

Kiersh, Edward. Photographs by Wallis, Stephen. *Where Are You Now, Bo Diddley?: The Stars Who Made Us Rock and Where They are Now*. Garden City: Doubleday & Company, Inc., 1986. 288 pages. Approximately 50 black-and-white photographs throughout.

So, where *have* they been? John Sebastian, betrayed by the counterculture after a drug bust, has had only one hit ("Welcome Back") since the glory days of the Lovin' Spoonful. Pop star icon Tommy James has battled and overcome an amphetamine addiction and continues to write and perform. Doug Ingle of Iron Butterfly has become a house painter—and seems genuinely pleased with the change of pace. These 44 journalism pieces tell generally depressing sagas of drug addiction, greed, and tenuous fandom; but at least we know these performers have lived long enough to approach middle age. A fine curio item that could have used some discographical information.

Lydon, Michael. *Rock Folk: Portraits from the Rock 'N' Roll Pantheon*. New York: The Dial Press, 1971. 200 pages. Approximately 50 black-and-white photographs throughout.

By fate, this is a weird book: Hendrix and Joplin died around press time. Both are covered here, as are randomly selected artists Chuck Berry, Carl Perkins, B.B. King, Smokey Robinson, Grateful Dead, and The Rolling Stones. Lydon's reflections don't stand the test of time.

Obrecht, Jas (Editor). *Masters of Heavy Metal.* New York: Quill (an imprint of William Morrow, Inc.), 1984. 192 pages. Approximately 80 black-and-white photographs throughout.

The text consists of material edited from the pages of *Guitar Player* magazine from 1968 to 1983. Surprise, surprise: the book begins with Jimi Hendrix and follows with Jimmy Page, Ritchie Blackmore, Ted Nugent, Judas Priest, Eddie Van Halen, and Randy Rhoads. Quirky and non-essential, particularly if you read the magazine religiously during the aforementioned time period.

Rivelli, Pauline and Levin, Robert (Editors). Introduction by Alfred Arnowitz. *Giants of Rock Music.* New York: Da Capo, 1981. 126 pages. One sixteen-page black-and-white photo insert. (Originally published in 1970 as *The Rock Giants* by Thomas Y. Crowell Publishers.)

Eighteen pieces on 1960's rock and roll, the majority of which were contributions from Frank Kofsky and Jay Ruby. The interviews with Frank Zappa, Donovan, Roger McGuinn, and Creedence Clearwater Revival are of historical significance, although Jutta Ney's conversation with John and Yoko is poorly handled. The book even prints a line indicating Ney's lack of preparation for the assignment ("I'm trying to think of things to put together in my mind"). Not top drawer.

Schaffner, Nicholas. *The British Invasion: From the First Wave to the New Wave.* New York: McGraw-Hill, 1983. 316 pages. Approximately 300 black-and-white photographs, covering almost every page. The Transatlantic Gold (Top Twenty Singles 1964-1980). The British Rock Diary (1963-1980). Selected Bibliography. Index.

Introduction to British beat groups, with extra special treatment afforded to The Beatles, The Kinks, The Rolling Stones, The Who, Pink Floyd, T.Rex, and David Bowie. The Dave Clark Five, The Animals, Billy J. Kramer, and other verifiable "first invasion" groups are lumped into the collection of "hot hundred," which includes "second" and "third" wave acts such as The Clash, Elvis Costello, and Led Zeppelin. Eric Clapton is also garbled into the hot hundred, under his own entry and under The Yardbirds—but not for Cream. Poor organization and methodology bury some very fine arti-

cles by Schaffner and by contributors such as David Keeps and Wally Podrazik.

Sumrall, Harry. *Pioneers of Rock and Roll: 100 Artists Who Changed the Face of Rock.* New York: Billboard Books (Watson-Guptill), 1994. 308 pages. Approximately 100 full-page black-and-white photographs throughout. Index.

Magazine-length profiles of 100 selectively chosen artists who, according to the author, "have had the greatest impact on the music as an art form." When it comes to narrowing down such a list, the decisions almost always become fuzzy. Certainly, The Beatles, The Kinks, Elvis, The Stones, and The Doors all belong, as do Jimi Hendrix, Janis Joplin, U2, The Velvet Underground, R.E.M., and so on. But when it comes down to it, if the Crazy World of Arthur Brown (who only made one album) and Neil Sedaka (who didn't have that much influence on rockers) are included, one can cite any one of a number of more crucial pioneers as missing: Kiss, Blondie, Leonard Cohen, Joe Cocker, etc. And then the ladies of the 1970's are totally shafted: Linda Ronstadt, Carly Simon, and Carole King. In spite of the limited nature of the selection, the essays themselves are well-written and largely informative, though with only bare bones highlights of the artists' top albums and singles (only five of each for The Beatles).

Tobler, John and Grundy, Stuart. *The Guitar Greats.* New York: St. Martin's Press, 1984. 192 pages. Approximately 100 black-and-white photographs throughout. Index.

Profiles of 14 of some of the world's most gifted electric guitarists, including B.B. King, Eric Clapton, Jeff Beck, Pete Townshend, Jimmy Page, Ritchie Blackmore, Joe Walsh, Brian May, and others. Not to deny the talents of the above, but what about deceased legends (Jimi Hendrix) and still active heroes (Dave Davies, Eddie Van Halen, and Keith Richards)? Fans of Clapton, Beck, and Page can obtain much of the same information from the metal publications listed in the Magazines section.

Tosches, Nick. Foreword by Samuel Beckett. *Unsung Heroes of Rock: The Birth of Rock in the Wild Years Before Elvis.* New York: Harmony Books (Crown), 1991. 276 pages. Approximately 40 black-and-white photographs throughout. What That Was (chronology). Archaeologia Rockola (discographies). Old Noise, New Plastic (CD releases). Index.

Tosches, determined to shock and alarm, begins this edition of *Unsung Heroes* with a new foreword that takes a reprehensible jab at Elvis ("another dead fuck"). After a nonsensical bit of rubbish from Samuel Beckett and an Introduction that goes overboard in attempting to prove folks were rocking and rolling in the 1940's, Tosches comes through with 25 enlightening pieces on artists, such as Jesse Stone, Louis Jordan, and Screamin' Jay Hawkins, who helped shape rock and roll before Elvis came on the scene. One major failing is the book's inclusion of only two women, Ellie Mae Morse and Wanda Jackson. Another flaw is that the author can't control himself from torching his subjects: Big Joe Turner is branded "a big fat fuck"; and Johnny Ace "blew what little brains he had to kingdom-come." Insensitive.

White, Timothy. *Rock Lives: Profiles and Interviews.* New York: Henry Holt and Company, 1990. 808 pages. Approximately 60 black-and-white photographs throughout. Bibliography. Index.

Collection of profiles and interviews spanning White's admirable rock mag career through *Crawdaddy!, Penthouse, Musician,* and several others. The 57 male and three female subjects (four if you count Fleetwood Mac) are organized in three sections: pioneers (Robert Johnson, Elvis, etc.); pilgrims (Bill Haley, Mick Jagger, etc.); and progeny (Michael Jackson, Bruce Springsteen, etc.). The candid discussions with the likes of Pete Townshend (who speaks out about his homosexuality), George Harrison, and Billy Joel are highly recommended for the rock masses. The bare biographical articles about other artists (John Lennon, Jim Morrison, etc.) tell us nothing we don't already know. A conversations-only package would have been of wider relevance.

Weinberg, Max with Santelli, Robert. *The Big Beat: Conversations With Rock's Great Drummers.*

See: Part Two: Publications on Artists A TO Z, Springsteen, Bruce: Written Works.

CHART DATA

Bronson, Fred. *The Billboard Book of Number One Hits 3rd Edition.* New York: Billboard Books (Watson-Guptill), 1992. 824 pages. 800 black-and-white photographs. Artists Index. Title Index.

Rather than simply list the hits one on top of another, this exciting volume devotes an entire three-column page and a photo to every number one hit from Bill Haley's "Rock Around the Clock" in 1955 to Vanessa Williams' "Save the Best for Last" in 1992. Each entry lists the catalog number, artist, writer(s), producer(s), date the song hit number one, length of time at the top, plus a list of top five songs for that week. The text gives special insights into the makings of the songs, band and personal histories, current perceptions, and more. The book also has cross-references galore, and the photos and text are neatly designed. Untitled back matter contains the following lists: biggest jumps to number one; biggest falls; most number ones by artist, writer, producer, and label; and most weeks at number one by artist and song. I won't divulge record holders—you're on your own to find a copy.

Bronson, Fred. *Billboard's Hottest Hot 100 Hits: Revised and Enlarged Edition.* New York: Billboard Books (Watson-Guptill), 1995. 498 pages. Approximately 150 black-and-white photographs throughout. Index to the Top 5,000 Hits.

The sell-line reads: "Facts and figures about rock's top songs and song makers with the 5,000 biggest singles from 1955 to the present." This book presents myriad chart miscellany for the DJ and serious chart fan: the top songs by major artists (ranging from The Beatles to Dionne Warwick); the writers (Carole King to Jimmy Webb); the producers (Quincy Jones to Narada Michael Walden); the labels (A&M to Virgin); and more. Though with a little effort this information could probably be culled from Bronson's other chart data books, why bother figuring it out yourself? This work solves questions such as "what are the top thirty songs by Leiber and Stoller?" with a mere flip of the page. I question however, the omission of George Martin under the "producer" section. Bronson's rationale for coming up with his top list of 5,000 hits makes sense—though some fans might be upset by where their favorite songs now fall ("I Want to Hold Your Hand" doesn't make the top 150?).

Gambaccini, Paul; Rice, Tim; and Rice, Jonathan. *British Hit Albums.* New York: Billboard Books (Watson-Guptill), 1992. 416 pages. Approximately 100 black-and-white photographs throughout. Facts and Feats.

This volume does to albums (now CDs, but we'll let it pass) what *British Hit Singles* (below) does for singles. The book begins with a "Year by Year Chronology," which is followed by the alphabetical listings. Release dates, catalog numbers, weeks on the chart, and highest position are provided for each artist. The distinctly British format and style are not a hindrance to the book's appeal among American audiences, although an index of album titles would have been helpful. All in all, a must for the serious-minded chart-watcher. Would *you* believe Elvis Presley has 95 hit albums in the U.K.? (Keep in mind that at the time The Beatles had 25!)

Gambaccini, Paul; Rice, Tim; and Rice, Jonathan. *British Hit Singles 8th Edition.* New York: Billboard Books (Watson-Guptill), 1991. 408 pages. Approximately 100 black-and-white photographs throughout. British Hit Singles by Title. Facts and Feats.

The British chart system is fascinating and demands serious study against the American; one can spend hours comparing American chart successes versus those across the Great Pond. Why, for example, did T.Rex have such blazing success in England but not in the U.S.? Why did it take Elton John nearly 20 years to chart a number one in his home country when he has seven numbers ones in the States? And how on earth could Cliff Richard have more top ten hits in England than both Elvis and The Beatles? In true Guinness fashion, this book presents the information with authority. The book only has two setbacks as a reference: the song index (foolishly titled "British Hit Singles by Title") is placed before the "British Hit Singles Facts and Feats."

Hoffman, Frank and Albert, George. Preface by George Albert. *The Cash Box Album Charts, 1975-1985.* Scarecrow Press, 1987. 546 pages. Appendixes.

Typewritten chart listing from *Cash Box* magazine that was actually published *prior* to the volume on 1955-1974 (see below). Oddly, the entire book is an artist-by-artist and album index, listing chart positions as a broad laundry list. Perhaps unique for its time, but com-pletely outmoded by chart data books in the 1990's.

Hoffman, Frank and Albert, George. Preface by George Albert. *The Cash Box Album Charts, 1955-1974.* Scarecrow Press, 1988. 512 pages. Appendixes.

This book does the same for the years 1955-1974 as the previously published *Cash Box* guide (see above) does for 1975-1985. Difficult to use, none too attractive.

Jancik, Wayne. *One-Hit Wonders.* New York: Billboard Books (Watson-Guptill), 1990. 432 pages. Approximately 200 black-and-white photographs. Artist Index. Song Index. The Runners-Up. More One-Hit Wonders.

Jancik—a psychotherapist, of all occupations—boasts one of the largest record collections in the country (over 130,000 albums and singles). Here he tackles one hit wonders—any recording act that placed only one 45 RPM single on Billboard's top 40 chart. One time pairings, such as Donna Summer and Barbra Streisand, are not included. That still makes for a diverse range of fly-by-night charters, from the unfamiliar (Ernie Maresca, The Detergents, and Marmalade) to the novelty (Bill Dana as "Jose Jimenez," Tracey Ullman, and Weird Al Yankovic) to the surprisingly familiar (Eric Burdon and War, Jimi Hendrix, and Derek and the Dominoes). This is a fun book that treats its overlooked subjects with refreshing respect.

McAleer, Dave. *The All Music Book Of Hit Albums: The Top 10 U.S. and U.K. Album Charts from 1960 to the Present.* San Francisco: Freeman-Miller, 1995. 352 pages. Approximately 100 black-and-white photographs throughout. Listings by Artist. Listings by Title.

Comparative analysis of U.S. and U.K. songs from each side of the Atlantic. A combination of concepts in titles from Guinness and Billboard, this work has the advantage of listing chart data from both countries directly opposite each other. Listings include album, artist, label, weeks on the chart, peak position, and symbols for platinum and gold. On the borders are mini-photos and trivia tidbits, which are nothing special. Despite an ugly gridlike format and uncomfortable design, this book offers answers to some immediate research and trivia queries.

Reed, Dafydd; Mazell, Barry; and Osborne, Roger. *The Complete NME Singles Charts*. London: Boxtree, 1995. 688 pages. Approximately 100 black-and-white photographs throughout. Title Index. Artist Index.

A revised edition of *40 Years of NME Charts* (which is still listed on the title page), this hefty work includes NME chart data from November 1952 to December 1994. Entries are prepared in timeline fashion, recording top 11 hits from week-to-week and providing only the bare information on who recorded the song and on what label. Some photographs and notes are included. Not particularly attractive on the inside or out—and it doesn't include data on record holders—but this is still the direct source to NME chart information.

Rosen, Craig. *The Billboard Book of Number One Albums: The Inside Story Behind Pop Music's Blockbuster Records*. New York: Billboard Books (Watson-Guptill), 1996. 434 pages. Approximately 425 black-and-white photographs throughout. Appendix.

A follow-up of sorts to Bronson's study of number one songs (see above), this book contains one-page profiles of all 424 number one albums starting in 1956 with *Elvis Presley* and ending, rather befittingly, in 1995 with The Beatles' *Anthology 1*. (Of course, this has already since dated, since The Beatles now have their record seventeenth number one with *Anthology 2*.) Those who feel disheartened with the ultra-pop orientation of the singles charts might be comforted in knowing virtually every other album here is a general rock and roll album. In the 1990's, number ones have come from Pearl Jam, R.E.M., The Eagles, Alice in Chains, Smashing Pumpkins, and many others. The essays are complemented with listings of the top five for that week, plus quick information on label, producer(s), song line-up, release date, and weeks at number one; each page has a photo. Valuable for researchers and fun for browsers.

Whitburn, Joel. *The Billboard Book of Top 40 Albums: Revised and Enlarged 3rd Edition*. New York: Billboard Books (Watson-Guptill), 1995. 402 pages. Approximately 150 black-and-white photographs throughout. The Record Holders: Top Artists and Album Achievements.

The sell line reads: "The complete chart guide to every album in the top forty since 1955."

The format of this work is similar to the Gambaccini book on the British album charts (see above). There are some significant improvements here to that successful work. Each artist name is designed in a different color for easier visual accessibility. The entries contain incisive group line-ups and bare-bones facts, along with album listings that cite highest chart positioning, weeks on the charts, single releases from the albums, and labels with catalog numbers. Though this is a wonderful reference tool—and the record holders section covers a great deal of ground—an index of album titles should have been provided. Aside from Whitburn's book on top 40 hits (see below), his chart data has also been spun-off into the following titles, packaged by various publishers: *Top 1000 Singles 1955-1992*; *Top 1000 x 5*; *Pop Hits 1940-1954*; *Top Pop Albums 1955-1992*; *Billboard's Top Ten Charts 1958-1995*; *Top Pop Singles 1955-1993*; and *Daily #1 Hits 1940-1992*.

Whitburn, Joel. *The Billboard Book of Top 40 Hits 6th Edition*. New York: Billboard Books (Watson-Guptill), 1996. 832 pages. Song Index. Record Holders.

The sell-line reads: "Fascinating trivia and complete chart data about the artists and their songs 1955 to the present." The book alphabetically lists all artists who ever had top forty hits, and then supplies information for the date their songs made the charts, their highest positions (plus weeks at number one if they reached that mark), total weeks on the chart, and record labels and numbers. Group line-ups and vital facts are briefly noted. The records section lists the top singles, top artists and leaders by decade up through 1995. This book is a must-have for fans of the charts, as a researcher can at last access information to *all* top forty hits—not just those that made number one; one can finally find listings for groups such as The Kinks, Led Zeppelin, and The Who. One can even dig up Frank Zappa's only top forty hit ("Valley Girl"). The song index should have come at the *end* of the book to save page flipping while searching for songs.

CHRONOLOGIES

De Noyer, Paul (consultant editor). *The Story of Rock 'N Roll: The Year-by-Year Illustrated Chronicle*. Miami, FL: MBS, 1995. 304 pages. Approximately 350 color and black-and-white photographs, covering every page. Top 5 U.K. Albums. Top 5 U.S. Albums. Index.

Slick, colorful rendering of rock's evolution and history from 1954-1994. Through somewhat meandering prose—and way too many distracting boldface names within the text—the book conveys the bare facts, which we've all seen before. The book's main appeal lies in its entertaining sidebars on bands and events, from the release of the *Sgt. Pepper's Lonely Hearts Club Band* LP, to movie tie-ins, to glitter rock, to Jim Morrison's collapsing on stage. For teens only.

Editors of *Rolling Stone*. Foreword by Peter Wolf. *Rolling Stone Rock Almanac: The Chronicles of Rock and Roll*. New York: Macmillan, 1983. 372 pages. Approximately 250 black-and-white photographs throughout. Milestones. Index.

A fine early study of rock from January 1954 to December 1982. The chronological data includes at least a half dozen events for each month, with useful week-ending chart data on the bottoms of pages. The blurbs for each filled-in date are concise and informative, with bold type for artist names. Though dated, this book is closer to its target than Nite's work (see below), but doesn't have the sensationalistic qualities of Tobler's work. For quick research on factoids spanning 1954-1982.

Laufenberg, Frank. Edited by Hugh Gregory. *Rock and Pop Day by Day*. New York: Sterling, 1992. 392 pages. Index of Names. (Released in the U.K. by Blandford [Cassell].)

This day-by-day chronology of birth and death dates spans the music industry in over 4,000 entries. "Hits of the day" are supplied in boxes throughout the book. The criteria for inclusion is very vague; it seems odd to find entries for Enrico Caruso and Tommy Dorsey in a work so clearly defined as "rock" and "pop." Other entries, such as the October 30 listing for the Orson Welles' broadcast of "War of the Worlds" (1938) seem truly off the mark. Of interest primarily to DJ's who need to tell listeners of birth and death dates of the rich and famous.

Nite, Norm N. Foreword by Dick Clark. *Rock On Almanac: The First Four Decades of Rock `N' Roll 2nd Edition*. New York: HarperCollins, 1992. 582 pages. Approximately 400 black-and-white photographs throughout. Glossary. Index of Performers.

Noted radio broadcaster Norm N. Nite charts the course of rock and roll from the 1950's to the 90's. For each year, Nite summarizes the main musical events, followed by debut artists, month-by-month chart hits, top singles, TV shows, Oscar winners, deaths, and more. This is a well-intended ode to pop culture, but unfortunately there's too much coverage of film/TV/sports/other news and not enough on music and the bands themselves. As this edition was published in the early 1990's, alternative, indie, and grunge bands have been completely ignored. Young fans will tap the snooze button.

Rees, Dafydd and Crampton, Luke. *Rock Movers and Shakers: Revised and Enlarged Edition*. New York: Billboard Books (Watson-Guptill), 1991. 586 pages. 100 black-and-white photos throughout.

The title and sell line of this book ("An A to Z of the People Who Made Rock Happen") are somewhat oblique. A more apt title might have indicated that this is an alphabetical compendium of chronologies of major performers and groups. Each artist entry lists band members on top with instruments played; this is followed below by a thorough listing of day-by-day events (birth dates, album releases, awards, prison stints, and so on). Emphasis is on sales and chart successes, though other rare pieces of information are also mentioned. Researchers will undeniably be pleased with the exhaustive coverage on everyone from Cowboy Junkies to Suzi Quatro—but many will be disconcerted about the lack of indexing and cross-referencing (e.g., there are no see also refs under The Beatles, for example, to alert readers to the entries on the members' solo careers; and there is no cross-reference entry for The Partridge Family relating to the existing David Cassidy entry). Photo placement is also a bit lacking; a photo spread of the Bee Gees, Chuck Berry, Jon Bon Jovi, and David Bowie is in the C's, some 30-plus pages after the B's end.

Tobler, John. *This Day in Rock: Day by Day Record of Rock's Biggest News Stories*. New York: Carroll & Graf, 1993. 384 pages. Approximately 400 black-and-white photographs, covering every page.

This work starts with a great idea—a thorough news flash history of rock events related to days of the calendar year—but the author executes the concept rather foolishly. Rather than begin the timeline from 1955 and proceed chronologically, this book opens with January 1 and ends with December 31, providing news articles along the way. Thus the reader has to already know offhand that Gary Glitter announced his retirement on January 28 in order to know to look it up in that spot (and find out what year that was in). There is no index to help you find your way around. Though its tabloid flavor is entertaining at times, this book would have served better as a daily planner.

Uslan, Michael and Solomon, Bruce. Foreword by Dick Clark. *Dick Clark's The First 25 Years of Rock & Roll.* New York: Delacorte, 1981. 466 pages. Approximately 250 black-and-white photographs throughout. Index.

Lackluster year-by-year account of rock and roll, with profiles of 125 some-odd artists and indiscriminately selected studies on those who defined the "sound" of that year (e.g., The Doors for 1967 and Blood, Sweat and Tears for 1969). This leaves some major acts as one-paragraph mentions (The Kinks, under "British Invasion") or as just plain misses (Journey). Some write-ups are overtly critical while others are not, evidently revealing the authors' biases. This may be the way Clark, Uslan, and Solomon remember the first 25 years of rock, but most fans will not be impressed.

CRITICAL/ANALYTICAL COMMENTARY

Heylin, Clinton (Editor). *The Penguin Book of Rock & Roll Writing.* New York: Viking (Penguin Group), 1992. 682 pages. Ten original drawings by Ray Lowry.

Heylin has gathered in one volume an "oracle-cum bible in just 200,000 words and 80 testaments." Some of the giants are here (Jon Landau, Paul Williams, and Greil Marcus), while others (Robert Hilburn, Peter Guralnick, and Dave Marsh) are not. Fans will enjoy pieces written by musicians such as Ian Hunter, Lou Reed, Lenny Kaye, and Frank Zappa. Running the full gamut of experiences from pre-rock writing in the 1950's to rock's casualties (predating Kurt Cobain), the criticism in this book will make you wince, roll your eyes—and also revel in rock's ability to evolve, grow, and poke fun at itself.

Kent, Nick. Foreword by Iggy Pop. *The Dark Stuff: Selected Writings in Rock Music 1972-1995.* 347 pages. (First published in Great Britain in 1994 by Penguin.)

Nick Kent, primarily known in England for his journalism and reviews in the *New Musical Express*, has essentially spent a career entering the minds of rock's most haunted male figures: Brian Jones, Brian Wilson, Jerry Lee Lewis, Sid Vicious, Kurt Cobain, Syd Barrett, et. al. Yet Kent eschews the concept that the people gathered in this volume were chosen based on the fact that they are drug casualties—after all, the Smiths are included. In pieces about the aforementioned, as well as today's favorites such as Guns N' Roses and Iggy Pop, Kent achieves his goal of showing what these musicians are like in person.

Loder, Kurt. *Bat Chain Puller: Rock & Roll in the Age of Celebrity.* New York: St. Martin's Press, 1990. 380 pages. 36 full-page black-and-white photographs throughout.

Loder pinched the title from a tune by Captain Beefheart (with verbal permission). His essays (with a few interviews), reprinted from the pages of *Rolling Stone*, are intended to represent the flipside of pop culture in the tradition of Greil Marcus. In reality, these are Loder's views on rock stars themselves: the two sides of Mick Jagger; the downslide of The Who after Keith Moon's death; the comic genius of Frank Zappa; and so on. Loder manages to get more out of his subjects than most interviewers, actually prying a semblance of genuine banter from Bob Dylan. And yet, while we can excuse the out-of-place Sean Connery piece (most fans of 1960's rock seem to have an affection for James Bond), why include the one on Don Johnson? Good rock and roll reportage outweighs the book's general lack of unity.

Love, Robert (Editor). Introduction by Jann S. Wenner. *The Best of Rolling Stone: 25 Years of Journalism on the Edge.* New York: Doubleday (division of Bantam Doubleday Dell), 1993. 512 pages.

A collection of 37 pieces spanning the magazine's 25-year history. The authors introduce their own articles, providing present-day reflections on the stars or events at hand. All but four of the original articles are abridged. Here you can find a variety of critiquing, from Robert Greenfield's backstage look at The

Stones on tour in 1971 to an attempt at "unteenybopping" David Cassidy in Robin Green's 1972 piece "Naked Lunch Box." The last 14 articles relate more to people and happenings in politics and counter-culture than rock and roll. Well put together, if slightly stuffy.

Marcus, Greil. *Mystery Train: Images of America in Rock 'N' Roll Music*. New York: Plume (Penguin Group), 1990. 282 pages. Notes and Discographies. Index.

First published in 1975, this unusual study focuses largely on four artists—The Band, Sly Stone, Randy Newman, and Elvis Presley—and how they impacted on American culture. The obvious question is: Why Randy Newman alongside these other musical giants? Most of Marcus' pronouncements rate closer to criticism than social commentary, but his observations carry immense weight (e.g., on Sly: "[he] made music no one had heard before"). The Elvis section, left in the sorry state of present tense from the first edition, reads strangely.

Williams, Paul. *Outlaw Blues: A Book of Rock Music*. New York: E.P. Dutton & Co., Inc., 1969. 192 pages. Eight black-and-white photographs throughout. Discography.

Paul Williams' first book, most of which was originally seen in the pages of his brainchild, *Crawdaddy!* (see Magazines). Williams is among the few rock journalists who writes from his gut, not his ego; he assesses Donovan, Buffalo Springfield, Bob Dylan ("Tom Paine himself"), The Doors, and Brian Wilson in words that will excite anyone who has been listening to album-rock radio since the late 1960's. More photos and additional prose would have made *Outlaw Blues* a classic.

DICTIONARIES AND ENCYCLOPEDIAS

Bane, Michael. *Who's Who in Rock*. New York: Facts On File, Inc., 1981. 260 pages. One hundred black-and-white photographs throughout. Index.

A straightforward A to Z of rock music up through the early 1980's, and therefore too dated to be of much use for the hard-core rock fan. The book is completely lacking in discographies, bibliographic information and cross-referencing. On the other hand, the entries are so concise and accessible they do make the book worthwhile for one who knows

absolutely nothing about rock. But why include Cheech and Chong in a rock who's who?

Bianco, Dave. *Who's Who in New Wave Music: An Illustrated Encyclopedia 1962-1982 (The First Wave)*. Ann Arbor, MI: Pierian Press, 1986. 420 pages. Approximately 175 black-and-white photographs throughout. Appendixes. Glossary. Indexes: Personal Name Index; Record Label Index; Song & Album Title Index; Geographic Index.

Listy encyclopedia that provides the bare details for bands ranging from The A's to Zoom. Each entry includes where and when formed, style, personnel, chronology, history, and discography. The appendixes feature sections on record companies, bibliography, musical terminology, artists grouped by musical style, and more. Consistently handled and thoroughly researched, this book is immensely useful, though somewhat dry. Fans of New Wave would want some anecdotes on bands such as The Urinals, Penetration, and F-Word. Equal coverage of both underground groups and chart-breakers.

Clarke, Donald (editor). *The Penguin Encyclopedia of Popular Music*. New York: Penguin, 1989. 1,378 pages. Index.

How does this compare to works by Rolling Stone and Harmony? In the illustrative department, not at all. Doesn't the publisher realize that the rock image is almost on the same level of importance as the music, and that even researchers like to see a face when turning the pages? This work also doesn't include the detailed discographical information of *The New Rolling Stone Encyclopedia* (see Romanowski, below), although the major albums seem to be mentioned in the essays. Entries are compact and fully cross-referenced; longer entries keep the one-paragraph format, so you'll probably get blinded reading the four-page double-column articles, such as the one on Elvis. Somewhat dated, excessively dry and rather Euro-American in focus.

Clifford, Mike. *The Harmony Illustrated Encyclopedia of Rock: Seventh Edition*. New York: Harmony Books (Crown), 1992. 208 pages. Approximately 425 color and black-and-white photographs, covering every page.

Despite the seventh edition labeling—this book was first published in 1988—*The Harmony*

Illustrated Encyclopedia of Rock is still a 1980's artifact in terms of design, content, and coverage. The photos are colorful, but they're stiff publicity shots, not representations of live performances. Many vital 1990's artists such as Pearl Jam and Stone Temple Pilots were unknown when this book came out, and it's hard to look at it without feeling the history of rock ended with U2. The entries—which include many cross-references, concise histories, and some chart/discographical information—also ring like blasts from the past. Glitzy without a purpose.

Cross, Colin with Kendall, Paul and Farren, Mick. *Encyclopedia of British Beat Groups & Solo Artists of the Sixties.* London: Omnibus Press (division of Book Sales Limited), 1980. 96 pages. Approximately 100 black-and-white photographs, covering every page. Index.

Uninformed eyesore of an encyclopedia, with entries ranging from four lines (Babylon) to The Beatles (3¼ columns). The write-ups do not contain birthdates or discographies; the information is sketchy and boring. Although the copyright is 1980, some entries (such as The Kinks) don't even have information stretching past 1975! The photos are so faded that few of the musicians in the pictures even have faces. Grade F-.

DiMartino, Dave. *Singer-Songwriters: Pop Music's Performer Composers, From A to Zevon.* New York: Billboard Books (Watson-Guptill), 1994. 306 pages. Approximately 150 black-and-white photographs throughout. Index.

According to author Dave DiMartino, singer-songwriters are those who "...do it all—the artists who write the music that they themselves perform." This is right on the money in the sense that DiMartino further qualifies his definition by weeding out those who aren't pop and those who haven't quite gone solo, and by including only those who are known equally for writing and performing. DiMartino thus intentionally leaves out a seminal singer/songwriter—Ray Davies—who up to 1994 hadn't ventured out solo that much (but has since that time). For reasons unexplained, DiMartino also omits Prince, who seems to fit the author's criteria for inclusion. Then again, in addition to the obvious, some interesting names do crop up: Tim Buckley, Leonard Cohen, Jim Croce, Neil Diamond, Arlo Guthrie, Ian Hunter, Randy Newman, and Warren

Zevon. As a pleasant surprise, Tracy Chapman and Melissa Etheridge both made the cut. The entries read extremely well, but chart data is limited to only a handful of singles and albums. Fun for browsing, but not for in-depth research on all of pop's great singer-songwriters.

Gammond, Peter. *The Oxford Companion to Popular Music.* Oxford and New York: Oxford University Press, 1991. 742 pages. Index of People and Groups. Index of Shows and Films. Index of Songs and Albums.

An overtly academic and poorly devised pop encyclopedia that is not unlike *The Da Capo Companion to 20th Century Poplar Music* (see below). As in that volume, entries span everything from jazz, reggae, and blues, to rock, country western, and folk. Needless to say, rap and alternative music are non-existent here. Decisions on many entries seem to have no rhyme or reason. The Who, for example, is afforded an entry, as is Roger Daltrey as soloist; however, there isn't one for Pete Townshend as soloist. Meanwhile, there is an entry on Boy George, but not an entry or even a cross-reference for Culture Club. The essays on major artists are generally way too brief and often focus on all of the wrong recordings. Only good for basic birth and death data.

Hardy, Phil and Laing, Dave. *The Da Capo Companion to 20th Century Popular Music.* New York: Da Capo, 1995. 1,216 pages. Index of Song and Album Titles.

First published in 1990 as *The Faber Companion to 20th Century Popular Music* (and updated since), this book includes over 22,000 entries on popular artists spanning rock, pop, Broadway, rap, jazz, and everything else considered "popular music" except, perhaps, classical music. Entries are slightly British in tone and style, but not nearly as stodgy or overtly critical as *The Guinness Encyclopedia of Popular Music* (see Larkin, below). Entries include birth data, lengthy bios (mentioning many key records)—but not discographical or chart lists. Within the articles on each entry, cross-references to other full entries are printed in boldface. With a handy index in the back, this is a good source to fans of eclectic 20th century music, but certainly not 1990's alternative.

Heatley, Michael (Editor). *The Ultimate Encyclopedia of Rock.* New York: HarperCollins, 1993. 352 pages. Approximately 350 color and black-and-white photographs, covering nearly every page. Rock Chronology. Most Successful Chart Albums. Index. (First published in 1993 in Great Britain by Virgin Books Limited.)

Competition mainly for Harmony's illustrated encyclopedia (see above), this book has the benefit of a much better photo selection, an easier-to-follow design, and an index. Still, it doesn't have the discographical details or depth of information. The division of musicians into A to Z sections on roots, who's who, and legends is a disaster of epic proportions. Without checking the index, how is one to know in what category to find an artist? More of a PR-piece for Virgin Books than a real rock encyclopedia.

Jasper, Tony and Oliver, Derek. *The International Encyclopedia of Hard Rock and Heavy Metal.* New York: Facts On File, Inc., 1983. 400 pages.

A good source to find the bare minimum on your favorite and lesser-known headbangers: who are they, where are they from, are they worth looking for, and what are their key albums. Years of groups' formation and demise are not supplied for every band, which may be excusable given the relative obscurity of many included. There is no excuse, however, for not including photos. Wouldn't you like to see what Heavy Pettin', Samson, Cirith Ungol (credited herein with the great honor of having the worst heavy metal album ever), and Hellenbach look like?

Larkin, Colin (editor). *The Guinness Encyclopedia of Popular Music: Concise Edition.* Enfield, Middlesex (England): Guinness Publishing Limited, 1993. 1,296 pages. Approximately 100 full-page black-and-white photographs throughout. Bibliography. Index.

Originally published as a three-volume set, this hefty reference may have fewer entries than other volumes included herein ("only" 3,000), but the essays themselves are generally longer, even for non-giants. In addition to detailed background information, the Guinness encyclopedia also includes selected album releases and books. The text is distinctly British in tone, and reflects U.K. tastes in the artists and their

releases; most fans would have preferred a more evenhanded approach and less criticism—even when positive. Still, there are many entries here you will not find in other pop encyclopedias (albeit mostly British): Lora Logic, Steve Gadd, and Diamond Head, to name a few.

Larkin, Colin (general editor). *The Guinness Who's Who of Heavy Metal.* Enfield, Middlesex (England): Guinness Publishing Limited, 1992. 286 pages. Approximately 100 full-page black-and-white photographs throughout.

This heavy metal who's who kicks butt over Jasper's work (see above) on the same subject. Beginning with a superb glossary of heavy metal terminology ("Euro-rock," "Satanic metal," etc.), this book provides solid information on all major HM bands from Aaronsrod to ZZ Top (though mistakenly identified as "Z.Z." with periods). The entries are generally concise—only one paragraph on average, although major bands, such as Metallica, stretch to two. Larkin also offers readers some album releases at the end of entries. Despite the fact that there is a shot of Spinal Tap, the photo coverage is so-so; but bear in mind that the Jasper book didn't have *any* pictures. While the text and design could have been jazzier, this is still an authoritative reference work for serious headbangers.

Larkin, Colin (general editor). *The Guinness Who's Who of Sixties Music.* Enfield, Middlesex (England): Guinness Publishing Limited), c.1994. 352 pages. Approximately 100 black-and-white photographs throughout.

A slice of the pie from Guinness Publishing's larger, all-inclusive encyclopedia (see above). If you own the more comprehensive work, you don't need this one.

Morehead, Philip D. with MacNeil, Anne. *The New International Dictionary of Music.* New York: Penguin, 1992. 624 pages. Approximately 225 line drawings throughout. Glossary of Musical Terms in Four Languages.

In case you were wondering, Philip D. Morehead is music administrator of the Lyric Opera of Chicago, not the name of the new drummer for Spinal Tap or a character in a James Bond movie. This basic dictionary contains concise definitions of terminology spanning all areas of music, and what seems to be just as much space devoted to capsule identi-fiers of musicians. While there is some cover-age of major rock musicians—e.g., The Beatles, The Stones, The Who—you won't find much in the way of substance. The entire entry for U2: "Irish punk band formed in 1978 in Dublin." More means less.

Naha, Ed (compiler). *Lillian Roxton's Rock Encyclopedia*. New York: Grosset & Dunlap, 1978. 566 pages. Two eight-page black-and-white photo inserts. Index.

First published in 1969(!), this relic—created all those years ago by journalist Lillian Roxton—has the distinction of being the first established rock encyclopedia. Useless today for either discographical or biographical data, this book is still a trip for information on 1960's artists as the data was perceived in 1978. For The Animals: "The Animals' sound was incredibly black..." For Abba: "All systems are go for this Swedish entourage and their top-ten oriented sound." Only for collectors.

Paraire, Philippe. *50 Years of Rock*. Edinburgh, Scotland: Chambers, 1992. 246 pages. Approximately 75 black-and-white photographs throughout. Index.

Essentially, a translation and an update of a French publication, *50 Ans de Musique Rock*, this "compact reference" is an embarrassing work on any level. Divided into sections on the blues, early rock, English sounds, and commer-cial rock, the artist profiles offer hardly any discographical/biographical information, but a lot of rhetoric. For The Kinks: "Because of the length of their career (or some say, lack of inspiration), The Kinks have also experimented with hard rock, disco, and New Wave. Should they be condemned for their eclecticism?" John Lennon is branded "symbol and martyr"—a statement that would make even acolytes laugh out loud. Rubbish.

Romanowski, Patricia and George-Warren, Holly (editors). *The New Rolling Stone Encyclopedia of Rock & Roll*. New York: Fireside (Simon & Schuster), 1995. 1,120 pages. Approximately 200 black-and-white photos throughout.

First published in 1983, this exhaustive refer-ence spans the 1950's-early 90's rock, with some coverage of rap, hip-hop, alternative, country, soul, and blues. The 1,800 useful bio-graphical entries are supplemented with broad

definitions of musical terms and genres. Boxes highlight Grammy winners, Rock and Roll Hall of Fame inductees, festivals, and other related information. Each biography contains original band line-ups and album discogra-phies (with plus and minus signs used to indi-cate personnel changes). The writing in this revised, revamped package is rewardingly non-critical and tight—just the facts. Fans who purchased earlier editions and have long wait-ed to see entries on Pearl Jam, Nine Inch Nails, and 2 Live Crew will not be disappointed, but those hoping to find depth of coverage on alternative and indie bands will be.

Shaw, Arnold. *Dictionary of American Pop Rock*. New York: Schirmer, 1982. 440 pages. Index.

One of the early dictionaries to combine music terminology with brief entries on pop/rock performers. Articles on groups are surprisingly critical in tone (Paul McCartney "seems con-tent to write bubble-gum, romantic ballads"), which is unnecessary in a dictionary. A poor place to look up information on artists, since scores of musicians from Richie Havens to Elvis Costello are missing. Believe it or not, the complete entry on Jimi Hendrix reads: "See the `black Elvis.'"

Stambler, Irwin. *The Encyclopedia of Pop, Rock and Soul*. New York: St. Martin's Press, 1989. 896 pages. Two 16-page black-and-white photo inserts. Appendix A: Recording Industry Association of America, Inc.: Gold and Platinum Record Awards. Appendix B: National Academy of Recording Arts and Sciences Grammy Winners by Category. Appendix C: Academy of Motion Picture Arts and Sciences Award Nominations and Winners in Music. Bibliography.

This old chestnut has appeared in various forms since it was first published in 1974. Despite the fact that it is still buried in a previ-ous decade—and is far more pop and rock than it is soul—fans of classic rock and roll from AC/DC to Warren Zevon will derive pleasure from the highly readable (and often lengthy) essays. This book does not contain discographical lists for artists, but it does offer extensive cross-referencing and information on gold/platinum and Grammy winners in the back. The photo inserts are negligible.

Stancell, Steven. *Rap Whoz Who: The World of Rap Music*. New York: Schirmer, 1996. 340 pages. Approximately 125 black-and-white photographs throughout. Index.

A comprehensive survey of the best known rappers, deejays, promoters, and composers—whether black or white. In addition to lucidly written entries on rap stars from Above the Law to YZ, Stancell provides selected discographies, photos, issue-related sidebars ("MC Ren: On Islam and Gangsta Rap") and flavorful definitions ("gangsta," "gang banger," etc.). The ultimate guide to a much-neglected subject. Highly recommended.

Suter, Paul. *HM A-Z: The Ultimate Heavy Metal Encyclopedia*. London: Omnibus Press (division of Book Sales Limited), 1985. 112 pages. Approximately 100 black-and-white photographs, covering every page.

Skimpy encyclopedia of headbanging music, with entries on approximately 150 top acts. Coverage is less than satisfactory; the book omits notable lesser-known HM bands but throws in pop groups such as REO Speedwagon, who never quite fit the heavy metal title. Other decision-making also seems fuzzy, in that there is a write-up on 1960's giant Cream but not The Kinks, whose power chords inspired the genre. The photos are drudging publicity shots unsuitable for a book that should have had some punch. Not recommended.

Warner, Jay. Foreword by Frankie Valli. *The Billboard Book of American Singing Groups: A History 1940-1980*. New York: Billboard Books (Watson-Guptill), 1992. 560 pages. Approximately 50 full pages of photos.

This enormous book divides American vocal groups A to Z into five decades, plus contains an additional section for "the a cappella era." The author defines a vocal group as being "three or more people singing in harmony—more than a duet and less than a chorus." This opens the floodgates for quite a wide range of performers; there will be those who have difficulty accepting 1940's vocal groups such as The Andrew Sisters and The Pilgrim Travellers in the same book with The Platters, The Ronettes, The Mamas and the Papas, and Crosby, Stills and Nash. Most of the decisions do seem to make sense, though it seems funny to include The Archies and not other television

tie-in acts (e.g., The Monkees and The Partridge Family). Biographies are painstakingly thorough (with some emphasis on chart success), as are the lists of single releases for each artist. Listen to what Frankie says in his foreword: "I've never been so thoroughly entertained while being informed." Sadly, no index or bibliography is provided for this otherwise superb work.

Westband, Eric and Marks, Craig. *Spin Alternative Press Record Guide: The Essential Artists of Punk, New Wave, Indie Rock, and Hip Hop*. New York: Vintage (Random House), 1995. 468 pages. Approximately 350 color and black-and-white photographs throughout. The Top 10 Alternative Albums. Index.

Just so we have this straight: This book is all punk, New Wave, indie, and hip-hop—*plus* pop artists such as Madonna who happen to have some alternative sounds in their music. The outcry for an encyclopedia on alternative rockers from Patti Smith to Courtney Love was a powerful one, but this encyclopedia fails to convince the reader of its distinctions about who belongs and who doesn't. Perhaps when it comes to alternative music, no list could possibly please everyone. The only outright omissions in the alternative heading as defined here, it seems, are so-called dinosaur rockers, from Elvis to Led Zeppelin. In any event, this reviewer has difficulty seeing entries on David Bowie and Kiss but not Marc Bolan or Gary Glitter; AC/DC but not Metallica; Abba but not Frank Zappa. For staple alternative artists such as The New York Dolls, The Breeders, Roxy Music, X, Nirvana, and so on, this book does deliver the goods, replete with discographies and some color images. Combine this with *The New Rolling Stone Encyclopedia of Rock* (see Romanowski, above) and we may have something.

York, William. *Who's Who in Rock Music*. New York: Charles Scribner's Sons, 1982. 413 pages. Appendix: Record Label Abbreviations.

Bare-bones, non-illustrated listing of artists, with entries only including musician line-ups and record releases (up through the early 1980's). Way past its prime—although it's one of the few books to offer record label names and addresses. Useless, despite its 12,000 entries.

DISCOGRAPHIES AND COLLECTIBLES

Henkel, David K. *Official Price Guide to Rock and Roll Magazines, Posters, and Memorabilia.* New York: House of Collectibles (Random House), 1992. 614 pages. Approximately 250 black-and-white photographs throughout; one glossy eight-page color insert. Fan Clubs. The Rock and Roll Hall of Fame. Index.

The first edition of this guide that cites over 10,000 magazines, 750 posters and various other collectibles, and fan publications. After opening sections on the history of teenybopper and rock magazines and advice on how to evaluate and protect your collection, there is a lengthy alphabetical listing of rock and teen magazines. The author only cites the name of the magazine with issue number and bands covered, plus a general range of commercial value. Unfortunately, no history or description of the magazine's focus is provided. For the section on rock posters, there are special sections on various types of San Francisco art, all of which identify artist, date of creation, dimensions, and prices based on whether the piece is a poster, a handbill, or a postcard. This book has an odd assortment of data that strangely includes extra inserts on collecting The Beatles, The Buckinghams, Kiss, and Annette Funicello, but misses biggies such as Elvis Presley, The Monkees, The Rolling Stones, and The Partridge Family. A mixed bag.

Hounsome, Terry. *Rock Record 3rd Edition: A Collectors' Directory of Rock Albums and Rock Musicians.* New York: Facts On File, Inc., 1987. 740 pages. Index. (Published in the U.K. by Blandford [Cassell].)

The quintessential rock album catalog, with entries alphabetized A to Z by artist and albums listed below. Each album citation lists (through a complex coding system) instruments played, musicians featured, country of origin, and catalog number. Collectors kill for this item which, unfortunately, is out of print as of this writing because the immense book could no longer be condensed into one volume. Recently, Hounsome has self-published various directories in the United Kingdom—including this title, which is now called *Rock Record 6 Album File.*

No author. *The Official Music Master Albums Catalog Edition 18.* Hastings, East Sussex (England): Music Master (division of MBC Information Service), 1991. Unpaginated (over 1,000 pages).

First published in 1971, this is a massive guide to every album and cassette release in the United Kingdom. Coverage includes rock, jazz, classical, folk, rap, and just about everything else under the sun. This longtime British classic thus lists over 10,000 releases from AB Sounds to ZZ Top, with entries indicating title, songs, format (LP or cassette), and catalog number. Unfortunately, chart positions and information on U.S. counterparts are not provided. Researchers may be ticked that all albums beginning with numbers appear at the top of entries, a situation any typesetter or database expert should easily resolve in the 1990's. This is otherwise a superlative reference for anyone interested in U.K. releases.

Osborne, Jerry. *Official Price Guide to Records: Eleventh Edition.* New York: House of Collectibles, 1995. 1,226 pages. Approximately 100 black-and-white reproductions of album covers throughout.

"The ultimate guide to record collecting, with more than 100,000 prices listed!," this is an invaluable reference source for those who want to dust off their record collections and determine if cashing in the vinyl will be enough for a down payment on a house. Promotional issues and foreign releases are not included, while bootlegs are cited but not priced. Those monetary values supplied only take into consideration near mint condition. Priceless, as it were, though a chore to use for non-collectors. The green cover of the eleventh edition actually makes the book look like a baseball card pricing guide.

Rees, Tony. Foreword by Ken Kessler. *Rare Rock: A Collector's Guide.* Poole, Dorset (England). Blandford Press, 1985. 348 pages. Approximately 200 black-and-white reproductions of album covers.

A mid-1980's encyclopedia of hard-to-find albums, EPs, singles, flexis, and cassettes, as well as compilations, flexipop, SFX, NME tapes, and non-album tracks. Each entry, alphabetized from Abba to Zappa, includes: first recordings; American/British singles and albums; and a heading aptly titled "odds and sods." To show just how dated this is, there is no information on Culture Club or ZZ Top. Until another edition comes along, only for collectors of material pre-1984.

Umphred, Neal. *Goldmine's Rock 'n Roll 45 RPM Record Price Guide 3rd Edition.* Iola, WI: Krause Publications, 1994. Approximately 200 black-and-white reproductions of records throughout. 864 pages.

With *Goldmine* magazine's unsurpassed reputation among collectors (see Magazines), it's a natural for a book to appear bearing its imprimatur. This exhaustively researched and easy-to-comprehend work accomplishes even more for 45s than Osborne's (see above) does for albums. Author Neal Umphred includes values for over 30,000 45s, EPs, and picture sleeves, including promotional and novelty releases. A nice advantage of this book is the inclusion of prices for both very good as well as near-mint. Highly recommended.

MISCELLANEOUS REFERENCE

Bego, Mark. *The Rock Almanac.* New York: Macmillan, 1996. 308 pages.

General assortment of rock lists, not nearly as substantive (or as fun) as Marsh's work (see below), but still useful in certain areas. The book contains a bare rock chronology, inductees into the Rock and Roll Hall of Fame, Elvis movies, weird marriages, rock festivals, famous cross-dressers, rock TV shows, and more. Some sections, such as "Rock Stars Who Drowned in Their Own Vomit," sound better than they really are (since there are only two cases, Mama Cass and Jimi Hendrix). An index might have made this a handy reference source.

Dolgins, Adam. *Rock Names from Abba to ZZ Top: How Rock Bands Got Their Names.* New York: Citadel, 1995. 252 pages. Approximately 50 line drawings throughout.

First published in 1993 and revised here, this clever book presents the history and evolution of hundreds of band names. While you may have known that Cream was so-titled because the three musicians considered themselves the "cream" of British blues players, you certainly didn't know that Bread arrived at its group name because the musicians were once caught in traffic behind a Wonderbread truck—or that the Pogues derived from *pogue mahone*, which in Gaelic means "kiss my arse." The kind of rock reference that should be encouraged: concise, informative, and fascinating.

Gray, Michael. *Bibliography of Discographies: Volume 3: Popular Music.* New York: R.R. Bowker & Company, 1983. 206 pages. Periodicals Cited. Index.

Unique guide to discographies in print, including journals, magazines, and books. Artists span pre-1955 popular music, rock, contemporary pop, bluegrass, hillbilly, country, show and film music, and folk, plus several useful label discographies (e.g., Chess). Both discographical sections of books and complete books are cited. Entries list author, title, year and, where relevant, page numbers. Handy, though dated.

Haggerty, Gary. *A Guide to Popular Music Reference Books: An Annotated Bibliography.* Westport, CT: Greenwood Press, 1995. 212 pages. Appendix A: Individual Discographies. Appendix B: Individual Bibliographies. Appendix C: Electronic Resources. Index.

Concise library edition guide to popular music literature, spanning jazz, rock, pop, blues, and country. The emphasis here is on non-artist titles—bibliographies, dictionaries, and encyclopedias; discographies; almanacs; yearbooks; etc.—although there are also appendixes covering discographies and bibliographies. The author includes general bibliographic data with ISBN number and Library of Congress Cataloguing number; this is followed by a brief, non-critical summary, with citations indicating magazine reviews at the end. For libraries with extensive music collections.

Hoffman, Frank and Cooper, B. Lee. *The Literature of Rock Vols. I-III.* Metuchen, NJ and London, England: Scarecrow Press, 1981 (vol. I); 1986 (vol. II); and 1995 (vol. III). Vol. 1: 580 pages; Vol II: 337 pages; Vol. III: 1,004 pages. Index.

Lists of books and magazine articles encompassing everything in pop music from rhythm and blues, to the beat era, to doo-wop, to British Invasion, to American renaissance (whatever that means) to special areas of music such as glitter/glam rock and Christian music. While the scope of this book is very broad—and it includes many hard-to-find articles—it's virtually impossible to find anything specific without trenching through the index. Worse, there are no descriptions for any of the works cited. Volume III, which spans 1984-1990 and includes "additional material for the period

1954-1983," is the only volume of the three that holds up today.

Leyser, Brady. J. *Rock Stars/Pop Stars: A Comprehensive Bibliography 1955-1994.* Westport, CT: Greenwood Press, 1994. 304 pages. Sources. Subject Index. Author Index. Title Index.

Yet another library edition bibliography from Greenwood (see Haggerty, above), this one is more focused on rock and has the benefit of reaching well into the 1990's. This volume lists raw bibliographic data (title, author, publisher, where published, year of publication, and when published) for books, which are divided into the following categories: bibliography, caricatures/cartoons, chronology, collectibles, concordances, correspondence, criticism, dictionaries/indexes/encyclopedias, discography, fiction, film, interviews, pictorials, song lyrics, writings, and a few others here and there. An easy-to-use laundry list of publication data related to rock and roll.

Marsh, Dave and Bernard, James. *The New Book of Rock Lists.* New York: Fireside (Simon & Schuster), 1994. 602 pages.

First published in 1981, this amazing compendium—with contents consisting of no less than eleven pages—includes chapters on wisdom, money, record companies, promotion, production companies, awards, firsts, criticism, art, film, and a vast range of other subjects. By their very nature, the lists are all over the place—from rock and roll photographers, to songs about The Beatles, to discredited theories ("rock died between 1959 and 1964"), to the greatest quintets (in which AC/DC is ranked above The Animals, The Band, and The Beach Boys!), to rockers who really did pump gas, to Max Weinberg's favorite drummers in bands (with Ringo Starr at the top of the list). While all of this offers much enjoyment, there's equally as much to frustrate rock fans: ludicrous criticism (Janis Joplin is identified as "not a great blues singer"); and flat-out errors (John Lennon is identified as the screamer in "Helter Skelter," when clearly it was Paul McCartney). Fortunately, the positive far outweighs the negative.

Schinder, Scott and the Editors of *Rolling Stone.* *Rolling Stone's Alternative Rock a Rama: An Outrageous Compendium of Facts, Fiction and*

Critiques of Alternative Rock. New York: Delta (Bantam Doubleday Dell), 1996. 492 pages. Index.

Perhaps to atone for shortchanging alternative music in *The New Rolling Stone Encyclopedia of Rock & Roll* (see Dictionaries and Encyclopedias: Romanowski), this chunky compendium from the editors of *Rolling Stone* includes everything bragged about in the subtitle and more: humorous lists of "supergroups we hope never happen"; trivia data such as five ex-Nirvana drummers excluding Dave Grohl; personal opinions from various experts on the most influential recordings and performances; and more. With solid contributions from Neil Strauss, Clinton Heylin, Ira Robbins, and many others, this handy book can be read, browsed, or used purely for reference information. For real gritty detail on the alternative attitude and message, this book will serve for years to come. One minor point: Joan Jett's list of favorite new bands won't mean squat to alternative fans.

Taylor, Paul. *Popular Music Since 1955: A Critical Guide to the Literature.* Boston, MA: G.K. Hall & Co., 1985. 536 pages. Periodicals. Glossary. Indexes: Author Index; Title Index; Subject Index. ((First published in Great Britain in 1985 by Mansell Publishing Limited.)

One of the better academic bibliographies of popular music (although not apparent it is a bibliography until the subtitle), with sections on general works, social/artistic aspects of popular music, etc., plus titles specifically connected to artists. Coverage spans rock, folk, and jazz and other areas of popular music recognized by the mid-1980's. Each entry, divided by category, includes author, title, publication data, ISBN number, and a brief, slightly critical blurb (only occasionally exceeding three sentences). This work is particularly strong on British publications, but is evidently only current through the early 1980's.

PICTORIALS

Byford, Phil. *The Boys Who Rock.* No city (Netherlands), 1982. 92 pages. 100 color photographs, covering every page.

Color photographs of about 50 rockers from AC/DC to Frank Zappa, with perhaps a paragraph of text about each. Why include Hall & Oates, Michael Schenker, and Saxon and none of The Beatles? Junk with a sequel, *The Girls Who Rock* (not found).

Drate, Spencer. Foreword by Roger Dean. *Rock Art, CDs, Albums & Posters*. Glen Cove, NY: PCB Books, 1993. 160 pages. Approximately 175 color and black-and-white reproductions of albums, CDs, and posters, covering nearly every page.

A tribute to the masters of rock art, this book is organized not by rock musician, but by the folks who painted, drew, photographed, sketched, designed, and/or assembled images for CD and record sleeves, as well as for posters and other items that have since become collectible. From Martyn Atkins' covers for alternative bands such as Depeche Mode, to Carol Bobolts' thoughtful photo of Tracy Chapman on her debut album, to the cartoon fantasies in Roger Dean's work for Yes, this book is a thoughtful and highly appealing survey of these much-neglected craftspeople. The screened photographs of the artists themselves are tastefully subdued. Well done.

Farren, Mick and Snow, George. *Rock N' Roll Circus: The Illustrated Rock Concert*. London: Big O Publishing Limited, 1978. 120 pages. Approximately 150 black-and-white illustrations, covering every page.

Don't be fooled by the title: This isn't about The Rolling Stones' recently released television performance. This awful book tries to do way too much all at once, chronicling festivals, musicians in studio, bands in performance, foibles, etc., and ends up simply sending the message that rock stars are screw-ups. The book stoops to an all-time low of sexism (true, it was the 1970's), with a two-page spread of naked groupies inside a chapter on female bands entitled "Old Ladies, Road Ladies, and Oh Shit I Forgot Your Name." Sleazy and avoidable.

Grushkin, Paul D. Artworks photographed by John Sievert. *The Art of Rock: Posters from Presley to Punk*. New York: Abbeville Press, 1987. Approximately 316 pages. Over three hundred color plates. The Poster Shops. "Tiny Folio" edition.

"A spectacular visual and oral history" that lives up to its billing. The posters really do span all of rock and roll history—that is, classic rock and roll: Otis Redding; the Ike and Tina

Revue; Dylan and Baez; The Beatles; Big Brother and the Holding Company; Jimi Hendrix (are you surprised?); The Rolling Stones (in the 1970's, perhaps the best period for their related art); and even a few 1980's groups, such as The Ramones. Each work includes title, artist, and the show for which it was exhibited. A pint-sized tribute to rock's artistic giants: David Singer, Stanley Mouse, Carl Lundgren, Rick Griffin, et. al.

Hammond, Harry and Mankowitz, Gered. *Pop Shots*. New York: Harper & Row, 1984. 160 pages. Approximately 150 color and black-and-white photographs throughout.

Harry Hammond was a staff photographer for Britain's *New Musical Express*; Gered Mankowitz was a key figure in rock art, having photographed over 50 album covers and snapped seminal photographs for magazines all over the world. This book may have too much of the "fuddy-duddy factor"—namely, Hammond's early shots of Sinatra, Crosby, and the Poni-Tails—but picks up with The Beatles, The Stones, Kate Bush, and others. Most of the shots seem too posed by 1990's standards and are not glossy enough to catch your attention. Of historical importance, but flattened by larger, more recent pictorial works.

No author. *Rolling Stone: The Photographs*. New York: Fireside (Simon & Schuster, Inc.), 1989. One hundred oversized color and black-and-white photographs.

This collection of eye-catching photographs, culled from the covers, interiors, and related photo sessions of *Rolling Stone* magazine, spans the realm of American pop culture: rock stars, film actors, and politicians, as well as notable writers, artists, and comedians. Some of the world-famous photographers whose works are presented here include Richard Avedon, Herb Greene, and Annie Leibovitz. Flipping the pages, you can see John Lennon crouched naked on top of a fully-clad Yoko; Pete Townshend leaning his head on his bloodied hand; Brian Wilson standing, flab-flexed on a piano stool; and a ghastly Alice Cooper with a snake wrapped around his head. As a coffee-table book, this one pretty much has something for everyone's taste. Who would think that in the same book you would have a choice of nude photos of Janis Joplin, Lisa Bonet, and Nastassja Kinski?

No author. *Sex & Drugs & Rock & Roll*. London: Bobcat Books (division of Book Sales Limited), no date. 192 pages. Approximately 400 black-and-white photographs, covering every page.

The quintessential rock orgy book, this pictorial consists of carnal and druggie photos of rockers from the 1950's to the 90's. Yes, you can find some chesty women from Elvis films, but what most eyes will turn to are the shots of John & Yoko, Mick & Jerry, et. al. blissfully in the buff, as well as some plain crude shots of artists such as Patti Smith, Angus Young, and The Dead Boys (who try to hide their penises between their legs to make it seem as if they have female genitalia!). Needless to say, there are also many spotlight hounds (the Knebworth Streaker) and giddy groupies willing to show skin for the camera. Good for a tingle.

Pollock, Bruce and Wagman, John. Foreword by Pete Fornatale. *The Face of Rock & Roll: Images of a Generation*. New York: Holt, Rinehart and Winston, 1978. 184 pages. Approximately 200 color reproductions of album covers. Index of Artists. Index of Photographers, Illustrators, and Designers.

Very, very 1970's book of rock and roll covers, with some accompanying text. There's a chunk on Dylan, a section on The Beatles (which is really solo), and lots of other trendsetting designs from the Everly Brothers to *Saturday Night Fever*. A couple of pictures are needlessly repeated in different sections. There is something here to bring almost anybody back to the days of albums past, but who is asking to go?

Russell, Ethan A. *Dear Mr. Fantasy: Diary of a Decade*. Boston: Houghton Mifflin, 1985. 256 pages. Approximately 200 glossy color and black-and-white photographs throughout.

A collection of snapshots taken by professional photographer Ethan Russell, who worked closely with John and Yoko in the late- 1960's, but also captured The Rolling Stones, The Doors, Mary Hopkin, Linda Ronstadt, and many others. Since Russell was present for the filming of both *The Rolling Stones' Rock and Roll Circus* (never aired) and *Let It Be*, this book is probably of key interest to both Stones and Beatles fans. Many of the pieces stand the test of time.

Sandison, David. *Rock Visions: The Art of David Oxtoby*. New York: Dutton, 1988. 80 pages. Approximately 85 original color and black-and-white paintings, drawings, lithographs, and watercolors, covering every page.

A retrospective on the magic of David Oxtoby, noted English painter. Oxtoby mingled with artists such as Roy Orbison, Rod Stewart, and Elton John, and clearly had an eye for capturing the rock spirit and attitude. His studies of Carl Perkins, Chuck Berry, Buddy Holly, and Otis Redding are nothing short of brilliant. (His Daltrey, however, looks too much like a caricature for this reviewer's taste.) Many of these portraits should be hanging in The Rock and Roll Hall of Fame (if they aren't already).

White, Timothy. *Rock Stars*. New York: Stewart, Tabori & Chang, 1984. 288 pages. Approximately 150 full-page glossy color and black-and-white photographs throughout.

The opening color pages of The Beach Boys, The Stones, The Beatles, and Elvis tell you right away what you're in for: a high-quality glossy photo book, starting from rock's roots. In fact, author Timothy White has provided a wonderful section on "ancestors," which traces back to Robert Johnson and then includes brief profiles of Chuck Berry, Ray Charles, Little Richard, Sam Cooke, et. al. A chapter on "descendants" spotlights The Beatles, Jim Morrison, The Stones, Bowie, The Sex Pistols, etc. The pages on "inheritors" is an early 1980's fluke, with coverage leaning toward the pop side with artists such as Annie Lennox, Prince, and Michael Jackson. There are many omissions here—from Orbison to Joplin to U2—but the photo selection helps forget some of the scattershot coverage.

Wolman, Barry. Preface by Jann Wenner. *Classic Rock & Other Rollers*. Santa Rosa, CA: Square Books, 1992. 142 pages. Approximately 145 glossy black-and-white photographs throughout.

Collection of photos by Barry Wolman, *Rolling Stone*'s first photographer. Once again, here are the legends from the late 1960's to the end of the following decade—Janis Joplin, Pink Floyd, Jimi Hendrix, Phil Spector—as well as a few country greats, groupies, and literary figures. Not as collectible a package as works by Linda McCartney (see McCartney, Paul: Written Works), but attractive and well-executed nonetheless.

Woodward, Fred (Editor); DeCurtis, Anthony (Text). *Rolling Stone Images of Rock & Roll*. New York: Little, Brown and Company, 1995. Unpaginated (approximately 216 pages). Approximately 200 color and black-and-white photographs, covering every page.

From the two endpaper images (both Johnny Cash and Kurt Cobain giving the photographer the finger), rock lovers know they are in for a visual treat. From the youthful, raw sexuality of The Beatles to the dangerous, sweaty posturings of Elvis, Jim Morrison, and Jerry Lee Lewis, this book is crammed with energetic and graphically satisfying portraits of top rockers—some of whom are very close up and/or half naked. Work by Dennis Keeley, Annie Leibovitz, Bob Seidemann, Astrid Kirchherr, Dennis Hopper, and numerous others help put the balls back in rock and roll. And dig Alice Cooper with a tarantula on his cheek!

QUIZBOOKS AND QUOTEBOOKS

Cohen, Scott. *Yakety Yak*. New York: Fireside (Simon & Schuster), 1994. 192 pages. Approximately 175 black-and-white photographs throughout.

The sell-line for this book reads "The midnight confessions and revelations of thirty-seven rock stars and legends," but this really is just a lively compendium of quotes and personal tastes of randomly selected artists. It's wonderful to see that author Scott Cohen picked a handful of poetic stars (Patti Smith, Lou Reed, and Leonard Cohen), but it's a puzzle how he arrived at some timeless rockers (Neil Young, Bob Dylan, James Brown) while barely touching British Invasion acts. In spite of all this, there are wonderful quotes from neglected artists such as Screaming Jay Hawkins and Lenny Kravitz. Idiosyncratic.

Foster, Ron. *Pure Gold: Rock & Roll Trivia Questions*. Austin, TX: Historical Publications, 1995. 192 pages. Approximately 75 black-and-white photographs throughout. Index.

This quizbook offers more of a tease to rock fans than either work attributed to Presley Love (see below). The questions are funnier ("Who was Mr. Nudy?") and the suggested answers (to a different question: "This is obviously a trick question—good grief") more cleverly constructed. Foster actually seems to have had *fun* putting this together: Points are

awarded for answering questions correctly, while scorecards (with handicaps provided based on lower age!) tabulate how well you've done. Fluffy sidebars (the author's interaction with various artists, such as The Shirelles) and photos, although not reproduced well, appear throughout. Light entertainment.

Kohut, Joe and Kohut, John J. *Rock Talk: The Great Rock and Roll Quote Book*. London: Faber and Faber, 1994. 216 pages. Sources. Index.

Rock quotes divided into thematic sections such as the business, critics, festivals, women in rock, and several others. The quotes have been chosen based on their shock/humor value (from a fan who sent Mick Jagger a piece of chewed gum: "Please Mick. Chew some and send back") but others have been culled from other quotebooks (Johnny Cash: "Prison audiences are the best audiences in the world"). The yellow cover is terrible, and there are no photographs; still, out of the 600 quotes, there are about 50-75 gems.

Love, Presley. *The Classic Rock Quiz Book: From The Animals to Frank Zappa*. New York: Carol, 1995. 292 pages.

Non-illustrated trivia book for fans of classic rock artists from the 1950's to present. The first section covers groups A to Z, with typically five questions for run-of-the-mill artists (America) and up to 20 for the top brass (The Beatles). The second section features questions about lyrics and song titles. All questions are multiple choice, although many are so easy (e.g., "Who was The Beatles' manager?") any rock fan over 12 would be able to answer them without such assistance. Only for beginners.

Love, Presley. *Rock Lyrics Quiz Book*. New York: Carol, 1995. 248 pages.

So you think you know the words to your favorite rock songs? This book puts you to the test. Through sections spanning Elvis, The Beatles, early rock, American rock, the British Invasion, dance/party rock, and various other topics, this book probes your knowledge through various multiple choice and bonus questions. If you have any difficulty with these relatively easy questions, you should probably expand your record collection immediately. If you only own CDs and not any records, you've discovered the problem already. Also note the later quiz book (see above) attributed to Presley Love.

Robbins, Ira. *Test Your Rock I.Q: the 60's: Folk Rock and Acid Rock, Bubblegum and Woodstock: 250 Mindbenders from Rock's Glory Decade.* New York and Boston: Little, Brown and Company, 1993. 122 pages. Approximately 25 pen-and-ink drawings throughout.

Light fun for fans of 1960's rock, with 250 quizzes divided into sections such as "Previously Known As" (original band names), The Beatles, British Invasion, San Francisco, and more. Questions vary in format from multiple choice, to matching up the columns, to simple question-and-answer. Robbins has assembled a quotebook that will be too easy for experts, but challenging to those who only recognize Eric Clapton as the guy who did some soft songs on MTV's "Unplugged." The cute drawings were created by Nick DeBenedetto.

Worth, Fred L. *Rock Facts: The Ultimate Book of Rock and Roll Trivia.* New York: Facts On File, Inc., 1985. 416 pages. 50 black-and-white photographs throughout. Index.

The sell line reads: "The inside story of over 1,500 of rock and roll's best kept secrets!" Worth explains in his introduction that this work is neither an encyclopedia nor a compilation of biographies, but rather, a compilation of stuff one wouldn't find in other books. The book is organized alphabetically and includes entries on song titles, group names, and unusual subjects ("children of rock stars"). While some tidbits are very intriguing (Grace Slick is a descendant of John Cabell Breckinridge, the United States' youngest vice president at 36), criteria for inclusion is fuzzy (how could there not be separate entries for The Doors or Jim Morrison?) and some of the information is either too obvious (that Arlo Guthrie's song "Alice's Restaurant" and film of the same name are autobiographical) or too old news (Paul McCartney owns rights to 90 percent of Buddy Holly's titles) to make this worth seeking out.

RECORD GUIDES

Christgau, Robert. *Robert Christgau: Rock Albums of the 70's: A Critical Guide.* New York: Da Capo, 1981. 472 pages. Rock and Roll: A Basic Library.

As music critic for *The Village Voice*, Robert Christgau was one of rock's most recognized and authoritative voices. In 50 words or less, he reviews and rates all releases from the 1970's. It almost goes without saying that this is quality work and has historical significance; however, since it doesn't reflect CD packages (especially for remixes, sound quality, etc.), it's unlikely to be of that much help for the serious fan. It also seems that, using today's perspective, Christgau has deducted many more grades from his original reviews than he's added on.

Christgau, Robert. *Robert Christgau's Price Guide: The 1980's.* New York: Da Capo, 1994. 520 pages. Appendices.

Village Voice critic Robert Christgau follows up his work on the 1970's (see above) with a similar treatment on the 1980's. Once again, Christgau sums up his opinions on some 3,000 albums—about 50 words apiece—with expansive coverage of rock, pop, country, blues, and other areas. Christgau doesn't list song line-ups or musicians, but does provide letter ratings and record labels. For the general audience, Christgau is on-target panning The Rolling Stones' *Undercover* and, to my pleasant surprise, awarding John and Yoko's *Milk and Honey* a solid "A." Christgau does for records what Leonard Maltin does for movies.

DeCurtis, Anthony and Henke, James; with George-Warren, Holly (editors). *Rolling Stone Album Guide: The Definitive Guide to the Best of Rock, Rap, Jazz, Blues, Country, Soul, Folk & Gospel.* New York: Random House, 1992. 838 pages.

Originally published in 1979 as *The Rolling Stone Record Guide* (with Dave Marsh as editor), this one-time classic is really an all-new book, with band descriptions and critical essays rewritten and updated for the 1990's. Many critics and rock fans have already pointed out the sad fact that this book slights many alternative/indie/grunge bands; however, one cannot ignore the fact that the format of the book—with albums and star ratings on top—is the prototype for all album guides. The band star delineations in this edition are a puzzle, often giving greatest hits compendiums (such as those for The Doors) higher marks than the original classic albums. Since this book has not quite caught up with the CD age, it fails to live up to its hype as "invaluable" and "indispensable."

Erlewine, Michael; Bogadanov, Vladimir; and Woodstra, Chris. *All Music Guide to Rock: The Best CDs, Albums, and Tapes*. San Francisco, CA: Miller Freeman, 1995. 974 pages. Artist Index.

A gargantuan reference for the serious, eclectic music buff, this book includes artist/album reviews not dissimilar in format to *The Rolling Stone Album Guide* (see DeCurtis, above), with star ratings for albums and concise career summaries. In addition to the A to Z artist listing, this work contains weighty sections in the back on rock styles, influences, and reference material (producers, bootlegs, fanzines, books, catalogs, magazines, etc.). Incisive and thorough, without anything too one-sided to complain about. Remarkably all-encompassing.

Guterman, Jimmy. *The Best Rock and Roll Records of All Time: A Fan's Guide to the Stuff You Love*. New York: Carol, 1992. 208 pages. Approximately 75 black-and-white photographs throughout.

While this collection is better than Guterman's lament for the "worst" records (see below), this is still a haphazard high school list of titles. He considers Rod Stewart's *Every Picture Tells a Story* the best album *ever*? Over *Exile on Main Street* and *Please Please Me*? You know you're in trouble when The Kinks' *Greatest Hits* is included in the top hundred, but not one of their album masterpieces, such as *The Village Green Preservation Society*. Meanwhile, there's nothing from Pink Floyd, Led Zeppelin, The Doors, or for that matter, any 1980's and 90's bands. Any author producing a book of this kind deserves some leeway for personal taste and idiosyncrasy, but this only shows a complete blindness to reality.

Guterman, Jimmy and O'Donnell, Owen. *The Worst Rock and Roll Records of All Time: A Fan's Guide to the Stuff You Love to Hate*. New York: Carol, 1991. 254 pages. Approximately 75 black-and-white photographs throughout.

Iconoclastic dogma from Guterman and O'Donnell, in which the authors attack much-beloved classic rockers with little cause—and even less effect. It's easy to agree with the authors that Crosby, Stills, Nash and Young's *American Dream* is by far their worst product and that Bruce Willis' *The Return of Bruno* is pure drivel. But U2's *The Unforgettable Fire*? The Doors' *Alive, She Cried*, and Blood, Sweat and Tears' self-titled album? Anything by the Village People, Bay City Rollers, Menudo, and even Styx would have been more suited to this kind of selection. And hasn't Paul McCartney suffered enough attacks to not warrant being dumped in the has-been pile? Unfunky.

No author. *Schwann CD Review Digest 1996 Annual*. Santa Fe, NM: Schwann, 1996. 812 pages. Show Composer Index. Title Index. Reviewer Index.

Massive work, organized by artists, that culls quotes about their respected records from magazine and fanzine reviews. Each album includes further information, such as catalog number, label, musician line-ups, and, in many instances, songs appearing. A special feature is the book's attention to bootlegs and rare releases. A strong, unbiased reference source. Since the book comes out annually, be certain you are purchasing an edition that has the reviews you want.

Robbins, Ira A. *The Trouser Press Record Guide: The Ultimate Guide to Alternative Music*. New York: Collier (Macmillan Books), 1991. 764 pages. Sources.

The fourth edition of this classic, which was first published in 1985. If you are into alternative music and only have the *Spin Alternative Press Guide* (see Dictionaries and Encyclopedias: Westband) on your shelf, hit the bookstore immediately. With over 2,500 artists critiqued and 9,500 albums, CDs, and cassettes reviewed, *The Trouser Press Record Guide* is the best retrospective of the alternative music scene ever published. Author Ira A. Robbins provides detailed coverage of the most famous (Nirvana) and the most obscure (KMFDM), with hard-to-find data on CD availability, format, release date, and country of origin, as well as highly entertaining (and critical) histories worked into the album commentaries. For Adam Ant: "After that triumph [*Friend or Foe* LP], time for another bad album? No problem! *Strip* is pathetic." Star ratings are not indicated on top, but that would have been silly anyway; you get the gist of it from the summary. Highly recommended, if only to read about a band called X—that's not the one based in L.A. with Exene Cervenka. Past due for an update.

Sinclair, David. *Rock on CD: The Essential Guide.* London: Kalie Cathie Limited, 1992. 464 pages. Bibliography. Index.

Decidedly incomplete and dated guide to rock music available on CD. Where are The Kinks? Janis Joplin? The format is way too British for an American market; instead of a heading for "where formed," it's actually written as "convened"! The reviews of the CDs themselves are superficial. Non-essential.

Williams, Paul. *Rock and Roll: The 100 Best Singles.* New York: Carroll & Graf, 1993. 240 pages.

Williams, now back in place producing *Crawdaddy!* (see Magazines), has pulled together his choice 100 singles from 1937 (Robert Johnson) to 1991 (Nirvana). One has to forgive bizarre selections like Tears for Fears' 1984 hit "Shout," but laud choices such as "Waterloo Sunset" from The Kinks, "Good Vibrations" from The Beach Boys, and "Thank You (Falettinme Be Mice Elf Again)" from Sly and the Family Stone. And who would ever have thought that The Sex Pistols would make a published list of best singles? Williams is unmatched in his ability to pinpoint the mysterious "hook" that makes a song distinctive and sets it above the average song. A connoisseur's dream.

SPECIAL SUBJECTS

CONCERT EVENTS/FESTIVALS

(See also Part Two: Publications on Artists A to Z: Geldof, Bob)

Fuller, John G. *Are the Kids All Right? The Rock Generation and Its Hidden Death Wish.* New York: Times Books, 1981. 262 pages.

An analytical history of violence and self-destruction as linked to rock and roll. Fuller's work deals in particular with the hysteria at The Who's 1979 concert at Riverfront Stadium in Cincinnati, which resulted in several deaths. Fuller apparently doesn't know much about the groups he is writing about (Kiss is described as "inappropriately named"), and his theory that rock is *only* about death is somewhat offensive. Fuller ignores the fact that the teenage need for rebellion may simply be an unleashing of anger against the older generation, not necessarily a call for suicide. No, the kids aren't all right: after rock came grunge.

Hillmore, Peter. Introduction by Bob Geldof. *Live Aid: World-Wide Concert Book.* 192 pages. Approximately 250 color and 75 black-and-white photographs throughout.

A celebrity feast of the famous Live Aid mega-concert of July 13, 1985. All proceeds of the book and the event went towards African famine relief. Every photo contains a clever time clock in the upper right indicating exactly when each artist performed (and thus the moment of the photograph). There are some preparation photos, as well as posed shots and backstage giggles from performers such as Paul McCartney and David Bowie. The Who and Led Zeppelin reunions and Tina Turner's scorching performance in the sun are among the highlights.

Makower, Joel. *Woodstock: The Oral History.* New York: Doubleday (Bantam Doubleday Dell), 1989. 362 pages. Approximately 150 black-and-white photographs throughout. Appendix. Index.

Ill-conceived tribute to the Woodstock Festival, with special attention devoted to the four visionary organizers/producers: Michael Lang, John Roberts, Artie Kornfeld, and Joel Rosenman. Their reflections are intermingled with oral history from Woodstock laborers and attendees. Unfortunately, the musicians interviewed (e.g., Richie Havens) are few and far between and are afforded little book space. The index is one of the worst ever rendered.

Rosenman, Joel; Roberts, John; and Pilpel, Robert. *Young Men With Unlimited Capital.* New York and London: Harcourt Brace Jovanovich, 1974. 214 pages.

The story of three men—Joel Rosenman, John Roberts, and Robert Pilpel—who funded the Woodstock festival in 1969. These guys talk about themselves, talk about each other, and then allow room for others involved to talk about them. What's with all the talking? A boring play-by-play of the back office happenings that simply doesn't hold a candle to what transpired on stage. Dullstock.

Selvin, Joel. Photos by Marshall, Jim. *Monterey Pop.* San Francisco: Chronicle Books, 1992. 106 pages. Approximately 100 glossy black-and-white photographs throughout; one glossy 16-page color insert.

Twenty-fifth anniversary celebration of the Monterey Festival, which ushered in the Summer of Love in 1967 and was an artistic breakthrough for a number of performers.

From June 16-18, 1967, diverse artists such as Eric Burdon and The Animals, Simon and Garfunkel, The Mamas and the Papas, Buffalo Springfield, The Who, Otis Redding, Jimi Hendrix, and several others made history. And let's not forget Janis Joplin who, with Big Brother and the Holding Company, virtually stole the show. Contains some excellent portraits of the musicians, with engaging commentary by Selvin. A solid tribute.

Spitz, Bob. *Barefoot in Babylon: The Creation of the Woodstock Music Festival.* New York: W.W. Norton & Company, 1989. 516 pages. Twenty Years Later. Index.

This epic novel on the evolution of the Woodstock Festival was first published in 1979 and updated for the 20th anniversary of the event. Spitz's descriptions of the burdensome planning, fundraising, and artist headhunting are compelling and highly amusing. In one memorable passage, production manager John Morris wears Pete Townshend down and hires The Who to play at the event for a paltry $12,500. (Blood, Sweat and Tears received $15,000.) The drugs, sex, nudity, mud, and miles of bewildered flower children are not the focus here; this is strictly a tale of the preparation leading up to a major event. No photos included in this edition.

Young, Jean and Lang, Michael. *Woodstock Festival Remembered.* New York: Ballantine, 1979. 128 pages. Approximately 150 black-and-white photographs throughout; one 48-page glossy color insert.

A visual document of the Woodstock Festival, at last told in participation with the man who did most of the footwork for the management team: Michael Lang. This book does not pretend to be a minute-by-minute account of the event or a study of its significance; it's simply Lang's reflections on Woodstock some ten years after (no pun intended). The real draw, of course, are the behind-the-scenes photos of performers: Janis Joplin, Mountain, Arlo Guthrie, Blood, Sweat and Tears, Crosby, Stills, Nash and Young, etc. As expected, lots of mud, nudity, rain-drenched crowds, and, by the end, garbage. Of interest for the little details, such as the story behind why Iron Butterfly didn't perform at the festival (and why Lang didn't care).

FILM

Burt, Rob. *Rock and Roll in the Movies.* Poole, Dorset (England): Blandford Press, 1983. 208 pages. Approximately 300 black-and-white photographs throughout; one 16-page color insert. Index.

Photo study not only of rock films, but also of those cinematic landmarks such as *Rebel Without a Cause* and *High School Confidential* that inspired rockers and teens for generations. The book, divided into sections on image, heavy petting, Presley, Brit films, beach films, The Beatles, and the late 1960's concert documentaries, continues up through The Who's *The Kids Are Alright* in 1979. If you can deal with shots from films starring Elvis, Tommy Steele, and Cliff Richard—and couldn't care less about film and video in the years since 1983—this book is for you. Most people would cringe at the photo spreads of Henry Winkler from *Lords of Flatbush* and "Happy Days."

Crenshaw, Marshall. *Hollywood Rock: A Guide to Rock `N' Roll in the Movies.* New York: HarperCollins, 1994. 352 pages. Approximately 100 black-and-white photographs throughout. Appendix: More Rock Films; Concert Films and Rockumentary; Rock Actors Filmography. Cameo Glossary. Where to Find It. Performer Index.

Musician Marshall Crenshaw not only has had a noteworthy musical career, he also is something of a student of rock and roll. Here Crenshaw has created an encyclopedic review guide of rock-related films, with entries on all of your favorites from *The Buddy Holly Story* to *True Stories.* Each A to Z entry includes: ratings for music, attitude, and fun (one to five stars); a cast list; studio; producer; director; screenwriter; running time; and mention of whether it's color or black-and-white. Adding depth to the entries are extra tidbits on key scenes, lines, cameos, and songs. While the information is accurate, some of the reviews (written by reviewers, not Crenshaw) are skewed—four stars for music/attitude/fun for *Great Balls of Fire* but only two for all the same categories for *Alice's Restaurant*? Overall, however, this is the most reflective summary of rock celluloid yet produced.

Jenkinson, Philip and Werner, Alan. *Celluloid Rock: Twenty Years of Movie Rock.* London: Lorrimer Publishing, 1974. 136 pages. Approximately

100 black-and-white photographs throughout; one four-page color photo insert. Filmography. Index.

Lesser treatment of rock films, with emphasis placed on all of the wrong movies; some truly major ones (*A Hard Day's Night*) are given short shrift. The photos are cropped so poorly that Eric Burdon (in *Monterey Pop*) is virtually decapitated. The first ten minutes of *Beach Blanket Bingo* hold more entertainment value.

Sandahl, Linda J. *Rock Films: A Viewer's Guide to Three Decades of Musicals, Concerts, Documentaries, and Soundtracks 1955-1986.* New York: Facts On File, Inc., 1987. 240 pages. Two hundred over-sized photographs. Index of Film Titles. Index of Names. Index of Song Titles. (Published in Great Britain by Blandford [Cassell] as *Encyclopedia of Rock Music on Film*).

Coffee-table reference that is fun to browse; after doing so, however, one is left with the sad feeling that all rock films are truly dumb and fans even dumber for enjoying them. Each listing supplies information such as year, studio, running time, director, producer, screenwriter(s), musical performer(s), songs performed, soundtrack title, and label, followed by a rather amateurish and under-written review/summary. The entire write-up for the Elvis film *Come and Go* reads: "Here El[sic] is a treasure-hunting deep-sea diver. Pretty poor cast, feeble music."

WOMEN AND ROCK

Betrock, Alan. *Girl Groups: The Story of a Sound.* New York: Delilah, 1982. 176 pages. Approximately 175 black-and-white photographs, covering nearly every page.

Before feminists can load their artillery to complain about the subject (and title) of this book, Alan Betrock defends his work with an immediate explanation/disclaimer. He explains that the book is not about "women in rock" or "girls in rock," it's the story of the styles and accomplishments of female singing groups of the 1950's and 60's—e.g., The Chantels, The Shirelles, The Crystals, The Marvelettes, The Ronettes, Martha Reeves and the Vandellas, and, of course, The Supremes. Betrock supplies an adequate history of these groups and their influence, as well as details of their interaction with their producers, songwriters, and collabo-

rators. Features some excellent photos of ever-grinning performers, but also some unsightly (and phony) reproductions of old albums in the corners.

Evans, Liz. *Women, Sex and Rock and Roll.* London: Pandora (HarperCollins), 1994. 276 pages. Approximately 20 black-and-white photographs throughout.

Fifteen women rockers speak out about their careers, as well as their dealings in the predominately male music industry. From veterans (Marianne Faithfull) to contemporary stars (Kat Bjelland Gray of Babes in Toyland), these rockers expose a tradition of hypocrisy and stereotypes. As Dolores O'Riordan of the Cranberries remarks, "I take the piss out of being a sexy woman." Candid and refreshing, though not quite as much fun as Juno's work (see below).

Garr, Gillian G. Preface by Yoko Ono. *She's a Rebel: The History of Women in Rock and Roll.* Seattle: Seal Press, 1993. 468 pages. Two eight-page photo inserts. Index. (Published in Great Britain by Blandford [Cassell].)

This is the first book by Garr, a freelance journalist and senior editor of the rock music paper *The Rocket.* Here she adroitly writes about a much-neglected subject in the field of pop music: the female rocker. The narrative begins with Willie Mae ("Big Mama") Thornton (author of Janis Joplin's "Ball and Chain" and the first to record "Hound Dog," which later became a classic for Elvis) and carries the history from the so-called "girl groups" of the late 1950's to rockers in the 90's. One might question the lack of blues/jazz background orientation prior to the 1950's and the omission of a few rock queens (Stevie Nicks, for example), but these are minor complaints.

Juno, Andrea (editor). *Angry Women in Rock: Volume 1.* New York: Juno Books, 1996. 224 pages. Approximately 250 black-and-white photographs, graphics, and drawings, covering every page. Healing Prayer Borders.

With a title like that, does a man dare open this book and scan the pages? This ultra-hip work provides profiles of legends and cutting-edge women in rock, including Chrissie Hynde, Joan Jett, Jarboe, Fanny, Candice, and many others. Each artist section includes a lengthy interview, a discography, and a rundown on the performer's musical equipment. If you have any doubt as to whether these women mean business, check out the various photos of women proudly waving phallic symbols. A gutsy, attractive volume, with more titles on the way.

Katz, Susan. *Superwomen of Rock.* New York: Grosset & Dunlap, 1978. 136 pages. One 12-page black-and-white photo insert.

Profiles of a half dozen rocking ladies of the 1970's: Debby Boone, Olivia Newton-John, Rita Coolidge, Linda Ronstadt, Steve Nicks, and Carly Simon. For the time capsule.

No author. *New Women in Rock.* New York: Delilah, 1982. 96 pages. Approximately 125 color and black-and-white photographs throughout.

Raucous portraits of 70 rock stars up through the early 1980's, with lots of busy photos that fall somewhere between Katz's "superwomen" of rock image (see above) and Juno's ballsy "women are rock conquerors" ideal (see above). The major problem with this work is the implication in the title that it only includes "new" women when, in fact, veterans Bette Midler, Patti Smith, and Marianne Faithfull are prominently featured. Still, if you're a fan of Danielle Dax of the Lemon Kittens, Gaye Advert of the Adverts, and Lydia Lunch, you might want to give a look. At least women of the Debby Boone and Marie Osmond variety are not to be found herein.

O'Brien, Lucy. *She Bop: The Definitive History of Women in Rock, Pop, and Soul.* New York and London: Penguin, 1996. 466 pages. Approximately 75 black-and-white photographs throughout.

A narrative history of women in pop music, starting with the roots in the blues and continuing on through the jazz age. O'Brien fills in some gaps from Garr's work (see above) and, in fact, writes more fluidly. O'Brien not only takes readers further into the worlds of 1950's dream babes (Dusty Springfield), 60's rock chicks (Janis Joplin), 70's punksters (Patti Smith), 80's media manipulators (Madonna), and 90's anything-goes players (Courtney Love), she also tackles issues such as lesbianism, the true story behind women and reggae, and the accomplishments of women as folkies. As valuable as Garr's book.

Orloff, Katherine. *Rock 'N Roll Woman.* Los Angeles: Nash Publishing, 1974. 198 pages. Approximately 30 full-page black-and-white photographs throughout.

Interviews with a dozen rocking women from the early 1970's, with a smattering of background biography provided by the author. Some of the artists are barely memories today (e.g., Nicole Barclay, Toni Brown, Terry Garthwaite), while others (e.g., Bonnie Raitt, Linda Ronstadt, Carly Simon) have since broadened their appeal and musical legacy. In her explanation for how women were selected for inclusion, Orloff brands Carole King "a housewife who writes songs" and doesn't even mention Tina Turner. Not terribly useful.

Raphael, Amy. Foreword by Deborah Harry. *Never Mind the Bullocks: Women Rewrite Rock.* London: Virago Press, 1995. 242 pages. Approximately 12 black-and-white photographs throughout. Bibliography.

A collection of interviews with contemporary rockers, not unlike Evans' work (see above). This time, the subjects are Courtney Love; Sonya Aurora Madan and Debbie Smith (Echobelly); Bjork; Nina Gordon and Louise Post (Veruca Salt); Gina Birch (Raincoats); Kim Gordon (Sonic Youth); Ellyott Dragon (Sister George); Huggy Bear; Tanya Donelly (Belly); Pam Hogg (Doll); Kristin Hersh; and Liz Phair. Raphael's introductions and passages leading into the interviews are clumsily written, if enthusiastic. Readers would do best to ignore them entirely and skip to the words uttered by the performers. Courtney Love: "When Tatum O'Neal got an Oscar, I was fucking jealous." Since there isn't much in the way of discographical and biographical material, this is only suited to those researching the aforementioned artists.

Shevey, Sandra. *Ladies of Pop Rock.* New York: Scholastic, 1971. 112 pages. Approximately 50 black-and-white photographs throughout.

A combination of narrative history with profiles of several key rockers. Blow the dust off this educational publication if you need commentary on Buffy Sainte-Marie, Melanie, Bonnie Bramlett, Florence LaRue Gordon, and Roslyn Kind. Otherwise, don't unbury the dead.

MAGAZINES

Acoustic Guitar. The String Letter Press, Publishers, 412 Red Hill Avenue #1, San Anselmo, CA 94960. Published bimonthly. Averages 114 pages. Black-and-white illustrations; some color in ads.

Complete guide to modern acoustic guitar playing that spans all areas of contemporary music, preeminently rock, but also country, blues, jazz, and folk. Includes music sheets, playing tips (for beginner and pro), artist profiles, product reviews, occasional book reviews, and classifieds.

The American Music Press. 325 10th Street, San Francisco, CA 94103. Published monthly. Averages 46 pages (oversized). Black-and-white photographs throughout.

"Northern California's free music paper" covers all of the San Francisco rock scene and some major contemporary bands. Includes local and international news, artist profiles, CD reviews, local gigs, and countless classifieds.

A.P. Alternative Press. P.O. Box 17136, N. Hollywood, CA 91615-9817. Published 12 times a year. Averages 120 pages. Color and black-and-white illustrations throughout. Often comes with a cassette.

Subtitled "New Music Now." Contains new alternative releases (artist, project, label), rock news, music reviews, an "in literature" page, and some chart information. Staple artists include Nirvana, The Cure, Smashing Pumpkins, Counting Crows, Blind Lemon, Nick Cave, and Sonic Youth. Lots of coverage of newcomers, though veterans such as Chrissie Hynde and Kiss appear in the pages.

The Aquarian Weekly. Arts Weekly, 7 Oak Place, Montclair, NJ 07042. Published weekly. Averages 65 pages (oversized). Black-and-white photographs throughout.

Underground news source that's been around since 1969; the bannerline reads "rock and roll freedom now." Touches on rap, hip hop, country, and other areas, but really focuses on standard rock and roll, New Wave, punk, and indie music. Staples: U2, Lollapalooza, Liquid Jesus. Contains special Jerseybeat sections.

Bass Frontiers. Information Revolution. 6739 San Acer Way, Rio Linda, CA 95673. Published bimonthly. Averages 58 pages. Color and black-and-white photographs throughout.

Magazine that emphasizes rock bassists (Geddy Lee, Gene Simmons, et. al.), but also covers "session aces" and jazz legends. Sections include news, product updates, reviews, classifieds, and profiles.

Bassics. 924 Sea Cliff Drive, Carlsbad, CA 92009. Published three times a year. Averages 46 pages. Black-and-white photographs throughout.

"The magazine for the modern bassist" contains features on hot bassists, reviews (recordings, products, books), and departments (news, classified, etc.). Covers all musical areas.

Bass Player. Miller Freeman, Inc., P.O. Box 57324, Boulder, CO 80322-7324. Published monthly. Averages 96 pages. Color and black-and-white photos throughout.

Magazine for the bass player and bass lover, with emphasis on rock artists (Geddy Lee of Rush, Nikki Sixx of Motley Crue) and talented side players (Hutch Hutchinson, Bonnie Raitt's bassist). Some coverage of Latin music, country, and jazz. Features include profiles on bass legends, essays on new trends and artists, and lessons from pros. Also includes bass news, product and gear profiles, workshops (for beginners and more advanced players), chord charts, reviews, classifieds, and more.

Billboard. Subscription Dept. P.O. Box 2011, Marion, OH 43306-2111. Published weekly. Averages 110 pages (oversized). Color and black-and-white photographs throughout.

"The international newsweekly of music, video and home entertainment" lists awards, sales, company mergers, etc., as well as weekly results on chart hits, CD's, radio airplay, and video rentals and sales. All areas of music are covered: classical, country, jazz, R&B, dance, Latin, rap, album ("classic") rock, and adult contemporary. Also has exclusives on the international scene: tour grosses, charts, corporate news, and more. Special columns include "Words and Music" (mostly publishing rights) and "Chart Beat" by Fred Bronson. Timothy White is *Billboard* magazine's Editor-in-Chief.

B-Side. P.O. Box 1860, Burlington, NJ 08016. Published bimonthly. Averages 50 pages. Black-and-white and color illustrations throughout.

Magazine focusing on the lighter side of contemporary music, with over a dozen artist profiles and interviews throughout. Also contains news on techno, electro, experimental, and dance music, as well as CD reviews. Staples: Tori Amos, Cocteau Twins, Peter Murphy.

Cake. 3028 Ewing Avenue South, Suite #201, Minneapolis, MN 55416. Published sporadically. Averages 26 pages (unpaginated and oversized). Black-and-white photographs throughout.

Protean magazine marked by its distinctive back cover, which is upside down (and sometimes referred to there as "upside down cake").

The music coverage changes considerably from issue to issue. Is it New Wave? Punk? Alternative music? Lots of comics, artists profiles, CD reviews, and strange illustrative matter. Bands have ranged from the mega-successful (Teenage Fanclub, Smashing Pumpkins, and Pearl Jam) to lesser-known artists and groups (Crush, Steve Albini, Velocity Girl).

Cash Box. 345 West 58th Street, Suite 15W, New York, NY 10019. Published weekly. Averages 27 pages. Black-and-white illustrations throughout.

"The music trade magazine" contains news (divided by East Coast and West Coast), talent review (of concerts), film and video reviews, and coverage of the international scene. *Cash Box* charts include weekly singles and albums divided by pop, R&B, urban (rap and hip hop), Christian country, contemporary Christian, and country.

CD Review. P.O. Box 588, Mount Morris, IL 61054. Published monthly. Averages 80-90 pages. Black-and-white and color photographs throughout.

Eclectic CD publication ("the best in new music") covering rock and roll, jazz, blues, classical, and country. In addition to reviews, contains features on performers, music roundups, and audio equipment. Reviews supply ratings for both performance and sound quality. Releases special issues, such as *CD Review's Guide to New Country Music.*

Circus. Circus Enterprises Corporation, 805 Third Avenue, 28th Floor, New York, NY 10002. Published monthly. Averages 86 pages. Color photographs throughout. Pull-out color poster.

"America's rock magazine," a rock staple from the hippie years of the late 1960's through today, is essentially for males in their late teens. Today the focus is on mainstay rock groups, with a slight emphasis on hard rock and grunge. Features include: album, group and tour profiles, video games, sheet music, song lyrics, and music gear. Staples: U2, Pearl Jam, Soul Asylum, Anthrax.

CMJ: New Music Monthly. 11 Middle Neck Road, Suite 400, Great Neck, NY 11021. Published monthly. Averages 60 pages. Color photographs throughout. Usually comes with a free CD sampler.

"The consumer guide to new music." Contains reviews of dozens of brand-new CD's each month in all areas of contemporary music. Also offers video and dance reviews. The CD sampler features about 17 hot tracks, which are described in the last pages of the magazine.

CMJ: New Music Report. 11 Middle Neck Road, Suite 400, Great Neck, NY 11021. Published weekly. Averages 60 pages. Black-and-white photos throughout, mostly CD covers.

Weekly trade magazine for eclectic tastes. Contains dozens of reviews, as well as chart listings, hot airplay tracks, and songs to come in the industry. See also *CMJ: New Music Monthly,* above.

Cover. P.O. Box 1215, Cooper Station, New York, NY 10276. Published monthly. Averages 64 pages. Black-and-white photographs throughout.

"The underground national" includes advertising for art and performances, as well as profiles of underground artists and occasional interviews. Equal emphasis on "fashion/art/online/film/rock." Staples: Patti Rothberg, Collective Soul.

Crawdaddy!. Box 611, Glen Ellen, CA 95442. Published quarterly. Averages 16 pages. Pen-and-ink drawings throughout.

Founded in 1966 by a 17-year-old kid named Paul Williams, *Crawdaddy!* was the first national rock magazine in the United States. (*Rolling Stone,* below, followed one year and a half later.) Williams quit in 1968, and the magazine was continued by other editors until it folded in 1979. Williams resurrected it in 1993 in the form of this quarterly fanzine. Consists of lengthy reviews, mostly CD releases from classic rockers. Almost each issue contains something with Dylan's name in it.

Creem. T. Edwards Publishing Limited, 28 West 35th Street, New York, NY 10010. Published monthly except for September and November. Averages 82 pages. Color and black-and-white illustrations throughout.

Over the years, this rock staple has changed considerably; it's now closer in design to British publications and *Rolling Stone* than its traditional competitors *Circus* and *Hit Parader.* Includes rock news, concert profiles, CD reviews, sporadic book reviews, and more. Mostly coverage of hard rock, punk, and heavy metal; some alternative, New Wave, and hip hop.

Details. 632 Broadway, New York, NY 10012. Published monthly. 144 pages. Color and black-and-white illustrations throughout.

Magazine geared towards a male audience, with a wee-bit of music coverage and issues devoted exclusively to music. Includes fashion, sports, fad crazes, essays on topical subjects, books, comics, etc. Special coverage, it seems, of sexy female rock and rollers, e.g., Traci Lords, Chrissie Hynde, Stevie Nicks.

Discoveries. Arena Publishing, Ltd., 17230 13 Mile Road, Roseville, MI 48066. Published monthly. Averages 146 pages (oversized). Black-and-white photographs throughout.

Subtitled "the record collector's marketplace." Lengthy catalog with coverage of the 1950's-70's classic rocker, with a tip of the hat to country, rhythm and blues, and soul performers. Contains profiles of artists and CD reissues, but the main attraction is the 25,000 or so rare record and CD listings from private distributors and collectors. Lots of Elvis and Sun Records performers.

DJ Times. 25 Willowdale Avenue, Port Washington, NY 11050. Published monthly. Averages 90 pages. Color and black-and-white photographs throughout.

"The international magazine for the professional disk jockey" includes articles on the hottest trends and performers, as well as ample advertising and reviews of audio equipment. Spotlights new releases and mixes.

EQ. Miller Freeman, 2 Park Avenue Suite 1820, New York, NY 10016. Publication varies. Averages 146 pages. Color and black-and-white photographs throughout.

"The project sound and recording magazine" includes various articles on stereo and recording equipment. Some coverage of innovative classic rockers, e.g. Brian Wilson.

The Face. Third Floor Block A, Exmouth House, Pine Street, London EC1R O3L. Published monthly. Averages 186 pages. Color and black-and-white photographs throughout.

British pop culture magazine covering music, sports, film, fashion, and pop culture in general. Staple artists vary.

Fiz. P.O. Box 67E10, Los Angeles, CA 90067. Published bimonthly. Averages 110 pages. Black-and-white photographs throughout.

The cover reads: "A blah blah blah blah magazine." Fanzine on contemporary indie and alternative music. Contains interviews and reports on the underground scene, comics, classifieds, etc.

Flipside. P.O. Box 60790, Pasadena CA 91116. Publication varies. Averages 60 pages (unpaginated). Black-and-white photographs throughout.

Fanzine for the fan of underground hard and alternative rock. You'll find some reportage on groups such as Smashing Pumpkins and Nirvana, but most of the bands are little known—and may stay that way, given their names: Minutes of Nausea, Barnyard Slut, Bassholes, Anus the Menace, and...you get the idea.

f Magazine. 1133 Broadway Suite 1220, New York, NY 10010. Published biweekly. Averages 32 pages (unpaginated). Black-and-white photographs throughout.

Magazine of the contemporary hard rock/alternative scene, with radio chart information, listings for new albums, artist profiles, interviews, concert schedules, and news. Staples: Babes in Toyland, Stone Temple Pilots, Nine Inch Nails, and Jesus Lizard.

Forced Exposure. P.O. Box 9102, Waltham, MA 02254. Published quarterly. Averages 146 pages. Some black-and-white photographs.

Lengthy fanzine on alternative and underground rock. Contains in-depth interviews and pages full of record, book, and video reviews. Some articles pertain to contemporary issues, such as child abuse. The magazine ends with a mail order section.

Goldmine. Krause Publications, 700 East State Street, Iola, WI 54990. Published biweekly. Averages 200 pages (oversized). Black-and-white illustrations throughout.

"The collector's record and compact disc marketplace" for classic rock lovers has been in existence since 1974. Mail order advertisers offer rare albums, fanzine subscriptions, CDs, videos, posters, autographs, books, and anything else rock-oriented and collectible. Each issue focuses on a couple of late 1950's-70's rock artists, with either interviews, catalog summaries, or general histories. Contains reviews of CDs and reissues. Periodically contains book reviews. Special coverage of British invasion bands (e.g., The Beatles, The Kinks, Manfred Mann, The Who), but folk, country, jazz, blues, and Motown stars also get their due. Each year *Goldmine* releases a special Beatles issue.

Guitar Player. Miller Freeman, P.O. Box 50376 Boulder, CO 80323-0376. Published Monthly. Averages 150 pages. Color and black-and-white photographs throughout.

Glossy magazine for electric guitar players and aficionados. Includes several sections on guitar gear (repairs, new products, chord transcriptions), tips from pros, and ample classifieds, but balances these out with profiles of contemporary mainstream rock, metal, and alternative bands. Staples: Metallica, Butthole Surfers.

Guitar School. Harris Publications, Inc., 1115 Broadway, New York, NY 10010. Published six times a year. Averages 138 pages. Color illustrations throughout early sections.

Magazine for the "brutal" rocker, with ample coverage of headbanging legends such as Alice in Chains, Megadeth, Metallica, Anthrax, and Slayer. Contains interviews, artist profiles, and numerous guitar song sheets. Harris Publications also releases special spin-off issues, such as *Guitar School Presents Thrash Guitar.*

Guitar Techniques. Popular Publications Limited, Alexander House, Forehill, Ely, Combs CB7 4AF England. Published monthly. Averages 98 pages. Color and black-and-white photographs throughout. Often comes with a CD-ROM.

"The guitar monthly in a class of its own" contains profiles of the greatest classic rock guitarists of all time: Clapton, Beck, Blackmore, and many others. Includes reviews, news, profiles, chord transcriptions, and more.

Guitar World. Harris Publications, Inc., 1115 Broadway, New York, NY 10010. Published monthly. Averages 190 pages. Color and black-and-white illustrations throughout.

"The guitar alternative" focuses on hard rock and heavy metal. Includes interviews, information on equipment, and advice for guitarists. Contains an average of 40 pages of song transcriptions and album reviews. Special issues (one is called *Guitar World Presents Guitar Legends*) feature in-depth interviews with, and song lyrics of, rock's elite (usually three musicians per issue). Staples: Ace Frehley, Ozzy Osbourne, Soundgarden, Metallica, Jimmy Page.

Hit Parader. Hit Parader Publications, Inc., 40 Violet Avenue, Poughkeepsie, NY 12601. Published monthly. Averages 100 pages. Color illustrations throughout. Pull-out poster.

Geared mostly toward contemporary hard rock and heavy metal, though there's plenty on dinosaurs such as Kiss and Aerosmith. Staples: Pearl Jam, Metallica, Anthrax, Deep Purple. Contains a video game review; a handful of song lyrics; and "video view."

hm. 6614 Bradley Drive, Austin, TX 78723. Published bimonthly. Averages 78 pages. Color and black-and-white photographs throughout.

"Your hard music authority" is geared to more of a college and above audience rather than junior high/high school. Includes brief news, gear information, interviews, reader surveys, trading, reviews, and more. Staples are not the traditional Megadeth, Kiss, Led Zeppelin, et. al.

Hypno. Hypno Industries, 914 Westwood Blvd. Suite 524 Los Angeles, CA 90024. Published monthly. Averages 64 pages. Color and black-and-white photographs throughout.

"The voice of pop culture" contains articles on musicians, actors, artists, and photographers. Also spotlights trends in sexual attitudes and movies. Staples: The Cure, Alanis Morissette.

ice. P.O. Box 3043, Santa Monica, CA 90408. Published monthly. Averages 24 pages. Black-and-white photographs throughout.

"The CD news authority" is a glossy stapled packet that includes sections on news, release dates, and the marketplace, as well as separate sections on jazz, country, blues, and multimedia. Staples: Pearl Jam, Soundgarden, The Rolling Stones.

i-D. 5th Floor, Seven Dials Warehouse, 44 Earlham Street, London WC2H 9LA England. Published monthly. Averages 80 pages. Color illustrations throughout.

British publication with coverage of "i-DEAS, FASHION, CLUBS, MUSIC, PEOPLE." Issues vary on different themes and topics—e.g., beauty, clothing, comedy, artists, futuristic sex (cyborg suits!), etc.—though each touches on the music industry, film, video, and books. Contains a wild mix of photos. Staples: U2, R.E.M.

Ill Literature. P.O. Box 480275, Los Angeles, CA 90048. Publication varies. Averages 156 pages. Black-and-white photographs throughout.

Alternative/hard rock magazine that includes news, interviews, and profiles, as well as hundreds of CD reviews. Staples: Dismember, Cannibal Corpse, Iron Maiden.

Keyboard. Miller Freeman, Inc., 600 Harrison Street, San Francisco, CA 94107. Published monthly. Averages 184 pages. Color and black-and-white illustrations throughout.

Practical keyboard magazine for the eclectic musician. Includes: reviews, ads, and recommendations on products; advice on how and where to buy synthesizers, digital and acoustic equipment, electronic pianos and antiques; and playing tips from pros. Some history of the piano, but not much on rock and roll.

Kulture Deluxe Magazine. 715 J Street #306, San Diego, CA 92101. Published bimonthly. Unpaginated (approximately 80 pages). Color and black-and-white illustrations throughout.

"The music magazine of skill and chance" is a wacky tribute to pop culture, with space devoted to offbeat musicians (Country Dick Montana), TV shows ("Mystery Science Theater 3000"), sex, and more. Includes interviews, profiles, and comic strip art. Staples: Iggy Pop, Meat Puppets.

Live!. 3701 Wilshire Boulevard, Los Angeles, CA 90010. Published monthly. Averages 112 pages. Color and black-and-white photographs throughout.

Dubbed "everything entertainment," this magazine covers today's mainstream music scene and, to a lesser degree, films, television, and sports. Includes features on rock groups and performers, special events (e.g., concert festivals), human interest stories, and more. Staples: Hootie and the Blowfish, Bruce Springsteen, Ashley Judd.

Livewire. J.Q. Adams Productions, Inc., 28 West 25th Street, New York, NY 10010. Published bimonthly. Averages 80 pages. Color illustrations and black-and-white photographs throughout. Comes with pull-out poster.

According to the sell-line, "the only metal mag that doesn't suck." Includes tour coverage and interviews with today's top metal bands. Mostly for teen males who are into tattooed musicians. Staples: Anthrax, Scorpions, Kiss, Van Halen, Metallica.

Lollipop. P.O. Box 147, Boston, MA 02123. Publication varies. Averages 82 pages. Black-and-white photographs throughout.

The "music entertainment magazine" includes articles on outrageous underground bands such as China Drum. Includes brief blurbs on a number of bands, as well as films, videos, comics, and zines.

Magnet. 258 W. Trenton Avenue, Morrisville, PA 19067-2041. Published bimonthly. Averages 98 pages. Color and black-and-white illustrations throughout.

The best of up-and-coming and lesser-known alternative music, with interviews, record reviews, fanzines, label profiles, imports, reissues, and more. Many artist profiles contain complete discographies. Staples: Robert Pollard, Superconductor.

MaximumRockNRoll. P.O. Box 460760, San Francisco, CA 94146-0760. Published bimonthly. Averages 80 pages (unpaginated). Black-and-white photographs and xeroxes throughout.

Fanzine and catalog for grunge rockers, punk rockers, and heavy metalers. Includes: bizarre

news; interviews; and album, movie, and book reviews. Actually reviews other zines (non-music related).

Melody Maker. IPC Magazines Limited, King's Reach Tower, Stamford Street, 26th Floor, London SE1 9LS, England. Published weekly. Averages 60 pages (oversized). Black-and-white illustrations with color inserts spreads.

Major weekly British rock tabloid/news information source that's been in existence since the 1960's. Ample coverage of classic rockers and modern grunge, hard rock, heavy metal, New Wave, hip hop, and rap. Includes several news columns, gig guides, question-and-answer pieces with rock stars (American and British), British charts, CD and video reviews, classifieds, movie reviews, and more. Staple artists vary, but The Cure, Nirvana (Kurt Cobain), Hole, Axl Rose, and Soundgarden frequently fill the pages.

Metal Edge. TV Picture Life, Sterling/MacFadden Partnership, 35 Wilbur Street, Lynbrook, NY 11563. Published monthly. 122 pages. Color and black-and-white illustrations throughout. Contains pull-out poster.

"Hard rock's No. 1 photo magazine" features the stars of heavy metal, acid rock, and grunge. Artists run the gamut of headbanging guitar music: Aerosmith, Kiss, Stone Temple Pilots, Motley Crue, Metallica, Van Halen, Def Leppard, Soundgarden, and Alice Cooper, to name a few. Contains lots of color spreads, "metal wire" (news), fanzine listings, and a music exchange.

Midi. GW Publishing Company, 313 Washington Street, Suite 450, Newton, MA 02158. Published bimonthly. Averages 108 pages. Black-and-white and color illustrations throughout.

"Written for the mind of the musician." Magazine for the virtual reality musician and songwriter, and those wanting to keep up with the latest technological innovations (keyboards, synthesizers, drums, etc.). Issues include interviews with musicians, product reviews, and even a glossary ("a listing of words that make you go `huh?'").

Mobile Beat. P.O. Box 309, East Rochester, NY 14445. Published bimonthly. Averages 114 pages. Color and black-and-white photographs throughout.

"The DJ magazine" includes articles of interest to rock and pop disk jockeys. Includes sections on equipment, music (news and charts), performing (club and video), and more.

Modern Drummer. P.O. Box 480, Mt. Morris, IL 61054- 0480. Published monthly. Averages 160 pages. Color and black-and-white photographs throughout.

"The world's most widely read drum magazine." Contains information on innovative drum equipment, tips from pros, sheet music, and numerous interviews with today's drummers. The emphasis is clearly, though not exclusively, on modern rock and roll drummers (e.g.: Dave D'Abbruzzese of Pearl Jam; Jimmy Chamberlain of Smashing Pumpkins; and Matt Cameron of Soundgarden). Also contains some CD, book, and video reviews.

Music Connection. 4731 Laurel Canyon Blvd., N. Hollywood, CA 91067. Published biweekly (every other Thursday). Averages 56 pages. Black-and-white photographs throughout.

The "West Coast trade magazine" contains a calendar of events, news, radio information, audio/video reports, night life, club and disc reviews, and more on the California music scene.

Musician. P.O. Box 1923, Marion, OH 43305. Published monthly. Averages 100 pages. Color and black-and-white photographs throughout.

Rock magazine from BPI Communications (Billboard Music Group). Leaning is slightly toward "classic rock"—members of The Who, Led Zeppelin, Queen, Springsteen, etc., though you'll also find coverage of 1990's groups, such as Stone Temple Pilots. Back sections feature updates on drum, guitar, and keyboard equipment. Some CD reviews.

The Music Paper. Sound Resources, Ltd., P.O. Box 304, Manhasset, NY 11030. Published monthly. Averages 46 pages (oversized). Black-and-white illustrations throughout.

Self-described as "the most complete music magazine available anywhere." Emphasis on mainstream classic rock from the 1970's, 80's,

and 90's. Interviews and profiles have included Aerosmith, Billy Joel, Soundgarden, Alan Parsons, Squeeze, and The Scorpions. Contains studio news, industry file, advice for musicians (bass, drums, electric guitar), product reviews, and record reviews.

Muzik. IPC Magazines Limited. King's Reach Tower, Stamford Street London SE1 9KS England. Published monthly. Averages 202 pages. Color and black-and-white photographs throughout.

"The new testament of club culture" features news, reviews, and awards, plus a lengthy club guide. Ample photo and chart information. Covers dance music from rap to digital music to pop. Staples vary from issue to issue.

New Musical Express (NME). IPC Specialist Group, 25th Floor, King's Reach Tower, Stamford Street, London SE1 9LS England. Published monthly. Averages 62 pages (oversized). Color and black-and-white photographs throughout.

British music newspaper that reports current trends and news in the rock scene. Includes U.K. chart information, profiles of legends and comeback artists, brief news flashes, TV and movie highlights (U.K. releases only), and more. Staples: Paul Weller, The Sex Pistols, The Cure, Nick Cave.

Option. Sonic Options Network, Inc., 1522-B, Cloverfield Blvd., Santa Monica, CA 90404. Published bimonthly. Averages 162 pages. Color and black-and-white illustrations throughout.

Subtitled "music alternatives." Magazine of today's alternative music but with a twist; while most of the bands lean toward punk alternative rock (The Posies, The Breeders, Iggy Pop, etc.), there is also significant treatment of alternative jazz, country, rap, and Latin music. Features include in-depth artist profiles, essays on broad topics such as psychedelic revivalism, and nearly 50 pages of reviews. Staples: Nirvana and Hole. Occasionally includes a UHF style supplement.

Paper. 529 Broadway, New York, NY 10012. Published monthly. Averages 131 pages. Color and black-and-white photographs throughout.

"The most stolen magazine with the cutest readers" contains features covering the full spectrum of pop culture. Includes features on music, fashion, film, TV, and more. Staple artists vary.

Plazm. 625 SW 10th, Portland, OR 97205-2788. Published three times a year. Averages 72 pages (unpaginated). Black-and-white and two-color tints throughout.

Offbeat fanzine that is an art designer's dream—you'll find every typeface and font ever created here, and sometimes it's upside down. Includes, essays, poetry, stories, interviews, and other literary forms not quite recognizable. Each issue has at least one article on a punk or rock artist, e.g., Iggy Pop.

Pulse!. Tower Records/Video, Pulse!, 2500 Del Monte St. Building C, West Sacramento, CA 95691. Available at Tower Record, Video, and Book outlets. Published monthly (every last Friday) except December. Averages 100 pages. Color and black-and-white photos throughout.

Music publicity magazine put out by Tower Records/Video music chain. The cover designs and staple subjects vary from issue to issue. Ample coverage of all areas of pop music (mostly in different issues): hard rock, alternative, heavy metal, rap/hip hop, punk, heavy metal, etc. Contains: profiles of performers on tour and new releases; equipment information (stereo and video); CD, film, and video reviews; and lots of colorful ads.

Puncture. P.O. Box 14806, Portland, OR 97214. Published quarterly. Averages 82 pages. Black-and-white illustrations throughout.

"Magazine of music and the arts." Coverage of the current rock, indie, alternative, and New Wave scenes. Includes numerous band profiles and CD reviews, as well as arts and books, shows, and world beat.

Q. Mappin House, 4 Winsley Street, London W1N 7AR England. Published monthly. Averages 144 pages. Color and black-and-white illustrations throughout.

"The modern guide to music and more" can be found at some newsstands in the U.S. Emphasis is on punk and New Wave. Staples: The Velvet Underground, The Cure, U2, Billy Idol. Includes reviews of new CDs and re-releases; also reviews books, films, videos, and concerts.

Raygun. Raygun Publishing, Inc., 2812 Santa Monica Blvd. Suite 204, Santa Monica, CA 90404. Published ten times a year. Averages 112 pages (unpaginated). Color and black-and-white photos and graphics.

"The Bible of music and style" is mostly for men; also seen as *raygun* and *Ray Gun.* Infamous for its use of excessive typefaces and superimposed images. Something of a "zine" for underground music and tastes. Staples: Soundgarden, Depeche Mode, Butthole Surfers, Porno for Pyros.

Request: The New Music Magazine. Request Media, Inc., 75000 Excelsior Blvd., Minneapolis, MN 55426. Published monthly. Averages 86 pages. Color and black-and-white photographs throughout.

This eclectic magazine features "modern rock metal rap country jazz world music blues R&B." Includes essays, interviews, and profiles of past and present artists, as well as: CD reviews; separate summaries of the metal, rap, country, jazz, blues, R&B, and indie scenes; and "media mix" reports on videos, games, and fanzines.

RIP. LFP Inc., 8484 Wilshire Blvd. Suite 900 Beverly Hills, CA 90211. Published monthly. Averages 80 pages. Color and black-and-white illustrations throughout.

Magazine of the contemporary hard rock, alternative, and punk rock scenes. Includes rock news, CD reviews, and artist profiles and interviews. Staples: Metallica, Smashing Pumpkins, Soundgarden.

Rock & Rap Confidential. Box 341305, Los Angeles, CA 90034. Published 10-12 times annually. Averages eight pages. Not illustrated.

Reports little-known news tidbits pertaining to the rock, rap, and hip-hop scenes. Specializes in controversial and topical issues (e.g., music censorship, concert violence, etc.). Has regular reader's polls, as well as occasional CD, video, and book recommendations. Author Dave Marsh is editor, writer, and book producer; Sandra (Sandy) Choron is associate editor.

Rolling Stone. 1290 Avenue of the Americas, New York, NY 10104-0298. Published monthly. Averages 110 pages. Color illustrations throughout.

The quintessential rock magazine, *Rolling Stone* was created in 1967 by Jann S. Wenner in San Francisco. Today the focus is primarily on contemporary leading bands and performers (U2, Soul Asylum, Pearl Jam), although every once in a while a longtime veteran (Clapton, Dylan, Costello, et. al.) appears on the cover. News items span rap, funk, soul, etc. Some essays on politics and social issues, as well as album and film reviews, and some chart information. Famous for the "Rolling Stone interview," as well as numerous classic book publications bearing the imprimatur.

Scrawl. P.O. Box 205, New York, NY 10012. Published quarterly. Averages 42 pages. Black-and-white photographs throughout.

Hardcore rock magazine, with each issue containing three to five profiles of lesser-known contemporary groups that have a dangerous attitude (e.g., Lunachicks). Also includes CD and book reviews.

Screamer. Screamer Subscription Department, McMullen & Yee Publishing, Inc., P.O. Box 70015, Anaheim, CA 92825-0015. Published biweekly. Averages 78 pages. Color and black-and-white photographs throughout.

"The world's loudest rock n' metal magazine" contains CD reviews and features on the classic metal bands and artists. Two other columns of interest: "Bass-ics" from Megadeth bassist David Ellefson; and "Drum Track" from Quiet Riot drummer Frankie Banali. Staples: Ozzy Osbourne, Kiss, Soundgarden.

Seconds. 24 Fifth Avenue Suite 405, New York, NY 10011. Published bimonthly. Averages 80 pages. Black-and-white photos throughout. Occasionally comes with cassette sampler.

The "Table of Malcontents" in this magazine lists the in-depth interviews with artists in the pages that follow. Artists range from Robert Plant, Todd Rundgren, Nick Cave, and Leonard Cohen to Butthole Surfers, Z, and Hair & Skin Trading Co. Somehow George Clinton and Billy Idol also fit in. The question most asked in interviews: What music do you fuck to?

Select. Tower Publishing, Tower House, Sovereign Park, Market Harborough, Leics LE16 England. Published monthly. Averages 110 pages. Color photographs throughout.

England's offbeat "pop Babylon" rock magazine does receive good distribution in the U.S. Contains features on concerts, profiles of cutting-edge groups (Teenage Fanclub, New Order, Smashing Pumpkins), and reviews of CDs (old and new), films, video, and books (mostly rock and pop culture).

Sin International. Nolan & Howland Productions, P.O. Box 9428, San Diego, CA 92109. Published monthly. Averages 82 pages. Color tints and black-and-white illustrations throughout.

Punk/metal magazine with plenty of comic strip art and illustrations suggesting sado-masochism and torture. Contains interviews with fringe bands, such as Sky Cries Mary, The Muffs, and Paw. Some campy reviews of reissued albums.

Sod. Independent Media International, Inc., 1069 Pinegate Drive, Kirkwood, MO 63122. Published four times a year. Averages 68 pages. Black-and-white photos and drawings throughout.

Sod stands for "sounds of death"; it's billed as "the international magazine of extreme music, art & film." Lots of skulls, corpses, dismemberment, and guns to heads. And, yes, there are a few CD reviews also. The bands are pure morbid "black" heavy metal—Venom, Rotting Christ, Bleed, Satan, Skeleton of God, Necrophobic...and let's not forget Genitorturers. For suicidal sado-masochistic rockers.

Soma. 285 Ninth Street, San Francisco, CA 94103. Published bimonthly. Averages 88 pages. Black-and-white and color illustrations throughout.

"Left coast culture" magazine, with reports on trendy events and personalities in San Francisco, and, to a lesser degree, Seattle. Coverage of contemporary alternative rock, fashion, dance, movies, videos, and, of course, sex. Club and restaurant listings. Some reviews. Artists have ranged from The Buzzcocks to Mickey Dolenz (ex-Monkee).

Spin. P.O. Box 420193, Palm Coast, FL 32142-0193. Published monthly. Averages 100 pages. Color throughout.

Publication from Bob Guccione, Jr., reporting on music (mostly rock and alternative; slight coverage of rap and country), movies, media, and pop culture. Lots of glitzy ads. Staples: Pearl Jam, U2, Red Hot Chili Peppers, and whatever alternative groups are hot.

Streetsound. Street Media Ventures, 333 W. 52nd Street, Suite 1003, New York, NY 10019. Published monthly. Averages 66 pages. Black-and-white illustrations throughout.

"Field guide" for DJ's to all types of today's music: rock, rap, reggae, soul/funk, alternative, jazz, etc. Includes CD ratings and reviews, essays on today's rock trends, unreleased tracking (for DJ's), U.K. reviews, and fanzine listings.

Teen Machine. Sterling/MacFadden Partnership, Inc., 35 Wilbur Street, Lynbrook, NY 11563. Published bimonthly. Averages 80 pages. Black-and-white and color photographs throughout. Large pull-out color posters.

For teenage girls only: coverage of bubblegum pop, rap, hip hop, and contemporary soul, though it usually has ample coverage of TV studs. Staples: Jason Priestley, Kriss Kross, Janet Jackson, and, well, you know the rest. Contains advice columns, interviews, and ads for much-needed products (Arrid Teen Image deodorant!).

Tiger Beat. Sterling/Macfadden Partnership, 35 Wilbur Street, Lynbrook, NY 11563. Published bimonthly. Averages 90 pages. Black-and-white and color photographs throughout. Large pull-out color posters.

Fanzine for teenybopper girls (12-16 age range), with emphasis on night-time soap stars (from "Beverly Hills 90210") and some coverage of pop stars (Janet Jackson).

The Village Noize. 48-54 213th Street, Bayside, NY 11364-1234. Published sporadically. 50 pages per issue. Black-and-white photographs throughout.

Magazine on contemporary rock, with a leaning toward punk, New Wave, and avant-garde. Staples: Iggy Pop, Tom Waits, U2, Sonic Youth. Contains interviews with new bands, updates on those that have seemingly faded from the scene, and "record" reviews.

Vintage Guitar. P.O. Box 7301 Bismarck, ND 58507. Published monthly. Averages 208 pages (oversized). Black-and-white photographs throughout; color in ads.

The *Goldmine* (see above) of magazines for guitar aficionados, with ample advertising devoted to rare collectible guitars. Also includes: meaty interviews with guitar virtuosos; profiles of stars; tips from pros; record reviews; book reviews; and more. Staples: Chet Atkins, Spencer Davis.

Vox. IPC Magazines Limited, IPC Specialist Group, King's Reach Tower, Stamford Street, 25th Floor, London SE1 9LS, England. Published monthly. Averages 154 pages. Color and black-and-white illustrations throughout.

British rock magazine, with color spreads on news events, CD releases, tours, and artist profiles. Each issue contains hundreds of reviews: CDs, films, books, and videos. Predominant coverage of contemporary bands (Crash Test Dummies) and classic rockers (The Stones, The Who). Also includes sections on dance music, reggae, blues, country, folk, jazz, and even classical. Extra sections often concern unreleased material and recommend CDs with explicit content.

Warp. P.O. Box 469019, Escondido, CA 92046. Published quarterly. Averages 80 pages. Color and black-and-white illustrations.

"Skate, snow, surf, sound," but not necessarily in that order. Issues vary in terms of target male age group; some are for the 18-21 crowd and others for 22-26. Focus on skiing, surfing, skateboarding, sledding—and other activities beginning with the letter "s", and involving balancing on a piece of wood—with some coverage of modern rock, such as Smashing Pumpkins and Pearl Jam.

Wax. Croxted Mews, 286A-288 Croxted Road, London SE24 9BY England. Published monthly. Averages 98 pages. Color and black-and-white illustrations throughout.

"A celebration of dance music and club culture," this magazine includes coverage of the European (English and German) dance scene, with emphasis on techno-pop. Includes profiles, interviews, and reviews. Staple artists vary.

The Wire. 45-46 Poland Street, London W1V 3DF England. Published 11 times per year. Averages 74 pages. Black-and-white illustrations throughout with some color.

The sell-line of this British publication (that certainly can pass for American) reads: "adventures in modern music." General music magazine, with coverage of classic rock and roll, jazz, Latin music, and alternative music. Contains current and future musical trends, profiles on artists, CD reviews, and film/video reviews. Occasionally includes a *Sight and Sound Wire* insert, focusing on old and new movie soundtracks and film composers.

Wolf Marshall's Guitar. Cherry Lane Magazines, Inc. 10 Midland Avenue, Port Chester, NY 10573-1490. Published monthly. Averages 170 pages. Some color. Pull-out color poster.

Magazine "for the practicing musician" from a division of music publisher Cherry Lane; emphasis is predominantly heavy metal. Profiles on great guitarists, interviews, and loads of song transcriptions. Staple guitarists: Steve Vai, Jeff Beck, and Jimmy Page. Staples: Metallica, Kiss, Aerosmith, Anthrax.

BLUES

Blues Access. 1455 Chestnut Place, Boulder, CO 80304. Published seasonally. Averages 62 pages. Black-and-white photographs throughout.

Contains nothing but the blues: interviews with blues legends and contemporary musicians; numerous CD reviews; and obituaries. Special coverage of festivals, clubs, and new releases.

Blues Review. Rt. 2 Box 118, West Union, WV 26456. Published bimonthly. Averages 96 pages. Black-and-white and color illustrations throughout.

"The world's largest Blues publication devoted to the listener and musician whose musical passion is the full spectrum of the Blues" includes features on a half-dozen contemporary blues artists, as well as columns (general essays) and departments (reviews and classifieds).

Blue Suede News: House Organ of the Church of Rock and Roll. Box 25, Duvall, WA 98019-0025.

Published quarterly. Averages 64 pages. A few black-and-white photographs.

Publication focusing on the roots of rock—blues, soul, etc.—and rock itself. Essays and updates on legends, especially those that influenced others or have faded from memory (Charles Brown, Solomon Burke, etc.). Regularly contains prominent book reviews, as well as review sections for videos and CDs.

Chicago Blues Magazine. P.O. Box 81614, Chicago, IL 60681-0614. Published quarterly. Averages 28 pages. Black-and-white photographs throughout.

"America's contemporary blues journal" tips its hat to the legends, but its main focus is on modern performers and current news. As of this writing the coverage is only local, although the editors have plans to expand it nationally. Contains interviews, profiles, and CD reviews.

Living Blues. Subscription Department, 301 Hill Hall, The University of Mississippi, University, MS 38677-9836. Published bimonthly. Averages 128 pages. Color and black-and-white photographs throughout.

"The magazine of the African-American blues tradition" highlights blues-related activities throughout the country, with articles and reports on festivals, school programs, benefits, and more. Includes profiles of blues artists both past and present, CD reviews, festival calendars, radio chart listings, and more.

COUNTRY

Country America. P.O. Box 55091, Boulder, CO 80322. Published monthly. Averages 96 pages. Color and black-and-white photographs throughout.

The "real country/real music/real America" magazine concerns contemporary country stars, with a slight emphasis on female performers. Staples: Shania Twain, Tim McGraw.

Country Mirror. 6 West 18th St. Second Fl., New York, NY 10011. Published sporadically. Averages 82 pages. Color and black-and-white photographs throughout. Often comes with a pull-out poster.

Profiles of today's top country performers, from Billy Ray Cyrus to Shania Twain. Includes calendars of events, quotes, news, and complete stat sheets on stars.

Country Music. Silver Eagle Publishers, 329 Riverside Avenue, Westport, CT 06880. Published bimonthly. Averages 96 pages. Color and black-and-white illustrations throughout. Pull-out poster.

Magazine of the mainstream country music scene. Includes a lengthy people section, record reviews, artist profiles, chart listings, and more. Staples: Conway Twitty, Larry Gatlin, Vince Gill.

Country Song Roundup. 40 Violet Avenue, Poughkeepsie, New York 12601. Published monthly. Averages 70 pages. Color and black-and-white illustrations throughout. Come with a pull-out poster.

Contains profiles of country's modern-day superstars, song lyrics, classified ads, advice on song writing, and album reviews. Staples: Garth Brooks, Alan Jackson, Kelly Willis.

Country Weekly. P.O. Box 37070, Boone, IA 50037-0070. Published monthly. Averages 58 pages. Color and black-and-white illustrations throughout.

"Your country music and entertainment magazine" features coverage of past and contemporary country stars, with a special focus on pop crossover artists: Garth Brooks, The Everly Brothers, Mary Chapin Carpenter, and others. Departments include late-breaking news, the week in country music, reviews, chart information, and more.

The Journal of Country Music. 4 Music Square East, Nashville, TN 37203. Published three times a year. Averages 60 pages. Black-and-white photos throughout.

Publication from the Country Music Foundation that covers country legends as well as current stars. Emphasis is clearly on the Nashville scene. Many photos are given full page or two-page spreads. Most issues contain interviews and numerous book reviews.

The Journal of the American Academy for the Preservation of Old-Time Country Music. Silver Eagle Publishers, 329 Riverside Avenue, Westport, Connecticut 06880. Published 6 times a year (February, April, June, August,

October, December). Averages 34 pages. Black-and-white illustrations throughout.

Co-publication of *Country Music* magazine (see above) and the Country Music Society of America. Includes profiles of legends (nothing contemporary), recommended recordings, record dealers, and more. Staples: The Carter Family, Hank Williams, Roy Acuff.

Music Country News. Music City News Publishing Co., P.O. Box 22975 Nashville, TN 37202-2975. Published monthly. Averages 46 pages. Color and black-and-white illustrations throughout.

"The voice of country music" includes lengthy profiles of a half-dozen hot country stars and usually one old time legend. Includes fan clubs, reviews, album sales, classifieds, and more.

New Country. 86 Elm Street, Peterborough, NH 03458. Published monthly. Averages 74 pages. Color and black-and-white photographs throughout. Comes with a CD.

Focus is on the hottest stars of today's country music. Features include profiles of performers, music reviews, guides through Nashville, and more. Artists vary, but Vince Gill, Shania Twain, Waylon Jennings, and Shenandoah frequently appear in the pages.

FOLK

Dirty Linen. P.O. Box 66600, Baltimore, MD 21239- 6600. Publication varies. Averages 122 pages. Black-and-white photographs throughout; one color insert.

"Folk, electric folk, traditional, and world music" brings folk into the 1990's, with coverage of books, concerts, new releases, rare recordings, tour schedules, and more. Also includes profiles of a wide range of mellow artists spanning the globe, from Seamus Egan to Arlo Guthrie.

Discover Music Magalogue. Aztec Corporation, 705 S. Washington St., Naperville, IL 60540-6654. Published quarterly. Averages 48 pages. Black-and-white photographs throughout.

Catalog featuring articles on past and present folk artists, with special attention to The Kingston Trio. Offers new and collector's item records and CDs through mail order. Aztec Corporation also publishes *Rediscover: The Joy of Music* catalog and *Popular Folk Music Today* folk catalogs.

Sing Out!: The Folk Song Magazine. Sing Out Corporation, 125 East 3rd Street, Bethlehem, PA (no zip). Published quarterly. Averages 150 pages. Black-and-white photographs throughout.

Magazine sponsored by the non-profit Sing-Out Corporation, which was formed to preserve cultural diversity and heritage of all traditional folk music. Coverage is international and spans the ages. Includes: profiles of major and lesser-known artists; CD and book reviews; guitar, banjo, and harmonica instruction; chord sheets; rare tapes; festival and camp listings; and more. The mid-1960's debates over whether Dylan sold out still continue!

JAZZ

Coda Magazine. Coda Publications, Box 87, Station J, Toronto, Ontario M4J4X8 Canada. Averages 40 pages. Some black-and-white photographs throughout.

"The journal of jazz and improvised music." Includes profiles on legendary and modern jazz musicians, as well as book reviews, interviews, and CD reviews. Exclusive coverage of Canadian jazz artists.

Down Beat. Maher Publications, P.O. Box 906, Elmhurst, IL 60126-0906. Published monthly. 70 pages. Black-and-white and color illustrations throughout.

"Jazz, blues & beyond," with a leaning to jazz. Contains profiles on both newcomers and jazz legends. Features annual reader's polls, CD reviews, festival coverage, occasional guitar transcriptions, video reviews, and more.

Jazziz. 3620 N.W. 43rd Street, Gainesville, FL 32606. Published bimonthly. Averages 100 pages. Color and black-and-white photographs throughout.

This "art for your ears magazine" is geared to the "adult" connoisseur of classic jazz. Contains profiles of great musicians (George Benson) and bands (even big bands, such as Horace Silver), as well as book and audio reviews. Some coverage of Latin music.

JazzTimes. 8737 Colesville Road, Fifth Floor Silver Spring, MD 20910-3921. Published ten times annually. Averages 90 pages. Color and black-and-white photos throughout.

"America's jazz magazine" covers both modern and classic jazz, with emphasis on the former. Contains profiles, as well as reviews of CD's, books, videos, and equipment. Features contests, quizzes, etc. For the jazz listener and musician. Staples: Miles Davis, George Benson.

Straight CD Chaser. 6 Hoxton Square, London N1 6NU England. Publication varies. Averages 78 pages. Color and black-and-white photographs throughout.

"The magazine of world jazz live" includes coverage of jazz in films, as well as on CD, vinyl, and live. Includes profiles, interviews, and reviews. Staple artists vary.

Strictly Jazz. P.O. Box 492008, College Park, GA 30349. Published monthly. Averages 32 pages. Black-and-white photographs throughout.

"Your total jazz source" includes CD reviews, artist profiles, birthdates, jazz directory (across the U.S.), jazz radio stations, and chart information. Staples: Joe Sample, Bobby McFerrin.

RAP AND HIP-HOP

Beat Down. P.O. Box 1266, New York, NY 10274. Published monthly. Averages 62 pages. Color and black-and-white photographs throughout.

The magazine that purports "culture for the mind, heart, and soul." Contains articles on issues ranging from street violence to feminism in hip-hop. Ample coverage of rap and hip-hop artists, with interviews, profiles, and CD reviews. Staples: DJ Stretch Armstrong, Ice-T.

The Best of Rap & R&B. Word Up! Publications, Inc., 63 Grand Street, Suite 230, River Edge, NJ 07661. Publishes six issues per year. Averages 80 pages. Tinted black-and-white photographs throughout; contains a 4-page color insert. Come with at least one color pin-up or poster.

Geared exclusively to rap and hip-hop fans, though there are exceptions (Janet Jackson). The coverage of R&B only extends to current soul/funk performers such as Lenny Kravitz.

Provides vital statistics on up-and-coming rappers and some reviews. Staples: Jade and LL Cool J.

Black Beat. Sterling/Macfadden Partnership, 35 Wilbur Street, Lynbrook, New York 11563. Published monthly. Averages 85 pages. Color pin-ups and pull-out posters; black-and-white photos otherwise.

Contains profiles on rap, soul, and pop stars; articles on the L.A. and New York music scenes; fashion and advice columns; and more. Some issues contain song lyrics and rap rhymes. Staples: LL Cool J, Kriss Kross, Janet Jackson, Bobby Brown.

Ego Trip. P.O. Box 8447, Long Island City, NY 11101. Averages 66 pages. Unspecified publication schedule. Black-and-white photographs throughout; color in ads only.

"The arrogant voice of musical truth" features articles on sex, rap, fashion, and various aspects of the international music scene. Includes interviews, profiles, CD reviews, book reviews, and more. Staples: Sepultura, Beenie Man.

4080. 2550 Shattuck Avenue Suite 107, Berkeley, CA 94704. Published monthly except July and August. Averages 72 pages. Color and black-and-white photographs throughout.

Hip-hop magazine containing artist profiles, letters, music reviews, comics, and essays on hip-hop culture. Staples: Suga T, Erick Sermon.

Rap Pages. LFP, Inc., 8484 Wilshire Blvd. Suite #900, Beverly Hills, CA 90211. Published monthly. Averages 84 pages. Color and black-and-white photographs throughout.

Rap/hip-hop magazine with lengthy essays on street life and violence, racism, the music industry, and more. Also includes profiles of contemporary musicians and DJ's, with some CD reviews, and lyrics. Staples: Ice-T, Public Enemy.

Rap Sheet. 2270 Centinela Avenue, Box B-4, Los Angeles, California 90064. Published monthly. Averages 40 pages (opens up newspaper size). Color and black-and-white photographs throughout.

Up-to-the-minute reports and profiles on rap artists, DJ's, and clubs; essays on the social relevance of rap. Occasional film and music reviews. Refuses "graphic illustrations of weapons or violence." Special issue for Black History Month. Staples: Ice Cube, KRS-One, Queen Latifah.

Rock & Rap Confidential. See Rock and Roll: Magazines.

The Source. 594 Broadway, Suite 510, New York, NY 10012. Published monthly. Averages 80 pages. Color and black-and-white illustrations.

"The magazine of hip-hop music, culture & politics." The publisher considers this publication "the only independent voice of the hip-hop nation." Contains stories and profiles on the hip-hop and rap scene; CD, book, and video reviews; and coverage of the street scene, sports, and reportage of rap controversies.

Spice!. Starlog Entertainment, P.O. Box 435, Mt. Morris, IL 61054-0132. Published eight times a year. Averages 62 pages. Color and black-and-white photographs throughout. Often comes with a pull-out poster.

Rap/hip-hop magazine, predominately geared to a teen audience. Equal coverage of males and female artists ranging from Sista to Lord Finesse. Includes interviews, color spreads, and contests.

Touch. 51 Hoxton Square, London N1 6PB England. Averages 66 pages. Published monthly. Color and black-and-white photographs throughout.

"The street culture and music monthly" is a colorful British rap/hip-hop magazine with attention to both European and American artists. Includes interviews, profiles, and reviews, as well as write-ups on audio equipment. Staples: Mark Morrison, Beenie Man.

True. 65 Clerkenwell Road, London EC1R 5BH England. Published monthly except July/August and December/January. Averages 98 pages. Color and black-and-white photographs throughout.

Rap magazine with outrageous photographs of stars, as well as some bizarre advertising. Includes essays and photo spreads on African-American musicians and athletes. Staples: Ice-T, Nas.

Urb. 1680 North Vine, Suite 1012, Los Angeles, CA 90028. "Slapped together" monthly. Averages 82 pages (oversized). Color and black-and-white illustrations throughout.

"The future of global hip-hop and dance culture" contains up-to-date club information (primarily on the west coast), film and video reviews, CD reviews, and more. Special sections on dance and local happenings. Staples: The Beastie Boys, Saafir, The Murk Boys.

Vibe. Time Inc., Ventures, Time & Life Building, Rockefeller Center, New York, NY 10020-1393. Published monthly (except for combined December/January and June/July issues). Averages 160 pages. Color and black-and-white illustrations throughout.

Music and pop culture magazine founded by Quincy Jones that covers contemporary pop, hip-hop, rap, funk, R&B, and soul. Also contains exclusives on films, up-and-coming movie stars, and fashion. Ample film, video, and CD reviews. Performers have included Queen Latifah, Janet Jackson, Jade, Salt-N-Pepa, and Dr. Dre.

Word Up!. Word Up! Publications, Inc., 210 Route 4 East, Suite 401, Paramus, NJ 07652. Publishes 13 issues per year. Averages 80 pages. Color and tinted photographs throughout. Pull-out posters and pin-ups.

Colorful rap publication for the younger crowd with lots of pin-ups. Contains roughly a dozen profiles on rap musicians, averaging 2-3 pages each, plus music and fashion news, reviews, and a word search. Staples: LL Cool J, The Fugees, The Guru (from Gang Starr), Kriss Kross.

REGGAE

The Beat. Bongo Productions, P.O. Box 65856, Los Angeles, CA 90065. Published bimonthly. Averages 86 pages. Black-and-white photographs throughout.

Coverage of reggae and music from Africa, the Caribbean, and other parts of the world. Features include national beat, reggae update, technobeat, African beat, and more. Also includes news and reviews, new releases, and chart information. Staples: Bob Marley, Tony Rebel, Beenie Man.

Reggae Report. P.O. Box 2722, Hallandale, FL 33008. Published unspecified number of times per year. Averages 42 pages. Black-and-white illustrations throughout, with some color.

Coverage of reggae music today, with concert reportage, artist profiles, listings of new releases, world report, and CD reviews. Artists have included Eddy Grant, UB40, and Pliers.

Reggae Times. The Beverley Hills Centre, Suite #1, 94N Old Hope Road, Kingston 6, Jamaica, W.I. Published bimonthly. Averages 56 pages. Color and black-and-white photographs throughout.

"Your reggae bimonthly" is produced directly from the source in Kingston, Jamaica. Each issue profiles local and international reggae stars from past and present, and includes news, Jamaican tourism, and even essays on the New York scene. Staples: Peter Tosh, Bob Marley, Beenie Man.

PART TWO:
PUBLICATIONS ON ARTISTS A TO Z

ABBA

BIOGRAPHIES

Oldham, Andrew; Calder, Tony; and Irwin, Colin. *Abba: The Name of the Game.* London: Sidgwick & Jackson, 1995. 248 pages. One glossy eight-page color insert; one glossy eight-page black-and-white photo insert. Discography. Index.

Co-written by Andrew Oldham — former manager of The Rolling Stones, of all people— this extremely pro-biased biography tries to show that Abba was much more than a Scandinavian pop group in bottom-squeezing jump suits. So what is the quintet up to these days? Frida had a hit solo album a few years back and then fell out of the spotlight to marry a Dutch prince; Agnetha (who hasn't spoken to Frida for over a decade) had numerous proposals after her split from Bjorn and ended up marrying a surgeon; Benny has become something of an ornithologist, but keeps one foot in the recording studio; and Bjorn is now a computer consultant. A somewhat slow-going bio, strictly for fans.

PICTORIALS

Snaith, Paul. *Abba: The Music Still Goes On.* London: Castle Communications, 1994. 184 pages. Approximately 150 color and black-and-white photographs throughout. Discography.

Attractive, glossy photo book that can't really compare to Tobler's work (see below), despite its many full-page color photos. Anni-Frid (Frida) Lyngstad and Agnetha Faltskog look as glimmering as ever. A good alternative for those who can't find Tobler's book.

Tobler, John. *Abba Gold: The Complete Story.* Pinewood Studios, England: Century 22 Limited, 1993. 160 pages. Approximately 300 color and black-and-white photographs, covering every page. Discography. Index.

A year-by-year photo album of Abba, whose members hailed from Sweden and Norway. The singers gleam carefully posed smiles in nearly every shot, and the happy-go-lucky "I love life" giddiness is revoltingly outmoded to those who prefer to forget the 1970's. The

album coverage also seems like a perpetual déjà vu: How many greatest hits records can a group have? For ardent fans, however, there is quite a lot to savor. The unique black cover emulates the CD design, which has the same name as this book. The formation of Abba from two different bands (Hootenanny Singers and the Hep Stars) makes for interesting reading. If "Dancing Queen" is in your hit parade, go for the gold.

OTHER TITLES OF INTEREST

Abba as told to Borg, Christer. *Abba.* Knutsford, Cheshire (England): Pemberton, 1977.
Edgington, Harry. *Abba.* London: Magnum, 1978.
Lindvall, Marianne. *Abba: The Ultimate Pop Group.* London: Souvenir Press, 1977.
No author. *Abba Annual, 1976.* Knutsford, Cheshire (England): Pemberton, 1977.
Tobler, John. *Abba for the Record.* Knutsford, Cheshire (England): Pemberton, 1980.
Ulvaeus, Bjorn and Andersson, Benny. *Abba: A Lyrical Collection 1972-1982.* Iver, Buckhimshire (England): Century 21, 1982.
York, Rosemary. *Abba in Their Own Words.* London: W. H. Allen, 1982.

PAULA ABDUL

BIOGRAPHIES

Catalano, Grace. *Paula Abdul: Forever Yours.* New York: Signet (Penguin Group), 1990. 160 pages. One eight-page black-and-white photo insert. Appendices: Discography, Videography, Paula's Vital Statistics, Awards, Secret Facts.

Catalano portrays Abdul as the antithesis of Madonna: clean, clever, and classy. With a scholarship to Cal State at Northridge waiting in the wings, Abdul was signed on as cheerleader for the Los Angeles Lakers. Though only five foot two and a virtual unknown, Abdul made some savvy connections with The Jackson 5 and their sister Janet, and in no time was choreographing the dancing in some of that family's most famous videos and performance routines. Lacking vocal training and experience, Abdul still had to prove herself in the recording studio as a singer—which, through great determination, she did. Recommended for young teen fans, who finally have an idol whose feet are on the ground.

PICTORIALS

Williams, W.B. *The Paula Abdul Story.* New York: Wise Publications (Music Sales Corp.), 1990. 32 pages. 25 color and black-and-white photographs, covering every page.

The L.A. Laker cheerleader turned choreographer, dancer, and singer grins and smiles gleefully through this innocuous pictorial. Abdul is an eyeful, even in some amateurish black-and-white cut-outs stuck in the middle. If crammed together, the text itself could probably fit into a two-page magazine spread—with room for photos!

YOUNG ADULT

Ford, M. Thomas. *Paula Abdul: Straight Up.* New York: Dillon Press (Macmillan Publishing Company), 1992. 72 pages. Approximately 50 color photographs throughout. Index.

Role model time: Abdul is again cast as a woman who reached the heights of success on her own through hard work and setting her sights high—without knocking people down along the way. M. Thomas Ford cites her strong family relationships and dedication to her education as central reasons for her having made the big time. While no one is *that* perfect, it's still refreshing to see a children's book that doesn't have to skirt issues such as promiscuity, drug use, and so on. "...Abdul's fans will enjoy the numerous attractive photographs..." —*School Library Journal.*

OTHER TITLES OF INTEREST
Tager, Miriam. *Paula Abdul.* New York: Dell Publishing, 1992.
Part of Dell's "Who's Hot" series.

AC/DC

BIOGRAPHIES

Dome, Malcolm (editor). Introduction by Dave Mustaine. *AC/DC: The Kerrang! Files.* London: Virgin Publishing Limited, 1995. 256 pages. Approximately 75 black-and-white photographs throughout. Discography.

Not a biography per se, but a compilation of heavily edited articles drawn from *Kerrang!* magazine, which was spawned by the now defunct *Sounds.* After a gushing Introduction by Megadeth's Dave Mustaine, the book charts AC/DC's course from the band's formation in Sydney, Australia to the height of its bratty stardom in the late 1970's and early 80's. Shots of the musicians mooning and gaping at the camera fill the pages almost as much as the hype on *Kerrang!* magazine itself. Generally poor, despite the labors taken to make it cohesive.

Huxley, Martin. *AC/DC: The World's Heaviest Rock.* New York: St. Martin's Press, 1996. 210 pages. Approximately 50 black-and-white photographs throughout. AC/DC Album Discography.

Author Martin Huxley gives credit where it's due: AC/DC never caved in and composed soft ballads; the group never jumped on a bandwagon for a good cause; and the band didn't absorb an iota of influence from their contemporaries to reflect changing trends in the music industry. Huxley's treatment of this hard rock band is as straightforward and no-pretense as AC/DC itself. Huxley does a respectable job tracing how the brothers Young—Angus and Malcolm—moved from Scotland to Australia and, influenced by The Easybeats, turned to a life of gritty rock and roll. Recommended over Dome's work (see above).

PICTORIALS

Bunton, Richard. *AC/DC: Hell Ain't No Bad Place to Be.* London: Omnibus Press (division of Book Sales Limited), 1982. 96 pages. Approximately 75 black-and-white and eight color photographs throughout. Discography (includes bootlegs).

To coin a Kinks' phrase, AC/DC lead guitarist Angus Young was a "schoolboy in disgrace"—and he dressed the part (cap, short trousers, rumpled shirt, and tie) for much of his early musical career. This book approaches the history of the schoolboy motif with some measure of intelligence, but it's unsatisfactory as a general pictorial history of AC/DC. The photos, many of which are too dark or are out of focus, hide the musicians' faces—which, come to think of it, may be a blessing in disguise. Done dirt cheap.

No author. Introduction by Chris Welch. *AC/DC Photo Book*. London: Omnibus Press (division of Book Sales Limited), 1983. Unpaginated (approximately 128 pages). Approximately 130 color and black-and-white photographs, covering every page.

As the title suggests, this is exclusively a photo book, except for an introductory essay by Chris Welch. The shots are predominately of the band circa 1970's-early 80's. Annoying as hell, and that's the way the band would prefer it.

Putterford, Mark. *AC/DC: Shock to the System*. London: Omnibus Press (division of Book Sales Limited), 1992. 96 pages. Approximately 100 black-and-white photographs throughout; four pages of color throughout. Discography.

Glossy photo book on the infantile Aussies that erroneously claims to be the "first" biography of the band. The photos are not bad, but who needs to see these guys' faces *so* close? Only slightly better than *AC/DC Photo Book* (see above), but only because at least there's a modicum of information here.

OTHER TITLES OF INTEREST
Holmes, Tim. *AC/DC*. New York: Ballantine, 1986.

ROY ACUFF

TITLES OF INTEREST
Dunkleberger, A.C. *King of Country Music: The Life Story of Roy Acuff*. Nashville: William, 1971.
Schlappi, Elizabeth. *Roy Acuff: The Smoky Mountain Boy*. Gretna, LA: Pelican, 1978.

ADAM AND THE ANTS

TITLES OF INTEREST
Maw, James. *The Official Adam Ant Story*. London: Futura, 1981.
No author. *Adam and the Ants Annual*. Knutsford, Cheshire (England): Pemberton, 1982.
No author. *Adam and the Ants Superstar*. Knutsford, Cheshire (England): Pemberton, 1982.
Vermorel, Fred. *Adam and the Ants*. London: Omnibus Press (division of Book Sales Limited), 1981.
Welch, Chris. *Adam & the Ants*. London: Star Books, 1981.
West, Mike. *Adam and the Ants*. Manchester, England: Babylon Books, 1981.

BRYAN ADAMS

PICTORIALS

Robertson, Sandy. *Bryan Adams*. London: Bobcat Books (division of Book Sales, Limited), 1986. 48 pages. 24 pages of color illustrations; 24 pages of black-and-white photographs. Discography.

Canadian-born rocker Adams is given mediocre treatment in this collection of photos for the teenage fan. Against some downright awful background icons, there are photos of Adams singing with Tina Turner, posing in leather, and performing live with his band. Aside from pointing out songwriting hits penned by Adams and songwriting collaborator Jim Vallance (e.g., "Rock and Roll Hell" by Kiss), this book cuts like a butter knife.

FANZINES AND FAN CLUBS

Bad News. #406-68 Water Street, Vancouver, B.C. Canada 46B 1A4.

Fan club that offers an 8x10 autographed color photo, an exclusive club button, a newsletter (four issues per year), and a press kit pamphlet. The club sponsors contests and reserves concert seating for members. The glossy 12-page newsletter, also called *Bad News*, contains black-and-white photographs, random notes, book reviews, interviews, album reviews, a member page, want ads, and more. The press kit is a 16-page pamphlet featuring reprinted newspaper articles, a discography, and a Bryan Adams biography (year-by-year chronology). The cost of membership is $20 per year.

WRITTEN WORKS

Adams, Bryan. Photographs by Catlin, Andrew. *Bryan Adams*. Buffalo, NY: Firefly Books, 1995. 108 pages. Approximately 110 color and black-and-white photographs, covering every page.

High-quality oversized photo book not only created with Adams's cooperation, but with his participation and credit as author. Adams actually only contributes a few reflective lines here and there attached to illustrative material. Accompanying a black-and-white photo of Adams sitting on a piece of equipment is the following laid-back description: "The studio looked right down on the sea. At night it was like living on a Cabana because of the fresh air—the air conditioning was what came in over the ocean." Adams fans will rejoice at the unpretentious tone and magnificent photos.

OTHER TITLES OF INTEREST
Fredericks, Darlene. *Bryan Adams.* New York: Ballantine, 1987.

AEROSMITH

BIOGRAPHIES

Huxley, Martin. *Aerosmith: The Fall and Rise of Rock's Greatest Band.* New York: St. Martin's Press, 1995. 200 pages. One eight-page glossy color insert; approximately 50 black-and-white photographs throughout. What It Takes (Discography).

Is Aerosmith the greatest of all still-active dinosaur rock bands? Rolling Stones' fans may not think so. Nevertheless, it is conceivable that Tyler and company are what they cast themselves as: an American garage band with the electricity of British noisemakers such as Cream, The Yardbirds, and Led Zeppelin. Martin Huxley faithfully summarizes the band's history, notably how the group had the staying power to overcome drugs and rock cinema's most notable turkey (*Sergeant Pepper's Lonely Hearts Club Band*), but he never rises above making this an outsider's account. Note that the title rips off Mark Putterford's earlier work (see Pictorials, below).

FANZINES AND FAN CLUBS

Aero Force One. Dept. Pick, P.O. Box 882494, San Francisco, CA 94168.

Aerosmith fan club offering members access to exclusive concert tickets, travel packages, the Aerosmith hotline, special contests, and exclusive merchandise. New members also receive a kit containing collectibles and souvenirs, a membership card, a band biography/discography, a color photo, and more. The club's newsletter contains interviews, photos, pen-pals, and more. The cost of membership is $16 U.S.; $23 elsewhere.

PICTORIALS

Dome, Malcolm. *Aerosmith: Life in the Fast Lane.* Chessington, Surrey (England): Castle Communications, 1994. 112 pages. Approximately 50 glossy full-page color and black-and-white illustrations throughout. Appendix (compilation albums).

According to author Malcolm Dome, Aerosmith is as "American as John Wayne, Mom's Apple Pie, and the Stars & Stripes." Ayeh. While attempting to jazz up this ultra-glossy photo book with ridiculous metaphors, Dome misses the point that Tyler follows in the tradition of Mick Jagger as a charismatic, thick-lipped rock performer, while the band itself continues from where harder-edged British rock-blues gods left off. If you want LOUD, look no further; you'll hear Tyler's shrill screams in your head as you flip the pages. The title isn't really a rip-off of The Eagles' song, but of Eddy McSquare's *Low Life in the Fast Lane* (see Guns N' Roses: Pictorials). Get a grip.

Putterford, Mark. *The Fall and Rise of Aerosmith.* London: Omnibus Press (division of Book Sales Limited), 1991. 80 pages. Approximately 100 black-and-white photographs, covering every page; 20 pages of color throughout. Discography.

Putterford focuses primarily on the late 1980's comeback of this dynamic, controversial band. Steve Tyler sneers, tongue-wags, and shows us his tonsils in a number of exciting photographs—which rely more heavily on black-and-white than color. The copy is straight out of the magazines and heavily weighted with quotes from the band. An attractive package from Omnibus Press, slightly better handled than Dome's work (see above).

ALABAMA

PICTORIALS

Morris, Edward. *Alabama.* Chicago: Contemporary Books, 1985. 108 pages. Approximately 75 black-and-white photos throughout. Discography. Index.

Pictorial history of the country/rock band, complete with an "Alabama Almanac" of

Events, tour photos, and a look at the group in studio and on tour. A good find for the fan, with exhaustive biographical details of all major Alabama band members: Jeff Cook, Randy Owen, Teddy Gentry, and Mark Herndon. And yes, it tells you lead singer Owen was, in fact, born in Alabama (Adamsburg, to be exact).

OTHER TITLES OF INTEREST

Steinbach, Sheila. *Alabama*. Port Chester, NY: Cherry Lane Books, 1986.

ALAN PARSONS PROJECT

FANZINES AND FAN CLUBS

The Avenue. 65 Front Street West, Suite 0116, Box 201, Toronto, Ontario M5J 1E6 Canada.

Twelve-page newsletter with "up-to-date news on Alan Parsons and his projects." Includes: letters from fans, collectibles, profiles of peripheral musicians, photos, and more. The cost per issue is $3.50 in the U.S. and Canada; elsewhere, $4.25 per issue. Subscriptions (four issues) cost $12.50 in the U.S.; $15.50 elsewhere.

THE ALARM

TITLES OF INTEREST

Taylor, Rick. *The Alarm*. Woodstock, NY: Beekman, 1992.

ALICE IN CHAINS

FANZINES AND FAN CLUBS

Alice in Chains Fan Club. P.O. Box 61475, Seattle, WA 98121.

Fan club that offers both "mailing list" and "fan club" packages. The former provides information on merchandise and touring (for $2), while the latter offers the same plus photos, guitar picks, posters, stickers, and more ($12 one-time fee in the U.S.; $15 one-time fee elsewhere). The club also supplies data sheets featuring question and answer with the band, profiles of each member, and a chronology.

THE ALLMAN BROTHERS BAND

BIOGRAPHIES

Freeman, Scott. *Midnight Riders: The Story of the Allman Brothers Band*. New York: Little, Brown and Company, 1995. 344 pages. Two glossy black-and-white photo inserts. Sources. Selected Discography. Fan's Notes.

Southern boys Gregg and Duane Allman lost their father when he was shot to death by an unemployed combat vet (for reasons that remain undetermined). The brothers spent some time in a military school and then moved to Daytona Beach, Florida. Over the years, they formed several bands (The Kings, Escorts, The Hour Glass, and Allman Joys), until Duane's memorable guitar work on Wilson Pickett's version of "Hey Jude" led to underground recognition. The Allman Brothers' unsurpassed reputation as a live band came to several screeching stops with Duane Allman's death in a motorcycle accident, Gregg's cocaine addictions, and the band's infamous internal squabbles. This rock biography sidesteps the usual publicity hype and supplants it with solid, reliable fact. Essential reading for anyone who has ever grooved to the band's legendary Fillmore performances.

FANZINES AND FAN CLUBS

GABBA: Georgia Allman Brothers Band Association. P.O. Box 870, Macon, GA 31202-0870.

Non-profit foundation that is "dedicated to the preservation and promotion of the Allman Brother's[sic] Band musical heritage in Georgia." The group provides community services in the Georgia area, is affiliated with the Georgia Rock and Roll Hall of Fame, and hosts annual Allman Brothers Band festivals. Members receive a certificate and updates on the organization's activities. To become a supporting member, send $15.

PICTORIALS

Nolan, Tom. *The Allman Brothers Band: A Biography in Words and Pictures*. New York: Sire Books (Chappell Music Company, 1976). 56 pages. Approximately 30 full-page black-and-white photographs throughout. Appendix.

Destitute "words and pictures" treatment in Sire and Chappell's music book series. The generic photos are too few, while the type is extremely too small. Purportedly firsthand quotes from figures such as Geraldine Allman (the brothers' mother), producer Johnny Sandlin, guitarist Dicky Betts, and others are loosely strung together and fail to establish why the band has proven so durable, despite tragedies and the usual rock foibles. Not nearly enough attention is paid to the late Duane Allman. For must-haves only.

TORI AMOS

PICTORIALS

No author. *Tori Amos: Pink Earthquakes.* London: Vinyl Experience, c.1996. Unpaginated (approximately 48 pages) Approximately 50 color and black-and-white photographs throughout. Tori Amos Selected Discography.

Multi-colored, album-shaped promotional book that accentuates Amos' cute-as-a-button red hair and baby blue eyes. Amos doesn't do much performing here—save a few token tinkles on a keyboard—but fans (and most red-blooded males) won't mind a quick look.

Rogers, Kalen. *Tori Amos All These Years: The Authorized Illustrated Biography.* London: Omnibus (division of Book Sales Limited), 1994. 116 pages. 150 color and black-and-white photographs throughout. Discography.

Slightly more informative than *Pink Earthquakes* (see above), but not nearly as pink, this book does offer quite a lot in terms of childhood photographs, little-known details, and discography. In love with The Beatles during her childhood, Amos was something of a prodigy on the piano. Her eccentricities occasionally took over, however, and after performing a classical piece, she would imagine she was talking to the original composer—generally asking if he or she liked her interpretation. Until an actual biography comes along, this attractive and colorful book will serve.

St. Michael, Mick. *Tori Amos.* Miami, FL: MBS, 1996. 120 pages. Approximately 75 color and black-and-white photographs throughout. Discography. Chronology. Index.

CD-format book covering all aspects of Amos's life and career. This nicely designed and illustrated book is priced just right at $7.99.

THE ANIMALS

AUTOBIOGRAPHY

Burdon, Eric. *I Used to Be an Animal, But I'm All Right Now.* Boston: Faber and Faber, 1986. 224 pages. Approximately 20 black-and-white drawings throughout.

The lead singing Animal speaks out about fame, fortune, groupies, and what it's like to hit the skids after blockbuster success. Burdon also recorded a solo song and album of the same title in 1988. Each chapter opening bears the same odd drawing of Burdon singing with a bat (or some other such winged creature) on his head. Highly recommended as a source for details on the ups-and-downs of the man many consider to be rock's greatest white blues singer. Unfortunately, this classic is out of print.

FANZINES AND FAN CLUBS

The Eric Burdon Connection Newsletter. Phil Metzger, 448 Silver Lane, Oceanside, N.Y. 11572.

Eighteen-page newsletter providing up-to-date information on Eric Burdon's recent performances and recordings. Includes reproductions of black-and-white photos, interviews with Burdon, sections written by subscribers, "classyfieds"[sic], and more. Offers *The Eric Burdon Scrapbook,* which contains exclusive information on Eric Burdon with The Animals and with War. Write for subscription information.

ANTHRAX

FANZINES AND FAN CLUBS

NFC: The Official Anthrax Fan Club. P.O. Box 254, Kulpsville, PA 19443.

Club that offers live demo tapes, discographies, profiles, newsletters, and tour itineraries. The cost is $10 in the U.S. and $15 abroad.

ARROWS

BIOGRAPHIES

Harry, Bill. *Arrows: The Official Story.* London: Everest Books Limited, 1976. 144 pages. One glossy eight-page black-and-white photo insert.

Arrows (not *The* Arrows) were yet another discovery of Mickie Most, the man who produced The Animals' masterpiece "House of the Rising Sun" and brought Suzi Quatro to the world's attention. Author Bill Harry takes a break from writing about The Beatles (see their entry for several of his works), became an Arrows publicity agent, and penned this rah-rah biography in the hopes of cashing in on the group's then-running TV series. Three David Cassidy look-alikes in search of a following.

ASIA

See Yes.

BABES IN TOYLAND

BIOGRAPHIES

Karlen, Neal. *Babes in Toyland: The Making of a Rock and Roll Band.* New York: Times Books (Random House), 1994. 296 pages. One eight-page black-and-white photo insert.

Unique behind-the-scenes look at how these young women—Kat Bjelland, Lori Barbero, and Maureen Herman—started off on their quest for fame and fortune. Author Neal Karlen (whose credits include having written a rock opera with Prince!) attended corporate meetings at Warner Brothers Records, watched the group in the recording studio and hung out in the wings while they performed, to produce this biting commentary of the music business. It will be interesting to check the band out a few years down the line, and see if Kat ever becomes the soul singer she longs to be (such as Billie Holiday) or if she'll "sell out" like she naively thinks the girl groups of the 1960's did. Considering this book is a device to further the

trio's career, the quality of the photos should have been better.

BACHMAN-TURNER OVERDRIVE

(See also Guess Who, The)

BIOGRAPHIES

Melhuish, Martin. Introduction by Michael Watts. *Bachman-Turner Overdrive: Rock Is My Life This Is My Song.* Toronto/New York: Metheun/Two Continents, 1976. 178 pages. Approximately 80 black-and-white photographs throughout. Discography.

The band's little-known saga began in Winnipeg, Canada, where Randy Bachman was guitarist with his first supergroup, The Guess Who. With Burton Cummings, Bachman co-wrote classics such as "American Woman" and "These Eyes." Guilty at not spending enough time at home with his family, he quit the band (causing a furor in the music world) and became a Mormon. His next group, Brave Belt, did not make much of a mark and he and his bandmates—brother Robbie, Fred Turner and Blair Thornton—changed musical direction to form BTO. Soon they would be one of the top bands of the mid-1970's, with hits such as "Takin' Care of Business." Early on, the author of this book labeled Bachman-Turner Overdrive a "heavy metal" band which, over time, has proven inaccurate. The discography is incomplete, lacking Bachman's Guess Who albums and even years for recordings. Overall, though, a decent authorized biography.

JOAN BAEZ

AUTOBIOGRAPHY

Baez, Joan. *And a Voice to Sing With: A Memoir.* New York: Summit, 1987. Two eight-page black-and-white glossy photo inserts and numerous original drawings. 384 pages. Index.

In her autobiography, Baez traces all aspects of her eventful life: her childhood travels across the globe to Baghdad, Switzerland, California, and New York; her involvement in numerous causes (e.g., civil rights marches, tax dodging to protest the draft); the development of her voice ("Mine was a plain girl's voice...."); and more. While her writing style has matured over the years, it's also become slightly condescending; her passage about "Live Aid" seems like a direct attack against modern musicians for not living up to the expectations of Woodstock. (She does recount one humorous moment in which she mistook Sheena Easton for Madonna.) She also tends to overlook her feelings about the past and future of folk music. Baez's drawings are surprisingly effective, and the photos are top-notch. "...self-indulgent, yet nevertheless fascinating..." —*Booklist*.

BAEZ FRIENDS AND FAMILY

Baez, Sr., Joan. Foreword by Joan Baez. *Porridge: Memoirs of Somalia.* Santa Barbara, CA: John Daniel, Publisher, 1985. 96 pages. Approximately 20 black-and-white photographs throughout.

Joan Baez Sr., the mother of Joan and Mimi Baez, and wife of a noted physicist, is also a humanitarian and author in her own right. In this book, she invites readers along on her travels to Somalia, where she and a few others provided famine relief to refugee camps. Baez Sr. had actually been inspired to go on this mission by actress Liv Ullmann. The author's descriptions of the children are poignant and not cloying; worth a look for those with a special interest in the Baez family's activities and human rights issues. "A highly personal but revealing look at the problem of world hunger"—*Booklist*.

GENERAL REFERENCE

Swanekamp, Joan. *Diamonds & Rust: A Bibliography and Discography.* Ann Arbor, MI: Pierian Press. 1980. 76 pages. Approximately six black-and-white reproductions of album covers. Bibliography section: Author Index; Title Index; Subject Index; Periodicals Index. Recordings section: Album Chronology; Songs Released as Singles; Composer Index; Song Title Index.

A concise guide to Baez in print and on record. The bibliography, which is arranged chronologically, lists dozens of newspaper articles and other literature by or about Baez spanning the years 1961-1977. Each citation features a four-

five line description, with some indication of the work's slant and value. The discography takes the alphabetical approach and includes information such as catalog number, year and song titles. While obviously published before Baez's records were issued on CD, this volume might still be handy to collectors of her vinyl. The title of this book is from the Baez song of the same name.

WRITTEN WORKS

Baez, Joan. *Daybreak.* New York: Dial Press Inc., 1968. 160 pages.

"An intimate journal" composed by the singer at the height of her notoriety in the late 1960's. The book was dedicated "...to the men who find themselves facing imprisonment for resisting the draft." Not really an autobiography in the same sense as her later work (see above), this is a collection of dreams and remembrances (a good portion from childhood) that are accentuated with beautifully written nostalgia in the vein of Harper Lee. Fans of Baez will want to dig up this volume, as will historians seeking flavored writing from the period. Look for her furtive ode to Bob Dylan, "The Dada King." Simultaneously naive and charming.

Baez, Joan. *Joan C. Baez: And Then I Wrote.* New York: Big 3 Music Corp., 1979. 352 pages. Approximately 60 original pen-and-ink drawings throughout.

Drawings, poetry and sheet music, as chosen and arranged by Baez herself. The poems in part one are repeated in part two (the sheet music section); users have the option of reading the works for artistic value or studying the chords for performance. Baez's drawings in this volume do not constitute anything more than childish stick figures. Strictly for devotees.

YOUNG ADULT

Garza, Hedda. *Joan Baez.* New York: Chelsea House, 1991. 120 pages. Approximately 50 black-and-white photographs throughout. Discography. Chronology. Further Reading. Index.

Part of the "Hispanics of Achievement" series from Chelsea House, this richly detailed book for young readers is an excellent introduction to Baez's life and influence. The book expertly outlines the rocky political climate of the 1960's and how folk music, with Baez as one of its leading spokespeople, helped pave the way for social change. Garza splices such chapters with those of Baez's diverse background, which is comprised of Mexican American and Scottish lineage. Not merely a recycling of Baez's autobiography or of 1960's social commentaries, this is a highly original portrait of a singer with some Latin American roots who speaks out against social injustices. Recommended.

OTHER TITLES OF INTEREST

Baez, Albert and Baez, Joan Sr. Illustrations by Joan Baez. *A Year in Baghdad.* Santa Barbara, CA: John Daniel & Co. Publishers, 1988.
Travel memoir from Joan Baez's parents.
Heller, Jeffrey. *Joan Baez: Singer with a Cause.* Chicago, IL: Children's Press, 1991.
Part of Children's Press' "People of Distinction" series.

THE BAND

(See also Hawkins, Ronnie; Lightfoot, Gordon: Critical/Analytical Commentary)

AUTOBIOGRAPHY

Helm, Levon with Davis, Stephen. *This Wheel's on Fire: Levon Helm and the Story of The Band.* New York: William Morrow and Company, Inc., 1993. Two glossy 8-page black-and-white photo inserts. 320 pages. Sources. Index.

Released the same year as Hoskyns' brilliant biography (see below), Helm's autobiography is just as worthwhile for the insider's firsthand ruminations of his years as drummer, composer and singer in The Band. Helm, who worked on a cotton farm in an area he describes as being "near Scratch Arkansas" (which has a better ring to it than Helena, Arkansas), poetically relives his fascination with drums ("the sound of cymbals and the snare drum popping was synonymous with Saturday night and good times"), the nurturing The Band received from crude showman Ronnie Hawkins, and the pain he felt hearing boos while he backed Bob Dylan's first electric sets. It's unavoidable that this book overlaps with Hoskyns' work; however, Helm's modest, warm voice makes the reader feel present at the events being described. "...one of the most readable, enjoyable books about rock 'n' roll"—*Goldmine.*

BIOGRAPHIES

Hoskyns, Barney. *Across the Great Divide: The Band and America.* New York: Hyperion, 1993. 440 pages. Two eight-page glossy inserts. Notes. Discography. The Very Best of the Band (A Very Personal Selection). Index.

As most of us know, four of members of The Band—Richard Manuel, Rick Danko, Robbie Robertson, Garth Hudson—hailed from America's northern neighbors, Canada. Their drummer, Levon Helm, sprang from Helena, Arkansas and was "Mr. Downhome Apple Pie." This expansive and highly enjoyable volume is a sweeping epic of a group searching for its musical direction and identity. First, they were the support group for Ronnie Hawkins; in the mid-1960's they were the back-up band for Dylan when he turned electric; finally, when the decade drew to a close, they came into their own with the release of two innovative albums. Other high points included The Band's performance at the Woodstock Festival and the film *The Last Waltz.* This landmark book, which provides some of the stranger theories behind Richard Manuel's 1986 suicide, is "A fine meditation on the Canadians who mythologized America"—*Esquire.*

THE BANGLES

PICTORIALS

Hogan, Peter. *The Bangles.* London: Omnibus Press (division of Book Sales Limited), 1989. Unpaginated (approximately 16 pages). Approximately 32 color photographs, covering every page. Discography.

There's very little to discover about this California band here, except that the four musicians are stunning. Guitarist Susannah Lee Hoffs looks particularly lovely throughout. Take a quick peak when no one is looking and gently place back on the shelf.

BAUHAUS

BIOGRAPHIES

Shirley, Ian. *Dark Entries: Bauhaus and Beyond.* Wembley, Middlesex (England): SMF, 1994. 192 pages. One glossy eight-page black-and-white photo insert. Discography.

The indie sensation that struck chart success with "Bela Lugosi's Dead" is the subject of this interesting biography. Although Bauhaus split in 1983 and went out on their own, Peter Murphy—predicted to be the group's only con-tinuing star—was actually outsold by his for-mer bandmates (David J., Kevin Haskins and Daniel Ash) who went on to form Love and Rockets and other musical ventures. An excel-lent study of a short-lived band. The title of this book was another hit for the group.

THE BAY CITY ROLLERS

BIOGRAPHIES

Paton, Tam with Wale, Michael. *The Bay City Rollers.* New York: Berkley Medallion Books, 1975. 160 pages. One 16-page black-and-white photo insert.

Promotional book from Paton, the group's manager. Wale, his collaborator, was a noted TV personality. The book doesn't supply any names, dates, or places; we only find out that Leslie McKeown, Derek Longmuir, Alan Longmuir, Stuart John "Woody" Wood, and Eric Faulkner were from Edinburgh, Scotland and that they had one hit with "Keep on Dancing." The rest is pretty much dribble about the individual band members' likes and dislikes. Did you know that Leslie has a taste for potato soup, Irish stew, and beef stovies?

OTHER TITLES OF INTEREST
Allen, Ellis. *The Bay City Rollers.* St. Albans: Panther, 1975.
Golumb, David. *The Bay City Rollers Scrapbook.* London: Queen Anne Press, 1975.
No author. *Bay City Rollers Annual, 1975.* Knutsford, Cheshire (England): Pemberton, 1974.

THE BEACH BOYS

AUTOBIOGRAPHY

Wilson, Brian with Gold, Todd. *Wouldn't It Be Nice: My Own Story.* New York: HarperCollins, 1991. 398 pages. Two glossy black-and-white photo inserts. Index.

Brian Wilson, bassist, songwriter, producer, and founder of the Beach Boys, wrote his life story after his long recovery from various addictions and his successful solo comeback LP. The musical genius behind the boys of summer has not exactly lived an exclusive life of blondes, babes, and surf: he barely survived relations with his abusive father; he had life-threatening addictions to alcohol, drugs, and food; and he lost his brother Dennis in 1983 in a surfing accident. Unfortunately, virtually every other piece of information in this book is of dubious fact. Mike Love, Audree Wilson (Brian's mother), Carl Wilson (Brian's brother), and several others filed separate defamation suits against Brian, his psychotherapist Dr. Eugene Landy (for undue influence), and/or publisher HarperCollins, which resulted in Brian's undisclosed settlement to Mike Love and this book's expulsion to out-of-print obliv-ion. Best left unread, except by scholars of the band. Wilson's grim expression on the cover says it all.

BIOGRAPHIES

Gaines, Steven. *Heroes & Villains: The True Story of the Beach Boys.* New York: New American Library, 1986. 374 pages. Two glossy 16-page black-and-white photo inserts. Index.

The title—if taken literally—does not do the band justice, though it's taken from the name of a Beach Boys' hit. Author Steven Gaines delights in the darker side of two members of the band: Brian Wilson (his psychological prob-lems) and Dennis Wilson (addictions to sex and drugs). He even thanks the former's psy-chiatrist for an interview (isn't the doctor/patient relationship sacred?). This biog-raphy is more concerned with tabloid issues—e.g., Dennis Wilson's friendship with Charles Manson and model Rocky Pamphlin's affair with Brian's wife Marilyn—than anything sub-stantive on the band's history and musical legacy. Bad vibrations.

White, Timothy. *The Nearest Faraway Place: Brian Wilson, the Beach Boys and the Southern California Dream.* New York: Henry Holt and Company, 1994. 416 pages. Two glossy eight-page black-and-white photo inserts. Bibliography. Index.

A highly ambitious survey of The Beach Boys, against the social and cultural backdrop of Southern California. White provides an avalanche of detail on the Wilson family's move out West, a history of the region and of the brothers' rise to fame—all silhouetted by recreational symbols of past eras: sports cars, skateboards, go-cart races, etc. By focusing on the peripheral areas, White shirks attention to major events such as Dennis Wilson's death (only one and a quarter pages), and only clouds the Brian Wilson mystique, which readers can better access through the artist's autobiography (see above). The title of the book is from an instrumental track on the Beach Boys' *20/20* LP. "...the author's account of the recording industry's evolution in Los Angeles is both lucidly written and instructive"—*The New York Times*.

DISCOGRAPHIES, RECORDING GUIDES, AND COLLECTIBLES

Elliott, Brad. *Surf's Up! The Beach Boys on Record, 1961-1981.* Ann Arbor, MI: Pierian Press, 1982. 496 pages. Approximately 100 black-and-white photographs throughout. All This Is That (Index).

Influenced by Castleman and Podrazik's classic *All Together Now* (see Beatles, Discographies: *The End of The Beatles?*), Elliott has assembled numerous lists of data: recordings organized by U.S. release date; world releases; song charts (with singer, backing musicians, and entry numbers); promotional records; and chart listings. Running times, label numbers, recording dates, and producers are identified. The photos consist mostly of album cover shots. As usual with the Pierian Press guides, the information is all in here somewhere—it's just a chore to find it and a major headache to decipher the section headings. The book is well indexed (thankfully) and should be of use to Beach Boys' mavens, despite the years it's been on the shelf.

FANZINES AND FAN CLUBS

Beach Boys Australia Magazine. P.O. Box 106, North Strathfield 2137 NSW Australia.

Quarterly Australian fanzine first published in 1985. The 32-page booklet contains a couple of black-and-white photographs, updates in the rock world, reprinted interviews with Beach Boys' members, letters, and more. Among the contributors is author David Leaf. The cost per issue is $5. Subscription is $18 U.S.; $20 U.K and Europe; and $14 Australia.

Beach Boys Fan Club. P.O. Box 84282, Los Angeles, CA 90073.

Founded in 1973, this official club recognized by the band offers a button, a bumper sticker, a membership card, and five news sheets per year that list Beach Boys tour dates, recording information, and classifieds. The cost is $5 per year in the U.S. and $8 abroad.

Endless Summer Quarterly. P.O. Box 470315, Charlotte, NC 28247.

Founded in 1987, this quarterly magazine contains interviews, music and video reviews (including bootlegs), photographs, and up-to-the-minute news on Brian Wilson and the group. The cost of subscription is $20 U.S.; $24 Canada and Mexico; and $26 Europe and South America.

Friends of Dennis Wilson. 1381 Maria Way, San Jose, California 95117.

Fan club devoted to Dennis Wilson that was created in 1983 and at the time was endorsed by the drummer himself. Publishes *Dennymania*, a 36-42 page pamphlet containing reproduced black-and-white photographs, pen pals, birthday buddies, news, book reviews, poetry by club members, trading information, other fan clubs, Beach Boys concert information, album reviews (of work by The Beach Boys, Jan & Dean, and other surf groups), and more. The cost of membership is $8 per year; if you sponsor a friend, you earn a free lifetime membership.

The Mike Love Fan Club. c/o Patricia Ferrelli, 114 Gov. Winthrop Road, Somerville, MA 02145.

Fan club that offers members merchandise and a membership card. The club publishes *The*

Mike Love Fan Club Newsletter, a quarterly, 16-page stapled packet that includes: photocopies of black-and-white photographs; reviews of albums and concerts; interviews with Mike Love; classifieds; and more. All profits go to the charity of Mike Love's choice. The cost of membership per year is $7 U.S.; $8 elsewhere.

Surfer's Rule. Attn. Gren Turegatan, c/o Goran Tannfelt, 71 114 38 Stockholm, Sweden.

First printed in 1983, this Swedish Beach Boys fanzine is written completely in English. The 20-page stapled booklet contains photocopies of black-and-white photographs (mostly record sleeves and women in bathing suits), news, record releases, books, and more. The cost is $10 for three issues U.S.; £5 for two issues U.K.

PICTORIALS

Anthony, Dean. *The Beach Boys.* New York: Crescent Books (division of Harmony), 1985. Unpaginated (approximately 60 pages). Approximately 65 color and black-and-white photographs, covering every page.

Promotional book published a couple of years after Dennis Wilson's death. Non-informational, to say the least—only a dozen pages have any copy whatsoever—and the cover is dreadful. The book offers only a handful of genuinely exciting performance shots taken during the 1970's and early 80's (e.g., a couple with Ringo Starr on drums). Let this one get caught in the undertoe.

Barnes, Ken. *The Beach Boys: A Biography in Words and Pictures.* New York: Sire Books (Chappell Music Company), 1976. 56 pages. Approximately 25 full-page black-and-white photographs throughout. Appendix (discography).

Anachronistic "words and pictures" study of the Beach Boys, and one that is top-heavy on the former. With the subsequent release of Brian Wilson's autobiography (see above) and more elaborate color-filled pictorials, this book has become obsolete. There is hardly any mention of Brian Wilson's psychological struggles or his early conflicts with his abusive father. Needless.

Leaf, David. *The Beach Boys.* Philadelphia, PA: Courage Books (Running Press), 1985. 208 pages. Approximately 250 black-and-white photographs, covering every page.

First published in 1978, this is a Brian Wilson-exclusive Beach Boys biography/pictorial study, with insufferably bad photocopies of photos. Rather than provide an updated edition of the earlier book, the producers have instead tacked on a 16-page synopsis summarizing activities 1978-1985 that doesn't match the rest of the text in terms of tone or typesize. In fact, much of this epilogue deals with problems the author faced while dealing with the dysfunctional band. A marginal purchase.

Milward, John. *The Beach Boys: Silver Anniversary.* Garden City: Doubleday & Company, Inc., 1985. 240 pages. 200 color and black-and-white photographs, covering every page.

A thoughtful photo tribute to the boys, with an oversized portrait on just about every page. The mix of black-and-white and color images is effective in showing various aspects of the musicians' collective nature. In a startling close-up shot, Brian Wilson's face is split across a two-page spread. The captions are brief but revealing. Fun, fun, fun.

Preiss, Byron. *The Beach Boys.* New York: Ballantine Books, 1979. 160 pages. Four 16-page glossy color inserts; 100 black-and-white photographs throughout. Chronological Discography.

"The Authorized Biography of America's Greatest Rock and Roll Band" does not seem to have any evidence of being authorized—and fails to serve as a biography. The author has crammed the group's early development into the first four pages, and has overburdened the pages with quotes from the band, engineers, producers, etc. The saving grace is in the imaginative four color inserts, one of which contains the complete lyrics from the *Pet Sounds* LP. Released years before Dennis Wilson's death and prior to Brian Wilson's drug recovery.

Priore, Dominic. *Look! Listen! Vibrate! Smile!.* San Francisco: Last Gasp, 1994. 299 pages. Approximately 350 reproductions of black-and-white photographs.

A revised edition of the meaty 1985 book of the same name, this work—which features Beach Boys' album art and copy on the front and back—contains reprinted articles, promotional art, essays from experts such as Paul Williams, and insights into the group's studio sessions. This strident book brims with excitement, but is all over the place in focus: Browsers can find song lyrics and some wonderful clips, but when it's all over it doesn't amount to anything. Quite simply, this is the equivalent of about 200 fanzines all in one—which may be more than enough for the buff. Mostly of interest for the vintage magazine and newspaper pieces, a few of which compare The Beach Boys with The Beatles.

QUIZBOOKS AND QUOTEBOOKS

Wise, Nick. *The Beach Boys: In Their Own Words.* London: Omnibus Press (division of Book Sales Limited), 1994. 112 pages. Approximately 100 black-and-white photographs throughout.

Author Wise adds a quality volume to Omnibus Press' "in his/their own words" series. Compared to earlier titles in the series, this one has a significantly improved design, with a more legible typeface and a more aesthetic photo layout. Quotes have also been well selected, although they aren't coordinated as smoothly as they might have been. (The early days and group origins fall into several sections.) Fans will no doubt race to the feuds between Mike Love and Brian Wilson (both of whose words combined constitute 75% of the book). Love on Wilson: "He's a paranoid schizophrenic, and he feels guilty because he cheated me out of millions of dollars and credit for things." That about says it all.

OTHER TITLES OF INTEREST
Golden, Bruce. *The Beach Boys: Southern California Pastoral.* San Bernardino, CA: Borgo, 1991.
Green, Carl and Sanford, William R. *The Beach Boys.* New York: Macmillan Children's, 1986.
Ribowsky, Mark. *The Beach Boys.* New York: Simon & Schuster, 1986.

THE BEATLES

(See also Harrison, George; Kaufman, Murray; Lennon, John; McCartney, Paul; and Starr, Ringo)

BEATLEMANIA

Bedford, Carol. *Waiting for the Beatles: An Apple Scruff's Story.* Poole, Dorset (England): Blandford Press, 1984. 296 pages. Two eight-page glossy black-and-white photo inserts. Index.

The Apple Scruffs were the ultra-devoted female fans who waited outside the Apple offices to catch a glimpse of The Beatles. George Harrison dedicated his song "Apple Scruffs" to the ladies, while Paul was inspired to write "She Came in Through the Bathroom Window" when this author and another girl once illegally entered his home. Bedford innocently asserts that the Scruffs would never offend any of the Beatles and stood by to "protect them." There was even an unwritten code of Apple Scruffian behavior (e.g.: "Don't pick George's roses!"). Readers will no doubt flip past pages with long gaps between Beatle appearances. Bedford is surprisingly unschooled about the Beatles music, getting the title wrong to no less a classic than "Yellow Submarine." Published in the U.S. in 1984 by Sterling.

Catone, Marc A. Foreword by Tom Schultheiss. *As I Write This Letter: An American Generation Remembers the Beatles.* Ann Arbor, MI: Greenfield Books (division of Pierian Press), 1982. 236 pages. Approximately 75 line drawings throughout.

In hundreds of letters written between 1979-1980, fans express their feelings about their fab heroes. Many of the anonymous letters (only initials and city are provided) state the same thing and fail to demonstrate any detailed knowledge of The Beatles' music—shortcomings which suggest that Catone should have solicited more letters from repeat Beatlefest attendees. Drab drawings and a lazy design make this one easy to forget.

Conger, Mary Mack. *Sweet Beatle Dreams: The Diary of Mary Mack Conger.* Kansas City and New York: Andrews and McMeel, 1989. 88 pages. Approximately 100 black-and-white photographs throughout.

Mary Mack Conger (then just Mary Mack) was 14 years old when she traveled from Iowa to Chicago to see The Beatles perform. From 1964-1965 she kept a diary, in which she scribbled down her deepest thoughts about her beloved pop stars. The giddiness is terminal as Mary considers false fanzine rumors (that Paul married Jane Asher), celebrates Beatles birthdays (with real cake), and counts down her favorite songs (which typically only include a couple of Beatles songs anyway). Conger thinks she has accomplished a work comparable to Anne Frank's diary, but she must still be dreaming.

Mitchell, Carolyn Lee with Munn, Michael. *All Our Loving: A Beatles Fan's Memoirs.* London: Robson Books, undated (circa 1988). 150 pages. The glossy four-page black-and-white photo inserts. Bibliography.

Mitchell was 17 when she first saw the Beatles on "The Ed Sullivan Show"; five years later she was so obsessed with seeing a Beatle in person she trekked to London and stalked Paul McCartney at his home at 7 Cavendish Avenue. Things started to get hairier when she pursued Paul all of the way to his Cambeltown farm, and allegedly left with a nose bloodied by the cute Beatle himself. Was Paul really responsible for the assault? We'll never know. Mitchell makes no attempt to piece together what really did transpire on that day, although she seems to "forgive" Paul for whatever he may or may not have done. The rest is the usual puppy dog Beatles adulation.

BEATLES FRIENDS AND FAMILY

Best, Pete and Doncaster, Patrick. *Beatle: The Pete Best Story.* New York: Dell, 1985. 192 pages. Approximately 100 black-and-white photographs throughout.

The man "who almost was a..." tells of his role in the early days as the Beatles' drummer. Born in wartime, India, the son of a boxing promoter, Pete Best was a smart lad who almost fell into a career as a teacher until he, like most other teenage Liverpudlians, was drawn to skiffle music. His mother Mona (shortened to Mo) founded the Casbah Club, where The Quarry Men performed some of their earliest gigs. Best provides some keen firsthand accounts of the boys scrounging around in Germany trying to get laid and "make show" (stir the audience with wild antics)—and how he shared drumsticks with Rory Storm and the Hurricanes' Ringo Starr. Just as a recording date at EMI was set, the "bombshell" hit and Pete was out and Ringo in. Best reminds us that he was a close mate of John, Paul, and

George, and, despite harboring some understandable ill feelings, reports he shed some tears when he heard of Lennon's passing. The drummer-turned-businessman easily wins over his readers.

Clayson, Alan and Sutcliffe, Pauline. Foreword by Iain Softley. *Backbeat: The Real Life Story Behind Stuart Sutcliffe: The Lost Beatle.* London: Pan Books and Sidgwick & Jackson, 1994. 198 pages. One glossy eight-page black-and-white photo insert; one glossy eight-page color photo insert. Notes. Appendices: Chronology; Exhibitions; Television Documentaries; Discography.

The true, unadulterated story of Stu Sutcliffe, a founding Beatle who had no aptitude as a bassist, but had tremendous skill as a painter. Sutcliffe's friendship with John Lennon, romance with German photographer Astrid Kirchherr, and his death at 21 caused by cerebral paralysis have become legendary among Beatlefiles, but the real focus here is on Sutcliffe's artistic legacy. Pauline Sutcliffe, Stuart's sister, had access to diaries and sketchpads, while Ringo biographer Clayson (see Starr, Ringo: biographies) had the knowledge of how to put it all together. Clayson's prose is too dense for a casual readership, but more patient readers will reap the rewards from the period detail and observation by firsthand witnesses. Iain Softley, who directed the 1994 film *Backbeat* upon which this book is based, wrote the foreword.

Coleman, Ray. *The Man Who Made the Beatles: An Intimate Biography of Brian Epstein.* New York: McGraw-Hill, 1989. 400 pages. Two eight-page glossy black-and-white photo inserts. Index.

Ray Coleman captures the full spirit of the man who made the Beatles. Epstein, or "Eppy" as he was affectionately dubbed, was a suave, sensitive, determined, ego-driven, and bored man with an artistic drive that needed to be released—and The Beatles were his master creation. (He also managed Cilla Black, Billy J. Kramer, the early Moody Blues and others.) Coleman accurately represents the difficulties Epstein must have had being Jewish and a closet homosexual in 1950's and early 60's England. There are revelations at every turn of the page, including that Epstein was well aware of The Beatles several months before "My Bonnie" ever reached his record shop.

Coleman "...writes fluently, objectively and with warmth..."—*Publishers Weekly*.

Epstein, Brian. *A Cellarful of Noise*. New York: Pyramid, 1965. 128 pages. One 16-page black-and-white photo insert.

This memoir is from the man who struggled to bring The Beatles fame and was left with nothing to do once they'd achieved it. The title refers to the Cavern Club, where Brian saw John, Paul, George, and Pete (Best) perform for the first time. While the book (ghostwritten by publicist Derek Taylor) does reveal Brian's love for the group, his sensitivity, and aspects of his meticulous nature, the end result is a vapid promotional piece for The Beatles. Still, one can find points of interest, such as his comment on John Lennon: "Sometimes he has been abominably rude to me...." The book ends on a painfully ironic note, given that Epstein died of a sleeping pill overdose only three years after the book was published: "Tomorrow? I think the sun will shine tomorrow." Reisssued in 1984 by Popular Culture Ink.

Martin, George and Hornsby, Jeremy. *All You Need Is Ears*. London: Macmillan London Limited, 1979. 286 pages. Three glossy eight-page black-and-white photo inserts. Index.

Legendary Beatles' producer George Martin was a carpenter's son from Drayton Park, England. Like his father, he too became an expert craftsman—although his future lay in the realm of recorded sound: first with comedians, such as Peter Sellers, and then with rock music, most notably The Beatles. Martin doesn't smudge The Beatles' reputations in his autobiography; instead he conveys his first-hand impressions of them, which is all we really need. On Ringo: "...he's a solid rock drummer with a super steady beat." Martin is surprisingly unfunny for a man who has worked with such humorous people; however, his insights into the creation of contemporary music make this an enjoyable read to anyone interested in the process of recording.

Taylor, Derek. *As Time Goes By*. London: Davis Poynter Limited, 1973. 160 pages.

The topsy-turvy memoirs of The Beatles' former publicist Derek Taylor who, here, can't seem to put together two cohesive paragraphs about his life in the music industry. Taylor was also publicist at times for The Beach Boys, The

Doors, and Paul Revere and the Raiders—and he has little, if anything, in the way of anecdotes and observations. Saddled with run-on sentences, meaningless ramblings ("There were about eight things wrong with working for The Beatles and one of them is that there aren't any Beatles any more...") and generally pitiful self-reflections ("I am a lazy cunt..."), *As Time Goes By* should be left back in 1973. It's hard to believe *Fifty Years Adrift* (see below) was written by the same individual.

Taylor, Derek. Edited by George Harrison. *Fifty Years Adrift*. Guildford, Surrey (England): Genesis Publications, 1984. 542 pages. Approximately 200 black-and-white photographs, drawings, engravings, and reproductions of newspaper articles throughout; four glossy eight-page color and black-and-white photo inserts.

Magnificent, high-quality autobiography—the second from Derek Taylor (see *As Time Goes By*, above). The gold trim and Monterey concert ticket bookmark are only the start: This title has a wealth of unseen photos (both glossy and extremely fine standard print) and other documents, many of which directly relate to The Beatles and Apple. Taylor's childhood in Liverpool during wartime is fascinating, as is his detail about previous jobs in newspaper publishing. Yet fans should pounce on the insider sections concerning The Beatles' rise to fame in Liverpool and England. Harrison's involvement in the project is speculative, but he does receive quite a lot of attention throughout. A beautiful, comprehensive edition in which the signatures on letters and documents look more real than the originals. Beatles fans should lock it up in a display case.

Taylor, Derek. *It Was Twenty Years Ago Today: An Anniversary Celebration of 1967*. New York: Fireside (Simon & Schuster), 1987. 256 pages. Approximately 100 black-and-white photographs throughout; two glossy eight-page photo inserts. Chronicle of Events. Discography. Bibliography.

Reflections of the era as pulled together by Taylor, The Beatles' publicist. Naturally, the story unfolds through the creation, release, and impact of *Sgt. Pepper's Lonely Hearts Club Band*. The result is a slightly skewed history that reduces the impact of contributions by San Francisco acts. Taylor still has a knack for hyping The Beatles; ultimately, however, he fails to connect with the scene going on outside celebrity circles. Unpleasantly designed, with the black-and-white photos buried in the margins. "...may work better in a visual medium than as a book"—*Booklist*.

Williams, Allan and Marshall, William. *The Man Who Gave the Beatles Away*. New York: Macmillan, 1975. 216 pages. One glossy 24-page black-and-white photo insert.

Allan Williams fancies himself as having been the first Beatles manager, which he clearly was not. First a salesman and then a small-time coffee club owner (he founded the Jacaranda, usually shortened to Jac), Williams acted as booking agent for The Beatles and landed them their early gigs in places such as the Grosvenor Ballroom and the Top Ten club in Hamburg, Germany. Williams never caught on to what The Beatles were about ("I thought the Beatles were a right load of layabouts") and has a fairly low opinion of John Lennon (described here as "macabre" and "perverse"), which is justified by the fact that the group stiffed him commissions. One cannot justify his claim that Brian Epstein only recognized The Beatles' appeal because he was a homosexual. Unsavory and, more often than not, inaccurate.

BIOGRAPHIES

Brown, Peter and Gaines, Steven. *The Love You Make: An Insider's Story of The Beatles*. New York: McGraw-Hill, 1983. 448 pages. Two black-and-white photo inserts. Index.

Brown, the best man at John and Yoko's wedding (he's even mentioned in "The Ballad of John and Yoko") and former director of Apple Corps., should have known better than to write this muck. The book begins with a melodramatic description of Cynthia Lennon coming home to find Yoko Ono wearing her bathrobe, and goes on about Cynthia for another two chapters until finally beginning the story of how The Beatles were formed. From there it's a continuous ride downhill: strict trash of drugs, booze, infidelities (John's boasting of having slept with, among countless others, Joan Baez, Eleanor Bron, and Maureen Cleave), mismanagement, and more, without hardly a mentioning of the group's charm or talent. Paul McCartney made a public outcry against the book's implications of John's homosexual relations with manager Brian Epstein.

Cepican, Bob and Ali, Waleed. *Yesterday...Came Suddenly: The Definitive History of the Beatles*. New York: Arbor House, 1985. 288 pages. Two 16-page black-and-white photo inserts. Sources.

An unimpressive history of The Beatles, with plentiful quotes (particularly from early musicians and friends, such as Tommy Moore, drummer for The Silver Beatles) but nothing in the way of supportive material. The authors stick to the old formula stories and even get a few details wrong (stating that John had publicly broken down upon being told of Stuart Sutcliffe's death, which apparently wasn't the case). The inserts are nothing to speak of, and the book doesn't contain a discography or index.

Davies, Hunter. *The Beatles*. New York: McGraw-Hill Book Company, 1985. 426 pages. One 38-page black-and-white photo insert. Original song sheets, letters, artifacts throughout. Beatles Records. Beatles Places. Beatles Memorabilia. Beatles Books. Index.

The only authorized biography of The Beatles, originally titled *The Beatles: The Authorized Biography*, has been ripped off by countless writers and journalists since it was first a best seller in 1968. This 1985 "2nd revised edition" doesn't hold up at all. Davies has inserted a long-winded introduction and several updates at the back of the book, but the interior is the original, unrevised text from the first printing. This leads to several outdated and misleading statements, including that John's MBE "rests in Mimi's bungalow" (when it is common knowledge he returned the award to Buckingham Palace in November, 1969). Further, The Beatles admitted to having edited many of the more lurid passages to keep their names clean while they were still trying to sell new records. Some truly remarkable period quotes from immediate players (e.g., Freddie Lennon, John's dad) and rare jottings of lyrics are this edition's only saving graces.

Doney, Malcom. *Lennon and McCartney*. London and New York: Midas Books and Hippocrene Books, 1981. 128 pages. One glossy eight-page black-and-white photo insert. Discography.

Fans will be dismayed by this approach to The Beatles' story, which tells the bare elements through only John and Paul's points of view. If it had concentrated exclusively on their songwriting contributions, this may have made more sense; but as a survey of the band, you can't help feel George and Ringo have been shafted. An abbreviated telling condensed from other sources, and not worth the two-hour read.

Hutchins, Chris and Thompson, Peter. *Elvis Meets the Beatles.*

See Presley, Elvis: Biographies.

Norman, Philip. *Shout! The Beatles in Their Generation.* New York: Warner Books, 1981. 528 pages. One 30-page black-and-white photo insert. Index.

An exhaustive biography—a national best-seller—summarizing how the Beatles affected (and were affected by) the 1960's. The book is clear, objective, and thankfully, avoids the gossipy path of other biographies. In his "Author's Note," Norman concedes he could not get anywhere near The Beatles for interviews while researching the book; this does not, however, diminish the quality of this detailed work. Fans will enjoy the well-selected part titles, the chapter-opening quotes, and the detailed coverage of peripheral players, such as Magic Alex. "You're plunged into the middle of a story that's nothing less than thrilling...."—*Publishers Weekly.*

O'Donnell, Jim. *The Day John Met Paul: An Hour-by-Hour Account of How the Beatles Began.* New York: Penguin, 1996. 180 pages. Sources. Bibliography. Index.

First self-published in 1994, this is a novelesque telling of how the world's most famous musical partnership came to pass. O'Donnell sets the stage for this tumultuous event by describing the rich history of Liverpool and the sudden influence of rock on the community—which, on July 6, 1957, culminated with an annual church fete and its first rock performers: The Quarry Men. This book suffers from excessively melodramatic literary devices (alliteration: "Lennon listens. He listens and learns. He listens and learns from a Liverpool lad"), which may make older readers cringe. On the other hand, younger fans will no doubt be disappointed that there are no illustrations. "...an inspired idea becomes a lost opportunity because Jim can't brake a descent into distracting minutiae and self-indulgent purple prose"—*Beatles Fans Unite.*

CHRONOLOGIES

Lewisohn, Mark. *The Beatles Day by Day: A Chronology 1962-1989.* New York: Harmony Books (division of Crown Publishers, Inc.), 1990. 240 pages. Two eight-page glossy black-and-white photo inserts. (First published in Great Britain in 1987 as *The Beatles: 25 Years in the Life 1962-1987* by Sidgwick & Jackson.)

Straightforward chronology of events, beginning on October 1, 1962 (the day Brian Epstein signed The Beatles) to December 19, 1989 (Paul attending a Performing Rights Society luncheon). It's a puzzle why Lewisohn didn't choose to start the chronology much earlier, with birth dates and such. All concert and recording dates are here, as are other little-known details of The Beatles career. An excellent survey, but if you're looking for U.S. recording and release dates you'll have to turn to Allen Weiner's work (see Discographies and Recording Guides below). Also, there's nothing in the way of extras here except the black-and-white inserts.

Lewisohn, Mark. Foreword by George Martin. *The Complete Beatles Chronicle.* New York: Harmony (division of Crown), 1992. 368 pages. Approximately 400 black-and-white and color photographs throughout. Discography. Peak Chart Positions. Date/Composer Index of EMI Recordings. Chronology of U.K. Radio Appearances. Chronology of U.K. TV Appearances. Session/Live Performance Recordings Broadcast by BBC Radio. Other Engagements Played. Engagements Not Played. Where They Played. What They Played. Name Index.

With the heaping success of Lewisohn's earlier works, it's no surprise Harmony would want to churn out a follow-up. This thick reference is a day-by-day of The Beatles' artistic production, including their recordings and appearances on stage, radio, television, and in film. The publisher has provided small graphic icons to visually indicate which medium the group attended to on each day. The result is actually a tri-product of Lewisohn's earlier works, *The Beatles Live!*, *The Beatles Recording Sessions*, and *The Beatles Day by Day*, with several additional lists thrown in the back. Some fans might feel gypped by the repetition, but the "...dozens of stunning, rare Beatles photos, session notes, letters, and other visuals...are, in

themselves, worth the price of the book"
—*Goldmine*.

Schultheiss, Tom (compiler and editor). *A Day in the Life*. Ann Arbor, MI: Pierian Press, 1980. 336 pages. Six black-and-white photographs throughout. Index.

By intent, a "bare bones" day-by-day of The Beatles that opens with a curious introduction by Schultheiss, who concedes that *anything* published on The Beatles is laden with errors and fanciful embellishments. Beyond a shadow of a doubt, this chronology has the earliest starting point for any Beatles' chronology—1807—which marks the birth of Blind Lemon Preston, a fictional character who appeared in a *National Lampoon* parody. Readers would have been better served without such trivialities.

CRITICAL/ANALYTICAL COMMENTARY

Dowlding, William J. *Beatlesongs*. New York: Fireside (Simon & Schuster), 1989. 320 pages. Appendix 1: The Great Songwriting Contest. Appendix 2: Songs for Others. Appendix 3: Unreleased Recordings. Bibliography. Song Index.

Those seeking answers to the most impenetrable questions may get sucked into this analysis of The Beatles' music. For example, who played what instrument on each track? Which songs did they themselves like as an end product? And, what this book chiefly assails, who was the more prolific Beatles composer—John or Paul? Author William J. Dowlding chronologically lists every Beatles' song with headings for authorship, where recorded, instrumentation (who played what), and comments. He supports each bit of information with his source, so if he has printed a mistake we at least know who to blame. In attributing composer credit, Dowlding seeks to do the impossible: divide up the percentage Lennon and McCartney (or anyone else) contributed to a tune. (Thus, for "Drive My Car," McCartney receives a ".7" and Lennon a ".3.") Foolish.

Hertsgaard, Mark. *A Day in the Life: The Music and Artistry of the Beatles*. New York: Delacorte Press (Bantam Doubleday Dell), 1995. 434 pages. Approximately 25 black-and-white photographs as chapter openers. The Released Recordings of The Beatles. Research Notes. Bibliography. Notes. Index.

Building on Lewisohn's classic (see Discographies and Recording Guides), Hertsgaard illuminates The Beatles' magic by getting back to the basics: their music. Like Lewisohn, Hertsgaard had access to the sacred vaults at London's Abbey Road Studios, and he traces the songs' evolutions with similarly engaging results. Hertsgaard's notes, intended to show beyond a shadow of a doubt that his facts are of a provable nature, are not without holes (a comment that McCartney was displeased with Ringo's drumming on the first recording of "Love Me Do" is unsubstantiated), but, for the most part, his observations are of superior quality—especially in regard to the dynamics of the Lennon-McCartney songwriting team. "...this well-crafted bio delivers on its promise to make the Beatles' music the central subject"—*Publishers Weekly*.

Horn, Martin E. *The Music of the Beatles*. Bound Brook: Big Eye Publications, 1984. 112 pages. 50 black-and-white photographs throughout.

This softbound publication contains, as a narrative, reviews of every Beatles single and album. The critiquing is only on the most basic level ("I Want to Hold Your Hand" is described as "a great song") and some comments are simply a question of taste rather than musical insight (regarding "Till There Was You": "Wimpy ballads like this can't do very much for a rock and roller's reputation"). Not much.

Kelly, Michael Bryan (aka "Doc Rock"). *The Beatle Myth: The British Invasion of American Popular Music, 1956-1969*. Jefferson, NC: McFarland & Company, Inc., Publishers, 1978. 221 pages. Afterword with Bobby Vee. Appendix A: Chronologies. Appendix B: Roots of the British Invasion. Appendix C: A Chronological "Yeah Yeah Yeah" Discography. Bibliography. Index.

Doc Rock, as Kelly is dubbed, takes on a task that is the equivalent of a boxer lowering his guard and daring his larger opponent to deliver a free slug at the chin: harpooning myths related to The Beatles and the 1960's British Invasion. Kelly proclaims he's a Beatles fan who just wants the truth told—and seems to accept that this isn't exactly the best way to get him on a panel at Beatlefest. No, he asserts, The Beatles didn't invent the words "yeah, yeah, yeah"; no, they weren't the first Brits on the U.S. charts; and no, they didn't overpower the careers of American male vocalists. Kelly force-feeds the reader miles worth of Top 40 chart information—as well as numerous lists, graphs, and charts that foreshadow Ross Perot—and the results are condescending and misguided. "A marginal purchase..."—*Library Journal*.

Kozinn, Alan. *The Beatles*. London: Phaidon Press, 1995. 240 pages. Approximately 75 black-and-white photographs throughout. Further Reading. Selective Discography. Index.

Kozinn had the misfortune of having his book published alongside Hertsgaard's (see above). Both works attempt to stick directly to the music and steer clear of the path previously created by gossip mongers. Kozinn, the *New York Times* music critic, succeeds admirably in defining The Beatles' magical synergy and ability to borrow from the past and create something entirely their own. Kozinn strives to bring fresh insights into the group's studio innovations, focusing more on the non-commercial aspects of their output. The glossy paper and illustrations make this somewhat more exciting to behold than Hertsgaard's work, but both merit equal attention. "Kozinn is a thorough, persuasive guide through The Beatles' musical bridges, crescendos, odd bars and dialogue loops"—*Publishers Weekly*.

MacDonald, Ian. *Revolution in the Head: The Beatles Records and the Sixties*. New York: Henry Holt and Company, 1994. 388 pages. Chronology. Recommended Further Reading. Select Bibliography. Glossary. Index of Songs. Index of Main Text. (Originally published in Great Britain in 1994 by Fourth Estate Limited.)

Exhaustive scholarship on every Beatles' track, including both originals and covers, demonstrating how The Beatles created the tunes and exploring their meaning in the 1990's. MacDonald lists line-ups, composer(s), recording dates, and U.S. and U.K. release dates, and then pieces apart the songs in blurbs ranging from one paragraph ("Boys") to five ("Strawberry Fields Forever"). The author's same-page footnotes are blinding, and though he is knowledgeable about the released music, he doesn't have the insider information of a Mark Lewisohn, or even of the average bootlegger, for rare tracks. MacDonald's tone rarely rises out of a professorial voice, which will either entrance you or put you to sleep. "Eye-opening..."—*Q*.

Madow, Stuart and Sobul, Jeff. *The Colour of Your Dreams: The Beatles' Psychedelic Music*. Pittsburgh, PA: Dorrance Publishing Co., 1992. 116 pages. Appendix A: Discography of Beatles Psychedelic Music. Appendix B: Key Occurrences Between 1966-1968. Bibliography.

An analysis of The Beatles' psychedelic music, from early experimentations with backwards music and tape loops ("Rain") to quintessential examples that ushered in 1967's Summer of Love ("Strawberry Fields Forever"). The author unsteadily correlates The Beatles' work of this period with that of those they influenced, and falls into the trap of trying to find the "story" of intentionally oblique songs such as "Lucy in the Sky with Diamonds." The three-four line paragraphs in a 116-page work suggest this is only an outline for a larger, more substantive treatment.

Mellers, Wilfrid. *Twilight of the Gods: The Music of the Beatles*. New York: Schirmer Books (division of Macmillan Publishing Co., Inc.), 1973. 215 pages. Glossary. Eight-page black-and-white photo insert. Discography. Index.

At the time of publication, a landmark work in that it was among the first to treat The Beatles' music as a serious contribution to western culture. Twenty plus years later and this title seems a bit dated and slightly British for an American readership. Inexplicably, song titles are in italics with all words except the first in lowercase. The description of "Any Time at All" as "one of the blackest, most Negroid of early Beatle songs" turns politically correct lingo a century backwards. The two-page discography is a joke by 1990's standards. Too rigorous for the average reader.

Neises, Charles P. *The Beatles Reader: A Selection of Contemporary Views, News and Reviews of the Beatles in Their Heyday*. Ann Arbor, MI: Pierian Press, 1984. 216 pages. Further Reading.

Part of the vast "Rock & Roll Remembrance Series" from Pierian Press, *The Beatles Reader* consists of twenty-plus writings on The Beatles spanning the 1960's and 70's. Writers include David Frost, William J. Buckley, Terence O'Grady, Jonathon Cott, and others. The five sections concern news stories, analysis of three classic albums (*Rubber Soul, Sgt. Pepper's Lonely Hearts Club Band*, and *The Beatles*, aka *The White Album*), varied critical viewpoints, reviews of two movies, and the Beatles as soloists. A more comprehensive, less idiosyncratic compendium would have had given this collection better shelf life.

O'Grady, Terence. *The Beatles: A Musical Evolution*. Boston: Twayne Publishers (division of G.K. Hall), 1983. 216 pages. Notes and References. Selected Discography. Selected Bibliography. Index.

A follow-up of sorts to Mellers' study (above). The text contains incisive information on The Beatles' influences, early recording sessions, and concerts, and then goes head-on into exploring the music itself, complete with chord progressions. As expected, non-music fans would need a glossary to understand much of the jargon that runs throughout. Who on earth wants to deal with terminology and phrases such as "ostinato-based," "harmonic suavity," and "each beat subdivided in triplets"? For music history students only. Replaces O'Grady's earlier *The Music of the Beatles: From 1962 to Sgt. Pepper's Lonely Hearts Club Band*.

O'Grady, Terence. *The Music of the Beatles: From 1962 to Sgt. Pepper's Lonely Hearts Club Band*.

See: *The Beatles: A Musical Evolution*, above.

Riley, Tim. *Tell Me Why: A Beatles Commentary*. New York: Vintage Books, Inc. (division of Random House, Inc.), 1988. 426 pages. Selected Bibliography. Index.

An attempt to offset some of the highbrow writing of Mellers' and O'Grady's works (both above). While the language is certainly easier for the average fan to chew on, the commentary will probably be spit out. Riley is simply wrong on several counts. He claims that all of The Beatles, save Ringo, had straight middle-class upbringings. As George Harrison attests in his autobiography, he also grew up in poverty, struggling to keep warm in the winter months. The Beatles' unreleased recording "How Do You Do It" is mistitled "How Do You Do" throughout (apparently Riley never heard the song). Riley even claims "*Revolver* stands at the pinnacle of what The Beatles can do." Should The Beatles have quit at that point and not recorded *Sgt. Pepper's Lonely Hearts Club Band*? Originally published by Knopf, 1988.

Turner, Steve. *A Hard Day's Write: The Stories Behind Every Beatles' Song*. London: Little Brown & Company, 1994. 208 pages. Approximately 150 glossy black-and-white and 50 glossy color photographs throughout. Chronology. Discography. Bibliography. Index.

In *A Hard Day's Write*, author Steve Turner sifts through the origins of 186 songs written by The Beatles themselves (in other words, excluding covers), featuring background on the real figures, places, and events that triggered the composers' creative juices. Some, such as "Strawberry Fields Forever" (a children's community home run by the Salvation Army) and Tara Browne's car crash for "A Day in the Life" ("he blew his mind out in a car"), are common knowledge. Others, such as that Smokey Robinson inspired "This Boy" and that the disappearance of teenage runaway Melanie Coe led to "She's Leaving Home," are less obvious. Turner's work sparkles when there is something to say, but falls flat for songs in which the germinations were more tenuous. Further, the book doesn't address unreleased Beatles' songs or those Lennon-McCartney wrote for others. Lovingly produced and full of eye-catching photos, this book merits a B+ for its detailed insights into Beatles source material.

DICTIONARIES AND ENCYCLOPEDIAS

Friede, Goldie; Titone, Robin; and Weiner, Sue. *The Beatles A to Z*. New York: Metheun, 1980. 248 pages. 100 black-and-white photographs. Tours, Beatles Special Performances, Addresses.

Nifty encyclopedic paperback that somehow manages to fit in concise entries for everything pertaining to the Fab Four, both as a group and solo: songs, records, people, places, song characters (Polythene Pam), and so on. The book dated quickly, however, as it was published just before Lennon's assassination. Eager young Beatles fans might want to dig this one up to find out the historic significance of things such as Narita International Airport (where Paul was taken into custody for possession of marijuana in 1980). In certain respects, more carefully prepared than Harry's *The Ultimate Beatles Encyclopedia* (see page 76).

Harry, Bill. *The Beatles Who's Who*. New York: Delilah Books (Putnam), 1982. 192 pages. Approximately 100 black-and-white photographs throughout. Index.

Insufferably bad A to Z of people in The Beatles' lives. The entries are not alphabetized, so readers have to first consult the index to find any piece of information. In many cases, such as with electronics guru Magic Alex, the flipping back and forth will prove fruitless. Entries contain obvious oversights and careless misinterpretation of fact. A low point in music reference. Harry fared much better with his still-flawed encyclopedia (see below).

Harry, Bill. *The Ultimate Beatles Encyclopedia*. New York: Hyperion, 1992. 720 pages. Over 300 black-and-white photographs scattered throughout. (First published in Great Britain in 1992 by Virgin Books.)

The greatest advantage of this encyclopedia is that it contains entries on hundreds of fourth level players peripheral to The Beatles' scene, e.g., Brian Lewis (Apple employee). To the book's further credit, the entries are accessible, fully cross-referenced, and loaded with rare photos. As you flip through the pages, however, you'll spend more time nit-picking than enjoying the content. First, there's next to nothing on The Beatles' solo music. Second, why an entry for some films (*Candy*) but not others (*Imagine*)? Third, why isn't there an entry for the BBC? Or Marc Bolan (among Ringo's closest friends)? Or Alan White (Plastic Ono Band drummer)? Despite an overwhelming amount of inconsistencies, omissions, and errors, overall it is "...clearly one of Harry's better efforts"—*Goldmine*.

DISCOGRAPHIES, RECORDING GUIDES, AND COLLECTIBLES

Anjoorian, Jason. *The Beatles Japanese Record Guide*. Shrewsbury, MA: Jason Press, 1994. 216 pages. Approximately 500 black-and-white photographs, covering every page. Appendix A: Title Translations. Index.

Acknowledging that the main interest among collectors in North America is U.S. and U.K. releases, author Jason Anjoorian prevails upon buyers to stop fearing Japanese albums and become educated about a thing or two. In simple terms, he explains for the layperson the distinctions in Japanese pressings, label varia-

tions, and pricing for yen-marked items. For both Beatles and solo Beatles releases, Anjoorian identifies catalog numbers, release dates, song line-ups, monetary value, and other important details. In the back, there are crucial song translations from the Japanese. The book's multitude of photo reproductions (some of which are truly unique) and spurts of information make this essential for anyone seeking knowledge about Japanese Beatles recordings. "...no one will argue against the obvious and numerous positive merits of this outstanding work"—*Goldmine*.

Augsburger, Jeff; Eck, Marty; and Rann, Rick. *The Beatles Memorabilia Price Guide*. Radnor, PA: Wallace-Homestead Book Company, 1994. 232 pages. Over 400 black-and-white illustrations throughout; one eight-page color insert.

A comprehensive guide to Beatles memorabilia that was first published in 1988 and is now more up-to-date than other comparable works. Artifacts are arranged in the following sections: general memorabilia (clothing, tickets, jewelry, etc.); publications (books, magazines, sheet music, etc.); and record promotional items (posters). Easy-to-use with an uncluttered design, this is a very good resource for collectors, especially since it includes a great deal of handy advice on how to beware of counterfeits and test for condition. "...Beatles fan[s] of all ages will enjoy the countless hours just spent browsing through this volume"—*Goldmine*.

Berkenstadt, Jim and Belmo (aka Belmer, Scott). Foreword by Adrian Belew. *Black Market Beatles*. Burlington, Ontario (Canada): Collector's Guide Publishing, 1995. 240 pages. Approximately 225 black-and-white reproductions of album covers. Appendix A: Glossary. Appendix B: List of Beatles Bootlegs Organized by Manufacturer. Appendix C: Photo Survey of Bootleg Trademarks and Logos. Appendix D: Bootlegger's Family Trees. Reference Books.

Reputedly all-you-need-to-know about Beatles bootlegging, this book includes six semi-illicit chapters from self-proclaimed experts Berkenstadt and Belmo. The two examine the history of bootlegging, delve into the process of how it is typically accomplished and cite other top artists who are likely bootleg candidates (e.g., Bob Dylan and The Rolling Stones) before getting into the core of the subject: Beatles bootlegs. Each pirate record is described in chronological order, from the earliest recordings of The Quarry Men to the final *Abbey Road* sessions. A follow-up section containing interviews with bootleggers affords these characters way too much limelight. Given the various Beatles *Anthology* releases, casual fans will most likely have little interest in this book; collectors and scholars would need it for the reference shelf.

Carr, Roy and Tyler, Tony. *The Beatles: An Illustrated Record*. New York: Harmony (division of Crown), 1978. 128 pages. 200 black-and-white and color illustrations, covering nearly every page. U.S. Discography.

Lavishly illustrated year-by-year discography of the boys, but by no means comprehensive (no mention of bootlegs, single releases, EPs, etc.). Carr provides producer and release dates (it's unclear whether they refer to U.S. or U.K.) for each LP; on the sides are general events in The Beatles' lives with random quotes. The write-ups on the LPs are overtly critical and occasionally downright crabby ("Octopus's Garden": "a remake of `Yellow Submarine' with further subnautical noises and little else to commend it"). Age-old and overtaken by Lewisohn's works, both graphically and in terms of research content. An index would have helped.

Castleman, Harry and Podrazik, Walter J. *All Together Now: The First Complete Beatles Discography, 1961-1975*. Ann Arbor, MI: Pierian Press, 1976.

See: *The End of the Beatles?*.

Castleman, Harry and Podrazik, Walter J. *The Beatles Again?*. Ann Arbor, MI: Pierian Press, 1977.

See: *The End of the Beatles?*.

Castleman, Harry and Podrazik, Walter J. *The End of the Beatles?*. Ann Arbor, MI: Pierian Press, 1985. 554 pages. Approximately 150 black-and-white photographs throughout. Indexes and Instructions.

Castleman and Podrazik, the dynamic duo of Beatles research, were among the first of the dedicated Beatles' researchers to pull together lists of recordings, releases, bootlegs, and so

on. Their first work, *All Together Now*, was originally published in 1976. *The Beatles Again* was issued in 1977, continuing where the earlier book left off. Divided into five sections, this updated version includes the following meaty sections: chronological discography; background on records peripherally connected to The Beatles (by friends, such as Harry Nilsson); bootleg records; essays on unreleased recordings and publications; and massive Indexes (e.g., songs by the band and solo). Poorly formatted and haphazardly arranged, this work is a trial to use because you need to have the earlier volumes to find out about the years preceding 1977. Nevertheless, it is a staple for beginning collectors, if supplemented by the classics by Allen Wiener and Mark Lewisohn (see below for both). And no, it's not the end!

Cox, Perry and Miller, Michael. *The Beatles Price and Reference Guide for American Records*. Phoenix, AZ: Cox-Miller, Ltd., 1986. 362 pages. Over 1,000 black-and-white reproductions of album covers; one four-page color insert. Glossary.

A catalog of pricing information, including singles, LPs and EPs, with rating systems for price (circa mid-1980's), gradings, catalog numbers, and special jacket cover details. The song titles can only be detected if you strain your eyes at the reproductions of the disks, which have been photographed too dark. Giuliano's work (see below) contains high-quality color shots that put this book to shame; however, that book does not include pricing information. Cox and Miller know their stuff, but non-collectors will be turned off by the advertising in the back. In 1983, Cox collaborated on a similar book with Joe Lindsay entitled *The Complete U.S. Record Price Guide*.

Downes, Jonathan. *Take This, Brother, May It Serve You Well: An Incomplete Guide to the Unreleased Music of the Beatles*. No city: Spanish Train Publications, 1988. Unpaginated (approximately 192 pages).

Amateurish self-publication, loaded with typos, that attempts to catalog unreleased recordings such as "What's the New Mary Jane" (incorrectly titled in this work) and bootleg albums. Downes' book is difficult to read and manage, especially considering that the bootlegs are not arranged in any particular order and are not indexed. Without catalog numbers or labels for bootlegs, the use for this work is virtually nil. Take this, brother, and serve it you know where.

Fenick, Barbara. Photographs by Kolodziej, Rick A. *Collecting the Beatles: An Introduction & Price Guide to Fab Four Collectibles, Records & Memorabilia Volume 2*. Ann Arbor, MI: Pierian Press, 1985. 280 pages. Approximately 200 black-and-white photographs throughout. Appendix One: The Auctions at Sotheby. Appendix Two: Collecting and the Computer. Appendix Three: Additions to the Price Guide. Glossary. The Resource Guide: An Address List for Collectors. Questionnaire.

First published in 1982 as volume one, this valuable guide to collecting not only offers you advice on various Beatles-related products, it provides sound explanations to the layman about condition, authenticity, prices, and much more. Price ranges (now very dated) are supplied for albums (including promotional releases, bootlegs, etc.), novelties, books, magazines, jewelry, movie items, comics, and more. Many of the items, as photographed by Kolodziej, are fascinating to browse through: Beatles high-back tennis shoes; an Apple Corp. paperweight; official German documents on John Lennon; etc. Collectors will need to own both volumes one and two, as obviously not everything is repeated from volume to volume. Handy, despite its casual assemblage.

Giuliano, Geoffrey. *The Beatles Album: 30 Years of Music and Memorabilia*. New York: Viking Studio Books, 1991. 256 pages. Approximately 800 color and black-and-white album covers, photographs, paintings, etc., covering every page.

Illustrated amalgam of Beatles record sleeves, with chapters on: group LPs; solo LPs; bootlegs; singles; EPs and picture covers; acetates; flexi-discs; tapes and compact discs; picture discs, colored vinyl, and maxi-singles; etc. The visual flip-side to Allen Wiener's work (see below), this book fails to provide specific release dates in the U.S. or the U.K., and therefore has limited reference value. One page devoted to five Beatles back covers seems unnecessary, as does the rather flimsy memorabilia section (where are the lunch boxes and wigs?). The chapter on Apple Records, highlighting artists such as Badfinger, Mary Hopkin, The Iveys, etc., has greater significance. Thankfully unburdened by Giuliano's

usual pontificating, this book contains "...minimal text or other commentary..."—*Booklist*.

Howlett, Kevin. *The Beatles at the Beeb: The Story of Their Radio Career*. London: British Broadcasting Corporation, 1982. 128 pages. Approximately 50 black-and-white photographs throughout. Beatles Books. Discography. With a Little Help from My Friends. Index.

Between March 1962 and 1965, The Beatles appeared on over 50 radio shows on BBC radio, for which they recorded an astounding 88 different songs (69 of which appear on *The Beatles Live at the BBC* double CD). At the time of this book's release, the songs were available only in bootleg, which meant only collectors would have had interest; now that the CDs are out, the information included here is less than one can find in the CD's accompanying booklet. The show's co-producer, Kevin Howlett, reprints host Brian Matthew's on-the-air conversations with the boys, but he doesn't provide any fresh insights into their musical creations or working methods.

Lewisohn, Mark. Introductory interview with Paul McCartney. *The Beatles Recording Sessions: The Official Abbey Road Studio Session Notes 1962-1970*. New York: Harmony Books (division of Crown), 1988. 204 pages. More than 350 color and black-and-white photographs throughout. Discography. Index. Glossary.

The official diary of The Beatles recordings at EMI—painstakingly researched by Lewisohn, teeming with rare archive photos, and beautifully designed in the shape of an album cover. Each recording session reveals the musician line-up, time of recording, producer, engineer, and so forth. Lewisohn's notes and descriptions are filled with brilliant revelations and insights into the sessions. (Why *didn't* The Beatles release the "searing" Lennon vocal "Leave My Kitten Alone" in the 1960's?) The McCartney interview—quite a coup—provides much insight into rare tracks ("Thinking of Linking") and the inner workings of the Lennon/McCartney songwriting team. An absolute must-have for The Beatles fan who wants to know what he or she is listening to: a masterpiece.

McCoy, William and McGeary, Mitchell. *Every Little Thing: The Definitive Guide to Beatles Recording Variations, Rare Mixes & Other Musical Oddities 1958-1986.* Ann, Arbor, MI: Popular Culture Ink, 1990. 368 pages. Approximately 100 black-and-white reproductions of records and album covers. Glossary. Bibliography. Song & Record Title Index. People, Places & Things Index. Label & Record Number Index.

A mammoth exploration into rare Beatles tracks, citing every version of every song known to exist, and highlighting fine distinctions made among mono, stereo, and quadraphonic versions. The authors investigate various rumors that have circulated about Beatles' recordings, which results in formidable conclusions. Notably, they speculate about why a respected drummer like Bernard Purdie would claim to have drummed on 21 early Beatles tracks, when all evidence indicates otherwise. Intriguing issues like this aside, the book contains a great deal of information that is not presented in user-friendly form. Details on rare tracks from *The White Album* are mixed in with facts about earlier recordings with Tony Sheridan and "The Star Club Tape." A section on "records most collectors will never own" has dated badly, since several of those songs appear on *Anthology.* Needless to say, Popular Culture Ink does its usual superlative job pulling together reference material in the back, including a glossary, a bibliography, and indexes. A trial to sift through, but worthwhile for patient collectors.

Reinhart, Charles. Foreword by Wally (Walter) Podrazik. *You Can't Do That! Beatles Bootlegs & Novelty Records.* Ann Arbor, MI: Pierian Press, 1981. 412 pages. Approximately 50 black-and-white reproductions of bootleg covers. Appendix: Everything You Always Wanted to Know about Bootlegs But Were Too Busy Collecting Them to Ask.

A comprehensive bootleg guide for the collector, with the good, the bad, and the ugly all side by side. The author provides systematic and highly useful background information on the bootlegging process, and gives serious advice on what to look for (and steer clear from). Sections, which include both group and solo recordings, are divided into bootlegs, counterfeits, and novelties. There are substantial indexes for bootlegs and novelties organized by personal names, song and album

titles, cover versions, topics, and more. The Appendix (written by Tom Schultheiss) is a fine essay on the issues involved in bootlegging. Reliable collectors highly recommend this work, in spite of the errors and oversights one might expect from a book of this magnitude.

Russell, Jeff P. *The Beatles Album File and Complete Discography.* London: Blandford Press (division of Cassell), 1989. 310 pages. Approximately 100 black-and-white reproductions of album covers. Appendices: the Alternative Versions; the Unreleased Tracks; the Non-Album Tracks. Discography. Index.

First published in 1982 (under various titles, including *The Beatles on Record*) and updated again in 1989, this is a clear, if basic, presentation of recording data on British and American releases. The descriptions of each track and the recording processes involved pale in comparison with Lewisohn's work (see above), as here we only have composer, running time, line-ups, and a concise, one-paragraph description. Liverpudlian author Jeff Russell does not provide source material for any of the tracks.

Schwartz, David. *Listening to the Beatles: An Audiophile's Guide to the Sound of the Fab Four Volume 1: Bootlegs and Singles; and Volume 2.* 336 pages (each). Approximately 100 black-and-white photographs throughout. Glossary. Song and Record Title Index. People, Places and Things Index.

Volume 1 of this set is a quality-gauging source to Beatles bootlegs and singles—two areas that don't necessarily mesh. In his ratings of the records, author David Schwartz isn't looking for artistic merit on the part of The Beatles, but rather, for sound characteristics of the bootlegs put out by the different companies. In the bootleg section, titles are divided by 7-inch and 12-inch records. In the commercial singles section, the focus is on international mass-market releases. Volume 2 covers audiophile records only. In both volumes, charts rate the recordings in order of quality. Highly sophisticated material only digestible for collectors with acute hearing.

Stannard, Neville. Edited by Tobler, John. *The Beatles: The Long and Winding Road: A History of The Beatles on Record*. New York: Avon, 1982. 240 pages. Approximately 150 black-and-white reproductions of albums covers and graphics. Appendices: cover versions; "Paul is Dead" clues; unreleased recordings; Hamburg recordings; bootlegs; the British Market Research Bureau chart; song recording dates; Christmas records. Bibliography. Index.

Divided into two parts (British releases and then American), this discography chronologically introduces every Beatles single and LP up through the early 1980's, excluding solo material. Entries are numbered and contain song timings, composer(s), lead singer(s), sleeve notes, catalogue numbers, tidbits of history, and notable cover versions. Albums are distinguished from singles by bold type. The work has its limited uses, but one should be skeptical when an author concedes that the song timings may not be accurate. Additionally, the book should have utilized year headings to provide immediate recognition. Difficult to sort through and not worth the effort.

Stern, Michael; Crawford, Barbara; and Lamon, Hollis. *The Beatles: A Reference & Value Guide*. Paducah, KY: Collector Books (division of Schroder Publishing), 1993. 142 pages. Approximately 400 color photographs of collectibles, covering every page.

An attractive representation of Beatles memorabilia, excluding books, records, and fanzines. Each item is matted on a sky-blue background and dated (where possible), with pricing information for good, excellent, and mint conditions. (In other words, if it's tattered, it's not worth much in the commercial sense.) All of the extraordinary pieces here—including bootybags, buttons, and scarves—look to be in the mint category and have been clearly photographed, so print details on the surfaces can be read. Unfortunately, the book is not indexed, so readers will need to do quite a bit of rummaging. Good fun, even if you're not a collector.

Wallgren, Marc. *The Beatles on Record*. New York: Fireside (Simon & Schuster), 1982. 336 pages. Approximately 300 black-and-white reproductions of album covers throughout. Appendix I. Appendix II. Appendix III. Index.

Basic information on every official Beatles and solo Beatles release up through early 1982. The photos take up much of the space on each page, although catalog number, release date, a one-two paragraph description, and chart-data details are also included. Wallgren is a pro and clearly knows his Beatles, but later writers have delved much deeper into the stories behind the songs, the recordings of the tunes, and the availability of unreleased tracks. Does not stand the test of time.

Wiener, Allen J. *The Beatles: The Ultimate Recording Guide*. Holbrook: Adams, Inc., 1994. 596 pages. One hundred black-and-white photographs of album covers. Appendices of The Beatles as Supporting Players and Videocassettes and Laser Discs. References/Recommended Periodicals. Song and Record Title Index.

A complete recording chronology and discography of the group, from the first recordings of The Quarry Men to all solo efforts. Includes live recordings, unreleased songs, bootlegs, special releases, alternate versions, and even solo contributions to the works of other musicians (Carly Simon, Eric Clapton, et. al.). A special advantage is that it is the only volume to catalog all of the above, plus releases in both the United States and the United Kingdom. Originally published in 1986 as *The Beatles: A Recording History* by McFarland & Company Inc. "Perhaps no other Beatles researcher has gone as far in determining the minute differences between versions of Beatles recordings and releases, and where they can be found" —*Goldmine*.

FANZINES AND FAN CLUBS

BEATLanta. P.O. Box 2062, Stockbridge, GA 30281.

This Atlanta Beatles fan club is completely based on member participation. The club sponsors events such as record and CD shows, picnics, concerts (1960's stars), and its own Fab Four Fest. To get on the mailing list, send a self-addressed stamped envelope to the above address.

Beatlefan. P.O. Box 33515, Decatur, GA 30033.

Founded in 1978, this illustrated Beatles magazine consists of approximately 34 pages and contains: in-depth interviews; Beatlenews; recording, merchandising, publishing, and expo advertising; classifieds; pen pals; and more. Over the years, interview subjects have included Paul McCartney, Yoko Ono, Ringo Starr, and many others in The Beatles family. Alan Kozinn, Wally Podrazik, Bill Harry, and Mark Wallgren are among the expert contributors. Published bimonthly. $15 per year in the U.S.; $25 in the U.K., Western Europe and Latin America; $27 elsewhere. Payable in U.S. currency only.

Beatlefest Mail Order Catalogue. Beatlefest, P.O. Box 436, Westwood, NJ, 07675-0436. Also available at annual Beatlefest (Meadowlands Hilton, Secaucus, NJ).

Full color Beatles-only memorabilia catalog offering: videos, books, ties, t-shirts, socks, jewelry, keychains, posters, album art, mugs, information on the annual U.S. Beatlefest, and more.

The Beatleletter. Attn. James N. McNally, P.O. Box 13, St. Clair Shores, MI 48080.

Quarterly newsletter for serious collectors of the Beatles and related artists. Each 18-page packet contains photocopies of black-and-white photographs, news on all releases from The Beatles (group and solo), bootlegs, books and more. The cost of subscription is $7 U.S.; $10 Canada and Mexico; $12 elsewhere. Payable in U.S. dollars only to James N. McNally.

Beatlemania. BM Publications, PSF 565 99011, Erfurt, Thuringen, Germany.

Bimonthly German fanzine consisting of 52 pages. Intended for die-hard collectors (although not printed in English), this stapled booklet does not actually offer merchandising or collectibles. The cost of one-year subscription is 30 deutsche marks.

Beatles Club Wuppertal. Paulussenstrafle 7 4239 Wuppertal Germany.

Founded in 1986, this club claims to be the largest and oldest Beatles fan organization in Germany. The club publishes *A Ticket to Write*, a 28-page quarterly magazine printed exclusively in German. The cost of membership is 35 deutsche marks (DM) U.S.; 25 DM Europe.

Beatles Fans Unite Fan Club. P.O. Box 5012, Cicero, IL 60650-0123.

Non-profit fan club established in 1982 that has since become international. Members receive

six newsletters per year (plus a Christmas issue), a membership card and a special gift. Holds three club get-togethers per year. *Beatle News*, the 20-page, one-sided stapled newsletter contains updates, birthday features, original poetry, pen pals, photocopies of photos, book reviews, and more.

Beatles Museum. Heinsbergstrafle 13 D-50675 Koln-Zentrum Cologne Germany.

Fan club affiliated with The Beatles Museum in Cologne, Germany. Offers an international catalog of rare Beatles collectibles, notably CDs, LPs, EPs, singles, and bootlegs. The collection spans Japan, the Netherlands, England, Australia, Canada, Germany, Italy, and many other countries. "Best customers" are invited to join the club for free, but the cost of individual items remains the same.

Belmo's Beatleg News: The International Newsletter for Collectors. Belmo Publishing, P.O. Box 17163, Ft. Mitchell, KY 41017.

Begun in 1987, this 12-page stapled newsletter reviews new Beatles bootlegs, as well as all such material from The Beatles solo. The packet also includes drawings, photocopies of cover art, other Beatles news, essays on rare tapes and recordings, and more. The cost of six issues is $17.50 North America; $20 Europe. Payable by money order, check (U.S. bank), or cash (at your own risk).

bu Magazine. P.O. Box 602, 3430 AP Nieuwwegein, the Netherlands.

Aka *beatles unlimited Magazine*, this glossy booklet—available in several languages, including English—contains Beatles news, book reviews, record/CD reviews (including bootlegs and work from other artists), black-and-white photographs, chart listings, and information on the annual International Beatles Convention. Published bimonthly. $27 per year in U.S., payable by personal check only.

Good Day Sunshine. P.O. Box 1008, Mar Vista, CA 90066- 1008.

Eighty-page, illustrated fanzine that purports to be the "largest fan club magazine in the U.S." First issued circa 1980, *Good Day Sunshine* contains behind-the-scenes news, interviews with key Beatles-related figures (engineer Geoff Emerick, producer Jeff Lynne, and publicist Derek Taylor), articles on memorabilia, a bootleg column, and more. Contributors have included Jeff Augsburger and Wally Podrazik. Published five times per year. $15 for one year U.S.; $18 Canada; $24 elsewhere.

Le Club du Sgt. Pepper. 10 cite Delpal, 7800 Versailles France.

Founded in 1988, this club publishes *Abbey Road Magazine*, a 34-page stapled booklet exclusively in French with a color cover, black-and-white photographs throughout, articles updating new Beatles releases and more. Write for pricing information.

The London Beatles Fan Club. 4 Oaklands, Constance Road, Whitton, Twickenham, Middlesex TW2 7JQ England.

Fan club formed in 1988 "to enable Beatles fans to get together to share their love of the best group ever." Members become involved in a free pen pal service and are invited to regular social events such as video shows, quiz nights, and parties. The club publishes *Abbey Road*, an 80-page bound booklet containing black-and-white photographs, editorials, Beatles news, anniversary reports, articles on new releases, concert and appearance notes (of the solo Beatles), essays on inner-circle players (such as Neil Aspinall), and much more. The cost of subscription is $25 U.S.; £11 U.K.; £12 elsewhere in Europe. In the U.S. only, payable by U.S. dollar checks to Esther Shafer or Richard Porter. Everywhere else, payable by a check to the above club name drawn on a British bank, an international money order, or in cash.

The 910. P.O. Box 114, Princeton Junction, NJ 08550.

A twelve-page "international journal for Beatles scholars and collectors." Each stapled packet contains overtly critical essays and reviews of Beatles releases and bootlegs—often in the form of dialogues among the various contributors—meticulous notes about rare tracks, alternate versions, special releases, collector's items, and performances. The contributing editor and publisher is Doug Sulpy, while other writers have included Alan Pollack and Ray Schweighardt. The cost of a six-issue subscription is $22.50 U.S.; $25 Canada and Mexico; $34 Europe. The price per issue is $3.95 U.S. (prices vary for back issues).

Octopus' Garden. Attn: Beth Foster, 21 Montclair Avenue, Verona, NJ 07044.

Sixteen-page newsletter founded in 1991 that provides concert and album reviews and Beatles news. Accepts stories, comics, and poetry from subscribers. A special emphasis on guess which Beatle—Ringo! The cost is $12 for new members and $8 for renewals.

Sgt. Beatles Fan Club. Apdo, Correos 7.250 50080 Zaragoza, Spain.

Spanish fan club that offers members special cassette releases (Spanish artists recording Beatles songs), key chains, and other collectibles. The club publishes *The Beatles' Garden*, a quarterly, glossy (exclusively Spanish) magazine with a color cover, color and black-and-white illustrations, translated interviews (conducted by notable authors such as Mark Lewisohn and Robert Freeman), updates on recordings, and more. Also publishes filler newsletters in-between magazine releases. The cost of membership is $30 (cash by registered mail only).

Sgt. Peppers Club. c/o Edmund Thielow, August-Bebel- Strabe 6 08371 Glauchau, Germany.

German fan club tied to its own Beat(les) Museum. Offers fans rare books and CDs for purchase. Write for more details.

Tokyo Beatles Fan Club. 4-6-14-304 Toyotama-Kita, Nerima-ku, Tokyo #176 Japan.

Japanese fan club (aka *TBFC*) that publishes *Tokyo Beatles Fan Club Magazine*, which contains both Japanese and English. The 98-page booklet features a color cover, black-and-white photographs throughout, examinations of rare recordings and releases, profiles of solo Beatles' activities, interviews, book reviews, news, and much more. The cost of an annual, four-issue subscription is $27.

The Working Class Hero. B. Whatmough, 3311 Niagara Street, Pittsburgh, PA 15213.

Originally begun in the late 1960's as *Beatle Peace Followers*, this club merged for a spell with *Beatles Live In Pepperland* until it took its present name in the early 1970's after the Lennon song (although it focuses on all four Beatles). The club publishes a quarterly fanzine of the same name. The cost of membership is

$10 per year U.S.; $15 elsewhere. Payable, by money order only, to: Sue Link. Write for more information on the zine's contents.

FILM

Gross, Edward. *The Fab Films of the Beatles*. Las Vegas, NV: Pioneer, 1990. 160 pages. Approximately 60 black-and-white photographs throughout. The Videos: A Guide.

Atrocious "films of" study, devoid of any color and without any visible knowledge of The Beatles' movie career. The first part covers films starring The Beatles; this is followed by various sections on screen projects featuring John, Paul, George, or Ringo. Entire sentences have been garbled (either by bad writing, editing, typesetting, or all three combined), while all of John Lennon's video work with Yoko has been entirely overlooked. Out of sheer ignorance, Gross savages several classic Beatles' songs ("I'll Be Back"), but it's this book that merits drubbing.

No author. *The Beatles: The Yellow Submarine*. London: Vinyl Experience Limited, 1994. Unpaginated (approximately 48 pages). Approximately 50 color photographs, covering every page.

Beautiful background shots and outtakes from The Beatles beloved animated feature. This book includes photographs of the artists at work, plus The Beatles themselves mingling with life-size cardboard cutouts of their alteregos. As it contains little text, this book only succeeds as a visual reminder of the film's charm.

Orton, Joe. Introduction by John Lahr. *Up Against It*. London: Eyre Metheun, 1979. 70 pages.

The complete screenplay to *Up Against It*, which began as a project commissioned by Walter Shenson (who produced The Beatles' first two films). English comic playwright Joe Orton (*Loot*) was first scheduled to rework a script called *Shades of a Personality*, but his ideas expanded and he came up with this script. The farce, which would have cast The Beatles as subversives, was never produced. Orton himself died on the day he was scheduled to discuss shooting the film with Shenson. (Orton was struck on the head with a hammer by his homosexual lover.) This script is full of Orton's bizarre, macabre sense of humor and

sexual innuendo (especially the title!), and is well worth a read for fans of the playwright or anyone wishing to speculate how The Beatles might have carried this off.

Sinyard, Neil. *The Films of Richard Lester*. Totowa: Barnes & Noble Books, 1985. 174 pages. One eight-page black-and-white photo insert. Filmography. Index.

An incisive, critical examination of the British director's craft, from *The Running, Jumping & Standing Still Film* to *Superman III*. About ten pages are devoted to Lester's Beatles' films *A Hard Day's Night* and *Help!*. Sinyard is stuffy but generally knows what he's talking about: he praises "Can't Buy Me Love" as the "greatest sequence" in the earlier film; and he finds unified meaning to the chaos in *Help!* (the concept of sacrifice and loss). Sorry Beatles fanatics—there's nothing about cut footage. Would you believe a photo of Superman is on the cover?

Yule, Andrew. *The Man Who "Framed" the Beatles: A Biography of Richard Lester*. Introduction by Paul McCartney. New York: Donald I. Fine, Inc. 384 pages. Approximately 75 black-and-white photographs throughout. Filmography. Deleted Scene From *A Hard Day's Night*. Index.

What does Richard Lester himself think of having his 35-year film career reduced to two Beatles films? The book has some information on The Goons (a Lennon favorite) and some fresh anecdotes pertaining to The Beatles in films, but as a biography of Lester it falls flat. The captions sport goofy quotes that are laughably unfunny. On the positive side, the McCartney intro *is* funny (if The Beatles were The Marx Brothers, he considered himself Zeppo); the book also contains Paul McCartney's cut solo scene from *A Hard Day's Night*. "...Yule's direct access to the director himself [is] the greatest strength of this work"—*Goldmine*.

GENERAL REFERENCE

Fulpen, H.V. *The Beatles: An Illustrated Diary*. New York: Perigee Books (Putnam Publishing Group), 1982. 176 pages. Over 300 black-and-white photographs throughout.

In this highly illustrated volume—which inaccurately claims to boast "over 1,000 photographs"—Fulpen splices chronologies of The Beatles' history with dozens of special features pertaining to the band. There is no real rhyme or reason to the selection of features, some of which include: a history of Ringo's drums (why, then not one also on Paul's bass?); the Paul is Dead hoax; engineer Norman (nicknamed "Normal" by Lennon) Smith; Pete Best; etc. The book uses the same dust jacket image as on Miles' *The Beatles in Their Own Words* (see Quizbooks and Quotebooks, below). Check out Lewisohn's works (see Chronologies, above) for more up-to-date—and better packaged— chronological data.

Harry, Bill. *Paperback Writers: The History of the Beatles in Print.* London: Virgin Books Limited, 1984. 192 pages. Approximately 150 reproductions of book and magazine covers. Index.

This time around, tireless Beatles writer Bill Harry chronicles Fab Four literature, with substantial sections on books, comics, music books, fanzines, and more. Titles in the book section are arranged chronologically—not by author, title, or subject—so either you have to know when a book was published or else consult the index. Harry's summaries are by intent critical, and he provides star ratings (one as the lowest and five as the highest) for each title. This system proves rather senseless, since most of the books receive three to five stars. As a case in point, Brown and Gaines' tabloid gusher (see Biographies, above), receives three stars, which is two and a half too many. Harry also faces a conflict of interest in the sense that he reviews several of his own books, generously awarding them either four or five stars. Inferior in comparison with McKeen's and Terry's respective bibliographic works (see below for both).

No author. Forewords by Tom Schultheiss (volume one) and Wally Podrazik (volume two). *Beatlefan: The Authoritative Publication of Record for Fans of the Beatles, Volumes 1 & 2 (1978-79-1980)* and *Volumes 3 & 4 (1981-1982).* Ann Arbor, MI: Pierian Press, 1985 and 1986 (respectively). Volume one: 298 pages. Volume two: 794 pages. Index (each volume). Approximately 1,000 black-and-white reproductions of photos and miscellaneous artwork.

If you own both of these volumes, you are in possession of a fantastic amalgam of Beatles news, factoids, classifieds, letters, puzzles, interviews, discographical information, publications, etc. *Beatlefan* (see Fanzines, above), then dubbed "the fanzine Beatle fans have been waiting for," was first issued in December 1978 and was launched with an exclusive interview with ex-Wings drummer Joe English. Highly recommended, especially considering that the early issues overlap with John Lennon's death.

McKeen, William. *The Beatles: A Bio-Bibliography.* Westport, CT: Greenwood Press, 1989. 182 pages. Index.

An information-packed source that breaks down into two parts: The Beatles' lives, works, influences, and demise; and discography, bibliography, performances, films, television, concerts, and chronology. Difficult to read due to its miniscule type size and crammed-together paragraphing, but well worth the effort if you need one reference for quick access to Beatles factoids. Antiquated given the releases of the BBC material on CD and The Beatles *Anthology* documentary and related releases, and incomplete in the sense that it overlooks bootlegs, videos, and all solo material.

Reinhart, Charles. *The Book of Beatles Lists.* Chicago: Contemporary Books, Inc., 1985. 230 pages. 25 black-and-white photographs scattered throughout.

This collection of lists can be used for quick research or for finding juicy morsels of information. Although haphazardly organized and lacking access points (no subheadings or index), one can randomly find quite a lot of miscellany here: all Quarry Men members; 20 clues linking the group Klaatu with The Beatles; specific brands of equipment used by the group; and aliases used by The Beatles (George called himself "Son of Harry" on Dave Mason's "If You've Got Love"). The book is not without typos, as well as omissions: Elton John is missing from the list of Brian Epstein-related clients; and "Leave My Kitten Alone" is not on the list of unreleased songs. Some lists also seem quite irrelevant (*Rolling Stone* writer Brant Mewborn's "15 Best of the Beatles").

Schaffner, Nicholas. *The Beatles Forever.* New York: Cameron House, 1977. 222 pages. Approximately 200 black-and-white photographs; one four-page color insert. All

Together Now (rare singles collection). Every Little Thing (discography). With a Little Help from Their Friends (interpretations, tributes, and cash-ins). Popularity Contests. Bibliography. Index.

Fun-filled tribute that was a near classic in the 1970's. There's something for everyone here: general history, anecdotes, tour song line-ups, song lyrics, chart information, collectibles, superb shots of album covers (including rarities and bootlegs), and ample solo information. Schaffner does good research and has some interesting interpretations of many Beatles' songs (specifically, he found a Dylan Thomas influence for "Penny Lane"). Still has pizazz.

Terry, Carol D. (compiler and editor). Foreword by Tom Schultheiss. *Here, There and Everywhere: The First International Beatles Bibliography, 1962-1982.* Ann Arbor, MI: Pierian Press, 1985. 284 pages. Approximately six pages of photographs. Author Index. Title Index. Subject Index.

A huge undertaking to say the least, this is a comprehensive list of Beatles-related literature from all around the globe. Sections cite books, fan magazines (active and ceased), magazine articles, newspaper articles, reviews of books, reviews of recordings, sheet music books, special addresses, and more. As is typical for Pierian Press publications, the book contains several useful codes and closes with substantial indexes. An excellent launching point for Beatles research up through the early 1980's, though without any descriptive material on the publications themselves. "...for large general reference collections and academic libraries"— *Library Journal.*

INTERVIEWS

Giuliano, Geoffrey and Giuliano, Brenda. Foreword by Charlie Lennon. *The Lost Beatles Interviews.* New York: Dutton (Penguin Group), 1994. 400 pages. Two glossy 16-page black-and-white photo inserts. Afterword by Timothy Leary. Index.

Misguided collection of conversations involving the Beatles (group and solo), friends, relatives, and fellow musicians. Charlie Lennon, John's uncle, praises Giuliano's work to the hilt in the foreword, while Timothy Leary wraps up his 1960's acid dream in the afterword. The pieces sandwiched in between these bookends

contain moments of insight into The Beatles' personalities and famed wit, but their lack of source material makes one very suspicious. Giuliano tells us the date of each interview and, occasionally, where it took place; however, as in many cases he doesn't provide a full bibliography or state whether he transcribed the material from a printed source, the radio, a bootleg, etc., we can't be certain of the author's accuracy or faithfulness to the original texts. Incredibly biased toward the end, with Giuliano stepping in and out of the interviewer role to lash out against Yoko, John, and Paul. "...the book lacks narrative coherence"— *Publishers Weekly.*

Somach, Denny; Somach, Kathleen; Gunn, Kevin. Introduction by Scott Muni. *Ticket to Ride.* New York: William Morrow & Company, Inc., 1989. 316 pages. Over 50 black-and-white illustrations throughout.

The sell-line reads: "A Celebration of the Beatles Based Hit Radio Show." On WNEW-FM radio (102.7 in New York City), disc jockey Scott "the Professor" Muni hosted a weekly radio show titled "Ticket to Ride" in the late 1980's. The program, which featured rare recordings, history and Beatles-related news, spawned this book of excerpted interviews. Though most of the passages are brief (some as short as a paragraph), the range of people is astounding: all four Beatles (at different times), Pete Townshend, Smokey Robinson, Sid Bernstein, Eric Burdon, Cynthia Lennon, Roy Orbison, Billy Preston, etc. Also, many of the comments—such as Phil Collins' statement that, uncredited, he had played drums on Harrison's *All Things Must Pass* LP—are good nuggets for mavens. Muni fans have the additional treat of his foreword and long-time association with the Beatles; those in the anti-Muni league should stay clear.

LIVERPOOL AND LONDON

Evans, Mike and Jones, Ron. *In the Footsteps of the Beatles.* Liverpool (England): Merseyside County Council, 1981. 72 pages. Approximately 50 black-and-white photographs and maps throughout.

A guide through the streets and sites of Liverpool, starting at Oxford Street Maternity Hospital (where John Lennon was born) and ending with Neston Village Institute (one of the halls where The Beatles performed). Each location has a one paragraph history, plus italicized instruction on where to proceed next. Not all that attractive or informative, Liverpool tourists would do just as well buying a tour pamphlet from a local Liverpool shop.

Harry, Bill. *Mersey Beat: The Beginnings of the Beatles*. London: Omnibus Press (division of Book Sales Limited), 1977. 96 pages. Reproductions of photographs.

In their formative years, The Beatles had a major ally: Bill Harry, editor of *Mersey Beat*, "Merseyside's Own Entertainments Paper." Harry could always be counted on to get the group into a column, either by announcing a booking or by publishing a contribution from a Beatle himself. As usual, John's writings are hilarious ("...a man appeared on a flaming pie and said unto them `From this day on you are Beatles with an A'..."). Pieces from Brian Epstein, Paul McCartney, and Pete Best can also be found. The pages themselves are replicas of the original newspaper stock; the photos are pretty good, considering. A fan's dream source for rare clips, such as Stu Sutcliffe's obituary.

Leach, Sam. *Sam Leach's Follow the Merseybeat Road*. Liverpool England: Eden Publications, 1992. 34 pages. Approximately 50 black-and-white photographs and drawings, covering every page; one color map.

Sam Leach, Liverpool music promoter and early pal of the Beatles, "follows the Merseybeat Road"—an obvious allusion to *The Wizard of Oz*. Crudely written and with little thought to organization or presentation, the book is lifted toward acceptability on the basis of Leach's warm, friendly observations and non-judgmental recollections. Despite appearing in several photos with The Beatles (from the early days and even in more recent ones with Paul McCartney), Leach doesn't hype himself or his connections with The Beatles. Neither magical nor colorful, but of passing interest to fans of Liverpool culture. The drawings were rendered by Steve Barwise, a student from Liverpool Art College (John Lennon's old school).

Leigh, Spencer. Charts by Frame, Pete. *Let's Go Down to the Cavern: The Story of Liverpool's Merseybeat*. London: Vermillion & Company, Ltd (Hutchinson Publishing Group), 1984. 216 pages. One glossy 16-page black-and-white photo insert. Discography.

Liverpudlian Spencer Leigh takes on a bit more than he can handle with this combination Merseybeat history and biographical study of 1960's Liverpool bands. Major acts such as Rory Storm and the Hurricanes and Cilla Black are only afforded 2-3 pages, and we don't find out how these artists interrelated or what they are doing today. Overtly British (only U.K. releases are mentioned) and shamefully under-researched. Dank, like the Cavern club itself.

Scheler, Max and Kirchherr, Astrid. Afterword by Mike Byrne. *Liverpool Days*. Guildford, Surrey, England: Genesis Publications, 1994. 122 pages. Approximately 125 black-and-white and blue-tinted photographs, covering every page.

Limited edition photo collection (2,500 signed by the two photographers), encased in a lovely clothbound slipcase. The photos are exclusively from 1964—the point at which The Beatles finished up their Cavern club dates and began work on the film *A Hard Day's Night*—and integrate moody images of youth in Liverpool with upbeat moments of The Beatles and other Liverpool bands, such as Arrows, The Merseybeats, and The Undertakers. Do not expect to find any of Kirchherr's earlier shots of The Beatles in Hamburg, Germany. An intimate visual feast.

Schreuders, Piet; Lewisohn, Mark; and Smith, Adam. Foreword by Derek Taylor. *The Beatles London: The Ultimate Guide to Over 400 Beatles Sites in and Around London*. New York: St. Martin's Press, 1994. 128 pages. Approximately 250 black-and-white photographs, covering every page. Index. (First published in Great Britain in 1994 by Reed Consumer Books, Inc.)

A guidebook to the London hot spots frequented by The Beatles in their heyday, 1963-1970. If one only associates The Beatles with Liverpool, he or she is overlooking the fact that at the time all members of the group lived and worked in London, the center of England's recording industry. Among the 400 sites are locales where The Beatles were photographed or captured on film or video, or else places that have become associated with one or more of them in a significant way, such as Montpelier Square (the former location of the Playboy Club, at which The Beatles attended parties). Overall, wise decisions seem to have been made about what to include and exclude. The book is arranged by street name, but the index in the back divides locations by topic (shops, restaurants, theaters, etc.) and contains several maps, so chances are you will have no difficulty finding what you're seeking. "All in all, the ultimate `Magical Mystery Tour'"—*Goldmine*.

PICTORIALS

Barrow, Tony. *P.S. We Love You: The Beatles Story 1962-63*. London: Mirror Books, 1982. 48 pages. Approximately 60 black-and-white and 15 color-tinted photographs, covering every page.

Promotional book focusing on the years 1962-63, when the group just returned to Liverpool from Germany and began their climb toward national and international stardom. Skims the surface.

Benson, Harry. *The Beatles: In the Beginning*. Edinburgh and London: Mainstream Publishing Company, 1993. 128 pages. Approximately 200 black-and-white photographs, covering every page.

Excellent photos of The Beatles, starting with their 1964 Paris tour and including a few from their "Ed Sullivan Show" appearances, George and Patti's honeymoon in Barbados (what was Benson doing there anyway?), and their final concert in Candlestick Park in 1966. The most satisfying shots are those of John and Paul composing what would ultimately become "I Feel Fine" on the piano. Captures some of The Beatles' magic, but the subject coverage is sporadic. "Benson's photographs are very appealing..."—*Goldmine*.

Cahill, Marie. *The Beatles: A Pictorial History*. London: Brompton Books, 1990. 112 pages. Approximately 125 color and black-and-white photographs, covering every page. The Albums of The Beatles. Index.

Photo book whose only distinction is that it may rank as the *tallest* Beatles book published. Otherwise, standard promotional fluff.

Editors of *Life*. *The Beatles: From Yesterday to Today*. New York: Time, 1996. 128 pages. Approximately 150 color and black-and-white illustrations, covering every page.

After *Unseen Beatles* (see Whitaker, below), is there an unprinted Beatles image in existence that would make all other Beatles books obso-

lete? There is always the possibility one or several such photos could materialize—but this book doesn't contain anything on that level. These shots are all vaguely familiar, except that a few from the early period have been blown up with a glossy effect. Young fans drawn in by the *Anthology* releases might want a peek at this, although Beatles fans will probably be upset that 1995-96 photos of George, Paul, and Ringo tacked-on in the back make them look kind of crusty. Synthetic.

Evans, Mike. *The Art of the Beatles*. New York: Beech Tree Books (division of William Morrow and Company, Inc.), 1984. 144 pages. Approximately 175 color and black-and-white photographs, paintings, drawings, and works in other medium. Index of Artists and Authors. (First published in Great Britain in 1984 by Anthony Blond.)

Intended as a companion to a Beatles art exhibition at the Walker Art Gallery, Liverpool in 1984, this collection of visual art features works by Cynthia Lennon, John Lennon, Dezo Hoffmann, Andy Warhol, Robert Freeman, and many others. Some rarities will be most welcome pieces for Beatlefiles: Anne Mason's portrait of John Lennon in his art school days; and the legendary "hotel" painting by all four Beatles. Repeats a good deal from other pictorials, but its all-inclusiveness allows it to better represent the universality of The Beatles' image and message. Don't waste your time looking for memorabilia here.

Ewing, Jon. *The Beatles*. Miami, FL: MBS, 1996. 120 pages. Approximately 75 color and black-and-white photographs throughout. Discography. Chronology. Index.

CD-format book covering all aspects of The Beatles' career. A fine package, priced just right around $7.99.

Freeman, Robert. Foreword by Paul McCartney. *Yesterday: The Beatles 1963–1965*. New York: Holt, Rinehart and Winston, 1983. 96 pages. Over 100 black-and-white photographs, covering every page.

Paul McCartney wrote in his foreword to this fine photo-compilation: "I have a feeling that his [Freeman's] photos were amongst the best ever taken of the Beatles." Agree or disagree, one cannot deny the brilliance of Freeman's album cover shots, from the infamous grainy headshots on *Meet the Beatles* to the moody inverted image on the *Rubber Soul* LP sleeve. The other pictures are mostly the standard concert and film outtakes, but there are a few interesting personal studies of the four individually (especially one of John in his art studio).

Greenwald, Ted. *The Long and Winding Road: An Intimate Guide to the Beatles*. New York: Michael Friedman Publishing, 1995. 124 pages. Approximately 125 color and black-and-white photographs, covering every page.

Photo-factbook with lots of color sections containing biographies, records, concert appearances, movies, bibliography, and even a family tree. It's all been done before and in greater detail, but breezy fun.

Hoffmann, Dezo. *The Beatle Book*. New York: Lancer Books, 1964. Unpaginated. Approximately 75 black-and-white photographs throughout.

Photos and text exclusively from 1964, as executed by The Beatles' primary photographer, Dezo Hoffmann. A collector's relic, if you can get hold of a copy, but you'll be much better off with Hoffmann's coffee table book *With the Beatles* (see below), in which the photos are much larger and printed with greater care. This one does have intentional omissions for PR sake, including basic facts such as that Ringo replaced Pete Best as Beatles' drummer and John married Cynthia because he had gotten her pregnant.

Hoffmann, Dezo. *The Beatles Conquer America: The Photographic Record of Their First American Tour*. New York: Avon Books, 1984. 160 pages. Approximately 250 black-and-white photographs throughout.

Hoffmann once again slices up his photographic experiences with the early Beatles. This time, his focus is on the first American tour in 1964, which was actually preceded by a whirlwind set of gigs in France. In America, The Beatles are mobbed at the airport, incite female ecstasy in The Ed Sullivan Theater, meet the press and then fill stadiums in Washington and Miami. In the last chapter, the boys return to London where they meet up with the same flashbulbs and police-held crowds. *With the Beatles* (see below) offers greater diversity.

Hoffmann, Dezo and Maugham, Patrick. *Life with the Beatles*. Albany, NY: Highlight Publications, 1964. 24 pages. Approximately 40 black-and-white photographs, covering every page; one color spread.

Early Hoffmann compilation that is really a collectible fanzine. The boys look cute, as expected, circa 1964. See Hoffmann's *With the Beatles*, below.

Hoffmann, Dezo. *With the Beatles: The Historic Photographs of Dezo Hoffmann*. New York: Omnibus Press (division of Book Sales Limited), 1982. 128 pages. Approximately 150 black-and-white photographs, covering every page.

Hoffmann was The Beatles' court photographer of sorts from 1962 to 1964, and took many of the sensational photographs that brought the group to the world's attention. He was present for their first recording sessions, their last Cavern Club gig, and for loads of concert and television appearances. Most notable, however, are the goofy and serious portraits of the boys (both individually and as a foursome), which by now have been seen just about everywhere. Still fun.

McCartney, Michael. *Remember: The Recollections and Photographs of Michael McCartney*.

See: McCartney, Michael; Pictorials.

No author. *The Beatles Book*. London: Omnibus Press (division of Book Sales Limited), 1985. 176 pages. Over 100 black-and-white photographs throughout. Filmography.

Essay-filled photo book, with articles contributed by such notables as David Fricke, Nicholas Schaffner, Milton Okun, Dave Marsh, Lenny Kaye, and others. A portion of David Scheff's final interview with John Lennon (excerpted from *Playboy*) is included, as are conversations with, and/or profiles of, Paul, George, and Ringo. While certainly not *the* Beatles book—most of the articles have dated considerably and there are few post-1967 photos—there is enough here to rope in an ardent Beatlefile.

No author. *The Beatles: For the Record*. Knutsford, Cheshire (England): Totem Books (division of Collins), 1982. 96 pages. Approximately 125 color and black-and-white photographs throughout.

Piecemeal history of The Beatles, with individual biographies, chronological spreads, and many colorful photos. All gloss, no substance.

No author. *The Beatles Tear-Out Photo Book*. London: Oliver Books, 1993. Unpaginated (approximately 48 pages). Approximately 20 color photographs throughout.

Cheesy photo book, with the added benefit of being able to tear out pages. The cover image of The Beatles from *Help!* immediately dates things. Of interest, perhaps, to very young fans.

No author. *The Beatles Up-to-Date*. New York: Lancer Books, 1964. Unpaginated (approximately 128). Approximately 100 black-and-white photographs throughout.

Early promotional book (obviously *not* up-to-date!) that simply reflected public opinion of The Beatles' personalities: John the "literate" one; Paul the "cute" one; George the "great stone face"; and Ringo the loveable clown. Nearly half of the book is devoted to then competitive bands, such as Gerry and the Pacemakers and The Searchers.

Pascall, Jeremy (editorial consultant) and Burt, Robert (compiler). *The Beatles: The Fabulous Story of John, Paul, George and Ringo*. London: Octopus Books Limited, 1975. 92 pages. Approximately 200 color and black-and-white photographs throughout.

Trudging mid-1970's photo book, with nine predictably superficial essays on subjects such as Brian Epstein, the group's films, headlines, and The Beatles' break-up. Negligible. Issued in paperback in 1976 as *The Beatles: The Story in Rock* and later redone in 1983 as *The Beatles: The Fab Four Who Dominated Pop Music for a Decade*.

Ranson, Arthur (drawings) and Allan, Angus P. (text). *The Beatles: Their Story in Words and Pictures*. London: ITV Books, 1982. 52 pages. Approximately 400 comic strip drawings, covering every page; a dozen black-and-white photographs on the last pages.

Notable comic strip history of The Beatles, based on the *Look-in* picture strip, "The Story of the Beatles." Ranson has a sharp, accurate eye for depicting The Beatles; they don't look overly cute or grating. Much better than you'd expect; a good way to pass The Beatles story on to your kids.

Robertson, John. *The Complete Guide to the Music of the Beatles*. London: Omnibus Press (division of Book Sales Limited), 1994. 138 pages. Approximately 125 color and black-and-white photographs throughout. Track Listing.

CD-format book covering the high points of the Beatles' career. "A nifty idea: a handy, CD-sized (5-inches x 5½ inches) carry-along guide to The Beatles' official releases"—*Goldmine*.

Schaumberg, Ron. *Growing Up With the Beatles: An Illustrated Tribute*. New York: Pyramid Publications (Delilah), 1976. 160 pages. Approximately 300 black-and-white photographs, covering every page. Comes with a color poster.

A "personal valentine" to The Beatles from a fan raised in a suburb of Kansas City. Schaumberg evidently thought that by mixing his own family photos with standard Beatles history, he would live the ultimate fantasy. Other fans probably won't derive that much pleasure from reading this, however. Schaumberg not only places himself alongside The Beatles, he feels urged to serve as their critic as well, lambasting "Strawberry Fields Forever" because he doesn't get the lyrics. Amateurish.

Scheler, Max and Kirchherr, Astrid. Afterword by Mike Byrne. *Liverpool Days*.

See: Liverpool and London.

Spence, Helen. Foreword by Alan Freeman. *The Beatles*. New York: Crescent Books, 1981. 96 pages. 125 black-and-white photographs, covering every page. (First published in England by Colour Library International Limited, circa 1981.)

Messy promotional booklet that opens with a skimpy discography and an incomplete tour and concert roster. What follows is 80 pages of cut-and-paste Beatles history, supported by some exciting performance shots circa 1965-66 that would have been better handled elsewhere. Don't look for sense in Alan Freeman's foreword, which also seems to have been badly edited.

Stokes, Geoffrey. Introduction by Leonard Bernstein. *The Beatles*. New York: The New York Times Book Co., 1980. 246 pages. Approximately 150 black-and-white photographs, covering every page; twelve pages of color in two inserts.

Headlined by an Introduction from incomparable maestro Leonard Bernstein—which is actually rather perfunctory—Stokes' *The Beatles* remains one of the most accessible, original Beatles pictorials. Shrouded by Andy Warhol's timeless, colorful cover art of all four Beatles (opening up in front and back to reveal George and Ringo), the book is set in gargantuan type and exults in The Beatles larger-than-life aura. The enlarged photographic proportions allow one to detect a brooding coolness in George Harrison at age five and the already in-place loveable charm of Ringo as, with beer in hand, he attempts to act older than his 15 years. A staple for fans who prefer to avoid seeing any Beatle post-1970. "Superb..."*The Village Voice*.

Tobler, John. *The Beatles*. New York: Exeter Books, 1984. 192 pages. 80 color and 160 black-and-white illustrations, covering every page. Bibliography. Filmography. Discography. Index.

Photo history of The Beatles that stretches into their solo years and concludes with information on posthumous Lennon releases. There are only a few photos here that haven't been seen elsewhere, although the coverage of the early years and of the musicians' solo appearances may be of some interest. (See page 117 to see Ringo as a convincing Frank Zappa in *200 Motels*.) Tobler's writing is spotty in this mediocre package.

Vollmer, Jurgen. *Rock `N' Roll Times: The Style of the Early Beatles and Their First Fans*. Woodstock: The Overlook Press, 1983. Unpaginated (approximately 60 pages). Approximately 50 black-and-white photographs, covering nearly every page.

Vollmer was a friend of The Beatles in the early days, and took numerous photographs of the band performing in various clubs in Hamburg, Germany. While not as haunting or timeless as photos taken by Stuart Sutcliffe's lover, Astrid

Kirchherr, these photos are of historical interest. The second half of the book contains pictures of the Hamburg rock scene, including some up-close carnal moments. Vollmer is perhaps most noteworthy as the photographer of the cover image on John Lennon's *Rock `N' Roll* album.

Whitaker, Bob. *The Unseen Beatles*. San Francisco: HarperCollins San Francisco, 1991. 160 pages (oversized). Over 100 black-and-white photographs; 16 color photos throughout. (First published in the U.K. in 1991 by Conran Octopus Limited.)

In terms of time frame, the photos in this collection just follow Freeman's (in *Yesterday*, see above), from late 1965 through 1966. Whitaker is noted for having shot the back cover for *Revolver* and the infamous butcher photo on the recalled *Yesterday and Today* sleeve. The photos in this book are nothing special except for the fact that they are unseen—The Beatles at work on their only joint painting, George psychedelicizing his house, John as family man with Cynthia and Julian, etc.

POST-BEATLES

Blake, John. *All You Needed Was Love: The Beatles After the Beatles*. New York: Perigee Books (G.P. Putnam's Sons), 1981. 288 pages. 50 black-and-white photographs throughout.

All four Beatles are given equal attention in this narrative history of the band from their difficult break-up through John Lennon's death in 1980. There's nothing here any Beatles fan hasn't heard before, and, to be sure, *no one* wants to read any more about Linda McCartney's pathetic first attempts at keyboards. Loads of staple solo albums are neglected, including Wings' *Band on the Run* and John and Yoko's *Double Fantasy*. There are also some shameful typos, namely the misspelling of singer Eric Burdon's name (as "Burden"). Not what you need.

DiLello, Richard. Foreword by Wally Podrazik. *The Longest Cocktail Party: An Insider's Diary of the Beatles, Their Million-Dollar Apple Empire and Its Wild Rise and Fall*. Ann Arbor, MI: Pierian Press, 1983. 340 pages. Approximately 75 black-and-white photographs throughout. Appendix 1: The Beatles from 1962. Appendix 2: Beatles Tour Information. Appendix 3: A Beatle

Discography. Appendix 4: Happy Birthdays. Index.

First published in 1972, this diary of The Beatles and Apple was compiled by DiLello, a member of the band's PR office, but by no means a close confidante of the Fab Four. Refreshingly, the author's goal was not to retread tales of greed, lust, and bad business acumen, but to center on the fresh, creative side of the enterprise, in all its naive glory. Hangers-on, druggies, and would-be musicians/poets/electronic geniuses and their ilk flood the pages and drive The Beatles to the brink of disaster. An unusual behind-the-scenes tale, full of rare press releases, financial statements, and photos.

McCabe, Peter and Schonfeld, Robert D. *Apple to the Core: The Unmaking of the Beatles.* New York: Pocket Books (division of Simon & Schuster, Inc.), 1972. 200 pages. One eight-page black-and-white photo insert.

"The truth that's never been told before about the break-up of The Beatles" suffers from the fact that we don't know any of the authors' sources. The book details the evolution of The Beatles, the rocky last few months of Brian Epstein's management, and the band's side-choosing between Allen Klein and Lee Eastman (Linda's father). The authors provide a fair assessment of the roles played by Yoko and Linda, and do not pin the blame of the group's break-up on one or all. Paul's self-interview on his *McCartney* LP, in which he announces The Beatles' break-up, is strangely downplayed. More hype than new information.

Woffinden, Bob. *The Beatles Apart.* London: Proteus Books, 1981. Unpaginated (approximately 142 pages). Approximately 80 black-and-white and 20 color photographs throughout. Discography. Bibliography.

Senseless portrait of The Beatles, beginning with the "anticlimax" of events following the *Sgt. Pepper's Lonely Hearts Club Band* LP. Woffinden doesn't search for clues to why The Beatles broke up (or simply didn't know them) and we are left with a story that omits important details of business dealings with Apple and Allen Klein. Some color spreads scattered throughout only marginally lift this from bargain basement status.

QUIZBOOKS AND QUOTEBOOKS

Bennahum, David. *The Beatles...After the Break-Up: In Their Own Words.* London: Omnibus Press (division of Book Sales Limited), 1991. 128 pages. Approximately 125 black-and-white photographs throughout. Bibliography.

Intelligent assemblage of Beatles quotes, all uttered subsequent to The Beatles' break-up in 1970. The musicians talk about the split, business, solo work, drugs, family, each other, etc. Surprisingly, there isn't a chapter devoted solely to John Lennon's death. Contains some excellent photos and some beefy, well-balanced quotes from all four musicians, taken out of context and without source material. Ironically, many of the quotes in which Paul, George, and Ringo disassociate themselves are now immaterial (since the three have now collaborated).

Hockinson, Michael J. Foreword by Tom Schultheiss. *Nothing is Beatleproof: Advanced Beatles Trivia for Fab Fanciers.* Ann Arbor, MI: Popular Culture Inc., 1990. 442 pages. Approximately 125 black-and-white photographs throughout. Song and Record Title Index. Personal and Group Name Index. Name Index. Places and Things Index. Date Index.

Comprehensive 50-chapter quizbook exclusively for Beatlefiles with incredible recall. Each section includes 25-35 extremely difficult questions, followed by fully explanatory answers. Can you name Sgt. Pepper's hometown from the Bee Gees' film, the musician dubbed by publicist Derek Taylor as "the American Beatle," or the first three names of Ringo's old group Rory Storm and the Hurricanes? The only Beatles quizbook to be so fully indexed, this one is recommended for hardcore aficionados only. Published by St. Martin's Press in 1990 in paperback as *The Ultimate Beatles Quiz Book.*

Miles. *The Beatles: In Their Own Words.* London: Omnibus Press (division of Book Sales Limited), 1978. 128 pages. Approximately 75 black-and-white photographs throughout.

A stone age compilation of quotes that by now have been seen everywhere—and in many cases placed in context of the full interviews. The book, which doesn't provide introductions to any of the quotes, is divided into seven sections: the story, press conferences, songwriting, the songs, the films, drugs, and politics. While all four Beatles have their moments of verbal hilarity (Ringo: "I started to be an engineer but I banged me thumb the first day"), the book is lightweight and pointless.

RELATED WORKS

Shipper, Mark. *Paperback Writer: The Life and Times of the Beatles.* New York: Grosset & Dunlap, 1978. 254 pages. Approximately 25 black-and-white photographs throughout.

Hilarious spoof ("the spurious chronicle of their rise to stardom, their triumphs and disasters, plus the amazing story of their ultimate reunion") that pokes fun not at The Beatles but at all of the fiction that's been written about them. Shipper's outlandish story opens with McCartney's having had a solo career *before* joining The Beatles. Other ludicrous details follow—occasionally supplemented with clever same-page footnotes—that tell about Brian Epstein's prior career as a plumber; how Del Shannon was once The Beatles' lead guitarist; and that The Beatles recorded cover versions of "Shake Your Booty" and The Doors' "Peace Frog." This minor classic concludes with a December 7, 1979 reunion (ironically, one year and a day before Lennon would be murdered) in which The Beatles are reunited, only to receive second-billing to Peter Frampton! An earlier passage about Bob Dylan teaching John Lennon how to write a song can't be missed.

TOURBOOKS

Lewisohn, Mark. Foreword by Tim Rice. *The Beatles Live!: The Ultimate Reference Book.* New York: Henry Holt and Company, 1986. 208 pages. Approximately 100 black-and-white photographs, including clippings, letters, ticket stubs, posters, etc. Live Engagements Venue Index. Free disc. (First published in Great Britain, publisher unnamed.)

In his Introduction, Lewisohn pronounces that his previous work was "hailed as the most important slice of Beatles research ever." True—but so much for humility. Still and all, Lewisohn has culled some remarkable information on The Beatles' live engagements, all organized in an easy-to-follow chronological format. He provides in-depth commentary for each section, as well as useful song lists and travel itineraries. The free disc contains The

Beatles' first-ever Beatles interview in 1962. "Lewisohn ties the entire effort together with a snappy narrative charting The Beatles' career in general"—*Booklist.*

Lefcowitz, Eric. Photos by Marshall, Jim. *Tomorrow Never Knows: The Beatles Last Concert.* San Francisco, CA: Terra Firma, 1987. 102 pages. Approximately 76 black-and-white photographs throughout.

On August 29, 1966, The Beatles played their final stadium concert in Candlestick Park, San Francisco. Lefcowitz and Marshall have packaged a concise guide to the show and other events of 1966, including the brouhaha caused by Lennon's remarks on Christianity. Tidbits such as Candlestick Park history and The Beatles' 1966 North American tour schedule take up central book space that should have been devoted to more goods on the performance itself. Some interesting photos of Joan Baez going gaga over The Beatles add novelty to an otherwise mediocre photo-journal.

WRITTEN WORKS

Aldridge, Alan (Editor). *The Beatles Illustrated Lyrics Volumes 1 and 2.* Boston: Houghton Mifflin, 1991. 128 pages. Over 200 original color and black-and-white drawings, paintings and photographs. Index.

Surrealistic and imaginative art rendered to the accompaniment of the lyrics to over 100 Beatles songs. Far more inspired than a collection of *Yellow Submarine* outtakes, this book contains some of the very best pieces ever created relevant to Beatles concepts—and with insider knowledge into lesser-known Beatles recordings and compositions. (The names of some of the works include: "Love of the Loved," "Come and Get It," "Like Dreamers Do," "That Means a Lot," etc.). The image depicting "Yesterday" is of a squelched cigarette inside a sunnyside-up egg (which most fans will immediately recognize as an allusion to the song's first title, "Scrambled Eggs"). Kudos to all of the artists, who include Hans Ulrich, Marcia Hercovitz, Barry Smith, and David Bailey. Note: Contains sexually explicit images.

Brautigan, Richard. *The Beatles Lyrics Illustrated.* New York: Dell, 1975. 208 pages. Insert containing 104 black-and-white photos. Index.

A very basic lyric book containing all released

Beatles songs by Lennon/McCartney, Harrison, and Starr. Songs written for others and not recorded by the band ("Nobody I Know" by Peter and Gordon) are also included. Pale in comparison to lyric books that have original, imaginative graphics and color drawings. The book sorely lacks release dates, composer credits (distinguishing Lennon/McCartney from Harrison and Starr), lead singer identification, album references, and just about everything else.

Campbell, Colin and Murphy, Allan. *Things We Said Today: The Complete Lyrics and a Concordance to the Beatles' Songs, 1962-1970.* Ann Arbor, MI: Pierian Press, 1980. 386 pages. Approximately 20 black-and-white reproductions of handwritten song lyrics. Listener's Guide to Songs. Song Index to Albums.

Lyrics to The Beatles' 189 original compositions, identified line-by-line and catalogued into a major Bible-like concordance. The idea sounds better than the results: Is there really a point to finding out how many dozen Beatles' songs used the words *go*, *is*, and *are*? Things really get out of hand as the authors cite every "nah" from "Hey Jude." To make matters irreparable, the lyrics themselves are suspect (the number 909 is written out in "One After 909," which is nonstandard) if not flat-out wrong ("In," the first word of "Penny Lane," is missing). A botched job.

YOUNG ADULT

Sutton, Margaret. *We Love You Beatles.* New York: Doubleday, 1971. 50 pages. Original color illustrations throughout.

Cute illustrated story of The Beatles for kids six and under. The drawings are of the psychedelic *Yellow Submarine* period; one image even depicts Paul spread out in a bathtub strumming on a guitar. Fun, although parents will have to fill in a lot a gaps; for one thing, the book doesn't mention The Beatles' break-up!

Zanderbergen, George. *The Beatles.* Mankato, MN: Crestwood House, 1976. 48 pages. Approximately 30 black-and-white and color illustrations throughout.

Part of Crestwood's spotlight series, this history of The Beatles in 48 pages is written for fans in the 8-11 range. Your eight-year-old will pick up on some of the obvious errors herein, and will certainly not be impressed with the photo selection. The only thing written about the animated feature *The Yellow Submarine* is that "It was a big hit in America." Call for the Blue Meanies.

OTHER TITLES OF INTEREST

Adler, Bill. *Dear Beatles.* New York: Grosset & Dunlap, 1964.

Adler, Bill. *Love Letters to the Beatles.* New York: Putnam & Sons, 1964.

Alico, Stella H. *Elvis Presley-The Beatles.* West Haven, CT: Pendulum Press, Inc., 1979.

Bacon, David and Maslow, Norman. *The Beatles' England: There Are Places I'll Remember.* No city: 910 Press, 1982.

Baker, Glenn A. *The Beatles Down Under: The 1964 Australia & New Zealand Tour.* Ann Arbor, MI: Popular Culture, Inc., 1985.
Part of Pop Culture Ink's "Rock 'N' Roll Remembrances" series.

Benson, Joe. *Uncle Joe's Record Guide: The Beatles.* No city: Benson J. Unlimited, 1990.

Bicknell, Alf and Marsh, Garry. *Baby You Can Drive My Car.* No city: No. 9 Books, 1989.
The autobiography of Alf Bicknell, The Beatles' one-time chauffeur. George Harrison wrote the foreword.

Blessing, Adam. *Out of the Mouths of Beatles.* New York: Dell, 1964.

Braun, Michael. *Love Me Do: The Beatles Progress.* New York: Penguin, 1964.

Bugliosi, Vincent. *Helter Skelter.* New York: Bantam, 1982.
Best-selling novel based on Charles Manson's cult murders; among his victims was Sharon Tate, actress and wife of director Roman Polanski. Paul McCartney's song inspired Manson, but Brits recognize that a helter skelter is a spiral slide for kiddies. The book was adapted to a two-part television drama in 1976.

Burke, John. *A Hard Day's Night.* No city: Pan Books, 1964.
Novelization of The Beatles' movie A Hard Day's Night.

Cepican, Robert. *The Long and Winding Road: Beatles from Beginning to Break-Up.* New York: Putnam, no date.

Clesi, Teresa. *The Beatles.* Cos Cobb, CT: Ariel Books, 1994.
Goldmine commented: "...it didn't take long for a mini-book on the Beatles to materialize."

Clifford, Mike. *The Beatles.* New York: Smithmark (Penguin USA), 1991.

Connolly, Ray. *The Beatles Years.* New York: Macmillan, 1972.

Cott, Jonathan and Dalton, David. *The Beatles Get Back Together*. No city: Apple, 1970.

Courtney, Richard G. *I Never Saw a Beatle*. Cross Bridges Company, 1986.

Cowan, Philip. *Behind the Beatles' Songs*. New York: Putnam, 1978.

Davis, Edward E. *The Beatles Books*. No city: Cowles Educational Corporation, 1968.

De Blasio, Edward. *All About the Beatles*. New York: Bantam, 1964.

Delano, Julia. *Beatles Album*. New York: Smithmark (Penguin USA), 1992.

DeWitt, Howard A. *Beatle Poems*. Bountiful, UT: Horizon, 1987.

Di Franco, Philip. *A Hard Day's Night*. New York: Chelsea House, 1976.

Friedman, Rick. *The Beatles: Words Without Music*. New York: Grosset & Dunlap, 1968.

Gibson, Bob. *The True Story of the Beatles Illustrated*. New York: Bantam Books, 1964.

Gilles, D.B. *The Girl Who Loved the Beatles*. No city: Dramatists Play Service, 1990.

Giuliano, Geoffrey. *The Beatles: A Celebration*. New York: St. Martin's, 1986.
 School Library Journal *commented: "Another book about the Beatles, but this one is definitely worth the shelf space even in its oversize format."*

Goodgold, Edwin and Carlinksy, Don. *The Complete Beatles Quiz Book*. New York: Warner, 1975.

Grove, Martin A. *Beatle Madness*. No city: Manor Books, 1978.

Hamblett, Charles. *Here Are the Beatles*. No city: Four Square Books, 1964.

Harry, Bill. *Beatlemania: An Illustrated Filmography*. New York: Avon, 1985.
 Also known as The History of the Beatles on Film.

Harry, Bill. *Book of Beatle Lists: Everything You Ever Wanted to Know and Never Thought of About the Fab Four*. New York: Sterling, 1985.

Hemenway, Robert. *The Girl Who Sang With the Beatles*. New York: Knopf, 1970.

Hine, Al. *Help!*. New York: Dell, 1965.
 Novelization of the Beatles' film.

Hoffmann, Dezo. *The Beatles Up To Date*. No city: Lancer Books, 1964.

House, Jack. *Beatles Quiz Book*. No city: William Collins Sons, 1969.

Humphrey-Smith, Cecil R.; Heenan, Michael G.; and Mount, Jennifer. *Up the Beatles' Family Tree*. No city: Achievements Limited, 1965.

Keenan, Debra (Deborah). *On Stage with the Beatles*. Mankato, MN: Creative Education, 1975.

King, LRE. *Do You Want to Know a Secret?*. No city: Storyteller Productions, 1988.

King, LRE. *Fixing a Hole: A Second Look at the Beatles' Unreleased Recordings*. No city: Storyteller Productions, 1989.

King, LRE. *Help! A Companion to the Beatles Recording Sessions*. No city: Storyteller Productions, 1989.

King, LRE. *It's All Too Much: A Beatles Recording Checklist*. No city: Storyteller Productions, 1993.

Kirwan, Larry. *Mad Angels: The Plays of Larry Kirwan*. Mt. Vernon, NY: 47 Books, 1994.
 Collection of plays, opening with Kirwan's well-received Liverpool Fantasy, which speculates on what might have been if The Beatles had split up after only their second single.

Larkin, Rochelle. *The Beatles Yesterday...Today... Tomorrow*. New York: Scholastic, 1974.

Loewen, L. *The Beatles*. No city: Rourke Corp., 1989.

Palmer, Tony. *All You Need Is Love*. No city: Weidenfeld & Nicholson/Chappell & Company, 1976.

Pirmanten, Patricia. *Beatles*. Mankato, MN: Creative Education, 1974.

No author. *26 Days That Rocked the World*. No city: O'Brien Publishing, 1978.

Noebel, Reverend David A. *Communism, Hypnotism and the Beatles*. No city: Christian Crusade, 1965.

Patterson, R. Gary. *The Walrus Was Paul: The Great Beatle Death Clues of 1969*. Nashville, TN: Dowling Press, 1996.

Podrazik, Walter. *Strange Days: The Music of John, Paul, George & Ringo Twenty Years On*. Ann Arbor, MI: Popular Culture, Inc., 1993.
 Part of Pop Culture Ink's "Rock `N' Roll Reference" series.

Powlowski, Gareth. *How They Became the Beatles: A Definitive History of the Early Years 1960-1964*. New York: NAL, 1990.

Rayl, Salley. Photographs by Carl Gunther. *Beatles 64*. New York: Doubleday & Co., 1989.

Reeve, Andru. *Turn Me On, Dead Man: The Complete Story of the Paul McCartney Death Hoax*. Ann Arbor, MI: Popular Culture Ink, 1994.
 Goldmine *commented: "Reeve expertly re-examines the origins of the rumors, studies all of the `clues' (from the obvious to the not-so; some 70 clues in all!) and contemplates the ramifications of this incredible story."*

Rosenbaum, Helen. *Beatles' Trivia Quiz Book*. New York: NAL, 1978.

Scaduto, Anthony. *The Beatles Yesterday Today and Tomorrow*. New York: Signet, 1968.

Schaffner, Nicholas. *The Boys from Liverpool*. New York: Routledge, 1980.

Scharoff, Mitch. *The Beatles: Collecting the Original U.K. Pressings 1962-70*. Self-published.
 Goldmine *commented: "...Scharoff's 64-page guide will be helpful to anyone trying to pursue those [original British] pressings, particularly the novice import collector."*

Shaumburg, Ron. *Growing Up With the Beatles*. No city: Pyramid Books, 1976.

Shepherd, Billy. *The True Story of the Beatles*. New York: Beat Publications (Bantam), 1964.

Southall, Brian. *Abbey Road: The Story of the World's Most Famous Recording Studio*. New York: Sterling, 1986.

Spencer, Helen. *Beatles Forever*. New York: Outlet Book Company, 1991.

Stannard, Neville. *The Beatles: Working Class Heroes*. New York: Avon, 1984.

Stern, Michael. *The Beatles*. Paducah, KY: Collector Books, 1993.

Sulpy, Doug. *Illegal Beatles: Archival Back Issues, 1989-90*. Princeton Junction, NJ: The 910, 1994.
Sequel to Illegal Beatles: Back Issues, 1986-1988 (see below). Goldmine commented: "...may prove helpful in determining which purchases one can afford to live with or without."

Sulpy, Doug. *Illegal Beatles: Back Issues, 1986-1988*. No city: Storyteller Productions, 1992.
Sulpy's original fanzine was Illegal Beatles, which became The 910 (see Fanzines, above). This book reprints articles from the zine during the aforementioned years.

Sutcliffe, Stuart. *Stuart: The Life and Art of Stuart Sutcliffe*. Guildford, Surrey (England): Genesis Publications, Limited.
Limited edition publication that includes Sutcliffe's high-quality paintings.

Taylor, Alistair. *Yesterday: The Beatles Remembered*. London: Sidgwick & Jackson, 1988.
Taylor was assistant to Brian Epstein, The Beatles' manager.

Taylor, John A. *Beatles*. New York: Smithmark (division of Penguin USA), 1992.

Tobler, John. *Meet the Beatles*. New York: Smithmark (Penguin USA), 1990.

Turner, J. Lancelot. *Turn Me On Dead Man*. No city: Stone Garden, 1969.

Wilt, Max. *The Beatles in Yellow Submarine*. New York: Signet, 1968.
Companion to the 1968 animated feature.

Woyer, Paul. *The Beatles: The Ultimate Encyclopedia*. Edison, NJ: Book Sales, Inc., no date.

Yenne, Bill. *The Beatles*. Stamford, CT: Longmeadow, 1994.
Goldmine commented: "A straight reprint of a promotional book first published in 1989 by Gallery Books."

JEFF BECK

See Yardbirds, The.

THE BEE GEES

FANZINES AND FAN CLUBS

Bee Gees Quarterly. Att. Renee Schreiber, P.O. Box 2429, Miami Beach, FL 33140.

Worldwide fan club that provides members with a Bee Gees fact sheet, a membership card, color and black-and-white postcards, access to the Bee Gees hotline, and subscription to the quarterly newsletter. *Bee Gees Quarterly* includes new releases, black-and-white photographs, touring information, personal appearances, pen pals, classified ads, question and answer, contests, and much more. The club is an active supporter of the Andy Gibb Memorial Foundation. The cost of membership is $18 per year U.S. (check or money order); $20 Mexico and Canada (international money order drawn on a U.S. bank); and $22 overseas (international money order drawn on a U.S. bank). Make payable to Renee Schreiber.

PICTORIALS

The Bee Gees. As told to Leaf, David. *Bee Gees: The Authorized Biography*. London: Octopus Books Limited, 1979. 160 pages. Approximately 175 black-and-white photographs, covering every page. Appendix (Discography, Awards). Comes with a pull-out color poster.

A detailed account of the musical lives of the Gibb brothers. Despite the obvious absence of their voices in the text, Barry, Robin, and Maurice share author credit with Leaf and hold full copyright on the book. However, their stamp of approval and cooperation is visible through the mountainload of rare photos, several of which include the trio's teenage performing days on Australian TV's "Bandstand" (equivalent to the U.S. "American Bandstand"). Fans will enjoy the book's many little-known tidbits; for example, their original name was almost Rupert's World, and the group had to fight manager Robert Stigwood to allow "Stayin' Alive" to serve as the theme song for *Saturday Night Fever*. For disco lovers everywhere.

YOUNG ADULT

Pryce, Larry. *The Bee Gees*. New York: Chelsea House, 1980. 140 pages (pocket-sized). One 16-page glossy black-and-white photo insert. Discography. (Originally published in Great Britain in 1979 by Granada Publishing.)

In the first chapter (ridiculously titled "The Long and Winding Road") of this pint-sized bio, we discover that the brothers were born on the Isle of Man to a musical family. Skipping over their childhoods, the next chapter takes us right to the boys' Beatles-derivative first recordings. Lo and behold, they became buddies with Robert Stigwood of NEMS (artist agency run by Beatles' manager Brian Epstein) and the hits followed. So much for revelations. The description of the film *Sgt. Pepper's Lonely Hearts Club Band* is laughable: "As a colorful fantasy it works, from the opening scene right up to the amazing and joyous grand finale." Back to the time warp.

Schumacher, Craig. *The Bee Gees*. Mankato, MN: Creative Education, 1979. 32 pages. Approximately 12 black-and-white photos throughout.

This entry in the "Rock 'n Pop Stars" series starts out okay, with a crisply written history of the band from their Isle of Man roots. Unlike other juvenile works on the group, this publication mentions their brief 1969 split caused by Robin Gibb's desire to become a solo act (which evidently didn't pan out). In the last chapter, misinformation prevails, notably in regard to the public reception to the film *Sgt. Pepper's Lonely Hearts Club Band* (labeled here as "a box office success everywhere"). Fortunately, neither the film nor this book is much in circulation these days.

Stevens, Kim. *The Bee Gees*. New York: Quick Fox (Music Sales), 1978. 92 pages. 75 black-and-white photos throughout. Discography.

Quickie picture-book from Quick Fox, with emphasis on the Bee Gees' formula and inner-workings. The author actually defends the group's "goody-goody" image. At least, Stevens asserts, "the Bee Gees could never be accused of projecting the ultra-straight conservatism of a Debby Boone or the Osmonds." Inexplicably, bare biographical data (where

they were born, their educations, their family, etc.) is not included, and there are only two paragraphs about Andy Gibb in here. The photos add some variety to a neatly designed package.

OTHER TITLES OF INTEREST
English, David. *The Legend: The Illustrated Story of the Bee Gees*. No city: Salem House, 1984.
Munshower, Suzanne. *The Bee Gees*. New York: Putnam, 1978.

PAT BENATAR

PICTORIALS

Fissinger, Laura. *Pat Benatar*. Mankato, MN: Creative Education: 1983. 32 pages. Eight black-and-white photographs throughout.

Part of Creative Education's "Rock 'n Pop Stars" series, *Pat Benatar* has little to offer. Even young fans are sure to be disappointed with a book that only has one hundred words per page and barely two handfuls of photos. Mistakes crop up at every turn, not only regarding Benatar's life; the author states that Long Island is part of New York City, which is not quite true (it's part of New York State). You better run.

OTHER TITLES OF INTEREST
Magee, Doug. *Benatar*. London: Proteus, 1984.

CHUCK BERRY

AUTOBIOGRAPHY

Berry, Chuck. Foreword by Bruce Springsteen. *Chuck Berry: The Autobiography*. New York: Harmony (Crown), 1987. 352 pages. 100 black-and-white photos throughout. Recording Sessions. Discography/Filmography. Index.

One can't help but feel that Berry was trying too hard to write his autobiography and was in dire need of a collaborator. Details of his life are missing, some passages are just plain confusing, and we don't really get a sense of his emotions during traumatic events, such as his two arrests (in 1958 for violating the Mann Act and in 1978 for not paying taxes). Still, in spite of this book's many shortcomings, it *is* from rock and roll legend Chuck Berry himself—and he comes off as quite an unembittered survivor. We learn he was born on 2520 Goode Avenue in St. Louis MO, gained his rock and roll beat from his parents' Baptist rhythms, developed the "duck walk" as a child to humor choir members, and learned guitar chords from *Nick Mannaloft's Guitar Book of Chords*. Well worth it, though keep in mind that the author only read six hardbacks in full in his entire life.

DISCOGRAPHIES, RECORDING GUIDES, AND COLLECTIBLES

DeWitt, Howard A. *Chuck Berry: Rock 'N' Roll Music*. Ann Arbor, MI: Pierian Press, 1985. 292 pages. Approximately 100 black-and-white photographs throughout. Bibliographic Essay. Index.

Part biographical analysis and discographical survey, this book—which was first published in 1981—is a much-needed study into the persona and legendary musical contributions of Chuck Berry. DeWitt doesn't focus on Berry's legal, marital, and financial difficulties, but on the master's guitar genius, brilliance in the recording studio, influence (notably on English artists, such as John Lennon), and flair for capturing the needs, woes, and yearnings of teens in the late 1950's. The second part lists: Berry's singles, EPs, and LPs released in the U.S., the U.K., and even places such as Holland, Sweden, and West Germany; cover versions; Berry-influenced songs; motion picture soundtracks and albums; and miscellaneous lists (foreign tours, Berry's favorite songs, etc.). "...an outstanding research tool..."—*Choice*.

PICTORIALS

Reese, Krista. *Mr. Rock N' Roll*. London and New York: Proteus, 1982. 128 pages. Approximately 50 black-and-white photographs throughout; eight color photos throughout. Discography.

Forgettable study of Berry that strays all too regularly from its subject. Why are we reading about F. Scott Fitzgerald in the opening chapter when we should leap right into the history of rhythm and blues? The graphics are also a major disappointment: there are far too few pictures of a pre-1960 Berry; in many cases the images are way too dark; and icons of couples dancing at the bottoms of pages look more like

spilled ink splotches than passable design elements. Unsightly printing errors and a half-hearted discography only make matters worse. A duckwalk into shallow water.

THE B-52S

(See also R.E.M.: Athens, GA)

PICTORIALS

Martini, Della. *The B-52's*. New York and London: Music Sales Corporation, 1990. 32 pages. Approximately 35 color and black-and-white photographs, covering nearly every page.

This book could have been subtitled "wardrobes and hairstyles from hell." Except for a mentioning of band memeber Ricky Wilson's death (presumably due to AIDS), *The B-52's* is a fanzine on a band that gets a kick wearing outrageous duds and sporting frightful-looking beehives. A tambourine or two aside, the players don't really *look* much like musicians. If you have the impulse, flip to page 22 to see their unidentified bare butts. Wacky and stylish without a cause.

OTHER TITLES OF INTEREST
Schneider, Fred. Illustrations by Scharf, Kenny. *Fred Schneider and Other Unrelated Works*. No city: Arbor House, 1987.
   Booklist *commented this is a: "...silly, whimsical, 9-inch-square paperback...a tossed-off, take-it-or-leave-it proposition."*

BIG COUNTRY

FANZINES AND FAN CLUBS

All of Us. Att. James D. Birch, 201 Gay Street #4, Denton, MD 21629.

Fanzine strictly for North American fans that claims support from the band and its management. The 32-page booklet contains black-and-white photographs, album reviews, member articles and comments, profiles, some merchandising, an Internet Directory, and more. The cost of four annual issues is $12 per year.

THE BLACK CROWES

PICTORIALS

Black, Martin. *The Black Crowes*. London: Omnibus Press (division of Book Sales Limited), 1993. 64 pages. Over 100 color and black-and-white photos, covering every page. The Black Crowes Discography.

The first book-length photo retrospective on the "American band whose brand of blues, soul, and rebel attitudes have brought both sleaze and idealism back into rock and roll." The Black Crowes took adversity by the balls and made a name for themselves by refusing to cow-tow to Miller Lite, the sponsor of the 1991 ZZ Top Tour, for whom the band opened. Their remarks on overcommercialization led to their getting booted off the tour, but advanced their reputation as a band with integrity. Despite lacking early biographical details (where did these guys come from?), this book has enough charismatic photos to hold fans until something more comprehensive comes along.

BLACK FLAG

See Rollins Band.

BLACK SABBATH

See Osbourne, Ozzy.

BLONDIE

PICTORIALS

Bangs, Lester. *Blondie*. New York: Delilah/Fireside (Simon & Schuster), 1980. 96 pages. Approximately 100 color and black-and-white illustrations throughout.

Music critic Lester Bangs first became involved with Blondie when he gave their debut album a rave review back in 1977 in *The Village Voice*. He followed their progress over the next three years, and while he admits he didn't go gaga over all of their work during this time, he relents somewhat by admitting the group is "avant-garde enough to be obscure." Hardcore fans will be disappointed by a pop writer who is so candid, but those who have an interest in American punk—or simply dig ex-Playboy bunnies who front rock and roll bands—may find some pre-Madonna entertainment here.

OTHER TITLES OF INTEREST

Bardach, Ann. *Blondie*. New York: Simon & Schuster, 1980.

Harry, Deborah and Stein, Chris. *Making Tracks: The Rise of Blondie*. New York: Dell, 1982.

No author. *Blondie*. Manchester, England: Babylon Books, 1979.

No author. *Blondie*. London: Omnibus Press (division of Book Sales Limited), 1980.

Schreurs, Fred. *Blondie*. London: Star Books, 1980.

BLOOD, SWEAT AND TEARS

See Kooper, Al.

MICHAEL BLOOMFIELD

PICTORIALS

Ward, Ed. *Michael Bloomfield: The Rise and Fall of an American Guitar Hero*. Port Chester, NY: Cherry Lane, 1983. 136 pages. Approximately 100 black-and-white illustrations throughout; six pages of color in the Epilogue. Discography.

Michael Bloomfield first came to the public's attention as the lead guitarist of The Paul Butterfield Blues Band—the group that backed Dylan when he went electric at the 1965 Newport Folk Festival. Bloomfield was also a musician in two other cult blues-rock-oriented bands of the late 1960's and early 70's, The Electric Flag and KGB, and his impresario guitar can be found on film soundtracks such as *The Trip*. *Michael Bloomfield* provides a wide range of photos of bluesmen, Bloomfield's family, contemporaries and rock and folk festivals; it also has an authentic flavor for the Chicago blues scene and contains some classic encounters with blues and rock players (B.B. King, Al Kooper, Mitch Ryder, etc.). Those who don't mind the near-neglect of Bloomfield's last solo albums (they're only mentioned in the Discography) will be rewarded.

BLUE OYSTER CULT

FANZINES AND FAN CLUBS

Blue Oyster Cult International Fan Club. P.O. Box 931324, Los Angeles, CA 90093.

Fan club that offers a quarterly newsletter, *Morning Final Newsletter*, which comes with an exclusive club photo and a bumper sticker. Features include Covert Cult (unreleased songs), Kingdoms of the Radio (live shows and radio broadcasts), Singles Bar (collecting 7" singles), Press Eject and Give Me the Tape (bootlegs), as well as news, interviews, and other miscellany. The fan club also produces the *Blue Oyster Cult Lyric Book*, a spiral bound book with Blue Oyster song lyrics ($22 U.S; $28 elsewhere). The cost of the newsletter is $18 for four issues in the U.S. and $22 outside.

THE BLUES BROTHERS

BELUSHI FRIENDS AND FAMILY

Belushi, Judith Jacklin. *Samurai Widow*. New York: Carroll & Graf Publishers, Inc., 1990. 428 pages. One glossy 24-page black-and-white photo insert.

In these crosscut memoirs, John Belushi's widow pours out her emotions during the seven years subsequent to her husband's death. Hounded by the callous press, sold out by author Bob Woodward (see Biographies, below), and left to start all over again at 31, Judith Jacklin Belushi recounts her pain, anguish, and ultimate fascination with what really did happen to John Belushi in his final hours. The book successfully counters monstrous tabloid depictions of John with examples of his sensitive, affectionate side (e.g., he was the kind of guy who would towel dry his wife after a shower). We can all be assured that by book's close Ms. Belushi did remarry and start life anew. "Belushi is willing to do what many writers can't or won't—let the reader see their pain"—*Booklist*.

BIOGRAPHIES

Woodward, Bob. *Wired: The Short Life and Fast Times of John Belushi*. New York: Simon & Schuster, 1984. 462 pages. One 16-page black-and-white photo insert.

Sensationalized portrait of Belushi, assisted at first by widow Judy Jacklin Belushi. Jacklin was actually betrayed by Woodward, who had assured her he was only putting together a series of articles for *The Washington Post*, not an all-out biography. As expected, Woodward focuses on Belushi's many excesses—cocaine, pot, LSD, quaaludes, and food—not Belushi the comedian, film actor, singer, and husband. The results were a best seller and, in 1989, a flop of a film. Offensive and often cited as hugely inaccurate and exaggerated, this book will hopefully fade as Belushi's legend continues to grow.

PICTORIALS

Cader, Michael (editor). Photographs by Buskin, Edie. *Saturday Night Live: The First Twenty Years*. Boston and New York: Houghton Mifflin, 1994. 264 pages. Over 500 color and black-and-white photographs throughout. Index.

An extraordinarily colorful history of the show that introduced the talents of Gilda Radner, Chevy Chase, Bill Murray, Steve Martin, John Candy, Eddie Murphy, John Belushi, Dan Aykroyd, and so many others to national attention. Fans of the durable NBC show can instantly recall the hosts, comedy sketches, incredible musical acts (three solo Beatles on separate occasions, Paul Simon, The Rolling Stones, The Kinks, etc.) and wonderful characters created by the "not ready for prime time players." While Belushi's various alter egos are prominent here, there is surprisingly little reference to The Blues Brothers—not a solitary photo of Jake and Elwood—or even one of Belushi doing his uncanny Joe Cocker at Woodstock impression. Only Blues Brothers fans will notice the difference, however, as this is an otherwise definitive tribute.

OTHER TITLES OF INTEREST
Jacklin, Judith. *The Blues Brothers: Private*. New York: Putnam, 1980.
Mitch, Miami. *The Blues Brothers*. No city: Jove, 1980.

THE BLUES PROJECT

See Kooper, Al.

BLUR

PICTORIALS

Holorny, Linda. *Blur: An Illustrated Biography*. London: Omnibus Press (division of Book Sales Limited), 1995. Unpaginated (approximately 64 pages). Approximately 75 glossy color photographs, covering every page. Discography.

Extremely fluffy pop bio of the quintet, who struck big in the U.K. with singles such as "Country House" and "The Great Singles Escape." The photos are very colorful—red and green galore—but this book hardly sets Blur above Menudo status. One more for the bubblegum factory.

Lester, Paul. *Blur*. London: Hamlyn (imprint of Reed Consumer Books Limited), 1994. 80 pages. One hundred color and black-and-white photographs, covering every page.

Sponsored by England's *Melody Maker* magazine, *Blur* is a photo exposé of the titular band. Originally known as Seymour, the group changed its name to Blur because the former was "too airy-fairy." The youths have had several hits in the U.K. (starting with "She's So High"), but as of yet haven't connected on this side of the Atlantic. If you're into alternative music in the vein of Echo & the Bunnymen, The Stone Roses, and My Bloody Valentine—with a touch of flowery Syd Barrett psychedlicism—check this out.

WRITTEN WORKS

Postle, Paul and Blur. *Blurbook*. London: HarperCollins, 1995. Unpaginated (approximately 128 pages). Approximately 150 color and black-and-white photographs, covering every page.

Highly visual photo book that edges out Holorny and Lester's respective works (see above) because of the band's involvement in the project. Not that there is anything here in terms of information; the book primarily consists of quotes from band members and many never-before-seen photos. But the images are quite a contrast to the aforementioned works, revealing the boys' charisma and stage presence, as opposed to pretty boy teen idol wimpiness. Without a discography of any kind and only photo locations serving as headings, this book's appeal is limited to ardent U.K. fans.

MARC BOLAN

BIOGRAPHIES

Bramley, John and Shan. Photographs by Morris, Keith. *Marc Bolan: The Legendary Years*. London: Smith Gryphon, 1992. 128 pages. One glossy 32-page black-and-white photo insert. Discography. Top Twenty Singles Profile: The Legendary Years 1970-4. Songs' Anthology A to Z. Diary Dates: 1968-77.

Not really a biography, this is a cut-and-paste job of quotes—some fresh, but many simply restated from other publications. The Bramleys, then organizers of the Marc Bolan Fan Club, can't seem to translate their enthusiasm for Bolan into anything digestible for those who only know T.Rex's "Bang a Gong (Get It On)." However, Keith Morris' photo insert instantly brings to life Bolan's elfin magic, capturing him goofing off with mates Elton John and Ringo Starr. It looks like these boys must have had some wild parties—so why weren't they described in the text? The discographical sections are U.K.-only.

Paytress, Mark. *Twentieth Century Boy*. London: Sidgwick & Jackson, Limited, 1992. 294 pages. One glossy eight-page black-and-white photo insert. Appendix One: Marc Bolan and T.Rex: A Recorded History. Appendix Two: Sources. Appendix Three: Bibliography. Index.

The master of glamour rock (or, as he preferred, "cosmic" rock) is given a warm and balanced treatment by Paytress. Though he was too young to see Bolan perform—and even admitted to feeling indifferent to his later recordings—Paytress shows how the artist carved a niche in one direction, yet unintentionally paved the way for the punk, alternative, and New Wave scenes. With rare objectivity, Paytress traces how the Jewish lad born Mark Feld rose from the middle-class borough of Hackney, Stoke Newington to prominence as an undisputed rock legend. The photo insert contains some fine early stills. Essential.

DEATH OF BOLAN

Dicks, Ted (editor). *Marc Bolan: A Tribute.* London: Essex House Publishing 1978. Unpaginated (approximately 120 pages). Approximately 50 black-and-white photographs throughout. Discography.

Reflections on Bolan from friends, relatives, musicians, and journalists, released one year after the glam rocker's death. The book begins with a zodiac profile of Bolan the Libra, as prepared by an astrologer who allegedly was not told the name of her subject—yet somehow was on the mark about several of his characteristics. This is followed by a chronological series of quotes that tell the Bolan story, many of which were culled from newspapers and magazines (although only some contain sources). Speakers are only identified the first time mentioned (and there isn't a "who's who"), so readers will have to flip back to the first reference for names such as E.P. Fallon (Bolan's publicist). Sheet music is provided for several Bolan classics, but this material is incongruous with the rest of the book. Strictly for diehards.

OTHER TITLES OF INTEREST
Bolan, Marc. *The Warlock of Love.* No city: Lupus, 1969.
Bramley, John. *Marc Bolan: The Illustrated Discography.* London: Omnibus (division of Book Sales Limited), 1983.
Sinclair, Paul. *The Mark Bolan Story.* London: Omnibus Press (division of Book Sales Limited), 1982.
Tremlett, George. *The Marc Bolan Story.* London: Futura, 1975.
Williams, Dave. *Marc Bolan: The Motivator.* No city: Silver Surfer, 1985.

MICHAEL BOLTON

PICTORIALS

Randall, Lee. *Michael Bolton: Time, Love, and Tenderness.* New York: Fireside, 1993. 128 pages. Approximately 75 black-and-white photographs throughout; one eight-page color insert. Index.

Standard photo history of the singer boosted by crisp photos and a stunning color insert. The book attempts to present a fair image of Bolton—admitting to the critical flack he's received over the years—though the text still reads like fanzine copy and doesn't live up to its hype as the "inside story." We are repeatedly reminded that at one time Bolton opened for acts such as Krocus and Ozzy Osbourne—whose fans would be more upset to learn this? For the lovesick.

FANZINES AND FAN CLUBS

Bolton Behind the Scenes. P.O. Box 679, Branford, CT 06405.

A 22-page magazine with a color cover, black-and-white photographs, and a color pull-out poster. Approved by Bolton, the magazine includes profiles of his band members, updates on Bolton's softball activities, news on charity involvement, question-and-answer with Bolton, and more. The cost is $22 for four issues U.S. and Canada; $28 elsewhere.

The Gold Club. P.O. Box 679, Branford, CT 06405.

Gold Club members receive a Gold Club membership card, which entitles them to purchase preferred seating at concerts, discounts on mail merchandise, photos, a pin, a bio sheet, a bumper sticker, personal facts, access to the hotline phone number, and e-mail news flashes. The one-time membership fee is $50 U.S. and Canada; $55 elsewhere.

The Michael Bolton Official International Fan Club. P.O. Box 679, Branford, CT 06405.

Members receive 8x10 photos, a bio sheet, a pin, a membership card, personal facts, e-mail news flashes, and *Bolton Beat* newsletters. The eight-page packet contains black-and-white photographs, information on CDs, photo gallery, collectibles, pen pal exchange, and more. Dues are $22 in the U.S. and Canada; $28 elsewhere.

BON JOVI

BIOGRAPHIES

Bowler, Dave and Dray, Bryan. *Bon Jovi: Runaway*. London: Boxtree, 1995. 164 pages. One four-page glossy black-and-white photo insert. Sources.

The first full-length biography of Bon Jovi, this book may only have limited appeal to fans—simply due to the later existence of other books that have more illustrative or discographical material. Jon Bongiovi, a teenage runaway from Perth Amboy, New Jersey, was the son of a hairdresser (his father) and a former Playboy bunny (yes, his mother). Raised in the Roman Catholic church, Jon sought refuge in Jersey bar rock—a movement paved by Bruce Springsteen. That Bon Jovi became a success despite his rebellious nature may be a testament to his spirit, but is not necessarily the best message to give teenagers.

PICTORIALS

Bateman, Bill. *Bon Jovi*. Miami, FL: MBS, 1994. 120 pages. 125 color illustrations, covering every page. Discography. Chronology. Index.

CD-format book covering all aspects of Bon Jovi's life and career. This nicely designed and illustrated book is priced just right at around $7.99.

Dome, Malcolm. Photographs by Weiss, Mark. *Bon Jovi: Faith and Glory*. Chessington, Surrey (England): Castle Communications, 1994. 160 pages. Over 200 color and black-and-white photographs, covering every page.

Atmospheric, colorful rendering of the Bon Jovi saga, from the group's Jersey bar club days to their mega-selling albums. Author Dome promises to avoid pitfalls such as gossip, innuendo, and blatant band butt-kissing and, for the most part, he is successful. Aside from misspelling Asbury (as in Southside Johnny and the Asbury Jukes), the goofs are kept to a minimum. For female fans, there are lots of angles of Jon Bon Jovi's sweaty shoulders and hairy chest. (Some female fans would probably settle for the other dudes, who in terms of looks all appear capable of fronting their own bands.) Dome mistakenly avoids

including a discography, which is essential for this kind of treatment.

Wall, Mick. *All Night Long: The True Story of Bon Jovi*. London: Omnibus Press (division of Book Sales Limited), 1995. 96 pages. Approximately 125 color and black-and-white illustrations, covering every page. Discography.

It seems that everything Malcolm Dome does for Castle Communications (see above), Mick Wall (or another British journalist) must then follow-up with the same for Omnibus Press. This pictorial promises to deliver "the true story" of the "heavy metal glamour boy," but there is very little new to tell. We only discover that Jon Bon Jovi is what he seems: "a nice guy." Visually extravagant and featuring some superb graphic images on the chapter titles, this book has some advantages over Dome's work, notably that it has a discography.

YOUNG ADULT

Eichhorn, Dennis P. *Bon Jovi*. Seattle: Turman Publishing Company, 1987. 76 pages. 30 black-and-white photographs throughout.

Attention young Bon Jovi fans—here's just what you want: a bio of your favorite group that's three-quarters glossary. *Not*. Every chapter in *Bon Jovi* concludes with a glossary of terms which, under ordinary circumstances, could be a nice idea from a teacher's perspective; but the words are so common (e.g., "albums") and the definitions so obvious (e.g., for drummer: "person who plays drums") that even a five-year-old headbanger would say, "Hey, you calling me dumb?"

OTHER TITLES OF INTEREST
Bon Jovi. *Bon Jovi*. New York: Putnam, 1988.
McSquare, Eddy. *Bon Jovi: An Illustrated Discography*. London: Omnibus Press (division of Book Sales Limited), 1990.

THE BOOMTOWN RATS

See Geldof, Bob.

DEBBY BOONE

AUTOBIOGRAPHY

Boone, Debby with Baker, Dennis. *Debby Boone: So Far*. Nashville, TN: Thomas Nelson Publishers, 1981. 192 pages. One glossy 16-page black-and-white photo insert.

Boone, known to most as either the singer of the monster 1977 hit "You Light up My Life" or as the daughter of singer Pat Boone, shows her rebellious side, while still spreading the word of her love for Jesus. Boone claims to have had a strict upbringing by her father, who wouldn't allow her to wear make-up, prevented her from dating until she was in her late teens, and repeatedly embarrassed her by complaining to her teachers that the books being read were pornographic. Meanwhile, Debby actually admits to having smoked, imbibed alcohol, and watched such controversial films as *Easy Rider*. Move over, Drew Barrymore!

OTHER TITLES OF INTEREST
Boone, Debby. *Bedtime Bugs for Little Ones*. Eugene, OR: Harvest House, 1988.
Boone, Debby. *Hug Along Songs #1 and 2*. No city: Gold, 1992.
Boone, Debby. *Snow Angel*. Eugene, OR: Harvest House, 1991.
Boone, Debby. *Tomorrow Is a Brand New Day*. Eugene, OR: Harvest House, 1989.
Eldred, Patricia M. *Debby Boone*. Mankato, MN: Creative Education, 1979.

PAT BOONE

FANZINES AND FAN CLUBS

National Pat Boone Fan Club. Ms. Chris Bujnovsky, 1025 Park Road, Leesport, PA 19533.

Fan club that is recognized by Pat Boone and enjoys his active participation. Publishes a quarterly newsletter, *Then & Now*, which offers recordings, videos, and collectibles, and has sections called Pat's Calendar (appearances) and Bits & Pieces (brief trivia). Members also receive a photo membership card and a letter from Boone himself. Annual subscription is $10; $12 in Canada and elsewhere. Payable in U.S. currency only.

OTHER TITLES OF INTEREST
Boone, Pat. *A New Song*. London: Lakeland, 1972.
Boone, Pat. *25 Years With the Boone Family*. Nashville, TN: T. Nelson, 1979.

DAVID BOWIE

BIOGRAPHIES

Douglas, David. *Presenting David Bowie!*. New York: Pinnacle Books, 1975. 220 pages.

Empty, fluffed-up introduction to David Bowie that isn't even on the same level as Tremlett's work (see below), released at the same time. Douglas evidently never had access to Bowie and was simply retreading material from magazines and newspapers. Not illustrated and not very interesting.

Edwards, Henry and Zanetta, Tony. *Stardust: The David Bowie Story*. New York: McGraw-Hill Book Company, 1986. 436 pages. Two eight-page glossy black-and-white photographs. Selected Bibliography. Discography. Index.

According to *Stardust*, David Bowie knew from his teen years that he wanted to be a "pop star." This surprisingly long process (it took seven years of performing for him to have a hit with "Space Oddity") is treated here as more a result of expert grooming (from a host of lovers and friends) than of Bowie's talent or musical ability. While it is true that Bowie's image-making and flamboyant style constitute a large part of his success, this book shortchanges him in terms of his abilities as a composer, singer, and icon. Don't we want to know at least some of the cultural significance of Bowie's "Young Americans" and "Rebel Rebel"? As a laundry list of strung together events and sexual affairs, this might serve; but what's missing is the man behind the dramatic wardrobe and multiple stage personae.

Gillman, Peter and Gillman, Leni. *Alias David Bowie: A Biography*. New York: Henry Holt and Company, 1986. 512 pages. Eight four-page black-and-white photo inserts. Discography. Index.

"Alias" is a well chosen word to describe David Bowie; like Bob Dylan, he's manufactured a public image that he alternately uses to his advantage and then rejects when he needs to bail out. Is David Bowie really like Ziggy Stardust or the alien in the film *The Man Who Fell to Earth*? The Gillmans have taken pains in this marvelous biography to set some facts straight. Contrary to Bowie's tall tales, he never "absorbed" black music through his upbringing in Brixton. (The Gillmans' demographic research showed there were hardly any black people in Brixton at all). The authors also explore with great care the real "taboo" subject—mental illness, which was associated with several of Bowie's direct relatives. "No biography of rock star David Bowie has explored the artist's beginnings so thoroughly as this one..."—*Booklist*.

Hopkins, Jerry. *Bowie*. New York: Macmillan, 1985. 285 pages. Two glossy black-and-white photo inserts. Discography. Index.

Leaden biography that fails to bring forth Bowie's creative, narcissistic brilliance. Sentences such as "David was an individualist, studiedly" on the surface seem to have meaning, but actually leave the reader baffled. Crucial aspects of Bowie's early life are left unprobed, as are elements of Bowie's self-mythologizing (how he created his last name, for example). This underwritten, uninvolving bio ends on the bizarre note of David Bowie's December 8, 1980 performance in Hong Kong, when he played "Imagine" in tribute to John Lennon, who had been assassinated that very day—an event that should have been incorporated earlier. The Gillmans' bio (see above) is better in every respect.

Tremlett, George. *The David Bowie Story*. New York: Warner, 1975. 160 pages. One 16-page black-and-white photo insert. Chronology.

Hyper mid-1970's bio on "the boy, the man, the pop star, the cult hero." Author George Tremlett charts Bowie's Brixton boyhood, search for musical identity, and earth-shattering success with "Space Oddity" without penetrating an inch into the artist's chameleonlike elusiveness. Tremlett has a tendency to slip in too many references about his own interviews with Bowie, which disrupt the flow of the narrative. An old story.

BOWIE FRIENDS AND FAMILY

Bowie, Angela and Carr, Patrick. *Backstage Passes: Life on the Wild Side with David Bowie*. New York: G.P. Putnam's Sons, 1993. 352 pages. One 16-page glossy black-and-white photo insert. Discography. Index.

Angela Bowie's 1980 divorce agreement contained a gag clause stipulating that she could not discuss her "open marriage" with David for ten years. Unfortunately, the gag was removed and she regurgitated her guts out in this tell-all barf bag. Ms. Bowie felt compelled to elaborate on virtually every one of the couple's sexual entanglements (heterosexual, homosexual, and lesbian) and entreat us to a fanciful description of what stud Bowie and his "Lance of Love" are like in bed. Things remain on basically the same level of intelligence in digressive chapters about the author's run-ins with now dead rock stars (including Jimi Hendrix, Keith Moon, and John Bonham). "Sex and drugs far outweigh the rock and roll..."—*Publishers Weekly*.

CHRONOLOGIES

Cann, Kevin. *David Bowie: A Chronology*. New York: Fireside (division of Simon & Schuster, Inc.), 1983. 240 pages. One 16-page glossy black-and-white photo insert; 30 black-and-white line drawings throughout. Appendix One: Filmography. Appendix Two: Single Releases and Catalogue Numbers. Appendix Three: U.S. Catalogue Numbers. Further Reading. (First published in Great Britain in 1983 by Hutchinson Publishing Group Unlimited.)

This British-slanted listing of events and dates is enlivened by occasional anecdotes, magazine excerpts, and an above-average glossy spread. Entries are concise and cover all aspects of Bowie's recording and performing career up through the *Let's Dance* LP in 1983. There's just enough elaboration on his friendships with the likes of Lou Reed, John Lennon, John Paul Jones, and Oona Chaplin (Charles' widow). Given that it's a chronology, the book could desperately have used an index; how can one find anything in here unless one happens to know the date (and in that case, why use the book?).

CRITICAL/ANALYTICAL COMMENTARY

Matthew-Walker, Robert. *David Bowie: Theatre of Music*. Buckinghamshire, England: The Kensal Press, 1985. 198 pages. 50 full-page black-and-white photographs scattered throughout. Select Discography. Filmography. Select Bibliography. Index of Music and Album Titles. Index of Persons.

Matthew-Walker defines Bowie's work as "strongly visual"—and actually does the artist's theatricality justice throughout. Divided into three parts—the man (biography), the music (1964-1985), and the artist (producer and actor)—*Theatre of Music* examines, in easily understood terms, the production values, performance quality, and artistic development of every Bowie track since his earliest recordings with The King Bees. Matthew-Walker's writing is unpretentious and engaging, as in a remarkable passage about how "Let's Dance" takes listeners "by the scruff of the neck" into its vision of pleasure. A highly intelligent work; recommended for the serious fan.

DISCOGRAPHIES, RECORDING GUIDES, AND COLLECTIBLES

Carr, Roy and Murray, Charles Shaar. *Bowie: An Illustrated Record*. New York: Avon (division of Hearst), 1981. 120 pages. Approximately 300 color and black-and-white illustrations, covering every page. Bootlegs. Guest Shots, Productions, Cover Versions.

Carr's series of oversized recording guides continues (see Beatles, The) with this investigation into David Bowie's oeuvre up until 1981. Each release includes producer, release date, catalog number, personnel of musicians, and a page of critical description about the recordings. Most interesting are the pages devoted to Bowie's early years and recordings with The King Bees and The Manish Boys. Contains some excellent photos and rare album sleeves, but Carr's views on glitter rock are long outmoded (and may have been in 1981 as well). The book concludes with a selection of what the authors considered to be the most interesting Bowie bootlegs, as well as listings of guest appearances and cover songs. Marginal.

Charlesworth, Chris and Hoggard, Stuart. *Bowie Changes: The Illustrated David Bowie Story*. London: Omnibus Press (division of Book Sales

Limited), 1983. 86 pages. 75 black-and-white photographs throughout.

The title implies that this is an illustrated biography, but it's far from it. The opening chapters provide basic information on Bowie's life, which are followed by a combined listing of singles and LPs. (Bootlegs are included but not identified as such.) Descriptions are critical in tone but do not address sound/recording quality. There is no key to entry format, so researchers have to figure out what the floating dates, label numbers, and performers signify; songwriters are uncredited, and cover groups are only sporadically mentioned (e.g., where is Mott the Hoople for "All the Young Dudes"?). Dated and unreliable.

FANZINES AND FAN CLUBS

Best of Bowie Now. P.O. Box 9103, 1006 AC Amsterdam, Holland.

Membership to this international fan club entitles fans to: a black-and-white poster; a reduction in entrance fee to the annual or biannual meeting; possibility of free advertising; and entrance into contests. Also publishes four illustrated magazines a year, printed in English, which provide Bowie news, member contributions, reviews, and more. The cost in the U.S. is $27 per year.

PICTORIALS

Charlesworth, Chris. *David Bowie: Profile*. London and New York: Proteus Publishing Group, 1981. 96 pages. Approximately 200 color and black-and-white photographs, covering every page. Discography.

Charlesworth, Bowie's ex-public relations man, presents this unnecessary profile of Bowie, which contains splatterings of wild 1970's photos. Many of the shots are simply photocopies of originals, and are way too dark, smudged, and out-of-focus; they seem to be have been selected based on their suggestiveness, i.e., a good portion reveal the star in skintight, see-through outfits or in colored underwear resembling a Speedo. Not so much a pictorial as a poor caricature of an artist who deserves a classier treatment.

Gett, Steve. *David Bowie*. Port Chester, NY: Cherry Lane Books, 1985. 48 pages. 50 color and black-and-white photographs throughout.

How can a pictorial actually make David Bowie look bland? Somehow, this one accomplishes the feat. The three magazine-like spreads that open the book—"dancing in the moonlight," "the cracked actor," and "future legend"—are formulaic and clichéd. Evidently, the book producers felt they needed *something* to fill up the final two thirds of the book and tossed in a very basic chronology of Bowie's life and career to supplement the photos. Forget it.

Miles. *David Bowie Black Book*. London: Omnibus Press (division of Book Sales Limited), 1984. 144 pages. Approximately 200 black-and-white photographs throughout. Discography.

Unusual photo book that sticks rather rigidly to the black motif on both the jacket and interior page designs. Those readers expecting to find lists of Bowie's sexual conquests will be disappointed; the title is just a design gimmick. The sections chart Bowie's career year-by-year, without reporting anything new about the star. With only a handful of quality photos, this one is not worth the effort a decade-plus later.

No author. *Bowie Lives and Times: Bootleg Records Illustrated*. No city (England): Babylon Books, 1978. Unpaginated (approximately 52 pages). Approximately 75 black-and-white reproductions of photographs, album art, and comic strips.

An embarrassing fanzine compendium containing a chronology, some comic strip art ("Suffragette City"), a discography, reproductions of newspaper articles, a discography— and what seems to be a great deal of paid advertising. A complete goose chase, with precious little on bootlegs.

Marchbank, Pearce. *Bowie Pix*. No publication information provided. 32 pages. 64 black-and-white photographs, covering every page.

Bowie is depicted here in his usual variety of poses and costumes. Each photo, supported by a lone Bowie quote, takes up a page and is silhouetted with a repetitious sky blue border. The end result is what appears to be a Bowie modeling portfolio. Look at all the money Bowie saved!

Thompson, Dave. *David Bowie: Moonlight Daydream*. London: Plexus, 1987. 224 pages. Over 200 black-and-white photographs, covering nearly every page. The Bowie Files: Live Performances, Stage, and TV Appearances; The Bowie Songbook; World Discography; Other Artists' Songs Performed and Recorded; Films, Theatre, and Video.

Oversized combination pictorial history and recording guide that catalogs Bowie's career up through the Glass Spider Tour in 1987 (in progress as of press-time). The photos, particularly of the early period, are a stand-out, although not in color: Bowie at 15 playing sax; onstage with George Underwood, the man who socked David in the eye over a row about a girl, leaving the future star with his trademark paralyzed pupil; young Zowie Bowie (David's son); and infinitely more. In terms of Bowie's personal life, readers are advised to read the Gillmans' work (see Biographies, above) instead. While not as glittery as the more color-filled works listed herein, this book might be appreciated by the ultra-devoted fan.

QUIZBOOKS AND QUOTEBOOKS

Miles. *Bowie: In His Own Words*. London: Omnibus Press (division of Book Sales Limited), 1980. 128 pages. Approximately 100 black-and-white photographs, covering every page.

Bowie is quoted here on topics covering everything from rock and roll to sex (which isn't exactly what one would consider an impressive range). On the former, he says: "I was never a rock 'n' roll singer." On the latter, he comments: "Well, if I ever get sent to prison, I'll know how to keep happy." Most of the comments are good throwaways—just Bowie out to hoodwink the media and fans. The photos are of inferior quality.

TOURBOOKS

Flippo, Chet and O'Regan, Denis. Introduction by David Bowie. *David Bowie's Serious Moonlight: The World Tour*. Garden City: Doubleday & Company, Inc., 1984. 256 pages. Over 200 color photos, covering every page.

If you're looking for a book showing Bowie at his controlled best, this one of the 1983 Serious Moonlight Tour is a must. The photos—of Bowie and his band, set-ups, props, crew members, stadiums, fans, and stars he met along the way (e.g., in Japan, singer Sandi)—are highly original and feature some exceptional camera-work and excellent color printing. All of these are accentuated with subtle "moonlight" designs and graphics. Bowie's introduction about the restrictions he faced in Singapore is nothing less than thrilling. An interview with Bowie, the song sheet for "Let's Dance," and a letter from a young fan are thrown in for good measure. Lots of fun.

Kamin, Philip and Goddard, Peter. *David Bowie: Out of the Cool.* New York: Beaufort Books, 1983. 128 pages. Approximately 200 color and black-and-white illustrations, covering every page.

Serviceable photo book of Bowie's Serious Moonlight Tour, with approximately 200 photos of Bowie in action on stage. Kamin has captured the blonde (and occasionally redheaded) superstar in a variety of poses, costumes, hairstyles (variations on sweaty, slick, and plain messy), facial expressions, mannerisms—and even Hamlet-reminiscent props (a skull). The usual Kamin/Goddard formula made enticing by the apropos book subtitle.

Rock, Mick. *Ziggy Stardust: Bowie 1972/1973.* New York: St. Martin's Press, 1984. Unpaginated (approximately 120 pages). Approximately 100 black-and-white photographs, covering every page; two glossy color inserts.

Rather belated synopsis of Bowie's 1972/1973 Ziggy Stardust Tour. Bowie's metamorphosis into the fictional Ziggy character—replete with glamour rock makeup, silky fashions, alien marks on the forehead, and some unabashedly feminine frocks—is clumsily summarized by author Mick Rock, who makes an unforgivable attempt to blend elements of the Ziggy legend with quotes from Bowie and his band about the tour. A haphazard mix, occasionally off-putting, with only a couple of standout photographs in the color inserts.

YOUNG ADULT

Claire, Vivian. *David Bowie! The King of Glitter Rock.* New York: Flash Books, 1977. 80 pages. Approximately 100 black-and-white photographs throughout. Discography.

Reprehensible photo book intended for the young reader. Author Vivian Claire latches onto Bowie's then-prevalent political views, which

included an admiration for Adolf Hitler. (The explanation of this is unclear, but it seems Bowie was impressed with the way The Fuhrer could manipulate a crowd.) Not recommended.

OTHER TITLES OF INTEREST

Currie, David. *Bowie: Glass Idol.* London: Omnibus Press (division of Book Sales Limited), 1991.

Currie, David. *David Bowie: The Stardust Interviews.* London: Omnibus Press (division of Book Sales Limited), 1990.

Fletcher, David J. *David Bowie: The Discography of a Generalist.* No city: Fergeson F. Productions, 1980.

Juby, Kerry. *David Bowie: In Other Words.* London: Omnibus Press (division of Book Sales Limited), 1990.

Kelleher, Ed. *David Bowie: A Biography in Words and Pictures.* No city: Chappell (Sire Books), 1977.

Pitt, Ken. *Bowie: The Pitt Report.* London: Omnibus Press (division of Book Sales Limited), 1991.

Thomson, Elizabeth and Gutman, David. *The Bowie Companion.* New York: Da Capo, 1996.

BOY GEORGE

See Culture Club.

BOYZ II MEN

BIOGRAPHIES

Henderson, Rita Elizabeth. *Boyz II Men Success Story: Defying the Odds.* Los Angeles: Aynderson Press, 1995. 128 pages. Approximately 30 black-and-white photographs throughout. Chronology.

Introductory biography to the hugely successful singing quartet from Philadelphia. The Boyz give hope to the younger generation, as somehow they escaped from the drug-infested slums of that city and went on to break chart records held by Elvis Presley and Michael Jackson. The opening chapters profiling each member are well-written, despite the fact that such a format leads to some redundancies. Henderson reports the full story of the tragedy of road manager Roderick "Khalil" Rountree, who was shot to death in 1992. Recommended in conjunction with the book by the Boyz themselves (see Written Works, below).

FANZINES AND FAN CLUBS

Boyz II Men International Fan Club. P.O. Box 884448, San Francisco, CA 94188.

Boyz II Men fan club that offers access to preferred tickets, exclusive Boyz II Men merchandise, travel packages, and the Boyz II Men hotline. New members receive an identification card, a group photo, and various mailings. The cost of membership is $19.95 U.S.; $24.95 Canada and Mexico; and $29.95 elsewhere.

WRITTEN WORKS

Boyz II Men. *Boyz II Men: [Us to You].* San Francisco: Collins, 1995. 112 pages. Approximately 125 glossy color photographs, covering every page.

Glossy, color-filled photo book capturing the Boys on stage, back stage, rehearsing, traveling, and looking like a bunch of friendly, fun guys. In well-handled sections called "private time," each group member (Shawn Stockman, Michael McCary, Nathan Morris, and Wanya Morris) chat about their upbringings, fame, gospel, money, and other topics. The four bring forth a strong message of family and religion, which seems believable, if a bit pre-packaged. Surprisingly, there is no discography mentioning their chart successes and record-breaking singles—or is this a sign of humbleness? While obviously not written by the quartet, the book contains significant evidence of the Boys' cooperation and personalities, and fans should deem it as a must-purchase for display.

OTHER TITLES OF INTEREST

Hardy, James E. *Boyz II Men.* New York: Chelsea House, 1996.

Shay, Regan. *Boyz II Men.* New York: Dell, 1992.

BILLY BRAGG

TOURBOOKS

Salewicz, Chris. Photographs by Boot, Adrian. *Billy Bragg: Midnights in Moscow.* London: Omnibus Press (division of Book Sales Limited), 1989. 96 pages. Approximately 100 black-and-white photographs throughout. Discography.

In the early 1980's, Billy Bragg served in the English military and fought in the Falkland

Islands war, which many English people felt Margaret Thatcher had started only to gain votes for her re-election as British Minister. This sentiment was shared by young Bragg, who subsequently became a Socialist and studied Soviet culture as his musical career took off. In 1988, Bragg, accompanied by Chris Salewicz and photographer Adrian Boot, went to the Soviet Union, performed with the musicians, and observed the society firsthand. This unusual book uncomfortably mixes the trio's accounts with some history and lore of European, American, and Soviet politics and pop culture.

GARTH BROOKS

BIOGRAPHIES

Morris, Edward. *Garth Brooks: Platinum Cowboy.* New York: St. Martin's Press, 1993. 198 pages. One glossy eight-page black-and-white photo insert. Discography. Chronology.

Shallow study of the "platinum cowboy" (blech!) that doesn't do much except reinforce the concept that Brooks is a humble, nice guy who happened to take the music industry by storm. Author Edward Morris portrays Brooks as a lover of women, but omits mentioning Brooks' cheating heart. Meanwhile, the entire concept of Brooks as the charismatic performer who put the balls back in country is also lost. Since St. Martin's issued this as an attractive but slim paperback—only 179 pages comprise the biography—fans wanting something definitive biography should probably hold on to their britches and wait.

PICTORIALS

Mitchell, Rick. *Garth Brooks: One of a Kind, Workin' on a Full House.* New York: Fireside (Simon & Schuster), 1993. 128 pages. 100 black-and-white photographs; one glossy eight-page color photo insert. Index.

Well-written, popular account of the "old, fat, bald cowboy" who sold 20 million records in only a three-year span. Mitchell is quick to point out Brooks' humbleness, but also shows a characteristic usually overlooked: his sense of humor. ("A great concert," Brooks remarks, "is like any great sex, where you get wild and frenzied, then turn around quick to something gentle, tender, and slow, and then get wild and crazy again.") Fans will enjoy this fluffy treatment.

Randall, Lee. *The Garth Brooks Scrapbook*. New York: Citadel Press (Carol Publishing Group), 1992. 208 pages. Approximately 175 color and black-and-white illustrations throughout.

Garth Brooks rock and roller? This phenomenally popular country artist with some crossover pop appeal grew up listening to Led Zeppelin, Pink Floyd, Journey, Boston, James Taylor, Dan Fogelberg—and even Kiss. He went down the country road because he didn't think "there's any style better than country music as far as letting the lyrics stand out." (He also would have looked pretty silly in glam rock makeup!) Randall's photo-biography has some inspired passages and many excellent color shots for Brooks' fans, but the text is laden with irrelevant sidebars (a treatise on the Aquarius astrological sign) and corny shots from school yearbooks that don't even include the star himself.

OTHER TITLES OF INTEREST
Burke, Bronwen. *Garth Brooks*. New York: Dell, 1992.
Gomer, Celeste R. *Garth Brooks: An Unauthorized Biography*. No city: Country-Song Round-Up, 1993.
McCall, Michael. *Garth Brooks*. New York: Bantam, 1991.
Tallman, Edward. *Garth Brooks: Straight from the Heart*. New York: Macmillan, 1993.

BROS

TOURBOOKS

Black, Susan (editorial research). *Bros Live!*. London: Omnibus Press (division of Book Sales Limited), 1989. Unpaginated (approximately 42 pages). Discography. Comes with a full-color poster.

Visual documentation of Bros' first "world" tour, which included 37 performances in England, Australia, and Japan (no other locales are mentioned, except Hawaii, where they only vacationed). The boys are compared to the Beatles, Michael Jackson (who, like Bros, had Pepsi as a sponsor), and Wham!, although this

is unconvincing, since only one or two shots show screaming fans. Fodder for desperate teenyboppers.

OTHER TITLES OF INTEREST
Hrano, Mike. *Bros: The Big Push*. New York: Beekman, 1991.

BOBBY BROWN

See New Edition.

JAMES BROWN

CRITICAL/ANALYTICAL COMMENTARY

Rose, Cynthia. *Living in America: The Soul Saga of James Brown*. London: Serpent's Tail, 1990. 190 pages. Index.

Cynthia Rose has immense enthusiasm for her subject and describes James Brown with gusto (she dubs him "the Andy Warhol of 20th century sound"). While there's much skill in her analysis, she rarely devotes more than a couple of paragraphs to Brown's classics. She interviewed a small handful of musicians who worked with, or were influenced by, Brown (e.g., trombone player Fred Wesley, bandleader Pee Wee Ellis, and rapper Afrika Bambaata), but these are not enough to create a complete picture of Brown's soul saga. The book does not contain a discography or photos, both of which are crucial; the index only lists names, not songs or albums. If you can overlook these flaws, it's a "...compelling mix of journalism and cultural history"—*Publishers Weekly*.

OTHER TITLES OF INTEREST
Brown. James and Tucker, Bruce. *James Brown: The Godfather of Soul*. New York: Thunder's Mouth Press, 1990.
Brown's autobiography. Booklist *commented: "Brown tells his story of survival and artistic achievement with pride and humor."*

JACKSON BROWNE

PICTORIALS

Wiseman, Rich. *Jackson Browne: The Story of a Hold Out*. Garden City: Doubleday & Company, 1982. 178 pages. Approximately 75 black-and-white photographs throughout. Discography.

Remember the days when Jackson Browne had that boyish, non-threatening look and was your sister's secret crush? Well, he still looks like that...but this book captures young "Jackie" Browne when he was incredibly youthful and parted his hair to the side (as opposed to his trademark bangs). The elements of biography are poorly prioritized here; for example, we learn all about his grandfather, "master printer" Clyde Browne, but we are not informed of Browne's reaction to his wife Phyllis' suicide in 1976 (the date isn't even provided). However, this is a good reminder of Browne's dedication to anti-nuclear causes in the late 1970's and early 80's. Hold out for something better.

JIMMY BUFFETT

PICTORIALS

Humphrey, Mark with Lewine, Harris. *The Jimmy Buffett Scrapbook*. New York: Citadel Press (Carol), 1993. 208 pages. Over two hundred color and black-and-white photographs.

Sue me. I don't get the Parrothead cult in the way I can understand, for example, Grateful Deadmania. But *The Jimmy Buffett Scrapbook* is an orgy of colors and tastes that should please fans of the performer immensely. Buffett's idols—Spike Jones, Marlon Brando, Lord Buckley, Ernest Hemingway, and many others that don't seem to mesh but somehow do—are all amply covered here amidst a backdrop of fluorescent parrots and Caribbean imagery (e.g., pirates, calypso music, etc.). Naturally, blues and 1960's folk music also fit in. The book is filled with exquisite reproductions of covers from old novels, album covers (not only from Buffett), and magazines that are printed on high-quality paper stock one hardly sees these days. Recommended.

WRITTEN WORKS

Buffett, Jimmy and Buffett, Savannah Jane. Illustrations by Davis, Lambert. *The Jolly Mon*. New York: Harcourt Brace Jovanovich, 1988. Unpaginated (approximately 32 pages). Approximately 30 color drawings throughout.

Buffett and his eight-year-old daughter Savannah produced this exceptional best seller about a wonderful fellow named the Jolly Mon, who finds a magical guitar and fills the island of Bananaland with joy. The story involves moments of danger—such as when the Jolly Mon meets up with pirates who happen to be music critics—and some fine moments of fantasy—such as when he is rescued by a talking dolphin (a recurring image in several of Buffett's works). The music sheet to Buffett's famous song of the same name is in the back. Enchanting, and a splash better than the Buffetts' second children's book (see *Trouble Dolls*, below). "The Jolly Mon's smile is winsome"—*Booklist*.

Buffett, Jimmy. *Tales from Margaritaville: Fictional Facts and Factual Fictions*. New York: Fawcett (Ballantine Books), 1989. 240 pages.

Fourteen short stories by Buffett, four of which tip over to the autobiographical side. Cowboys, football coaches, seafarers, and musicians abound, as do men named Kirk (one of whom is a captain) and animals with literary names (a horse named "Mr. Twain"). Buffett's first best seller has moments of irrepressible humor (in "Off to See the Lizard," Godzilla plays mascot to a football team) and a laid back tone that will pass over readers like a rejuvenating Caribbean breeze. By the time the wind has passed, readers will feel great but will have remembered little. "Buffett's material is as evocative and colorful as his music"—*Booklist*.

Buffett, Jimmy and Buffett, Savannah Jane. Illustrations by Davis, Lambert. *Trouble Dolls*. New York: Harcourt Brace Jovanovich, 1991. Unpaginated (approximately 32 pages). Approximately 30 color illustrations, covering every page.

The second collaboration between Buffett and his daughter tells the story of a girl named Lizzy who, with the help of her Guatemalan trouble dolls, must find her father, who has crashed in a seaplane expedition. A wondrous, environmentally correct children's adventure, filled with Davis' lovely pastels that do justice to the Florida Everglade trappings. Ever-present are Buffett's parakeets and other recurring Caribbean symbols. The complex language and lengthy text make this suitable for kids eight and above with superior reading skills. "A satisfying tale with great visual appeal"—*Booklist*.

Buffett, Jimmy. *Where is Joe Merchant?* New York: Avon, 1992. 400 pages.

Light and entertaining "novel tale" by Buffett that doesn't really make much attempt at plausibility. The story concerns a pilot named Frank Bama who is convinced by his on-and-off-again flame Trevor Kane to seek out her brother, 1960's rock star Joe Merchant, who had been presumed dead years earlier. The writing is full of humor, lush details of the Caribbean, and some wonderfully oddball characters (including a former rock groupie named Desdemona who talks to spirits through a dolphin), but some might find the plot predictable and some of the passages rambling. On the whole, this number one best seller makes good summer reading. "You don't have to be a Parrothead to enjoy this wacked-out tale"—*Atlanta Journal and Constitution*.

YOUNG ADULT

Buffett, Jimmy and Buffett, Savannah Jane. Illustrations by Davis, Lambert. *The Jolly Mon*.

See: Written Works.

Buffett, Jimmy and Buffett, Savannah Jane. Illustrations by Davis, Lambert. *Trouble Dolls*.

See: Written Works.

KATE BUSH

DISCOGRAPHIES, RECORDING GUIDES, AND COLLECTIBLES

Goodwin, Robert. *The Illustrated Collector's Guide to Kate Bush*. Bowlington, Ontario (Canada): Collector's Guide Publishing, 1991. 142 pages. Approximately 300 black-and-white photographs of album covers and records.

By "collector's guide," the author primarily refers to albums, CDs, laser discs, videos, and bootlegs—not posters, key chains, boxer shorts, and other merchandising. For each release, Goodwin provides a one-paragraph description—informational in content, not critical—which is followed by catalog numbers for each country of issuance. Oddly, song titles are not mentioned. On the positive side, nearly every album and CD is represented by a photo. Closing sections encompass books, fanzines, and programs. All in all, this only skims the surface of Bush's work.

FANZINES AND FAN CLUBS

American Kate Bush Society. Ernest Heramia, 167 Central Avenue, East Providence, RI 02914.

Networking and service organization for North American fans of Bush that publishes various fanzines and organizes get-togethers and outings among members. *One Step on the Water* is a 20-page stapled packet featuring stories, poetry, reproductions of black-and-white photographs, drawings, open letters, and more—all written by the Society's Amateur Publishing Association. The cost of membership is $10 U.S.; $20 overseas. Make checks payable to Ernest Heramia.

Homeground: The International Kate Bush Fanzine. P.O. Box 176, Orpington, Kent BR5 3NA England.

This international fanzine claims to be the oldest established Kate Bush publication in production, having been in existence since 1982. The fanzine's "aim is to provide a service of news and information about Kate and her music, and to provide a platform for review and discussion of Kate's work on a world-wide basis." The oversized, 32-page magazine contains beautiful glossy black-and-white photographs and original art, news, publications, reviews, letters, ads, fanzines, pen pals, and more. The cost of four issues is £12.75 U.S. and Canada; £8.25 United Kingdom; £8.90 Europe; and £13.55 Australia and Japan.

PICTORIALS

Cann, Kevin and Mayes, Sean. *Kate Bush: A Visual Documentary*. London: Omnibus Press (division of Book Sales Limited), 1988. 96 pages. Approximately 100 black-and-white photographs throughout; 16 pages of color scattered throughout. Discography. Miscellaneous Lists and Trivia. Useful Contacts.

Respectable photo chronology of Kate Bush, with picture spreads of her childhood, her family's farmhouse in East Wickham, England, and the star recording at EMI. Bush is sly and knowing in the photos and does fit the authors' bill as a "windswept beauty." While the authors have never had access to the singer, they are knowledgeable about the subject and cram a generous amount of information in the back sections.

OTHER TITLES OF INTEREST
Bush, Kate. *Leaving My Tracks*. London: Sidgwick & Jackson, 1982.
Kerton, Paul. *Kate Bush*. London: Proteus, 1980.
Vermorel, Fred. *Kate Bush: The Secret History (and the Strange Art of Pop)*. London: Omnibus Press (division of Book Sales Limited), 1983.

THE BUZZCOCKS

CHRONOLOGIES

McGartland, Tony. *Buzzcocks: The Complete History*. London: Independent Music Press, 1995. 160 pages. Two glossy eight-page black-and-white photo inserts. Chronology. Discography. Buzzcocks Family Tree.

This short-lived Manchester punk band (1976-1981) was one of the first to make it big on an independent label—and inspire an entire generation of musicians in the 1980's and 90's. The quintet—Howard Trafford, Peter McNeish, Garth Davies, and Steve Diggle—released the hits "Orgasm Addict" and "What Do I Get," but split primarily due to financial woes. This strangely assembled book uncomfortably combines biography, chronology, and discography, making it useful for quick details, but not the whole picture. Optional.

THE BYRDS

(See also Crosby, Stills, Nash and Young; Parsons, Gram)

TITLES OF INTEREST
Rogan, Johnny. *Timeless Flight: The Definitive Biography of the Byrds*. No city: Hallenbook, 1991.
Scoppa, Bud. *The Biography of the Byrds*. New York: Scholastic, 1972.
Scoppa, Bud. *The Byrds*. New York: Quick Fox, 1971.

CAN

BIOGRAPHIES

Bussy, Pascal and Hall, Andy. *The Can Book*. Harrow, Middlesex (England): SAF, 1989. 192 pages. Approximately 75 black-and-white photographs throughout. Discography.

For those unfamiliar, Can was a German techno-pop group from the late 1960's to the end of the 70's featuring Holger Czukay, Michael Karoli, Jaki Liebezeit, Irmin Schmidt, and Damo Saluski. A hard-to-classify blend of The Velvet Underground, Jimi Hendrix, and Frank Zappa, this rather strange group reunited in 1986 for one more album. Fans of avant-garde rock might enjoy this book, at least to search for the roots of what was to come later on in alternative music.

CAPTAIN AND TENNILLE

TITLES OF INTEREST
Spada, James. *Captain & Tennille*. Mankato, MN: Creative Education, c.1976.

MARIAH CAREY

BIOGRAPHIES

Nickson, Chris. *Mariah Carey: Her Story*. New York: St. Martin's Griffin, 1995. 154 pages. One glossy eight-page black-and-white photo insert. Chronology. Index.

With five consecutive number one singles on the Billboard charts—a record not even matched by Elvis or The Beatles—Carey seems ripe for profiling. Raised by a lower-middle class divorcée, Carey had a natural singing talent as a child. She was discovered a few years later by Tommy Mottola, who founded Champion Entertainment, paved her recording career, and ultimately became her husband. This self-proclaimed "Cinderella" story is heavily padded with statistics on single-parent families and biographical information on other female artists that would have made more interesting copy elsewhere. In this setting, these distractions only serve to point out the author's lack of firsthand material.

FANZINES AND FAN CLUBS

Mariah Carey Official International Fan Club. P.O. Box 679, Bramford, CT 06405.

Members of this club receive 8x10 photos, a personal fact sheet, a pin, a membership card, newsletters, access to the hotline phone number, e-mail news flashes, and more. The club's illustrated, six-page newsletter contains a lengthy letter from Carey herself, in which she discusses her charity work and recent recordings. Also featured are contests, pen pals, and photo gallery. The cost of membership is $22 per year for U.S. and Canada; $28 elsewhere.

THE CARPENTERS

BIOGRAPHIES

Coleman, Ray. Foreword Herb Albert. *The Carpenters: The Untold Story.* New York: HarperCollins, 1994. 360 pages. Two glossy 16-page black-and-white photo inserts. The Carpenters on Record. Index.

Deeply moving portrait of Karen and Richard Carpenter, the brother and sister combo who charmed a generation in the early 1970's with their brand of soft, melancholy tunes. Karen's long battle with anorexia nervosa—which is believed to have claimed her life in 1983—take up much of the story, but other woes, such as Richard's sleeping pill addiction, are also part of the larger picture. Painful to say the least, this book is recommended for fans of the duo,

as well as for anorexia sufferers and their families. British Lennon biographer Coleman has an impressive grasp of American society and culture (though a little too much enthusiasm for the Carpenters' performance for President Nixon while he was in the White House). "Well-researched, well-written and less gossipy than most celebrity bios..."—*Publishers Weekly.*

JIM CARROLL

WRITTEN WORKS

Carroll, Jim. *The Basketball Diaries.* New York: Penguin, 1995. 214 pages.

First published in the U.S. in 1978 by Tombouctou Books, this underground classic consists of Carroll's journal entries spanning the years 1963-1966. The future poet and rocker was only 12-15 when he wrote these passages, which tell of his teenage experiences in New York City and of his involvements with drugs, sex, crime, and sports. A *Catcher in the Rye* for the 1970's, with distinct influence from Jack Kerouac, and some very disturbing scenes of substance abuse. Avoid the film adaptation—which updated the story to the 1990's—but by all means give this a read.

Carroll, Jim. *The Book of Nods.* New York: Viking Penguin, 1986.

See: *Fear of Dreaming.*

Carroll, Jim. *Fear of Dreaming.* New York: Penguin Books, 1993. 276 pages.

A compilation of works by Carroll, including the full text to his first book, *Living at the Movies*; selections from *The Book of Nods*; a chunk of uncollected works spanning 1973-1985; and 16 new works from the years 1989-1993. Carroll's poetry covers a broad spectrum, from city life ("Leaving N.Y.C.") and hallucinogenic drugs ("The Blue Pill") to allegory ("Five Irresponsible Students at Zen") and art ("Post-Modernism"). Works are dedicated to Ezra Pound, Jack Kerouac, Phil Ochs, and several other Carroll influences. Highly recommended for fans of the poet, but not a substitute for *The Basketball Diaries* (see above).

Carroll, Jim. *Forced Entries: The Downtown Diaries 1971–1973*. New York: Penguin Books, 1987. 184 pages.

The follow-up memoir to the classic *Basketball Diaries* (see above), this work spans Carroll's activities post-1960's and the hippie generation. (Curiously, he opens the book pointing out that he shares his birth date with Jerry Garcia.) Carroll has a flair for finding humor in the most perverse situations (his girlfriend picking bouncing genital crabs out of his crotch), but of greater interest are his experiences with a cast of characters that includes Andy Warhol. The story takes an unexpected turn as Carroll escapes to California to sort himself out. Haunting.

Carroll, Jim. *Living at the Movies*. New York: Grossman Publishers, 1973.

See: *Fear of Dreaming*.

THE CARS

PICTORIALS

Goldstein, Toby. *Frozen Fire: The Story of the Cars*. New York: Contemporary Books, Inc., 1985. 134 pages. 75 photographs throughout; one eight-page glossy color insert (at the back of the book). U.S. Discography. Videography.

Author Goldstein has written a faithful history of the band, replete with excellent black-and-white and color photography from Ebet Roberts. Goldstein cleverly sums up the Cars' place in pop history by distinguishing how they function in a hotel room, as compared with hard rock and punk bands: Instead of completely demolishing the room like The Who or The Sex Pistols, they might simply slant a wall picture or tilt a lampshade. Don't look for basic facts such as birth dates—you won't find them. However, as a nicely packaged start-up kit for Cars fans, this will do.

Kamin, Philip and Goddard, Peter. *The Cars*. New York: McGraw-Hill Book Company, 1986. 96 pages. Approximately 75 color and black-and-white illustrations throughout. Discography.

Stylish photo book on the Boston band that treats them as "normal" rock publicity hounds, but with a certain mystery about them—notably in the tricky lyrics to Ric Ocasek's tunes. Writer Goddard did more research here than is his usual, examining the band's overlooked meticulousness, diversity, and artistic relationship with Andy Warhol (who directed some of their videos). Superb concert and recording shots by Kamin, taken on "exclusive" Canon cameras and equipment. The book sorely lacks a videography, given the band's reputation in this area.

THE CARTER FAMILY

DISCOGRAPHIES, RECORDING GUIDES, AND COLLECTIBLES

Christie, Keith G. *Carter Family Discography*. Nashville, TN: Records Associates, 1964. Unpaginated (approximately 28 pages).

Sloppy, dated vanity press publication that is barely typewritten. Sections are divided by studio (Acme, American, etc.) and contain release dates, catalog numbers and not much else. A section on radio transcriptions is buried in the middle. Don't bother.

GENERAL REFERENCE

Atkins, John (Editor). *The Carter Family*. London: Old Time Music, 1973. 60 pages. Approximately 60 black-and-white photographs and reproductions of programs, playbills, etc. Discography.

An "Old Time Music" booklet containing cut-and-paste reproductions of photos, a general bio of the family, and a comprehensive discography (by Alec Davidson). The research and background material are top-notch, and help overcome the many shortcomings of presentation.

YOUNG ADULT

Krishef, Robert K. and Harris, Stacy. *The Carter Family*. Minneapolis: Lerner Publications, 1978. 64 pages. 20 black-and-white photographs scattered throughout. Recordings of the Carter Family. Index.

Part of the "Country Music Library," this is a well done and succinct history of the legendary family, beginning with the birth of Alvin Pleasant Carter in 1891 in a part of Maces Springs, Virginia known as "Poor Valley." The photos are rare and neatly bordered. The only visible flaw: There are no years provided for record releases.

JOHNNY CASH

AUTOBIOGRAPHY

Cash, Johnny. *Man in Black*. Grand Rapids: Zondervan, 1975. 246 pages. One 24-page glossy black-and-white photo insert.

Cash's "story in his own words" is a forum for the country legend as he comes to terms with his amphetamine addiction and spreads his love of Christianity. There are snippets of information throughout that could have been of significant interest—ranging from his childhood experiences working on a cotton crop to his interaction with the likes of Elvis and Carl Perkins at Sun Records—but these are not given enough attention or embellishment. Fans can only look forward to seeing Cash's reprinted compositions throughout.

BIOGRAPHIES

Carpozi, Jr., George. *The Johnny Cash Story*. New York: Pyramid Books, 1970. 128 pages. 16-page glossy black-and-white photo insert.

Slight bio of the legendary country singer, with emphasis on Cash's recovery from drug addiction in the mid-1960's and his triumphant 1969 Madison Square Garden performances. The author mentions interesting facts about Cash, such as his fear of snakes and tendency to over-perspire, but does not go into any great detail. In the end, we yearn for more information about Cash's contemporaries, collaborations, and his influence on the country and folk scenes.

Conn, Charles Paul. *The New Johnny Cash*. New York: family Library, 1973. 94 pages. One 16-page glossy black-and-white photo insert.

"The inspiring true story of a great singer who found an even greater faith" was issued in 1973 to coincide with Cash's film *The Gospel Road*. This is a retread of past biographies, but with a bent on Cash's religious affiliations and his friendships with Billy Graham and Reverend Billy Snow. In the end, this is more about the author's love of Jesus Christ than Cash's.

Wren, Christopher. *Winners Got Scars Too: The Life and Legends of Johnny Cash*. New York: The Dials Press, 1971. 230 pages.

Listless rendering of the Cash story, devoid of photos and any color whatsoever. The author focuses way too much on how Cash's success story and his performance at the White House (presumably for then-President Richard Nixon, although his name is strangely omitted) were the culmination of the American Dream for the son of a Depression-era cotton farmer. The book's one saving grace (if you'll forgive the pun) is that it doesn't hype Cash's newborn religion to the same extent as other bios.

DISCOGRAPHIES, RECORDING GUIDES, AND COLLECTIBLES

Smith, John L. Foreword by Johnny Cash and Johnny Western. *The Johnny Cash Discography*. Westport, CT: Greenwood Press, 1984. 203 pages. Bibliography. Index.

Part one of Smith's three-volume series of discographical works on Johnny Cash with Greenwood Press (see below). More about the actual recording sessions than discography, this book examines Cash's body of work starting with his early Sun recordings, identifying players on all his singles and albums up through the early 1980's. Not much here in terms of personality, and anyone conducting research will need to have all three volumes.

Smith, John L. *Johnny Cash Discography and Recording History, 1955-1968*. Los Angeles: University of California, undated. 48 pages. Four black-and-white photographs. Appendix A: Johnny Cash Songbooks & Folios. Appendix B: Feature Films & Television Appearances.

A catalog of Cash recordings, sponsored by the John Edwards Memorial Foundation, and something of a precursor to his trilogy with Greenwood Press (see above and below). Album listings only include song titles and catalog numbers; there are a few footnotes at the bottoms of pages, usually to indicate label misspellings and alternate tracks released in other countries. Running times, chart positions, studio musicians, etc. are not provided. As old as the hills, as they say, and not comprehensive enough for complex research. Go with Smith's more recent discographies.

Smith, John L. Foreword by Marty Stuart. *The Johnny Cash Discography, 1984-1993.* Westport, CT: Greenwood, 1994. 336 pages. Appendix A: Pre-1984 Sessions. Appendix B: Billboard Chart Entries. Index.

More hardcore discographical material from Smith, this is the intermediary volume in his trilogy with Greenwood Press (see above and below). Sessions are chronological and contain: name, date, and address of recording studio; label; composer; notes; musician line-ups; and more. Not particularly pretty to look at, but researchers can gain wide insights into the diversity of Cash's talents looking at these lists. Some may be surprised to discover that Cash actually recorded a couple of Elvis Costello songs in 1984. Valuable.

Smith, John L. *The Johnny Cash Record Catalog.* Westport, CT: Greenwood Press, 1994. 256 pages. Appendix. Index.

The third in Smith's trilogy with Greenwood Press, intended to supplement the earlier works. The book, focusing exclusively on releases, is divided into four parts: singles, EPs, LPs, and CDs. All sections are arranged by label (CBS, A&M, etc.) and then by catalog number. Smith is diligent including international releases and annotating the lists (stereo vs. mono, etc.). Highly useful, but researchers will be spending most of their time plodding through the indexes searching for titles. Frustrating for those who don't own the earlier volumes.

YOUNG ADULT

Hudson, James A. *Johnny Cash: Close-Up.* New York: Scholastic Book Services, 1971. 96 pages. Approximately 20 black-and-white photographs throughout.

Antiquated young adult bio on the country legend. The book may have some special value to those who have interest in Cash's family life, since a good portion of the story concerns the birth of his son, John Carter. The author adroitly deals with Cash's arrests, drug problems, and various squabbles with The Grand Ole Opry. Optional.

DAVID CASSIDY

See Partridge Family, The.

SHAUN CASSIDY

(See also Partridge Family, The)

TITLES OF INTEREST
Schumacher, Craig. *Shaun Cassidy.* Mankato, MN: Creative Education, 1979.
Part of Creative Education's "Rock 'n Pop Stars" series.

NICK CAVE (& THE BAD SEEDS)

BIOGRAPHIES

Johnston, Ian. *Bad Seed: The Biography of Nick Cave.* London: Little, Brown and Company, 1995. 344 pages. One glossy 16-page black-and-white photo insert. Discography. Index.

Superb, thoroughly detailed biography of Nick Cave, the tall, slender lead singer of The Birthday Party, The Boys Next Door, and ultimately The Bad Seeds. Author Ian Johnston shows that Cave is more than just a rocker: He's also a novelist, poet, lyricist, and film actor with a unique vision and charisma. Born in Melbourne, Australia, Cave first became involved in music through glam rock: David Bowie and Marc Bolan. Like most young stars, he was a delinquent, the kind of kid who would pull down a girl's knickers in public. "Gripping and well-written..."—*Q.*

TOURBOOKS

Milne, Peter. Introduction by Nick Cave. *Fish in a Barrel: Nick Cave & the Bad Seeds on Tour.* London: Tender Prey, 1993. 110 pages. Approximately 75 black-and-white photographs throughout.

Extremely entertaining series of images tracking Nick Cave & the Bad Seeds on tour circa 1993 in Japan, Europe, and Australia. The pictures are stark, glossy black-and-white, and reflect the photographer's desire to snap people when they least expect it. (In his

Introduction, Cave asserts Milne's brilliance but stipulates he's "basically interested in people's suffering"). The book sports fascinating outtakes of the band doodling backstage, sleeping on trains, tinkering in the recording studio, tonguing female fans at night clubs, and looking just plain exhausted. Although the pictures are uncaptioned, a closing interview between Milne and Cave explains some of the goings-on. Essential for Cave fans.

WRITTEN WORKS

Cave, Nick. *And the Ass Saw the Angel*. New York: HarperCollins, 1992. 252 pages.

Cave's first novel is an imaginative and offbeat biblical allegory set in a strange, swampy place called the Ukulore Valley. The main character, Euchrid Eucrow, is a mute who can communicate with animals; to the reader he uses a bizarre backwoods dialect ("ah" for "I" and "mah" for "my"). Among the assorted weird characters is Beth, a holy child who thinks Euchrid is Jesus, and a fellow unfortunately named Kike. "Although Cave's manic effort will not lure traditionalists, it may snare the more adventurous"—*Publishers Weekly*.

Cave, Nick. *King Ink*. Los Angeles: 2.13.61 Publications, 1993. 196 pages. Index. (First published in Great Britain in 1993 by Black Spring Press, Ltd.).

Nick Cave, the founder of The Birthday Party and more recently The Bad Seeds, presents his own collection of lyrics, sketches, and other writings. All of the works are divided into a dozen unifying chapters. "Dead Joe" combines a cheery Santa-like rhythm with lyrical details of a car crash. "Pleasure is the Boss" reflects on blind servility. Various sketches (or playlets), such as "Gun Play #3,") tell of erotic, violent interactions between couples. Throughout the book one can find reproductions of Cave's typewritten manuscript, with globs of crossouts and notations. While not nearly as imaginative as Jim Morrison's works or as clever with wordplay as those of Lou Reed or Bob Dylan, Cave's writings manage to shock and manipulate among the best of them.

OTHER TITLES OF INTEREST
Brokenmouth, Robert. *Nick Cave: The Birthday Party & Other Epic Adventures*. London: Omnibus Press (division of Book Sales Limited), 1996.

HARRY CHAPIN

BIOGRAPHIES

Coan, Peter M. *Taxi: The Harry Chapin Story*. Port Washington: Ashley Books, Inc., 1987. 480 pages. One 24-page black-and-white photo insert. Discography.

Harry Chapin had many titles: "poet laureate of cab drivers," "founder of the story song," and "crusader for human decency." He was also a restless philanderer, a driven "star tripper," and perhaps one of the worst drivers of our time. (His driver's license was revoked shortly before his life-ending car accident in 1981.) Author Peter Coan befriended Chapin before his death and, though suffering through the latter's tardy arrivals, had his support and approval on this biography. The book is affectionate and revealing, describing at length positive and negative criticism of Chapin and even reporting the mind-blowing news that Chapin's wife Sandy wrote most of the lyrics to "Cat's in the Cradle." Unfortunately, *Taxi* does not contain a table of contents, any source material, or an index. "For general, not academic, music libraries"—*Choice*.

OTHER TITLES OF INTEREST
Chapin, Harry. *Looking...Seeing*. No city: Thomas Cromwell Company, 1977.
Collection of poetry by Chapin.

RAY CHARLES

AUTOBIOGRAPHY

Charles, Ray and Ritz, David. *Brother Ray: Ray Charles' Own Story*. New York: Da Capo Press, 1992. 348 pages. One eight-page black-and-white photo insert. Discography and Notes.

What a musician, what a life—and what an autobiography. Brother Ray lets loose his life story with cheerful, uninhibited confidence and verisimilitude. You feel like you are in the room with Charles as he tells all: his childhood woes (how he couldn't save his baby brother from drowning, his gradual blindness, his mother's death); influences (Nat King Cole and Art Tatum); and legal hassles (dope arrests, paternity suits). One memorable passage involves how boys in his school for the blind made intricate maps so they could find their way to the girls' dormitory. The voice of the man, occasionally lascivious, is also present as he details his philosophies on sex, music ("I never considered myself part of rock and roll"), racial prejudice, and even Israel. While lacking in illustrative material and dates here and there, this is the prime source to get to know the man himself. First published in 1978 by Dial Press.

YOUNG ADULT

Mathis, Sharon Bell. Illustrated by Ford, George. *Ray Charles*. New York: Thomas Y. Crowell, Company, 1973. 32 pages. Approximately 25 original pencil drawings throughout.

Foots, the name by which other kids tormented Ray Charles as a child, is afforded this sympathetic and encouraging picture-book. Author Sharon Bell Mathis tells how Charles overcame the traumas associated with his childhood blindness, and learned through practice and training how to play a number of musical instruments; he required neither for his naturally gifted soulful singing voice. Ford's pencil drawings have not held up over the years and do little to illustrate the emotions involved; today, kids would want some color pictures.

OTHER TITLES OF INTEREST
Ritz, David. *Ray Charles: Musician*. New York: Chelsea, 1994.

CHARLIE DANIELS BAND

TITLES OF INTEREST
Daniels, Charlie. *The Devil Went Down to Georgia*. Atlanta, GA: Peachtree, 1986.

CHUBBY CHECKER

RELATED WORKS

Dawson, Jim. *The Twist: The Story of the Song and Dance That Changed the World*. Boston and London: Faber and Faber, 1995. 176 pages. One 16-page black-and-white photo insert.

A comprehensive tracing of the origins of the most famous dance craze of this century. "The Twist" stands as the only non-Christmas song to hit number one twice; Hank Ballard recorded it, but it was Chubby Checker's version that struck gold—thanks to Dick Clark's constant plugging on his various dance and radio shows. Dawson reveals many controversies about the song that might shock fans of the record; researchers of early American pop would want to give it a look.

CHER

(See also Sonny and Cher)

BIOGRAPHIES

Quirk, Lawrence J. *Totally Uninhibited: The Life and Wild Times of Cher*. New York: William Morrow & Company, 1991. 304 pages. Three eight-page black-and-white photo inserts. Filmography. Selected Discography. Selected Bibliography. Index.

The tabloid war on Cherilyn Sarkisian continued into the 1990's with this tell-all installment from Lawrence J. Quirk. Sonny Bono once again is portrayed as the 1960's diminutive pop Svengali (although not quite so enthralling in the sack), with Cher as his sleazy, nymphomaniac sidekick who only has one pair of panties. Cher's other lovers—David Geffen, Gregg Allman, Gene Simmons, Val Kilmer, Josh Donen (director Stanley's son), et al.—are branded like bulls in a pen, although as Quirk portrays things we're never too sure who is the bull and who is the cow. Cher's career as solo singer is almost completely buried amidst the gust of extremist reviews of her films. "Quirk at times is driven to gaga screen-mag lapses into vulgarity..."—*Kirkus*.

Taraborrelli, J. Randy. *Cher: A Biography*. New York: St. Martin's, 1986. 322 pages. Four eight-page black-and-white inserts.

Taraborrelli defines Cher as an oddball entertainer whose talents haven't yet been appreciated; but only shortly after this book was published she received some genuine recognition by winning an Academy Award (for the film *Moonstruck*). Taraborrelli can't be excused for the errors that pop out every few pages (Roger Moore is incorrectly identified as James Bond in *You Only Live Twice*) or for failing to uncover Cher's mask: her glitzy, rebellious, self-centered, stray-cat mystique. "...as flat as last night's champagne and as deep as a *People* magazine profile"—*Library Journal*.

CHRONOLOGIES

St. Michael, Mick. *Cher: The Visual Documentary*. London: Omnibus Press (division of Book Sales Limited), 1993. 96 pages. Approximately 125 color and black-and-white photographs, covering every page. Discography.

Sex symbol. Rock star. Fashion victim. Movie star. Millionairess. The woman of many titles (and even more outfits) is the subject of this excessively illustrated day-by-day chronology of events. Cher's name is of such epic stature that entire pages in this book are devoted to that alone. If this book serves one purpose, it shows that Cher can change clothes faster than the best of them. If you need the bare facts about Cher (or just Cher nearly bare), you might want to give this a try.

QUIZBOOKS AND QUOTEBOOKS

Goodall, Nigel. *Cher: In Her Own Words*. London: Omnibus Press (division of Book Sales Limited), 1992. 96 pages. Approximately 100 black-and-white photographs throughout.

Cher gets in both the first and the last word in this collection of quotes and pictures. Sections include growing up, making it, men, marriage, music, stage, fashion, etc. A chapter called "The Things They Say about Me" is rebuffed by the star in "The Things Cher Says about Them." Here's what she has to say about Madonna: "She's not beautiful and she's rude." Readers will without question race ahead to the section on men (which has subheadings on various lovers, such as Val Kilmer, Gene Simmons, et. al.). Spicy.

WRITTEN WORKS

Cher and Haas, Robert, M.S. *Forever Fit: The Lifetime Plan for Health, Fitness, and Beauty*. New York: Bantam (division of Bantam Doubleday Dell), 1991. 342 pages. Approximately 20 black-and-white photographs throughout. Appendix I: Forever Fit Recipes. Appendix II: Forever Fit Computer Software. Appendix Three: Food Composition Tables. Appendix IV: Bibliography. Index of Recipes.

A complete fitness factfile designed for busy women over 40. Full of tables with caloric and fat content, recipes, exercise regimes, tips on beauty and cosmetics, etc., the book attempts to convince any woman that she could look like Cher before the microwave stops revolving. While Cher *does* look marvelous in the photos, she's really only posing while smeared with heavy makeup and airbrush photo effects: She doesn't exactly look like Richard Simmons sweating with the pouchy masses. Slickly packaged and needful of a video supplement.

OTHER TITLES OF INTEREST
Bego, Mark. *Cher*. New York: Pocket, 1986.
Jacobs, Linda. *Cher: Simply Cher*. St. Paul, MN: EMC, 1975.

CHICAGO

TITLES OF INTEREST
O'Shea, Mary. *Chicago*. Mankato, MN: Creative Education, 1975.
Part of Creative Education's "Rock 'n Pop Stars" series.

LOU CHRISTIE

FANZINES AND FAN CLUBS

Lou Christie Fan Club. P.O. Box 748, Chicago, IL, 60690-748.

Publishes *Lightning Strikes: The Lou Christie Newsletter*, which consists of 44 pages covering all aspects of the artist. Each issue is packed with black-and-white photos, reprints of newspaper articles and reviews, studies of Lou Christie history, chart information, and more. Members also receive bulletins, merchandise, photos, contest entrances, etc. The cost of membership is $10 per year in the U.S.; $12 for Canada; and $14 everywhere else (U.S. currency only).

ERIC CLAPTON

(See also Cream; Yardbirds, The)

BIOGRAPHIES

Coleman, Ray. *Clapton! An Authorized Biography.* New York: Warner Books, Inc., 1985. 368 pages. Approximately 75 black-and-white photographs scattered throughout. Eric Clapton's Career Moves. Discography. Index. (First published in Great Britain in 1985 by Sidgwick & Jackson Limited as *Survivor! The Authorized Biography of Eric Clapton.*)

Clapton may be God in the eyes of many of his fans, but he's a troubled, lonely artist in search of his identity. He failed miserably as an art student, briefly pursued a career in stained glass, and then found the calling that would propel him to fame: blues guitar. Clapton's addictions to alcohol and heroin, longing for Pattie Harrison (wife of his best friend, Beatle George), and battles for artistic integrity (leaving The Yardbirds because they were becoming too commercial) are part of rock lore. Coleman's biography relays these familiar trappings with sensitive authority and has the advantage of firsthand quotes from the likes of Pete Townshend, Steve Winwood, Jack Bruce, and Clapton himself. The book's only flaw lies in its redundant chiming about Clapton being a paradox of both humble and conceited virtues.

Pidgeon, John. *Eric Clapton: A Biography.* No city: Century Hutchinson/Vermillion, 1987. 123 pages. One eight-page black-and-white photo insert. Discography. Index.

A revised edition of Pidgeon's 1980 mass-market paperback, primarily covering Clapton's career as a guitarist in supergroups and as a soloist. The book shirks basic information about his childhood and family background, and fails to penetrate important details of his character and years coping with drug addiction. Even Clapton's accomplishments as singer/songwriter are overlooked in favor of the usual hype about his guitar mastery. God should have been treated with better care.

Sandford, Christopher. *Clapton: Edge of Darkness.* London: Victor Gollancz, 1994. 322 pages. Two glossy eight-page photo inserts.

Appendices: 1. Chronology. 2. Eric Clapton's Groups 1963-94. Sources and Chapter Notes. Index.

With recent biographies from Coleman, Schumacher, and Shapiro (see above and below for all) and Roberty's staple collection of photo books (see below), is there really a need for another—and one that doesn't even contain a discography? Author Christopher Sandford has a flair for the dramatic in telling Clapton's story, and in many cases succeeds better in capturing the man himself—his musical genius, his professorial demeanor, his blues pretensions, his inner battles for soulful music vs. commercialism. and his prodigious lusts. Sandford even brings to light several unseen aspects of Clapton's personality, such as his sense of humor, notably by fondness for slapstick. A sound alternative to those wanting a sense of Clapton the man.

Schumacher, Michael. *Crossroads: The Life and Music of Eric Clapton.* New York: Hyperion, 1995. 388 pages. Two eight-page glossy black-and-white photo inserts. Source Notes. Selected Discography. Appendix: Eric Clapton's Bands.

Just when you thought Clapton had experienced the world up through the end of the 1980's, all of a sudden his life turned around again with 1990's events such as the death of his young son Conor out a New York City window, his successful stint as George Harrison's sideman in Japan, and the Grammy avalanche stirred by his MTV *Unplugged* CD. Schumacher's laid-back bio is a recommended continuance of the decade following Coleman's biography (see above). A few trivial errors here and there are worth overlooking.

Shapiro, Harry. *Eric Clapton: Lost in the Blues.* New York: Da Capo, 1992. 226 pages. One 32-page black-and-white photo insert. Discography. Groupography. Sources. Index. (First published in 1992 in Great Britain by Guinness Publishing Limited.)

Incorrectly dubbing Clapton "the first musician to be tagged a guitar hero" (what about Chuck Berry?), author Harry Shapiro fails to add anything new to the already weighty literature existing on Clapton. Shapiro waters down the pages on Clapton's heroin addiction, and it's only in the very last paragraph of the narrative that he attempts to probe the reasons for Clapton's popularity. The photo insert, while extensive in terms of number of pages, doesn't compare to the visual material in Roberty's works (see below)—and the same can be said for the discographical sections. Middling.

CHRONOLOGIES

Roberty, Marc. *Eric Clapton: The New Visual Documentary*. London: Omnibus Press (division of Book Sales Limited), 1990. 128 pages. Approximately 125 black-and-white photographs, covering every page.

Lavishly illustrated day-by-day of events that have shaped Clapton's career. Beginning in October 1963 and Clapton's first rehearsals with the Yardbirds—unfortunately, no earlier details of his childhood and art school days are included—the book charts his recordings, concerts, famous meetings with other stars, and more. In many cases, only a venue is identified. If you only need activities up through the end of the 1980's, this book will serve. Published in the U.S. under the title *The Eric Clapton Scrapbook* (Crown, 1994).

DISCOGRAPHIES, RECORDING GUIDES, AND COLLECTIBLES

Roberty, Marc. *Eric Clapton: The Complete Recording Sessions 1963-1992*. London: Blandford (Cassell), 1993. 192 pages. Approximately 75 black-and-white photos throughout. Discography. Guest Sessions. Videography. Bootlegs. Index of Song Titles.

Clapton is a good subject for a discography, and author Roberty (editor of *Slowhand*, see Fanzines below) does an admirable job of culling information on recording sessions from The Yardbirds, Cream, John Mayall, Derek and the Dominoes, and Blind Faith, as well as solo work and occasional contributions to music by George Harrison, Dr. John, The Rolling Stones, etc. In the British edition the photos are either too dark or too faded (although the U.S. edition is slightly improved). Those who don't care about aesthetics will treasure this volume and will keep it close at hand next to their CD set of Clapton's *Crossroads*. Published in the U.S. by St. Martin's Press in 1993.

Roberty, Marc. *Eric Clapton: The Man, the Music and the Memorabilia*. Limpsfield, Surrey (England): Paper Tiger (Dragon's World), 1994. 226 pages. Approximately 500 color and black-and-white reproductions of album covers, posters, magazines, memorabilia, etc. Bootlegs. Discography. Index.

Companion-piece to Roberty's fine recording guide (see above), this publication concentrates on the visual end of Clapton recordings, with excellent depictions of album and poster art. The meatiest part of the work consists of Clapton biography, which alternates with tour date listings. A section called "Moonlighting" is especially vital, given Clapton's prodigious and varied session work; thus even obscure contributions to the works of Lovin' Spoonful, Howlin' Wolf, Buddy Guy, and many others are duly noted—although not cited alphabetically. Fans will search back and forth through this book for hours, continuously getting sidetracked from the intended destination; for the most part, the distractions are well worth it. Roberty once again proves to be the Discographer Laureate of Clapton recordings.

FANZINES AND FAN CLUBS

Slowhand: The Quarterly Magazine for Eric Clapton Fans. P.O. Box 488, Pelham, N.Y. 10803.

Twelve to fourteen-page fan magazine on Clapton, with comprehensive news, tour information, backstage interviews (with sidemen, such as harp player Jerry Portnoy), concert reviews, quotes from fans, and miscellaneous subscriber contributions. Some photocopies of black-and-white photographs. The cost for four issues is $20 (payable by check or money order); add $5 if out of the U.S.

INTERVIEWS

Turner, Steve. *Conversations with Eric Clapton*. London: Abacus, 1976. 116 pages. Three glossy eight-page black-and-white photo inserts. Discography.

Rock writer Steve Turner had the unusual fortune of being friends with the doctor who helped Eric Clapton overcome his heroin addiction in the early 1970's. Turner struck up some conversations with the suddenly garrulous guitarist, who opens up here about his temporary layoff from recording, his junkie habits, the writing of "Layla," details of recordings with The Yardbirds and Cream, groupies, and many other topics. Clapton is forthright about what was then a sensitive area, his friendship with George Harrison: "It's a lively friendship. It's never boring." As good as any *Rolling Stone* interview, with three superior glossy inserts.

PICTORIALS

Giuliano, Geoffrey; Giuliano, Brenda; and Black, Deborah Lynn. *The Illustrated Eric Clapton.* London: Sunburst Books, 1994. 96 pages. Approximately 75 color and black-and-white photographs throughout.

The Giulianos et al. celebrate the life and legend of Eric Clapton through a wide range of photos and some straightforward photo spreads on his musical excursions with The Yardbirds, John Mayall, Cream, Blind Faith, Derek and the Dominoes, and as a perennial sideman and soloist. The early black-and-white and color shots represent The Yardbirds and Cream with befitting respect, but many of the more recent photos of Clapton in the 1980's and 90's have been enlarged to full-page with blurry results. Lightweight.

Roberty, Marc. *The Complete Guide to the Music of Eric Clapton.* London: Omnibus Press (division of Book Sales Limited), 1995. 152 pages. Approximately 125 color and black-and-white photographs throughout. Index.

CD-format book by Robertson that actually competes with a similar work of his (see below) distributed by MBS! This one offers a grander selection of photos, the other more information in the back: Take your pick.

Roberty, Marc. *Eric Clapton.* Miami, FL: MBS, 1996. 120 pages. Approximately 75 color and black-and-white photographs throughout. Discography. Chronology. Index.

CD-format book covering all aspects of Clapton's life and career. This nicely designed and illustrated book is priced just right at $7.99.

Roberty, Marc. *Slowhand: The Life and Music of Eric Clapton.* New York: Crown, 1993. 192 pages. Approximately 250 color and black-and-white photographs throughout. Discography. Index. (First published in Great Britain in 1991 by Octopus Books.)

Another gushing but respectable Clapton photo book from Roberty, who has virtually cornered the market on his subject. This one is basic visual candy, with photographic spreads on The Yardbirds, John Mayall's Bluesbreakers, Cream, Derek and the Dominoes, Blind Faith, and Slowhand as soloist. This book overlaps to some degree with almost all of Roberty's other works, so if you own any of those you can easily pass on this. Despite the fact that this was first published in England in 1991, the text has been updated to 1993 for U.S. release. "A must for rock `n' roll fans. Roberty follows Clapton's career from his earliest days with The Yardbirds to his latest solo efforts"—*School Library Journal.*

QUIZBOOKS AND QUOTEBOOKS

Roberty, Marc. *Eric Clapton: In His Own Words.* London: Omnibus Press (division of Book Sales Limited), 1993. 96 pages. Approximately 100 black-and-white photographs, covering every page.

Clapton is quoted at length on topics ranging from his early days, art school, Cream, guitars, women and marriage, drugs, etc. One chapter, "Eric by His Peers," reverses things and prints what others say about him. (Unfortunately, George Harrison is not included in this section.) Clapton's words don't leap out like those of a Dylan or a Lennon, but occasionally he does have a stand-out. (On ex-wife Pattie Boyd Harrison: "The lady can draw a lot out of people.") Assembled by veteran Clapton writer Roberty (see works, above), this "in his own words" treatment should be gobbled up by fans of Clapton and lovers of rock and roll in general.

RELATED WORKS

Nizami. *The Story of Layla & Majnun.* London: Luzac & Co. Limited, 1966. 222 pages.

Written by Persian poet Nizami sometime in the 12th century, this classic love story tells of a young fellow named Qays who is separated from his true love, Layla, and becomes so insane from the parting that he is dubbed Majnun—meaning "madman." Sound familiar? This superb tale, possibly based on a true story, inspired Eric Clapton to pen the gut-wrenching song "Layla" as a love call to Pattie Boyd Harrison, who was then married to his best friend, George Harrison. Clapton did ultimately win her over—somehow maintaining his friendship with George—but that marriage didn't last either. Who ever said rock stars' lives matched parables? This beautiful translation by Dr. R. Gelpke is long overdue for revision.

OTHER TITLES OF INTEREST

Garrett, George. *Eric Clapton's Lover and Other Stories from the Virginia Quarterly Review.* Charlottesville, VA: University Press of Virginia, 1990.

Roberty, Marc and Welch, Chris. *Eric Clapton: The Illustrated Discography.* New York: Beekman, 1990.

Weiler, Fred. *Eric Clapton.* New York: Smithmark (Penguin (USA), 1992.

PETULA CLARK

TITLES OF INTEREST

Kon, Andrea. *This Is My Song: Biography of Petula Clark.* London: Comet, 1984.

THE CLASH

PICTORIALS

Miles. *The Clash.* London: Omnibus Press (division of Book Sales Limited), 1978. 52 pages. Approximately 75 black-and-white photographs, covering every page. Discography.

The "sole survivors of the summer of '77" are the focus of this difficult-to-follow photo book. The pages are designed with shaky black-and-white backgrounds superimposed on the text and on the photos, which make both aspects too hard to absorb. The book's numerous quotes —it could easily have passed for one of Omnibus Press' "in their own words" titles—are good for an occasional laugh, but do not serve as a replacement for genuine insight. The most value can be derived from a passage called "The Story of the Clash," written by Joe Strummer.

No author. *The Clash: The New Visual Documentary* London: Omnibus Press (division of Book Sales Limited), 1992. 112 pages. Approximately 100 black-and-white photographs, covering nearly every page.

Fudged biography of The Clash, with some good illustrative material—although nothing on the same level as Smith's work (see below). A hack job, resurrected with only minor revision from an earlier 1983 printing. The only evident update seems to be the (unnamed) author's plea for The Clash "to resist the money and calls for a Clash reunion." Untimely.

Smith, Pennie. *The Clash: Before & After.* Boston: Little, Brown and Company, 1980. Unpaginated (approximately 160 pages). Approximately 150 black-and-white photographs throughout.

Revealing black-and-white portraits of The Clash, who posed for Pennie Smith in the late 1970's. The boys wear oddball punk Mafioso outfits and ham it up onstage and off: in one photo, Joe Strummer bites his thumbnail; in another, Mick Jones sucks on a wet cigar. Photographer Smith complements the images with brief, witty captions not intended for informational value. Entertaining and surprisingly harmless, although the package would have been significantly improved with glossy paper.

Yewdall, Julian Leonard. Introductory text by Nick Jones. *Joe Strummer with the 101'ers & the Clash.* London: Image Direct, 1976. Unpaginated (approximately 76 pages). 65 glossy black-and-white photographs throughout.

Slightly larger than pocket-size collection of glossy photos of Joe Strummer dating back to when he was with The 101'ers and on to his days with The Clash. Thus the book contains some raw performance shots of Strummer in action circa 1974-76. A gig list is provided in the back. If you don't own Smith's work (see above), this could prove a valuable addition to your collection.

OTHER TITLES OF INTEREST

Tobler, Miles. *The Clash.* New York: Beekman, 1991.

PATSY CLINE

BIOGRAPHIES

Bego, Mark. Introduction by Carlene Carter. *I Fall to Pieces: The Music and Life of Patsy Cline.* Holbrook, MA: Adams Publishing, 1995. 258

pages. Two glossy 16-page black-and-white photo inserts. Discography and Recording History. Bibliography. Index.

The ever-prolific Bego—who published his Bonnie Raitt autobiography within a year of this work (see Raitt, Biographies)—harkens back to an even more legendary, fragile performer. Born in Gore, Virginia, Cline was sexually abused by her father at eleven years of age. Despite it all, she became quite a rambunctious child and an outgoing performer. Cline survived a near-fatal car crash just as her career was just taking off, but was not so fortunate when she perished in an airplane crash not many years later. This book covers the depressing basics of Cline's life, but this is more or less a hack job compared to Jones' and Nassour's respective works (see below).

Jones, Margaret. Introduction by Loretta Lynn. *Patsy: The Life and Times of Patsy Cline*. New York: HarperCollins, 1994. 336 pages. One 16-page black-and-white photo insert. Notes. Discography. Index.

Patsy Cline had more than her share of trials and tribulations: she was sexually abused as a child by her father; she was physically beaten by her husband Charlie; and she tried in vain to find happiness in various torrid affairs. Although meticulously footnoted to give the aura of scholarship, this book is not done with nearly as much affection as Nassour's work (see below) and is not nearly as credible. Given Cline's continued popularity and the numerous tabloid aspects of her life, it's certain this won't be the last of the so-called comprehensive biographies on her life and legacy.

Nassour, Ellis. *Honky Tonk Angel: The Intimate Story of Patsy Cline*. New York: St. Martin's Press, 1993. 288 pages. One 24-page black-and-white photo insert. Discography. Index.

One of the most influential country singers of all time, Patsy Cline hailed from Winchester, VA. Her appearances on "Arthur Godfrey and His Talent Scouts" and Dick Clark's "American Bandstand" made her a recognizable pop figure with crossover hits such as "Walkin' After Midnight" and "I Fall to Pieces." Although not exactly the best-looking singer on the circuit, Cline developed a hugely successful career, which ended abruptly with her tragic death in a plane crash in 1963. Author Ellis Nassour, who first published this book in 1988, tells of

the real Patsy Cline: a multi-talented, guttermouthed, immensely likable woman who couldn't hang on to her relationships or friendships. "Nassour, obviously an enamored fan, successfully proves his thesis that Patsy Cline was the first female country singer to cross the line into pop and blues"—*Booklist*.

THE COASTERS

(See also Leiber and Stoller)

BIOGRAPHIES

Millar, Bill. *The Coasters*. London: W. H. Allen & Co. Limited, 1974. 208 pages. One eight-page black-and-white photo insert. Where Are They Now? Jerry Leiber-Mike Stoller Compositions. Discography.

The Coasters, who recorded classics such as "Yakety Yak," "Sweet Georgia Brown,"" Searchin'," and "Charlie Brown" were a crossover doo-wop group in the 1950's who blended rhythm and blues with the campy humor of Jewish songwriter/producers Jerry Leiber and Mike Stoller. Millar's biography cogently explains the slightly confusing formation of the group (they partially evolved from The Robins) and shows how The Coasters signaled major changes in rock and roll: black artists working with white; white audiences listening to black music; etc. Millar also brings to the foreground the roles of other players, such as King Curtis (the "fifth" Coaster). Generally stands the test of time.

JOE COCKER

BIOGRAPHIES

Bean, J.P. Foreword by Joe Cocker. *Joe Cocker: With a Little Help from My Friends*. London: Omnibus Press (division of Book Sales Limited), 1990. 204 pages. Two glossy eight-page black-and-white photo inserts. British Discography. Index.

The only biography of the Sheffield blues rocker is authorized by Cocker, who supplies a one-page foreword. Like many young English lads, Cocker was inspired by skiffler Lonnie

Donegan before finding his soul in the music of Ray Charles and Jerry Lee Lewis. Author J.P. Bean has done adequate research and has tracked down the right people, but his summary of Cocker's musical experiences with the Cavaliers, Vance Arnold and the Avengers, The Grease Band, and Mad Dogs and Englishmen reads like the life of a dreary accountant—with some alcohol, heroin, and PCP thrown in. There's even less enthusiasm and detail provided for Cocker's legendary recordings (e.g., the title) and performances (e.g., Woodstock). Note that the discography is limited to U.K.-only.

LEONARD COHEN

(See also Lightfoot, Gordon: Critical/Analytical Commentary)

BIOGRAPHIES

Dorman, L.S. and Rawlins, C.L. *Leonard Cohen: Prophet of the Heart*. London: Omnibus Press (division of Book Sales Limited), 1990. 284 pages. One glossy 16-page black-and-white photo insert. Bibliography. Discography.

This rather daunting biography focuses more on Cohen as literary figure than as musician, which is actually sensible, since that is how Cohen began his career back in the late-1950's. Cohen authorized this book and made himself open for interviews and questioning. The authors took full advantage of the opportunity and placed their subject under the closest scrutiny—in fact, so close as to narrow Cohen's height to the exact centimeter and observe the grays on his temples. Nothing seems too petty for these researchers to mention; we are bombarded with more details about Cohen's childhood synagogue, his early influences (Ezra Pound), and the finer points of his poetry than we'll ever need to know. Read up on all of Cohen's writing (see Written Works, below) and then, if you have a strong eyeglass prescription, dive into this.

Nadel, Ira. *Leonard Cohen: A Life in Art*. Toronto, Ontario (Canada): ECW Press, 1994. 160 pages. Approximately 20 black-and-white photographs throughout. Chronology. Discography. Works Consulted.

Part of the "Canadian biography series," this concise work traces the life of Canada's "rock n' roll Lord Byron": poet, novelist, singer, and songwriter. Nadel's workmanlike prose conveys the story with efficiency, from Cohen's European Conservative Jewish heritage to his upbringing in Canada, early poetry writing career, stabs at folk music, commercial floundering in the 1970's, and rebirth in the 1990's as an acknowledged pop renaissance man. Nadel also sifts through Cohen's complex work and themes ranging from eroticism to traditional Judaism; ultimately, it reads more like a textbook than a real biography.

CRITICAL/ANALYTICAL COMMENTARY

Gnarowski, Michael (Editor). *Leonard Cohen and His Critics*. New York: McGraw-Hill Ryerson, Limited, 1976. 172 pages. Selected Bibliography.

For the serious student of Cohen's writing and music—with a distinct emphasis on the former—this book contains: reviews of Cohen's first seven books (up through *Selected Poems*, see Written Works); five commentaries on his role as pop artist; and another seven on his status as "literary phenomenon." Includes thought-provoking pieces from Milton Wilson, Ed Kleinman, George Browering, Richard Goldstein, Stephen Scobie, and others. A worthwhile collection for those highly familiar with Cohen's work and themes.

WRITTEN WORKS

Cohen, Leonard. *Beautiful Losers*. New York: Random House, 1993. 307 pages.

First published in 1966, Cohen's first novel (which still contains some poetic elements) is an unusual, erotic allegory of betrayal among two men and a woman. Somehow, all sins are redeemed by a 17th century Iroquois virgin. Cohen returns to his two favorite subjects: God and sex. See also *Stranger Music* below.

Cohen, Leonard. *Book of Mercy*. Toronto, Canada: McClelland and Stewart, 1984. 113 pages.

This short collection of poems express inner struggles for spiritual enlightenment and redemption. One work, "Israel"—an all-out assault on that country's militarism—will no doubt alarm a constituency of his fans. A solemn, rather depressing volume, including "You Who Pour Mercy into Hell" and "We Cry Out." See also *Stranger Music* below.

Cohen, Leonard. *Dance Me to the End of Love.* New York: Stewart, Tabori & Chang, 1995. Unpaginated (approximately 32 pages). Approximately 32 original color cutouts and paintings.

Primarily intended for children, this beautiful meeting of two great artistic visions—Leonard Cohen and Henri Matisse—combines Cohen's titillating words to the song "Dance Me to the End of Love" with Matisse's recognizable cutouts and paintings. The two together create a remarkable synergy of dance as pleasure, symbolizing love, harmony, elegance, and friendship. A clever way to introduce folk music and 20th century art to kids up to middle school age. Highly recommended.

Cohen, Leonard. *Death of a Lady's Man.* New York: Viking Penguin, 1978. 216 pages.

Cohen unleashes some fiery words of macabre passion in this late 1970's collection of poetry. In many works, such as "The Beetle" and "This Marriage," he follows-up with a paragraph of additional poetic commentary. A year earlier Cohen released a similarly titled album, *Death of a Ladies' Man,* with the pluralization of the word "ladies." See also *Stranger Music* below.

Cohen, Leonard. *The Energy of Slaves.* New York: Viking Penguin, 1972. 127 pages.

Early 1970's collection of works in which Cohen puts a new spin on a recurring topic: vice. Cohen masterfully conveys images of lust ("I Perceived the Outline of Your Breasts"), avarice ("My Greed"), and other sins. See also *Stranger Music* below.

Cohen, Leonard. *The Favourite Game.* Toronto, Canada: McClelland and Stewart, 1970. 256 pages.

First published in 1963, this provocative semi-autobiographical novel concerns a young Jewish man, Lawrence Breavman, who—like Cohen a few years before this book—is on his way to becoming a folk singer and poet. Through vignettes stretching from Breavman's rich Montreal childhood to his adulthood, the story brings us inside the dynamics of various relationships (most notably, a mistress named Shell) that ignite the artist's creative juices. Cohen's second novel is sexy, but with a smattering of dark humor.

Cohen, Leonard. *Flowers for Hitler.* Toronto, Canada: McClelland and Stewart, 1964. 80 pages.

Cohen's third book of poetry, perhaps his most controversial, includes a number of works with themes relating to Nazi Germany. Poems such as "Opium and Hitler" and "All There Is to Know about Adolph Eichmann" are irascible and funny. See also *Stranger Music* below.

Cohen, Leonard. *Let Us Compare Mythologies.* Toronto, Canada: McClelland and Stewart, 1970. 80 pages.

Cohen's dazzling first collection of poetry—written when the artist was still a student at Columbia University—was originally published in 1956 (McGill Poetry Series). From the opening bareness of "Poem" to the coitus interruptus of "The Fly," this work paved the way for Cohen's move from poet to beat performance artist to folk performer. Many works concern the relationships between Jews and gentiles. See also *Stranger Music* below.

Cohen, Leonard. *Parasites of Heaven.* Toronto, Canada: McClelland and Stewart, 1966. 80 pages.

Cohen's fourth book of poetry includes "Suzanne" and "Avalanche," both of which later became his songs. (Judy Collins also recorded the former.) Also featured in this volume are "I See You on a Greek Mattress," "One of Us Cannot Be Wrong," and "The Stranger Song." See also *Stranger Music* below.

Cohen, Leonard. *Selected Poems, 1956-1968.* New York: Penguin, 1968. 245 pages.

Early retrospective of uncollected works spanning the mid-1950's to the late 60's. Includes "A Person Who Eats Meat," "The Reason I Write," and "You Live Like a God." See also *Stranger Music* below.

Cohen, Leonard. *The Spice Box of the Earth.* New York: Viking Press, 1961. 80 pages.

Cohen's second collection of poetry concerns themes such as loss ("For Anne"), dreams ("Morning Song"), and sin-cleansing ("I have Two Bars of Soap"). Enriching. See also *Stranger Music* below.

Cohen, Leonard. *Stranger Music: Selected Poems and Songs*. New York: Vintage Books (division of Random House, Inc.), 1993. 416 pages. Index of Titles. Index of First Lines.

A "greatest hits" collection of Cohen's poetry and songs that span Cohen's career from 1956 to the early 1990's. In addition to containing lengthy excerpts from his earlier poetry collections—*Let Us Compare Mythologies, The Spice Box of the Earth, Flowers for Hitler, Parasites of Heaven, Selected Poems, 1956-1968, Beautiful Losers, The Energy of Slaves, Death of a Lady's Man,* and *Book of Mercy* (see above for all)—this retrospective also includes lyrics from nine of his eleven albums (including *Songs of Leonard Cohen, New Skin for the Old Ceremony,* and *Various Positions*) and eleven previously unpublished poems. Students may prefer to tackle each of the original books individually and compare them with the slightly altered revisions found herein; fans of Cohen's music need look no further than this wonderful volume. "...there is no fat in Cohen's landscape—only passion, longing, anger, pain, wonder, and cynicism, all laid bare"—*Billboard*.

YOUNG ADULT

Cohen, Leonard. *Dance Me to the End of Love*.

See: Written Works.

OTHER TITLES OF INTEREST
Leeker, Robert and David, Jack. *The Annotated Bibliography of Canada's Major Authors: Margaret Atwood, Leonard Cohen, Archibald Lampman*. New York: Macmillan, 1981.

NATALIE COLE

TITLES OF INTEREST
Cole, Natalie. *Little Dog*. No city: Children's Art Foundation, 1975.
Jacobs, Linda. *Natalie Cole: Star Child*. St. Paul, MN: EMC Publishers, 1977.

NAT KING COLE

BIOGRAPHIES

Gourse, Leslie. *Unforgettable: The Life and Mystique of Nat King Cole*. New York: St. Martin's Press, 1991. 309 pages. One glossy 16-page black-and-white photo insert. Bibliography. A Discographical Survey. Index.

The most recent Cole biography retreads much of the same material covered in Haskins' work (see below). However, Gourse eloquently defines Nat King Cole's unforgettable qualities: "his breathiness made his low-key delivery of a lyric sound heady; the older he got and the more he smoked, the deeper, hoarser, huskier, and more hypnotic he sounded." Gourse's same-page footnotes are useful, although occasionally long-winded and tiresome. "This volume, promising much, is in fact inferior" —*Booklist*.

Haskins, James with Benson, Kathleen. *Nat King Cole*. New York: Stein and Day, 1984. 204 pages. One glossy 16-page black-and-white photo insert. Discography. Index.

Fluid study of Nat King Cole that fills in the gaps in Maria Cole's work (see Cole Friends and Family, below). Haskins does a fine job outlining Cole's Chicago roots and his development from jazz pianist to pop crooner. Haskins also points out that Cole took it on the chin from the National Association for the Advancement of Colored People (NAACP), who called him an Uncle Tom because he didn't protest loud enough against the discrimination set against him from television networks and segregating venue owners. Ultimately, Haskins has created a picture of a talented artist who made understandable career compromises in order to make it in a white-dominated music industry.

COLE FRIENDS AND FAMILY

Cole, Maria with Robinson, Louie. *Nat King Cole: An Intimate Biography*. New York: William Morrow & Company, Inc., 1971. 184 pages. One eight-page black-and-white photo insert. Discography.

Maria Cole, Nat King Cole's widow, wrote this story a few years after her husband's death in

1965 due to lung cancer. The two had a long romance, which began when they met at a club date back in 1946. Although other girls had their sights on Nat, Maria played it cool and let him make the move; when he did, she discovered he was already married. Nat divorced his first wife, married Maria (they had five children, the second of whom is singer Natalie), and he pursued a successful singing and acting career. Maria casts her late husband as a gullible, gentle fellow, prone to ulcers and unable to say "no" to anyone. Fans of his music will appreciate her warm candor; some may be annoyed by her divisive remarks against more hardcore rock and roll.

JUDY COLLINS

AUTOBIOGRAPHY

Collins, Judy. *Trust Your Heart: An Autobiography*. Boston: Houghton Mifflin, 1987. 276 pages. Two 16-page glossy black-and-white photo inserts. Discography.

The inspiration behind the songs "Suite: Judy Blue Eyes" (Crosby, Stills and Nash) and "I'll Keep It with Mine" (Bob Dylan) is just what you'd imagine in prose: sweet, good-natured, and poetic without being frothy. In her autobiography, which switches from the past to her 1985 journal entries, Collins sends out the distressing word that she may not want to sing again. Her story otherwise conveys details of her relationship with her blind father; illnesses, such as childhood polio; legal hassles, such as her lost custody battle for her child; and her sometimes turbulent romances (e.g., Stephen Stills). Collins is flattering almost to a fault about her folk contemporaries; she admits, for example, to having "always envied Joan Baez's sleek figure and black hair." Trust Collins' heart and read.

WRITTEN WORKS

Collins, Judy. *Voices*. New York: Clarkson, Potter, 1995. 48 pages. Approximately 50 original watercolors, covering every page. Comes with a CD.

Autobiographical tri-package, combining a 13-song CD, an accompanying songbook, and a compact book of Collins' original art and jot-

tings. All three are equivalent high points to this multimedia delight. Parents will love introducing Collins's music to their kids, and will probably sing along with them while flipping through the lyrics and pointing out the artist's fine watercolors. Available on both book and music store shelves. Highly recommended.

YOUNG ADULT

Claire, Vivian. *Judy Collins*. New York: Flash Books (division of Music Sales Corporation), 1977. 78 pages. Approximately 50 black-and-white photographs throughout. Discography.

Vivian Claire does a monumental job on this small-scale biography of Collins. She presents an equal balance of material on the singer's background, persona, political/social causes, relationships, and music. Collins' relationship with her piano teacher Dr. Brico will certainly make music teachers feel a little warm inside. Collins herself looks striking and/or introspective in several eye-pleasing photos. A well-rounded, if dated, introduction for young fans.

OTHER TITLES OF INTEREST
Andersen, Hans Christian. *Thumbelina*. New York: Knopf, 1990.
  Abridged edition of the Andersen story, with a contribution by Judy Collins.
Chorao, Kay. *The Baby's Bedtime Book*. New York: Dutton, c. 1989.
  Contains a contribution by Judy Collins. Followed by The Baby's Good Morning Book (see below).
Chorao, Kay *The Baby's Good Morning Book*. New York: Dutton, 1990
  Contains a contribution by Judy Collins. School Library Journal commented: "Cheerful, brilliantly colored illustrations spread through the pages like the first rays of summer sun in this refreshing collection of short poems for children."
Collins, Judy. Illustrated by Dyer, Jane. *My Father*. New York and Boston: Little, Brown & Company, 1989.
  Publishers Weekly commented: "Based on the lyrics of folk singer Collins's well-known song, this appealing picture book takes a nostalgic look at a daughter and a childhood made radiant by `my father's dreams' of an ideal life."
Collins, Judy. *Shameless*. New York: Pocket, 1996.
  Novel by Judy Collins.
Packard, William. *The Poet's Dictionary: A Handbook of Prosody and Poetic Devices*. New York: HarperCollins, 1989.
  Contains a contribution by Judy Collins.

PHIL COLLINS

(See also Genesis)

TITLES OF INTEREST
Goldstein, Toby. *Phil Collins*. New York: Ballantine, 1987.

Kamin, Philip. *Phil Collins*. Milwaukee, WI: Hal Leonard, 1985.

Nance, Scott. *Genesis of Phil Collins*. No city: Movie Publisher Services, In., 1991.

Waller, Johnny. *The Phil Collins Story*. Milwaukee, WI: Hal Leonard, 1986.

THE COMMODORES

See Richie, Lionel.

SAM COOKE

BIOGRAPHIES

Wolff, Daniel, with Crain, S.R.; White, Clifton; and Tenenbaum, G. David. *You Send Me: The Life and Times of Sam Cooke*. New York: Morrow, 1995. 424 pages. Two glossy eight-page black-and-white photo inserts. Discography. Notes and Sources. Selected Bibliography. Index.

The first comprehensive biography of Rock and Roll Hall of Fame member Sam Cooke— and a long overdue one at that. Wolff et. al., have plowed through Cooke's brief but eventful life, from his early gospel hits, his crossover chart successes ("Only Sixteen," "Twisting the Night Away," etc.), to the death of his infant son, a near-fatal car accident, and his own bloody death. The book also enlightens readers to Cooke's little-known entrepreneurial abilities, in that he began his own record label and negotiated ground-breaking artist contracts in the early 1960's. The conclusion of the story— Cooke's demise—presents some faint evidence that Cooke may have been the victim of a mob hit, and was not a slain attempted rapist. Whether this is a fact or the aggrandizing of a dead legend will perhaps never be known; in either event, it's excellent fodder for a TV movie.

PICTORIALS

McEwen, Joe. *Sam Cooke: A Biography in Words & Pictures*. No city: Sire Books (Chappell Music Company), 1977. 46 pages. Approximately 40 black-and-white photographs, covering nearly every page.

"The man who invented soul" is the focus of this tribute in Chappell's "words and pictures" series. Born in Clarksdale, Mississippi, Cooke began singing gospel at a very young age with The Soul Stirrers. As a pop soloist, he wrote and recorded some of the industry's most timeless hits, including "You Send Me" and "Bring It on Home to Me." While this book does little to solve the mysteries surrounding Cooke's controversial death (he was allegedly killed after attempting to rape one woman and physically attacking another; the second victim, who shot him to death, was acquitted on self-defense), it's one of the few books centering on his monumental contributions to popular music.

ALICE COOPER

TITLES OF INTEREST
Cooper, Alice. *The Last Temptation of Alice Cooper*. New York: Marvel Entertainment, 1996.

DeMorest, Steve. *Alice Cooper: Alice Cooper*. New York: Popular Library, 1974.

Gaines, Steven. *Me, Alice: The Autobiography of Alice Cooper*. New York: Putnam, 1976.
Alice Cooper's early autobiography, as told to Steven Gaines.

ELVIS COSTELLO (AND THE ATTRACTIONS)

CRITICAL/ANALYTICAL COMMENTARY

Gouldstone, David. *Elvis Costello: God's Comic*. 196 pages. New York: St. Martin's Press, 1989. Appendix: The Best of Elvis Costello. Bibliography. Index. (First published as *Elvis Costello: A Man Out of Time* in England, c.1989, by Sidgwick & Jackson Limited.)

A "critical companion to his [Costello's] lyrics and music," this is by far a deeper investigation into the latter rather than the former. This is a shame, because Costello has composed some beautiful lyrics over the years that demand some attention. Gouldstone's greater problem, however, is in his smug, unsubstantiated references to other artists (James Taylor is branded "pitiful") and the general absence of connection-making to various rock traditions—or at least how Costello eschews certain trends. While some of Gouldstone's interpretations have merit (the theme "disintegrating love," for one), most fans would do better listening to the music and coming up with their own conclusions.

FANZINES AND FAN CLUBS

Elvis Costello Information Service. Primulastraat 46, 1441 hc, Pumerend, Netherlands.

This fanzine was first published in 1979, and in 1982 it merged with a British Costello fanzine. The 28-page booklet contains information on Costello's performances, photocopies of black-and-white photos, reprinted articles, bootlegs, a quiz, and even an index in the back. Offers a 344-page book entitled *Going Through the Motions*, which integrates biography, lyrics, concerts, an index of songs, and various illustrated material. The cost for six issues: U.S. $17; Canada $25; and U.K. £12.60.

PICTORIALS

Reese, Krista. *Elvis Costello: A Completely False Biography Based on Rumor, Innuendo and Lies.* London and New York: Proteus Publishing, 1981. 128 pages. One four-page color insert and 40 black-and-white photographs throughout. Discography.

Printed on page one is a letter written from Jake Riviera, the man who signed Elvis Costello up in 1977, to the author: "...I will do everything in my power to prevent you from writing a book about Elvis Costello." What ever happened to freedom of the press? Judging by the title and subtitle (which seems to be a cheeky reaction to Riviera), at least it can be said that Reese has a terrific sense of humor. While you won't find anything deep about Costello—Reese states that "details of his early life are scarce"—the tone of the book is loads of fun; all of the chapters are from Costello titles or lyrics, including "I Want to Bite the Hand That Feeds Me."

WRITTEN WORKS

Thomas, Bruce. *The Big Wheel: Rock & Roll and Roadside Attractions.* Boston and London: Faber and Faber, 1991. 184 pages.

The story of a rock band on the road, written by the ex-bassist of The Attractions. Is this a novel, a travelogue, or a true rendering of events involving Elvis Costello and his band? Well, it's actually a combination of all three. Despite the absurdities of rock and roll life—late night sexual escapades, drinking, drug-taking, and pesky fans—the narrator (most obviously, Thomas himself) is in a chronic state of boredom. As the Singer (most obviously, Costello) remarks, "a bored person is a boring person." The narrator condescendingly observes the goings-on of his fellow musicians and reflects on aspects of his past; the shocker is there is hardly any music here at all, only the frequent click of channel-changing on the TV. A highly stylized and accomplished work that leaves readers somewhat depressed. "Imagine a rock 'n' roll star with shades of Marcel Proust's introspection, Hunter Thompson's sensibility and William Least Moon's ability to relate atmosphere"—*Publishers Weekly.*

OTHER TITLES OF INTEREST
Jones, Allan. *Elvis Costello: The Man Who Would Be King.* New York: Grove/Atlantic, 1988.

THE COWSILLS

(See also Partridge Family, The)

FANZINES AND FAN CLUBS

Cowsills Fan Club. P.O. Box 83, Lexington, MS 39095.

Fan club to the real-life singing family that inspired "The Partridge Family" TV show, offering a quarterly newsletter, an 8x10 photo, and a membership card. The 12-page newsletter, *Cowsill Connection,* contains reprints of newspaper articles, photocopies of black-and-white photos, reading lists, record lists, book reviews, and more. The cost of membership is $10 per year (check or money order).

THE CRAMPS

TITLES OF INTEREST

Johnston, Ian. *The Wild Wild World of The Cramps*. London: Omnibus Press (division of Book Sales Limited), 1990.

THE CRANBERRIES

FANZINES AND FAN CLUBS

The Cranberries Official International Fan Club. P.O. Box 679, Branford, CT 06405.

Members of this club receive 8x10 photos, a personal bio of the group, newsletters, e-mail, news flashes, and more. The two-page newsletter contains black-and-white photographs, updates on the band in studio, and more. The cost per year is $22 in the U.S. and Canada; $28 elsewhere.

PICTORIALS

Bailie, Stuart. *The Cranberries: In Your Head*. London: Omnibus Press (division of Book Sales Limited), 1995. 80 pages. Approximately 100 color and black-and-white photographs, covering every page.

Glossy magazine study of the quartet, with 90% of the photos and text focusing on singer and composer Dolores O'Riordan. In fact, we don't get very much past the first names of the other band members, Noel, Mike, and Feargal. To coin author Stuart Bailie's favorite phrase, his intent here is to "get into O'Riordan's head"; by book's end, however, all he's succeeded at accomplishing is a broad listing of events up through and including Woodstock 94. Marginal purchase for fans.

Carran, Mick. *The Cranberries*. London: Omnibus Press (division of Book Sales Limited), 1995. 48 pages. Approximately 60 glossy color and black-and-white photos throughout. Discography.

Flimsy but colorful magazine-length book on the Cranberries. While few can dispute the back ad copy that the Cranberries are "Ireland's biggest musical export since U2," non-fans will be turned off by the hyperbole

that pervades the interior text. Less than what's in Blailie's work (see above), and that's leaving out quite a lot.

CRASH TEST DUMMIES

BIOGRAPHIES

Ostick, Stephen. *Superman's Song: The Story of Crash Test Dummies*. Kingston, Ontario (Canada): Quarry Press, 1995. 204 pages. Approximately 50 black-and-white photographs throughout.

The world's most famous Dummies, who made their mark on David Letterman's "Late Show" and on "Saturday Night Live," are the subject of this revealing, if premature biography. The Canadian quintet, led by baritone Brad Roberts, has already earned Grammy nominations, played packed houses, won over the critics, and had a smash single with "Superman's Song." Author Stephen Ostick points out that the group has attained this great success in spite of the fact that their name misleads the public into thinking the group is a grunge or punk band and has no ear for melody. Whether fans really need 204 pages on Crash Test Dummies so early in their careers is speculative, but author Stephen Ostick—who first brought the group attention in the *Winnipeg Free Press*—delivers enough information to make it worth their while.

CREAM

(See also Clapton, Eric)

PICTORIALS

Welch, Chris. *Cream: Strange Brew*. Chessington, Surrey (England): Castle Communications, 1994. 176 pages. Approximately 150 color and black-and-white photographs throughout.

Over 25 years after Cream's break-up, a publisher finally realized this short-lived supergroup deserved some kind of attention in print. Unfortunately, this book doesn't live up to expectations. Welch's hackneyed writing is supported with many quotes by the trio themselves—several of which are repeated large, magazine-style, just to fill up space. The photographs, which consist of TV appearances, large outdoor concerts, rare publicity stills, and images of psychedelia, will appeal to fans who have grown accustomed to Ginger Baker's ghoulish appearance. Incredibly, the book does not contain a Clapton/Baker/Bruce discography—a grievous oversight. Sour cream.

CREEDENCE CLEARWATER REVIVAL

TITLES OF INTEREST
Hallowell, John. *Inside Creedence*. New York: Bantam, 1971.

MARSHALL CRENSHAW

See Selected General Reference: Special Subjects, Film.

JIM CROCE

TITLES OF INTEREST
Jacobs, Linda. *Jim Croce: The Feeling Lives On*. St Paul, MN: EMC Publishing, 1976.

CROSBY, STILLS, NASH AND YOUNG

(See also Young, Neil)

AUTOBIOGRAPHIES

Crosby, David and Gottlieb, Carl. *Long Time Gone: The Autobiography of David Crosby*. New York: Doubleday, 1988. 489 pages. One 14-page glossy black-and-white photo insert.

Crosby overcame years of drug abuse and even a prison sentence in order to come full circle with his cathartic tale. We are given an elaborate sense of Crosby's talents as a vocal harmonist, as well as a taste for his hobbies and joys, such as sailing. His weaknesses, of course, were cocaine and sex with young girls. There were also two traumas—one, his being booted out of The Byrds, and two, the tragic death of his beautiful 1960's nymphette, Christine Hinton. Crosby's writing, like his singing voice, is honest, warm, and laid-back;

it blends in harmonically with text from Gottlieb and the words of friends, teachers, relatives, and musicians. You have to admire a performer who is willing to share so many unpleasantries, including shocking photos of himself at lowest-ebb. "...a harrowing tale"— *Publishers Weekly*.

Taylor, Dallas. Introductions by David Crosby and Graham Nash. *Prisoner of Woodstock*. New York: Thunder's Mouth Press, 1994. 242 pages. One glossy 16-page black-and-white photo insert. Index.

The autobiography of Dallas Taylor, Crosby, Stills, Nash and Young's drummer who, like bandmate Crosby, became something of a junkie and nearly lost his life. Taylor had met the boys when they were attending a Lovin' Spoonful recording session. He joined CSN&Y and did not mind taking a backseat to the talented harmonists, riding the 1960's wave that culminated with the Woodstock Festival. The fast life took its toll on Taylor, and in 1984 he even attempted suicide; in 1989, he was diagnosed with a liver disease, which required an immediate transplant. Once again his old mates came to the rescue: CSN held a concert to raise money for his surgery. A unique view of a cool side player, but not to serve as a substitute for Crosby's work (see above). "This autobiography-cum-cautionary tale candidly explores the `dark side' of the music industry"—*Publishers Weekly*.

BIOGRAPHIES

Zimmer, Dave. Photographs by Ditz, Henry. Foreword by Graham Nash. *Crosby, Stills & Nash: The Authorized Biography*. New York: St. Martin's Press, 1984. 268 pages. Approximately 200 black-and-white photographs, covering nearly every page; one glossy eight-page color insert. Discography.

The only full-length biography of CSN is actually authorized by the trio, which makes this of great interest to fans. (Neil Young did not lend his support to this project, but there is some coverage of his work with Crosby, Stills, Nash and Young.) In choppy passages, author Dave Zimmer tells the story of the musicians' diverse upbringings (Stills, Florida; Crosby, Southern California; and Nash, England), followed by sections on their activities with their first major bands: The Byrds (Crosby), The Hollies (Nash), and Buffalo Springfield (Stills and Young). Wonders abound, including a desire by Nash to record with George Harrison (which hasn't happened yet). Hey, George—Crosby, Stills, Nash and Wilbury?

CHRONOLOGIES

Rogan, Johnny. *Crosby, Stills, Nash & Young: The Visual Documentary*. London: Omnibus Press (division of Book Sales Limited), 1996. 176 pages. Approximately 175 black-and-white photographs, covering every page; one glossy 16-page color insert. Discography. Unreleased Compositions.

In between writing assignments on Morrissey and Marr (see Smiths, The), Johnny Rogan moves back further in rock history while tackling the pop world's ultimate harmonizers. In an era during which music critics take perverse pleasure thrashing Woodstock bands, it's wonderful to see such care taken in a book on CSN (and sometimes Y). As Rogan points out, this day-by-day study is long overdue, and neither he nor the publisher wastes the effort. The book covers the bases on all four members' movements, starting with Crosby's birth in 1941 and ending with his liver transplant at the end of 1994. Listings for performances include set lists, while the color insert features many exciting psychedelic performance shots. Worthwhile for both casual and serious fans.

YOUNG ADULT

Armstrong, Robert H. *Crosby, Stills & Nash*. Mankato, MN: Creative Education, 1983. 32 pages. Six black-and-white photographs throughout.

This entry in the "Rock 'n Pop Stars" series is typically superficial and skimpy, with a few scant basics of the CSN story, but little explanation on the Woodstock Festival and the hippie generation. Any child would probably wonder why only Graham Nash is depicted on the book's cover.

CROWDED HOUSE

BIOGRAPHIES

Doole, Kerry and Twomey, Chris. *Crowded House: Private Universe*. London: Omnibus Press

(division of Book Sales Limited), 1995. 122 pages. Approximately 75 black-and-white and color photographs throughout. U.K. Discography.

The first and only biography of the New Zealand band headed by brothers Tim and Neil Finn. The two were actually born in the small town of Te Awamutu, but the boys were educated in a Catholic school in Auckland. This high-quality biography borders on pictorial format, and it's a shame the publishers didn't go all-out and throw in even more color and enlarge the images. Only time will tell if this band will sustain itself past its first four albums; in any event, this superior book should hold fans off until newer developments surface.

CULTURE CLUB

AUTOBIOGRAPHY

Boy George with Bright, Spencer. *Take It Like a Man: The Autobiography of Boy George*. New York: HarperCollins, 1995. 500 pages. Two glossy eight-page black-and-white photo inserts. Index.

Boy George provides conclusive evidence that it's tough to be a poof. Aware he was "different" from other boys at an early age, young George O'Dowd from the London suburbs had more interest in curlers, make-up, lip gloss, and high heels than in boys activities such as girl watching and sports; as he grew older, he became interested in sexually androgynous rockers such as Marc Bolan and David Bowie. George withstood the taunting from his peers, confronted his family's traditional values, and went down his own path, which culminated with his creative and romantic partnership with Jon Moss, Culture Club's drummer. After the band had a string of hits ("Karma Chameleon," among others), it dissolved and the Boy became a junkie. The Boy claims to have recovered, reassessed his musical direction, and found religion, which must be a frightful thought for parents of churchgoing boys. "The drug chapters are less entertaining than the drag chapters"—*The New York Times*.

BIOGRAPHIES

Ginsberg, Merle. *Boy George*. New York: Dell, 1984. 192 pages. One ten-page black-and-white photo insert.

Nineteen eighty four should be dubbed the "Year of the Boy"—at least in terms of the volumes written about Boy George that particular year. This slapdash retread of magazine material offers nothing special; we don't gain any insights into Boy George's psyche and there is even less substance on his music. The book clumsily asserts that George prefers to be "ambiguous" about his sexuality—he's not "a complete poof." The photos in the insert are designed on graph paper, with unaesthetic results.

Robins, Wayne. *Boy George and Culture Club*. New York: Ballantine Books, 1984. 148 pages. One glossy 16-page black-and-white photo insert. Discography, Videography, Fan Club Information.

Newsday writer Wayne Robins adds some spark to Ballantine's series on pop stars (see Duran Duran: Biographies). Robins tells a concise history of glam rock and punk rock, which builds up to George's rebellious need for public spectacle and ability to ignite fashion trends. While researching the book, Robins attempted to find out the Boy's make-up secrets by speaking to top artists in the field. Predates the group's decline and the Boy's junkie habits but, for what it's worth, it's one of the better treatments from the era.

CRITICAL/ANALYTICAL COMMENTARY

Rimmer, Dave. *Like Punk Never Happened: Culture Club and the New Pop*. London and Boston: Faber and Faber, 1986. 196 pages. Approximately 50 black-and-white photographs throughout. Sources.

Intelligent British account of the "New Pop" phenomenon of the mid-1980's that ushered in Culture Club, Duran Duran, Adam Ant, Spandau Ballet, and several others. The focus of this book is Culture Club, but the author admits it just as easily could have been about Duran Duran and have focused "more about video, less about the press and dressing-up." This is one of the few books about Boy George and the band that doesn't hype the image and make the group seem ridiculous. Author Dave Rimmer, then a writer for *Smash Hits* maga-zine, ties Boy in with the tradition of ever-changing pop culture starting with Elvis and moving on to The Beatles, Marc Bolan, David Bowie, The Sex Pistols, The Clash, etc. The title is aptly chosen.

PICTORIALS

Brompton, Sally. *Chameleon: The Boy George Story*. Tunbridge Wells, Kent (England): Spellmount Limited, 1984. 160 pages. Approximately 150 black-and-white photographs throughout; one 116-page color insert.

Early attempt at a Boy George bio, with the usual over-the-top emphasis on illustrative matter and fashion trends. The photos may actually be enough to draw in fans, however, since there are numerous rarities here, particularly covering the early years. You can see George's school headmaster, his mother, his father, his sister, his brother, as well as many sites from his past. One photo of Boy George with actor Robert Mitchum (who reportedly wanted to "adopt" him) will make you do a double-take. Some anecdotes from George's young adulthood add flavor lacking in George's autobiography (see above).

David, Maria. *Boy George and Culture Club*. No city: Greenwich House, 1984. Unpaginated (approximately 32 pages). Approximately 40 color and black-and-white photographs, covering every page.

Glossy photo book that is divided into black-and-white and color sections. As the Boy dons his usual pink frocks and various hats worn only by color-blind rabbis, the rest of Culture Club unenthusiastically plays along by sporting baseball uniforms, overalls, tanktops, and other unsightly outerwear. Shlock.

Dietrich, Jo. *Boy George and Culture Club*. London: Proteus, 1984. 32 pages. 10 color illustrations and 50 black-and-white photographs.

The usual on Boy George and company: little in the way of information, a lot in the way of color and design. There is some interesting coverage of Boy George's macho-bent family (at one time his father ran a boxing club and his brothers were boxers). This one also provides a long-awaited explanation as to where Culture Club's trademark Orthodox hat and Star of David came from (drummer Jon Moss is Jewish). Neatly packaged but skimpy.

Gallo, Armando (photographer). *The Boy George Fact File*. London, England: Omnibus Press (division of Book Sales Limited), 1984. Unpaginated (approximately 40 pages). 30 color illustrations, covering every page. Discography. Comes with a full-color poster.

Vainglorious photos showing the Boy with his ghastly red hat, multi-colored garb, and non-matching floppy sneaks. Barely a fact to be found in this file. Welcome to the circus!

No author. *Boy George and Culture Club*. No city (U.K.): Multimedia Publications, 1984. Unpaginated (approximately 72 pages). Approximately 75 color photographs, covering every page. Discography. The Boy George File.

Fluffy picture-book with barely any text and captioning. Boy George is revealed in all of his early 1980's colors; after so many years the shock effect of his cross-dressing has worn off and the image alone is simply dull. The other Culture Club band members don't even seem to know how to pose as extras. A photo of George with his mother (dressed like him) is good for a chuckle. The releases in the Discography are undated.

OTHER TITLES OF INTEREST
Cohen, Scott. *Boy George*. New York: Berkley, 1984.
De Graaf, Kaspar and Garrett, Malcolm. *Culture Club: When Cameras Go Crazy*. New York: St. Martin's, 1983.
Gill, Anton. *Mad About the Boy: The Life & Times of Boy George & Culture Club*. New York: Owl Books (Henry Holt), 1985.

THE CURE

BIOGRAPHIES

Bowler, Dave and Dray, Bryan. *The Cure: Faith*. London: Pan Books, 1995. 198 pages. One glossy eight-page black-and-white photo insert. U.K. Discography. Sources. Index.

The story of The Cure is inextricably linked with that of its one constant member, Robert Smith. Smith continues to stand as the creative driving force behind the group that has managed to survive the 1980's and beyond, despite industry labeling and various battles between artistic integrity and pop commercialism. Authors Bowler and Gray have not created a

landmark work, nor have they succeeded in giving readers much in the way of anecdotal material or making this accessible to an American readership. Still, this minor biography sheds some light on The Cure's origins and ongoing development.

Thompson, Dave and Greene, Jo-Ann. *The Cure: A Visual Documentary*. London: Omnibus Press (division of Book Sales Limited), 1993. 112 pages. Approximately 125 glossy color and black-and-white photographs throughout. The Cure Discography.

First published in 1988, this is a day-by-day of The Cure's activities, essentially from December 1972 (Robert Smith's first receiving a guitar) to August 1992 (Robert getting a black eye at a concert in Mexico City). Only Smith's birth and childhood are mentioned in a few cursory introductory paragraphs. The listings themselves include performances, release dates, public appearances, and other miscellany. A few quotes and anecdotes appear in some of the entries, although they are nothing spectacular. The real draw here is the photos: Smith's hair seems to get woollier in every picture. For fans, a viable alternative.

DISCOGRAPHIES, RECORDING GUIDES, AND COLLECTIBLES

Butler, Daren. *The Cure on Record*. London: Omnibus Press (division of Book Sales Limited), 1995. 128 pages. Approximately 300 color and black-and-white photographs and reproductions of records and CDs. Glossary of Terms.

Sumptuous color retrospective of The Cure's releases, highlighted by representations of the group's CDs, album covers, promotional art, and more. Organized chronologically—and with little commentary from Butler—each piece contains mentioning of release date, catalog number, band line-up, and other details. The one page Glossary doesn't add much, especially since that space could have been better utilized for a song and record title index. In spite of its shortcomings, it's nevertheless a comprehensive and eye-catching compendium.

PICTORIALS

Barbarian; Sutherland, Steve; and Smith, Robert. *The Cure: The Imaginary Years*. London: Fiction Books, 1988. 128 pages. Approximately 125 black-and-white photographs, news clips, and graphics and 50 color illustrations, covering every page. Discography.

This aqua-embossed picture book (with a very difficult to read title) is a busy retrospective of The Cure, reputedly published with the band's authorization (which is not in evidence). Amidst the biographical details, readers will be distracted by cumbersome charcoal black-and-white designs smattered on the pages. The copy itself isn't exactly riveting either, generally introducing magazine-clipped quotes with a five-word line, e.g., "The tour moved on to Europe." Things improve drastically with a closing chapter containing cute childhood photos of each band member, accompanied by a fact-sheet (where born, family members, etc.). Promises more than it delivers. And yes, the first author name is correctly credited Barbarian.

Greene, Jo-Ann. *The Cure*. London: Bobcat Books (division of Book Sales Limited), 1986. 48 pages. Approximately 12 color and 50 black-and-white illustrations, covering every page. Discography.

Artsy photo montage of the techno-rock group, with some history accompanied by quotes from the usual rock mags. Many of the abstract illustrations and assorted colors work successfully, though some of the text, superimposed over graphics, is difficult to read. For young fans into The Cure's hair-splitting image.

WRITTEN WORKS

Smith, Robert. *The Cure: Songwords 1979-1989*. London: Omnibus Press (division of Book Sales Limited), 1989. 168 pages. Approximately 50 black-and-white photographs and graphics throughout.

A complete collection of Robert Smith's lyrics for The Cure, divided largely by one-to two-year periods. Some photos and graphics are provided throughout, but they lack flash and style. Smith's lyrics on the page are sure to offend many; "Killing an Arab," for obvious reasons; and "Heroin Face" for its unnecessarily condescending tone in assaulting a junkie.

As a counter-balance, there are works that have spiritual overtones ("Faith" and "Wailing Wall") and others that convey lusty celebration ("Hot! Hot! Hot!"). A more colorful, up-to-date edition is necessitated by The Cure's durability in the 1990's.

TERENCE TRENT D'ARBY

PICTORIALS

St. Michael, Mick. *Introducing Terence Trent D'Arby*. London: Zomba Books, 1988. 48 pages. Approximately 50 color and black-and-white photographs, covering nearly every page. For the Record: Discography.

A slim introduction to the star, with minimal biographical data. All we really learn in chapter one is that he's a preacher's son from New York City; a fact file tells us D'Arby's heroes include Duke Ellington, Marlon Brando, and Lauren Bacall. The pictures will please young fans; D'Arby struts his stuff throughout, and he is seen arm-in-arm with then-love interest Susanna Hoffs (of The Bangles). D'Arby's popularity hadn't quite crossed over to this side of the Atlantic at the time of publication, so we can only hope a better offering is on the way.

BOBBY DARIN

BIOGRAPHIES

DiOrio, Al. *Borrowed Time: The 37 Years of Bobby Darin*. Philadelphia: Running Press, 1981. 256 pages. Approximately 60 black-and-white photographs throughout. Appendix: Darin on Records; Songs Written by Bobby Darin; Bobby Darin on Film. Index.

Hitmaker Bobby Darin was born under an odd set of circumstances. The result of a teenage pregnancy, Darin was raised by his grandmother and told that she was his mother and his mother his sister. Al DiOrio's diffident biography doesn't explain how this secret was kept away from Darin for 32 years, or how he felt when he discovered the truth. The book also fails to explore Darin's emotions as he coped with his heart disease (caused by bouts of rheumatic fever) and the realization of his imminent death. DiOrio does not supply source notes, so we are left to wonder whether his assertion that Murray the K Kaufman's mother really inspired the song "Splish Splash" is fact or speculation. Not enough bubbles in this bathtub.

DARIN FRIENDS AND FAMILY

Darin, Dodd. *Dream Lovers: The Magnificent Shattered Lives of Bobby Darin and Sandra Dee*. New York: Warner Books, 1994. 406 pages. One 16-page black-and-white photo insert.

The marriage of Bobby Darin and Sandra Dee was anything but magnificent—except, perhaps, if you're into Hollywood soap opera. As kids, both stars had their share of trauma: Darin, who did not find out his sister was his mother until he was 32 and never learned the identity of his father, suffered from rheumatic fever, which led to heart trouble and ultimately claimed his life; Sandra Dee, the wholesome teen screen star, was the victim of sexual abuse from her step-father, which resulted in anorexia and, later, chronic alcoholism. The couple's son, Dodd Darin, confronts his family's demons—which persist to this day—"with touching honesty and grace"—*Los Angeles Daily News*.

GENERAL REFERENCE

Bleiel, Jeff. Foreword by Dick Clark. *That's All: Bobby Darin on Record, Stage & Screen*. Ann Arbor, MI: Popular Culture, Ink., 1993. 306 pages. Approximately 100 black-and-white photographs throughout. Appendices: Chronology; Discography; Bobby Darin's Films; Television Appearances; Songs Written by Bobby Darin; Darin Songs Recorded by Other Artists; Unreleased Tracks; Never-Recorded Songs Performed Live; Darin's Favorite Songwriters. Bibliography. Index.

Does Bobby Darin deserve his place in the Rock and Roll Hall of Fame? Author Bleiel states his case succinctly: Buddy Holly and Dion covered his songs; he had several indisputable rock classics (e.g., "Splish Splash"); and rocker Neil Young counted him as the artist he "most identified with." Downplaying Darin's Vegas years, Bleiel instead portrays the singer as a versatile, consummate artist who until the end hammered out "Mack the Knife" to a young, hip generation. Given that Darin had a respectable television and film career, the

numerous appendixes in the back of the book are highly valuable. While neither an extensive biography nor a comprehensive discography, this book is "...straightforward and laudably unsensationalistic..."—*Goldmine*.

DEACON BLUE

BIOGRAPHIES

Bowler, Dave and Dray, Bryan. *Deacon Blue: Just What I Feel*. London: Sidgwick & Jackson, 1995. 200 pages. One glossy eight-page black-and-white photo insert.

From 1987-1994, Deacon Blue had four hit albums and several successful singles in the U.K.—but not all that much success abroad. Authors Bowler and Dray theorize that the group's rise to prominence in their own country was due in no small part to the age of CDs; however, this does not prove that the group is merely a reflection of an electronic trend. The authors place Deacon Blue somewhere between gritty rockers à la Bruce Springsteen and slick performers such as Michael Bolton. There's quite a gap there, and one gets the feeling the authors are stretching beyond their reach. In any event, when the U.S. has a calling for this band, this book will be ready and waiting for them.

DEAD KENNEDYS

PICTORIALS

Fitzgerald, f-Stop (Editor). Written by Kester, Marian. *Dead Kennedys: The Unauthorized Version*. San Francisco: Last Gasp, 1983. 65 pages. Approximately 75 black-and-white photographs, covering every page. Discography.

Raucous exposé of the punk band featuring countless shots of fans storming the stage. Some lyrics are scattered throughout, including the band's popular ditty "Kill the Poor." The photos are lousy and the design hideous; most fans have probably checked it out already. If not, skip the book and read musician Biafra's editorial about the book on the inside back cover: "Overall we feel the book is fairly well done... Given a choice, however, we would have preferred it never came out."

DEAD OR ALIVE

PICTORIALS

Greene, Jo-Ann. *Dead or Alive*. London: Bobcat Books/Omnibus Press (division of Book Sales Limited), 1985. 48 pages. 12 color and 50 black-and-white photos throughout. Discography.

These Liverpool lads had long hair, played loud music, and most certainly would offend your parents' sensibilities. Time warp: 1985, not 1965, when Dead or Alive was hot on the charts with clean-cut singles such as "Black Leather" and "In Too Deep." Standard fanzine fare, although it's funny to read about "polysexual" singer Pete Burns' feud with Boy George.

CHRIS DE BURGH

TITLES OF INTEREST

Thompson, Dave. *Chris De Burgh: From a Spark to a Flame*. London: Omnibus Press (division of Book Sales Limited), 1987.

DEEP PURPLE

AUTOBIOGRAPHY

Gillan, Ian with Cohen, David. *Child in Time*. Miami Springs, FL: MBS, 1994. 212 pages. Two glossy eight-page color and black-and-white photo inserts. Index. (First published in 1994 in Great Britain by Smith Gryphon Limited.)

The lead singer of Deep Purple—who was not a founding member but joined in 1969—tells of his involvement with the hard rock band, culminating with Purple's 1993-94 world tour. Gillan describes his on-and-off relationship with the band as a bad habit that "he has loved in torment." Gillan discusses his early days in the 1960's, disastrous tours of the Middle East, groupies and drugs, but it's his dynamic rela-

tionship with guitarist Ritchie Blackmore and the creation of classics such as "Smoke on the Water" that will most interest fans. Essential for headbangers and dinosaur rock lovers.

PICTORIALS

Charlesworth, Chris. *Deep Purple: The Illustrated Biography*. London: Omnibus Press (division of Book Sales Limited), 1983. Unpaginated (approximately 96 pages). Approximately 100 color and 100 black-and-white photographs, covering every page. Albums.

Released at about the same time as Welch's photo book (see below)—and by the same publisher, no less—this is a somewhat more informed history and evolution of the band. On the back cover is a four-tier headshot spread of Deep Purple in its various phases; at the time of press, Jon Lord and Ian Paice were the only founding fathers still in the band. The interior is arranged year-by-year until the final chapter (the most important one, by most accounts), which encapsulates "1976 to present." The early years tell the fairly engaging story of how the band was formed; it's interesting to see how players such as Denny Laine (of The Moody Blues) and Arthur Wood (eldest brother of Ronnie Wood) figured in Deep Purple's story. As for the photos, some fans might get a kick seeing a Ritchie Blackmore photo circa 1968, in which he looks like the winner of a Neil Diamond look-alike contest! Recommended for metal-maniacs, in spite of its many limitations.

Welch, Chris. *Deep Purple HM Photo Book: Burn with Deep Purple*. London (England): Omnibus Press (division of Book Sales Limited), 1983. Unpaginated (approximately 96 pages). Approximately 100 color and black-and-white photographs, on every page.

This compilation contains lots of fine photos of "the world's loudest band" from their early days in the late 1960's (performing, posing, touring) through to the early 1980's. This is a waste because the photos aren't captioned or dated—and common folk won't know who they're looking at. The only text—buried in the back—is superficial magazine history. Burn the book, not the band.

DEF LEPPARD

BIOGRAPHIES

Crocker, Chris. *Def Leppard*. New York: Ballantine Books, 1986. 148 pages. One 16-page glossy black-and-white photo insert. Appendixes: Discography; Videography; Fan Club Information.

Crocker is game for this mass market treatment of the group he considers the "first great heavy metal band of the 1980's." Originating from Sheffield, the city many consider to be England's Pittsburgh, the boys began as Atomic Mass but changed the name when the other musicians witnessed Joe Elliott's drawing of a leopard in which the animal had an ear horn (a primitive hearing aid) pressed against its ear. (The removal of the "a" in Def goes unexplained here, although other publications have suggested it's a reference to the "Led" of Led Zeppelin.) Lightweight but with some high points.

PICTORIALS

Collingwood, Chris. *Def Leppard: No Safety Net*. Chessington, Surrey (England): Castle, 1994. 144 pages. Approximately 125 full-page color and black-and-white photographs throughout. Discography.

A thick magazine dripping with Def Leppard history and commentary. Collingwood has a sharp perspective on the band, but is rather on the wimpy side; how many times do we need to be reminded of Joe Elliott's puppy fat? The pictures don't do much to distinguish Leppard from other heavy metal bands, which is not helped by the group's British flag tops and bottoms. Optional for fans.

McGilly, Willy. *Def Leppard*. London and New York: Proteus Publishing, 1984. 32 pages. Approximately 40 color and black-and-white photographs, covering nearly every page.

The boys from Sheffield, England are credited for having succeeded at cranking out heavy metal at a time when punk was all the rage. This book has few trimmings and little detail; even for 32 pages it contains less than the average metal mag. Def Leppard may be among the better-looking heavy metal bands, but these photos are largely forgettable. Hey, is there really someone out there named Willy McGilly?

Rich, Jason. *Def Leppard*. Miami, FL: MBS, 1996. 120 pages. Approximately 75 color and black-and-white photographs throughout. Discography. Chronology. Index.

CD-format book covering all aspects of Def Leppard's career. This nicely designed and illustrated book is priced right at $7.99.

OTHER TITLES OF INTEREST
Fricke, David. *Def Leppard: Animal Instinct*. London: Omnibus Press (division of Book Sales Limited), 1990.

JOHN DENVER

AUTOBIOGRAPHY

Denver, John with Tobier, Arthur. Introduction by Harold A. Thau. *Take Me Home: An Autobiography*. New York: Harmony (division of Crown), 1994. 262 pages. Two glossy eight-page black-and-white photo inserts. Discography. Index.

The son of a military man, young John Denver had more of the quiet rebel in him than people realize. He moved around quite a bit during his childhood (to a handful of cities in Arizona and Texas), which led to his becoming a pacifist and an antagonist against his starchy dad. Denver even ran away once. In laid-back, soothing prose, Denver recounts his little-known ties in the 1960's to folk rockers (e.g., Jim McGuinn of The Byrds), his wives and lovers (yes, there were several), and his involvement with vital causes (e.g., The Hunger Project). Denver's affability shines throughout, a fact that will please his record-buyers. "This is a story with tremendous allure"—*The New York Times*.

BIOGRAPHIES

Dachs, David. *John Denver*. New York: Pyramid Books, 1976. 96 pages. Two eight-page black-and-white photo inserts. Discography, Songbooks, TV, Films, Awards.

"A warm biography of the folk composer, concert performer, conservationist, and TV personality." In other words, a 96-page mass market paperback hoping to cash in on the star's then thriving popularity. Amateurishly written and generally insulting to just about anyone's intelligence ("John wears glasses because he has to"), this has been completely outmoded by later biographies and, most especially, Denver's autobiography (see above). The back matter lists (discography) are outdated and contain less information than you could find in your own Denver record collection. Not recommended.

FANZINES AND FAN CLUBS

Free Spirit: The World Family of John Denver. c/o Karen Richmond, 3 Almond Walk, Hazlemere, Near High Wycombe, Bucks HP15 7RE England.

"The Official U.K. Club" offers a membership card, a club badge, a color photograph, a discography packet, and a subscription to the magazine of the same name. *Free Spirit* is a 20-page, glossy magazine with a color cover that contains Denver-related news, occasional contributions by Denver, member submissions, reprinted newspaper articles, and more. Books, t-shirts, CDs, sweatshirts, and other items are also available through the club. The cost per year is £18 U.S. (to receive the complete new members pack) and £14 in Europe.

Hearts in Harmony: World Family of John Denver. Attn. Carol Blevins, 1213 River Road, Quarryville, PA 17566-9757.

Founded in the mid-1980's, this quarterly journal covers all aspects of Denver's career. The 36-page stapled magazine includes a color front and back cover, black-and-white photographs throughout, concert updates, reprinted newspaper articles, excerpts from *Passages: The Quarterly Newsletter of the Plant-It 2000 Foundation*, discography, letters, merchandise, swap shop, question-and-answer, entry in raffles, and much more. The cost of subscription is $24 U.S.; $28 Canada; and $32 overseas. For an extra $2 fee, subscribers can become part of the "Fast News Network" and receive timely information between regular issues.

YOUNG ADULT

Fleischer, Leonore. *John Denver: The Man and His Music.* New York and London: Flash Books (division of Book Sales Limited), 1976. 80

pages. Approximately 65 black-and-white photographs throughout. Discography.

This book provides some Denver bio and details of his recording, concert, and television career (remember "An Evening with John Denver"?), but most of it reports on what the critics had to say. Words such as muzak, bland, corny, kitsch, and schmaltz are repeated throughout. Denver's rebuttals are in the last chapter. While honest criticism is certainly welcome, so much space is devoted to it many will be inclined to simply agree. The photos are downright awful reproductions from old newspaper clippings and books.

Jacobs, Linda. *John Denver: A Natural High.* St. Paul, MN: EMC Corporation, 1976. 40 pages. Approximately 25 black-and-white photographs throughout.

Rectangular juvenile book intended for fans eight and under. The text is highly readable and not too syrupy. Few songs are mentioned, however; in fact, only "Leaving on a Jet Plane" is discussed in detail. Ardent fans might enjoy reading this to their kids.

McGreane, Meagan. *On Stage with John Denver.* Mankato, MN: Creative Education, 1976. 48 pages. Eight black-and-white photographs throughout.

Subsequent to Creative Education's *John Denver* (see Morse, below) and in many respects a step down. Chapter titles and headings are designed in a bland yellow, the color also used in various graphic arc patterns scattered throughout. The focus is not "live Denver," as the title seems to imply; the text is fluffy fare, providing insight into a fragment of the artist's personality.

Morse, Charles and Morse, Ann. Illustrations by Keely, John. *John Denver.* Mankato, MN: Creative Education, 1975. 32 pages. Eight original watercolor drawings throughout.

Creative Education's "Rock 'n Pop Stars" series takes a gentler turn to the artistry of John Denver. The musician is portrayed as "a happy man," a fact that was only superficially true (see Denver's autobiography, above). For very young fans this probably won't make very much difference. The book also focuses on Denver's love of nature, camping, mountains, and animals. Simple and pleasant, but noticeably absent of any recording information or discography.

OTHER TITLES OF INTEREST

Denver, John. *The Children and the Flowers*. No city: Green Tiger Press, 1979.

Denver, John and Pidgeon, Jean (illustrator). *Alfie the Christmas Tree*. No city: National Wildlife Federation, 1990.

DEPECHE MODE

BIOGRAPHIES

Thomson, Dave. *Depeche Mode: Some Great Reward*. New York: St. Martin's Press, 1994. 274 pages. One glossy eight-page black-and-white photo insert. Discographies.

Depeche Mode receives an all-out biographical treatment here, which is surprising given that the musicians cannot be pinned down on anything. They began as a youth-club band, turned to synthesizers, and emerged as a post-punk band without a cause. Notably excluded from large fundraising galas such as Band Aid and Live Aid, one wonders what the musicians really do stand for. Dave Thomson astutely points out that Depeche Mode's contributions and chameleonlike approach pick up from where David Bowie and Bryan Ferry left off, and that somehow the group has managed an impressive fifteen-year durability. "...above the shortsighted band biographies typically written to capitalize on sudden popularity"— *Publishers Weekly*.

PICTORIALS

Corbijn, Anton. Introduction by Paul Morley. *Depeche Mode: Strangers: The Photographs*. London: Omnibus (division of Book Sales Limited), 1990. Unpaginated (116 pages). Approximately 100 black-and-white photographs, covering every page; about 20 color photographs throughout.

Oblique, moody photos taken by Anton Corbijn and published with the obvious intention of perpetuating the boys' enigmatic image. Suffice it to say, that goal is accomplished. The photos are not labeled—and the introduction doesn't afford a clue—so, unless you know the band quite well, this book is a mystery. Judging by the section headings "East" and

"West" and a snapshot of Kafka's gravestone, we can safely assume these pics were taken in Germany. After that, you're on your own.

NEIL DIAMOND

BIOGRAPHIES

Grossman, Alan; Truman, Bill; and Yamanaka, Roy Oki. *Diamond: A Biography*. Chicago: Contemporary Books, 1987. 235 pages. One glossy 12-page black-and-white photo insert. Compositions List. American Discography.

This biography only skims the surface of Diamond's low public profile and moody exterior. Born to Polish-Russian Jewish ancestry in Brooklyn, New York, Diamond was an introverted kid who sought refuge and cool status by joining a street gang. Interestingly, it was The Everly Brothers—not Elvis—who influenced him as a musician. While we still end up not knowing much more about Diamond than when we started, the book is slightly more direct about his struggles for recognition than Wiseman's biography (below); it also sports a much-needed composer list. Even so, the two books combined aren't as useful as a *People* magazine profile.

Wiseman, Rich. *Neil Diamond: Solitary Star*. New York: Dodd, Mead & Company, 1987. 324 pages. One 16-page black-and-white photo insert. Discography. Index.

Diamond receives a flat treatment in this synopsis of his life and career. Wiseman uncovers only a few little known facets of Diamond's life—his early interest in fencing and his botched screen test to star in the film *Lenny*—and the rest is uninspired public knowledge. The author points out that Diamond was ultra-conservative in the late 1960's (critical of musicians such as The Beatles who had suggestive lyrics), yet he doesn't comment about the hypocrisy of his being busted several years later for possession of marijuana. The discography doesn't separate Diamond's credits for other artists—a must given that songwriting is, debatably, his greatest asset. Keep in solitary.

FANZINES AND FAN CLUBS

The Diamond Connection. The Diamond Connection, P.O. Box 2764, Witham, Essex CM8 2SF England.

"Britain's brightest fanzine for Neil Diamond fans" contains articles by fans, wants and swaps, reviews, items of special interest, and updates on Diamond's latest performances and recordings. Published bimonthly, the 12-page, glossy fanzine costs $5 per issue or six issues for $25 in the U.S.; in the U.K., £2.50 per issue or six issues for £12.50.

YOUNG ADULT

O'Regan, Suzanne K. Illustrations by Keely, John. *Neil Diamond*. Mankato, MN: Creative Education, 1975. 32 pages. Six original watercolor and pencil drawings throughout.

One of the more nauseating installments in the "Rock 'n Pop Stars" series. The illustrations are embarrassingly bad (the artist couldn't really capture Diamond's facial structure or expressions) and the text is in dire need of a lower-calorie sweetener. Considering this was done closer to when Diamond was "rock/folk" rather than "adult contemporary," it should have been much livelier.

BO DIDDLEY

DISCOGRAPHIES, RECORDING GUIDES AND COLLECTIBLES

White, George R. *The Complete Bo Diddley Sessions*. Great Horton, Brandford (England): George White Publications, 1993. 92 pages. Approximately 50 photocopies of black-and-white photographs.

Self-published guide to the music of Bo Diddley, produced and published by George R. White. This study represents the only listing of Diddley's U.S. and U.K. releases, rare issues, BBC recordings (yes, he did perform on U.K. radio), guest spots on others' sessions, film/video appearances, and more. For each track, White also supplies the studio addresses where recorded, personnel, dates, and catalog numbers. Since it stands alone, this book has its uses until something more solid comes

along. Not typeset or indexed. "White has done a tremendous job..."—*Goldmine*.

OTHER TITLES OF INTEREST
White, George R. Foreword by Don Everly. *Bo Diddley: Living Legend*. Chessington, Surrey (England): Castle, 1995.

DION AND THE BELMONTS

AUTOBIOGRAPHY

DiMucci, Dion with Seay, Davin. *The Wanderer: Dion's Story*. New York: Beech Tree Books (division of William Morrow and Company), 1988. 224 pages. Three eight-page black-and-white photo inserts.

Dion DiMucci's image as the Italian street kid from the Bronx is pretty close to reality. Growing up on East 183rd Street, Dion went from eating spaghetti with his family and drinking egg creams at the soda shop to joining a street gang and becoming a heroin addict—all before he was fourteen years old. In this low-key autobiography, DiMucci tells of his rise to fame, his associations with numerous rockers (e.g., Bobby Darin, Sam Cooke, Buddy Holly), his movie career (working with actors such as Buster Keaton and Bert Lahr), and the back stories to his songs ("Little Diane" was inspired by a Jewish prayer). The book is full of key revelations; readers will probably surprised to find Dion in the company of early 1960's folk rockers such as Bob Dylan, Tom Paxton, and Phil Ochs.

DIRE STRAITS

PICTORIALS

Irwin, Colin. *Dire Straits*. London: Carlton Books, 1994. 120 pages. Approximately 125 color illustrations, covering every page. Discography. Chronology. Index.

CD-format book (in terms of size and shape) focusing on the "Sultans of Swing." This publication is remarkably well put together for a work of its kind, with high quality photos and text that is set against nicely blended color backdrops. Irwin's biography of the band is concise, but he gets in the essentials. One passage succinctly tells how Mark and David Knopflers' father was a Jewish Hungarian architect who had fled Nazi Germany to settle in various parts of the United Kingdom. Managing to squeeze in a discography, chronology, and index, this gift item is better than many rock pictorials four times its size.

Oldfield, Michael. *Dire Straits.* New York: Quill, 1984. 152 pages. One hundred black-and-white photographs, covering nearly every page. Discography. Index. (First published in 1984 in Great Britain by Sidgwick & Jackson Limited.)

Dire Straits are always at their most natural while playing live, hence fans will approve of the fact that most of the shots in this book were taken during concert performances between 1978 and 1983. The photos reproduced rather dark, though, and many are bordered by black lines for want of a more creative design. There are no shots of other musicians (e.g., Dylan) with the band. The book is labeled as having been "written in cooperation with the band," but the extent of this authorization is not explained.

OTHER TITLES OF INTEREST
Kamin, Philip. *Dire Straits.* Milwaukee, WI: Hal Leonard, 1985.
Matthews, Gordon. *Dire Straits.* New York: Ballantine, 1987.

WILLIE DIXON

AUTOBIOGRAPHY

Dixon, Willie with Snowden, Don, *I Am the Blues: The Willie Dixon Story.* London: Quartet Books, 1989. 260 pages. One glossy 116-page black-and-white photo insert. Appendix 1: Discography. Appendix 2: Willie Dixon Songbook. Appendix 3: Studio Contributions. Appendixes 4 and 5: Books and Films. Index.

An oral autobiography from the bluesman that opens with a useful map of Chicago, complete with blues landmarks. Dixon tells portions of his story, supported by italicized history from Snowden. Other personalities quoted include L.V. Dixon (Willie's brother), Buddy Guy, and Scott Cameron (Willie's agent). A larger than life fellow (both physically and musically), Dixon's first musical experience was in a

gospel quartet known as The Union Jubilee Singers. Arrested for stealing plumbing supplies, he escaped from prison and found his way to Chess Records with players such as Howlin' Wolf. This book is essential for blues aficionados and recommended to Led Zep fans, who should be aware that many of that band's classics were "inspired" by Dixon's genius. Reprinted in the U.S. in 1990 by Da Capo Press.

D.J. JAZZY JEFF AND THE FRESH PRINCE

TITLES OF INTEREST
Peeples, Freda. *D.J. Jazzy Jeff & the Fresh Prince.* New York: Dell, 1992.

DR. JOHN

AUTOBIOGRAPHY

John, Dr. *Under a Hoodoo Moon: The Life of the Night Tripper.* New York: St. Martin's Press, 1994. 264 pages. One 16-page glossy black-and-white photo insert. Index.

What better source to find New Orleans lingo such as voodoo, hoodoo, and gris-gris? Mac Rebennack, aka Dr. John—cocaine junkie, honkytonk pianist, composer ("Right Place, Wrong Time"), and producer—began his career as a sideman, working with musicians such as Frank Zappa, Iron Butterfly (whom he dubs "Iron Butterfingers"), and Buffalo Springfield. Dr. John is mysteriously cold about his associates; he saves the real anecdotes and praise for veterans such as Little Richard, Ray Charles, and Fats Domino. His boogie-beat style of writing has its moments—especially when we are treated to his word creations (e.g., "flusterations")—but after a while you'd just wish an editor had corrected at least *some* of his ungrammatical phrasings. For fans of Dr. John's brand of funk and rhythm and blues.

DONOVAN

WRITTEN WORKS

Donovan. *Dry Songs and Scribbles*. Garden City, NY: Doubleday & Company, 1971. Unpaginated (approximately 128 pages). Approximately 75 black-and-white photographs and original drawings throughout.

Just as it was becoming fashionable for rockers to publish books (Morrison, Dylan, etc.), Donovan felt his creative juices flowing as well. This book includes two sets of poetry—1964-65 and 1965-1970—and a section of prose, all of which is accompanied by photos and Donovan's simplistic doodles. Acid, acid everywhere: "...tangerine harlequins splashing from a pastel play moon twinkling skin of that girl..." Harmless, dreamy poetry, with an occasional knock against the queen. More mellow than yellow.

JASON DONOVAN

TITLES OF INTEREST
Black, Susan. *Jason Donovan*. Woodstock, NY: Beekman, 1990.

DONNY AND MARIE

See Osmonds, The.

THE DOORS

AUTOBIOGRAPHY

Densmore, John. *Riders on the Storm: My Life with Jim Morrison and the Doors*. New York: Delacorte Press (division of Bantam Doubleday Dell), 1990. 320 pages. Four glossy eight-page black-and-white photo inserts.

A cathartic memoir by The Doors' jazz-inspired drummer, which appropriately focuses more on the life, work, and excesses of Jim Morrison rather than on Densmore himself.

Densmore refers to Morrison as "mentor, nemesis, friend," and, of the three other band members, his relationship with the singer was the most strained. His numerous self-therapy letters to dead Morrison show a great deal of love for the man, but also frustration with his self-destructive behavior. "...indispensable for fans of one of rock music's most flamboyant and controversial groups"—*Publishers Weekly*.

BIOGRAPHIES

Hopkins, Jerry and Sugerman, Danny. *No One Here Gets Out Alive*. New York: Warner Books, 1980. 384 pages. Black-and-white photos. Discography and Filmography.

The first major biography of Jim Morrison, which became a national 9-month best seller and helped re-ignite the craze for Doors music. Love that open-chested Dionysian Morrison on the cover and spine! The book contains many juicy details, including his parents' reactions to hearing "The End" for the first time and Morrison's classic encounters with figures such as Janis Joplin and Andy Warhol. The authors took some critical flack for helping to promulgate the myths more than the man (particularly in reference to his death), but the book is surely "a must-read for any Doors fan—young or old—chock-full of spicy revelations"—*Los Angeles Times*. For those few who are unfamiliar: The title is a line in the Doors' song "Five to One."

Riordan, James and Prochincky, Jerry. *Break on Through: The Life and Death of Jim Morrison*. New York: William Morrow & Company, 1991. 400 pages. Two black-and-white photo inserts. Bibliography and Index.

A revealing and comprehensive biography that traces Morrison's life from navy brat to UCLA film student, poet, charismatic singer, sex symbol, and overweight barfly. Probably a more realistic—if less idolistic—investigation than Sugerman and Hopkins' work (see above) and almost as entertaining. "The book isn't part of the retro-craze for the 1960's, but an examination of one man's immersion into the dark and dangerous aspects of life and the poetry he flung back to us from the other side"—*Booklist*.

CRITICAL/ANALYTICAL COMMENTARY

Crisafulli, Chuck. *Moonlight Drive: The Stories Behind Every Doors Song.* Miami Springs, FL: MBS, 1995. 176 pages. Approximately 200 color and black-and-white illustrations throughout. Chronology. Discography. Index.

Unbelievably—given the extent of publications on The Doors—this is the first work that addresses The Doors' music exclusively. American critic Chuck Crisafulli studies every composition in The Doors' catalog from "Break on Through" to "An American Prayer," providing insights on how the songs were written and/or what elements inspired them. The details of the recording sessions themselves are not covered, but there are enough tidbits and rare photographs here to keep fans and researchers alike busy. Crisafulli stretches things by devoting ten paragraphs around a throwaway song such as "Do It," but his comments on "Shaman's Blues" are engrossing. The illustrative matter, consisting of both color and black-and-white photos and period artwork (ships, soldiers, etc.), make this an attractive and enjoyable read.

Fowlie, Wallace. *Rimbaud and Jim Morrison: The Rebel As a Poet.* Durham, NC: Duke University Press, 1994. 136 pages. Bibliography. Index.

Comparative analysis of French symbolist poet Rimbaud and rock poet Jim Morrison. Morrison actually corresponded with author Wallace Fowlie in 1968, complimenting him on his translation of Rimbaud's work. The similarities between the two historical figures, Morrison and Rimbaud, are striking: both poets died around 27; both were known for their erratic and rebellious behavior; and both took the view that being a poet meant expanding the senses to the fullest. Fowlie gets some of his facts on The Doors wrong (such as titles of songs), but he is very strong analyzing the written works of the respective poets. Recommended for disciples of either Morrison or Rimbaud.

DEATH OF MORRISON

Hopkins, Jerry. *The Lizard King: The Essential Jim Morrison.* New York: Charles Scribner's Sons (Macmillan Publishing Company), 1992. 272 pages. 50 black-and-white photos throughout.

A sequel of sorts to Hopkins' *No One Here Gets Out Alive* (see Biographies, above), mostly focusing on Morrison's death but also containing some interviews with journalists (e.g., Ben Fong-Torres). The justification for this work is that some of Hopkins' writing had to be cut from the earlier book to make room for Sugerman's portion of the manuscript. What's so bizarre is that, at the time of the previous book, Hopkins had no idea how Morrison died; he even wanted to release editions of *No One Here Gets Out Alive* with different endings! Now he claims that his coauthor Sugerman only recently confided to him that he knew all along Morrison had died of heroin overdose. What gives?

Seymore, Bob. *The End: The Death of Jim Morrison.* New York: Omnibus Press (division of Book Sales Limited), 1990. 96 pages. Approximately twenty black-and-white photographs throughout.

Is this finally the end-all to the saga of Morrison's death? Or is Mojo Risin' alive and guzzling a few beers at a roadhouse in Africa? The most important question: Is there a need for this slim volume after the droves of other books that cover much the same ground? Probably not. But the most fanatical Doors' followers will want to buy this one, if only to sort through the bizarre details all over again.

FANZINES AND FAN CLUBS

The Doors Collectors Magazine. c/o Three Dimensional Marketing, Inc., P.O. Box 1441, Orem, UT 84059-1441.

"The unofficial magazine for Doors collectors and fans" is a 60-page, glossy rock mag covering all facets of the group's legend. Includes black-and-white and color illustrations, "Dusky Jewels" (latest news), bootleg information, concert appearances of the ex-Doors and tribute bands, updates on the Morrison gravesite, CD and video reviews, auction items, fan forum (poetry, essays, and interviews with fans), classifieds, and much more. Published four times a year. The cost is $20 in the U.S.; $25 in Canada.

The Doors Quarterly Fanzine. Am Oelvebach 5, D. 47809 Krefeld-Stratum, West Germany.

Fan club that publishes a 74-page quarterly fanzine of the same name, holds fan club meetings, and provides members with a membership card. Founded in 1983, the club has support from Ray Manzarek. Over the years the magazine has featured interviews with Ray, Robby Krieger, and John Densmore, as well as Morrison friends Frank Lisciandro, Danny Sugerman, Patricia Kennealy, and others. It also contains black-and-white photographs, reprints of newspaper articles, transcripts from various writings and concerts, album and book reviews, and more. Editor von Rainer Moddemann is also author of a book entitled *The Doors*, available from Heel Publishers (Germany). Write for membership information.

Highway: Fanzine Del Doors. Tony Romanazzi, Via Agucchi N 18, 40131, Bologna, Italy.

Fifty-page Italian fanzine with extensive Italian (and a smidgeon of English) articles on The Doors and Jim Morrison in particular. Contains photocopies of photos and graphics, "Shaman's News," interviews, reprints of articles, and more. Write for subscription information.

Ship of Fools: A Doors Fanzine. P.O. Box 91, Floral Park, NY 11002.

Thirty-two-page newspaper that includes Doors news, interviews with band members (e.g. Ray Manzarek), special events, reproductions of black-and-white photographs, and more. The cost of subscription is $6 for one year (two issues).

MORRISON FRIENDS AND FAMILY

Huddleston, Judy. *This Is the End...My Only Friend: Living and Dying With Jim Morrison.* New York: Shapolsky Publishers, Inc., 1991. Bibliography and Discography. Index.

A fascinating account from Huddleston, a self-confessed obsessive Doors fan, and groupie who was only 17 when she first bedded down with Jim Morrison. Lots of kinky, wild (and occasionally abusive) sex, which may be a turn-on to certain fans. One of the better groupie bios, this by far outdoes Kennealy's work (see below). "An excellent biography of a true rock icon, this reviewer highly recommends this book..."—*Choice.*

Kennealy, Patricia. *Strange Days: My Life With and Without Jim Morrison.* New York: Dutton (published by the Penguin Group), 1992. 432 pages. One eight-page glossy black-and-white photo insert.

A pretentious memoir from the infamous "witch" who was "married" to Morrison through her Celtic coven. Kennealy, who takes special pride in the fact that she aborted Morrison's only child, has used the Morrison angle as an excuse to publish her opinions and tell as much about her own life story as possible. To put it bluntly, the ramblings in *Strange Days* are self-indulgent and bothersome. "Much ado about the high priestess, not enough about the Lizard King"—*Kirkus.*

Sugerman, Danny. *Wonderland Avenue: A True Rock 'N' Roll Saga.* New York: Morrow, 1989. 408 pages.

These "tales of glamour & excess" might seem to fall into the Selected General Reference section, but this book belongs here because it would only appeal to truly desperate Doors' fans. Sugerman befriended Jim Morrison when he was only twelve years old. After only a brief period of time, he was already working in The Doors' offices, answering fan mail, and getting Morrison a beer every now and then. Sugerman attempts to be candid about his own heroin addiction and ultimate fall over the edge, but this is sadly familiar territory and the reader doesn't know him well enough as a public figure to care.

PICTORIALS

Clarke, Ross. *The Doors: Dance on Fire.* Chessington (England): Castle Communications, 1993. 224 pages. Approximately 150 black-and-white and 20 color illustrations throughout. "Chronicles from an Obsession" by Rainer Moddemann. Discography.

And the question arises: How many more books will be released with titles from Doors' lyrics? (This title derives from "When the Music's Over.") A moody history with grainy black tapestry designs on nearly every page, *Dance on Fire* will satisfy some Doors' fans with its photo emphasis on the years 1966-1968 and excellent reproductions of documents such as Morrison's will. You won't see a fat, bearded Morrison here, nor will you find pix of his lovers, Pamela Courson and Patricia Kennealy. "...commendable enough to fans if not in the Danny Sugerman league"—*Select.*

Dalton, David. Foreword by Nick Tosches. *Mr. Mojo Risin': Jim Morrison, the Last Holy Fool.* New York: St. Martin's Press, 1991. 160 pages. Approximately 80 black-and-white and tinted photographs scattered throughout.

This one is for the teenage fan idolizing the Morrison mystique and for those seeking reassurance that he was a highly intellectual and serious poet. In between excessive literary namedropping (and frequent comparisons to another Dalton subject, James Dean), the author defines Morrison as a "teen idol, hippie, poet, lout" with "one of the great voices in rock." The photos are so-so and not helped much by pinkish tints. "Mr. Mojo Risin'" was Morrison's anagram in the song "L.A. Woman."

Hogan, Peter K. *The Complete Guide to the Music of the Doors.* London: Omnibus (division of Book Sales Limited), 1994. 112 pages. Discography.

CD-format book covering all aspects of The Doors' career. This nicely designed and illustrated book is priced right at around $7.99.

Jones, Dylan. *Jim Morrison: Dark Star.* New York: Viking Studio Books (Viking Penguin, a division of Penguin), 1990. 192 pages. Contains approximately 130 black-and-white and color photographs. Bibliography.

Another book that hoped to cash in on the 20th anniversary of Morrison's death. The book does not qualify as a biography, but it's somewhat more successful as a pictorial. The opening and closing chapters set in Père Lachaise—the French cemetery where Morrison is buried—are overkill. *Booklist* commented that this "unexceptional biography wisely highlights Morrison's looks with a portrait on just about every page."

Lisciandro, Frank. *Jim Morrison: An Hour for Magic.* London: Plexus, 1993. 160 pages. Approximately 100 color and black-and-white photographs throughout.

Frank Lisciandro was among Jim Morrison's closest friends, their association having begun when the former did some filmwork for The Doors (*Feast of Friends*). The second half of the book consists of photos exclusively of a bearded Morrison, which may serve the needs of fans of the *L.A. Woman* LP period. Morrison's

poetry is strewn throughout, including a rare work entitled "Ode to L.A. While Thinking of Brian Jones, Deceased." A few random anecdotes and reminiscences, such as Morrison's casual meeting with ballet legend Rudolf Nureyev, provide some authenticity to what is otherwise a bland pictorial.

Lisciandro, Frank. *Morrison: A Feast of Friends.* New York: Warner Books, 1991. 174 pages. Approximately 125 black-and-white and color illustrations throughout.

A remembrance of Morrison through a plethora of photographs and comments from friends. Some of the testimony is given by author Lisciandro, Vince Treanor, Fud Ford, January Jansen, and others who knew the singer intimately (perhaps better than The Doors band members). A solid oral pictorial on a rock legend, although the cover photo of a very young teen-idol Morrison (against a purple background) will most certainly turn some acid rockers off.

No author. *The Doors Tear-Out Book.* London: Oliver Books, 1993. Unpaginated (approximately 48 pages). Approximately 20 color and black-and-white photographs throughout.

Eighteen photographs of Morrison, both familiar and unfamiliar, with two dreary black-and-white group shots of The Doors. Many of the tear-sheets are poorly executed cut-outs, while others are badly cropped or have lousy color tones. A needless book that will no doubt be scooped up by pre-teen fans.

Sugerman, Danny. *The Doors Illustrated History.* New York: William Morrow & Co., 1983. 204 pages. Approximately 200 black-and-white and color illustrations, covering every page.

Lavishly illustrated oversized history of The Doors, with capsule summaries of concerts and related events. Excerpts from news stories are scattered throughout, in no particular order. A must for Doors' fans and a good addition to the libraries of those who own *No One Here Gets Out Alive* (see Biographies, above). Articles are contributed by Joan Didion, Digby Diehl, Charles Gardner, and others.

Tobler, John and Doe, Andrew. *The Doors*. London: Bobcat Books (division of Book Sales Limited), 1984. 128 pages. Approximately 125 black-and-white photographs, covering every page; 12 color illustrations throughout. Discography. Bibliography. Filmography.

Reprinted many times since 1984, this photo treatment adds little to existing literature. Bare facts, interspersed with quotes readily available in a number of sources, constitute most of the text. Those wanting yet another Morrison photo might be pleased that, except for one shot, the images are all of a youthful, slim Morrison (as opposed to a bearded, blimpish, boozy rock casualty). Young fans may derive some pleasure, but the lack of a cover illustration discourages browsing.

Wincenstein, Edward. *Images of Jim Morrison*. El Paso: Vergin Press, 1982. 94 pages. Approximately 100 black-and-white photos throughout.

A slim collection of snapshots of Morrison only, with minimal text. Recommended if you can find this second hand and need to have yet another photo collection on Morrison.

QUIZBOOKS AND QUOTEBOOKS

Doe, Andrew. *The Doors: In Their Own Words*. New York: Putnam Publishing Group, 1991. 96 pages. Approximately 100 black-and-white photographs, covering every page.

A fun rehash of old Doors' quotes. Although not as comprehensive as similar books on other groups (e.g., The Beatles and The Who), followers of the band will want to read statements taken out of context, such as: Robby Krieger—"`Touch Me' was originally `Hit Me,' but Jim said, `No way am I going to sing those lyrics'"; Ray Manzarek—"America hasn't produced anybody heavy in rock `n' roll as far as I'm concerned. Maybe Bob Dylan..."; John Densmore—"The whole first album was very quick—two weeks—because we had worked it up in the clubs"; and Jim Morrison—"The most loving parents and relatives commit murder with smiles on their faces."

RELATED WORKS

Huxley, Aldous. *The Doors of Perception & Heaven and Hell*. San Bernardino: Borgo Press, 1990. 185 pages.

As legend has it, this is the book that inspired Jim Morrison and keyboardist Ray Manzarek to name their group The Doors. The exact line in question has been a subject for debate, though it must be one of these two: "There are things that are known and things that are unknown; in between are doors" (from William Blake's poem "The Doors: Open and Closed," as quoted in Huxley's work) and "all the other chemical Doors in the Wall are labelled Dope...." Huxley's book is actually the author's study of consciousness expansion through mescaline, and is only of interest for the curious-minded and the intellectual substance abuser. Written in dense British, the text will probably soar over the heads of most young readers.

WRITTEN WORKS

Morrison, Jim. *The American Night: The Lost Writings of Jim Morrison Volume 2*. New York: Villard Books, 1990. 211 pages. Approximately 50 black-and-white photos of Morrison's original scrawl throughout. Index of First Lines.

More poetry from the Lizard King, covering life, sex, death, and religion, as well as some lyrics from Doors' songs. A continuation of *Wilderness* (see below) and including "An American Prayer" (also the name of a Morrison/Doors' album) and Morrison's Paris Journal, written during his final days. "The writing is uneven, ranging from clichéd, amateurish pieces to poetic works abounding with sensual or surrealistic imagery"—*School Library Journal*.

Morrison, Jim. *The Lords and The New Creatures, Poems*. New York: Simon & Schuster, Inc., 1971. 140 pages.

Originally published in 1969, this is the first mass-released collection of poems (in two sections) by the charismatic lead singer of The Doors. Many are simply brief (and bleak) reflections or loosely strung images on subjects such as drugs, movies, free love, inner torment, etc. The poems tend to be a bit sparse (often five to ten words on a page), but many are graphic and effective. Staple rock poetry.

Morrison, Jim. *Wilderness: The Lost Writings of Jim Morrison Volume 1*. New York: Vintage Books (division of Random House), 1988. Approximately 50 black-and-white photographs of Morrison's original scrawl throughout. 216 pages. Index of First Lines.

An assortment of poems and diaries penned by Morrison in various states of mind. For better or worse, it is not too difficult to imagine certain fresh pieces as Doors' lyrics. A second volume of "lost" writings was also mysteriously found and compiled in *American Night* (see above). Would Morrison himself have appreciated his rough works being carved up and published in such a commercial manner? Probably, although it is safe to assume he would have preferred that the compilations be placed in "poetry" sections (with Rimbaud, Frost, Longfellow, et. al.) and not alongside other rock publications.

No author. *The Doors Illustrated Lyrics 1965-1971*. London: Omnibus Press (division of Book Sales Limited), 1992. 80 pages. Approximately 40 black-and-white photographs throughout.

This book contains the lyrics to 59 some-odd original Doors songs, which comprise material from the six band albums released prior to Jim Morrison's death. The photos aren't bad, but they don't compare with those in Sugerman's work (see below). As in that title, there isn't a song index here either. It's always fun to read The Doors' songs (especially in the case of "Soul Kitchen," in which the words get drowned out), since you suddenly realize you've been singing the wrong lyrics for the past two decades. Not necessary if you own Sugerman's work.

Sugerman, Danny (Introduction). *The Doors Complete Illustrated Lyrics*. New York: Sterling, 1991. 224 pages. Approximately 100 color and black-and-white illustrations throughout.

A collection of lyrics by Morrison and company, with smatterings of journalistic prose throughout. The paperback edition of the book is published by Delta, under the slightly different title *The Doors Complete Lyrics*. The book is confusedly arranged in several parts and subdivisions, and not A to Z by song title. If you're into The Doors and want to croon along to the tunes while looking at some fine illustrative material, this is the book to get. "...giggle at the lyrics, snort and groan at the rock-criticese, ogle the pictures of Morrison's camera-loving puss, but by all means get this book for your library's contingent of one of rock's biggest cults"—*Booklist*.

OTHER TITLES OF INTEREST

John, Mike. *Jim Morrison and the Doors: An Unauthorized Book*. New York: Grosset & Dunlap, 1969.

Lisciandro, Frank. *Jim Morrison: Rattlesnakes, Whistles and Castanets*. No city: STMS, 1991.

Morrison, Jim, *American Prayer*. No city: Zeppelin Publishing, 1983.

Morrison, Jim. *Eyes: Poetry of Jim Morrison 1967-1971*. No city: Zeppelin Publishing, 1986.

Morrison, Jim. *IBM Oil: Asylum in a Danish Embassy Behind the Iron Curtain*. No city: Zeppelin Publishing, 1985.

Morrison, Jim. *Light My Fire*. No city: Zeppelin Publishing, 1978.

Ruhlmann, William. *The Doors*. New York: Smithmark (Penguin USA), 1991.

THE DRIFTERS

CRITICAL/ANALYTICAL COMMENTARY

Millar, Bill. *The Drifters: The Rise and Fall of the Black Vocal Group*. London: Studio Vista, 1971. 112 pages. Approximately 50 black-and-white photographs throughout. Further Readings. Notes. Appendix I: The Drifters' Lead Singers. Appendix 2: The Drifters' Hit Records 1953-70.

Clearly, this is not a biography of The Drifters, but a study of the group's development and their influence on popular music. Millar supplies a nutshell history of gospel, rhythm and blues, and black singing groups, which is followed by text about The Drifters' career and that of some of their contemporaries, such as The Clovers, The Inkspots, and The Coasters. Difficult to penetrate—in spite of its diminutive 112 pages—this book doesn't provide enough excitement about the players to make one overlook the fact that it's a quarter of a century old.

OTHER TITLES OF INTEREST

Allan, Tony. *Save the Last Dance for Me: The Musical Legacy of the Drifters, 1953-1992*. Ann Arbor, MI: Popular Culture Ink, 1993.

DURAN DURAN

BIOGRAPHIES

Goldstein, Toby. *Duran Duran*. New York: Ballantine, 1984. 150 pages. One glossy sixteen-page black-and-white photo insert. Appendixes: Duran Devotions; Did You Know...One Hundred Semi-Secrets; Some Things Duran Duran Told the Press. U.S. Discography, Videography, Fan Club Information.

A book of morsels for the younger fan. Author Goldstein provides some interesting background details not mentioned in other publications. For example, Hazel O'Connor is credited for having rescued the band from obscurity, by selecting them as her opening act. Other pieces of trivia include: Bowie, The Doors, and Chopin appear on Simon Le Bon's list of favorites; John Taylor is a Sean Connery 007 fan; and Le Bon appeared in TV commercials as a youth. Basic.

FANZINES AND FAN CLUBS

Carnival: The Duran Trade Magazine. c/o Kimberly Blessing, 930 Sassafras Circle, West Chester, PA 19382.

Sixteen-page packet, recommended by Duran Duran's management, that contains merchandise, collectibles, concert happenings, e-mail messages culled from the Internet, and more. Claims to maintain the largest database of Duran Duran discographical information, which is published annually. Quarterly issues are sold separately (no subscriptions) for prices ranging from $3-$5 in the U.S. and $4-$6 elsewhere (in U.S. currency only).

the ICON. P.O. Box 158, Allen Park, MI 48101-0158.

Large, glossy 38-page Duran Duran fanzine containing black-and-white photos, fans' letters and comments, band diaries (their comings and goings), album reviews, classifieds, contests, and more. The cost in the U.S. is $8 per issue or $30 per year; Canada/Mexico $9 per issue or $34.50 per year; U.K. and Europe $10 per issue or $38 per year.

PICTORIALS

Flans, Robyn. *Inside Duran Duran*. Cresskill: Sharon Starbook, 1984. 64 pages. Approximately 50 color and black-and-white illustrations throughout. Discography.

This photo book opens with a 1984 L.A. press conference, in which the five boys (all of whom are unrelated, though three are coincidentally named Taylor) are cheekily compared with The Beatles and their first U.S. interviews. How tacky can you get? The members of the band have obvious teen glamour, but the photos suffer from being blurry and/or out of focus. Stay outside.

No author. *Duran Duran: In Their Own Words*. London, England: Omnibus Press (division of Book Sales Limited), 1983. 34 pages. Approximately 30 full-page color photographs. Comes with a pull-out color poster.

Oddball entry in Omnibus' "in their own words" series, in that it has shrunken the quotes themselves to miniscule size and has cornered them in the margins (often on sides not facing the reader). Thus the emphasis is on the illustrative matter, which makes the boys look like The Bay City Rollers of the 1980's. As John Taylor ironically comments: "We seem to be getting stuck with this new romantic/nancy boy image." Don't ruin your vision squinting at the quotes.

TOURBOOKS

Kamin, Philip and Goddard, Peter. *Duran Duran Live*. Agincourt, Ontario (Canada): Metheun, 1984. 96 pages. Approximately 75 color and black-and-white photographs throughout.

The Kamin and Goddard photo/writing team go on the road again, this time to cover Duran Duran in the early 1980's. The copy has little to do with their live performances; the photos are not dated or captioned, so we have no idea which shows we are looking at. Fans may be able to overlook these shortcomings because the pictures capture the band members in action up-close.

O'Regan, Denis (photographer). *Duran Duran: Sing Blue Silver*. Milwaukee, WI: Hal Leonard, 1984. 80 pages. Approximately 100 color illustrations, covering every page; approximately 30 black-and-white photographs throughout. Comes with a pull-out poster.

Visual documentation of Duran Duran's enormous 1984 international tour, which spanned Australia, Great Britain, Japan, and North America. There is no captioning to accompany O'Regan's photos, although Roger Taylor contributes the back ad copy. The color photos are lively and energetic; the black-and-whites are incongruous, but still fun. In one picture, both Simon Le Bon and Nick Rhodes sit in a limo, each reading his own copy of Roman Polanski's autobiography. Optional for fans.

YOUNG ADULT

Martin, Susan. *Duran Duran*. New York: Julian Messner, 1984. 64 pages. Approximately 60 black-and-white photographs, covering nearly every page. How to Get in Touch with Duran Duran. Discography. Videography.

The band is in the spotlight at a time when they had three platinum albums and two Grammys under their belts. Three pages are devoted to the private lives of each of the five stars. The book supplies useful explanations of equipment (the WASP synthesizer) and is generously filled with photos. Some of the captions inaccurately state photo content and prove that the author wasn't at the events being described. Otherwise worthwhile.

OTHER TITLES OF INTEREST
Garrett, De Graff. *Duran Duran: The Book of Words*. Milwaukee, WI: Hal Leonard, 1984.
Vogrin. *Duran Duran Trivia Quiz*. Woodstock, NY: Hal Leonard, 1985

IAN DURY

RELATED WORKS

Dury, Ian; Paulin, Tom; and Dubes, Fanny (editors). *Hard Lines: Volumes 1, 2, 3*. London: Faber and Faber, circa 1983 (volume 1), 1985 (volume 2), 1987 (volume 3). Approximately 80 pages each.

British poetry selected by Dury, Paulin, and Dubes. Contributors among the three separate volumes include Pete Townshend, Alan

Beasdale, Shula Chiat, Frances Jessup, Ros Barber, and many others. The three volumes are marginal finds for Dury's fans, but may be of interest to readers of contemporary poetry.

BOB DYLAN

BIOGRAPHIES

Heylin, Clinton. *Bob Dylan Behind the Shades: A Biography*. New York: Summit Books (Simon & Schuster), 1991. 512 pages. One eight-page black-and-white photo insert. Notes. Dramatis Personae. Selected Bibliography. Sessionography 1961-1991. Index.

An authentic oral biography, expertly executed by Heylin (the cofounder of Wanted Man, "the British information office dedicated to Dylan"). Each chapter has a summary of events, followed by thousands of quotes by people "who were there" and broken up with explanatory passages. Heylin edited many of the quotes for ramblings, and his writings often smooth out clear-cut errors from the speakers. In one instance he gently points out that the memory of Echo Helstrom was "faulty" in regard to the process of how Dylan changed his name. The list of speakers is a Dylan who's who: Eric Von Schmidt, Robbie Robertson, Al Kooper, George Harrison, Joan Baez, Allen Ginsberg, etc. The Dramatis Personae section is a good supplement, although the couple of lines for each player only relates to Dylan. A good browse for Dylanographers.

Ribakove, Sy and Ribakove, Barbara. *Folk-Rock: The Bob Dylan Story*. New York: Dell Publishing Co., 1966. 128 pages. One 16-page black-and-white photo insert.

One of the first mass-released bios of Bob Dylan, this book is kind of humorous 30 years later. The authors pretty much swallowed up every Dylan statement as truth, even though it's now common knowledge he lied and embellished in nearly every interview. Dylan himself could not have been terribly happy with this book—especially the title, since he loathed the phrase "folk-rock." For those who must have everything.

Rowley, Chris. *Blood on the Tracks: The Story of Bob Dylan*. London/New York: Proteus, 1984. 160 pages. One eight-page glossy insert with both black-and-white and color photos. Discography.

This brief history of Dylan is clumsily written and really doesn't go anywhere that other Dylan bios haven't gone before. You don't find out anything about the man or the music here, although there is plenty slipped in about bootlegs. The last two chapters breeze through the late 1970's and early 80's, as if *Renaldo & Clara* is all that occurred in that time. The cover photo is awful.

Scaduto, Anthony. *Bob Dylan: An Intimate Biography*. New York: Signet (New American Library), 1971. 352 pages. One eight-page black-and-white photo insert. Discography (compiled by Sandy Gant). Index.

Young Dylan is pictured in this biography as, on the one hand, a "chubby-faced boy," a bullshit artist extraordinaire (he claimed to have been a hobo from Mexico, an orphan, a friend of Woody Guthrie's before he met the man, etc.), a rebellious slob, a hero worshipper (Woody and James Dean), an incredible egotist and, on the other, as a figure of incredible determination, originality, lyrical genius, and mythical vision. Most of the telling is fascinating, although sometimes the quotes (from inner circle people such as John Hammond, Joan Baez, and an old girlfriend from Minnesota named Echo) repeat or contradict themselves. A very early oral biography, and one that continues to be footnoted by researchers and gobbled up by fans. "Until Dylan writes his own story, this will be the one to read"—*Creem*.

Shelton, Robert. *No Direction Home: The Life and Music of Bob Dylan*. New York: Beech Tree Books (Morrow), 1986. 580 pages. Two eight-page black-and-white photo inserts. Select Bibliography. Song Index. Discography. Index.

Shelton, the *New York Times* folk critic in the 1960's and an old supporter and buddy of Dylan, tries to figure out Dylan where others fell short. Ninety percent of the book is on the early years—and fans wanting a comprehensive perspective will be disappointed. Shelton takes the space to briefly review every song on several Dylan albums, but there is no explanation as to whether these are his original or current views (or how they compare). Though the firsthand quotes and descriptions of the period are far more detailed than in Scaduto's bio (above), we are kept much further from the man's persona than in the former work. Useful for those tracing 1960's Dylan.

Spitz, Bob. *Dylan: A Biography*. New York: McGraw-Hill, 1989. 640 pages. Two eight-page glossy black-and-white photo inserts. Discography. Index.

A hefty bio that is unbalanced in coverage—nearly 450 pages on Dylan up through 1975 and less than one hundred covering the subsequent years through 1989. There is virtually nothing about the 1980's. And even in the early years there are essential details missing. Where, for example, is the description of Dylan's harmonica gig with Harry Belafonte? The writing and tone are monotonous and, sometimes, insulting for no reason whatsoever. He states "nothing exceptional is produced in folk music," and has caustic section titles (e.g., "That Weird Kid," "The Twerp," "Rolling Blunder") that will no doubt upset Dylan fans. Yuck. "Spitz covers no new ground here..." —*Publishers Weekly*.

CHRONOLOGIES

Heylin, Clinton. *Bob Dylan: Stolen Moments*. Romford, Essex (England): Wanted Man Publications. 420 pages. 50 black-and-white photos. Appendices: the Dylan acetates (1962-1971); Dylan on film; songs omitted from *Lyrics 1962-1985*; Dylan compositions; the missing audience recordings. Song Index.

Attractive chronology (and, to some extent, recording guide) on everything Dylan, including both personal events and dates for recordings, releases, and tours. The further readings, mistakenly buried in the introduction, are confusedly arranged and leave out vital bibliographic information. Not quite the "ultimate reference book" it claims to be (it could use much more than a simple song index), this is a valuable work nonetheless because of its completeness and easy access to information.

CRITICAL/ANALYTICAL COMMENTARY

Anderson, Dennis. *The Hollow Horn: Bob Dylan's Reception in the United States and Germany.* Munich (Germany): The Hobo Press, 1981. 280 pages. Notes. Works Consulted.

A typewritten study of Dylan criticism, with specific emphasis on the reaction to Dylan's first tour of Germany in 1978. The author would have benefited from the hand of an American editor; it reads as if written by someone unfamiliar with the English language. Narrow and unfocused.

Bauldie, John. *Bob Dylan & Desire.* Bury, Lancashire (England): Wanted Man, 1984. 58 pages.

Another in an ongoing series Wanted Man, from the British Dylan information service. This time around Bauldie himself critiques the classic *Desire* LP. Most of the text attempts to place the songs in a literal story-telling scenario, which would have been a marvelous idea had it been executed with a steadier hand. Bauldie's writing falters into redundancy and rambling; he skips over some of the tracks that deserve greater attention (e.g., "Mozambique" and "Hurricane"). Shameful.

Bowden, Betsy. *Performed Literature: Words and Music by Bob Dylan.* Bloomington: Indiana University Press, 1982. 240 pages. Appendix A: Texts and Recording Information for Performances Discussed. Appendix B: Dylan's Albums, Arranged by Date of Release. Appendix C: Practical Suggestions for Analysis of Performance. Notes. Bibliography. Index.

This work began as Bowden's English dissertation at the University of California at Berkeley. Not too stodgy or academic (though it isn't illustrated), this book is actually along the lines of some of Paul Williams' theses (see below); Bowden considers Dylan an "oral performer" in the grand sense, in that he is able to manipulate words and music to suit his mood and creative intention. For the billionth time, we can read about Dylan's "enigmatic use of pronouns"—a subject treated most conclusively in Day's work (below). Analytical and probing.

Day, Aidan. *Escaping on the Run.* Bury, Lancashire (England): Wanted Man, 1984. 36 pages. Index.

Delivered as an undergraduate lecture at the West London Institute of Higher Education,

this pamphlet—which was edited by Dylanographer John Bauldie—is full of complex insights into Dylan's albums. If you have Day's *Jokerman* (see below), there is no need for this work; Day developed and expanded his thesis for the later book, which is far more interesting.

Day, Aidan. *Jokerman: Reading the Lyrics of Bob Dylan.* Oxford, England: Basil Blackwell, 1988. 196 pages. Appendix (Dylan Chronology). Index.

This study analyzes selected Dylan works much the same way a professor of literature might critique Chaucer or Coleridge. Day's scope is only songs dealing with identity: the role of "I," "he," "she," and "they" in songs such as "Mr. Tambourine Man," "Isis," "The Ballad of a Thin Man," and a few others. *Q* magazine said it combines "sensitivity to poetry with an obvious love for the songs." Despite its affect, this book will be welcomed by those who want to see Dylan writings taken as serious poetry.

Dorman, James E. *Recorded Dylan: A Critical Review and Discography.* Pinedale, CA: Soma Press, 1982. 124 pages. Approximately five pen-and-ink drawings throughout. Selected Bibliography.

Ugly-looking and flimsy assessment of Dylan's work. Dorman, whose list of professions includes navy journalist, stock boy, cook, receiving clerk, and carhop, among others, doesn't analyze the music as much as he spews out his convoluted opinions. Another one from the heart that fails to satisfy.

Gray, Michael. *Song & Dance Man: The Art of Bob Dylan.* New York: St. Martin's Press, 1981. 240 pages. One hundred black-and-white and color illustrations scattered throughout. Index. (First published in Great Britain in 1972 by Hart-Davis, MacGibbon Limited.)

When first released, this book was a groundbreaking investigation into the significance and meanings behind Dylan's work and its literary and musical traditions. Now, two decades later, the competition for Dylan critiquing is fierce; many other writers have since dug deeper and have more structured theses (e.g., Aidan Day) than Gray. In fact, one may get frustrated with his unsubstantiated dismissiveness about certain classic tracks. ("Hurricane," for example, is demeaned as having "weak" lyrics compared to the music). At the time Robert Shelton, then with *The New York Times*, credited Gray for "showing just how important and complex an artist Dylan is...."

Hampton, Wayne. *Guerilla Minstrels: John Lennon, Joe Hill, Woody Guthrie and Bob Dylan.*

See: Lennon, John: Critical/Analytical Commentary.

Herdman, John. *Voice without Restraint: Bob Dylan's Lyrics and Their Background.* New York: Delilah Communications Limited, 1982. 164 pages. Notes. Selected Bibliography. Index.

Lucid analysis of Dylan's lyrics (up through the *Saved* LP) that, unlike some other works, does not take every quote from Dylan about his music literally. Author John Herdman does not leap to the conclusion that all song characters represent Dylan himself, and does not think it relevant to decide whether Mr. Jones in "Ballad of a Thin Man" is a newspaper reporter, a representative of the unhip world, a homosexual, or Dylan himself. (The point is, according to Herdman, he's someone who is vulnerable, exposed, and alone.) Refreshingly straightforward.

Karpel, Craig. *The Tarantula in Me: A Review of a Title.* San Francisco: Klonh, 1973. Unpaginated (approximately 36 pages). Approximately 20 black-and-white photocopies of black-and-white photos. Appendix: "Tarantella" music sheet.

Meaningless investigations into the symbolism and background of Bob Dylan's "novel" *Tarantula* (see Written Works, below). That is to say, not the work itself, but on the *title*—which strikes this reviewer as daft, since plainly the name was a throwaway. The writer truly loses his grip by analyzing different species of tarantula, and then manipulating the word itself to relate to ancient folklore and dance (e.g., the Italian ritual dance the "Tarantella"). Karpel ends by proposing why Dylan really wanted to suppress the book's publication, oblivious to the fact that it may have been because he realized it just wasn't very good.

McGregor, Craig. Introductory Foreword by Nat Hentoff. *Bob Dylan: The Early Years: A Retrospective.* New York: Da Capo, 1990.

410 pages. About a dozen black-and-white photos of album covers.

Exceptional collection of American essays, editorials, and news articles spanning 1962-1971. Pieces come from Robert Shelton, Sidney Fields, Studs Terkel, Jules Siegel, Robert Christgau, Ralph J. Gleason, and others. Hentoff's foreword includes a hilarious telling of Dylan's "rewrite" of his *Playboy* interview. Of key importance: the editorials from *Sing Out!*, in which the critics (Irwin Silber, for one) vent their rage or support for Dylan's switch to electric. Originally published by William Morrow & Company in 1972 as *Bob Dylan: A Retrospective.*

Mellers, Wilfrid. *A Darker Shade of Pale: A Backdrop to Bob Dylan.* New York: Oxford University Press, 1985. 260 pages. Two eight-page black-and-white photo inserts. Discography. Bibliography. Index. (First published in England in 1984 by Faber and Faber Limited.)

The first half of this backdrop links American folk music with its cultural heritage and history. The second half—the part Dylan fans will dive for (dubbed "Freedom, Belief and Responsibility")—goes through high points of the Dylan catalog and relates them to the American folk tradition, blues, gospel, and rock and roll. The "darker shade of pale," perhaps a reference to the Procol Harem song "A Whiter Shade of Pale," is the very mix of black-and-white musical inspiration in Dylan's work. Mellers attests that "writing words about music is a hazardous occupation"—but he does it much better than most academics.

Percival, Dave. *The Dust of Rumour.* London: X-Asity, 1985. 160 pages.

It's difficult to get past the amateurishness of this collection of British criticism on Dylan spanning 1964 to 1981. To begin with, the typing (and it *is* typed, not typeset) is atrocious— it's single-spaced and full of typos and missing words; even by self-publishing standards it's a disaster. The author makes good selections from the British press, including the *Guardian,* the *South Londoner,* and the *Daily Mirror,* but the lack of any editorial guidance shreds this potentially valuable work to ribbons. Go to the microfiche instead.

Percival, Dave. *Just a Personal Tendency.* London: X-Asity, undated (circa 1985). 168 pages. Several original pen-and-ink drawings by Dave Hoser.

Self-published critique of Dylan's *Empire Burlesque* LP (thankfully put together a bit better than *The Dust of Rumour,* see above), consisting mostly of Percival's random impressions of the individual songs, the album cover, the lyrics, the liner notes, etc. He also digresses somewhat to respond to Dylan's critics. For diehards of mid-1980's Dylan only.

Scobie, Stephen. *Alias Bob Dylan.* Alberta: Red Deer College Press, 1991. 192 pages. Notes. Works Cited.

An analysis of "alias" imagery in Dylan's work and private life, as symbolized by masks, ghosts, and shadows. To be certain, Dylan is constantly hiding his true self, and deliberately changes his sound, musical technique, and voice on creative impulse. It should be noted that Dylan's character's name in *Pat Garrett and Billy the Kid* is Alias. This book overlaps to some degree with Aidan Day's *Jokerman* (see above) and lacks the tight focus of the earlier publication. The text here varies from straight history, to rock criticese, to personal observation, to analytical commentary without a clear pattern holding anything together.

Thomson, Elizabeth and Gutman, David (editors). *The Dylan Companion.* New York: Delta (Bantam Doubleday Dell), 1990. Selective Bibliography. Discography. Index. (First published in London by Macmillan Limited.)

"A collection of essential writing about Bob Dylan" that includes nearly 50 short essays from a variety of sources. Familiar Dylan chroniclers Robert Shelton and Larry Sloman are here, but so are Bruce Springsteen (his oft-quoted Rock and Roll Hall of Fame speech), Joan Baez (a rather ugly image of a nose-picking Dylan excerpted from her book *And a Voice to Sing With*), Richard Williams (an on-target *New York Times* review of the *Oh Mercy* LP), and Pauline Kael (a scathing *New Yorker* review of the film *Renaldo & Clara:* "...even those who idolised him in the Sixties may gag a little"—ouch!). The mix of personages makes this a good addition to any Dylan library.

Williams, Paul. *Performing Artist: The Music of Bob Dylan: The Middle Years: 1974-1986.* Novato (CA) and Lancaster (PA): Underwood-Miller, 1990. 340 pages. One 12-page glossy black-and-white photo insert. Discography. Bibliography. Index.

The earlier volume (1960-1973, see below) achieved such success that this title was afforded some aesthetic improvements (e.g., the quality of the paper stock and the glossy photo insert). Williams picks up from where he left off in volume one (see below), touting that the Dylan of the 1970's and 80's was every bit as good as the one from the 1960's. He makes a case in point by providing a fascinating description of the "sound" and "unity of color" of the *Desire* LP (according to Allen Ginsberg, some songs hearken back to Hebraic chants). Williams' praise for the cinematic Dylan (the trashed *Renaldo and Clara*) and his Catholic phase will only be accepted by the stalwart fan. Still, this book ranks among the best. Look for the "late years"—in 2,001?

Williams, Paul. *Performing Artist: The Music of Bob Dylan: Volume One: 1960-1973.* Novato (CA) and Lancaster (PA): Underwood-Miller, 1990. 316 pages. One black-and-white photograph beginning each chapter. Discography. Bibliography. Index.

This is volume one of Williams' ongoing treatment of Dylan, covering the early years only. The author's approach is to call Dylan a performing artist rather than a poet or musician; his songs, like an artist's renderings (Picasso's *Guitar Player* was the example used) develop and change over the years with each new rendering. Williams, editor of *Crawdaddy!*, has the luxury of reflecting on other Dylan chroniclers (Shelton, Scaduto), and takes a stab at solving some of the Dylan discrepancies (he doesn't believe, as Dylan told Shelton, that he was "ill as a teenager"). Among the many lauds was *Library Journal:* "...an important addition to the voluminous analysis of Dylan."

DISCOGRAPHIES, RECORDING GUIDES, AND COLLECTIBLES

Begerau, Ernst-Otto. *Every Grain of Sand.* London/Munich/Chicago: Self-published, 1988. 96 pages.

Pamphlet for the most ardent tape collector and trader only, listing songs and albums with recording dates and running times. You know you're in trouble when the author admits in the introduction that his work contains "hundreds of errors"—and the first is on the same page (Michael Krogsgaard is spelled "Kroogsgard"). Don't say I didn't warn you.

Cable, Paul *Bob Dylan: His Unreleased Recordings.* New York: Schirmer (Macmillan), 1978. One half dozen black-and-white photographs throughout. Numerous recording tables. Index.

A listener and collector's guide to Dylan's unreleased recordings and bootlegs. Cable does a thorough job tracking down the history of these rare recordings and separating the good from the bad, though this book is now decades out of date. The author teeters uncomfortably between representing the hardened collector who needs everything and the credible researcher disapproving of those who do go overboard. For example, on Dylan's Bangladesh recordings he writes: "...this is one area where bootlegging really is somewhat unethical." Then why write this book?

Dunn, Tim. *I Just Write 'Em As They Come.* Painesville: NOT-A-CES, 1990. 256 pages.

Catalog of Dylan's songs, writings, and films in an easy-to-use A to Z format, with several useful discographies as appendixes: promotion/radio/test pressings; guest appearances, concert tapeography; filmography; Dylan co-writers; Dylan "almost weres" and "wish-it-were-sos," etc. Dunn repeats a good deal of information found in other works (from Clinton Heylin and Michael Krogsgaard), but he deserves high praise for the pains he took in crediting them.

Hoggard, Stuart and Shields, Jim. *Bob Dylan: An Illustrated Record.* No city (United Kingdom): Transmedia Express, 1978. 132 pages. Approximately 40 black-and-white photographs throughout. Bibliography. Index.

A much-sought after recording guide that, on the whole, is a disappointment. The first thing one notices is that 40 some-odd reproductions of album covers don't constitute an "illustrated" work (at least nothing to brag about in the title). Recordings are arranged chronologically, and include information such as producer, label, songs, and a brief (one paragraph) synopsis. Not worth the effort.

Krogsgaard, Michael. *Positively Bob Dylan: A Thirty-Year Discography, Concert & Recording Session Guide, 1960-1991.* Ann Arbor: Popular Culture, Inc., 1991. 500 pages. 50 black-and-white photographs. Index to Recorded Songs & Interviews; Index to Songs on Records and in Films; Index on Musicians; Chronological Index to Dylan Singles; Alphabetical Index to Dylan Singles; Index to Dylan Albums; Comprehensive Index to Commercially Released Recordings; Venue Index to Recorded Concert Performances; Geographic Index to Recorded Concert Performances; Label and Catalog Number Index; Index to Studio Sessions; Index to Recorded Radio and Television Broadcasts; Index to Recorded Interviews; Index to Recorded Press Conferences.

This massive discography and miscellany has undergone numerous revisions over the years, and has become a classic in the "rock and roll reference series" from Popular Culture Ink. The chronological listing of recording sessions is easy to follow, and the indexes package the information in every way imaginable. The photos and design are blah, but no one will care. At least the type is *large*. A staple on the Dylan collector's shelf. A revised and updated edition of *Master of the Tracks: The Bob Dylan Reference Book of Recording*, published in 1988 in Denmark by the Scandinavian Institute for Rock-Research. First introduced in 1981 by the Institute as *Twenty Years of Recording: The Bob Dylan Reference Book.*

Nogowski, John. *Bob Dylan: A Descriptive, Critical Discography and Filmography, 1961-1993.* Jefferson, NC: McFarland & Company, Inc., Publishers. 208 pages. Books by and about Dylan. Index.

Nogowski mixes discographical detail with consumer reviews in this unsteady recording guide. Sections include: albums; singles and collaborations with other artists; bootlegs; film and television; and radio. Each album entry breaks down into information on producer, where recorded, release date, chart position, outtakes, singles, the cover, liner notes, and then brief remarks on each song, complete with letter grades. Thirty plus years later, is it really productive to give Dylan's "Baby, Let Me Follow You Down" a C+? High school stuff.

Riley, Tim. *Hard Rain: A Dylan Commentary*. New York: Alfred A. Knopf, 1992. 358 pages. Discography. Index.

Riley scurries to Dylan's defense on a number of issues, ranging from the limitations of labeling him a nasal vocalist; to overgeneralizations about his being merely a Woody Guthrie clone; and to Joan Baez's assertion that his music conveys only "vagaries." Divided in ten sections—each of which groups together a bunch of Dylan records and tours—Riley probes the subtexts of Dylan's work with more intelligence than in his commentary on The Beatles (see Beatles, The: Critical/Analytical Commentary). However, readers will be annoyed by excessive typos and the book's lack of illustrative matter. "Riley reminds us how strong his [Dylan's] influence has been..."—*Booklist*.

Townsend, Phill. *Strangers and Prophets: The CD Bootlegs of Bob Dylan Volume I*. West Midlands, England: Next 2 Last Publications, 1992. 116 pages. One hundred photos of CDs, interiors, and posters. Matrix/Catalogue Numbers.

Limited edition catalog of CD bootlegs for the collector. Each bootleg listing takes up a page, and identifies its label, songs included, description of the cover and disk, disk running time, and performance listings (when known). A separate volume of appendices contains chronological notes on the recordings of the bootlegs, as well as indexes by: code, discs by title, sources, songs, and a brief bibliography. Not a bad package; if you have this, you'll need Volume II below.

Townsend, Phill. *Strangers and Prophets: The CD Bootlegs of Bob Dylan Volume II*. West Midlands, England: Next 2 Last Publications, 1994. 116 pages. Approximately one hundred photos of CD covers, disks and Dylan himself. Variants, Rarities, and Collectibles.

In the two years since Volume One (above) was issued, hundreds of new boots were released (two a week, according to the author)—and this book successfully picks up from where the first left off. This time around the CD reproductions are of much higher quality; you can see the fine details on the CDs themselves. As in the earlier catalog, the books are numbered. Volume III probably to come soon.

Wilson, Keith. *Bob Dylan: A Listing*. Toronto, Ontario (Canada): Bauer/Wilson, undated. Unpaginated (approximately 30 pages).

Typewritten list of Wilson's Dylan collection, including LPs, singles, EPs, bootlegs, contributions to others' records, etc. Don't bother.

DYLANEUTICS

Pickering, Stephen (alias Chofetz Chaim Ben-Avraham). *Bob Dylan Approximately: A Midrash*. New York: David McKay Company, Inc., 1975. 204 pages. Approximately 50 black-and-white photographs throughout, as well as designs of the Hebrew alphabet; color in the preliminary pages only.

This "portrait of the Jewish poet in search of God" is an oddity, but it's a sure purchase for Dylan worshippers. Pickering traces Dylan's 1975 tour with The Band through cities such as Chicago, Philadelphia, St. Louis, Los Angeles, etc. He relates everything Dylan does to Jewish texts and prayers, sometimes pausing to quote a rabbi "of blessed memory." Pickering eschews the fact that Dylan at times had shed aspects of his Judaism (e.g., changing his name from Zimmerman) and distorts many of Dylan's words for his fancy. This quirky book calls itself a *Midrash* (the collective of Jewish commentary) and touches on some aspects of the *Kabbalah* (the Jewish book of mysticism), but it's not worth having to run out and buy a Hebrew dictionary.

Thompson, Toby. *Positively Main Street: An Unorthodox View of Bob Dylan*. London: New English Library (NEL), 1972. 160 pages.

Memoir from Dylan fanatic Thompson telling of his visit to Dylan's roots in Hibbing, MN. The author writes with such childish enthusiasm it's almost embarrassing; he seems shocked to find that young Dylan was just an ordinary shy kid who had a baby sitter, didn't cut class in school, and was in a rock band. Thompson did manage to talk to the high school principal, Dylan's uncle, a mechanic, and many others, and have a certain rapport with Echo (Dylan's childhood sweetheart), but his reporting skills leave much to be desired. Thompson seems to have taken photos of his mecca, but, unfortunately, none of these are included in this edition. Anyone care to try to trek through the Pennsylvania Turnpike to search for Roger Maris' (another Hibbingite) roots? First published in the United States in 1971 by Howard McCann & Geoghegan, Inc.

Williams, Don. *Bob Dylan: The Man, The Music, The Message*. Old Tappan, NJ: Fleming H. Revell & Company, 1985. 160 pages. Approximately 20 black-and-white photographs throughout. Bibliography.

In 1979 it became public that Dylan had "accepted Christ" and was preaching his message. Suddenly, in the mid-1980's, Dylan released *Infidels*, and many felt his old disillusionments had returned to replace his newfound optimistic spiritual outlook. Williams, a Presbyterian pastor, is really just another fan as he digs for clues to prove that Dylan had not abandoned his faith. He writes that the generalizations about *Infidels* are "vastly oversimplified and one-sided," which may or may no be true—but isn't it up to Dylan himself to defend his faith (whatever it may be)? Really stretching it.

Williams, Paul. *Dylan—What Happened?*. South Bend, IN and Glen Ellen, CA: and books/Entwhistle Books, 1980. 128 pages. One 16-page black-and-white photo insert. Recommended Reading.

Another kick for Dylan on his quest for knowledge and spiritual fulfillment: Christianity. Back in 1979 Dylan became a born again Christian, and many of his recordings at the time (namely *The Slow Train Coming*) and various live performances reflected this newfound faith. In this work, Williams is quick to defend and support the inspirational, albeit fickle, musical legend: "He [Dylan] lets us in on his private relationship with the Lord." The strength of this work is in Williams' personal interpretations of Dylan's music; the drawback is that much of the significance here ended with the dissipation of Dylan's interest in Christianity in 1982.

FAN CLUBS, FANZINES, AND CATALOGS

My Back Pages: The Bob Dylan Bookshelf. P.O. Box 2 (North P.D.O.). Manchester, M8 7BL, England.

Monthly listings of Dylan-related books, magazines, fanzines, tour programs, and a few titles on other musicians. Orders must be prepaid, either in pounds sterling or U.S. dollars. Send a self-addressed stamped envelope for a reply to a query.

On the Tracks: The Unauthorized Bob Dylan Magazine. Rolling Tomes Inc., P.O. Box 1943, Grand Junction, CO 81502.

From Rolling Tome Inc.—the people who publish *Rolling Tomes—The Bob Dylan Collectors' Service* and *Series of Dreams* (see below for both)—and formerly *Isis* (no longer in print), comes this quarterly magazine, which is said to have the highest circulation of any Dylan magazine. In its 60 pages readers will find glossy color and black-and-white photographs, interviews with Dylan, profiles of related rock and folk stars, concert information, CD reviews, and much more. Among the Dylan literati featured are Paul Williams, Stephen Scobie, John Darcy, and Michael Krogsgaard. The cost of subscription is $24.95 U.S.; $27 Canada and Mexico; and $40 Europe. The cost per issue is $8.50.

Rolling Tomes: The Bob Dylan Collectors' Service. P.O. Box 1943, Grand Junction, Colorado 81502.

Quarterly catalog of literary Dylan miscellany, offering magazines, Dylanzines, in print and out of print books, rare records and posters, and more. The cost of subscription is $5 for four catalogs.

Series of Dreams. Rolling Tomes Inc., P.O. Box 1943, Grand Junction, CO 81502.

Monthly eight-page newsletter published by Rolling Tomes Inc. Provides subscribers with the latest Dylan news on books, concerts, bootlegs, CDs, and reprinted newspaper articles—much of which has been submitted by fans. The cost of subscription is $15 per year.

FILM

Pennebaker, D.A. *Bob Dylan: Don't Look Back*. New York: Ballantine Books, 1968. 160 pages. Approximately 200 black-and-white photographs, covering every page.

The written document of the Dylan documentary *Don't Look Back*, as directed by author Leacock (D.A.) Pennebaker. The book contains the complete written transcript of the film (which was shot without a screenplay) and features a great many fascinating stills you wish had been printed on glossy stock. Endlessly fascinating for capturing Dylan when he did this sort of thing, and for dramatizing his relations with Albert Grossman, Joan Baez, Donovan, and others. The stars' lingo (Baez: "I'm fagging out") is mesmerizing to read nearly three decades later. If you can't find this, however, repeated viewings of the film will suffice.

GENERAL REFERENCE

Dowley, Tim and Dunnage, Barry. *Bob Dylan: From a Hard Rain to a Slow Train*. New York: Hippocrene Books, 1982. 177 pages. One glossy four-page black-and-white photo insert. Bibliography. (First published in the U.K. in 1982 by Midas Books.)

Part of Midas Books' series on popular performers, this book was spawned by several talks Dowley had given to "a small group of people in Bethel Green, East London." The first half consists of background on Hibbing, MN, the Zimmerman clan, and Bob Dylan's rise to fame through his Woody Guthrie infatuation. Amidst the discussions of Dylan's protest years, his influence on U.K. rock, and his most successful LPs, the author makes abundantly clear Dylan's determination to follow his own drummer. The discography, which is incalculably dated, fills up the second half. Meatier information can be found elsewhere.

McKeen, William. *Bob Dylan: A Bio-Bibliography*. Westport: Greenwood Press, 1993. 308 pages. Index.

McKeen consulted the world's top Dylan authorities and produced this authoritative guide to conducting Dylan research. If the information you need to find isn't in here, most likely it will tell you where to look. Divided into five chunky sections—Portrait of the Artist, Bob Dylan's Songs and Influence, Bibliography, Performances and Chronology—the book provides a superior nutshell biography and a well-rounded study of Dylan's musical legacy, plus invaluable lists of songs (released, unreleased, and cover versions) and publications. More than the sum of its parts, *Bob Dylan: A Bio-Bibliography* should be course curriculum for anyone involved in Dylan academia.

Wissolik, Richard David (General Editor). *Bob Dylan—American Poet and Singer: An Annotated Bibliography and Study Guide of Sources and Background Materials 1961-1991*. Greensburg: Eadmer Press, 1991. 98 pages.

A concise bibliography of some 2,000 books and articles for the Dylan scholar. Articles and books are grouped together and alphabetized by author name. Listings tend to contain bare bibliographic data, but in some cases a sentence or two is provided to describe a book publication. The authors have supplied useful codes to indicate concert, film, book, and record reviews. Good for quick reference.

INTERVIEWS

Bauldie, John (editor). *Wanted Man: In Search of Bob Dylan*. London: Black Spring Press Limited, 1990. 228 pages. Eight-page black-and-white glossy photo insert. Some Bob Dylan Lists. Notes. Index.

These interviews were conducted by numerous journalists and writers over the years (including Clinton Heylin, Allen Ginsberg, Paul Williams, Miles, and others) and originally appeared in *The Telegraph* fanzine. The book contains brief, excerpted interviews with various personages, including Patti Smith, "the Girl from the North Country," Eric Clapton, Roy Orbison, and Tom Petty, as well as portions from speeches (Springsteen's speech inducting Dylan into the Rock and Roll Hall of Fame) and other miscellany. A section called "Some Bob Dylan Lists" cites trivialities such as 16 Dylan song lines taken from films, Dylan pseudonyms, etc. The book would have been more appealing with photos of the interview subjects (in addition to the glossies of Dylan). Given the diversity of figures included here (and the fact that it's more recent), this title is recommended over Gray and Bauldie's collection (see below).

Gray, Michael and Bauldie, John (editors). Introduction by Bob Willis. *All Across the Telegraph: A Bob Dylan Handbook*. London: Sidgwick & Jackson, Limited, 1987. 290 pages. One 12-page glossy black-and-white photo insert. Some Bob Dylan Lists. Notes. Index.

The word "handbook" is used in a broad sense here, because this book assumes more than the average fan's knowledge of Dylan and does not hone in on any one aspect of the man's life or musical career. Instead, the editors provide 48 journalistic pieces (mostly interviews) excerpted from the British Dylan fanzine, *The Telegraph*. Most of the writings are snippets that give brief insights into the Dylan puzzle. For example, was The Rolling Stones' Brian Jones the Mr. Jones in Dylan's "Ballad of a Thin Man"? The writings are arranged chronologically (not thematically) and were reprinted from the original sources without notations or updates from the editors. One interesting arrangement is that "Liam Clancy" by Bob Dylan precedes "Bob Dylan" by Liam Clancy. In spite of a few pearls here and there, the sum total is a bit of a hodgepodge.

PICTORIALS

Cott, Jonathan. *Dylan*. New York: Rolling Stone Press and Dolphin/Doubleday, Inc., 1984. 252 pages (oversized). Approximately 12 color photographs; approximately 150 black-and-white photographs throughout. Discography.

This "Rolling Stone Press" book still holds up over time. Though some of the photos have since been reproduced in subsequent publications (and on better quality paper), there are more than enough eyegrabbers (e.g., one in which Dylan is about to do a belly-flop in a pool) to make this one worth seeking out. The crystalline images of Dylan on the cover are somewhat incongruous with the artist's persona. "A first-class photo book"—*Boston Globe*.

Gross, Michael. Text by Alexander, Robert. *Bob Dylan: An Illustrated History*. New York: Grosset & Dunlap, 1975. 150 pages. Approximately 150 black-and-white photographs, covering every page. Chronology.

When released, this must have been a fun collection, but today it's just another book of Dylan photos—sans the trimmings, such as color, discography, etc. The authors rely heavily on Toby Thompson (see Dylaneutics, above) for information on Dylan's early years. Some of the captions draw some hasty conclusions: Why assume Dylan was funding the Jewish Defense League simply because he wore a yarmulke at the wailing wall in Jerusalem? Undistinguished.

Humphries, Patrick. *The Complete Guide to the Music of Bob Dylan*. London: Omnibus Press (division of Book Sales Limited), 1995. 152 pages.

CD-format book covering all aspects of Dylan's life and career. While this book doesn't have a discography or other extras in the back, it's nicely designed and priced right at around $7.99.

Humphries, Patrick and Bauldie, John. *Oh No! Not Another Bob Dylan Book*. Essex, England: Square One Books, Limited, 1991. 240 pages (oversized). 42 page color insert; approximately 150 black-and-white photographs throughout. Notes.

Oh yes—it *is* another one. But don't fear: it's among the best. The authors take the stance that, unlike other Dylan books, you are not expected to know everything about Bobby D before turning the first page. Though accessible to the Dylan beginner, the book will also be a major turn-on to the fan who has everything. The photos, notably in the color insert, are of superior quality; they pop off the page. The "notes" section mixes chronology, television and radio appearances, discography, interviews, unreleased recordings, bibliography, and concerts. Published in the United States in 1991 by Viking Penguin as *Absolutely Dylan*.

Kramer, Daniel. *Bob Dylan*. New York: Pocket Books, 1968. 216 pages. Over two hundred black-and-white photographs, covering nearly every page.

An oldie for certain, but worth seeking out for Kramer's candid and sensitive shots of a very young Dylan at home (on a swing, taking a long walk, reading the paper, playing chess, etc.). There are even a couple in which Dylan gives what looks like a very natural smile. Dylan's office claimed privacy infringement against Citadel's first release of this work, but their injunction plea failed. First published in 1967 by Citadel Press, Inc. Reprinted in 1991 by Carol Publishing under the title: *Bob Dylan: A Portrait of the Artist's Early Years*.

No author. *Bob Dylan*. No city: SCV Inc. and Brockum Company, undated. Unpaginated (approximately 32 pages). Approximately 30 color and black-and-white photographs throughout.

Oversized collection of Dylan photos and related graphics. Pages are smattered with Dylan non-sequiturs that have been selected presumably on comic effect alone: "Who said I can't act? Hahah. I mean, who?" For the avid collector only.

Rinzler, Alan. *Bob Dylan: The Illustrated Record.* New York: Harmony (division of Crown), 1978. 120 pages. Approximately 200 color and black-and-white photographs, covering every page.

Oversized album-by-album portrait of Dylan that evenly mixes color with black-and-white. The reproductions of album colors are exceptional, and if you're into the Dylan/Baez romance there is plenty to gawk at. The author's commentary is nothing special—typical gushing praise with lots of quotes lifted from other sources (e.g., see Biographies: Scaduto, Anthony). The book ends with the *Street-Legal* LP, so don't bother if you need something more recent.

Williams, Richard. *Dylan: A Man Called Alias.* New York: Henry Holt and Company, 1992. 192 pages (oversized). 12 pages of color scattered throughout; approximately 150 black-and-white photographs throughout. Bibliography. Index. (First published in Great Britain in 1992 by Bloomsbury Limited.)

Worthy of any Dylanite's coffee table, though not quite as sumptuous or as comprehensive as Humphries and Bauldie's pictorial above. Alias is Dylan's character in the film *Pat Garrett and Billy the Kid.* The photos from the early 1960's are a particular standout, as is the design; many pages have wonderful background drawings of Dylan. Essential for diehards.

QUIZBOOKS AND QUOTEBOOKS

Williams, Christian Bob. *Bob Dylan: In His Own Words.* London: Omnibus Press (division of Book Sales Limited), 1993. 112 pages. Approximately 100 black-and-white photographs, covering nearly every page.

Having undergone innumerable revised editions and reprints over the years (the earliest goes back to the late 1970's), this immensely popular collection of words and pictures was first credited to author Miles. There are some gems here (on songwriting: "I just sit down and the next thing I know it's there"), but the best quotes only cover the 1960's-80's; there's still very little of the 1990's in here. The range of subjects—early life, song and dance man, the real message, albums, films and books, etc.—will continue to please young fans.

RELATED WORKS

Carter, Rubin "Hurricane." *The Sixteenth Round: From #1 Contender to #45472.* New York: The Viking Press, 1974. 340 pages. One glossy eight-page black-and-white photo insert. Prize Fighting Record.

Rubin Carter, "the number one contender for the middleweight crown" (as Bob Dylan called him), tells the story of how he was framed for robbery and murder. The book inspired Dylan's classic saga "Hurricane" (although many of his facts were wrong) and is really a full autobiography of how a kid from the slums of Jersey became an enormously successful prize fighter—Carter had more knockouts than any other fighter of his time—only to have it ruined by a racist police force. Particularly relevant given events in L.A. in the 1990's. As Dylan was inspired, so might you be.

Guthrie, Woody. *Bound for Glory.*

See: Guthrie, Woody: Autobiography.

TOURBOOKS

Editors of *Rolling Stone. Knockin' on Dylan's Door: On the Road in '74.* New York: Pocket Books, 1974. 140 pages. One 24-page black-and-white photo insert. Songs Performed on the Tour.

Quickie collection of *Rolling Stone* articles (and one or two appearing elsewhere) summarizing the before, during, and after of Dylan/The Band's 1974 tour. The hubbub was created because it had been Dylan's first extensive tour since 1966, and it marked a return to his playing some of his original folk material. Nothing special here, except for an occasional critical zinger for posterity. Nat Hentoff wrote in a *Times* piece that at the time Dylan was "an undistinguished musician, vocally and instrumentally." Huh?

Muller, Harald and Lohse, Michael. *In the Summertime: A Bibliography of Articles on the Bob Dylan Concerts 1981.* West Germany: Hobo Press, 1981. Unpaginated (approximately 30 pages).

Reproductions of several articles published throughout Europe (Germany, France, England, and Italy) during Dylan's 1981 tour. The articles (and photos) are directly copied from their original forms (we do not know whether with or without permission) and are, of course, in the printed languages. Of limited value if you're in need of literature on this topic and can decipher several languages.

Shepard, Sam. *Rolling Thunder Logbook*. New York: Limelight Editions, 1977. 184 pages. Two hundred black-and-white photographs.

Period piece from playwright and actor Shepard, who had accompanied the Rolling Thunder Revue (Dylan, Joan Baez, Arlo Guthrie, Joni Mitchell, Allen Ginsberg, Roger McGuinn, and others) for a 22-city tour across the northeast in fall, 1975. Mostly visual snippits of the travels, with emphasis on the historic sights along the way (Plymouth) and told through Shepard's often acerbic wit (he refers to Dylan's new dog as a "puppy beagle bitch"). Apparently Shepard, who was originally commissioned as a screenwriter (for what ultimately became the film *Renaldo and Clara*), was given a bit of a runaround by Dylan and few of his contributions were used in the end product. For a more detailed history of the Revue, see Sloman's *On the Road with Bob Dylan* below.

Sloman, Larry. *On the Road with Bob Dylan: Rolling with Thunder*. New York: Bantam, 1978. 416 pages. One eight-page black-and-white photo insert.

This rolling tome delivers the goods on Dylan's 1975 Rolling Thunder Revue tour (which was actually on the road in October 1975 and then again in April 1976). Sloman himself had to constantly fight his way into Dylan's inner circle, and once there he proved himself a sharp observer. In the book, he takes us through how the concept of the Revue evolved; tells how musicians and groupies joined in; and reports many other intrigues that occurred throughout the tour. There are also many colorful insiders along the way, including Kinky Friedman, Sara Dylan, Ramblin' Jack Elliott, Ratso—and even Beattie Zimmerman (Dylan's momma). There are numerous intimate conversations among personnel (including a fascinating chat between Dylan and Rubin "Hurricane" Carter), and we get a good sense of the inner-workings of the *Desire* recording sessions and the shooting of the film *Renaldo and Clara*. Strongly recommended for fans of live Dylan.

WRITTEN WORKS

Dylan, Bob. *Lyrics, 1962-1985*. New York: Alfred A. Knopf, Inc., 1985. 532 pages. 120 original pen-and-ink drawings. Index of Songs, First Lines and Key Lines.

This mammoth collection contains, in chronological order and grouped by album title, transcribed song lyrics (no chords), liner notes, original drawings, and other miscellaneous writings by Dylan. The typeface is easy-to-read and appropriately reverential. There is no written commentary in this volume—not even an introduction (one page from Dylan would have sufficed)—but, then again, one can turn to any number of sources listed in the Critical/Analytical Commentary section above. The drawings are nothing special, except for the novelty that Dylan drew them. Certain writers (Stephen Scobie, for one) have complained that this book does not offer alternate lyrics and song variations for live performances, and is incomplete because it is missing 48 unreleased songs. These qualms aside, this is by far the most comprehensive book of Dylan lyrics in existence, and one that solidifies Dylan's place as the most influential bard in rock history. First published in 1973 as *Writings and Drawings*.

Dylan, Bob. *Tarantula*. New York: The Macmillan Company, 1971. 138 pages.

The novelty of this Bob Dylan "novel," or whatever you want to call it, wears thin after the first few lines of free verse. The publication history bears more significance than the work itself. First written, set to type, and hyped by the publisher in 1966, the galleys for *Tarantula* were put on hold while the artist considered "a few changes." After a prolonged delay, Dylan suffered a motorcycle accident and retreated to Woodstock for a physical and emotional recovery. In 1970, Dylan finally "agreed" to allow the book's publication (which, ironically, is no longer copyrighted in his name). Swirling with only a few sparks of Dylan's brilliance for words and imagery, *Tarantula* is an incoherent disaster—a half-baked high school creative writing assignment without the master's tunes, voice, guitar, and harmonica to lend credibility. First published in 1970 by MacGibbon & Kee; more recent editions include The Macmillan Company, 1972; and Viking Penguin, 1977.

YOUNG ADULT

Aaseng, Nathan. *Bob Dylan: Spellbinding Songwriter*. Minneapolis, MN: Lerner Publications Company, 1987. 56 pages. Approximately 30 black-and-white photographs throughout. A Timeline of Bob Dylan's Life.

Lucid study of Dylan that benefits from being more recent than Beal's work (see below). The author tosses in a reference to Dylan's participation in "We Are the World," which all-too-neatly demonstrates that the musician's humanitarianism wasn't limited to the 1960's folk scene. The timeline mentions album releases, though parents who want to introduce their kids to their album collections would probably need to have one of the stronger discographical guides (see above) close at hand. "...this will serve as an introduction to Dylan and his music..."—*Booklist*.

Beal, Kathleen. *Bob Dylan*. Mankato, MN: Creative Education, 1975. 32 pages. Six original watercolor drawings throughout.

Imaginative and colorful study of Dylan, published just after his 1974 tour. The psychedelic drawings are nicely done, if a throwback. Beal did commendable research of Dylan's early years, making reference to his old girlfriend Echo Helstrom and the "Dinkytown" folk scene in Minneapolis. Recommended.

Richardson, Susan. Introduction by Leeza Gibbons. *Bob Dylan*. New York: Chelsea House, 1995. 128 pages. Approximately 50 black-and-white photographs throughout. Further Readings. Chronology. Index.

Part of Chelsea House's "Pop Culture Legends" series—and with a positively repulsive glimmering Dylan on the cover—this book is an otherwise fine introduction to the artist for young students. After an unrelated series overview by Leeza Gibbons (of "Entertainment Tonight"), Richardson traces Dylan's roots from Hibbing, Minnesota to his worship of Woody Guthrie, his changeover to rock, his religious spurts in the 1970's, and his so-called return to causes in the 1980's ("Live Aid"). The last chapter, focusing on contemporary celebrations of Dylan, gives the erroneous impression that Dylan is like an eighty-year-old Charlie Chaplin, not a vital, enigmatic figure with some accomplishments still ahead.

OTHER TITLES OF INTEREST

Amendt, Gunter. *Reunion Sundown: Bob Dylan in Europa*. No city: Hobo, 1985.

Bauldie, John. *Bob Dylan & Desire*. No city: Wanted Man, 1984

Cartwright, Bert. *The Bible in the Lyrics of Bob Dylan*. No city: Wanted Man, 1985.

Dundas, Glen. *Tangled Up in Tapes*. No city: SMA, 1990.

Dylan, Bob. *Road Drawings*. New York: Random House, 1992.

Heylin, Clinton. *The Bob Dylan Interviews: A List*. No city: Quest, 1981.

Heylin, Clinton. *More Rain Unravelled*. London: Omnibus Press (division of Book Sales Limited), 1984.

Heylin, Clinton. *Rain Unravelled Tales: A Rumorography*. London: Omnibus Press (division of Book Sales Limited), 1982.

Heylin, Clinton. *Saved! The Gospel Speeches of Bob Dylan*. No city: Hanuman Books, 1990.

Heylin, Clinton. *To Live Outside the Law: A Guide to Bob Dylan's Bootlegs*. No city: Labour of Love, 1989.

Miles. *Bob Dylan*. No city: Big O, 1978.

Roques, Dominique. *The Great White Answers: The Bob Dylan Bootleg Records*. No city: Southern Live Oak, 1980.

Somogyi, De. *Jokerman & Thieves*. No city: Wanted Man, 1985.

Stein, George. *Bob Dylan: Temples in Flames*. No city: Palmyra, 1989.

Thomson, Elizabeth M. *Conclusions on the Wall*. No city: Thin Man, 1980.

Williams (no first name). *Bob Dylan: From a Slow Train*. No city: Gleneida Publishing, 1985.

Wurlitzer, Rudolph. *Pat Garrett and Billy the Kid*. New York: Signet: NAL, 1973.
Novel companion to the 1973 Peckinpah film, in which Dylan briefly appeared.

THE EAGLES

BIOGRAPHIES

Shapiro, Marc. *The Long Run: The Story of the Eagles*. London: Omnibus Press (division of Book Sales Limited), 1995. 166 pages. One glossy 16-page black-and-white photo insert. Discography.

Despite a career spanning nearly a quarter of a century, there wasn't a proper biography of The Eagles until this book came along. It's a puzzle why: Three of the key members—Glen Frey, Don Henley and Joe Walsh—have had successful solo careers and have had great impact on the rock scene in general. Author Marc Shapiro isn't up to the task of profiling this supergroup, however, neglecting key aspects of The Eagles' dynamics and lumping all of their solo work into one chapter. His access to two lesser band members (Randy Meisner and Bernie Leadon) doesn't bring us any closer to knowing The Eagles themselves. Shapiro's attempts at slang ("It wasn't *on* the cards" instead of "in the cards") is more disruptive than descriptive. It's evident this was hastily prepared in light of The Eagles' completed "Hell Freezes Over" tour.

OTHER TITLES OF INTEREST

Henley, Don and Marsh, Dave (editors). *Heaven Is Under Our Feet: A Book for Walden Woods*. New York: Berkley (Putnam), 1991.
    Kirkus *commented: "Sprinkled with passages by Thoreau, it's an attractive volume...."*
Swenson, John. *The Eagles*. No city: Ace Books, 1981.

EARTH, WIND AND FIRE

TITLES OF INTEREST

White, Verdine. *Playing the Bass Guitar*. No city: Almo, 1978.
    Instructional book from Verdine, the band's bassist.

ECHO AND THE BUNNYMEN

PICTORIALS

Cooper, Mark. *Liverpool Explodes! The Teardrop Explodes: Echo and the Bunnymen*. London: Sidgwick & Jackson Limited, 1982. 96 pages. Approximately 100 black-and-white photographs, covering every page. Discography. Index.

Why a dual pictorial on the Teardrop Explodes and Echo and the Bunnymen? Simple: both bands are from Liverpool; frontmen Julian Cope and Ian McCulloch were once in the same band, The Crucial Three; they had the same manager, Bill Drummond; and they rose to popularity amidst the declining punk scene. The two groups are forced into an off-the-wall and carefree image, but in the end, their antics (prancing onstage in diapers) come off as

harmless and sophomoric. Strictly for fans of the incestuous early 1980's Liverpool music scene.

OTHER TITLES OF INTEREST

Fletcher, Tony. *Never Stop: Echo and the Bunnymen*. Woodstock, NY: Beekman, 1990.

ELECTRIC LIGHT ORCHESTRA

TITLES OF INTEREST

Bevan, Bev. *The Electric Light Orchestra Story*. New York: Putnam, 1981.

DAVID ESSEX

BIOGRAPHIES

Tremlett, George. *The David Essex Story*. London: Futura Publications Limited, 1974. 144 pages. One glossy eight-page black-and-white photo insert. Appendix I: Chronology. Appendix II: Cast List and Synopsis for *That'll Be the Day*. Appendix III: Cast List and Synopsis for *Stardust*.

"A docker's son makes good," David Essex bounded on the rock and roll and film scenes in the early 1970's. This distinctly British book is a quickie intended to cash in on Essex's success with the latter. There's really not much going on here, except for a few light moments in which Essex mucks about with drumming buddies Keith Moon and Ringo Starr. One for the dust-bin.

GLORIA ESTEFAN

BIOGRAPHIES

Catalano, Grace. *Gloria Estefan*. New York: St. Martin's Press, 1991. 196 pages. One eight-page black-and-white photo insert. Discography. Videography.

Though not likely to inspire conga lines in the library stack aisles, this is a compelling tale of a popular young star overcoming personal traumas. Estefan's father, an ex-patriot Cuban and then U.S. soldier who was taken captive by the

Communists in the Bay of Pigs, served in Vietnam after his release and contracted multiple sclerosis from exposure to Agent Orange. In 1990, Gloria Estefan herself suffered a broken spinal vertebrae in a bus accident and underwent extensive surgery (that ultimately proved successful). Author Catalano's portrayal of Estefan's marriage (to Emilio Estefan, the founder of the Miami Sound Machine) reads as too idyllic to believe. A decent start for fans.

YOUNG ADULT

Stefoff, Rebecca. Introduction by Rodolfo Cordona. *Gloria Estefan*. New York: Chelsea House Publishers, 1991. 104 pages. Approximately 35 black-and-white photographs throughout. Discography. Chronology. Further Reading. Index.

Part of the "Hispanics of Achievement" series that also includes Raul Julia, Gabriel Garcia Marquez, and Roberto Clemente, this is a cultural study of Estefan and how she succeeded at introducing Latin music to a pop American audience. Stefoff successfully presents Estefan as an ideal role model; she succeeded with others (Miami Sound Machine) and independently, and recovered from her near-paralyzing spinal injury. The photos, which include shots of Cuban history and culture, add some value. "Standard, dependable biographical fare..." —*Booklist*.

OTHER TITLES OF INTEREST

Gonzalez, Fernando. *Gloria Estefan, Cuban American Singing Star*. No city: Milbrook, 1993.
Shirley, David. *Gloria Estefan: Entertainer*. New York: Chelsea House, 1993.

MELISSA ETHERIDGE

FANZINES AND FAN CLUBS

Melissa Etheridge Information Network. P.O. Box 884563, San Francisco, CA 94188.

Fan club that offers members access to preferred concert tickets, travel packages, the Melissa Etheridge hotline, contests, and merchandising. New members also receive a photo of Melissa, a biography, a discography, a membership card, subscription to the newsletter, and more. The cost of membership is $19 U.S.; $25 elsewhere.

EURYTHMICS

BIOGRAPHIES

Martin, Nancie S. *Eurythmics*. New York: Ballantine Books, 1984. 148 pages. One eight-page glossy black-and-white photo insert. Appendixes: Pop Quiz; Discography; Videography; Getting in Touch with Eurythmics.

Scotswoman Annie Lennox and Englishman Dave Stewart met in 1977, by way of introduction from a mutual friend. They formed a musical and romantic partnership almost on the spot and, in subsequent years, developed the innovative synthesizer sound that made Eurythmics perhaps the most respected duo of the early 1980's. Nancie Martin's study is ancient history, but it covers all pertinent information. For younger fans, Martin provides sidebars on instruments (e.g., the flute, synthesizers), stylistic movements (London fashion), and several brief charts (other Scottish pop stars). The book tactfully deals with Lennox's so-called "androgynous" physical characteristics.

O'Brien, Lucy. *Annie Lennox*. London: Sidgwick & Jackson, 1991. 214 pages. Two glossy eight-page photo inserts. U.K. Discography.

Lucy O'Brien admits that her subject is a bit young for a full-scale biography, but asserts that Lennox had 15 years of fame and has become "a pop star incarnate." An isolated child from a middle-class family in Aberdeen, Scotland, Lennox is a woman who has flourished against the odds. After her classical musical training at the Royal Academy proved a bust, she floundered in musical ventures until she met up with Dave Stewart, her collaborator and lover; the two became an avant-garde Sonny and Cher for the 1980's. Having shed Stewart, the Eurythmics, and her cross-dressing persona, Lennox stands in the 1990's as a supporter of myriad causes, a solo artist, a wife (to Israeli filmmaker Uri Fruchtman), and mother of two. "She appears to be a normal human being, which makes her the dullest of subjects"—*Publishers Weekly*.

PICTORIALS

Jasper, Tony. *Eurythmics*. Port Chester, NY: Cherry Lane, 1985. 128 pages. Approximately 100 black-and-white and 20 color illustrations, covering every page. Discography. (First published in Great Britain in 1985 by Zomba Books.)

Lacking any real substance, this book pales in comparison to Waller's pictorial (below). Tracing the group's history up through the 1984 world tour, Jasper doesn't have much to say about Eurythmics and thus ends with a dumb chapter containing quotes from fans. The only positive note: The pics of a beautiful young Annie Lennox with majestic long blonde hair. Sweet dreams can occasionally put you to sleep.

Waller, Johnny and Rapport, Steve. *Sweet Dreams: The Definitive Biography*. Wawatosa: Robus Books, 1985. 128 pages. One hundred black-and-white photographs, covering nearly every page; one 16-page color insert. Dave and Annie: The Discography.

Bearing the endorsement of Dave Stewart and Annie Lennox, this book is a real treat. Without presenting anything new or controversial, the authors keep the interest alive via a wealth of photos that tell the Eurythmics' story from childhood through the group's major albums and videos. Stand-out shots include Dave as a child on a rocking horse and Annie on her first day of school. As time passes, Dave resembles a beatnik folkie until the end of the 1980's, when he becomes Mr. Strange Avant-Garde. Annie, on the other hand, looks like a debutante flutist with classical aspirations, until she snips off her long blonde hair and turns pop. A strong survey.

THE EVERLY BROTHERS

DISCOGRAPHIES, RECORDING GUIDES, AND COLLECTIBLES

Hosum, John. *Living Legends: The History of the Everly Brothers on Record: An Illustrated Discography*. Seattle, WA: Forever Music, 1985. 64 pages. Approximately 75 black-and-white photographs throughout.

Vanity press discography of the Everly Brothers, tracing their releases up through their 1984 reunion tour. Since this is the only such work on the duo, it will have to serve; still, all of the sections (divided by studio) are so discordantly designed it's virtually impossible to find information. Worse, there isn't an Index. The "illustrated" aspect—out-of-focus album covers—doesn't help much. Scarcely annotated.

FANZINES AND FAN CLUBS

Everly Brothers Foundation. P.O. Box 309, Central City, Kentucky 42330-0309.

Non-profit organization that raises money for academic assistance to deserving causes in the Central City, Kentucky area (the Everlys' hometown). Sponsors the local Music Festival, at which the Everlys have appeared; has purchased land intended to serve as the site of the Everly Brothers Museum. Write for more information.

The Fun Club for Fans of the Everly Brothers. P.O. Box 3933, Seattle, WA 98124-3933.

This club has superseded *Everly Brothers International* in Holland—the former "official" club—which is now defunct. The current club, endorsed by the Everlys, began as *The Beehive*, but no longer carries that name. The club publishes *Heartaches & Harmonies* newsletter, which costs $15 for six issues in the U.S. and Canada; $20 elsewhere.

PICTORIALS

White, Roger. *Walk Right Back: The Story of the Everly Brothers*. London: Plexus, 1984. 160 pages. Approximately 200 black-and-white photographs, covering every page. Discography.

Photo tribute to rock's most famous brothers of the early 1960's that was postponed to cover Don and Phil's reunion concert in 1983. White tells the Everlys' story without much fanfare: Kentuckians by birth, they moved with their family through the American southwest to Shenandoah, Iowa and Knoxville, Tennessee. Influenced first by country and western tunes and then Elvis, the Everlys shifted to rock ballads and, with the help of songwriters Boudleaux and Felix Bryant (e.g., "Bye Bye Love," "Wake Up Little Susie"), became the idols of millions. Thankfully, White doesn't skip over the racy bits (speed addiction, failed marriages, quarrels), though he fails to get us inside the brother's working relationship. Recommended wholeheartedly to those who still swoon.

OTHER TITLES OF INTEREST

Dodge, Consuelo. *The Everly Brothers: Ladies Love Outlaws.* Starke, FL: Cin-Dav, 1991. Library Journal *commented: "Unfortunately, this `fanzine' masquerading as an unauthorized biography does not do them [the Everlys] justice."*

Karpp, Phyllis. *Ike's Boys: The Story of the Everly Brothers.* Ann Arbor, MI: Popular Culture Ink, 1988.

Sauers, John. *The Everly Brothers Rock N' Roll Odyssey.* New York: Putnam, 1986.

THE FACES

See Rolling Stones, The; Small Faces, The; Stewart, Rod.

ADAM FAITH

TITLES OF INTEREST

Faith, Adam. *Adam, His Fabulous Year.* London: Picture Story Publications, 1960.

Faith, Adam. *Poor Me.* London: Souvenir Press, 1961.

MARIANNE FAITHFULL

(See also Rolling Stones, The)

AUTOBIOGRAPHY

Faithfull, Marianne with Dalton, David. *Faithfull: An Autobiography.* Boston: Little Brown and Company, 1994. 310 pages. Two eight-page glossy black-and-white photo inserts. Index.

Poorly written and full of errors, oversights, and self-indulgent flights of fancy, *Faithfull* is extricated from its low plateau by the sheer tenacity of the author. Faithfull unrelentingly hits readers with the eye-opening details of her life: a three-decade long heroin addiction, her romance with Mick Jagger, dozens of love affairs (including one close call with Bob

Dylan), a miscarriage, anorexia—and that's just the beginning. Faithfull truly believes that she met Rolling Stone Brian Jones on the "other side" when she experienced her suicide-induced coma. It's absurd, and yet it all somehow makes sense in this singer's world. "...her co-author and editor look like they must have been on hard drugs themselves when they took this to the printer"—*Crawdaddy!*.

BIOGRAPHIES

Hodkinson, Mark. *Marianne Faithfull: As Tears Go By.* London: Omnibus (division of Book Sales), 1991. 216 pages. Three glossy eight-page black-and-white photo inserts. Discography.

Unauthorized biography of Faithfull that is nevertheless elegantly written and sticks to the facts. (Perhaps Faithfull should have consulted this book when compiling her autobiography; see above.) Hodkinson, who was a mere child in the 1960's, has the advantage of a fresh, objective distance from the events being told. He fully appreciates Faithfull's contributions to the era, which are all the more staggering considering she was only 22 at the close of the decade. Hodkinson explores her aristocratic lineage, her rebellious streak, the development of her singing career, and her legendary relationship with Mick Jagger (and how it was less a part of her life than most people think). Ultimately, Faithfull is portrayed to be a funny, charming icon, whose talents overshadow her dilettante image. "Thorough and intelligently written"—*New Musical Express.*

FAITH NO MORE

PICTORIALS

Chirazi, Steffan. *Faith No More: The Real Story.* Chessington, Surrey (U.K.): Castle Communications Limited, 1994. 152 pages. Approximately 50 color and black-and-white photographs throughout; original black-and-white graphics and drawings on every page. Discography.

Is this group heavy metal? Punk? Grunge? Alternative? Defying categorization, Faith No More carries on at least one straight rock and roll tradition: They simply don't give a shit. This "real story"—which relies heavily on the touting of "band cooperation"—is as raucous as it comes. Pill-popping, orgies, alcohol binges, and piss guzzling (yes, you're reading correctly) are commonplace activities for these guys, both onstage and off. Fanzine graphics and question/answer quotes from band members take up most of the book space. Crucial for fans—and almost as valuable for buffs of the Red Hot Chili Peppers (with whom Faith No More toured).

RICHARD FARIÑA

WRITTEN WORKS

Fariña, Richard. Introduction by Thomas Pynchon. *Been Down So Long It Looks Like Up to Me*. New York: Viking, 1966. 332 pages.

Richard Fariña, part of the mid-1960's folk-rock transformation, recorded three albums with his wife, Mimi Baez (Joan's sister). Fariña died in a motorcycle accident in 1966 after a party promoting the release of this book (which was reprinted in 1983). The story takes place on the campus of Cornell University amidst political and social demonstrations. Gnossos Pappadopoulis absorbs all of the goings-on, exploring drugs, sex, religion, and death in a way similar to many others from that era. A highly stylized and poetic tale, with plentiful mythological references to keep the academic-minded busy. Recommended for those with interest in the period.

PERRY FARRELL

TITLES OF INTEREST
Thompson, Dave. *Perry Farrell: The Saga of a Hypester*. New York: St. Martin's Press, 1995.

JOSÉ FELICIANO

TITLES OF INTEREST
Maymi, Carmen R. Edited by Maynes, J.O. *Hispanic Heroes of the U.S.A.: Roberto Clemente and José Feliciano*. St. Paul, MN: EMC Publishing, 1975. *Book three of EMC's young adult series on Hispanic heroes.*

FINE YOUNG CANNIBALS

PICTORIALS

Edge, Brian. *The Fine Young Cannibals Story: The Sweet and the Sour*. London: Omnibus Press (division of Book Sales Limited), 1991. 96 pages. Approximately 75 black-and-white photographs throughout. Discography.

The Cannibals originally agreed to sponsor this as an "official" band book, but dropped out when they read the actual manuscript. Perhaps they found it boring: Low-key and failing to capture Roland Gift's sensual side, the book contains phrases such as "salubrious surroundings"—which may have forced the musicians to actually consult a dictionary. Gift is commanding in several photos—many of which are green-tinted—although no captions are provided. If you're a fan in dire need, this book has intermittent pleasures.

ROBERTA FLACK

YOUNG ADULT

Jacobs, Linda. *Roberta Flack: The Sound of Velvet Melting*. St. Paul, MN: EMC Corporation, 1975. 40 pages. Approximately 30 black-and-white photographs throughout.

Part of EMC Corporation's "Women Behind the Bright Lights" series, this well-intended junior biography is too dated to be of much use. Published in the mid-1970's, this book only serves as a scan of the early phase of her career, during which time she had the hit songs "The First Time Ever I Saw Your Face" and "Killing Me Softly." The book discusses her integration of jazz, blues, and rock, but it doesn't mention any specific influences; it mentions her initial desire to become a classical singer and her previous career as an English teacher, but it doesn't convey her tastes in classical music or literature. All that's left is one terrific subtitle.

OTHER TITLES OF INTEREST
Morse, Charles and Morse, Ann. *Roberta Flack*. Mankato, MN: Creative Education, 1994.

FLEETWOOD MAC

AUTOBIOGRAPHY

Fleetwood, Mick with Davis, Stephen. New York: William Morrow & Company, 1990. *Fleetwood: My Life and Adventures with Fleetwood Mac.* 288 pages. Four eight-page black-and-white photo inserts.

Mick Fleetwood's colorful life story begins with the low-point of his life and career: the liquidation of his assets following bankruptcy. How could a man of such wealth and talent have ended up in this pitiable state? Fleetwood's adventures from top to bottom and back up again are riveting. We gain compelling insight into the makings of John Mayall's Bluesbreakers (of which Fleetwood was a member for six weeks) and accounts of the many intrigues within Fleetwood Mac itself, including Lindsey Buckingham's famous resignation tantrum and Stevie Nicks' drug addiction. To his immeasurable credit, Fleetwood is affable and objective and doesn't use book space to take pot-shots at his long-time associates. He is rather curt about his drumming technique (or is this humility?), which is the book's only disappointment. "Fleetwood emerges as hip and flip..."— *Publishers Weekly.*

BIOGRAPHIES

Celmins, Martin. Foreword by B.B. King. *Peter Green: The Biography.* Chessington, Surrey (England): Castle Communications, 1995. 234 pages. One glossy eight-page black-and-white photo insert. Sound Equipment. Discography. Sessionography. Reference Notes. Index.

So, you think Mick Fleetwood founded Fleetwood Mac? Nope. Virtuoso guitarist Peter Green did. Born in England of Ukrainian and Polish Jewish ancestry, Green was a natural guitarist (he never had a lesson) and became a session guitarist in England in the early 1960's. He had his first break when Eric Clapton left John Mayall's Bluesbreakers to form Cream, causing the group to be short a guitarist. Ultimately, Green had the urge to establish his own bluesy band, and in 1967 he joined up with drummer Mick Fleetwood, bassist John McVie, and guitarist Jeremy Spencer: Thus the first incarnation of Fleetwood Mac was born.

From 1967-1970, the group gradually shifted away from the blues, and by 1970 Green quit the group altogether. Green, who authorized this biography, has supplied the author with a number of wonderful anecdotes that make this book an engaging and informative read.

GYPSY: MYSTICAL LADY

Wincenstein, Edward. *Stevie Nicks: Rock's Mystical Lady.* Pickens, SC: Wynn Publishing, 1995. 122 pages. Approximately 50 black-and-white photographs throughout.

Gypsy, poet, romantic, and beautiful dreamer Nicks is the subject of this large type soul search. Wincenstein sees depth and spirituality to her work few others have recognized (others concentrate on her sex appeal or her Munchkinland voice), and cites a number of sources of her creative flow, including Scottish occultist Aleister Crowley, the book *Sacred Symbols of the Ancients*, and even tarot cards and astrology. A decent, if light, effort with some gorgeous photos of the pop queen up through the early 1980's.

PICTORIALS

Carr, Roy and Clarke, Steve. *Fleetwood Mac: Rumours n' Fax.* New York: Harmony (division of Crown), 1978. 124 pages. Over 100 black-and-white and color photographs throughout. Contains a Discography.

Oblong-shaped book that traces how Christie McVie, Lindsey Buckingham, Mick Fleetwood and Stevie Nicks overcame personal traumas and legal troubles to become superstars of rock and roll that pleases almost everyone from ages 15-45. A must for the hard core fan (Bill Clinton take note!), as its concert shots are well photographed and the text contains a good many surprises about the band.

Graham, Samuel. *Fleetwood Mac: The Authorized History.* New York: Warner Books, 1978. 104 pages. Approximately 75 black-and-white photos throughout.

Ordinary photo history, with decent quality shots taken during the height of Mac's success in the mid-to-late 1970's. One could probably do without this out of print title and opt for Fleetwood's magnificent pictorial listed below.

WRITTEN WORKS

Fleetwood, Mick. *My Twenty-Five Years in Fleetwood Mac*. New York: Hyperion, 1992. 204 pages. Approximately 200 color and black-and-white and color photographs, covering nearly every page. Discography. Index. Comes with a CD of new and rare tracks.

Attractive and valuable photo history from drummer Fleetwood himself, with shots of the band in studio and live, handwritten lyric sheets, album covers, postcards, memorabilia, and much more. A fine complement to Fleetwood's autobiography (see *Fleetwood*, above); while the biography is the more essential read, this is the one most will reach for because it has both exquisite eye and ear candy. The CD, the marvelous interior design and casing, and the comprehensive discography make it a great gift item for the fan and collector.

YOUNG ADULT

Armstrong, Robert H. *Fleetwood Mac*. Mankato, MN: Creative Education, 1983. 32 pages. Approximately ten full-page black-and-white photos.

Part of the "Rock 'n Pop" series from Creative Education, this picture and fact-book is highly readable for the fan ten years old and younger. Slightly more recent than the outpour of Creative Education titles in the 1970's, but still very dated. Most would say the band slipped after that point anyway.

OTHER TITLES OF INTEREST
Vare, Ethlie and Ochs, Ed. *Stevie Nicks*. New York: Ballantine, 1984.

THE FLYING BURRITO BROTHERS

See Parsons, Gram.

PETER FRAMPTON

BIOGRAPHIES

Katz, Susan. *Frampton!: An Unauthorized Biography*. New York: Jove Publications (Harcourt Brace Jovanovich), 1978. 190 pages. Approximately 100 black-and-white photographs throughout. Discography.

An inept, sycophantic biography of the pop star. For a character description of Frampton, we have the following: "He's wholesome. And above all, he's nice." For a description of fan excitement, we have a tale concerning a young girl who is desperate to have in her possession "one of Frampton's 237 chest hairs." Frampton's life story is buried in the middle of this nightmare, which is full of ghastly mistakes. Unauthorized and unimaginably bad.

PICTORIALS

Clarke, Steve. *Peter Frampton: The Man Who Came Alive*. No city: Bunch Books, 1976. 64 pages. 12 full pages of color tinted pages scattered throughout; 50 black-and-white photographs.

This "fascinating biography in words, interviews, and photographs" has one benefit: It was published prior to Frampton's film *Sgt. Pepper's Lonely Hearts Club Band* and you don't have to suffer through the obligatory stills from the notorious flop. The book offers several rare childhood shots of Frampton, as well as photos with The Herd, Humble Pie, and solo; Frampton does seem to be rocking in most of these poses. Hopelessly lacking depth and discographical information.

YOUNG ADULT

Adler, Irene. *Peter Frampton*. New York: Quick Fox, 1979. 96 pages. 60 black-and-white photographs throughout. Discography.

"A photo biography" of Frampton during the height of his "pretty boy" popularity in the 1970's. The author goes way too far trying to convince us of Frampton's boy next door wholesomeness. Most of the photos (which printed very muddy) display him with the disco/pop stars of the era: Donna Summer, Leif Garrett, Olivia Newton-John, et al. Show me the way to something better.

OTHER TITLES OF INTEREST
Daly, Marsha. *Peter Frampton*. No city: Ace, 1979.

CONNIE FRANCIS

AUTOBIOGRAPHY

Francis, Connie. Introduction by Dick Clark. *Who's Sorry Now?*. New York: St. Martin's Press, 1984. 336 pages. 50 black-and-white photos throughout; one 16-page insert. Discography.

In the interim "clean cut" years of pop in the late 1950's and early 60's, Francis was the superstar love-interest of Bobby Darin and the polished vocalist of 25 top 100 singles in a five-year period. Not to mention the fact she could sing her songs in nearly a dozen languages. Francis tells the horror of her brutal rape in Westbury, New York in 1974 and of her brother George's tragic murder, but the book ends on the uplifting note of her comeback in 1981. While this book leaves much for biographers to fill in (there's hardly anything about the police investigation into her rape and no mention of her years in psychiatric treatment), fans will still want to share in her triumphs and tragedies.

FRANKIE GOES TO HOLLYWOOD

PICTORIALS

Blair, Ian. *Frankie Goes to Hollywood*. Chicago: Contemporary Books, Inc., 1985. 70 pages. Approximately 75 black-and-white photographs, covering every page.

Poorly executed photo spread about the Liverpool band. Then again, at the time of writing, the author only had two Frankie Goes to Hollywood hits to go on: "Relax" and "Two Tribes." The writing is wretched fanzine copy, mixed with some quotes on topics such as homosexuality and fan mail. The last page bears the ominous thought: "This is the last book you'll ever read."

OTHER TITLES OF INTEREST
Jackson, Danny. *Frankie Say: The Rise of Frankie Goes to Hollywood*. New York: Simon & Schuster, 1985.

ARETHA FRANKLIN

BIOGRAPHIES

Bego, Mark. *Aretha Franklin: The Queen of Soul*. New York: St. Martin's Press, 1989. 342 pages. Two eight-page glossy black-and-white photo inserts. Discography. Aretha's Grammy Awards. Index.

Franklin was abandoned by her mother at an early age, and shortly thereafter had to live with the pain of her death. She was raised by her father, an affluent and charismatic Baptist minister, and was given the rare opportunity of befriending many artists in the Detroit talent mill: Mahalia Jackson, Smokey Robinson, Sam Cooke, et. al. At fifteen, she gave birth to a child; to this day, no one knows the circumstances surrounding the occurrence. Mark Bego does a magnificent job exploring the pieces of Franklin's life and Grammy-filled career, and lays off giving credence to mindless hearsay surrounding her many skeletons. Occasionally, Bego uses slang ("laid me out") to a fault. The excellent photos contribute to this "...well rounded-portrait"—*Booklist*.

YOUNG ADULT

Olson, James T. *Aretha Franklin*. Mankato, MN: Creative Education, 1975. 32 pages. Approximately 20 original watercolors throughout.

Under-par entry in the "Rock 'n Pop Stars" series, which highlights shooting star logos more than it does its subject. Some of John Keely's art designs—such as an image of Franklin superimposed over a church—are effective, but others—such as a superimposed spread of the singer in African garb—are too busy. More than two decades out of date.

OTHER TITLES OF INTEREST
Haskins, James and Benson, Kathleen. *Aretha: A Personal & Professional Biography*. No city: Madison, 1987.

ALAN FREED

BIOGRAPHIES

Jackson, John A. *Big Beat Heat: Alan Freed and the Early Years of Rock & Roll.* New York: Schirmer (division of Macmillan, Inc.), 1991. 400 pages. Two 16-page glossy black-and-white photo inserts. Notes. Bibliography. Index.

Dubbed "the King of the Moondogs," disc jockey Alan Freed was rock & roll's leading proponent in the 1950's and was among the first to fully promote the concept of black music for a white audience. To his credit, Freed defended the teens who were allegedly incited to riot by rhythm and blues-inspired rock; he also aggressively fought racial barriers at a time when walls were being built. Yet, as author Jackson relays, show biz became too much of a temptation for Freed and he fell prey to the great payola scandal—in which he and other jockeys accepted bribes to increase radio airplay of certain artists—and ultimately drowned in alcohol until his death in 1965 at 44. A coherent and effective portrait.

KINKY FRIEDMAN

WRITTEN WORKS

Friedman, Kinky. *Armadillos and Old Lace.* New York: Simon & Schuster, 1994. 240 pages.

In his most recent mystery, Friedman once again mixes the bare facts of his life with a comic mystery. Having completed work on *Elvis, Jesus and Coca Cola* (see below), Friedman decides he needs a break from the city and flees to Knoxville, Texas and his family's homestead. Yet there's still no relief for the Kinkster; his cat vanishes (a sure sign of trouble ahead), spies materialize everywhere, four ladies turn up dead, and our hero detective has "a lady sheriff" on his tail. Enjoyable fare.

Friedman, Kinky. *Elvis, Jesus & Coca-Cola.* New York: Simon & Schuster, 1993. 302 pages.

A tape containing footage of Elvis imitators is missing, and a trail of corpses follows. Amateur detective Friedman goes on the case, primarily because his lover Uptown Judy has vanished, causing his other girl, Downtown Judy, to figure out their relationship. Friedman's misplaced country drawl in New York City is funny, fresh, and unlike anything else you'll ever read. This novel featuring Friedman's usual cast of wackos is worth a gander.

Friedman, Kinky. *Frequent Flyer.* New York: Berkley Books, 1990. 298 pages.

First published in 1989 by William Morrow and Company Inc., this is yet another mystery with Friedman on the trail of a dangerous case. This time, he and Ratso (his Watsonlike sidekick) must solve a puzzle as to why John Morgan, an old buddy from the jungles of Borneo, had died—yet his body wasn't the one in the coffin. Friedman meets up with Morgan's luscious fiancee and some rather unfriendly neo-Nazis who want to make sure the Jewish cowboy doesn't ride again. Leisurely reading, made all the more entertaining thanks to Friedman's gift for slang and wordplay.

Friedman, Kinky. *Greenwich Killing Time.* New York: William Morrow & Company, 1986. 204 pages.

Friedman's first detective novel proves that the country rocker can spin a yarn among the best of them. When a buddy reporter finds a corpse down the hall, he calls on the amateur sleuth to help solve the crime. The chain of events takes place in New York's Greenwich Village, but occasionally the characters mosey on up to the Carnegie Deli for a corned beef on rye. Fans will love it.

Friedman, Kinky. *Musical Chairs.* New York: William Morrow & Company, 1991. 264 pages.

Friedman churns out another scorching mystery. This time, however, the murder hits close to home when a former guitarist for the Texas Jewboys stays for a spell at Friedman's apartment and is found dead in the shower. Kinky and Ratso, his unlikely Watson, trudge through the suspects, who include a lesbian dancer and the former manager of the Lone Star. Cigar-chomping fun.

Friedman, Kinky. *When the Cat's Away* New York: William Morrow & Company, 1988. 204 pages.

Friedman, always the cat lover, at first investigates not a murder, but the disappearance of a cat at the annual Cat Show at Madison Square Garden. Ultimately, of course, dead bodies appear, and the Kinkster must press his case even harder—battling Columbian cocaine cartels along the way. As New York as a bagel and lox from Zabar's—but through the eyes of a Texan with just a few too many sprinkles of prairie dust in his head—this book is cynical and edgy, without guts and gore across the page. A noir work bursting with Friedman's asides and wit.

OTHER TITLES OF INTEREST

Friedman, Kinky. *God Bless John Wayne.* New York: Simon & Schuster, 1995.

Friedman, Kinky. *Kinky Friedman Mysteries.* New York: Random House, 1995.

Collection of three Kinky Friedman mystery novels: *Greenwich Killing Time* (see Written Works, above), *A Case of Lone Star*, and *When the Cat's Away* (see Written Works, above).

PETER GABRIEL

(See also Genesis)

BIOGRAPHIES

Bright, Spencer. *Peter Gabriel: An Authorized Biography.* London: Sidgwick & Jackson, 1988. 232 pages. Two glossy eight-page black-and-white photo inserts. Discography.

Starting out by introducing an unlikely subject—Tony Stratton Smith, the head of Charisma Records—Spencer Bright takes a while to find his way into the Peter Gabriel story. A child with a wild imagination, Gabriel was born into a creative and unusual family (his mother played the piano, his father was an inventor). Bright investigates Gabriel's years with Genesis, his split with the band, his dedication to human rights issues, and his love life. At press time, Gabriel had separated from his wife, Jill, and was thus free to continue his romance with Rosanna Arquette. In this slow-paced bio, trivialities such as Gabriel's attendance at an Osmonds concert are given almost equal attention to his musical talents. Should have been better.

QUIZBOOKS AND QUOTEBOOKS

St. Michael, Mick. *Peter Gabriel: In His Own Words.* London: Omnibus (division of Book Sales Limited), 1994. 96 pages. Approximately 80 photographs throughout.

Gabriel is quoted on dressing up, Phil Collins ("Phil was the critical element in terms of the feel of the music"), the split with Genesis ("The pressure was accumulating"), his records, playing live, etc. The standard "in his own words" format from Omnibus doesn't allow you to get inside Gabriel, but the photos are outrageous; you can't help your curiosity and stare at photos of him with a stocking over his head, his face smeared with multi-colored make-up, or even those in which he appears downright clean. For the dedicated.

OTHER TITLES OF INTEREST

Gallo, Armando. *Peter Gabriel.* Woodstock, NY: Beekman, 1990.

MARVIN GAYE

BIOGRAPHIES

Davis, Sharon. Introduction by Martha Reeves. *I Heard It Through the Grapevine.* Edinburgh, Scotland: Mainstream Publishing Company, 1991. 304 pages. One eight-page black-and-white photo insert. Discography. Bibliography. Index.

This manuscript has a long history that actually began with some cooperation from Gaye himself. Author Sharon Davis also had some access to performers Martha Reeves and Dusty Springfield. However, she is less knowledgeable about the man himself than David Ritz (see below) and, in fact, relies heavily on his work. You have to wait until the end of the book for the biography's lone revelation, attested to by witness Lady Edith Foxwell: That Marvin Gaye could have survived the fatal bullet shot from his father, if the paramedics had reacted more quickly to the emergency. Some excellent narrative of Motown's greatest personalities helps establish a solid backdrop to what is otherwise redundant material.

Ritz, David. *Divided Soul: The Life of Marvin Gaye*. New York and Toronto: Paperjacks Limited, 1986. 420 pages. One 32-page black-and-white photo insert. Discography. Index.

Ritz, Marvin Gaye's friend and one-time collaborator (co-songwriter of "Sexual Healing"), interviewed numerous friends, family, and associates of the artist to research this exhaustive and often shocking tale. Gaye had a tragic and peculiar life indeed: he was physically beaten by his father (who actually shot him to death on April Fool's Day, 1984 and got off on a suspended manslaughter charge); he had incredible feelings of sexual inadequacy that led to the abuse of women and his frequenting prostitutes; and he had insurmountable jealousies of other artists, including Stevie Wonder and Lou Rawls. The happy times are non-existent here, but this is where to start if you want the unglamorous truth behind a tortured soul legend. "Gripping fare..."—*New Musical Express*.

BOB GELDOF

(See also Selected General Reference: Concert Events)

AUTOBIOGRAPHY

Geldof, Bob with Vallely, Paul. *Is That It?*. New York: Weidenfeld & Nicolson, 1986. 360 pages. One eight-page color photo insert; 75 black-and-white photographs throughout. Index.

Geldof's early life has the feel of James Joyce's *A Portrait of the Artist as a Young Man*. Geldof grew up as an Irish Catholic working-class rebel; he suffered the loss of his mother at a young age; he was frequently beaten by his father; and he worked in a butcher slaughterhouse until he hooked up with punk/New Wave music and became the leader of The Boomtown Rats. This man who once had questionable values has somehow become the music world's greatest champion of causes and the force behind the Band Aid and Live Aid concert events. Although Geldof comes off as self-righteous, his prose is absorbing and difficult to put down. "...a clear and honest sharing of a most colorful life"—*Booklist*.

PICTORIALS

Blundy, David and Vallely, Paul. Photographs by Herrmann, Frank. Introduction by Bob Geldof. *With Geldof in Africa: Confronting the Famine Crisis*. London: Times Books, 1985. 160 pages. Approximately 150 color photographs, covering nearly every page.

Another example of Bob Geldof putting his money where his mouth is: In 1985, he and a small entourage traveled across Africa from Timbuctoo to Addis Adaba to see famine and poverty conditions firsthand. Journalists Blundy and Vallely capture Geldof's experiences in words and color photographs—predominately scenes of hunger and deprivation. Geldof met various dignitaries along the way, but most of his travels involved mingling with the masses. Like Geldof, readers will be alarmed to discover how mismanaged famine relief funds really are. All proceeds from this Times/Band Aid publication went toward that very cause. Teeming with disturbing full-page photos of emaciated, diseased frames, but well worth the guilt trip.

RELATED WORKS

Guthrie, Woody. *Bound for Glory*.

See Guthrie, Woody: Autobiography.

OTHER TITLES OF INTEREST
Aaseng, Nathan. *Bob Geldof: The Man Behind Live Aid*. Minneapolis, MN: Lerner Publications, 1986.
Gray, Charlotte. *Bob Geldof: The Rock Star Who Raised 140 Million Dollars for Famine Relief in Africa*. Milwaukee, WI: Stevens, Gareth, Inc., 1988.
May, Chris. *Bob Geldof*. London: Trafalgar, 1989.
Stone, Peter. *The Boomtown Rats: Having Their Picture Taken*. London: Star Books, 1980.

GENESIS

(See also Collins, Phil; Gabriel, Peter)

FANZINES AND FAN CLUBS

Deutscher Genesis Fan Club. c/o. Helmut Janisch, Postfach 261 36002 Fulda, Germany.

German Genesis fan club founded in 1991. Membership entitles one to the quarterly fanzine, supplemental newsletters, and a "newcomer set" that includes a membership card. The glossy, 30-page magazine is exclusively German and contains black-and-white photographs, updates on past and present members, articles on new releases, collectibles, and more. The cost of membership is 50 deutsche marks (DM) U.S.; 40 DM Europe; and 30 DM Germany.

Dusk: Italian Genesis Magazine. P.O. Box 10 82100 Benevento Italy.

Founded in 1991, this 56-page Italian fanzine features a color cover, black-and-white photographs throughout, and coverage of all Genesis band members past and present. A less extravagant issue translates the Italian into English. The cost per issue is 8.000 Italian lire; a subscription of three issues costs 25.000 Italian lire.

Genesis Information Australia. P.O. Box 19, Mortdale NSW 2223, Australia.

Genesis and Phil Collins information service that offers a quarterly newsletter and details about purchasing collectibles such as t-shirts, posters, videos, CDs, tour programs, and more. The cost per year is $25 (Australian).

USA Genesis Fan Club. c/o R. Baxter, P.O. Box 562, Mays Landing, NJ 08330.

Fan club that offers members information related to Genesis, including details on past and present members and related bands: Phil Collins, Mike and the Mechanics, Anthony Phillips, Steve Hackett, Peter Gabriel, Mike Rutherford, and Tony Banks. Members receive photos, special offers, and subscription to the quarterly fanzine, *Supper's Ready*. The 12-page, stapled packet includes updates on CD releases, tour plans, cyber news, reviews, pen friends, trivia, reprinted newspaper articles, and photocopies of black-and-white photographs. The cost of membership is $15 annually.

The Waiting Room. Attn. Alan J. Hewitt, 174 Salisbury Road, Everton, Liverpool L5 6RQ England.

Begun in 1987, this quarterly magazine claims to be the longest-running Genesis magazine in existence. The cost of membership is £10 for one year U.S. and Canada; £6 U.K.; and £10 elsewhere in Europe. Send payments (international money order drawn on U.K. bank draft only) to: Mr. P. Morton, P.O. Box 1002, Sheffield, S6 6YS, England.

PICTORIALS

Gallo, Armando. *The Evolution of a Rock Band: Genesis*. London: Sidgwick & Jackson, 1978. 178 pages. Approximately 150 black-and-white photographs, covering every page; one 16-page color insert. Equipment. Index.

A visual history of Genesis up through the *Seconds Out* LP. Author Armando Gallo had access to the band—he can be seen goofing off with the musicians in a number of shots—and absorbed an impressive amount of information, particularly pertaining to the early years. The photos (e.g., Charterhouse, where Tony Banks and Peter Gabriel went to school) seem to have been selected with great care, although they weren't arranged with any game plan in mind. In addition to the overwhelming number of pictures of groupies, wives, and girlfriends, you can see Gabriel as a teenager with wavy hair—and even Phil Collins giving Gabriel the literal kiss-off (yes, on the lips). Recommended for listeners of 1970's Genesis.

Gallo, Armando. Introduction by Dan Jones. *Genesis: From One Fan to Another*. Omnibus Press (division of Book Sales Limited), 1984. Unpaginated (approximately 144). Approximately 400 color photographs, covering every page; two dozen black-and-white photographs throughout.

Glossy photo collection that is even more animated than Gallo's earlier book (see above). The band can be seen in their usual assortment of offbeat costumes, both onstage and off. Interestingly, the publishers printed the original color slides in their casings on the front and back covers—and even in portions of the interior pages. Dan Jones, who wrote the introduction, is just a Genesis fan who helped select the photos.

Kamin, Philip and Goddard, Peter. Introduction by Phil Collins. *Genesis: Peter Gabriel, Phil Collins and Beyond*. New York: Beaufort Books, 1984. 128 pages. 75 color and 25 black-and-white photographs, covering every page.

An assemblage of live photos of the group together and solo from the Kamin/Goddard team: Kamin handles the pictures, Goddard writes the words. The book is divided into the following sections: reunion concert 1982; Mike Rutherford and Tony Banks; Phil Collins; Peter Gabriel (with and without hair); and Genesis on Genesis. The arrangement of Rutherford and Banks up front in Part Two nicely downplays the large shadows cast by the dynamic Collins and Gabriel. Most of the shots are close-ups, with colored lights and stage smoke looming large in the backdrops. A dynamic and moody presentation that should please fans of Genesis, Collins, and Gabriel alike.

Welch, Chris. *The Complete Guide to the Music of Genesis*. London: Omnibus Press (division of Book Sales Limited), 1995. 134 pages. Approximately 115 color and black-and-white photographs throughout.

CD-format book covering all aspects of Genesis' career. This nicely designed and illustrated book is priced just right at around $7.99.

OTHER TITLES OF INTEREST

Gallo, Armando. *Genesis: I Know What I Like*. Woodstock, NY: Beekman, 1990.

Parkynn, Geoff. *Genesis: Turn It On Again*. London: Omnibus (division of Book Sales Limited), 1984.

GERRY AND THE PACEMAKERS

AUTOBIOGRAPHY

Marsden, Gerry with Coleman, Ray. *I'll Never Walk Alone* London: Bloomsbury, 1993. 178 pages. Two glossy eight-page black-and-white photo inserts. Discography. Index.

Marsden, the frontman of Gerry and the Pacemakers, has innumerable ties to The Beatles: he was born in the Dingle section of Liverpool, from whence Ringo hailed; his group was managed by Brian Epstein and produced by George Martin; The Pacemakers had a number one hit with the song The Beatles recorded and rejected ("How Do You Do It?"); and the musician ultimately married George Harrison's one-time girlfriend. Marsden's praise of "The Beats" (as he refers to them) overflows, except when discussing the sacking of drummer Pete Best. Chocked full of cheeky Liverpudlian humor, *I'll Never Walk Alone* (the name of another Pacemakers' hit) is a chipper ferry ride across the Mersey.

DEBBIE GIBSON

TITLES OF INTEREST

Gibson, Debbie. *Between the Lines*. Austin, TX: Eakin Press, 1989.

Reisfeld, Randi. *Debbie Gibson: Electric Star: A Guide to Understanding & Overcoming Bulimia*. New York: Bantam, 1990.

GARY GLITTER

BIOGRAPHIES

Tremlett, George. *The Gary Glitter Story*. London: Futura Publications, 1975. 144 pages. One 16-page black-and-white photo insert. Chronology.

At one time known as "the British Elvis Presley" (probably by those who said the same for Cliff Richard), Gary Glitter (born Paul Gadd) was the only Protestant boy attending a Catholic school. He knew as far back as 1958 that he wanted to be a rock star, but it took a failed marriage and years struggling in Germany before he finally hit big with "Rock and Roll Part II." Tremlett bears the distinction of having written the only biography of this faded glam-rocker; the information on his life and career up through 1975 is here, for those poor souls who need it.

THE GO-GO'S

FANZINES AND FAN CLUBS

Beatnik Beat: The Go-Go's Fanzine. 4960 Alamaden Expy #186, San Jose, CA 95118. U.K.: P.O. Box 129, Southport, Merseyside PR86UW, England.

Bimonthly fanzine, consisting of approximately 32 pages, with concert and studio information, as well as letters from fans, black-and-white photos, and some original art. Since its founding in 1993, the zine has enjoyed some cooperation from the Go-Go's and has had a few exclusive interviews. The cost in the U.S. is $3.50 per issue (make checks payable to Craig Ehr); in the U.K., £1.75 per issue (make checks payable to Paul Barber).

BERRY GORDY

AUTOBIOGRAPHY

Gordy, Berry. *To Be Loved: The Music, the Magic, the Memories of Motown*. New York: Warner Books, 1994. 432 pages. Four glossy 16-page black-and-white photo inserts. Released Compositions by Berry Gordy. Index.

The brilliant visionary who started it all for black artists was the son of a plastering contractor in Detroit. After almost pursuing a boxing career, Berry brought his fighting instincts to the music industry and paved the careers of several Motown legends: The Supremes, Marvin Gaye, Smokey Robinson, The Jackson 5, Stevie Wonder, The Four Tops, and countless others. Berry admits to the controversies involved in his personal and professional lives—that he fathered Diana Ross' child and that he had tyrannical control over his artists—but with the sub-context that he survived using the only means available to him as a black businessman in a white industry. Surprisingly affable tale from "...an African-American culture hero of historic stature"—*The New York Times*.

GORDY FRIENDS AND FAMILY

Gordy, Sr., Berry. Introduction by Alex Haley. *Movin' Up: Pop Gordy Tells His Story*. New York: Harper & Row, 1979. 144 pages. One five-page black-and-white photo insert.

Fondly referred to as "Pops" by all who knew him, Berry Gordy, Sr. was an executive at Motown Records, the company created by his pioneering son. Motown musicians such as Diana Ross and Marvin Gaye had enormous respect for the elder Gordy, and the two (with Stevie Wonder and Smokey Robinson) recorded the song "Pops We Love You" in his honor. This posthumously published autobiography traces the Gordy lineage to Native Americans and to southern plantation slaves down south. Gordy Sr.'s language is earthy and funny, particularly when he describes his childhood love of roasted eggs. He also recounts his odd jobs as a contractor, the family's move to Detroit, confrontations with racism, and more—but the story pretty much ends prior to his involvement in the music industry. Strong supplemental reading for Motown and Berry, Jr. scholars.

Singleton, Raynoma Gordy with Brown, Bryan and Eichler, Mim. *Berry, Me and Motown: The Untold Story*. Chicago: Contemporary, 1990. 345 pages. Two glossy eight-page black-and-white photo inserts. Index.

Raynoma Gordy Singleton was Berry Gordy Jr.'s wife and helped nurture the acts and the business that would make Motown the hit-making epicenter of the 1960's. While clear about Gordy's abilities as a charismatic leader, she is also brutally honest about his infidelities (including on their wedding night!), greed, jealousies, and spitefulness. During their torrid relationship, Gordy had his wife arrested by the FBI, allowed his psychopathic lover to torment her, and then left her penniless after their divorce. Singleton's battle to assert her independence gains our sympathy only up to a point; after a while readers will be baffled as to why she continues to allow herself to reappear in Gordy's life.

BILL GRAHAM

AUTOBIOGRAPHY

Graham, Bill and Greenfield, Robert. Afterword by David Graham. *Bill Graham Presents: My Life Inside Rock and Out*. New York: Doubleday (division of Bantam Doubleday Dell), 1992. 568 pages. Two glossy eight-page black-and-white photo inserts. Speakers. Index.

Posthumously published oral autobiography from the enigmatic concert promoter, and winner of the Ralph J. Gleason Music Book Award. Born Wolodia Gajonca, Graham escaped from Nazi Germany as a child, was adopted by U.S. foster parents, became a soldier before he was officially an American citizen, worked as a busboy in the Catskills, and, in 1965, hooked up with the happenings in San Francisco. Before long he was promoting local acts such as The Grateful Dead and The Jefferson Airplane and introducing The Doors and The Byrds to the scene. Able to dish it out (e.g., telling off Barbra Streisand) as well as take it (e.g., a microphone flung into his head by Jim Morrison), Graham was a powerful and irreplaceable figure in rock history. The thousands of lengthy quotes—from Bill himself, relatives, associates, and musicians—amount to a riveting epic tale.

BIOGRAPHIES

Glatt, John. *Rage & Roll: Bill Graham and the Selling of Rock*. New York: Carol Publishing Group, 1993. 306 pages. Two eight-page glossy black-and-white photo inserts. Notes and Sources. Index.

While Graham and Greenfield's definitive oral opus (see *Bill Graham Presents*, above) contains probably all you need to know about the impresario, this fine biography should not be overlooked as supplemental reading. Glatt's narrative has a quicker pace, so you absorb the highlights while at the same time gaining an even more rounded picture of Graham: a clever, creative, hyperactive, greedy, gambler who transplanted himself from New York to San Francisco to make a name for himself— always above the bands he hyped. This biography perhaps tells the wider truths of his conflicts with Chet Helms, Don King, and The Rolling Stones. "...a fast-moving, colorful and well-researched portrait..."—*Publishers Weekly*.

THE GRATEFUL DEAD

BIOGRAPHIES

Jackson, Blair. *Grateful Dead: The Music Never Stopped*. New York: Delilah Books (Putnam), 1983. 260 pages. 75 black-and-white photos throughout. Pull-out family tree. A Critical Discography.

Fanzine-like history of the band, organized haphazardly and with little in the way of inside information. The author's heart is in the right place, but the coverage is superficial and the writing rather strained. Descriptions of the albums in the text overlap in content, flavor, and tone with the reviews in the "Critical Discography" section. Young Dead fans might like the casual approach and the photos (some of which are rare). Fans are better directed to Jackson's excellent pictorial (see below).

Troy, Sandy. Foreword by Gene Anthony. *Captain Trips: A Biography of Jerry Garcia*. New York: Thunder's Mouth Press, 1994. 288 pages. Two sixteen-page glossy black-and-white photo inserts. Appendix A: An Early Garcia Song List. Appendix B: Astrological Chart and Interpretation. Notes. Bibliography. Index.

Captain Trips is not much different from any other general history of The Dead. The formative years are miniscule summaries of the basic events in Garcia's life: the loss of half his middle finger; his father's drowning; his dishonorable discharge from the Army; etc. Why aren't there quotes from childhood friends, relatives, teachers, and Army buddies to provide details and anecdotes? Despite a colorful jacket and two strong photo inserts, *Captain Trips* won't take you where want to go. *The New York Times* pointed out that it "serves to correct the impression that life for the rock group has been an unending round of parties, drug taking and music."

CHRONOLOGIES

Greene, Herb. *Dead Days: A Grateful Dead Illustrated History*. Petaluma, CA: Acid Test Productions, 1994. Unpaginated (approximately 120 pages). 100 color and black-and-white photos and graphics throughout.

"Commemorative edition" of a "perpetual datebook," this slender volume contains sentence bites of information—primarily club dates—listed chronologically on a day-by-day calendar. It's not exactly meant as a personal journal or as a daily planner, although it could have passed for either with a design change here and there. What it offers fans, though, are some excellent condition color illustrations that have been well selected, but may seem too familiar to Dead fans who have large libraries. If you need to know dates, check out *DeadBase* (see Discographies, below); if you want a photo book, there are countless variations listed below. This one just doesn't fill a niche.

CRITICAL/ANALYTICAL COMMENTARY

Womack, David. *Aesthetics of the Grateful Dead: A Critical Analysis*. Palo Alto: Flying Public Press, 1991. 192 pages.

Judging by this horrendous piece of critical hogwash, one might think no one has ever said a kind word about The Dead. The author acts as self-appointed spokesman for The Dead, in order to flatten the critics who had reported negatively on the band. Some who take it on the nose are Greil Marcus, Robert Hilburn, and, most solidly, Dave Marsh. From what I gather the group has a pretty thick skin and really couldn't care less what the critics have to say. This book manages to include a cliché on nearly every line; he even uses the phrase "idiot wind of pop criticism," something that relates quite appropriately to this book. Unaesthetic.

DEADHEADS AND GRATEFUL DEAD FRIENDS AND FAMILY

Grushkin, Paul; Bassett, Cynthia; Grushkin, Jonas. Preface by Jerry Garcia. *The Official Book of the Dead Heads.* New York: Quill (division of Morrow & Co.), 1983. 216 pages. Hundreds of color and black-and-white photos; many Dead-related drawings, doodles, graphic art, etc. Encore: Grateful Dead Tour List.

A pictorial celebration of the Deadheads themselves—dedicated fans and followers of The Grateful Dead since 1965. The book includes letters from Deadheads, some brief newspaper excerpts and a few lyrics, but the essence here is in the photos themselves, which are quite good. What one really gets to understand is the respect the band had for their cult flock. As Jerry Garcia put it, "I see the Dead Heads both as familiar faces in the audience and stars in their own right."

Harrison, Hank. *The Dead.* Millbrae (CA): Celestial Arts, 1980. 336 pages. Over 100 black-and-white photos throughout. Partial Discography. Astrological Charts.

Volumes two ("Under the Dragon") and three ("Sausalito Split") of an ongoing series (see below). Dubious as social history of the 1960's, but more than enough fun to hang in for the author's tales of The Dead's ultimate highs and lows. His often clumsy history of San Francisco, the Haight-Ashbury scene, etc. should be taken with major grains of salt, yet it is entertaining. Harrison was Phil Lesh's roommate on two occasions, and has keen insights into the personas of band members. The passage concerning Pigpen's gradual demise is particularly touching. *The Dead* is not a definitive biography, history, or social commentary by any means, but it is a unique relic Dead fans might want to dig up.

Harrison, Hank. *The Dead: Volume One.* Los Altos (CA): The Archives Press, 1990. 240 pages. 75 black-and-white photographs. Annotated Index.

Updated edition (the earlier editions were pub-

lished in 1972 and 1985) of the first in a three volume series from Harrison, one of the founders of the Haight-Ashbury community, former manager of The Warlocks and now perhaps best known as Courtney Love's father. Harrison is emphatic that this is not a biography of The Dead, but an "underground classic" of the Haight-Ashbury revolution. Why, then, the title? To cash in on The Dead market without supplying the goods on the band itself? Lots of rare photos here and some restored text that had been censored in earlier versions, but the writing is sloppy and the reflections lack accessibility to a modern readership. The follow-ups (combined in one volume above) are a significant improvement.

Keeney, Bradford. *Crazy Wisdom Tales for Deadheads: A Shamanic Companion to the Grateful Dead.* New York: Barrytown, Limited, 1996. 120 pages. Approximately 100 black-and-white pen-and-ink drawings and engravings throughout.

Jokey instruction manual, verging on condescending, that sheds spiritual guidance to those seeking to join The Grateful Dead's flock. Through ludicrous meditative exercises and rituals, Keeney pokes fun at the habits of Deadheads, while at the same time trying to show there is something to all this mumbo-jumbo. "Go visit a garden and take one pinch of dirt," advises Keeney, "Sprinkle this dirt over your *Crazy Wisdom Tales for Deadheads* and say out loud, `I hereby baptize my Shaman's Companion in the name of Mother Earth and all that provides a ground for becoming.'" Stories and passages involve acting like a Merry Prankster, tapping into your dreams, and building an ark. Taken literally—which some individuals may be inclined to do—may make this a rather dangerous volume. The laughs are never out loud.

Kelly, Linda. *Deadheads: Stories from Fellow Artists, Friends, and Followers of the Grateful Dead.* New York: Citadel (Carol Publishing Group), 1995. 244 pages. Approximately 50 black-and-white photographs throughout.

As Timothy Leary is quoted here as saying, "Shit! We were doing this thirty years ago, hanging around backstage," so too does this book seem oddly familiar and reminiscent of a slew of other Dead books. Fans, musicians, writers, and associates ranging from Dead lyricist John Perry Barlow to green grocer/

Deadhead Annie Harlow pass on their reminiscences of The Dead experience, from getting turned on, to getting tickets, to growing older, etc.—but this volume lacks the steam and originality of some other volumes, notably Blair Jackson's work (see Interviews). For those who intend to stay "on the bus" interminably.

Scully, Rock with Dalton, David. *Living With the Dead: Twenty Years on the Bus with Garcia and the Grateful Dead*. New York: Little, Brown, 1996. 381 pages. Two glossy eight-page black-and-white photo inserts. Index.

The Dead's former manager, Rock Scully, tells his version of the band's story. According to Scully, he had Garcia's blessing on the project—or at least the guitarist gave him encouragement to "tell the truth." Only insiders will be able to recognize whether the facts delivered here are on target or askew. To the objective viewer, Scully seems to be taking out his gripes on the late Garcia by rattling off the man's weight gains, staggering cholesterol level, blood toxicity, and inability to handle a relationship with a woman for years after his break-up with Mountain Girl in the 1970's. All of this seems to build up to Scully's own resentment for having been put under fire by The Dead entourage for allegedly plundering The Dead till. A bit fierce.

DEATH OF GARCIA

Gans, David (Editor). Foreword by Steve Silberman. *Not Fade Away: The On-Line World Remembers Jerry Garcia*. New York: Thunder's Mouth Press, 1995. 128 pages. Approximately 75 black-and-white photographs throughout.

When Jerry Garcia died, the Internet was flooded with tributes and comments on The Dead's legendary guitarist. Most of the cyberspace writers were Deadheads, but a few 1960's insiders (such as Ken Kesey and Wavy Gravy) sing a few notes of praise for their lost friend. Some of the quotes are shlocky (one Deadhead: "Jerry will be reincarnated as a long string of notes"), but a few passages translate successfully from the moment of initial shock to the present. Photo contributors include Richard McCaffrey, f-stop Fitzgerald, and Baron Wolman. Those who aren't on the Superhighway may want to check this out in print and see what they are missing.

DICTIONARIES AND ENCYCLOPEDIAS

Shenk, David and Silberman, Steve. *Skeleton Key: A Dictionary for Deadheads*. New York: Doubleday (division of Bantam Doubleday Dell), 1994. 388 pages. Appendices: The Dead Line (chronology); How to Tie-Dye; How to Become a Nethead; Profiles from the Zones (profiles of sources); Sources; Notes; Deadhead's Bookshelf.

Investigating Grateful Dead terminology, slang, songs, albums, metaphors, and key personnel, this language book is a cherishable commodity for fans, rock mavens, and linguists. *Skeleton Key* is full of detailed definitions, concise examples of usage, and amusing anecdotes (including quotes from band members). After reading, you'll find out how to avoid "the ick," know where the "Phil zone" is located, and discover the origins of "cherry Garcia." The book supplies loads of cross-references, a few black-and-white graphics and some useful discographical lists. While the nitpicky will find many glaring omissions—there isn't an entry for the general term "trip," for example—most are encouraged to get "on the bus."

Trager, Oliver. *The American Book of the Dead: A Grateful Dead Encyclopedia*. New York: Fireside (Simon & Schuster), 1997. 352 pages. 70 black-and-white photographs throughout. Index.

As much a discography and recording history of The Dead as it is a comprehensive A to Z encyclopedia, this unique book contains entries on all songs ever recorded and/or performed by The Dead, as well as on full-length Grateful Dead records, places, books, films, and biographical profiles on the musicians and their ilk. For albums, meticulous researcher Oliver Trager identifies record labels, catalog numbers, producers, song line-ups, and then follows with detailed summaries of their importance, along with a wealth of notes, anecdotes, and quotes. For songs, Trager includes information such as composers, the artists who covered them (before and after The Dead), synopses of their history, and even closing lines indicating the author's preferred live performances. The biographical entries (e.g., one on Canon's Jug Stompers, a jug band that inspired The Dead) are endlessly fascinating and historically relevant. The author and publisher have made the wise decision to illustrate lesser-known figures rather than overdoing the traditional cliché shots of Jerry on stage with guitar. A rare encyclopedia that should be savored from beginning to end. Essential.

DISCOGRAPHIES, RECORDING GUIDES, AND COLLECTIBLES

Scott, John W.; Dolgushkin, Mike; and Nixon, Stu. *DeadBase IX: The Complete Guide to Grateful Dead Song Lists*. Hanover, NH: DeadBase (P.O. Box 499-R, Hanover, NH 03755), 1996. 780 pages. Approximately 200 black-and-white photographs throughout.

A marvel by self-publishing standards: the most exhaustive, up-to-date, accurate and anal retentive discography/song list ever compiled. This annual publication is not only updated every year or so to catalog each year's concerts and recordings, but also to fill in old gaps on rare recordings and bootlegs—and make key design improvements. Contains: song lists, songs played, statistics, played/not played, every time played, places played, arena survey, Deadhead survey (absolutely fascinating, based on annual reader's surveys of Deadheads themselves), feedback results, tape trimmings, reviews, discography, GarciaBase, WeirBase, and Odds & Ends. In other words, every Dead recording and live performance is presented in every way imaginable. The format is complex, but easy enough to figure out with some time spent absorbing the introduction. If you are a collector or would-be collector, this is the place to begin—and end—your search for Dead information. For fans that own past editions, DeadBase also publishes a separate catalog of the year's Dead shows and recordings with the subtitle "The Annual Edition of the Complete Guide to Grateful Dead Song Lists."

FANZINES AND FAN CLUBS

Dupree's Diamond News: Documenting the Deadhead Experience. P.O. Box 936, Northampton, MA 01061.

Glossy eighty-page magazine published four times a year. Each issue contains black-and-white photographs, essays on recent concerts, interviews with Grateful Dead musicians, new releases, collectibles, song statistics, profiles of cool 1990's bands, classifieds, personals, tape trading, books, and much more. In 1996, the magazine published *Garcia: A Grateful Celebration*, a beautiful 104-page paperbound

tribute to Jerry Garcia that includes glossy color and black-and-white photographs, poetry from lyricist Robert Hunter and reflections from friends and musicians, such as David Crosby, Mountain Girl, Ken Kesey, and many others. The cost of the book is $10 in the U.S.; $14.95 in Canada; and £8.90 in the U.K. The cost of one year subscription to the magazine is $14 in the U.S.; $18 in Canada; and $26 in Europe. The cost per issue is $4.50 in the U.S.; $6.50 in Canada; and £4 in the U.K.

Relix: Music for the Mind. Relix Magazine, Inc., P.O. Box 94, Brooklyn, NY 11229.

Bimonthly magazine on The Grateful Dead, with a glossy color cover and black-and-white photographs throughout. Approximately 70 pages provide: various submissions by fans; feature articles on events, people, and places; stories on technological advancements; interviews with Grateful Dead band members and insiders; Bay area news; updates on artists from the psychedelic period; collectibles; book and CD reviews; and more. The cost of subscription is $34 for eight issues in the U.S.; $42 elsewhere. The newsstand price is $4 U.S.; $5.75 Canada; and £4.50 U.K.

Unbroken Chain. P.O. Box 49019, Austin, TX 78765-9019.

Quarterly, 34-page Grateful Dead fanzine that contains black-and-white photographs, interviews, Web comments and sites, recommended tapes, reviews, and more. The cost of subscription is $12 in the U.S.; $18 in Canada; and $25 elsewhere.

INTERVIEWS

Gans, David. Foreword by Blair Jackson. *Conversations with the Dead: The Grateful Dead Interview Book*. New York: Citadel Press (Carol Publishing Group), 1991. 352 pages. Two eight-page glossy black-and-white photo inserts.

A solid compilation of interviews with Dead-related figures spanning the years 1977-1991. Most of the interviews were conducted between 1981-1983. There are many juicy quotes to be found here: Robert Hunter comments that Bob Weir "uses a lyricist like a whore"; and Jerry Garcia bashes The Doors, stating that Jim Morrison was nothing but "a Mick Jagger imitation." Does Bob Weir feel The

Dead sets out to transmit a message? "Hell no," he retorts. Other interview subjects include acid guru Bear (Owsley Stanley), Mickey Hart, and Don Healy. Gans is a meticulous journalist, and he does an admirable job providing useful notes at the bottom of pages. Foreword writer Jackson co-interviewed a few of the subjects with Gans.

Jackson, Blair. *Goin' Down the Road: A Grateful Dead Traveling Companion.* New York: Harmony Books (division of Crown), 1992. 336 pages. 35 black-and-white photographs throughout.

Dead fans will appreciate this collection of material excerpted from *The Golden Road* fanzine, which is now defunct, but during its time was considered the top Grateful Dead rag. Articles, contributed mostly by Jackson, span February 1984-March 1991 and include interviews with Jerry Garcia, Donna Godchaux, Bob Weir, Phil Lesh, Bill Kreutzmann, Mickey Hart, and Robert Hunter. Each interview has a surprise or two; Godchaux, for example, said that she sang on two Elvis tracks, "Suspicious Minds" and "In the Ghetto." For good measure, Jackson supplies a "Roots" section (histories of songs The Dead covered), a Neal Cassady tribute, and more. "...get this book"—*Booklist*.

Reich, Charles and Wenner, Jann. *Garcia: A Signpost to New Space.* New York: Straight Arrow Books (distributed by Quick Fox), 1972. 260 pages. 50 black-and-white photographs.

Dated but thorough interview with Dead guitarist Jerry Garcia, portions of which were originally printed in *Rolling Stone*. This book offers Garcia's take on just about everything, including pot, sex, the hippie scene, music, playing guitar, his personal history, etc., and we find him to be a highly intelligent and sensitive philosopher. He's also quite funny—early, terrible choices for a band name included Emergency Crew and Mythical Ethical Icicle Tricycle. Twenty plus years later this book doesn't hold many surprises, but is a curio item since Garcia had co-copyright on it.

Troy, Sandy. Illustrations by Stanley Mouse. *One More Saturday Night: Reflections with the Grateful Dead, Dead Family, and Dead Heads.* New York: St. Martin's, 1991. 284 pages. 30 color illustrations and over 150 black-and-white photographs and graphic designs.

The story in Sandy Troy's book is really the terrific cover and brief flashes of interior art by Stanley Mouse—the master of 1960's psychedelic art executed primarily on posters and album covers. Mouse is also among the 19 people briefly interviewed in this book, most of whom fall under The Dead family or Deadheads category: Rock Scully (former Dead manager), Alec Levy (one time Dead booking agent), and even Tony Serra (a criminal defense lawyer and Dead fan). The Dead are only represented in two chapters: one grouping features Jerry Garcia, Dan Healy, Phil Lesh, and Ramrod; and another solely covers keyboardist Tom Constanten. Recommended for those wanting a peak at Mouse's creations and some rare photos, or those seeking interviews with figures peripheral to The Dead.

PICTORIALS

Brandelius, Jerilyn Lee. Foreword by Bill Graham. *Grateful Dead Family Album.* New York: Warner Books, 1989. 260 pages. Approximately two hundred color and black-and-white illustrations throughout.

Arguably, the best pictorial of The Dead ever put together—at the least, it's the most colorful. The rare photos (mostly taken by Brandelius herself) are superb and are printed on high quality, multi-colored paper. The design—notably the montages—is top-notch. Subjects are chronological and include The Merry Pranksters, orgies with Janis Joplin, Woodstock, trips to Egypt (quite extensive), New Year's Eve celebrations, and infinitely more. The book ends with a two-page spread on saving the rain forests. Perfect for any Deadhead in need of a visual trip.

Editors of *Rolling Stone. Garcia.* New York: Little, Brown, 1995. 240 pages. Approximately 200 color and black-and-white illustrations throughout. Garcia Discography.

Respectful photo tribute to the memory of Garcia, with generous illustrative material supplementing articles that had been published in *Rolling Stone* magazine over the past three decades. While the package is lovely to look at, the contents are difficult to read and there is no index; however, it's doubtful anyone will read all of the text from front to back anyway. Among the 23 or so fine pieces (all by men) that should not be missed are those by Ben Fong-Torres, Robert Hunter, and Jann Wenner.

A classy design, from the quotes on the endpaper to Garcia's handprint on the back cover. Recommended.

Gans, David and Simon, Peter. Foreword by Phil Lesh. *Playing in the Band: An Oral and Visual Portrait of the Grateful Dead.* New York: St. Martin's Press, 1985. 192 pages. One 32-page color insert; over 200 black-and-white photographs, covering nearly every page. Sources.

A thematically arranged pictorial history, with a generous offering of color and black-and-white photos. The "text" of the book consists of quotes from the band taken out-of-context and grouped together according to the knowledgeable, though idiosyncratic, whims of the authors. Dates and sources are intentionally not provided because "Seeing these words outside their usual contexts, the reader may find new angles from which to engage the ideas and images." The design of the book sometimes makes it difficult to distinguish between where a quote ends and where the authors' comments begin. For light browsing only.

Greene, Herb. Foreword by Robert Hunter. *Book of the Dead: Celebrating 25 Years with the Grateful Dead.* New York: Delacorte and Delta Books (division of Bantam Doubleday Dell), 1990. 160 pages. 100 black-and-white photographs throughout.

Over the years Greene, a commercial and later rock photographer, posed The Dead on a few occasions and captured them in stark black-and-white. While this may seem incongruous with the band's colorful, psychedelic image, it does present a different, introspective side of the group. Shots of Pigpen make him seem deceptively forlorn and sensitive. Ironically, in the more recent shots, the band seems to be having more naughty boy fun (performing surgery on drummer Mickey Hart with a saw). The photographs are of superior quality, but there are few shots from the 1970's through the mid-80's. Fans will also be disappointed by the lack of caption material. Others might see the book as a nifty change of pace for a Dead pictorial.

Jensen, Jamie. *Grateful Dead: Built to Last: 25th Anniversary Album.* London and New York: Plume (New American Library, a division of the Penguin Group), 1990. 96 pages.

Approximately 120 color and black-and-white photos, covering every page.

Concise pictorial history (the size of a tour book) with lots of blank space, which does make for a pleasant, though unoriginal, read. The photos tend to be crammed into the margins and are rather small (especially a shot of the 1967 "human be-in"). Reportedly, The Dead gave "full cooperation" for the book's publication. Certainly a better find than the Ruhlmann anniversary tribute listed below.

Ruhlmann, William. *The History of the Grateful Dead.* New York: Gallery Books ((W.H. Smith Publishers, Inc.), 1990. 96 pages (oversized). Full color and black-and-white illustrations throughout. Large color poster. Discography. Index.

Dubbing this photo treatment a "25th anniversary edition" and throwing in a color poster do not help bring it out of its place as a remainder (post-publication dung-heap) item. While there are a few rare and eye-catching photos, Deadheads will find the coverage superficial and the book design rather ordinary. The discography lists singles and albums by the group and by the members as soloists, but does not refer to any bootlegs or special releases.

Tamarkin, Jeff and Schreiner, David (editors). Introduction by Jerry Garcia. *Grateful Dead Comix.* New York: Hyperion, 1992. 120 pages. Approximately 250 original color panels, covering every page.

A greatest hits collection of comic strips largely conceived by The Grateful Dead themselves. Inexplicably, except for Garcia's introduction, The Dead remain humbly uncredited on the cover and title page. The Dead—specifically Garcia, lyricist Robert Hunter, Bob Weir, Phil Lesh, and Bill Kreutzmann—created the storylines or concepts for the strips, while professional artists such as Randall Bendt, Dan Steffan, Tim Truman, Dan Burr, Nina Paley, and host of others "interpreted" and "colored" them. The stories vary greatly in terms of styles and themes, taking on nightmarish tones in some, while cartoonish fantasies and autobiographical allegories in others. Deadheads who haven't purchased the comics can atone by seeking out this entertaining book. "...the book's dual appeal to comics aficionados and fans of the Dead makes it a natural for pop-culture collections"— *Booklist*.

QUIZBOOKS AND QUOTEBOOKS

Folker, Brian A. *Tell Me All That You Know: The Unauthorized Grateful Dead Trivia Book*. New York: Pinnacle (Kensington), 1996. 124 pages.

Slightly larger than a deck of playing cards, this quizbook is divided into 20 or so topics, ranging from geography to aliases to films to Jerry Garcia tribute. Questions are almost exclusively in a straight question-and-answer format, and the resolutions immediately follow each section. Some questions are on the easy end of the spectrum ("In what year did The Warlocks become The Grateful Dead?") while others demand broader knowledge ("What is the inscription on Pigpen's tombstone?"). Given this volume's small size and the absence of photographs, the appeal of this book is limited to fans of junior high and high school age.

No author. *The Wisdom of Jerry Garcia*. New York: Wolf Valley Books, 1995. Unpaginated (approximately 120).

Quickie cash-in quotebook, shot to press just after Garcia's death. Only younger fans will derive any value from this simplistic presentation, which waters Garcia's messages down to 10-20 word quotes (only one per page) and doesn't supply any sources. Garcia's wisdom is worthy of attention ("It's not enough to be good at your instrument—you also have to be able to get along with other musicians"), but one wouldn't want to see him on *Reader's Digest*'s "Quotable Quotables" page. If you have the urge, read this one in the bookstore aisle.

RELATED WORKS

Franzosa, Bob (editor). *Grateful Dead Folktales*. Orono: Zosafarm, Publications, 1989. 152 pages.

Yes, Jerry Garcia did spot the words "Grateful Dead" in *Funk and Wagnalls New Practical Standard Dictionary* and apply them to the name of his band. This collection of 13 international folktales bears no relation to the band itself (it is unknown which band members have actually read the stories), save the registered trademark of The Dead on the cover. These magical, ancient stories—from Italy, France, Iceland, Greece, and elsewhere—basically tell the same tale in ways unique to the respective cultures and the interpreters who set them down to paper. The common thread is that in each a young man pays the debts of an unburied corpse (or helps pay for the burial); later, the ghost of the "gratefully dead" corpse takes another form and helps the fellow succeed in a quest. Each story is engrossing.

Izumi, Alan Neal. Foreword by Robert Hunter. *Dead Tour*. Brooklyn: Relix Magazine, Inc, 1988. 172 pages.

Sophomoric mystery novel about a college senior who is enlightened to Dead Music and becomes entangled in stolen bootlegs and murder. Along the way he finds sex, love, and LSD, and learns how to dance at a Dead concert. The writing is choppy and full of clichés. For uninitiated Dead fans with low standards.

Rilke, Rainer Maria. Translated by Hunter, Robert. *Duino Elegies*. Eugene: Hulogos'i Communications, 1987. 120 pages. Approximately 20 original blockprints by Maureen Hunter.

Rilke wrote these ten elegies in German between 1912 and 1922. Robert Hunter, The Grateful Dead's lyricist, has supplied the original verse opposite his contemporary American English translations. Although the book doesn't provide literary commentary or historical background, Maureen Hunter's blockprints add some mood and flavor. The recommended translation remains Stephen Bender and J.D. Leishman's 1939 classic.

SAN FRANCISCO

Anthony, Gene. Foreword by Michael McClure. *The Summer of Love: Haight-Ashbury at Its Highest*. Millbrae: Celestial Arts, 1980. 184 pages. 275 black-and-white photographs; eight-page color insert. Dance Concerts. Index.

Pictorial history of the San Francisco scene, with rare shots and some psychedelic color to look at in the middle insert. Rare shots of Grace Slick, Jerry Rubin, Lenny Bruce, Janis Joplin, George Harrison, Bill Graham, Timothy Leary, and many others. A good visual companion to Perry's *The Haight-Ashbury* (see below).

McDonough, Jack. Foreword by Paul Kantner. *San Francisco Rock: The Illustrated History of San Francisco Rock Music*. San Francisco: Chronicle Books, undated. 228 pages. Three eight-page color inserts; 200 black-and-white photos throughout. Index.

Retrospective of the San Francisco rock scene, emphasizing, of course, the late 1960's. The first part hits the major artists (The Grateful Dead, The Jefferson Airplane, et. al.), while later sections cover impresarios, concert halls, music industry moguls, etc. The final A to Z portion profiles San Francisco-area rock musicians up through the present, including many artists who do not carry the Bay sound: Creedence Clearwater Revival, Sammy Hagar, Night Ranger, etc. This one should have gone either closer toward a narrative pictorial or an illustrated encyclopedia; as a combination of both, it fails miserably.

Perry, Charles. *The Haight-Ashbury*. New York: Vintage (Random House), 1984. 308 pages. Index.

The bands: Big Brother and the Holding Company, The Grateful Dead, The Jefferson Airplane, Country Joe and the Fish, and The Charlatans. The main substances: LSD, marijuana, and methedrine. The leaders: Timothy Leary, Jerry Rubin, and Ken Kesey and his Merry Pranksters. The hangouts: the psychedelic shop and 710 Ashbury ("the Dead House"). Where and when did all of this take place? San Francisco's infamous cross-section, Haight and Ashbury, between the years 1965-1967. This is good, simple reportage from Perry, capturing the spirit of the psychedelic era without the usual overdone nostalgia and heavy-handedness. However, you'll need other sources if you want illustrative matter. "There are portions of [this] exhaustively researched pop history that will blow your mind"—*The Fresno Bee*.

Selvin, Joel. *Summer of Love: The Inside Story of LSD, Rock & Roll, Free Love and High Times in the Wild West*. New York: Dutton (Penguin Group), 1994. 376 pages. One glossy eight-page black-and-white photo insert. The Music. The Players. Index.

Selvin assaults the concept that the "summer of love" in 1967 was a specific, blissful happening among people who knew what they were doing and what was going on around them.

And so follows this seasonally divided account of San Francisco's prominent players during the years 1965-1971. You know you're in for an iconoclastic account when the author begins chapter one with the one word sentence: "Dosed." Spirits never reach a high here, including in the photo insert, which indisputably has the ugliest photos of Janis Joplin (after being arrested in 1963 for shoplifting) ever taken.

TOURBOOKS

Nichols, Robert. *Truckin' With the Grateful Dead to: Egypt*. San Rafael: Moonbow Press, 1984. 132 pages. 38 color and black-and-white photographs in an insert. Appendix: Bibliography; Diagrams; Egyptian Periods and Dynasties; an Astrological Overview.

There is no doubt a book on The Dead's performances in Cairo, Egypt in September 1978 would be valued by Dead fans and rock astrologers. The three shows, which took place at the pyramids during a lunar eclipse, are one of those rare spiritual events in rock history that does seem planned out by the stars. Robert Nichols was part of The Dead's crew, and in a prime position to supply all of the details. Unfortunately, this book only provides us with the author's ridiculous descriptions of his trips to the pyramids and precious little about the band. The only interaction here is when Nichols creates an astrological chart for Bob Weir—which takes several chapters to build up to. The photos are horrendous, and the writing is uninspired.

WRITTEN WORKS

Cassady, Neal. Foreword and Notes by Carolyn Cassady. *Grace Beats Karma: Letters from Prison 1958-60*. New York: Blast Books, 1993. 224 pages.

Arrested for selling marijuana and even accused of being head of a smuggling ring, Cassady (later one of The Dead's lyricists) was imprisoned for two years at San Quentin. His wife supported him throughout the ordeal and corresponded with him regularly. Many of Cassady's letters are written in exaggerated biblical prose and contain the misspellings, grammatical errors, and a couple of crossouts from the originals. Of limited appeal to Grateful Dead fans.

Constanten, Tom. *Between Rock & Hard Places: A Musical Autobiodyssey.* Eugene: Hulogosi, 1992. 252 pages. Contains a few musical scores and astrological diagrams. Annotated Bibliography (books pertaining to keyboards); Compositions; Performances.

By the author's intent, hardly a biography at all—this book zips right past Constanten's childhood and first baseball game—but rather, a montage of images throughout the keyboardist's life. The primary interest here is on his stint with The Dead, which can mostly be found in chapter five: "Jerry [Garcia] is one of the most remarkable men of our times"; "Pigpen *looked* so mean..."; Phil Lesh is "the older brother I never had"; and so on. Constanten comes off as too much of a flippant prodigy for my tastes (quoting Jagger, Lord Buckley, and Chopin in a single bound), though young keyboardists might find some inspiration here.

Garcia, Jerry. *Harrington Street: An Anecdotal Personal History in Words and Pictures.* New York: Delacorte, 1995. Unpaginated (approximately 72). Approximately 60 color illustrations throughout.

Posthumous collection of Garcia's writings, original color art, and miscellaneous scribbles. Garcia's widow, Deborah, contributes a heartfelt note to the reader, while the publisher adds a longwinded publication history. The musician's childhood reflections will be lapped up by fans, especially painful images that depict Garcia's father's drowning in 1947. Colorful and imaginative—if a bit forced—all beautifully designed by Delacorte.

Garcia, Jerry. Edited by David Hinds. *J. Garcia: Paintings, Drawings and Sketches.* Berkeley: Celestial Arts, 1992. 96 pages. Approximately 70 prints of watercolors, pen-and-ink drawings and sketches.

A catalog of works by Garcia, who did briefly attend the San Francisco Art Institute. The pieces, mostly borrowed from private collections, are titled and accompanied by dimensions and mediums used. The artist cheekily remarks on the back cover, "I hope nobody takes them too seriously." Okay, I promise I won't—and I don't think there is much threat of the art world doing so either. Although some of the works are truly corny (a colored pencil drawing of a dinosaur called *Smile*), sev-

eral are pleasant and rather uplifting (*The Blue Iceberg*). Garcia admirers will want to own and display a copy.

Hart, Mickey with Stevens, Jay. *Drumming at the Edge of Magic: A Journey into the Spirit of Percussion.* New York: HarperCollins, 1990. 268 pages. One hundred black-and-white photographs; 50 color illustrations. Selected Readings. Discography.

Hart, one of The Dead's two percussionists, provides detailed history and spiritual enlightening for fellow drummers and others who feel the magic of the tom-tom. Both of Hart's parents were professional drummers, which serves as at least a partial explanation of his obsession with the instrument. It is also interesting to note that one of his gurus was Joseph Campbell, investigator of the relationship between man and myth. This is an attractive and well-written volume and quite a rewarding read. Where else might one find out that "the most distinctive *damarus* [drums] are made from human skulls"? For those concerned, the publisher did promise on the copyright page to plant two trees in the Central American rain forest for every tree needed to manufacture this book. "An accomplished and satisfying ramble through the lore of percussion...."—*Los Angeles Times*.

Hart, Mickey and Lieberman, Fredric, with Sonneborn, D.A. *Planet Drum.* New York: Harper San Francisco (division of HarperCollins), 1991. 228 pages. Approximately 250 color and black-and-white photographs and historic paintings, covering every page.

Quite simply, a brilliant sequel to *Drumming at the Edge of Magic* (above). This time Hart's collaborators are ethnomusicologists Fredric Lieberman, Ph.D., and D.A. Sonneborn. More so than the previous volume, this is a straight chronological pictorial history of the drum and its role in cultures throughout the world. Students of music will delight in flipping through the rich and diverse illustrations: photos of the drum as part of prehistoric society; as part of war; as part of Christianity; as part of tribal rights; and more. Though the book's focus intends to highlight international, centuries-old traditions, and the "sounds of the planet," rock and roll is not wholly neglected; there are photos of legends such as Buddy Rich, Gene Krupa, Keith Moon, Ginger Baker, and Ringo Starr.

Hunter, Robert. *A Box of Rain: Collected Lyrics of Robert Hunter*. New York: Viking Penguin (division of Penguin Books USA), 1990. 342 pages. Discography.

Hunter's lyrics for The Dead—as well as several for Jerry Garcia as soloist, The New Riders of the Purple Sage, Bob Dylan, The Jefferson Airplane and his own oeuvre—are collected in this substantive and melodious volume. The organization is, thankfully, A to Z by title, except for the "suites," which appropriately follow the main section. For a few (and perhaps not enough) of the works, the author supplies sparse notes on how he arrived at the lyrics. Although the discography section lists album release dates, composition dates are not provided. The big reward to be found for Deadheads is that the book includes complete versions of epic song-poems such as "Terrapin Station" and "Eagle Mall." The jacket art was done by Maureen Hunter, the author's wife. Hunter's lyrics read surprisingly well on the printed page, and Dead fans will not be disappointed by this collection.

Hunter, Robert. *Night Cadre*. New York: Penguin Books, 1991. 98 pages.

Contains several poems by Hunter, The Dead's best known outside lyricist. One won't be able to discern any mellow melodies for these 60 or so brief works, but the rhythm and tone capture images with effective passion. "Full Moon Cafe" is an excursion into lasciviousness; "C'Mere" pulls back into more of a teasing sex interlude; "Side Away from the Sun" delves into unrequited love altogether. The cover, executed by Maureen Hunter and depicting eight pensive skeletons in a purple haze, is mesmerizing.

Hunter, Robert. *Sentinel*. New York: Penguin, 1993. 154 pages.

Hunter's most recent collection of poetry, containing 35 all-new unprefaced works that predate Jerry Garcia's death. Includes "Black Sunflower," a reflection on lost time; "The Pool," a self examination that becomes a puzzle; and the titular "Sentinel," which consists of several guard "watches." Full of beauty and unpretentious power.

No author. *Dead Lyrics*. Germany: Self-published, 1985. 320 pages. Several original pen-and-ink drawings. Song Index. Guest Appearances.

The introduction begins: "This songbook is by no means a professional item." No kidding. There are over 300 songs included herein—including solo material from Garcia and Weir and a few lyrics from tunes that didn't make it to albums—and yet there aren't any permissions listed on the copyright page. In fact, *is there* a copyright page? Fans in need would do better to open up their bootleg collections and listen to the lyrics themselves.

Petersen, Robert M. Foreword by Robert Hunter. *Alleys of the Heart*. Eugene: Hulogosi Communications, Inc., 1988. 140 pages.

Petersen, who died in 1987, was one of The Dead's lyricists and a respected poet in his own right (as well as a jazz saxophonist and ex-con). This posthumous collection brings *Blue Petre & Other Poems*, *Far Away Radios* (originally published in 1980 by Ice Nine Publications), *Cabin Fever*, and *Dream of California* into one attractive, nicely flowing volume. There are wonderful odes to Janis Joplin and Pigpen ("He Was a Friend of Mine"), and even one entitled "For the Grateful Dead." Most of the poems, though, conjure up images of the West—log cabins, outdoors, coyotes, etc. Do not look for Petersen's Dead lyrics (e.g., "New Potato," "Caboose," "Cucamongo," and "Unbroken Chain"); they were excluded because they did not mesh with the tone of the poetry.

Weir, Bob and Weir, Wendy. *Panther Dream: A Story of the African Rainforest*. New York: Hyperion Books for Children, 1991. 40 pages. 40 original color illustrations by Wendy Weir. Key to illustrations. Glossary.

A poetic and beautifully executed children's story by Dead guitarist Bob Weir and his sister—financial consultant and painter Wendy Weir—that should be read to children and by adult deforestation mongers. Preserving the rain forests is a major concern of the entire Grateful Dead family and numerous other rockers, yet the reader is not clunked over the head with the theme here: only take from the rainforest what is needed to survive. As the panther says to Lokuli, the young hunter in the story, in reference to the forest: "Respect all life within it. If you need meat, take only enough to live on. Then life here can continue." *Booklist* raved: "...sure to heighten ecological awareness as it entertains."

YOUNG ADULT

Garcia, Jerry. *Harrington Street: An Anecdotal Personal History in Words and Pictures*:

See: Written Works.

Weir, Bob and Weir, Wendy. *Panther Dream: A Story of the African Rainforest*:

See: Written Works.

OTHER TITLES OF INTEREST

Brandelius, Jerilyn Lee. *The Grateful Dead Anthology*. No city: Ice Nine, 1979.

Cassady, Neal. *The First Third & Other Writing*. San Francisco: City Lights, 1971.

Gaskin, Stephen. *Haight Ashbury Flashbacks: Amazing Dope Tales of the Sixties*. Berkeley, CA: Ronin, 1990.

Greene, Herb. *Sunshine Daydreams: A Grateful Dead Journal*. San Francisco: Chronicle Books, 1991.

Greene, Jo-Ann. *Dead Or Alive*. Woodstock, NY: Beekman, 1990.

Greenfield, Robert. *Dark Star: An Oral Biography of Jerry Garcia*. New York William Morrow & Company, 1996.

Hall, Adrian. *The Story of the Grateful Dead*. Madison, WI: Magna Publications, 1993.
Select *commented: "...large pictures, big print and extreme brevity."*

Trist, Alan. Illustrations by Carpenter, Jim. *The Water of Life: A Tale of the Grateful Dead*. No city: Hulogosi Communications, 1990.
A children's book rendering the folk tale of the Grateful Dead, which inspired the name of the band. Booklist *commented: "...this handsome edition will appeal to older readers looking for hero tales."*

Weir, Bob and Weir, Wendy. *Baru Bay Australia*. New York: Hyperion Children, 1996.
Children's book from Bob Weir and his sister, available as a book or on cassette.

GREEN DAY

PICTORIALS

Ewing, Jon. *Green Day*. Miami, FL: MBS, 1995. 120 pages. Approximately 75 color and black-and-white photographs throughout. Discography. Chronology. Index.

CD-format book covering all aspects of Green Day's career. This nicely designed and illustrated book is priced just right at around $7.99.

Rogers, Kalen. *Green Day*. London: Omnibus Press (division of Book Sales Limited), 1995. 48 pages. Approximately 35 full page color and black-and-white photographs, covering every page. Discography.

Photos-only picture-book heralding the band that struck big at Woodstock II and made multiplatinum status with *Dookie*. Singer Billy Joe wears a shirt pointing at himself reading "stupid"; if you buy this expecting to find much information, turn the arrow and direct it at yourself.

THE GTO'S

(See also Zappa, Frank)

AUTOBIOGRAPHY

Des Barres, Pamela. *I'm with the Band: Confessions of a Groupie*. New York: Jove (The Berkley Publishing Group), 1988. 280 pages. Two 16-page black-and-white photo inserts.

In case you're wondering, The GTO's—that's Girls Together Outrageously—were a groupie girl group recorded by the even more outrageous Frank Zappa. Pamela Des Barres of The GTO's was the perennial groupie: she started out adoring Dion DiMucci, fell puppy-dog in love with Paul McCartney, and then actually started meeting—and subsequently having raunchy sex with—real rock stars, including Darryl (name misspelled here Daryl) DeLoach from Iron Butterfly, Noel Redding from Hendrix's Experience, Mick from you know what band, and a million others. Somehow she had a tryst with Jimmy Page and managed to avoid his whips. Kinky and brainless. "Flavorful as Juicy Fruit and almost as wet" —*Cream*.

Des Barres, Pamela. *Take Another Little Piece of My Heart*. New York: Berkley, 1993. One 16-page black-and-white photo insert.

Okay, Des Barres' first book (above) was perky and cute. By the sequel, however, her self-pronouncements that she is the "world's most famous groupie" and her giddy star gazings are flat. Her on-and-off relationships with members of Led Zeppelin don't make hot copy anymore; she even describes how aging has taken its toll on Jimmy Page. And her meetings with other musicians and celebrities—Ray Davies of The Kinks, for example—are scone and tea fare only.

THE GUESS WHO

(See also Bachman-Turner Overdrive)

BIOGRAPHIES

Einarson, John. *American Woman: The Story of the Guess Who*. Kingston, Ontario (Canada): The Quarry Press, 1995. 216 pages. Approximately 50 black-and-white photographs throughout. Discography.

The first of all Canadian Invasion artists (preceding The Band, Neil Young, and others), The Guess Who is known primarily for their 1960's classic tracks "American Woman" and "These Eyes." One of the group's key members, Randy Bachman, figured prominently in 1970's rock with his own band, Bachman-Turner Overdrive. This book, intelligently crafted by Einarson, shows that The Guess Who wasn't just another bubblegum group or dinosaur band; it literally kept the Canadian music industry afloat throughout the 1960's. The story of how Bachman came to write "American Woman" and its subsequent influence on both Canadian and American audiences (who mistakenly thought that the "woman" was the Statue of Liberty and a symbol of the Vietnam War) makes for fascinating reading. With some excellent photos and song lyrics opening chapters, this is quite a find for fans of the era. Unfortunately, the discography is limited to Guess Who albums.

GUNS N' ROSES

BIOGRAPHIES

Sugerman, Danny. *Appetite for Destruction: The Days of Guns N' Roses*. New York: St. Martin's, 1991. 266 pages. One glossy 16-page color insert; approximately 30 black-and-white photographs throughout. Index.

Claiming to have been "updated and expanded," this biography traces Guns N' Roses' career up through the early 1990's. Jim Morrison co-biographer Danny Sugerman (see Doors, The) sees Axl Rose as something of a Lizard King for the 1990's, a performer whose artistic vision is often clouded by his obsession with vice and the dark side. Sugerman has evidently been studying Morrison way too long and has his analogies mixed up. Further, he labels Guns N' Roses a modern-day Clash, whose street values were sacrificed in favor of money, fame, and glory. In any event, this is not the definitive biography of Axl, Slash, et al.; Sugerman's patronizing description of The Beatles' "Let It Be" says it all: tepid.

Wall, Mick. *Guns N' Roses: The Most Dangerous Band in the World*. London: Sidgwick & Jackson, 1993. One glossy eight-page black-and-white photo insert.

Guns N' Roses is defined by Mick Wall as a bunch of guys who like to party, drink, take drugs, and kill small animals. When not participating in the above, the band enjoys conjugating with groupies who have sex with one musician while the others pinch cash from her purse. Wall pronounces W. Axl Rose and Slash as "the Jagger and Richards of their generation," but this only seems valid in terms of the boys' sexual decadence and honesty about their sleaziness. Excellent fodder for the tabloids which, except for the observation that their release *Appetite for Destruction* contains the word "fuck" 20 times, fails to elucidate Guns N' Roses' place in the rock and roll pantheon. "The final sections are scrappy, mean-spirited and easily forgettable..."—*Booklist*.

FANZINES AND FAN CLUBS

Guns N' Roses International Fan Club. P.O. Box 884088, San Francisco, CA 94188.

Fan club offering access to the Guns N' Roses hotline, tour updates, news, preferred tickets, merchandising, and a fanzine. The cost of membership is $19.95 U.S.; $24.95 Canada and Mexico; and $29.95 elsewhere.

PICTORIALS

Bateman, Bill. *Guns N' Roses*. Miami, FL: MBS, 1995. 120 pages. Approximately 75 color and black-and-white photographs throughout. Discography. Chronology. Index.

CD-format book covering all aspects of Guns N' Roses' career. This nicely designed and illustrated book is priced just right at around $7.99.

Chin, George. *Guns N' Roses: The Pictures*. London: Omnibus Press (division of Book Sales Limited), 1994. 128 pages. Approximately 300 glossy color photographs throughout.

Just what the title suggests: a pictorial with little in the way of quotes and anecdotes. The front and back cover copy is laden with exaggeration (it claims to contain 500 photographs when many don't count since they are miniscule slides), but when it comes down to it, many of the stage photographs are pretty good—mostly due to the outrageous stage posturings of the band members. While neither Axl Rose or Slash is as gracefully acrobatic as David Lee Roth or as seductive as Jim Morrison, the entire band is raunchy in The Rolling Stones or Aerosmith vein. If you need a photo book on this band, you know what you're in for.

John, Robert. Foreword by W. Axl Rose. *Guns N' Roses: The Photographic History*. Boston: Little, Brown & Company. Unpaginated. Approximately 200 color and black-and-white photographs, covering every page.

Photographer Robert John is among W. Axl Rose's closest friends and had complete access to Guns N' Roses at the band's recording sessions, concerts, video shoots, and grungy timeouts. In the foreword, Rose calls John's photos "the best" ever of the band, which is really the only testimony a fan needs. Non-diehards will still be curious enough to check out the group's tattoos, nipple rings, leather apparel, and naughty t-shirt messages.

McSquare, Eddy. *Guns N' Roses: Low Life in the Fast Lane*. London : Omnibus Press: (division of Book Sales Limited), 1992. 88 pages. Approximately 100 color and black-and-white photographs, covering every page. Discography.

A magazine article spread out over a book, with many quotes in the "in their own words" (see Quizbooks and Quotebooks, below: Putterford) vein. While certainly enjoyable—many of the high-quality photos are full-page—some fans may not want to bother if they already own works containing more photos, quotes, or biography. Marginal.

No author. *Guns N' Roses in Person*. Port Chester, NY: Cherry Lane Music, 1989. 32 pages. Approximately 40 color and black-and-white photographs, covering every page. Comes with a pull-out poster.

Primarily for kids in their early teens, this is a general assortment of lyrics, photos, and essays on the lean, mean rock band. Excessive in hype, if nothing else.

No author. *Guns N' Roses Tear-Out Book*. London: Oliver Books, 1994. Unpaginated (approximately 48 pages). 20 color photographs throughout.

Twenty photos of Guns N' Roses—all in color, all live, and all with tear-out capability. You'll love it as a 12-year-old, and then at 13 you'll use the tear-sheets to line the bottom of your hamster cage.

Putterford, Mark. *Over the Top: The True Story of Guns N' Roses*. London: Omnibus Press (division of Book Sales Limited), 1993. 112 pages. Approximately 125 color and black-and-white photographs, covering every page. Discography.

A rehash of photos used in McSquare's book (see above). This pictorial opens with several pages of quotes from critics about the group, and then moves on to some history of Guns N' Roses' origins in Lafayette, Indiana. Guns N' Roses are depicted here as a hard-drinking, pill-popping band whose violent streak has nearly pulled them apart as much as it has united them. Consisting primarily of stage shots of Guns N' Roses in wild action, it's raunchier than McSquare's work, even though it overlaps tremendously.

QUIZBOOKS AND QUOTEBOOKS

Putterford, Mark. *Guns N' Roses: In Their Own Words*. London: Omnibus Press (division of Book Sales Limited), 1993. 96 pages.

Approximately 200 black-and-white photographs, covering every page.

Guns N' Roses are among the first of the 1990's bands to merit an "in their own words" treatment from Omnibus Press. This blown-up photo-quotebook contains sections on music, life on the road, sex/drugs/booze, women, and more. The musicians also reflect on themselves (Axl: "It was success that screwed us up") and on each other (Slash: "Axl is just another version of the Ayatollah"). The final section on what others think about them is a major disappointment, consisting of only a half dozen quotes that aren't all that interesting. Younger fans might enjoy this.

TOURBOOKS

St. Michael, Mick. *Guns N' Roses: Live!*. London: Omnibus Press (division of Book Sales Limited), 1991. Unpaginated (approximately 32 pages). Approximately 40 color photographs throughout. Guns N' Roses Discography. Comes with a color poster.

The "tour book" label is just another excuse to throw a few dozen photographs of the band together. St. Michael provides little in the way of description of the shows depicted in the photos. This one goes back to the beginning of the 1990's, so most fans will want something more recent and extensive.

OTHER TITLES OF INTEREST
Elliott, Paul. *Guns N' Roses: The World's Most Dangerous Rock Band*. New York: Morrow, 1990.

ARLO GUTHRIE

TITLES OF INTEREST
Eaton, Walter P. Illustrated by Bull, Charles L. and Drew, Donna. Foreword by Arlo Guthrie. *The Odyssey of Old Bill the Berkshire Moose*. Great Barrington, MA: Attic Revivals Press, 1996.
Guthrie's continuing fascination with "New England mooses"[sic] (see Guthrie, below) led to his contribution of the foreword to this work.
Guthrie, Arlo. *Alice's Restaurant*. New York: Grove Press, 1968.
Guthrie, Arlo. *Baby's Bedtime*. No city: BMG, 1990.
Children's book by the famed folksinger.
Guthrie, Arlo. Illustrated by Alice Brock. *Mooses Come Walking*. San Francisco: Chronicle Books, 1995.
Reflecting on the sudden flux of mooses[sic] to the New England area, Guthrie penned this children's

story. Illustrator Alice Brock—does anyone remember Alice?—is the very same Alice from Guthrie's classic folk song/tale "Alice's Restaurant."
Herndon, Venable and Penn, Arthur. *Alice's Restaurant: A Screenplay*. Garden City, NY: Doubleday, 1970.
Screenplay to the 1969 film, which starred Guthrie and was directed by Penn.

WOODY GUTHRIE

AUTOBIOGRAPHY

Guthrie, Woody. Introduction by Studs Terkel. *Bound for Glory*. New York: E.P. Dutton, 1976. 426 pages. About 50 pen-and-ink drawings by the author.

In his autobiography, which was first published in 1961 and originally titled *The Boomchasers*, the folk music hero tells his somewhat exaggerated story from childhood up through World War II—just before he struck fame. The book reads like a collection of vivid short stories of growing up in Depression-era America: tales of neighborhood bullies, town-tearing cyclones, and destitute hoboes. In a sense one can see why Bob Dylan related so much to these environs: Guthrie lived in an oil boomtown (Okema, Oklahoma), which was used and abused much the same way as Dylan's hometown (Hibbing, Minnesota) was plundered for its rich minerals. This book also inspired the name of the band The Boomtown Rats. Entirely rewarding; but be warned that only Terkel's gushing introduction refers to Guthrie's career as folk singer and songwriter.

CRITICAL/ANALYTICAL COMMENTARY

Hampton, Wayne. *Guerilla Minstrels: John Lennon, Joe Hill, Woody Guthrie and Bob Dylan*.

See: Lennon, John: Critical/Analytical Commentary.

WRITTEN WORKS

Guthrie, Woody. Edited by Dave Marsh and Harold Leventhal. *Pastures of Plenty: A Self-Portrait*. New York: HarperCollins, 1990. 260 pages. Approximately 100 black-and-white photographs, drawings and reproductions of lyrics throughout. Appendix. Index.

Another dive into the bottomless Guthrie archives, *Pastures of Plenty* is a treasure-chest of rare finds: a beautiful overleaf photo of Woody's wife, Marjorie; original letters (one from Guthrie to actor Paul Robeson, which was probably never sent); notes and entries from his datebook; poetry and songs; and countless anti-war statements. The book closes on a heart-wrenching note, as Guthrie began to deteriorate from Huntington's chorea and his works ("Oklahoma Nurse Girl") reflect his suffering. Marsh and Leventhal (Guthrie's manager) have done a masterful editing job on a book that "...gives new insight into the life and character of the beloved folk singer..."—*Publishers Weekly*.

Guthrie, Woody. *Seeds of Man: An Experience Lived and Dreamed*. New York: Dutton, 1976. 403 pages.

Guthrie was a terrific storyteller with a sensational ear for dialogue and a hawklike eye for character development. He wrote this book in Brooklyn in 1947-8, in an effort to expand on a shorter work entitled *Silver Mine*. Loosely based on a true story of Guthrie's search for a mine with his father (Charley), his father's youngish half-brother (Uncle Jeff), and his brother Roy, this is a funny, detailed account of an expedition through Big Bend of the Rio Grande. Guthrie is a marvelous humorist (Uncle Jeff is described as "a fiddling deputy sheriff") and his lengthy tale makes for pleasurable reading.

OTHER TITLES OF INTEREST

Klein, Joe. *Woody Guthrie: A Life*. New York: Knopf, 1980.

BUDDY GUY

BIOGRAPHIES

Wilcock, Donald E. and Guy, Buddy. Foreword by Eric Clapton. *Damn Right I've Got the Blues: Buddy Guy and the Roots of Rock and Roll*. San Francisco: Woodford Press, 1993. 152 pages. Over 120 black-and-white photographs throughout. Discography.

Buddy Guy is the guy many believe bridged the gap between rock and roll and Chicago blues. With the pulsating emotion of the blues and the smoking guitar feedback of psychedelic rock (that preceded Jimi Hendrix), Guy

influenced a wide range of *créme de la créme* rock artists, such as Clapton (who contributes the expected gushing foreword), John Mayall, Stevie Ray Vaughan, and countless others. The book, which is part blues/rock history and part oral biography, conveys both stories through firsthand quotes from personalities such as Ian Anderson (of Jethro Tull), Eric Burdon (of The Animals), and Noel Redding (of the Jimi Hendrix Experience), as well as ample photos and incisive text from the authors. The title was taken from the Guy album of the same name. "...a frank assessment of the life, many disappointments and rare hurrahs of Buddy Guy."—*The New York Times*.

BILL HALEY AND THE COMETS

BIOGRAPHIES

Haley, John W. and Hoelle, John Von. *Sound and Glory: The Incredible Story of Bill Haley*. Wilmington, DE: Dyne-America Publications, 1990. 250 pages. Approximately 100 black-and-white photographs throughout. Discography. Musicians. Songs Recorded by Bill Haley. Bill Haley's Firsts. Bibliography. Index.

John W. Haley, Bill Haley's eldest son, tells his father's story with historian John Von Hoelle. This is not a first-person account by any means (which is why it's included under "biographies" and not a "friends/family" heading), and Haley's presence doesn't do much to help characterize the man who put the "rock" in "rock and roll." Worse, we don't have any sense of what Haley was like as a husband or father. Though the authors have dug up some excellent photos, clippings, and memorabilia from the 1940's—when Haley was more of a hillbilly performer—the prose clumsily switches past and present tenses and incorporates wordy quotes that should have been edited down. A major disappointment.

Swenson, John. *Bill Haley: The Daddy of Rock and Roll*. New York: Scarborough (Stein and Day Publishers), 1982. 174 pages. 50 black-and-white photographs throughout. Discography. Index.

Bill Haley did not have the moves of Elvis, the guitar gimmickry of Chuck Berry, or the dramatic flair of Little Richard; but he is the originator of the first official rock record, "Rock Around the Clock," and a number of other classic rock tunes in the middle-1950's. Swenson is meticulous in tracing Haley's country music roots and does an excellent job showing how the singer moved up the top ranks of the music world and then watched the rest pass him by. The book sensitively addresses Haley's insecurities about his voice and guitaring ability, as well as his other personal traumas ranging from blindness in one eye to severe alcoholism. One can only wonder why this book didn't receive the packaging and distribution it deserved.

HALL AND OATES

FANZINES AND FAN CLUBS

The Daryl Hall-John Oates International Fan Club. P.O. Box 450, Mansfield, MA 02048.

Fan club that publishes the quarterly *The Rock & Soul Int'l Newsletter*, an 18-26-page stapled packet containing: Hall and Oates news; photos; tour dates and reports; contests; ads; pen pals; and more. The cost of membership is $8 per year in the U.S. and Canada; $10 everywhere else. Payable in U.S. funds to Diane Vaskas.

WRITTEN WORKS

Tosches, Nick with Hall, Daryl and Oates, John. *Dangerous Dances.* New York: Whole Oats Enterprises, 1984. 144 pages. Over one hundred black-and-white photographs throughout; 16 pages of color throughout.

Although it takes several pages to kick into gear, this "authorized biography" (assembled via 1984 interviews with Hall and Oates plus portions of their journals) is actually a major photo book for fans of the duo. Amidst cutouts of various peoples dancing in and out of sync, photos of Hall and Oates, and original doodlings by the former himself, Tosches tells of the boys' slow rise to fame (or, as John Oates calls it, the "tale of the invisible carrot") and their various phases of pop and disco. Hall's early band The Temptones (an obvious take on The Temptations) and years hanging out backstage at the Uptown Theater reveal a depth and

history previously unexplored. Fans will be disappointed, however, by the authors' failure to include any kind of recording information.

YOUNG ADULT

Fissinger, Laura. *Hall & Oates.* Mankato, MN: Creative Education, 1983. 32 pages. Five black-and-white photographs throughout.

Recycled kiddie-book that was part of Creative Education's "Rock 'n Pop Stars" series. Low on information, short on photos, and positively empty on discography. A waste.

OTHER TITLES OF INTEREST
Gooch, Brad. *Hall & Oates.* New York: Ballantine, 1980.

GEORGE HARRISON

(See also Beatles, The)

AUTOBIOGRAPHY

Harrison, George. *I Me Mine.* New York: Simon and Schuster, 1980. 400 pages. One black-and-white photo insert consisting of 48 plates. Song Lyrics. Index. (First 2,000 copies published in Great Britain by Genesis Publication Limited.)

A crucial collectible, as it is the closest thing to a Beatles autobiography. Of course, most of Harrison's writing was "as told to" Beatles insider Derek Taylor. George's dry wit is evident throughout; he begins his foreword by saying the book was originally going to be called *The Big Leather Job.* But he also seems to be resentful of what he went through as a Beatle—even to the point of whining about the experience being like *One Flew Over the Cuckoo's Nest.* He goes out of his way to deflate myths (claiming it was cigarettes, not pot, the boys smoked in the palace john) and doesn't express any of his feelings about his mates; Lennon, in fact, spoke out about his being omitted from the book in his 1980 *Playboy* interview. Fans won't be able to resist the original handwritten lyric sheets and George's accompanying notes, as well as the plentiful rare photos in the insert.

BIOGRAPHIES

Giuliano, Geoffrey. *Dark Horse: The Private Life of George Harrison.* New York: Dutton (Penguin Group), 1989. 242 pages. 50 black-and-white full-page photographs scattered throughout. Appendices: George Harrison's Family Tree; A Conversation; A Diary of Events; Solo Discography; Dark Horse Records; Hand Made Films. A Note on Sources. Index.

In *Dark Horse* (named after the Harrison tune), Giuliano attempts to get inside the mind and spirit of "the quiet Beatle," the one who keeps himself protected inside his Friar Park mansion. Harrison is more complex than one would think: generous to the needy; unashamed at his occasionally conflicting interests (self-denial vs. sexual gratification); and quite funny in a dry, naughty boy sort of way. This would have been a better book if it had been lengthier (certainly there is more to say about Harrison than only 242 pages) and the author hadn't gone out of his way to do some out of place Yoko bashing (he directly calls her a "bullish opportunist"). "This informative bio helps to fill in the blank spaces...in the life of one of the pivotal sidemen in contemporary pop history"—*Booklist.*

PICTORIALS

Giuliano, Geoffrey and Giuliano, Brenda. *The Illustrated George Harrison.* Secaucus: Chartwell Books, 1993. 96 pages. 117 color and black-and-white illustrations, covering every page.

Uninteresting photo-biography of Harrison, which apparently was dashed off in one afternoon. The Giulianos seemed to want to get this one over and done with, and didn't pay much attention to language or detail: Everything related to Harrison—from the gate of his mansion to Brian Epstein's office—is described as "posh" for want of any other description. Harrison's life in the 1990's is barely even addressed. For more on the Giulianos' treatments on the solo Beatles, see McCartney, Paul: Pictorials.

YOUNG ADULT

Michaels, Ross. *George Harrison: Yesterday and Today.* New York: Flash Books (Music Sales), 1977. 96 pages. 50 black-and-white photographs throughout. Discography.

An all-too incomplete study, even for a YA audience. The book doesn't present any case for the guitarist's virtues as a composer and artist. We are subjected to excerpts of only the most snide passages from Harrison's songs, and not the beautiful lyrics that can be found in classics such as "Something," "Here Comes the Sun," "Awaiting on You All," and "What Is Life." Errors can be detected on nearly every page: One caption cites Ringo as having been brought in as Beatles drummer as late as 1964!

OTHER TITLES OF INTEREST
Clayson, Alan. *The Quiet One: A Life of George Harrison.* London: Sidgwick & Jackson, 1990.

RONNIE HAWKINS

(See also Band, The)

AUTOBIOGRAPHY

Hawkins, Ronnie and Goddard, Peter. *Last of the Good Ol' Boys.* Toronto, Canada: Stoddart Publishing Co., 1989. 314 pages. Two eight-page black-and-white photo inserts. Appendix One: The Records of Ronnie Hawkins; Appendix Two: Q&A: With a Little Help from My Friends.

Ronnie Hawkins is perhaps best known as the godfather of The Band in their early formation as The Hawks. "Rompin' Ronnie" remains one of the rock era's greatest unknown showmen—both as a singer/songwriter and as a raunchy party animal. Crediting himself for having originated "the camel walk" (a predecessor to Michael Jackson's "moonwalk") and other onstage antics, Hawkins is quite a wild one off-stage as well. In one tale, David Clayton-Thomas (lead singer of Blood, Sweat and Tears) recalls a boozy orgy involving Hawkins and an 82-year-old woman! This wacked-out autobiography makes you want to head for the northern border and dive into the first Canadian roadhouse.

HAWKWIND

DISCOGRAPHIES, RECORDING GUIDES, AND COLLECTIBLES

Goodwin, Robert. *The Illustrated Collector's Guide to Hawkwind*. Burlington, Ontario (Canada): Collector's Guide, 1993. 176 pages. Approximately 300 black-and-white reproductions of CDs and album covers. Hawkwind Songs. Michael Moorcock Interview. David Brock Interview.

A guide through the 23-year history of the metal group Hawkwind, with separate sections on key recordings, personnel, family tree, concert dates, singles, EPs, and LPs. Further reference sections survey Hawkwind in print, CDs, and videos. Interviews with Hawkwind's Michael Moorcock (yes, that's his name) and David Brock end the book. The background information on the songs is rather limited, but the lists and the reproductions of the albums might serve as a simple checklist of releases. Unfortunately, there are no photographs of the band members themselves. Given Hawkwind's bizarre album-cover art, it would be nice to see a glossy color insert in the next edition.

RELATED WORKS

Butterworth, Michael. *The Time of the Hawklords*. Burlington, Ontario (Canada): Collector's Guide Publishing, 1995. 192 pages.

First published in 1976, this story was based on an idea by Hawkwind's Michael Moorcock. The characters are based loosely on members of Hawkwind and on their stage and recorded performances. This sci fi adventure takes place in the future—a post-nuclear London—where Hawkwind becomes the heroic Hawklords and battle evil forces. Pretty oblique stuff that would have succeeded better in comic book form.

JIMI HENDRIX (AND THE EXPERIENCE)

AUTOBIOGRAPHY

Redding, Noel and Appleby, Carol. *Are You Experienced?*. New York: Da Capo, 1996. 236 pages. One eight-page black-and-white photo insert. Index. (First published in Great Britain in 1990 by Fourth Estate Limited.)

We've heard from The Experience's drummer, Mitch Mitchell (see Written Works, below), so now it's time to read the bassist's story—which took some time to find a U.S. publisher. Noel Redding, from Hythe, Kent England, started out on the Jew's harp, worked his way up to violin, then followed with the mandolin—and went back down to the guitar and later bass. Redding's childhood is fittingly limited to his development as a musician, rather than describing his school activities and such. The book is rich in anecdotes, but not just about his involvements with Jimi Hendrix: there is also plenty about Keith Moon, The Monkees, Eric Clapton, The Animals, and more. Not as visually satisfying as his bandmate's work, but worthwhile nonetheless.

BIOGRAPHIES

Henderson, David. *'Scuse Me While I Kiss the Sky*. New York: Bantam Books, 1981. 386 pages. Over 100 black-and-white photographs, scattered throughout. Selected Discography.

Through extensive research in Seattle, London, Amsterdam, Vancouver, New York, and Los Angeles, Henderson has recreated Hendrix's youth, rise to fame, legendary performances, backstage intrigues (the groupie scene), and untimely death. There are many photos of young James Marshall Hendrix (who was originally dubbed Johnny Allen Hendrix by his mother), including playful shots of him in a football jersey and—believe it or not—his army photo (he was in the Screaming Eagles paratroopers). Some of the street lingo ("played his ass off") transfers from the speaker's to Henderson's prose, and detracts from the overall quality of the writing. While the monologues from Jimi's dad are worthy of inclusion, it's odd that there are no passages from anyone else. There is no biographical information on Mitch Mitchell (drummer) and Noel Redding (bassist) prior to their joining The Jimi Hendrix Experience. *Rolling Stone* hailed this as "The strongest and most ambitious biography yet written about any rock and roll performer." Previous editions were published by Doubleday, beginning in 1978, with the title *Jimi Hendrix: Voodoo Child of the Aquarian Age.*

Hopkins, Jerry. *Hit & Run: The Jimi Hendrix Story.* New York: Perigee (Putnam Publishing group), 1983. 336 pages. Approximately 75 black-and-white photographs throughout. Discography.

Lesser biography of Hendrix that cheapens the artist's reputation by highlighting his drug abuse, partying, and "hedonistic" attitudes. The book actually promises more than it delivers in those areas, teasing readers with inside information about Hendrix's "battles" with Mick Jagger over Marianne Faithfull (which amounts to less than common knowledge). Other books provide a great deal more about Hendrix's background and more original quotes from insiders. A rehash of other works that belittles Hendrix's place in 20th century music.

McDermott, John with Kramer, Eddie. *Hendrix: Setting the Record Straight.* New York: Warner Books, 1992. 364 pages. One glossy 16-page black-and-white photo insert. Appendix A: Architectural Layout of Electric Ladyland Studios. Appendix B: Legal Correspondence. Discography. Index.

Eddie Kramer was Hendrix's engineer for the recordings of albums such as *Are You Experienced?* and *The Cry of Love.* Posthumous Hendrix albums and CDs were issued without Kramer's assistance or that of Chas Chandler (the former Animals' bassist and Hendrix's manager) and are labeled here as inferior and damaging to Hendrix's reputation. The authors' intention in this book is to set the record straight, but other than the above and some inside information on the recording industry, it's a mystery as to what aspects of Hendrix's life or career they might be referring to. While there are significantly more firsthand accounts here than in Henderson's, the biography contains much less detail. The 16-page insert features many intimate shots taken by Linda McCartney.

Shapiro, Harry and Glebbeek, Caesar. *Hendrix: Electric Gypsy.* New York: St. Martin's Griffin. 1995. 770 pages. One glossy eight-page color insert; one hundred black-and-white photographs throughout. Reference Notes. Bibliography of Sources. Appendices. Index. (First published in 1990 in Great Britain by William Heinemann Limited.)

A serious biography of Hendrix, without the lengthy quotes and anecdotes found in Henderson's work (see above). Shapiro and Glebbeek's writing is far more elegant than Henderson's, but they don't have the grasp of the Seattle musical tradition or enough knowledge of Hendrix's family lineage. Much of the text on Hendrix's relationship with Monika Dannemann differs radically from descriptions found in her book (see Hendrix Family and Friends, below), but perhaps she's the one responsible for changing her versions of the stories. The chunky back sections, replete with discography, chronology, a family tree, books, films, etc. could constitute another book entirely; unfortunately, the design of these sections is not pleasant to the eye. "Sympathetic and comprehensive..."—*Publishers Weekly.*

CHRONOLOGIES

Brown, Tony. *Jimi Hendrix: A Visual Documentary: His Life, Loves and Music.* London: Omnibus Press (division of Book Sales Limited), 1992. 128 pages. Approximately 125 black-and-white and color photographs and documents throughout. Bibliography. Discography.

Highly illustrated day-by-day of events in Jimi's life. The first date actually traces back to circa 1783 and the birth of a "Mr. Kendrick," Jimi's great-great-grandfather (about which nothing is known). Author Tony Brown's summaries are concise, informative, and, on the whole, well selected, identifying concert appearances, interviews, noteworthy meetings with celebrities, etc. The listings are complemented by sensational blown-up photos that are either in light green or hazy purple (no, not just a coincidence). The closing Epilogue detailing Hendrix's final hours is among the clearest accounts available. Worthwhile.

CRITICAL/ANALYTICAL COMMENTARY

Murray, Charles Shaar. *Crosstown Traffic: Jimi Hendrix and the Post-War Rock and Roll*

Revolution. New York: St. Martin's Press, 1989. 248 pages. One glossy eight-page black-and-white photo insert. Discography. Bibliography. Index. (First published in Great Britain in 1989 by Faber & Faber.)

Serious account of Hendrix's influence on 1960's rock, on pop culture, and on the history of guitar playing. The first chapter, "The We Decade," summarizes events of the 1960's and explores how Hendrix's rendition of "Star Spangled Banner" captures the blood and fire of Vietnam more aptly than anything before or since. A biographical chapter on the man himself seems to have been written grudgingly. Chapters on Hendrix's womanizing and the race issue (black artists vs. white) are highly sophisticated and on target. For serious scholars of Hendrix's myriad contributions to rock, pop, soul, blues, jazz, rap, disco—and music he created not yet recognized. "...augments solid musical scholarship with astute social and historical commentary, and meets the challenge admirably"—*Publishers Weekly*.

DISCOGRAPHIES, RECORDING GUIDES, AND COLLECTIBLES

Matesich, Ken and Armstrong, Dave. *Jimi Hendrix: A Discography*. Tuscon, AZ: Purple Haze, 1982. 54 pages.

Self-published album-by-album guide to Hendrix's releases, collected in three sections: pre-Experience, Experience, and Bootleg. Each record includes recording date, musician line-up, songs, label, and notes. Not a bad source alone, but pales in comparison to discographies that appear in biographies (see Shapiro, above).

McDermott, John with Cox, Billy; and Kramer, Eddie. *The Jimi Hendrix Sessions: The Complete Recording Sessions, 1963-1970*. New York: Little, Brown and Company, 1995. 196 pages. Approximately 200 color and black-and-white photographs throughout. Selected Discography.

Unlike The Beatles, who had meticulous records kept in a vault at EMI Studios, the history of Jimi Hendrix's recordings (rough demos, unreleased tracks, early takes, etc.) has for the most part been lost or unrecorded. With the help of Hendrix's friend Billy Cox and one of his engineers, Eddie Kramer, John McDermott tries to piece together this 25-year-old puzzle, much in the same way Mark

Lewisohn tackled The Beatles (see Beatles: Discographies, Recording Guides, and Collectibles). The book begins with Hendrix's early 1960's studio work, but the bulk of it focuses primarily on solo efforts and recordings with The Experience 1966-1970. While details such as songs recorded and musician line-ups are not included in the headings for each day—and the book does not contain a song title index—this attractive book is highly relevant as a testament to Hendrix's larger-than-life presence in the studio.

FANZINES AND FAN CLUBS

Straight Ahead: The International Hendrix Fanzine. P.O. Box 965, Novato, CA 94948.

First begun in 1989, this fanzine claims support from former Hendrix associates Noel Redding, Billy Cox, Rosa Lee Brooks, and Juma Sultan. The 38-page, stapled fanzine includes photocopies of black-and-white photographs, interviews (Carlos Santana, Noel Redding, Al Hendrix, and others), CD and video reviews, classifieds, and much more. The cost of a one-year subscription is $26 for six issues; overseas $40, payable in international money order or a bank check in U.S. currency.

HENDRIX FRIENDS AND FAMILY

Dannemann, Monika. Introduction by U.J. Roth. *The Inner World of Jimi Hendrix*. New York: St. Martin's Press, 1995. 192 pages. Approximately 100 original color oil paintings and color photographs throughout.

Former ice-skating teacher Monika Dannemann alleges she was Jimi Hendrix's fiancée for two years, and was with him at the time of his death. Here she seeks to reveal the master guitarist's "inner world" and spiritual side through her brief reminiscences and anecdotes, which are supported by her original oil paintings. Dannemann succeeds at showing Hendrix as an impulsive, intuitive individual, as well as a musician, especially in recounting some of her private moments with him. In point of fact, the two were officially dating only a couple of hours after they met! A visceral delight, both unpretentious and non-trashy.

Willix, Mary. *Jimi Hendrix: Voices in Time*. San Diego, CA: Creative Forces Publishing, 1995. 208 pages. Approximately 125 black-and-white photographs throughout.

With the return of copyright of Hendrix's music to his family, the time seemed right for the Hendrixes to break their silence about their acclaimed clansmen. Over 75 personages from the Seattle area—relatives, friends, musicians, teachers, neighbors, etc.—reminisce about Jimi, some in a question/answer format and others in headings/text. More intimate and less sensational than other works, this is a past-due treasure trove for fans. It's fascinating to read quotes about Hendrix from his old school-teacher, Ralph Hayes: "I can't believe that gentleman went on to make the kind of music he made, because he was so shy." A cut above other rock remembrances.

PICTORIALS

Boot, Adrian and Salewicz, Chris. *Jimi Hendrix: Inside the Experience*. London: Boxtree, 1995. Unpaginated (approximately 192 pages). Approximately 200 color and black-and-white photographs throughout.

Once you get past the radiancy of this book's color cover, there isn't much in this photo book worth chewing on. While some photos of Hendrix exude his raw sexuality and the graphics are occasionally effective, the written pieces collected here don't constitute much of a book: reflections here, quotes there, and a smattering of lyrics lost in the shuffle. It's fun to browse the multi-colored pages, but in the end, Green and Sienkiewicz's work (see below) accomplishes a lot more. Optional.

Green, Martin I. (creator and producer) and Sienkiewicz, Bill. *Voodoo Child: The Illustrated Legend of Jimi Hendrix*. New York: Viking Penguin, 1995. 128 pages. Approximately 400 original glossy color panels, covering every page. Comes with an original CD.

Gorgeous cartoon history of Hendrix's life and career via the talents of Martin I. Green and illustrator Bill Sienkiewicz. The story unfolds through Hendrix's own voice as narrator, which succeeds admirably in presenting to the reader his personality and creating a "dream-work" of "words and pictures." The images of Jimi are effervescent and original, straying far enough away from the cliché images but not so

far as to lose semblance to the real Hendrix. The comic strip panels effortlessly switch gears while elucidating key moments in Hendrix's life, such as his father's return from fighting in World War II. The CD is icing on the cake. Highly recommended.

Hatay, Nona. *Jimi Hendrix: The Spirit Lives on Volume 1*. San Francisco: Last Gasp, 1983. 66 pages. Approximately 75 glossy black-and-white photographs throughout.

A tribute from a professional photographer who captured Hendrix live on several occasions from 1969 to the end of his life. Many of the images are psychedelic or surrealistic collages created by Hatay from original prints. Although not in color, these photographs manage to create an electric, neon effect that, more often than not, makes you want to look closer. The illustrative material is complemented with firsthand quotes from those who knew Hendrix, including drummer Mitch Mitchell, singer Eric Burdon, and soulman James Brown. Respectable.

Mann, Bruce. *Jimi Hendrix*. Miami, FL: MBS, 1994. 120 pages. Approximately 75 color and black-and-white photographs throughout. Discography. Chronology. Index.

CD-format book covering all aspects of Hendrix's life and career. This nicely designed and illustrated book is priced just right at around $7.99.

No author. *Jimi Hendrix Tear-Out Book*. London: Oliver Books, 1994. Unpaginated (approximately 48 pages). Approximately 20 glossy color and black-and-white photographs throughout.

Aside from a photo of Hendrix in wizard garb, all 20 of these shots have been seen before ad nauseam—unless you're under 12. Parents: If you can, sway your kids over to Green's comic strip biography (see above).

Nolan, Tom. *Jimi Hendrix: A Biography in Words and Pictures*. New York: Sire Books (Chappell Music Company), 1977. 56 pages. Approximately 65 black-and-white photographs, covering every page. Appendix: Discography.

Part of Chappell's "in words and pictures" series, this volume on Hendrix is a major disappointment. The photos are drab cutouts better reproduced elsewhere, while the text itself is almost wholly dependant on Chris Welch's (slightly) superior work (see below). The writing is boisterous to a fault: "...a guitar never heard on this side of the ionosphere. It walks! It talks! It wriggles on its body like a snake!" Purple and hazy.

Robertson, John. *The Complete Guide to the Music of Jimi Hendrix*. London: Omnibus Press (division of Book Sales Limited), 1995. 130 pages. Approximately 115 color and black-and-white photographs throughout.

CD-format book covering all aspects of Hendrix's life and career. Overlaps with Mann's CD-format book (see above), but each offers something of different appeal: This has more photos, the other more informational back sections.

Welch, Chris. *Hendrix: A Biography*. New York: Quick Fox (division of Book Sales Limited), 1978. 104 pages. Approximately 100 black-and-white photographs, covering nearly every page. Hendrix on Record.

Anachronistic photo book, which had first been published in 1972 and again in 1973. The book is poorly designed and contains only a handful of noteworthy photos (Hendrix with ex-Animal Chas Chandler). *Melody Maker* writer Chris Welch compresses events down to barely relevant quotes that are divided into chapters on peripheral players (such as Gary Stickells, Jimi's road manager). Below-par.

QUIZBOOKS AND QUOTEBOOKS

Brown, Tony. *Jimi Hendrix: In His Own Words*. London: Omnibus Press (division of Book Sales Limited), 1994. 96 pages. Approximately 125 black-and-white photographs throughout.

Collection of quotes by Hendrix divided into: various periods of his life (childhood, Army days, etc.); music (life on the road, songwriting, etc.); and assorted topics (religion, drugs, etc.). The quotes are supported with date and city only, not mentioning the form of media on which they were presented. This is a shame, since it would be nice to know tidbits such as that his remarks pertaining to Woodstock were stated on "The Dick Cavett Show" one week after the festival. The photos, in black-and-white only, do not compare to those in other books. Most fans will be disappointed that this

one doesn't reach at least 128 pages or include more than a couple of shots of The Experience.

STARCHILD

Knight, Curtis. *Jimi Hendrix: Starchild*. Wilmington, DE: Abelard Productions, Inc., 1992. 112 pages. Approximately 60 page throughout.

Musician Curtis Knight explores the paranormal surroundings of Jimi Hendrix, both before and after his death. Did Jimi the Sagittarian communicate with aliens living inside the inner Earth? Inquiring minds (like Knight) seem to want to know. Hastily packaged with photocopies of age-old newspaper and magazine photos, *Starchild* is full of so many typos and dubious information readers will become too dumfounded to be even slightly amused by it. The cover illustration actually makes this look like a coloring book!

WRITTEN WORKS

Hendrix, Jimi. Compiled by Nitopi, Bill. *Cherokee Mist: The Lost Writings of Jimi Hendrix*. New York: HarperCollins, 1993. 172 pages. Approximately 60 black-and-white photographs scattered throughout. Original handwritten lyric sheets.

The title is from the Hendrix song and refers to his part-Native American background. This collection contains 50 or so previously unpublished handwritten writings—including song lyrics, poems, sketches, and even a movie outline. A whopping 35 pages are taken up by prefatory material from Noe Gold, Bill Nitopi, Charles Blass, and Michael Fairchild. The works—all printed from the original sheets, including hotel stationery—are intensely erotic and full of the psychedelic imagery that made Hendrix the electric powerhouse of his era. All of the author's crossouts, edits, spellings errors, etc. are intact; it would have been better to typeset the works alongside the originals for an easier read. The photos are excellent and superbly arranged. "...both haunting and enlightening"—*Guitar*.

Mitchell, Mitch with Platt, John. *Jimi Hendrix: Inside the Experience*. New York: Harmony Books (Crown), 1990. 176 pages. Approximately 200 color and black-and-white photographs, covering every page. Set Lists. Tour Itinerary. Index.

Mitchell, the former drummer of The Experience, collaborated with journalist Platt to produce this colorful and memorable photo tribute. Mitchell's recollections are typeset in bold; Platt's text fills in the historical gaps. Mitchell's metamorphosis in the mid-1960's from a square drummer to a psychedelic sticks man with a full afro is astonishing. Hendrix's impact on him is unmistakable, and the same can probably be said for manager Chas Chandler, Eric Clapton, Brian Jones, Sly Stone, Stephen Stills, and many others. Occasionally funny and rich in period detail, this book deserves a prominent place on every rocker's shelf. Only shortcoming: It doesn't contain a discography.

OTHER TITLES OF INTEREST
Carey, Gary. *Lenny, Janis & Jimi*. New York: Pocket, 1975.

DON HENLEY

See Eagles, The.

HOLE

(See also Nirvana)

BIOGRAPHIES

Rossi, Melissa. *Courtney Love: Queen of Noise: A Most Unauthorized Biography*. New York: Pocket (Simon & Schuster), 1996. 266 pages. One eight-page black-and-white photo insert.

After being in and out of Courtney Love's circle, Melissa Rossi ultimately pulled this book together on her own (hence the strong disclaimer in the subtitle). Rossi originally had support from musician Rozz Rezabek, an old flame of Love, who agreed to provide letters and documents—but would only participate if Kurt Cobain's name wouldn't be mentioned! Rossi doesn't know the first thing about how to compile a biography, opening with a Seattle underground "who's who," which isn't alphabetized. The opening words of the book are a cacophonous "Fuck you," which may as well have been addressed directly at the reader. Rossi interweaves details of Love's drug abuses, delinquencies, whoriness, and suicidal tendencies with the singer's "baby doll" image, in the meantime overlooking Love's potential place in music history as a performer. The Hole apocrypha has only just begun.

PICTORIALS

Burrows, Tony. *Hole*. Miami, FL: MBS, 1996. 120 pages. Approximately 75 color and black-and-white photographs throughout. Discography. Chronology. Index.

CD-format book covering all aspects of Hole's career. This nicely designed and illustrated book is priced just right at around $7.99.

Wilson, Susan. *Hole: Look Through This*. London: UFO Music Books, 1995. 80 pages. Approximately 120 color and black-and-white photographs, covering every page.

The typical assortment of slutty photos supplemented with superficial text. The lone Kurt Cobain photo is pretty lousy, and there's hardly anything on the aftermath of his suicide (not to mention previous attempts on his life). Flagrantly superficial.

Wise, Nick. *Courtney Love*. London: Omnibus Press (division of Book Sales Limited), 1995. Unpaginated (approximately 48 pages). Approximately 50 color and black-and-white photographs, covering every page.

Trashy rag that cashes in on Courtney Love's notorious fame. The book does little to show any depth behind the stripper/groupie/clown turned singer/songwriter/mother/widow. If you want her physically exposed, however, look no further than this book. A sleazy treatment of a bitchy subject. Dead fans: Did you know Love's dad is author Hank Harrison (see Grateful Dead: Critical/Analytical Commentary)?

BUDDY HOLLY (AND THE CRICKETS)

BIOGRAPHIES

Amburn, Ellis. *Buddy Holly: A Biography*. New York: St. Martin's, 1995. 422 pages. Two glossy, 16-page black-and-white photo inserts. Notes. Discography. Index.

Four decades plus (and several publications) later, is there anything left to say about the life of a star who died at only 21 years of age? Plenty, at least according to biographer Amburn. For one thing, Holly was not the dorky, emaciated geek people seem to think of; in fact, as this book steadfastly seeks to prove, Holly was a horny, red-blooded, money-hungry, impetuous, delinquent set on success at all costs. Completing his own trilogy (see Joplin, Janis and Orbison, Roy: Biographies), Amburn has once again awakened the memory of a departed rocker only to scourge it with tenuous details of sexual escapades (actual gangbangs, although not referred to as such in those days), fisticuffs, and rabble-rousing. A harsh demythologizing.

Goldrosen, John and Beecher, John. *Remembering Buddy: The Definitive Biography of Buddy Holly*. New York: Penguin Books, 1987. 204 pages. One hundred black-and-white photographs scattered throughout. Session File. Discography. Chart File. Tour Dates. Index. Bibliography. (This edition first published in Great Britain in 1986 by Pavillon Books.)

This more-than-you-can-eat biography contains all you'll ever need to know on Buddy Holly: an in-depth biography of the man's roots (in the "buckle" of the Bible belt, Lubbock, Texas); background on his musical inspiration; a history of his brief rise to fame and tragic death; his widespread influence; and his complete recordings and concerts. The authors have made Holly a life's mission—and have cast a wide net in obtaining rare photos, documents (a fascinating essay Holly wrote in high school), and buried facts. One little known morsel is that The "Beetles" was actually considered as a band name before The Crickets. Well...all right! "...a must purchase for well-rounded pop music collections"—*Booklist*. Earlier editions of this book were published as *Buddy Holly: His Life and Music* by Popular Press, Charisma Books, and Granada Publishing.

CRITICAL/ANALYTICAL COMMENTARY

Laing, Dave. *Buddy Holly*. London: Studio Vista, 1971. 112 pages. Approximately 65 black-and-white photographs throughout. Notes. Discography.

Ancient study of Buddy Holly's musical legacy, introduced with weighty material on the Texas musical tradition and the burgeoning of rock and roll in the mid-to-late 1950's. With a slightly heavy hand and a touch of pomp, Laing examines the lyrical content, vocals, harmonies, instrumental solos, rhythm section, and other areas of Holly's music, but neglects to address his significant studio advances— which merit considerable attention given Holly was only in his early 20's at the height of his career (and on his death).

FANZINES AND FAN CLUBS

Crickets File. Pastime Publications, 412 Main Road, Sheffield, S9 4QL England.

Published since 1979, *Crickets File* claims to be the longest-running Crickets fanzine in existence. The fanzine is published four times a year and includes tour news, reviews, readers' letters, new releases, and more. The cost of membership is $11 U.S. and Canada; £5.50 U.K.; and £6 elsewhere in Europe.

GENERAL REFERENCE

Peer, Elizabeth and Peer, Ralph II. *Buddy Holly: A Biography in Words, Photographs and Music*. New York: Beer International, 1972. 148 pages. Approximately 50 black-and-white photographs throughout. Discography. Selected Bibliography. Index.

Muddled Holly retrospective, half biography and half sheet music for all of his original tunes. The authors went down to Lubbock, Texas to interview those who knew Holly or had information about him, but the results are less than comprehensive. Rave on.

PICTORIALS

Peters, Richard. *The Legend That Is Buddy Holly*. London: Souvenir Press Limited, 1990. 128 pages. Approximately 125 black-and-white photographs throughout. Buddy Holly: A Discography.

Decent photo-biography of one of rock's true icons, containing some fine photos and reproductions of documents such as Holly's hand-scripted copy of Edgar Allan (spelled by Holly as "Allen") Poe's "The Raven." Author Richard Peters also clarifies errors and exaggerations in the 1978 film *The Buddy Holly Story* (that would only matter to sticklers). Both the look and the text have dated considerably, but Holly fans should have this in their collections.

Tobler, John. *The Buddy Holly Story.* New York: Beaufort Books, 1979. 96 pages. Approximately 125 black-and-white photographs, covering every page. Discography.

Tobler gropes his way through the Buddy Holly tale, trying desperately to pass off for biography what others have at least put into English. The book was published hot on the heels of the 1978 film *The Buddy Holly Story* starring Gary Busey, and devotes a full chapter to it. Fans will appreciate the range of photos and reprinted newspaper clippings, as well as a chapter highlighting specific instances of Holly's influence on contemporary music. The yellow cover is among the ugliest ever slapped on a book.

RELATED WORKS

Denton, Bradley. *Buddy Holly Is Alive and Well on Ganymede.* New York: William Morrow & Company, 1991. 360 pages.

Oliver Vale was conceived on February 3, 1959 while Buddy Holly's song "Heartbeat" played on the radio—and, coincidentally, at the same moment Holly was incinerated in a fateful plane crash. Vale was born on December 8, a date that would live in infamy 21 years later as the day John Lennon was assassinated. Vale grows up consumed with his mother's "rock and roll religion" and actually takes over the nation's airwaves in order to broadcast Buddy Holly recordings. Somehow aliens and cyborgs fit in with this tale that interweaves events from Vale's childhood with the present. "...wild and crazy, action-packed satire"—*Booklist.*

BRUCE HORNSBY

TITLES OF INTEREST
Feldman, Sy. *Bruce Hornsby Hot House.* New York: Warner, 1995.

THE HOUSEMARTINS

PICTORIALS

Swift, Nick. *The Housemartins: Now That's What I Call Quite Good.* London: Book Sales Limited, 1988. 100 pages. Approximately 125 black-and-white photographs throughout. Discography.

This band, while "not quite as big as Jesus," is given a witty treatment by friend and confidante Swift. The Housemartins were originally from Hull, England, and had influence from The Beatles, Elvis Costello, and The Jam. Whether you like this book depends on your taste for the author's quirky sense of humor. On musician Norman Cook's joining the group: "A Housemartin sperm was being produced." Splendidly illustrated, with many pictures of the kids in their early heyday.

WHITNEY HOUSTON

BIOGRAPHIES

Bego, Mark. *Whitney!.* Toronto and New York: PaperJacks, 1986. 120 pages. One eight-page black-and-white photo insert. Discography. Videography. Chronology.

With her mother (Cissy Houston) and cousin (Dionne Warwick) both successful singers, it was a fait accompli that Whitney Houston would become a pop or soul vocalist herself. After lucking into a hugely successful modeling career (with the Click and Wilhelmina agencies), Houston launched her singing career with a series of high-note singles, tasteful videos, music awards, and a flurry of television endorsements. Mark Bego fudges himself as an insider by reprinting his interviews with corporate execs, publicists, and a peripheral musician here and there, but at this early stage in Whitney's career no one had anything terribly interesting to report. A stretch even at 120 pages.

Bowman, Jeffery. Introduction by J. Randy Taraborrelli. *The Totally Unauthorized Biography of Whitney Houston.* London: Headline Book Publishing, 1994. 340 pages. Two glossy eight-page black-and-white photo inserts.

The most acclaimed female singer of the 1980's and 90's is given the tabloid treatment by author Jeffery Bowman. Tormented as a child by other kids because of her light skin and straight hair, Houston survived a fluke accident—a wire getting stuck in her throat while goofing around with her brother—which almost ended her singing career before it began. Sympathetic details such as these flood the opening chapters, but then we get to the dirt, such as Houston's tempestuous relationship with husband/rapper Bobby Brown and her reputation for being stuck-up, illustrated by her refusal to show up at a function honoring Dolly Parton. (Implicitly, because she didn't want to publicly acknowledge that her hit song "I Will Always Love You" was handled equally as well by its composer.) Houston isn't exactly Madonna, however, and she just doesn't make juicy copy.

FANZINES AND FAN CLUBS

Whitney Houston Official Fan Club. Dept. Friend, P.O. Box 885288, San Francisco, CA 94188.

Whitney Houston fan club that offers members access to preferred concert tickets, travel packages, exclusive merchandise, and more. Members also receive a biography, a discography, a photo, a membership card, and subscription to the club newsletter, which contains interviews, photos, and contests. The cost of membership is $18 U.S.; $24 elsewhere.

YOUNG ADULT

Greenberg, Keith Eliot. *Whitney Houston.* Minneapolis, MN: Lerner Publications Company, 1988. 32 pages. Approximately 20 color and black-and-white photographs throughout.

Ultra-hype book for kids eight and younger, which casts Houston as beautiful, polite, dedicated, and talented—all of which are true—and then adds some genuine hyperbole by citing her "modesty." Still, children will have a hard time resisting the attractive violet cover and the flattering photos of Houston as her career was being launched. The last pages emphasize her non-party lifestyle, which some parents might find a relief compared to the barrage of controversies surrounding the Jackson family (including the women). "...it does provide a certain amount of entertainment value at an elementary level"—*School Library Journal.*

Wallner, Rosemary. *Whitney Houston: Singer/Actress/Superstar.* Edina, MN: Abdo & Daughters, 1994. 32 pages. Approximately ten black-and-white photographs throughout.

Part of the "Reaching for the Stars" series from Abdo & Daughters, this large print book may be enjoyed by fans hovering around six years of age; older kids would probably know more information than author Rosemary Wallner provides. Chapters run one to three pages in length and center on the film *The Bodyguard,* her relationship with husband/rapper Bobby Brown, and awards. The title lacks insight into Houston's personality and music.

OTHER TITLES OF INTEREST
Busnar, Gene. *The Picture Life of Whitney Houston.* New York: Franklin Watts, 1988.
Booklist *commented: "Fans of singer Whitney Houston, and they are legion, will be pleased by this compact biography."*

THE HUMAN LEAGUE

BIOGRAPHIES

Nash, Peter. *The Human League.* London: W.H. Allen & Co., Limited, 1982. 144 pages. One glossy four-page black-and-white photo insert. Discography.

The story of the Sheffield-based band that had aspirations to become the "English Abba," but instead became the top synthesizer/electronic drum group of the early 1980's. Fronted by crooner Phil Oakey, The Human League had its greatest success with its early LP *Dare,* which has since faded to oblivion. Although a little short on the visual end, this book is an intelligent and generally engaging work, hampered only by the band's inability to adapt to the 1990's.

OTHER TITLES OF INTEREST
Ross, Alaska. *The Story of a Band Called the Human League.* London: Proteus, 1982.

IAN HUNTER

See Mott the Hoople.

ICE-T

WRITTEN WORKS

Ice-T. As told to Siegmund, Heidi. *The Ice Opinion: Who Gives a Fuck?*. New York: St. Martin's Press, 1994. 200 pages. Approximately 20 black-and-white photographs throughout. Pimptionary/Glossary.

This book bears the proud distinction of being the only work herein to skip the innuendo altogether and go for the four-letter word in the title. Don't assume this is cutting-edge, however: The shock-value wears off pretty quickly through repetition on what seems to be every page of the text. Not intended as a biography—to be sure, there is very little of Ice-T's personal history here—but rather, this is a collection of lengthy articles by the notorious rapper (told through Siegmund) expounding his brash views on ghetto life, sex, crime, racism, and religion. When you read what Ice-T has to say about the survivalist mentality of ghetto life, you start to understand why his lyrics contain so much aggression against cops. Those who criticize Ice-T's lyrics and views might want to give this a look, if only to arrive at the conclusion that satire is always a stronger force against injustice than counter-hostility. "...Ice-T's book has the most appealing qualities of rap—verbal dexterity, imagination and bravado"—*Mademoiselle*.

BILLY IDOL

PICTORIALS

Wrenn, Mike. *Billy Idol: A Visual Documentary*. London: Omnibus Press (division of Book Sales Limited), 1991. 96 pages. Approximately 125 glossy black-and-white and 20 glossy color illustrations, covering every page. Discography.

Not much different than Omnibus Press' extensive "in their own words" series, this title benefits from a larger trim, an abundance of photos, glossy paper, and a format that incorporates both quotes and chronology. Fans of the star will go wild over photos of Idol—chains, leather, earrings, and tattoos, all for the same price. Unfortunately, the images are not captioned, so you have to look fast to catch Idol with other stars (such as the late Who drummer, Keith Moon). Is Idol punk, glam rock, or pop? Read for yourself to find out what the man himself has to say.

OTHER TITLES OF INTEREST
Gooch, Brad. *Billy Idol*. New York: Ballantine, 1985.
Russell, Kate. *Billy Idol*. New York: Simon & Schuster, 1985.

THE IMPRESSIONS

WRITTEN WORKS

Mayfield, Curtis. *Poetic License: In Poem and Song*. New York: Dove Books, 1996. 72 pages. Approximately 50 color drawings throughout.

Mayfield, a member of The Impressions and a successful soloist, had a lasting impact on rock, blues, soul, and gospel with songwriting credits such as "It's All Right" and "Amen." Mayfield has a strong connection to black history and spirituality, and the 72 poems and songs collected here reflect his continuing ties to ghetto life and religious expression. In "Miss Black America," he pays somber tribute to black women; in "Choice of Colors," he confronts race head-on; and in "I Loved and I Lost" he looks back forlornly on ended romance. David Soto's colorful drawings may seem directed to a young audience, but the works included herein are well suited to both kids and adults alike. Deeply felt and often moving.

INXS

TOURBOOKS

No author. *INXS: The Official Inside Story of a Band on the Road*. New York: St. Martin's Press, 1992. 80 pages. Approximately 120 color and 30 black-and-white photographs, covering every page. Chronology. Discography. Videography. Discography. INXS Tour Schedule 1990-91. X Tour Set Lists.

INX's 1990-91 X-factor tour spanned 80 cities across four continents and attracted 1.2 million fans. This authorless record (with vague mention of work done by Ed St. John) was the first document of the band's doings, and it has the luxury of INXS' support. The group contributed the foreword and a large share of original, semi-insightful quotes (singer Michael Hutchence: "I love being famous") throughout. The photo spreads are designed like *Rolling Stone* layout pages which, for the most part, pay off. Nicely done.

IRON BUTTERFLY

WOLFMAN JACK

AUTOBIOGRAPHY

Jack, Wolfman with Laursen, Byron. *Have Mercy! Confessions of the Original Rock 'n' Roll Animal.* New York: Warner Books, 1995. 364 pages. Four 16-page black-and-white photo inserts.

Born with the unlikeliest and blandest of names, Bob Smith, Wolfman Jack was a crucial figure for teen radio listeners in the early days of rock and roll. Young Bob was inspired by his family's maid, Frances (nicknamed Tantan), who taught him about gospel and how to put "soul" into his work. A high school dropout and on-and-off salesman, Smith latched on to working as a radio disc jockey and, over the years on XERB radio, fostered his classic persona, which he claims originated from his love of horror flicks. Despite the obligatory drugs, orgies, fistfights, and the passage of time, the Wolfman stood as a hip, humble icon—not far removed from his self-portrayal in *American Graffiti.* Sadly, the DJ died shortly after publication.

FANZINES AND FAN CLUBS

Iron Butterfly Information Network. Att. Rick Gagnon, Biografix, 9745 Sierra Avenue, Fontana, CA 92335.

A continuation of the Ironic Butterfly Fan Club, which ceased to exist in 1988, as did its newsletter, *Unconscious Power.* The network answers questions related to the band and offers Iron Butterfly related items for sale. Those who write must enclose a self-addressed stamped envelope for reply and in order to receive a membership certificate.

IRON MAIDEN

PICTORIALS

Halfin, Ross. *Iron Maiden: What Are We Doing This For?* London: Zomba, 1988. 128 pages. Approximately 400 color photographs and graphics, covering every page.

Photographer Ross Halfin tagged along with Iron Maiden for about a decade, during which time he produced what is perhaps the most exciting assortment of photos on the band available. Okay, so there's no text—only captions indicating dates and cities of performances. But despite the group's nasty image, Halfin has captured these guys having a blast, both on stage and behind-the-scenes. For an explanation of what these boys are doing this for (as hinted in the subtitle), look elsewhere; for some terrific photos, this will suffice.

JANET JACKSON

(See also Jackson 5, The)

BIOGRAPHIES

Andrews, Bart. Introduction by J. Randy Taraborrelli. *Out of the Madness: The Strictly Unauthorized Biography of Janet Jackson.* New York: HarperCollins, 1994. 306 pages. One 16-page black-and-white photo insert.

Andrews retreads the usual Jackson muck, with ample assistance from Michael Jackson biographer Taraborrelli (see Michael Jackson, biographies). Evidently neither feels Janet's story alone merits a reader's attention, so much of the hullabaloo concerns the usual junk about father Joe's various abuses of his wife and kids, sister La Toya's nude photos, cosmetic surgeries, molestation charges against Michael, etc. Janet's role in the dysfunctional Jackson clan is complete denial about her family's ills: Intentionally or not, she comes off as an uninteresting side player in her own biography. Fans would want more about Janet's trend-setting wardrobe, electric dance moves, chart-making vocal successes, and hot videos. This book fails to even supply a discography. Strictly off limits.

FANZINES AND FAN CLUBS

Friends of Janet. P.O. Box 884988, San Francisco, CA 94188.

Fan club that offers members access to the Friends of Janet hotline, preferred concert tickets, merchandising for purchase, contests, travel packages, and a newsletter containing interviews, photos, tour dates, and more. Members also receive a photo, a biography, a discography, and a membership card. The cost of membership is $19 U.S.; $25 elsewhere.

YOUNG ADULT

Mabery, D.L. *Janet Jackson*. Minneapolis, MN: Lerner Publications Company, 1988. 32 pages. Approximately 20 color and black-and-white photographs throughout.

Juvenile biography of Jackson that includes the minimum detail on her early years and her rise in the entertainment industry. The book sketchily tells of her success on TV with "Good Times" and of her brief marriage to James DeBarge. Unfortunately, it also predates much of Janet's success as a solo singer in the 1990's, resulting in only a couple of photos in which she looks like the glamorous video star of present. "...little substance between the pages"—*Booklist*.

OTHER TITLES OF INTEREST
Jackson, Janet and Jackson, Randy. *Ready & Fight*. St. Paul, MN: EMC, 1977.

LA TOYA JACKSON

(See also Jackson 5, The)

AUTOBIOGRAPHY

Jackson, La Toya with Romanowski, Patricia. *La Toya: Growing up in the Jackson Family*. New York: Dutton (Penguin Group), 1991. 262 pages. Two glossy 16-page black-and-white photo inserts.

The Jackson family did all they could to prevent the publication of this tell-all autobiography. Mainly they were upset about La Toya's harboring anger toward her father, Joe Jackson, who allegedly psychologically and physically abused all of his kids. Meanwhile, the man who fathered the Jackson 5 and two female mega-talents (the author and her sister, Janet) is portrayed here as a dominating hypocrite, stashing his lover and illegitimate child across town as he preached his family conservative Jehovah Witness values. La Toya writes candidly about her family (notably brother Michael's hypersensitivity), but one gets the distinct impression she's full of it when it comes to her naiveté on sex and her complete innocence at not knowing what was in store for her during her *Playboy* photo shoot. "...comparable to an episode from television's `A Current Affair'"—*Library Journal*.

MICHAEL JACKSON

(See also Jackson 5, The)

AUTOBIOGRAPHY

Jackson, Michael. *Moonwalk*. New York: Doubleday, 1988. 296 pages. Approximately 70 black-and-white photographs throughout; three glossy eight-page color inserts.

Published without the seemingly obligatory ghostwriter, *Moonwalk* is just what one might expect: a lightweight, straightforward retelling of events spreading the myth that both in public and in private Jackson is a happy, magical fellow. The then-29-year-old star fesses up to some resentment about his missed childhood, but he is not very forthcoming about his dominating father or his siblings. As for his love life, the highlight is a hand touch from Tatum O'Neal. Other women are not mentioned "because they are not celebrities and are unaccustomed to having their names in print." Even the most starblind fans will see through Jackson's smokescreens.

BIOGRAPHIES

Andersen, Christopher. *Michael Jackson Unauthorized*. New York: Simon & Schuster, 1994. 384 pages. Two glossy 16-page black-and-white photo inserts. Notes and Sources.

Andersen turns out what one would expect in

the wake of Jackson's $26 million molestation charge settlement and his brief marriage of convenience to Lisa Marie Presley: slick, tell-all tabloid fare. Andersen takes perverse pleasure in recounting every detail in the police investigation of Jackson's Neverland estate—and an even greater kick describing a strip search of Jacko himself. Painkiller addictions, hair-raising fires, child abuse, incest, skin disorders, cosmetic surgeries, emotional and physical breakdowns, and plenty of all-around strangeness (with children and zoo animals) pervade the text, and one wonders if there is anything left for Jackson to do that would raise an eyebrow. "...a sad book...the reader is left with the image of a selfish, publicity-obsessed star..." —*People*.

Bego, Mark. *Michael!*. New York: Pinnacle Books, 1984. 182 pages. Two 16-page black-and-white photo inserts.

An early 1980's press release with pretenses of serving as a biography, this book has one merit for fans blinded by Jackson's star power: there are no scandals, no hyperbaric chambers, no child-beating dads—and no mention of Jackson's traumatic teenage skin conditions. This tale reads as so idyllic it becomes absurd fiction, bordering on the Peter Pan and *E.T.* fantasies Jackson himself finds so alluring. Interviews with fashion designer Jill Klein and disco mixer John Jellybean Benitez serve as substandard filler.

Campbell, Lisa D. *Michael Jackson: The King of Pop*. Boston: Branden Books, 1993. 392 pages. One 16-page black-and-white photo insert. Appendix A: Michael Jackson and Jackson 5 Album Discography. Appendix B: Michael Jackson Videography. Appendix C: Michael Jackson Billboard Chart History. Appendix D: Michael Jackson's Number One Singles. Index.

Author Lisa D. Campbell goes on the record assaulting other biographers for getting their facts wrong on Michael Jackson. For example, she insists, The Jackson 5 were *not* discovered by Diana Ross, Gladys Knight, or Bobby Taylor (of Bobby Taylor and The Vancouvers). While this kind of clarification is useful, it detracts from the general coverage of what made Michael and family so popular: hard work, practice, bubbly charm, influence from James Brown (only one small paragraph here), and a taskmaster father. Badly written.

Latham, Caroline. *Michael Jackson: Thrill*. New York: Kensington, 1984. 192 pages. One 16-page black-and-white photo insert. Discography.

Lazily researched mass-market biography that is full of typos, errors, and just plain stupidity. Author Caroline Latham is at such a loss to say anything intelligent about Michael Jackson, she fills up space that should have been devoted to biography with her friends' impressions of why the star is so admired. Not helping matters is the fact that the title doesn't make any sense. Heap onto the junk pile.

Marsh, Dave. *Trapped: Michael Jackson and the Crossover Dream*. New York: Bantam, 1985. 260 pages. One eight-page black-and-white photo insert.

Not exactly the prototypical flashy trashcan bio, but instead a social and psychological profile of Jackson up through the mid-1980's, with plenty of musical criticism. Marsh fades in and out of a "Dear Michael" letter approach to demonstrate the extent of Jackson's mysteries and elusiveness, which produces less than satisfactory results. He also gives the star unasked for advice ("you could stand to lighten up"), which may be true—but reads as condescending. Below Marsh's usual standard.

Taraborrelli, J. Randy. *Michael Jackson: The Magic and the Madness*. New York, Ballantine, 1991. 624 pages. One 16-page black-and-white photo insert. Source Notes. Extensive Bibliography. Index.

On the cover of this mass market paperback is a blurb from a *Baltimore Sun* review: "More luscious scandal. More good dirt." Actually, this number one best-seller is a semi-fair investigation into the bizarre world of the performer up through 1990, with surprisingly detailed source notes and bibliographic information. Taraborrelli tackles myth versus fact with believable authority (though it is clearly dated, since molestation claims occurred years after the book's release). He asserts Jackson does not sleep in a hyperbaric chamber (it was a publicity hoax devised by Jackson himself to test how he could manipulate the media) and is quite a shrewd businessman (acing Paul McCartney out for rights to Northern Songs and The Beatles' music). Wait for a revised edition (or buy any recent tabloid) if you need the most up-to-date poop.

CHRONOLOGIES

Grant, Adrian. *Michael Jackson: The Visual Documentary*. London: Omnibus Press (division of Book Sales Limited), 1994. 184 pages. Approximately 175 color and black-and-white photographs throughout. U.K. Discography.

A year-by-year photo history of Jackson, opening with a handy (and illustrated) family tree. The text starts with Michael's birth (August 29, 1958) and breezes through major events in his life up through the release of *History*. The text deals with molestation charges and other unpleasant oddities in Jackson's life, but doesn't highlight them either; special boxes have been designed primarily to emphasize Jackson's dedication to causes and human rights issues. The photo reproductions are quite good, and so is the wealth of oversized quotes. Grant's most glaring pitfall is that she tends to unnecessarily cite her own role in the Jackson story. Otherwise, a non-tabloid alternative for those who still believe in the magic.

DISCOGRAPHIES, RECORDING GUIDES, AND COLLECTIBLES

Machlin, Milt. *The Michael Jackson Catalog*. New York: Arbor House, 1984. 128 pages. Over 125 black-and-white reproductions of merchandise, collectibles, and publications; two glossy eight-page color inserts. Appendix.

Collectors' guide for Michael Jacksonfiles that is divided into: merchandise (bubblegum cards, towels, shirts, etc.); collectibles (booklets, autographs, etc.); discography; publications; and Victory Tour paraphernalia. Prices (circa 1984) are provided for most items. The author has not included much on the early days of The Jackson 5, although there is slightly more on the later Jacksons (memorabilia from the 1984 Victory Tour). Contrary to the author's assertion, Jackson's mega-popularity has *not* filtered to a merchandising and collectible line of the same magnitude as The Beatles and Elvis. This is a rather slim volume lacking personality; Jackson seems just as waxy on a beach towel as he does in real life.

Terry, Carol D. Foreword by Tom Schultheiss. *Sequins & Shades: The Michael Jackson Reference Guide*. Ann Arbor, MI: Pierian Press, 1987. 508 pages. Approximately 200 black-and-white reproductions of album covers.

Indexes: Author Index, Title Index, Subject Index, Date Index, Publications Index, Record Number Index.

Part of the "Rock & Roll reference" series from Pierian Press, this book includes absolutely every detail one would need to know about Jackson's recordings up through April 1987. Author Carol Terry oddly opens with a bibliography (rather than place it in the back), which contains book titles, periodicals, articles, and more. A chronology follows, starting with 1903 and the birth of Michael Jackson's grandfather. The discography breaks releases down by both U.S. and U.K. releases under various combinations: The Jackson 5, The Jacksons, and Michael Jackson solo. Terry takes things further by listing collaborative efforts, reissues, multi-artist recordings, special formats, and broadcast and novelty records. The song list and indexes are of Pierian's usual high standards. The photos of album covers are nothing to speak of but, for discographical information, *Sequins & Shades* stands as the definitive volume.

FANZINES AND FAN CLUBS

Michael Jackson Fan Club: The Legend Continues. P.O. Box 1160, 2301 Eb Leiden, Holland.

Dutch fan club that provides to fans a membership card, a certificate, a surprise gift, and subscription to the quarterly fanzine, *Tribute*. The 40-page stapled packet, written in English, contains black-and-white photographs, Jackson news, information on charities, updates on Euro-Disney, and more. Write for price information.

PICTORIALS

Brown, Geoff. *Michael Jackson: Body and Soul*. Beaufort Books, 1984. 128 pages. 100 black-and-white photographs; two glossy eight-page color inserts.

Effervescent pictorial retrospective of Jackson's career, with better-than-usual photos and two lively color inserts. The book also contains a useful chapter on musical roots (James Brown, Sly Stone) and one on the Jackson family itself. If you are into 1980's Jackson hype, this is one of the better photo books you'll find. Fans might like that the scandals and intrigues of the 1990's had not occurred at the time of this book's release.

Chenery, John. *Michael Jackson: A View from Down Under*. Sidney, Australia: Little Hills Press, 1984. Unpaginated (approximately 56 pages). Approximately 50 glossy color and black-and-white illustrations, covering nearly every page. Comes with a full-color poster.

Aussie publication that, unfortunately, doesn't have any charm or personality from the folks down under. This rag could have been produced anywhere, with dated chapters on The Jackson 5 formation, the Victory Tour, and not much else. The inside is almost as horrible to look at as the *Thriller* still on the book's back cover.

Endrei, Mary J. *The Magic of Michael Jackson*. Cresskill, NJ: Sharon Starbook, 1984. 64 pages. Approximately 75 black-and-white and 20 color illustrations, covering nearly every page. Discography.

Sketchy profile of Jackson, with a then-understandable emphasis on the *Thriller* LP and its accompanying videos. A digressive chapter on choreographer Michael Peters takes attention away from the star himself, as does an interview with Jackson family confidante Steve Manning. The magic show ended a long time ago.

Honeyford, Paul. *The Thrill of Michael Jackson*. New York: William Morrow & Company, 1984. 64 pages. Approximately 75 color and black-and-white photographs throughout.

Straightforward pictorial work that begins with Jackson's upbringing in Gary, Indiana and traces his story to the Jacksons' *Victory* album and tour in 1984. Jackson smiles and struts in every photo, except for those of him at the Burn Center recovering from his Pepsi commercial fire. This virtually scandal-free book is a decent PR-piece that might still be enjoyed by kids for its color photos and breezy tone. Not for research or to serve as a biography.

No author. *Michael Jackson*. Port Chester, NY: Cherry Lane Books, 1984. Unpaginated (approximately 32 pages). Approximately 35 color photographs throughout. Discography. Comes with a color pull-out poster.

Collection of photos, all of which have been glossed with repulsive shades of pink. The images are in extreme close-up to Jackson's face, so you can see all of the fine details of his pubescent mustache (he was in his 20's at the time), although not a trace of his much-discussed skin condition/acne or reconstructive surgeries. Poor.

No author. *Michael Jackson Tear-Out Photo Book*. London: Oliver Books, 1993. Unpaginated (approximately 48 pages). 20 color photographs throughout.

Outside the snazzy cover, there isn't that much to pull in Jackson's fans. These tearsheets are mostly publicity poses of Jackson (with monkey, in trendsetting garb, etc.), but nothing terrible, charismatic, or familiar. Serves less of a purpose than Grant's tourbook (see below).

QUIZBOOKS AND QUOTEBOOKS

Dineen, Catherine. *Michael Jackson: In His Own Words*. London: Omnibus Press (division of Book Sales Limited), 1993. 96 pages. Approximately 100 black-and-white photographs, covering every page.

Jacko is quoted on topics such as the early days, songs, performing, films, his family, producers, celebrities, etc. The only problem here is that there seem to be more quotes *about* him than by him. The author's research hasn't yielded anything remarkable and, in fact, quotes such as "I was a veteran before I was a teenager" have been reprinted elsewhere ad nauseam. Published prior to Jackson's "marriage" to Priscilla, although it's doubtful Jackson has said anything worth quoting about the relationship anyway. A mixed bag.

Rowland, Mark. *The Totally Unauthorized Michael Jackson Trivia Book*. New York: Dell, 1984. 274 pages. Two 16-page black-and-white photo inserts. Discography. Appendix.

Since when is a pop trivia book ever authorized anyway? Quizmaster Rowland, hot on the heels of Jackson's early 1980's mega-stardom, cashed in with this mass-market quizbook divided into sections on Gary (Indiana), Motown, L.A., the Jackson Family, Tours, Records, *Thriller*, and more. Most of the questions are multiple choice, although there is one crossword puzzle. Surprisingly all-encompassing, with an educated range of questions for all difficulty levels. The topics also keep a good distance from Jackson, including both supportive and controversial issues. So, true or false: Did Michael Jackson ever admit to smoking marijuana?

TOURBOOKS

Grant, Adrian. *Michael Jackson: Live and Dangerous*. London: Omnibus Press (division of Book Sales Limited), 1992. Unpaginated (approximately 48 pages). Approximately 50 color photographs throughout. Comes with a full-color poster.

Color photos from Jackson's 1992 Dangerous tour. As a document of the tour, this is pretty barren; as a collection of close-up photos, some fans might be satisfied. Now will someone refresh my memory as to why Jackson had Band-Aids on three of his fingers and wasn't wearing his traditional glove?

WRITTEN WORKS

Jackson, Michael. Introduction by Elizabeth Taylor. *Dancing the Dream: Poetry & Reflections*. New York: Doubleday (division of Bantam Doubleday Dell Publishing Group, Inc.), 1992. 152 pages. Approximately 100 color photographs and drawings throughout; a half dozen black-and-white sketches throughout.

Jackson's second book (see Autobiography, above) combines high quality art and photos with prose and poetry by the "king of pop" himself. The author's naiveté and politically correct goodness abound: respect planet earth, tend to your children, keep dolphins out of fish nets, honor your mother, etc. His poetry is haplessly on a third grade emotional level, while his reflections on his artistry are bland clichés. How does he make his music? "It's like stepping into a river and joining the flow." Thanks for the insight. Kitsch, with many worthwhile dance action photos for Jackson fans.

YOUNG ADULT

George, Nelson. *The Michael Jackson Story*. New York: Dell Publishing Company, Inc., 1984. 192 pages. One eight-page black-and-white photo insert. Appendix (includes discography).

Innocuous bio that contains more about the Jackson family than Michael himself. The book avoids going for the traditional strangeness and hype, which is most definitely a plus for the YA market. Instead, there's quite a lot about his influences (Diana Ross, James Brown, et. al.), the *Thriller* LP, and his friendships at the time (including Paul McCartney and Katharine Hepburn). The back ad is one for the

time capsule: "...Michael, the shy, sensitive enchanter, who counts llamas, cockatoos—and Brooke Shields—among his first loves." Revised in 1987.

Halliburton, Warren J. *The Picture Life of Michael Jackson*. New York: Franklin Watts, 1984. 48 pages. 24 black-and-white photographs throughout.

Simplistic introduction to Jackson for fans eight and younger. Not bad considering all of the years that have gone by since the book's publication, but kids would probably prefer a more color-filled presentation.

Haskins, James. *About Michael Jackson*. Hillside, NJ: Enslow Publishers, Inc., 1985. 96 pages. Approximately 50 black-and-white photographs throughout.

Encased in a sleek black cover, this is a standard bio of the Gloved One, written in simple sentences (with long paragraphing) for fans ten and younger. Recurring E.T. photos and line drawings will be a puzzle for a new generation who did not grow up with the film and Jackson's children's album of that name; on the other hand, it will probably be sickening to those who did. Derivative fare, with some very obvious errors. "The black-and-white photos are standard shots found in many Jackson biographies"—*School Library Journal*.

Mabery, D.L. *This Is Michael Jackson*. Minneapolis, MN: Lerner Publications Company, 1984. 48 pages. Approximately 25 color and black-and-white illustrations throughout. Records and Awards.

Glossy picture book geared toward the eight-year-old that focuses on Jackson's popularity, awards, love of animals, and ties to Peter Pan. Hardly anything new, although the book is harmless entertainment for little ones who are fascinated with Jackson's mystique.

Matthews, Gordon. *Michael Jackson*. New York: Simon & Schuster, 1984. 64 pages. Approximately 40 black-and-white photographs throughout. Discography.

"He's Super Hot! Super Talented! Super Creative!" Yet another young adult paperback, published amidst the onslaught of Michael Jackson publications in 1984. This one lacks the color of some of the others, but does capture the excitement of Jackson's spectacular Grammy coup in the early 1980's. Basic.

McKissack, Patricia. *Michael Jackson, Superstar!*. Chicago: Children's Press, 1984. 96 pages. Time Line. Fact Sheet. Index.

Glossy, silvery-designed package for young fans. Many of the pictures and headings are framed with gray borders, which only works in some cases. A photo of Jane Fonda accepting her Academy Award in sign language is strangely included because the actress was "Jackson's friend." The glossy paper will be appreciated by kids, but the lack of color will not. A better treatment than Halliburton's (see above).

Nicholson, Lois P. Introduction by Coretta Scott King. *Michael Jackson: Entertainer*. New York: Chelsea House, 1994. 104 pages. Approximately 50 black-and-white photographs throughout.

Part of the "Black Americans of Achievement" series, this intelligent study traces the full scope of Jackson's musical career, and shows how he went from child performing star to seasoned veteran in only a few short years. Nicholson deals with Jackson's multifarious problems, from skin acne to his burn from the Pepsi commercial to his settlement over molestation charges, but the real attention is on his musical accomplishments. Chelsea House deserves credit for sticking to their guns and depicting Jackson as a role model, while still being forthcoming about controversies and public opinion. The book's beautifully designed cover means many repeat customers to the library shelves.

No author. Introduction by Robin Katz. *Michael Jackson*. New York: Gallery Books (division of W.H. Allen), 1984. Unpaginated (approximately 32 pages). Approximately 40 color photographs, covering every page. Discography.

One of the better studies of Jackson for children, ably assisted by an opening chapter containing bubbly pictures of The Jackson 5 playing their hearts out. The pages are nicely designed, with an emphasis on caption material over actual text.

OTHER TITLES OF INTEREST

Black, Susan. *Michael Jackson Live*. Woodstock, NY: Beekman, 1990.

Garland, Phyl. *Michael: In Concert, with Friends, at Play*. Woodstock, NY: Beekman, 1984.

Horwich, Richard. *Michael Jackson*. No city: Gallery Books, 1984.

Lee, Les. *Michael Jackson Scrapbook*. New York: Carol, 1992.

Levenson, David. *Michael Jackson: The Victory Tour*. Ann Arbor, MI: Crescent, 1983.

Magee, Doug. *Michael Jackson*. London: Proteus, 1984.

Marchbank, Pearce. *Michael Jackson Fact File and Official Lyric Book*. London: Omnibus Press (division of Book Sales Limited), 1984.

Parker, Lewis K. *Michael Jackson Trivia Book*. Middletown, CT: Weekly Reader Books, 1984.

Quill, Greg. *Michael Jackson Electrifying*. No city: Barson's, 1988.

Regan, Stewart. *Michael Jackson*. No city: Colour Library Books, 1984.

Rubenstein, Bruce. *Michael Jackson*. Mankato, MN: Creative Education, 1984.

Schiffman, Bonnie (photographer). *Michael Jackson*. London: Omnibus Press (division of Book Sales Limited), 1984.

Schuster, Hal. *The Magical Michael Jackson*. No city: Pioneer, 1990.

Schuster, Hal. *Michael Jackson: A Life in Music*. No city: Movie Publisher Services, 1990.

Wallner, Rosemary. *Michael Jackson*. Minneapolis, MN: Abdo & Daughters, 1991.

THE JACKSON 5

(See also Jackson, Janet; Jackson, La Toya; Jackson, Michael)

JACKSON FRIENDS AND FAMILY

Jackson, Margaret Maldonado with Hack, Richard. *Jackson Family Values: Memories of Madness*. New York: Dove Books, 1995. 240 pages. One glossy 16-page black-and-white photo insert.

Margaret Jackson, ex-wife to Jermaine Jackson (and mother of his two kids), tells all about her sordid and very strange encounters with the Jackson family. After years of aimless existence—running away from home as a teenager, drug rehabilitation, etc.—she began a relationship with Jermaine who, as she later found out when pregnant with his child, was already "happily" married. In this strange soap opera of events, Margaret was gradually accepted into the Jackson clan, where she encountered and witnessed rape, physical and emotional abuse, plastic surgery (including a particularly unpleasant description of Jermaine's cosmetic work), and numerous other horrors. (Surprisingly, she negates molestation claims against Michael Jackson.) Margaret's lesson to all? Avoid the Jackson men at all costs.

PICTORIALS

Pitts, Jr., Leonard. *Papa Joe's Boys: The Jacksons Story*. Cresskill, N.J.: Sharon Starbooks, 1983. 96 pages. Approximately 125 black-and-white photographs throughout.

As expected, Papa Joe—the patriarch of the Jackson clan—is introduced early on and quickly dismissed in favor of the real subjects: his five boys. Mama Jackson and the family's religious leanings (Jehovah's Witness) are omitted altogether. If you're into images of 1970's Jackson 5—especially Randy and Jackie, the two figures generally buried in their brothers' large shadows—this might hold some interest. From a historical viewpoint, one should look for a more recent pictorial with color photos, a complete discography—and at least a smidgen of insider's knowledge about the family. Issued in mass-market with the title *Those Incredible Jackson Boys*.

OTHER TITLES OF INTEREST

Gregory, James. *The Soul of the Jackson Five*. No city: Curtis, 1984.

Jackson, Katherine. *My Family, The Jacksons*. New York: St. Martin's Press, 1990.

Kamin, Philip and Goddard, Peter. *Michael Jackson and the Jacksons Victory Tour in '84*. New York: St. Martin's Press, 1984.

Manning, Steve. *The Jackson 5*. No city: Bobbs-Merill, 1976.

McDougal, Weldon A. *The Michael Jackson Scrapbook: The Early Days of the Jackson 5*. New York: Avon, 1985.

Morse, Charles and Morse, Ann. *Jackson Five*. Mankato, MN: Creative Education, 1975.

Motoviloff, Ellen. *The Jackson Five*. New York: Scholastic, 1971.

Taylor, Paula. *On Stage with the Jackson Five*. Mankato, MN: Creative Education, 1975.

MICK JAGGER

(See also Rolling Stones, The)

BIOGRAPHIES

Andersen, Christopher. *Jagger Unauthorized*. New York: Delacorte Press (Bantam Doubleday Dell), 1993. 440 pages. 64 photos in 32-page glossy black-and-white photo insert. Sources and Chapter Notes. Index.

By far the most comprehensive of all Jagger bios, this is also the sleaziest and the least plausible. Where is supportive evidence that Jagger bit and swallowed part of his tongue in a high school basketball game, thereby causing him to lose his "British veneer"? Or that as a teenager he lost his virginity in a hospital closet to a nymphomaniac, raven-haired nurse? Or that Stones' drummer Charlie Watts punched Jagger out in 1984? Sexual encounters with Carly Simon, Linda Ronstadt, Michelle Phillips (of The Mamas and Papas), David Bowie, and innumerable others are rattled off for posterity—and trash factor. Andersen's "source notes" do not provide specific substantiation to any of these claims. Unsurprisingly, Jagger was upset with the book and tried to block its release. No discography provided. "Grubbily entertaining, with the cultural weight of a *Sunday People* exposé of defective electric blankets"—*Select*.

Marks, J. *Mick Jagger: The Singer, Not the Song*. New York: Curtis Books, 1973. 190 pages. One 32-page glossy black-and-white photo insert.

This feeble early bio of Jagger fails to even cover the basics with care. Important events such as drug busts and Brian Jones' death are given only passing attention, bearing little relation to Jagger. The prose is so rambling you wonder how any publishing house could have set it to type. Completely useless.

Scaduto, Tony. *Mick Jagger: Everybody's Lucifer*. New York: David McKay Company, Inc., 1974. 375 pages. Two glossy eight-page black-and-white photo inserts.

Dylan biographer Anthony Scaduto (see Dylan: Biographies) wrote this early 1970's bio while the singer was wrapped up with Bianca and still searching for the "next thing" (which turned out to be disco). While not an insider's piece, a tell-all, or even a minutely researched study, Scaduto has impressive skill at analyzing Jagger's mixed composition: the soft, vulnerable surface; and the cruel, unscrupulous underside. An unsensational, well-written portrayal that is hopelessly dated and contains limited description of Jagger's stage antics, songwriting abilities, and vocal skills.

Schofield, Carey. *Jagger.* New York: Beaufort Books, 1985. 248 pages. One eight-page black-and-white photo insert. Selected Bibliography. Index.

Published just prior to Jagger's first solo release, *Jagger* will not satisfy any fan's need for information. Mick is once again treated as the shrewd, resourceful seducer who uses cleverness rather than pure intelligence to enforce his will. Ho-hum. What about his stage charisma and vocal nuances? Schofield virtually ignores the 1970's and 80's, and in telling earlier events lacks the raunchy tone requisite for a Stones-related bio. Nice cover art by Michael Sell.

Seay, Davin. *Mick Jagger: The Story Behind the Rolling Stone.* New York: Carol Publishing Group, 1993. 264 pages. One glossy eight-page black-and-white photo insert. Sources. Index.

Innocuous bio of Jagger that generally retreads information more fully developed in general biographies of The Rolling Stones. Not as gossipy as Andersen's bio (see above), which is a positive factor only on the surface; Jagger's relationships with Marianne Faithfull, Bianca Jagger, Jerry Hall, and numerous other women remain undeveloped. Innuendos come in unsubstantiated dribs and drabs, such as that Brian Jones and actor James Fox had affairs with Jagger. For all of the author's spouting about Mr. Lips being a private chameleon, he doesn't bring the reader an inch under the surface. The full story remains to be told.

QUIZBOOKS AND QUOTEBOOKS

Miles. *Mick Jagger: In His Own Words.* London: Omnibus Press (division of Book Sales Limited), 1982. 128 pages. Approximately 125 black-and-white photographs, covering every page.

The usual fluffy picture/quotebook from Omnibus Press. Some early 1960's photographs are sorrowfully integrated as jagged cut-outs, while others from that period are spotty and faded. One would do best to skip the sections on The Stones' story, lifestyle, the music business, etc. and plow into those on sex and marriage. If you don't laugh out loud reading Jagger's comments on rock and roll wives ("Aaaahhh—I hate 'em"), at least you'll be seduced by nude photos of Jagger with Jerry Hall.

OTHER TITLES OF INTEREST

Aldridge, John. *Satisfaction: The Story of Mick Jagger.* London: Proteus, 1984.

Blake, John. *His Satanic Majesty Mick Jagger.* New York: Henry Holt Inc., 1985.

Whitaker, Robert. *Mick Jagger Is Ned Kelly.* London: Corgi, 1970.
Tie-in to the 1970 film Ned Kelly starring Mick Jagger.

THE JAM

AUTOBIOGRAPHY

Foxton, Bruce and Buckler, Rick; with Ogg, Alex. *The Jam: Our Story.* Chessington, Surrey (England): Castle Communications, 1994. 208 pages. Two glossy 16-page black-and-white photo inserts; one 16-page glossy color insert. U.K. Discography.

Two of The Jam's three members tell their account of their meteoric rise to music stardom in the 1970's. The most glaring missing presence is that of Paul Weller, The Jam's guitarist and vocalist, who most people consider the focal point of the group. (In fact, his father, John Weller, was the group's manager.) This book is not written in first person, and it's difficult to decipher Foxton or Buckler's voice in the text (except for an occasional "Bruce remembers"). Though it's been more than a decade since The Jam has recorded together, this book has special resonance because it's not a sour grapes tell-all book. Weller split the group because he felt he had become too dominating to the others musically and couldn't handle the pressure of touring; Foxton and Buckler disagreed with the former, but couldn't argue the latter. An uncomplicated package, boosted by three glossy photo inserts.

BIOGRAPHIES

Hewitt, Paolo. *The Jam: A Beat Concerto*. London and New York: Omnibus Press (division of Book Sales Limited), 1983. 128 pages. 150 black-and-white photographs, covering every page. Jam 45's. Imports on '45. Jam 33's.

"The authorized biography" of the group is actually co-copyrighted in the name of the author and Jam leader Paul Weller. Weller only wrote a few opening words: "It must have been a difficult task to write The Jam's biography—there haven't been any drug busts, violent deaths, or mystical sojourns." This is all true, but it doesn't prevent the group from being an interesting study. Weller's secondary school report card is reprinted for some good laughs; there are lots of C's and D's and a comment from a science teacher that he was "a troublesome and destructive boy." Hence, rock and roll—via the perfect influences in The Beatles, The Kinks, and The Who. With lots of firsthand quotes and reprinted album reviews (mostly British), *A Beat Concerto* does justice to the musical legacy left by Weller, Rick Buckler, and Bruce Foxton, although the design (alternating green, blue, and olive borders in the margins) is an eyesore. Fans in the States may resent Weller's repeated disparaging remarks about America.

PICTORIALS

Watson, Lawrence and Hewitt, Paolo. *Paul Weller: Days Love Their Names and Time Slips Away 1992-1995*. London: Boxtree, 1995. 128 pages. Approximately 125 color and black-and-white photographs throughout.

A classy photo tribute to Paul Weller—exclusively as soloist during the years 1992-1995. Published on the cusp of Weller's having won the 1995 Brit award for Best Male Artist and the Ivor Novello Award for songwriting, this book takes us close inside Weller in the recording studio and during live performances. Photographer Watson had access to Weller amidst some very introspective moments, and the results pay off. Weller's works-in-progress and lyrics are scattered throughout. A strong complement to Foxton and Buckler's work (see Autobiography, above).

OTHER TITLES OF INTEREST
Honeyford, Paul. *The Jam: The Modern World by Number*. London: Eel Pie, 1980.

Nicholls, Mike. *The Jam: About the Young Idea*. Woodstock, NY: Beekman, 1990.

JEFFERSON AIRPLANE/ JEFFERSON STARSHIP

BIOGRAPHIES

Rowes, Barbara. *Grace Slick: The Biography*. Garden City: Doubleday & Company, Inc., 1980. 216 pages. Two eight-page black-and-white photo inserts.

A rebel, a free spirit, and an outsider since childhood, Grace Slick was the embodiment of 1960's San Francisco psychedelia. In this authorized biography, author Rowes takes us through the looking glass and into Slick's world of acid trips, naked groupie bodies, bad marriages, Be-Ins, alcohol-binges, and, of course, some of the Airplane's most influential acid rock of the period. A humorous passage involves a Great Society (Slick's first band) recording session with producer Sylvester Stewart (later, Sly Stone); Stewart thought the group's performance was so pitiful he couldn't control his laughter. The book is pretty interesting until 1971; after that, it becomes rather discursive and uninvolving. No discography or index provided.

OTHER TITLES OF INTEREST
Gleason, Ralph J. *The Jefferson Airplane and the San Francisco Sound*. New York: Ballantine, 1969.

WAYLON JENNINGS

BIOGRAPHIES

Denisoff, R. Serge. *Waylon: A Biography*. Knoxville, TN: University of Tennessee, 1983. 376 pages. Approximately 60 full-page black-and-white photographs throughout. Notes. Selected Bibliography. Discographies. Index.

Born in the West Texas panhandle, Jennings unintentionally became part of rock lore through his association with legend Buddy Holly and his unusual reputation for being an individualist in what was, up through the

1970's, a very narrow-minded country music community. Jennings, who played bass on Holly's first tour, was supposed to be on the fateful plane that crashed, but traded places with the Big Bopper at the last minute. (All, of course, perished.) Jennings struggled to make a name for himself in the years that followed, suffering through studio bureaucracy, bad management, and several failed marriages. Denisoff reveals how Jennings emerged a success with his integrity intact, an independent "outlaw" country artist with a rocker's heart. Recommended for libraries with a strong country shelf.

DISCOGRAPHIES, RECORDING GUIDES, AND COLLECTIBLES

Smith, John L. Forewords by Johnny Cash and Johnny Western. *The Waylon Jennings Discography*. Westport, CT: Greenwood Press, 1995. 376 pages. Bibliography. Sessions Index. Release Index.

Smith does for Jennings in one volume what it took him three for Johnny Cash (see Cash, Johnny: Discographies and Recording Guides). Cash's foreword is a handwritten blessing that makes you think this is a biography. In his piece, Western talks in-depth about his experiences with Jennings. Smith's text is divided into sessions, releases, and chart listings. The 850 sessions are arranged chronologically and contain studio, player line-ups, songs, composers, and notes. Releases, arranged by label, include catalog number, song names, and miscellaneous notes. The Billboard chart listing shows the positioning of all Jennings' songs and albums from when they first hit the list to when they went off. The appendixes in the back are good for quick search-and-find. An excellent, if overtly listy compendium.

PICTORIALS

Allen, Bob. *Waylon & Willie: The Full Story in Words and Pictures of Waylon Jennings and Willie Nelson*.

See: Nelson, Willie: Pictorials.

JESUS AND MARY CHAIN

TITLES OF INTEREST
Robertson, John. *Jesus and Mary Chain*. Woodstock, NY: Beekman, 1990.

JOAN JETT (AND THE BLACKHEARTS)

(See also Runaways, The)

FANZINES AND FAN CLUBS

La GaJette International. 3104 Willow Knolls #203, Peoria, IL 61604-1069.

Fanzine that includes copies of Jett-related articles, photos and interviews, as well as fans' reviews of the rocker's live shows. Published quarterly (February/May/August/November). Subscription costs $4 per year in the U.S. and $6 elsewhere; make checks payable to T. C. Cox.

BILLY JOEL

FANZINES AND FAN CLUBS

StreetLife Serenade. Wells Ink, P.O. Box 2075, Garden City, NY 11531.

The "newsletter for Billy Joel Fans" is a stapled 25-page packet containing black-and-white photos, news items, reprinted Joel interviews, tour information, profiles of Joel's musicians, souvenirs, classifieds, and more. Published four times a year. The cost is $10 in the U.S. and Canada; $20 elsewhere.

PICTORIALS

Geller, Debbie and Hibbert, Tom. *Billy Joel: An Illustrated Biography*. New York: McGraw Hill, 1985. 128 pages. Approximately 80 black-and-white photographs throughout; two eight-page color inserts.

Lightweight photo history of Billy Joel, with emphasis on his chart positions and upbeat successes. Well selected "street guy" quotes from Joel appear throughout the text in larger type. The end pages on Billy's wedding to Christie Brinkley seem just as dated as the chapter pertaining to his first wife, Elizabeth. (In fact, she takes up more photo space than Brinkley.) A "discography" concludes each chapter, which consists of less information than one can find the back of the average album cover. Strictly for fans.

YOUNG ADULT

Gambaccini, Peter. *Billy Joel: A Personal File*. New York: Quick Fox, 1979. 128 pages. 75 black-and-white photographs throughout. Discography.

The 1970's—when Billy Joel was just a hip punk from New York's "LonGuy-land" and Christie Brinkley was a fantasy away from him. The photos in this book might show young readers what Joel looked like in his semi-rebellious prime: a brash stand-up comic crossed with a poor man's Tony Danza. Gambaccini's biographical data and light analysis of songs are well handled. Those who prefer the pre-*Glass Houses* Joel will want to show their kids that the old days may not always have been good, but at least the music was *honest*; others will want something far more recent.

Gelfand, M. Howard. *Billy Joel*. Mankato, MN: Creative Education, 1983. 34 pages. Ten black-and-white photographs throughout.

Back in the early 1980's, the "Rock 'n Pop Stars" series turned its attention to the Piano Man. Starting way off base by repeating the age-old story of how three men each describe an elephant differently—implying, rather clumsily, that Joel represents something different to everyone—the book then briefly mentions his family history, including that his father was in a Nazi concentration camp in World War II—a detail that should have been given greater attention. Joel's songs and musical contributions are buried in this pitiably uneducated publication.

OTHER TITLES OF INTEREST
McKensie, Michael. *Billy Joel*. New York: Ballantine, 1984.

ELTON JOHN (AND BERNIE TAUPIN)

BIOGRAPHIES

Crimp, Susan and Burstein, Patricia. *The Many Lives of Elton John*. New York: Birch Lane (Carol), 1992. 310 pages. One eight-page glossy black-and-white photo insert; one four-page color insert. Discography. Sources. Index.

Crimp and Burstein's work has four distinct obvious advantages over Philip Norman's (below): it does not contain stereotypical references; it boasts a small color insert; it lists sources of information by chapter; and, at only 310 pages, it is much more digestible—and less stuffy—for casual readers. However, *The Many Lives of Elton John* lacks the meticulousness of Norman's tome. John himself is depicted as babyish, blaming his father for his childhood problems and throwing tantrums on New York radio over a mixed *New York Times* review of one of his performances. "Thinly done, though John makes it all easy reading" —*Kirkus*.

Newman, Gerald with Bivona, Joe. Introduction by Henry Edwards. *Elton John*. New York: Signet (New American Library), 1976. 188 pages. One 16-page black-and-white photo insert. Discography.

This ancient bio was written in the mid-1970's, when Elton John was the world's top hitmaker and champion wearer of strange glasses. Newman and Bivona's book begins shakily, with over-the-top fanzine prose and hype over John's performances at Los Angeles' Dodger Stadium. The writing improves slightly in the third chapter, where we get some unusual details, such as that John began his career singing back-up vocals on songs such as "He Ain't Heavy, He's My Brother" (The Hollies). Subsequent bios have dug much deeper.

Norman, Philip. *Elton John*. New York: Harmony (division of Crown), 1992. 520 pages. One 16-page glossy black-and-white photo insert. Discography by Mark Lewisohn. Index. (First published in Great Britain by Random Century Group Limited.)

It's a tragedy that this book is marred by needless political incorrectness. The author states that Grateful Dead and Bob Dylan concert-goers are "Hippies with paunches and bald patches." Rap fans are "fat boys in porkie hats." According to Norman, good-looking people are "somewhat lacking in imagination." Norman is not terribly subtle in his description of Bob Dylan as "hawk-nosed" either. The tragedy is that, these upsetting points notwithstanding, this book is the most comprehensive on the subject. The biographical material on Elton John insiders such as John Reid (his manager) and Bernie Taupin are exhaustive. We get a real "in the clubhouse" feel for what it was like to be a songwriter under the wing of Dick James (also the publisher of the Lennon/McCartney catalog). As usual, Lewisohn's discographical work is unmatched. Take off the shelf—but also take caution.

DISCOGRAPHIES, RECORDING GUIDES, AND COLLECTIBLES

DiStefano, John. With additional research by Dobbins, Peter. *The Complete Elton John Discography*. New Baltimore, MI: East End Lights, 1993. 66 pages.

A publication of the Elton John fanzine *East End Lights* (see Fanzines and Fan Clubs, below), this book is divided into three parts: singles and EPs; albums; and appearances. The singles section break down further into seven sections on U.S. and U.K. releases for singles and EPs (including promos); albums break down into six sections on U.S. and U.K. vinyl and CD releases; and appearances break down into two sections on John's guest appearances on others' releases and cover versions. Full of lists and catalog numbers, this work doesn't have high entertainment value; as a reference source, however, it is the only place one can find obscure information such as that Elton John played piano on three George Harrison tunes.

FANZINES AND FAN CLUBS

East End Lights. Box 760, New Baltimore, MI 48047.

Illustrated 24-page magazine for serious Elton John fans, with concert updates, black-and-white photos, reflections on his career and music, letters, and some collectibles (auction info.). Published quarterly. The cost of subscription is $20 per year; $5 at newsstands.

INTERVIEWS

Gambaccini, Paul. *A Conversation with Elton John and Bernie Taupin*. New York: Flash Books (division of Music Sales), 1975. 112 pages. Approximately 100 black-and-white photographs, covering every page. Singles. Albums.

Elton and his usually quiet lyrical partner Taupin team up for this dual interview with Paul Gambaccini, which was conducted when the dynamic songwriting duo was in its prime. After chapters in which the men summarize their careers, John and Taupin define their songwriting skills, explore the lyrical meanings behind their songs, and provide some insights into Elton's live performances. In many instances, John and Taupin bash other stars—including Carole King, Chuck Berry, and Donny Osmond—for being repetitive in their work, which is highly ironic given John's "adult contemporary" slant in the 1990's. Lots of flamboyant photos.

PICTORIALS

Tatham, Dick and Jasper, Tony. *Elton John*. London: England: Octopus Books, 1976. 92 pages. Approximately 100 color photographs, covering every page. Elton's Diary. Discography.

Outrageous photo book on Elton John that reminds one of exactly how far-out he was in the 1970's. Platform shoes, funky glasses (or goggles, depending), floppy fedoras, baggy trousers, a pin here and there—and always a smile, to show he's just goofing around. Where would Boy George have been without him? The text is third-hand copy, long outdated, while back sections on John's records and musicians contain little depth.

Tobler, John. *Elton John: 25 Years in the Charts*. London: Hamlyn (Reed Consumer Group), 1995. 208 pages. Over 200 color and black-and-white photographs throughout. Album Discography.

Attractive retrospective on John's professional career. The pages are beautifully designed, with an excellent mix of pastel colors and screened art in the backgrounds of many pages. Elton's outrageous costumes are ever-present, as are the infamous boots he wore for his role in the film *Tommy*—and sold for $11,000 at a Sotheby's auction! The book closes with Elton John kissing his Lion King Oscar (winner of Best Song). Unclear about John's musical direction in the 1990's (as John himself seems to be), but an appealing treat nonetheless.

QUIZBOOKS AND QUOTEBOOKS

Black, Susan. *Elton John: In His Own Words*. London: Omnibus Press (division of Book Sales Limited), 1993. 112 pages. Approximately 110 black-and-white photographs, covering nearly every page.

Congenial, fun-loving (and formerly outlandish) performer Elton John comes off as slightly acerbic in this collection of quotes covering a wide variety of subjects. On critics: "I resent the English press. I really don't like them. They're a bunch of liars, and for me they're the scum of the earth." On Rod Stewart: "He should stick to grave-digging, cos' that's where he belongs, six feet under." John also rants about relationships, songwriting, performing, diets, and other topics. Many photos are redundant in terms of subject matter and, in fact, some are thinly disguised repeats with different croppings. Optional for John fans.

TOURBOOKS

Nutter, David (photographer). *Elton: It's a Little Bit Funny*. Introduction by Bernie Taupin. New York: Penguin Books, 1977. 144 pages. Approximately 175 black-and-white and 12 color illustrations, covering every page.

Picture book, with minimal text, capturing John's 1976 world tour that smashed then-existing attendance records for London's Earl Court and New York's Madison Square Garden. Rock photographer David Nutter was present for most of the tour's breathtaking moments, including an oddball cocktail party, John waterskiing, John blowdrying his sparse scalp, John hot air ballooning, John bonging percussionist Ray Cooper, and John sharing the limelight with Kiki Dee. Good old Bernie Taupin contributes a lovely, poetic introduction called "On the Road," while Elton dedicates the book to Nutter "and to everybody else who picked me up off the floor!" A mid-1970's bash.

WRITTEN WORKS

Taupin, Bernie. Foreword by Elton John. *Bernie Taupin: The One Who Writes the Words for Elton John*. New York: Knopf, 1976. 144 pages. Approximately 80 black-and-white illustrations throughout.

The "complete lyrics from 1968 through to *Goodbye Yellow Brick Road*," many of which are represented by black-and-white illustrations, graphics, and collages from noted artists and performers, such as Joni Mitchell ("Talking Old Soldiers"), Charlie Watts ("Rocket Man"), and John Lennon ("Bennie and the Jets"). There's a fierce, burning sexuality to Taupin's words that almost gets lost in Elton's musical interpretations; fans of either half of the duo will very much enjoy seeing these early works down on paper. Unsurprisingly, co-edited by Alan Aldridge (see Beatles: Written Works).

OTHER TITLES OF INTEREST

Charlesworth, Chris. *Elton John*. Woodstock, NY: Beekman, 1990.

Jacobs, Linda. *Elton John: Reginald Dwight & Company*. St. Paul, MN: EMC, 1976.

Peebles, Andy. *The Elton John Tapes*. New York: St. Martin's, 1981.

Roland, Paul. *Elton John*. Woodstock, NY: Beekman, 1990.

St. Michael, Mick. *Elton John*. New York: Smithmark (Penguin USA), 1994.

Taylor, Paula. *Elton John*. Mankato, MN: Creative Education, 1975.

ROBERT JOHNSON

CRITICAL/ANALYTICAL COMMENTARY

Charters, Samuel. *Robert Johnson*. New York: Oak Publications, 1973. 88 pages. Approximately 30 black-and-white photographs throughout.

Uneven mix of biography, commentary, and guitar transcriptions of Johnson's compositions. Author Samuel Charters makes an effort to recreate Johnson's elusive life by going back to Robinsonville, TN, studying the places where Johnson hung out, and jogging the memories of some who (barely) recall the man. Only for guitarists seeking to learn the master's tunes.

GRACE JONES

TITLES OF INTEREST

Goude, Jean-Paul. *Jungle Fever*. London: Quartet, 1982.

TOM JONES

BIOGRAPHIES

Jones, Peter. *Tom Jones*. Chicago: Henry Regnery Company, 1970. 162 pages. Three glossy eight-page black-and-white photo inserts. Discography.

First Elvis, then The Beatles, and then—Tom Jones? If you can get past this version of rock and roll history—and it's doubtful anyone will—there is no way to swallow this author's constant hyperbole about Jones' masculinity and sex appeal. Even the most devoted fans of Mr. Lounge Act will head for another bar.

JANIS JOPLIN

BIOGRAPHIES

Amburn, Ellis. *Pearl: The Obsessions and Passions of Janis Joplin*. New York: Warner Books, 1992. 340 pages. Two eight-page black-and-white photo inserts. Coroner's Report. Discography. Bibliography. Index.

Judging by the title, this rather sleazy tale of Janis Joplin is just what one would expect: lots of graphic sex (both lesbian and heterosexual), drugs, and rock and roll. In that order. While it's plain that rock fans have a strange fascination with Joplin's excesses, this one just goes overboard. Do we really care that two of Janis' lesbian lovers, Kim Chappell and Peggy Caserta, both slept with Janis' male obsession, Kris Kristofferson? This one's desperately seeking some soul. "...he [Amburn] takes the well-trodden path—via a few pubescent incidences—to the 60's and the attendant scuzziness"—*Q*.

Friedman, Myra. *Buried Alive: The Biography of Janis Joplin*. New York: Harmony (Crown), 1992. 354 pages. One 16-page glossy black-and-white photo insert. Discography. Appendix: Permission Denied. Index.

Myra Friedman, Janis Joplin's publicist, first published this book in 1973 and revised it both in 1983 and again in 1992 with this edition. Friedman knew Joplin as well as anyone and sets the record straight in regard to many issues. The first—and most incredible—is that the singer had a "normal" childhood and was probably a virgin until the summer after she graduated from high school. Overweight with scraggly hair and suffering from skin problems, the overly trusting girl from Port Arthur, Texas never really fit in and constantly sought love and affection in all of the wrong places. A painful read to say the least, but starkly written. One complaint: We could have used an early family photo. (We only see her high school graduation picture.) "Written with a sympathetic intelligence, at times fiercely lyrical..."—*Time*.

Landau, Deborah. *Janis Joplin: Her Life and Times*. New York: Paperback Library (Coronet), 1971. 160 pages. One eight-page black-and-white photo insert. Discography.

Early mass-market biography that was published so close to Joplin's death you can still imagine her presence in Deborah Landau's descriptions: "She can come across as hot, temperamental, impulsive, she moaned and crooned, but mostly she shrieked...." Landau establishes a teenage Janis who was wild and somewhat rebellious, which is unsubstantiated here and differs radically from Friedman's more convincing work (see above). The story is told way too hastily, and many tales embellished in other works are missing here. Rock researchers needing period flavor may want to resurrect this one, but others should opt for something more comprehensive, objective, and recent.

FANZINES AND FAN CLUBS

Pearl: The Janis Joplin Fanzine. 178 Jarvis Street #506, Toronto, ON, Canada M5B 2K7.

Bimonthly, eight-page fanzine devoted to Janis with news updates, reprinted interviews, photocopies of photos, and more. The editor also offers to subscribers the *Janis Joplin Memorabilia Guide*, which includes listings of 4-tracks, 8-tracks, LPs, CDs, television appearances, videos, books, films, magazine and newspaper articles, concert performances, posters, postcards, autographs, etc. The cost of subscription for the fanzine is $6.50 per year for Canadian residents and $12 for American; overseas orders cost $17 per year. Make checks in Canadian currency and payable to: Sue Molyneaux. The *Memorabilia Guide* costs an additional $10 (for subscribers only, at the same address above, also payable to Sue Molyneaux).

GENERAL REFERENCE

Dalton, David. *Piece of My Heart: The Life, Times and Legend of Janis Joplin*. New York: St. Martin's Press, 1985. 288 pages. Approximately 75 black-and-white photographs throughout. Chronology.

First released in slightly different form in 1971 as *Janis* (Stonehill Books) this work, as the publisher describes, "brings back Janis's voice, her songs, her jangling bracelets and neon feathers, and the friends who were along for the ride." From the way it appears, Dalton knew Joplin well and chugged doubles of Jack Daniels with her one eight a.m. back in 1970. He is intrigued with the singer's sleaziness, and can't control himself from discussing her in the same tone as one who is recollecting an old whore. Somehow, he also works in nonsensical allusions to Zelda Fitzgerald. Pretty tacky stuff, but genuine fans might be charged by the author's descriptions of Joplin's wild hair and bluesy voice. "...much of the book is little more than sophomoric fluff..."—*Library Journal*.

JOPLIN FRIENDS AND FAMILY

Caserta, Peggy (as told to Knapp, Dan). *Going Down with Janis*. New York: Dell Publishing Co., 1973. 268 pages.

If you have a smutty mind and think the title of this book has a sexually explicit connotation—you're absolutely right. Peggy Caserta, Joplin's lesbian lover, plunges through the depths of the singer's lusts and addictions, from her speed and acid kicks to her relationships with Country Joe, Kris Kristofferson, Pigpen (of The Grateful Dead), and many others (both male and female). Gone entirely is the bluesy soul singer we knew and loved; she's replaced with a junkie, a sex addict, and an emotionally bereft woman who at least had amazing finesse injecting a needle into a chum's arm. Some rock fans will no doubt be titillated by passages describing Joplin's operatic cries of passion when Caserta brought her to climax; those likely to find offense—or pass judgment on Joplin's life—should stay clear.

Joplin, Laura. *Love, Janis*. New York: Villard Books (division of Random House, Inc.), 1992. 344 pages. Two eight-page black-and-white photo inserts. Sources. Index.

This intimate memoir will complement—but not supersede—the Friedman book (see Biographies, above). Laura Joplin, Janis' younger sister (by six years), fills in every minor incident of the singer's early years and shares many personal experiences, as well as rare early photos and letters. The chapters on her career and music seem to be retreads of other works, and the Janis pictured here is kind of unrealistically wholesome. Still, the author writes well and with genuine love and admiration for her famous sister. "This is quite a decent addition to the rock bio shelf, although my brother-in-law complains that it's lacking in the sordid detail dept."—*Forced Exposure*.

RELATED WORKS

Fleischer, Lenore. *The Rose*. New York: Warner Books, 1979. 256 pages.

Novelization based on Bill Kerby and Bo Goldman's screenplay for the 1979 film. Loosely drawn from the life of Janis Joplin, both the film and the book don't do justice to the real magic behind the performer or to the time period (ostensibly late 1960's). Characters such as her sleazy business manager Rudge (to rhyme with "sludge") and her lover, "piece of meat" Houston, are one-dimensional figures in an abysmal world full of drugged-out groupies and star users. Midler's powerful performance saved the film (barely), but it can't help the book.

JOURNEY

PICTORIALS

Flans, Robyn. *Journey*. Port Chester, New York: Cherry Lane Books, 1984. 48 pages. Approximately 50 color and black-and-white photographs, covering every page.

The popular 1980's band is given superficial treatment in this lightweight photo book. Fans will be disappointed by the shortage of coverage of the band's early days—notably Neal Schon's guitar work with Santana—and by the book's complete lack of discographical information. Fans would do much better finding an old *Hit Parader* magazine or reading their entry in *The New Rolling Stone Encyclopedia of Rock & Roll.*

JOY DIVISION

JOY DIVISION FRIENDS AND FAMILY

Curtis, Deborah. Foreword by Jon Savage. *Touching from a Distance: Ian Curtis and Joy Division.* London: Faber and Faber, 1995. 216 pages. One glossy eight-page color and black-and-white photo insert. Discography. Lyrics. Unseen Lyrics. Gig List. Index.

Kurt Cobain wasn't the first rock star with a young wife and child to take his life. Back in 1980, Ian Curtis, lead singer and composer of Joy Division, had hung himself—tormented by the pressures of performing and raising a family. Curtis's wife, Deborah, had been shunned by friends and musicians who didn't think it was hip for a rock and roller to have a pregnant wife; in this engaging book, she lets out her angst about her frustrations, her husband's long bouts of depression, suicidal tendencies, epilepsy, and brief but noteworthy career. An affectionate, insider's tale that also serves as a complete biography, complete with the artist's lyrics in the back.

PICTORIALS

Flowers, Calude. *New Order & Joy Division: Dreams Never End.* London: Omnibus Press (division of Book Sales Limited), 1995. 128 pages. Approximately 125 glossy black-and-white photographs, covering every page; one glossy 16-page color insert. Selected Discography, Videography, Bibliography.

A well-presented mix of photos and biography covering the band that began as Joy Division and, due to tragic circumstances, reformed as New Order. When singer Ian Curtis found himself unable to handle the pressures of stardom—and could not decide between his wife and his Dutch lover—he hanged himself, thus seemingly putting an end to one of the brightest bands of the 1980's. But the band members continued on undaunted, under the new title New Order. Solid history, excellent photos, compact packaging.

Johnson, Mark. *Joy Division: An Ideal for Living.* London: Bobcat Books, 1984. 126 pages. Approximately 125 black-and-white photographs, covering nearly every page.

Haphazard "scrap of information" about the original Joy Division. Without so much as a table of contents to guide us, the author and contributors catalog all of Joy Division's shows (with songs, dates, descriptions, etc.), as well as a discographical section that includes a smattering of analytical commentary. Some intriguing information here and there and some effective photos can't compensate for a lack of organization and direction.

OTHER TITLES OF INTEREST

Edge, Brian. *New Order & Joy Division: Pleasures & Wayward Distractions.* London: Omnibus Press (division of Book Sales Limited), 1989.

JUDAS PRIEST

PICTORIALS

Gett, Steve. Foreword by David Halford. *Judas Priest: Heavy Duty.* Port Chester, NY: Cherry Lane Music Co., Inc., 1984. 88 pages. One hundred color and black-and-white photographs scattered throughout. Factsfile. Priest Anthology (Chronology).

"The official biography" of Judas Priest is nothing of the sort; it's a pictorial magazine, with some background history of the band and album highlights. A black-and-white spread of "Kiddie Pix" and some flaming red pages make the band seem more like Culture Club than a group of headbangers. Not that the book doesn't have its rollicking metal moments, worthy of Spinal Tap satire. In one passage, a skeptical female journalist unzipped guitarist K.K. Downing's trousers to see if he is a natural blonde (which, she discovered, he is). And Downing's favorite actress? Linda Lovelace. Light duty.

KANSAS

AUTOBIOGRAPHY

Boa, Kenneth and Livgren, Kerry. *Seeds of Change: The Spiritual Quest of Kerry Livgren, Writer, Guitarist, and Keyboard Player with Kansas*. Westchester, IL: Crossway Books, 1983. 190 pages. One eight-page black-and-white photo insert. Notes.

The autobiography of musician Kerry Livgren, which evidently was put to paper primarily by writer Boa. Born in Topeka, Kansas (no surprise there), Livgren grew up fascinated with church organs, religious epics (*The Ten Commandments*), Nietzsche, and British groups such as The Yardbirds and The Kinks. This strange mix of tastes was further advanced with psychedelic rock and the visual explosion of the film *2,001: A Space Odyssey*, all of which combined somehow in his creative mind to give Kansas its unique progressive sound. Livgren and his collaborator are remarkably well read, tossing off Tolkien, Kerouac, and Yen master Alan Watts all within a few pages; fans may be disappointed, however, that this constitutes much more of the work than his recordings with Kansas.

MURRAY KAUFMAN

(See also Beatles, The)

WRITTEN WORKS

Kaufman, Murray. Forewords by Tony Bennett, Sybil Burton, Tucker Frederickson, and George Harrison. *Murray the K Tells It Like It Is*. New York: Holt, Rinehart and Winston, 1966. 128 pages. Approximately 50 photographs throughout, plus a miniature color comic insert: "Clark the `K'" (a Superman spoof).

Murray the K, famed disc jockey and pop philosopher who splashed The Beatles all over the radio airwaves on their early trips to America, wrote this naive sermon at the height of the British Invasion. Murray preaches anti-establishment mumbo-jumbo and interviews slinky teenage girls who reflect on The Beatles and Dylan as if they had worked on the records themselves. Good for the "camp time capsule," but not much else. And don't be impressed with the four forewords: They're only paragraph-long jacket copy blurbs.

LENNY KAYE

WRITTEN WORKS

Dalton, David and Kaye, Lenny. *Rock 100*.

See: Selected General Reference: Artist Profiles.

B.B. KING

BIOGRAPHIES

Sawyer, Charles. *B.B. King: The Authorized Biography*. London: Quartet Books, Limited, 1982. 274 pages. One glossy eight-page black-and-white photo insert. Appendices. Annotated Discography. Index. (First published in Great Britain in 1981 by Blandford Press.)

A "social" biography of B.B. King, legendary blues guitarist who has influenced countless players of his musical sphere, and many rock stars as well. Sawyer's "ax to grind" is his celebration of the death of Jim Crow—an honorable goal, but perhaps a bit heavyhanded one given the limitations of a single-personality biography. In part one, Sawyer recounts the daily, frenetic activities of B.B. King on the road and performing. In part two, he tackles the fascinating early years of B.B. King, from his roots on the Mississippi Delta, his mother's death when he was a boy, to the year's spent on his grandmother's farm and his search for bluesman Sonny Boy Williamson. Part three broadly outlines his musical talent and character development. The back of the book provides detailed research on southern plantations, statistics on lynchings, analysis of the King guitar solo, and more. An insightful and scholarly work.

OTHER TITLES OF INTEREST

King, B.B. and Ritz, David. *Blues All Around Me: The Autobiography of B.B. King*. New York: Avon, 1996.
King's long-awaited autobiography.

CAROLE KING

PICTORIALS

Cohen, Mitchell S. *Carole King: A Biography in Words & Pictures*. No city: Sire Books (Chappell Music Company), 1976. 56 pages. Approximately 50 black-and-white photographs, covering every page. Carole King Appendix: Goffin & King credits; albums and singles by Carole King.

Static collection of lousy photos and uninformed background text on the singer/songwriter's musical career. There is only a bare trace about King's family history (all we get is that her unnamed parents disapproved of her entering the music business) and even less on her later private life. Gerry Goffin, her husband and collaborator, is completely shafted. What's a nice Jewish girl doing in a book like this?

OTHER TITLES OF INTEREST

King, Carole. *You've Got a Friend*. Boulder, CO: Blue Mountain Press, 1978.

Taylor, Paula. *Carole King*. Mankato, MN: Creative Education, 1976.

KING CRIMSON

CRITICAL/ANALYTICAL COMMENTARY

Tamm, Eric. *Robert Fripp: From King Crimson to Guitar Craft*. Boston and London: Faber and Faber, 1990. 244 pages. Notes. Bibliography. Discography.

Guitarist Robert Fripp has had a magnificent and diversified career. A founding member of King Crimson—and the only constant member through its various incarnations 1969-1974 and a return during the years 1981-1984—he retreated from pop life at various points in his life to listen to music, study it, reflect on his craft—and even serve as a contributing editor for magazines such as *Musician*, *Player*, and *Listener*. Fripp's various sabbaticals and collaborations with David Bowie, Peter Gabriel, Daryl Hall, and others are noted here, but this isn't a biography or a namedropping tribute. Author Eric Tamm brilliantly splices together Fripp's musical concepts and theories about

guitar, only occasionally going overboard on musical techno-babble. Scholarly but enjoyable.

FANZINES AND FAN CLUBS

Book of Saturday. P.O. Box 221, Leeds, LS1 5LW, England.

Quarterly, 30-page fanzine containing convention news, articles on guitarist Robert Fripp, sound system advances, letters, King Crimson talk on the Internet, classifieds, and more. The cost is £10 for four issues (U.K.) and £14 in North America; checks must be payable in pounds and drawn from a U.K. bank.

THE KINGSMEN

RELATED WORKS

Marsh, Dave. *Louie Louie: The History and Mythology of the World's Most Famous Rock 'n' Roll Song; Including the Full Details of Its Torture and Persecution at the Hands of the Kingsmen, J. Edgar Hoover's F.B.I., and a Cast of Millions; and Introducing, for the First Time Anywhere, the Actual Dirty Lyrics*. New York: Hyperion, 1993. 296 pages. One glossy eight-page black-and-white photo insert. Maximum Louie Louie: A Discography. Index.

False subtitle advertising aside—conglomerate copyright ownerships prevented the reprinting of the correct "Louie Louie" lyrics—this book tackles both myth and fact behind Richard Berry's controversial and long-standing classic. Well over 1,200 recordings of "Louie Louie" exist, the most famous being the Kingsmen's version, while other standouts include those from Paul Revere and the Raiders and The Kinks. The song's changing hands, various interpretations, and obscenity trials make this an enlightening tale. Marsh is particularly adept at acknowledging the song's importance with just a note of appropriate "three chords and a cloud of dust" cheekiness. A book about one song is a risky proposition, and somehow Marsh "...pulls it off..."*Blue Suede News*.

KINGSTON TRIO

DISCOGRAPHIES, RECORDING GUIDES, AND COLLECTIBLES

Blake, Benjamin; Rubeck, Jack; and Shaw, Allan. Foreword by Nick Reynolds; Epilogue by John Stewart. *Kingston Trio on Record*. Naperville, IL: Kingston Korner, Inc., 1986. 272 pages. Approximately 125 black-and-white photographs throughout. Index.

Discography and recording guide on The Kingston Trio, assembled by Kingston Korner, Inc. (see Fanzines and Fan Clubs, below). Prior to discographical sections by the three credited authors are various interviews and essays by William Bush, Floyd Garrett, Paul Surratt, and Elizabeth Wilson. The photos are generally half or full-page, but the interviews (with Trio members Nick Reynolds and Dave Guard) take up the most book space—even more than the record sections. Fans of The Kingston Trio would want this book, but otherwise the appeal is fairly narrow due to its confused focus and lack of attention to its titular subject.

FANZINES AND FAN CLUBS

Kingston Korner Newsletter. Kingston Korner, Inc., 6 So. 230 Cohasset Road, Naperville, IL 60540.

Quarterly stapled pamphlet focusing on The Kingston Trio and related folk groups (such as The White Mountain Singers). Its eight pages include black-and-white photographs, editorials, Kingston Trio itinerary, news items, rare records, and more. The cost of subscription is $5 for four issues.

THE KINKS

AUTOBIOGRAPHIES

Davies, Dave. *Kink: An Autobiography*. London: Boxtree, 1996. 280 pages. One glossy 16-page black-and-white photo insert. Discography. Index.

The rivalry continues! Shortly after the release of brother Ray's work (see below), Dave Davies also felt the compunction to jump into the autobiographical fray. Unlike Ray, however, Dave opts for just the facts (as he sees them, of course), instead of creating a satirical plotline. The legendary guitarist was the typical rebellious rocker, impregnating a girl at 15 and joining his older brother's rock band. Dave recalls his early days learning the guitar and perfecting his craft in studio and on stage; needless to say, groupies and drugs are integral to his story. The straightforward flipside to Ray's work, with all the trimmings that his book failed to provide: a glossy photo insert, a discography, and an index. True Kinks fans will need to have this and *X-Ray*.

Davies, Ray. *X-Ray: The Unauthorized Autobiography*. Woodstock, New York: The Overlook Press, 1995. 420 pages.

Ray Davies' bizarre and occasionally brilliant autobiography is a highly imaginative self-investigation into the artist's psyche. Allegedly written by an automaton journalist raised by an Orwellian power structure known as "the Corporation," *X-Ray* fades in and out of the writer's voice and into Davies', thereby attempting to show up-close how a young social misfit evolved into a semi-paranoid, curmudgeonly rock and roller who battles corporate pinheads. In numerous passages, the journalist envisions himself as Davies and experiences his travails firsthand—from joining The Kinks onstage in 1965 to receiving a first-rate blowjob by a goddess-like brunette groupie. The book is shocking, funny, and innovative but, like the master's incomparable *Village Green Preservation Society* LP, one can never tell where the satire stops and the truth begins.

BIOGRAPHIES

Marten, Neville and Hudson, Jeffrey. *The Kinks: Well Respected Men*. Chessington, Surrey (England): Castle Communications Limited, 1996. 224 pages. One eight-page glossy black-and-white photo insert. U.K. Discography. References.

It's about time a book came out highlighting The Kinks' influence on contemporary music and culture: The authors here cite Blur as the most modern voice, but there a number of others, ranging from Paul Weller to The Pretenders. Unfortunately, this biography is only a rehash of what came before, from the Davies brothers' respective autobiographies (see above) to Johnny Rogan's biography and

Jon Savage's pictorial (see below for both). The language is not only stilted, it's also patronizing: Does any audience, American or British, need to have the slang word "bum" explained? The discography is U.K.-only and won't do fans here all that much good. Don't stop respecting The Kinks on this book's account.

Rogan, Johnny. *The Kinks: A Mental Institution.* London and New York: Proteus, 1984. 244 pages. One eight-page glossy black-and-white photo insert. Notes. Discography.

Slim bio of England's premier satirical rock band. The book relies heavily on secondary sources, and therefore we don't get anywhere near The Kinks themselves. Rogan only tells of incidents that are common knowledge, such as when Mick Avory speared a cymbal at Dave Davies, and that drummer Avory was almost a founding Rolling Stone. Rogan's sparse 191 pages of text—the rest are notes and discography—do not delve deeply enough into Ray's unique songwriting gifts, Dave's trendsetting guitar licks, and the always percolating love-hate relationship between rock's most controversial brother combination. Low budget.

CRITICAL/ANALYTICAL COMMENTARY

Bailey, Rebecca (editor). *The Kinks: Reflections on Thirty Years of Music.* Morehead, KY: Trillium Publications, 1994. 200 pages. Bibliography.

Paperbound collection of articles, essays, and interviews culled from a variety of sources ranging from *Guitar Play* to *Rolling Stone.* Editor Bailey, who began as a Beatles fan, moved over to The Kinks when she discovered Dave Davies' underappreciated guitar playing, Ray's ingenious lyrics, and the group's flair for nostalgia. She has brought together pieces that clearly cater to her personal taste: a rave about the band's return as a live act in 1975; a poem "The Guitarist" by Bailey herself (strictly fanzine material); interviews with Dave Davies, Mick Avory, Pete Quaife, and others; and album reviews, such as one of *Phobia.* Fans of Dave Davies will climb through the coconut trees with delight at the emphasis on his contributions, but all will be disappointed about the book's lack of illustrative material. Add it to your Kinks Kollection anyway.

Mendelssohn, John. *The Kinks Kronikles.* New York: Quill (division of William Morrow and Company), 1985. 208 pages. Approximately 20 black-and-white photographs throughout.

Mendelssohn, annotator of the classic Kinks' album *The Kink Kronikles,* is a major proponent of The Kinks up through the end of the 1960's and their early concept albums. Fans will drool over his gushings about songs such as "Waterloo Sunset" and "Days," but might cringe at his cannibalization of later rock standards such as "Catch Me Now I'm Falling" and "Destroyer." Interviews with Robert Wace (first manager), Shel Talmy (early producer), John Dalton (original bassist), et. al. only seem to add to the mess of contradictions surrounding the band. Not kinky enough.

DISCOGRAPHIES, RECORDING GUIDES, AND COLLECTIBLES

Hinman, Doug with Brabazon, Jason. *The Kinks Part One: You Really Got Me: An Illustrated World Discography of the Kinks, 1964-1993.* Rumford, RI: No publisher, 1994. 560 pages. Approximately 100 black-and-white reproductions of album covers and records. Indexes. Chart Placings. Glossary.

A self-published "labor of love" for author Doug Hilman, this limited edition book probes every area of Kinks' recordings. Hinman not only summarizes biographical details of the Davies brothers, Pete Quaife, et al., but does the same for auxiliary members (horn players, for example), backing singers, and all other realms of studio musicians. Tipping his hat to Podrazik and Lewisohn's respective masterworks (see Beatles, The: Discographies, Recording Guides, and Collectibles), yet neither has accounted for lists of players to this degree. The discographical sections on commercial releases in the U.S., the U.K., and continents as far-flung as Africa and South America are first-rate. Sections separating compact discs, promotional records, acetates, test pressings, and cover songs (by The Kinks and by others doing their material) are equally impressive. The only item not included is their live history—which no doubt Hinman is saving for part two. A rock and roll fantasy for Kinks lovers, although not nearly as illustrated as the title implies.

FANZINES AND FAN CLUBS

The Official Kinks Fan Club. P.O. Box 30, Atherstone, Warwickshire CV9 2ZX England.

Kinks fan club that provides members with a quarterly newsletter and one special glossy magazine around Christmastime. The 12-page stapled pack includes news, interviews, concert updates and a couple of reproductions of black-and-white photographs. The glossy magazine, at one time called *Now and Then,* is more expansive and covers Kinks and solo activities throughout the entire year. The cost of membership is $20 per year U.S. (payable by international money order only); £10 U.K. (check or postal money order); and £10 elsewhere in Europe (payable by Eurocheck or international postal money order).

PICTORIALS

Savage, Jon. *The Kinks: The Official Biography.* London: Faber and Faber, 1984. 176 pages. Approximately 100 glossy black-and-white and color tinted photographs throughout. Discography. Bibliography.

While not a true biography as its title implies, this retrospective of The Kinks is far more telling than Rogan's (see above). Savage sharply observes the social climate of the 1960's—even linking the roots of the word kinky to the Christine Keeler sex scandal and the British show "The Avengers"—and analyzes Ray Davies' lyrics with impressive fortitude. The Kinks' influences on The Beatles and Pete Townshend are duly noted. The book's excellent photos and wealth of lyrics (though not every gem is included: where's "Animal Farm"?) make this highly recommended to Kinks fans.

OTHER TITLES OF INTEREST
Schruers, Fred. *The Kinks.* New York: Viking Penguin, no date.

KISS

DISCOGRAPHIES, RECORDING GUIDES, AND COLLECTIBLES

Lesniewski, Karen and John. *Kiss Collectibles: Identification and Price Guide.* New York: Avon Books, 1993. 176 pages. Approximately 200

black-and-white photographs throughout; one glossy eight-page color insert. Index.

The Lesniewskis, who head The New England Kiss Collectors' Network and have organized various Kiss conventions over the years, are the ideal team to compile this quick reference guide. The early discographical chapters identify all releases, including vinyl, EPs, 45s, CDs, laser disks, and cassettes. They then proceed to merchandise ranging from posters and headbands to belt buckles and jigsaw puzzles. Books, magazines, fanzines, and clubs are also noted. Spliced in the middle is a flaming insert that does justice to the band's "hot" image. While Kiss never had the cult following of the more collectible icons such as Presley, The Beatles, or The Grateful Dead, this book has perks that will serve the intended legions.

OTHER TITLES OF INTEREST
Duncan, Robert. *Kiss.* Manchester, England: Savoy Books, 1980.

No author. *Kissed Kollector's Edition Book.* Ontario, Canada: Mount Olympus Enterprises, no date.

Swenson, John. *Kiss.* Feltham, England: no publisher, 1979.

Tamarkin, Peggy. *Kiss Diary: The Real Story.* No city: Almo, 1979.

AL KOOPER

AUTOBIOGRAPHY

Kooper, Al with Edmonds, Ben. *Backstage Passes: Rock 'N' Roll Life in the Sixties.* Briarcliff Manor, NY: Stein and Day, Publishers, 1977. 256 pages. Approximately 100 black-and-white photographs throughout. Discography. Index.

Al Kooper was an integral part of the 1960's rock scene, although not many 1990's listeners would be able to place his name. Session musician, keyboardist, composer, and innovator, Kooper was organist on Dylan's *Highway 61 Revisited* LP, a member of The Blues Project, and creator of the ultimate jazz-rock band, Blood, Sweat and Tears. (He quit and was replaced by bluesy Canadian crooner David Clayton-Thomas.) Kooper's tales of working with legends such as Dylan and The Stones make this inviting fare for fans of the era. The only distraction is co-writer Edmonds' bold-face comments, which get in the way of Kooper's storytelling.

KRAFTWERK

BIOGRAPHIES

Bussy, Pascal. *Man Machine and Music*. Wembley, Middlesex (England): SAF Publishing, 1993. 192 pages. One glossy eight-page black-and-white photo insert. Sources and Quotes. Discography.

Kraftwerk, the pioneers of "cybernetic rock" in the 1970's, were innovators of synthesizer music reflecting robotic human motion. Rock writer Paul Bussy interviewed the band's wizards, Ralf Hutter and Florian Schneider, to produce a remarkable study of this unusual German group. Bussy starts with a very basic history of rock, which is followed by the experimental exploits of The Can and Tangerine Dream. Both Hutter and Schneider were classically-trained musicians who, over a several-year period, fused their roots with Pink Floydian imagery and came up with a totally original sound. Fluid and thorough, this book is recommended for anyone interested in pop electronics.

KRISS KROSS

TITLES OF INTEREST
Raso, Anne M. *Kriss Kross Krazy*. New York: Bantam, 1992.

KRIS KRISTOFFERSON

PICTORIALS

Kalet, Beth. *Kris Kristofferson*. New York: Quick Fox (division of Music Sales), 1979. 96 pages. Approximately 75 black-and-white photographs throughout. Awards. Discography.

The story of Kris Kristofferson, up through the end of the 1970's: Army captain, Nashville songwriter, singer, movie star, guitarist, and (then) sex symbol. Kristofferson actually began as an English scholar (he received a degree from Oxford) and writer, but he suffered doubts when publishers turned down his early

manuscripts. After serving in the Army and paying his dues as a songwriter, Kristofferson made it big with the tune "Me and Bobby McGee," which has been successfully recorded by artists such as Janis Joplin (former lover) and Johnny Cash (his mentor). The simplistic writing level and large typesize make this only suitable for those around 12 years of age, who probably won't give two spits for Kristofferson's hunky pix with ex-wife Rita Coolidge.

K.D. LANG

BIOGRAPHIES

Robertson, William. *k.d. lang: Carrying the Torch*. Toronto, Ontario (Canada): ECW Press, 1993. 112 pages. Approximately 30 black-and-white photographs throughout. Works Consulted.

Early, slender Canadian biography of lang that more or less tells her story through headings and concise paragraphs, rather than chapters. The book sketchily presents information on her tomboy childhood, her early interests in sports and music, her climb to fame, and devotion to causes such as animal rights. With limited mention of lang's popularity in the United States (only a brief passage about an appearance at the Bottom Line in New York City), the coverage is pale in comparison with Starr's book (see below). Optional for fans.

Starr, Victoria. *k.d. lang: All You Get Is Me*. New York: St. Martin's Press, 1994. 272 pages. One glossy 16-page black-and-white photo insert. Discography. Index.

All you get is 100 percent pure k.d.: country/folk/jazz/pop chanteuse; vegetarian hellraiser; and outspoken lesbian who paved the way for a generation of young stars to come out of the closet. Lang, a tomboy from Consort, Alberta, Canada, began her climb to fame by implying she was Patsy Cline reincarnate—almost in the same way Bob Dylan used Woody Guthrie. Lang's career is still fairly young, thus the elements of her life in her first American biography are not as newsworthy as those of more media-hungry artists (e.g., Madonna). Starr can only tease about lang's lovers, rumored to range from Liza Minnelli to Madonna. "[the author's] account of the politics of sexual orientation, especially in the spotlight, is absorbing"—*Publishers Weekly*.

PICTORIALS

Bennahum, David. *k.d. lang*. London: Omnibus Press (division of Book Sales Limited), 1993. Unpaginated (approximately 32 pages). Approximately 32 color and black-and-white illustrations, covering every page. k.d. lang Discography.

Glossy-to-the-max pamphlet rush-released to cash-in on the success of the star's 1993 *Ingenue* album. The photos will draw fans in, but—if you'll excuse the reference to lang's animal rights advertisements—this one lacks meat. When the copy runs low, large type quotes are provided. This sparse treatment fails to capture why lang has become one of the preeminent musical figures of the 1990's.

QUIZBOOKS AND QUOTEBOOKS

Bennahum, David. *k.d. lang: In Her Own Words*. London: Omnibus Press (division of Books Sales Limited), 1995. 96 pages. Approximately 125 black-and-white photographs throughout.

k.d. lang hasn't been in the public eye for that many years, but already she has made her thoughts on issues from vegetarianism to sexuality quite clear. In many cases, lang's phrasings are cleverly turned: "The fact that anyone could say that AIDS is God's way of paying back homosexuals is really disturbing. If that's true, then lesbians are angels." A decent collection of quotes, with photos that are generally too dark. Lighter fare for those not wanting a full biography.

CYNDI LAUPER

PICTORIALS

Kamin, Philip and Goddard, Peter. *Cyndi Lauper*. New York: McGraw-Hill, 1986. 96 pages. Approximately 125 color and black-and-white photographs, covering every page.

A visual schlock-fest, with text and illustrative matter that self-consciously repeats itself throughout. One hideous close-up of Lauper caked with red and blue color on the eyes recurs several times, while Peter Goddard's prose rehashes the same mumbo-jumbo in virtually every chapter. How many times can one take reading about how Lauper was the "1980's Bette Midler" and the "Betty Boop of the pop era"? Kitsch.

Morreale, Marie and Mittelkauf, Susan. *The Cyndi Lauper Scrapbook*. New York: Bantam Books, 1985. 44 pages. Approximately 40 black-and-white photographs; one 16-page color photo insert. Fact Sheet. Discography.

Lauper is depicted as a childhood misfit, abused by nuns in a convent school and virtually neglected by her peers as a high school student. Of course, all of this is presumptuously told through the singer's point of view; there aren't any quotes from those who knew her to support the points made. While some of the pictures show the rebel in true comic form (there's even one with comedian Uncle Floyd, although he's unidentified), many are disappointing video outtakes. Scrap.

YOUNG ADULT

Crocker, Chris. *Cyndi Lauper*. New York: Julian Messner (division of Simon & Schuster), 1985. 64 pages. 20 black-and-white photographs throughout. Discography.

"Have fun with Cyndi"—or so says the cover of Chris Crocker's little package for young fans. Lauper's background, influences, early career (she worked as a Janis Joplin imitator for a while), songs, and fashion tastes are given superficial treatment. An entire chapter is devoted to the singer's bizarre mock feud with wrestling impresario Captain Lou Albano. Oy.

Greenberg, Keith Elliot. *Cyndi Lauper*. Minneapolis, MN: Lerner Publications Company, 1985. 32 pages. Approximately 20 color and black-and-white photographs throughout.

Glossy photo book for Lauper fans, with some light information about her boarding school days (in a convent), her relationship with her mother, her musical influences (The Beatles), and her musical training. Stuck in the 1985 time warp but it's "Just the sort of trivia that middle-schoolers, especially reluctant readers, will love"—*School Library Journal*.

Nicklaus, Carol. *The Picture Life of Cyndi Lauper*. New York: Franklin Watts, 1985. 48 pages. Approximately 40 color and black-and-white photographs throughout.

Silly, inferior photo book for kids, with a shortage of information on Lauper's contributions to music and video. Compares badly to young adult works by both Crocker and Greenberg (see above). "...the text is carelessly written..."—*Booklist*.

OTHER TITLES OF INTEREST

Green, Carl R. and Sanford, William R. *Cyndi Lauper*. New York: Macmillan, 1986.

Radlaur, Steve. *Cyndi Lauper*. New York: Ballantine, 1989.

LEAD BELLY

FANZINES AND FAN CLUBS

Lead Belly Society. P.O. Box 6679, Ithaca, N.Y. 14851.

Fan club designed "to appreciate & celebrate Lead Belly music." Publishes *Lead Belly Letter*, an eight-page newsletter that includes a chronology, session commentaries, resources, video, releases, and more. Subscription to the newsletter is $15; Canada $17.50; and $22 elsewhere.

LED ZEPPELIN

(See also Yardbirds, The)

BIOGRAPHIES

Gross, Michael. *Robert Plant*. New York: Popular Library, 1975. 160 pages. One 16-page black-and-white photo insert. Discography and Chronology.

Dated biography of "Led Zeppelin's Golden Boy" and "Rock's Heavy Metal Kid" that was sponsored by *Circus* magazine. The goofy cover illustration of Plant with a puckered face is liable to keep this one firmly buried in the back of library stacks. For early information, though, there is coverage of Plant's early groups, The Band of Joy and The Crawling Kingsmates (both with Zep drummer John Bonham).

Davis, Stephen. *Hammer of the Gods*. New York: William Morrow and Company, Inc., 1985. 352 pages. Three eight-page black-and-white photo inserts. Bibliography.

The lightning-bolt of a title says it all: Led Zeppelin was the quintessential hard rock band, the group that took the 1960's bluesy psychedelic rock of Cream and launched it into the heavy metal sounds of the 1970's. But music wasn't the only thing on the group's mind; their carousing and perverse sexual antics led some to believe that the musicians (or at least Page) sold their souls to the Devil à la Robert Johnson. Davis' biography overlaps with some of the decadent moments in Cole's work (see Led Zeppelin Friends and Family, below), but he provides readers with more detailed information on Zeppelin's recordings, performances, and overall impact than any other work in print. If you consider yourself a Zep fan and don't have a copy, you should be ashamed. Others beware: These Gods liked to party dangerously.

Yorke, Ritchie. *Led Zeppelin: The Definitive Biography*. Novato, CA and Lancaster, PA: Underwood-Miller, 1993. 342 pages. One eight-page glossy black-and-white photo insert. Discography. (First published in Great Britain in 1974 by Sphere Books as *The Led Zeppelin Biography*.)

This is far from definitive, though the author showered his tome with good quotes from Zep players and other musicians. Yorke has a superior knowledge of the music scene—with emphasis on the British—but he doesn't do anything to reveal the personalities of the four musicians. We find out that Robert Plant is a Leo and his favorite Zep song is "Going to California"—so what? And did the publisher really think we wouldn't notice the absence of a John Bonham photo?

CHRONOLOGIES

Kendall, Paul. *Led Zeppelin: A Visual Documentary*. New York: Delilah (distributed by Putnam Publishing Group), 1982. Unpaginated. 200 black-and-white and color photographs, covering every page. Albums. (First published in Great Britain in 1982 by Omnibus Press.)

Led Zep, day-by-day: The book begins with brief overviews of the band members, which are followed by a continuous chronology of the group through John Bonham's death and the release of the *Honeydrippers* LP. Entries for each date are typically a sentence or two long, and are interrupted by quotes from critics and the band members. The book crams in loads of photographs—up to six a page—and neatly juxtaposes black-and-white with color. The equivalent of about ten rock magazines, this book packs a visual wallop and is considered priceless among Zep fans. It could have incorporated a full discography: The "Albums" section doesn't list singles (okay, so Led Zeppelin wasn't a singles band), Page's recordings with The Yardbirds, or other outside recordings.

FANZINES AND FAN CLUBS

The Lemon Tree: The Robert Plant Fanzine and Information Network. c/o Liz Hames, 20 Ludford Crescent, Gainsborough, Linconshire DN21 1XB England.

Forty-page stapled booklet containing black-and-white photographs, lengthy essays on different phases of Plant's career, tour news, reprinted reviews and newspaper articles, letters, classified, and more. The information network means you will be sent all important news by first-class post. The cost of a four-issue subscription is £14 U.S.; £8 U.K.; and £10 elsewhere in Europe.

No Quarter Magazine: The Led Zeppelin Magazine. P.O. Box 23043, San Jose, CA 95153.

Glossy, 16-page Led Zeppelin magazine with black-and-white photographs, data on Page/Plant concerts (song lists, grosses, attendance, etc.), updates on insiders (e.g., manager Peter Grant, who died in 1995), books, CDs and records for collectors, fanzines, classifieds, marketplace (t-shirts and other collectibles), and more. The cost of subscription (six issues) is $20 U.S.; $24 Canada; and $32 elsewhere.

The Only One. 86 Main Street Suite 503, Dundas, Ontario (Canada) L9H 3V7.

Founded in 1994, this glossy, 16-page stapled packet features original black-and-white photographs, general news, editorials, concert reviews, live tape reviews, CD reviews, and personal and collector classifieds. A subscription of six issues per year costs $24 (same price everywhere); $5 for a sample issue.

Proximity: Led Zeppelin Collector's Journal. P.O. Box 45541, Seattle, WA 98145-0541.

Sixteen-page illustrated publication covering all aspects of Led Zeppelin's career, with emphasis on subjects of interest for the collector. Includes features on collectibles, current recordings, bootlegs, videos, books, fanzines, and old tours. The quarterly publication costs $3 per single issue and $12 per year; abroad, $6 per issue and $24 per year.

Tight But Loose. 14 Totnes Close, Bedford, MK40 3AX England.

This information service publishes a six-page newsletter that reports on all Page/Plant and Led Zeppelin news, including concerts, reprinted newspaper articles and detailed lists of songs performed live. Also publishes an annual 36-page glossy magazine of the same name, which features a color cover, black-and-white photographs, many reprinted newspaper articles and graphics from past and present, reflections on old albums and tours, some collectibles, and more. The cost of four issues of the newsletter and four issues of the magazine is $45 U.S./Canada; £18 U.K.; and £23 elsewhere in Europe.

LED ZEPPELIN FRIENDS AND FAMILY

Cole, Richard with Trubo, Richard. *Stairway to Heaven: Led Zeppelin Uncensored.* New York: HarperCollins, 1992. 392 pages. Two 16-page black-and-white photo inserts. Discography. Index.

In between play-by-play of his own cocaine addiction and failed marriage, Led Zeppelin's former tour manager takes us backstage, where the drugs and booze are plentiful, rowdy concertgoers get roughed up, and teenage blondes provide blowjobs to the three musicians as John "Bonzo" Bonham does his drum solo on stage. Richard Cole acts the part of sleazy cheerleader through most of the shenanigans, and typically eggs Bonzo on to behave recklessly—but cries like a baby when the joke is on him. (In one truly gross chapter Bonham tosses beans at Cole and his girlfriend while they are making love.) Worshippers of live Zep will love it; serious fans of their music will get a perverse tingle. "...as jaunty as a Broadway musical or the halftime show at the Rose Bowl"—*Booklist.*

PICTORIALS

Bunton, Richard and Mylett, Howard. *Led Zeppelin: In the Light*. London: Proteus, 1981. 96 pages. Approximately 75 black-and-white photographs, covering nearly every page, and 14 pages of color. Discography.

There was some awkward planning involved in this chronological pictorial, as all of the color pages are wasted in the first 62 pages, leaving nothing for the final third of the book. The quality of the illustrations goes drastically down at this point; some even appear to be reprints from newspapers and magazines. As a layperson's guide, an old Led Zeppelin-packed issue of *Circus* would serve better. Coauthor Mylett has an obvious affinity to Page, which is demonstrated to his advantage in *Tangents Within a Framework* (see below).

Clarke, Ross. *Led Zeppelin: Breaking and Making Records*. Oxted, Surrey (England): Kingsfleet Publications, 1992. 224 pages. Approximately 250 color and tinted black-and-white photographs, covering nearly every page. Discography. Gig List.

You know a book is in trouble when the title is inconsistent from the jacket to the inside pages. (The title page erroneously calls the book *Breaking and Making Records: A Tribute to Led Zeppelin*.) Things don't improve much within the book itself. Most pages are burdened with violet backgrounds and an excruciatingly difficult-to-read typeface. The writing is on a generic level, with linguistic problems (such as the word "allude" for "elude") surfacing on just about every page. If fans can overlook these major shortcomings, the rare photos and large-printed clippings may prove to be enough to rope in a few.

Cross, Charles R. and Flannigan, Erik. Photographs by Neal Preston. *Led Zeppelin: Heaven and Hell*. New York: Harmony Books (division of Crown), 1991. 208 pages. Over 200 color and black-and-white photographs throughout.

Five-part all-around tribute to the band, with text from Jimmy Cross and additional contributions by Jimmy Guterman, Dave Schulps, and Robert Goodwin. Full-page (no pun intended) photos by Neal Preston (and several others) work effectively in both color and black-and-white, though the majority are of the musicians one at a time. Chapters cover the band's blues inspirations, interviews (Schulps with Jimmy Page), collecting Led Zeppelin, tales from recording sessions (including a song-by-song breakdown), and a complete concert history. A standard discography would have been beneficial. An open-minded and unsensationalized treatment that thankfully doesn't go over the edge aggrandizing the memory of John Bonham.

Lewis, Dave. *The Complete Guide to the Music of Led Zeppelin*. London: Omnibus Press (division of Book Sales Limited), 1994. 104 pages. Approximately 100 color and black-and-white photographs throughout.

CD-format book covering all aspects of Led Zeppelin's career. Overlaps with Welch's CD-format book (see below), but each offers something of different appeal: This has more photos, the other more informational back sections.

Lewis, Dave. *Led Zeppelin: A Celebration*. London: Omnibus Press (division of Book Sales Limited), 1991. 120 pages. Approximately 150 black-and-white photographs, covering every page; one glossy 15-page color insert. Appendix 1: Chronology. Appendix 2A: Led Zeppelin Discography. Appendix 2B: Discography of Solo Material. Appendix 2C: Swansong Discography. Appendix 2D: Bootleg Discography. Appendix 3: Concert Listing. Appendix 4: Equipment File.

Hectic tribute to Led Zep, covering Page's guitar genius, Plant's early years, Led Zeppelin in studio, track-by-track analysis, collectibles, solo careers, and a number of discographical topics (in the appendix sections). The photo content, particularly the black-and-white shots, is quite good—except for the album-by-album section, in which the sleeves are reproduced rather small. Most of Lewis's comments on the songs themselves are synonymous with "a classic," but this may suit some fans. One hundred randomly selected collectibles are buried in the middle of the book, only two dozen of which are visually represented. The purplish front cover gives the false impression that this is a songbook. A lot of effort for readers, considering that the information can be found elsewhere.

McSquare, Eddy. *Led Zeppelin: Good Times, Bad Times*. London: Bobcat Books, 1991. 64 pages. Approximately 75 color and black-and-white photographs throughout. Discography.

The usual hype on the quintessential dinosaur band, punctuated with some dynamic live shots and crisp photos of John Bonham beating his drums. Some Led Zeppelin pictorials herein have done better, most have done worse.

Mylett, Howard. *Jimmy Page: Tangents Within a Framework*. London: Omnibus (division of Book Sales Limited), 1983. 96 pages. About 80 black-and-white photographs throughout, with six pages of color. Discography.

A blown-up magazine on the genius of Jimmy Page, with spreads on nearly every phase of his career. In a tight three-column space the book manages to cover it all, album by album. For historians there is a list of Page's uncredited contributions to many rock classics between 1963 and 1964 (ranging from "Gloria" by Them to "Sunshine Superman" by Donovan), and for fans there are lots of quotes from members of Zeppelin. There is a shortage of information on Page's private life, but teenage fans probably won't give a damn: The photos make up for it.

Preston, Neal. *Led Zeppelin Portraits*. New York: Harper & Row, 1983. Unpaginated (approximately 96 pages). Approximately 60 black-and-white photographs, mostly full-page.

Preston had "complete access" to the band between 1975 and 1979 and captured them backstage and while performing. Most of the photographs are portraits of one band member at a time, with emphasis on Robert Plant and Jimmy Page. John Bonham tips his bowler hat every now and then, but John Paul Jones is in less photos than Zep manager Peter Grant. The dark, fuzzy quality evidently fits in with what Page had in mind (conveying "Power, Mystery, and the Hammer of the Gods"), and for that reason this makes a nice contrast to more colorful photo compilations. See, mom? They aren't so dangerous.

Welch, Chris. *Led Zeppelin*. Miami, FL: MBS, 1996. 120 pages. Approximately 75 color and black-and-white photographs throughout. Discography. Chronology. Index.

CD-format book covering all aspects of Led Zeppelin's career. This nicely designed and illustrated book is priced just right at around $7.99.

QUIZBOOKS AND QUOTEBOOKS

Kendall, Paul. *Led Zeppelin: In Their Own Words*. London: Omnibus Press (division of Book Sales Limited), 1995. 144 pages. Approximately 150 black-and-white photographs, covering every page.

First published in 1981, this quotebook has been reprinted and repackaged many times since then. Unfortunately, neither the photos nor the quotes have been improved—all are too dark, grainy, out-of-focus, or slightly askew. Closing sections on solo careers and reunions are tack-ons that still look ancient. Don't be fooled by the attractive color cover: This remains a 1981 product.

TOURBOOKS

Mylett, Howard. *Led Zeppelin: From the Archives*. Self-published, no date. Unpaginated (approximately 48 pages). Approximately 50 black-and-white photographs throughout; one glossy four-page color insert.

Miscellaneous Led Zeppelin live photos spanning the group's entire career 1969-1980. The black-and-white photos are way too faded, while the color doesn't do anything. A magazine posing as a book. Mylett fared better with his other tourbook (see below).

Mylett, Howard. *On Tour with Led Zeppelin*. London: Mitchell Beazley (an imprint of Reed Consumer Books), 1993. 176 pages. Approximately 200 color photographs, covering nearly every page. Concert Log.

A collection of articles focusing on Led Zeppelin as a live act, from a piece by Chris Welch in October 1968 to the group's last performances in 1980 (with all four original members). Writers Welch, Nick Logan, Roy Carr, Chris Charlesworth, and others made their careers by tracking Zep on the road, and succeeded in raising the group above heavy metal bands who just played loud, without the guitar mastery, international musical influences, and flavored poetic imagery. The pictures vary in quality; some were shot out-of-focus from what seems to be a home camera, while others are intense fluorescent stagelit shots. One of John Bonzo Bonham flailing his hair (and drumsticks) is particularly memorable. Fans who witnessed Zep's powerhouse live show will need to have a copy, as will those who continue to settle for the tracks on *The Song Remains the Same* double-LP.

Ratner, L. Foreward[sic] by Dave Lewis. *Led Zeppelin: Live Dreams*. Chicago, IL: Margaux Publishing, 1993. Unpaginated (approximately 192 pages). Approximately 200 glossy color and black-and-white photographs throughout. Sources. Comes with a CD.

With its $80 price label and snazzy black packaging, one would have high hopes for this book/CD compendium. Opening up the plastic wrapping and the box, you'll find an oversized book that has an attractive cover featuring metallic upraised lettering and a CD containing 14 Led Zeppelin songs covered by Michael White. The interior of the book is a major disappointment: One might be able to overlook glaring errors such as the misspelling of the word "foreword" on the title page, but not the fact that quality is seriously lacking here. The photos span only a dozen Led Zeppelin performances 1971-1977, and many—way too many—are blurry and out-of-focus. John Bonzo Bonham is buried in the photos until the end of the book. To make matters worse, Ratner's descriptions of the shows are amateurish. Save your money—or buy Cross or Preston's pictorials (see above) instead.

Rey, Luis. *Led Zeppelin Live: An Illustrated Explanation of Underground Tapes*. Owen Sound, Ontario (Canada): The Hot Wacks Press, no date (c.1995). 336 pages. Approximately 100 black-and-white photographs throughout.

This cheaply-made publication might serve for those looking for information on Led Zeppelin's live performances or on the bootleg recordings of these shows. From Led Zeppelin's first performance in fall 1968 to their last show in 1980, this book is fairly complete in terms of factoids such as where the events took place, the lengths of shows, track lists, and notes about who did what. Author Rey is not at his best when critiquing the band's performance, but at determining if the soundboard and speaker systems were up to snuff at the show. Far from a work of art, but useful for collectors.

OTHER TITLES OF INTEREST

Burston, Jeremy. *Led Zeppelin: The Book*. London: Proteus, 1982.

Godwin, Robert. *The Illustrated Collector's Guide to Led Zeppelin*. Burlington, Ontario (Canada): Collector's Guide Publishing, no date.

Halfin, Ross. *The Photographers: Led Zeppelin*. Los Angeles, CA: 2.13.61, c.1995. *Collection of shots by 23 top Zeppelin photographers. According to* The Only One *fanzine (see above), this is among the best of all Led Zeppelin pictorials.*

Kamin, Philip. *Led Zeppelin*. Milwaukee, WI: Hal Leonard, 1986.

Ruhlmann, William. *Led Zeppelin*. Stamford, CT: Longmeadow, 1992.

Welch, Chris. *Led Zeppelin: Heavy Metal Photo Metal Book*. London: Omnibus Press (division of Book Sales Limited), 1983.

BRENDA LEE

FANZINES AND FAN CLUBS

Brenda Lee International Fan Club. Pat O'Leary, P.O. Box 2700, Murfreesboro, TN 37133-2700.

Fan club offering various material on Brenda Lee, including comprehensive discography packets (separate for national and international), merchandising (jackets, t-shirts, etc.), stat sheets, an autographed color photo, a bumper sticker, a newsletter, and a membership card. The 16-page newsletter is published quarterly and contains detailed tour itineraries, recent photos, and more. The cost of membership in the U.S. is $12 per year; $15 in Canada; and $18 elsewhere.

JERRY LEIBER AND MIKE STOLLER

PICTORIALS

Palmer, Robert. Introduction by John Lahr. *Baby, That Was Rock & Roll: The Legendary Leiber & Stoller*. New York and London: Harcourt Brace Jovanovich, 1978. 136 pages. Approximately 100 black-and-white photographs, covering every page. Recordings of Works by Leiber and Stoller. Chronological Listing of Records Produced by Leiber and Stoller.

The rock-writing duo who penned "Hound Dog," "On Broadway," "Charlie Brown," and countless other hits recorded by artists ranging from Peggy Lee to The Rolling Stones deserves much better than this half-attempt at a tribute. The author cuts back and forth from the various artists who recorded Leiber and Stoller's music, but doesn't supply enough about their background, collaborative process, and artistic relationship. Leiber and Stoller get buried amidst the oversized photos of rock stars. Some song lyrics are provided. The back matter material will prove useful for rock archivists.

THE LEMONHEADS

PICTORIALS

St. Michael, Mick *The Lemonheads*. London: Omnibus Press (division of Book Sales Limited), 1994. Unpaginated (approximately 64 pages). Approximately 100 black-and-white and color illustrations throughout. Discography.

Cut-and-paste photo book on the Boston band, with magazine-style copy dwarfed by the assortment of illustrations slapped on the pages. St. Michael addresses why The Lemonheads covered "Step by Step"—a tune made famous by New Kids on the Block—and singer Evan Dando's admiration for Gram Parsons—but coverage is generally light. Discriminating readers will opt for True's work (see below), even though only this title has a discography.

True, Everett. *The Lemonheads: The Illustrated Story*. London: Hamlyn (Reed Consumer Books), 1994. 80 pages. Approximately 100 color and black-and-white photographs, covering every page.

Described by author Everett True as "three affable, intelligent, easy-going boys," The Lemonheads are a unique band in the sense that they took on the macho-homophobic rock world with the song "Gay Heart" (interestingly inspired by actor Johnny Depp, who dubbed his home a "big gay place") and haven't yet disgraced themselves in public. True has the advantage of having met the group's singer Evan Dando on a few occasions, and he does

have a few interesting observations on the band. The photos are plentiful, including a few of Dando with singer Juliana Hatfield. Recommended (slightly) over St. Michael's work, but still not definitive.

JOHN LENNON

(See also Beatles, The; Lennon, Julian; Ono, Yoko)

BIOGRAPHIES

Coleman, Ray. *Lennon: The Definitive Biography*. New York: HarperCollins, 1992. 766 pages. Approximately 75 black-and-white photographs throughout. Chronology. Index. (First published in Great Britain in 1984 in two volumes: John Winston Lennon, 1940-1966; and John Ono Lennon, 1967-1980.)

Does this one live up to its title? Not quite—but it's as close as one is likely to get to definitive. Coleman has genuine love and affection for Lennon, plus the ability to represent paradoxical virtues of the man as both peacemaker and teenage street fighter. In addition to gathering hundreds of anecdotes (John's remark after a near plane crash: "Beatles and children out first!"), Coleman has pulled together an impressive array of photos, letters, postcards, documents (wedding certificates), and first-hand testimony (ex-girlfriends, Aunt Mimi, etc.). "You get a markedly more sane approach to the man than the hysteria of the legend"—*Creem*. First published in the U.S. in 1986 by McGraw-Hill.

Connolly, Ray. *John Lennon: 1940-1980*. Glasgow: Fontana Paperbacks, 1981. 190 pages. Four glossy black-and-white photo inserts.

Biography of Lennon that was released a year after his death. Chillingly, Connolly was scheduled to have interviewed John Lennon on December 9—the day after he was shot. Connolly's efforts are well intended, but he really doesn't have any sense of what Lennon's music was about. He criticizes John's contributions to *Revolver* ("largely disappointing") when in reality John was making the artistic experiments ("Tomorrow Never Knows") that pushed the group into another dimension. Packed with meaningless statements, redundancies (on New York: "It was cosmopolitan") and clichés.

Goldman, Albert. *The Lives of John Lennon*. New York: Morrow, 1988. 720 pages. Two eight-page black-and-white photo inserts. Sources. Index.

The flipside of Coleman's biography (above), this rank-smelling reputation-breaker is a pathetic collection of misinformed gossip and innuendo. Goldman's John Lennon is a hypocrite extraordinaire, a man of masks, a child bully, a flagrant phony, and an impressionable twit. Lennon is also dubbed an anorexic, an anal retentive neat freak, a dyslexic, a murderer, a plagiarist, and a homosexual. Goldman has utter contempt for his subject and blames almost all of the world's problems on him, including the death of his friend, Stu Sutcliffe. Fans, friends, and family protested these 720 pages of slop, but without success. The worst kind of fiction. "For those who hated him..."—*Research and Reference Book News*.

Ryan, David Stuart. *John Lennon's Secret*. London and Washington: Kozmik Press Centre, 1982. 255 pages. Approximately 60 full-page black-and-white photographs throughout. John Lennon's Favourite Lyrics. John Lennon's Compositions. Bibliography. Index.

What's the secret? What is there to know about John Lennon that hasn't already been thrown into the bonfire? This tepid biography doesn't follow through on its tease of a title, nor does it know where it is going in terms of musical commentary. The author falls into the trap of overgeneralizing that Paul wrote the music for The Beatles songs and John the words. No need to go past the genealogical table at the beginning of the book.

Wootton, Richard. *John Lennon: An Illustrated Biography*. London: Hodder and Stoughton, 1984. 128 pages. Approximately 50 black-and-white photographs throughout. Index.

Rocky British biography of Lennon, targeted primarily at young teens. Only two chapters (out of ten) focus on John's solo activities and life with Yoko. Barren of any quotes or period details—and with little exciting in the way of illustrative material—this is a dreary telling of what most would consider to be an event-filled life. "No new information here..."—*School Library Journal*.

CRITICAL/ANALYTICAL COMMENTARY

Editors of *Rolling Stone*. Edited by Cott, Jonathan and Doudna, Christine. *The Ballad of John and Yoko*. Garden City, NY: Dolphin Books (division of Doubleday & Company, Inc.), 1982. 320 pages. Two glossy eight-page black-and-white photo inserts; 50 photographs throughout. Index.

A heavyweight collection of *Rolling Stone* essays and interviews spanning 1968 (the magazine's first interview with John Lennon) to Lennon tributes in the early 1980's. The book unfolds chronologically, including separate bios of John and Yoko's childhoods, profiles of their bed-in for peace, the Toronto concert, Lennon's solo work, etc. The contributions, which were supplied by the usual highfalutin *Rolling Stone*/rock literati—Ben Fong-Torres, Ritchie York, Jann Wenner, Ralph J. Gleason, et. al.—typically demonstrate the magazine's dedicated support of Lennon's causes (e.g., his immigration battles). Superb.

Hampton, Wayne. *Guerilla Minstrels: John Lennon, Joe Hill, Woody Guthrie and Bob Dylan*. Knoxville, TN: University of Tennessee Press, 1986. 306 pages. One 16-page black-and-white photo inserts. Selected Bibliography. Index.

Hampton, a professor of political science, tackles the subject of protest singing through cultural studies of John Lennon, Joe Hill, Woody Guthrie, and Bob Dylan. Laden with fallacies (Hampton follows the theory that "Lucy in the Sky with Diamonds" stands for LSD, which John Lennon emphatically denied) and misobservations (that Joan Baez was "past her prime" at Woodstock), this book demeans the four icons as they become lost in the author's academic quagmire. "Tighter editing would have eliminated some of the extravagant tone and errors of language..."—*Choice*.

Robertson, John. *The Art and Music of John Lennon*. New York: Birch Lane (division of Carol Publishing), 1991. 218 pages. Appendix 1: Interviews. Appendix 2: Letters. Appendix 3: Discography. Index. (First published in England in 1990 by Omnibus Press.)

John Robertson is the pseudonym of "a distinguished British music writer." So why hide? Well, whoever the author might be, he or she does a decent enough job cataloguing Lennon's musical, literary, and artistic works from his childhood (Lennon's high school and art college creation *The Daily Howl*) to Yoko's December 1980 recordings. The book, printed in an unpleasant typeface for narrative, does not address criticism of Lennon's work or provide much insight past literal history. Additional appendices on films and books would have been a benefit.

Sauceda, Dr. James. *The Literary Lennon: A Comedy of Letters.* Ann Arbor: The Pierian Press, 1983. 200 pages. A half-dozen pen-and-ink drawings. Index to titles.

This was the first critical commentary devoted exclusively to Lennon's non-musical output. Dr. Sauceda makes many interesting, if highbrow, connections between Lennon's writing and that of James Joyce and Lewis Carroll. He methodically analyzes every piece of prose and drawing, with headings for overview, key themes, and interpretation. The writing is unpretentious, although the author seems to go too far in citing the need for his book. Since only a handful of drawings are reproduced here, readers should have copies of Lennon's works handy. The book also includes a funny limerick John wrote for *The Gay Liberation Book* (see Related Works, below), Lennon's sole book review (in the *New York Times* for *The Goon Show Scripts*), and some of Lennon's writings for *Mersey Beat* (Bill Harry's Liverpool magazine).

Shevey, Sandra. *The Other Side of Lennon.* London: Sidgwick & Jackson, 1990. 244 pages. Two glossy eight-page black-and-white photo inserts. Bibliography. Index.

An assault on John Lennon that is so-off track one can't help think the author is writing about someone else. Lennon is described as "not a particularly creative person" and "the ultimate cock-rocker past his prime"; and his writings (e.g., *In His Own Write*, see Written Works, below) are labeled, among other things, as "crude, lewd [and] adolescent." All of Shevey's impressions are based solely on one 1972 interview, which isn't even reprinted here. Her absurd repudiation of commonly accepted facts (such as that Beatles' manager Brian Epstein was *not* homosexual) is only exceeded in stupidity by her creation of a few incidents (such as her suggestion that John Lennon may have killed Brian Epstein over a dispute regarding Beatles' percentages). Heinous.

Thomson, Elizabeth and Gutman, David (editors). *The Lennon Companion: Twenty-Five Years of Comment.* New York: Schirmer Books (division of Macmillan, Inc.), 1987. 274 pages. Two glossy black-and-white photo inserts. Selected Bibliography. Discography. Index.

The editors have gone at length to avoid tampering with the 60 or so essays and reviews included in this retrospective volume, so you don't have to worry about it being a puff-job. The book contains an abysmal piece from Lloyd Rose in which he calls Ray Coleman's book *Lennon* (above) "one of a series of generally terrible biographies of Lennon"; Gloria Steinem's spirited article on her first meeting with John Lennon; and even Maureen Cleave's controversial story containing Lennon's alleged attack on Christianity. Other works come from Noel Coward, Andrew Sarris, Wilfred Mellers, and others. It's somewhat jarring that some of the part titles refer to Beatles' songs not written by Lennon (e.g., George's "Only a Northern Song"). "...a unique collection..."—*Booklist.*

Wiener, John. *Come Together: John Lennon in His Time.* New York: Random House, 1984. 380 pages. One eight-page glossy black-and-white photo insert. An Interview with Yoko Ono. Chronology. Notes. Index.

While conducting his research for this book, Wiener made a Freedom of Information request to the Federal Government to obtain documents regarding the Nixon administration's harassment of John Lennon in the early 1970's. The government's final disclosure ("26 pounds of files") isn't decisive proof of wrongdoing, but it does paint an incriminating picture of a paranoid government and FBI. Wiener humorously points out that the FBI took on the role of rock critic, critiquing the song "John Sinclair" as "lacking Lennon's standards." A thoughtful, and often ironic, study of the political ramifications of Lennon's music.

DEATH OF LENNON

Beckley, Timothy Green (editor). *Lennon: Up Close & Personal.* No city: Sunshine Publications, Inc., 1980. 160 pages. Approximately 50 black-and-white photographs scattered throughout. Chronology.

Paperback released to cash-in on Lennon's death. The writing is a bit too informal and cloying (though perhaps well-meaning), rehashing stuff that can be found in any one of a number of other Lennon books listed herein. The back endpaper is of some curious interest, actually reprinting Yoko's statement to the press on December 10, 1980: "I told Sean what happened. I showed him the picture of his father on the cover of the paper and explained the situation...."

Bresler, Fenton. *Who Killed John Lennon?*. New York: St. Martin's Paperbacks (Press), 1989. 354 pages. One eight-page black-and-white photo insert. Bibliography. Index. (First published in Great Britain by Sidgwick & Jackson Limited.)

The sell-line reads: "The Shocking Expose of the Lennon Murder Cover-Up." Was Mark David Chapman a "lone nut"—or were CIA, FBI, and presidential forces responsible for slaying John Lennon while he was on the comeback trail? While it's common knowledge that Lennon was a political activist in the late 1960's and early 70's —he held a rally for radical John Sinclair and befriended the likes of Abbey Hoffman and Jerry Rubin—Lennon had, for all intents and purposes, ceased his political noisemaking. Why on earth would incoming President Ronald Reagan see him as a threat in 1980? Bresler's conviction that Chapman was "brainwashed" via phone suggestions from the U.S. government is unconvincing. This book is of interest only to the assassination-minded. Oliver Stone, are you reading? "Bresler builds an entirely circumstantial case without a shred of hard evidence..."—*Publishers Weekly*.

Fogo, Fred. *I Read the News Today: The Social Drama of John Lennon's Death*. London: Rowman & Littlefield, 1994. 186 pages. Bibliography. Index.

An academic treatise on the impact and relevance of John Lennon's death, smugly referred to here as a "social drama" (an expression coined by one Victor Turner). Fogo examines the baby boomers of the 1960's, along with their relationship to The Beatles, in an attempt to show why many believed Lennon's death signified "the end of the 1960's." Diffusive and not all that interesting, especially when it's clear that 1960's survivors were not the only ones who mourned John Lennon's death. "...while many readers will no doubt find this work engaging and thought-provoking, others may simply tire along the way"—*Goldmine*.

Jones, Jack. *Let Me Take You Down: Inside the Mind of Mark David Chapman, the Man Who Killed John Lennon*. New York: Warner, 1992. 348 pages. One eight-page black-and-white photo insert. Bibliography.

Through extensive interviews, Jones has pieced together the bizarre life of Mark David Chapman and the chain of events that led to his murder of a rock legend. Some of the coincidences presented here are pretty spooky. For one thing, Chapman had spotted actress Mia Farrow shortly before he shot Lennon and took this as a sign. (Farrow had acted in *Rosemary's Baby*, which was set in the Dakota apartment building, where Lennon lived; the director of that film was Roman Polanski whose wife, Sharon Tate, was murdered by Charles Manson—the insane cult leader inspired to commit his atrocities by The Beatles' songs "Helter Skelter" and "Piggies.") Jones makes the mistake of relying on dubious testimony from Frederic Seaman, Lennon's former assistant, who many people believe broke into Yoko's apartment and stole Lennon's journal. (Seaman was one of several who claim Lennon had a "death fixation.") Should Lennon fans read this? Probably not, because "it gives us more than we would ever care to know about a notorious nobody"—*The New York Times*.

No author. *A Tribute to John Lennon 1940-1980*. London and New York: Proteus Publishing Co., 1981. Unpaginated (approximately 96 pages). Twenty black-and-white photographs scattered throughout.

This small book from Proteus excerpts approximately 75 newspaper and magazine articles and essays written subsequent to Lennon's death. Insightful, emotional, and nostalgic, these pieces cry out love for an artist in every sense of the word. "I am privileged to have known him," wrote Ray Connolly of the *Liverpool Daily Post*. "...everyone, it seemed, feels diminished by his death," commented *Punch*. Clive Barnes, then of the *Chicago Sun-Times*, wrote, "He was funny, he was sweet and he was generous.... He was an apostle of freedom. A man of infinite delicacy." For Lennon fans, this collection is almost as good as having the original clippings.

DICTIONARIES AND ENCYCLOPEDIAS

Harry, Bill. *The Book of Lennon*. New York: Delilah Communications Limited (distributed by the Putnam Publishing Group), 1984. Unpaginated (approximately 128 pages). Approximately 75 black-and-white illustrations throughout.

People, places, performances, records, films, publications, and personal facts about John Lennon—all A to Z within each of those respective sections. Harry's knowledge of obscure Beatles-related personages is immense, but he is careless as a compiler and researcher; he makes no attempt to explain his criteria for entry inclusion or the general parameters of the book. Hence, there are many glaring omissions. In the people section, where is Julia Baird, John's half-sister? In the performances section, he rattles off many Lennon-related songs, but where are "Meat City," "Nowhere Man," "Ticket to Ride, and so many others? The design of the book leaves much to be desired; the last line of every page is so low, text is nearly cut off. Harry's goal was to present a full picture of Lennon outside the gossip/scandal books, yet how could he with so much apparently missing?

FANZINES AND FAN CLUBS

Lennon International. 1 Wellington Avenue, St. Ives, Cambs, PE 17 6UT, England.

Founded in 1989, this irregularly published fanzine comes in a "video-style" box with a newsletter, cassette, photograph, and other items. Write for more information.

INTERVIEWS

Sheff, David. Edited by Barry Golson. *The Playboy Interviews with John Lennon and Yoko Ono*. New York: Playboy Press, 1980. 193 pages. One glossy eight-page black-and-white photo insert.

An expertly handled conversation with the couple, which was conducted over a period of three weeks in September of 1980, and released in segments in *Playboy* magazine. Little did anyone realize how valuable these interviews would be: Only three months prior to his death, Lennon expounded on virtually every important subject, from The Beatles' reuniting ("Why should The Beatles give more? Didn't they give everything on God's earth for ten years?") to death ("I worship the people who survive"). Full of irony, special insights, and spurts of Lennon's unique humor. This probably marked the only time in history *Playboy* readers flipped to the interview *before* ogling at the centerfold.

LENNON FRIENDS AND FAMILY

Baird, Julia with Giuliano, Geoffrey. Foreword by Paul McCartney. *John Lennon: My Brother*. New York: Henry Holt and Company, 1988. 156 pages. John Lennon's Family Tree. A Lennon Chronology.

It was an odd circumstance, to say the least: Lennon was raised by his Aunt Mimi, while his two younger half-sisters lived with his mother only two miles away. Just as John was getting old enough to spend time with his mother (and squeezing his band into her bathroom for grueling practice sessions!) she was hit by a car. Half-sister Julia Baird tells the Lennon story through her perspective, which is plaintively sentimental. Baird had infrequent contact with the Lennons over the years and has never even met Yoko. As far as one can see, this book only adds one new twist to the Lennon myth—that there was actually a *third* Lennon half-sister, who was given up for adoption and has never been heard from since. "Photos are included, but few of them do anything to establish Lennon's presence in the family"—*Booklist*.

Green, John. *Dakota Days: The True Story of John Lennon's Final Years*. New York: St. Martin's Press, 1983. 260 pages. One eight-page black-and-white photo insert.

An attempt to prove that Lennon's "househusband" excuse for his five years of domestic solitude was all a load of hogwash. Green, the Lennons' personal Merlin and tarot card reader, asserts Lennon was actually covering up his identity crisis and creative block. He smugly recounts how he advised the Lennons on everything from investing in cows to whether their baby would be born deformed; one wonders why—if he had genuine skill at premonition—John Lennon isn't alive today. Written in the style of one overlong conversation, this book is not of interest to either the fan or the Lennon myth basher.

Lennon, Pauline. *Daddy, Come Home: The True Story of John Lennon and His Father*. London: Angus & Robertson (division of HarperCollins), 1990. 210 pages. One glossy eight-page photo insert.

As history originally had it, Freddie Lennon was rock's quintessential deadbeat dad: He chose his love for the sea over his responsibilities to his wife and child (John). Pauline Lennon, Freddie's last wife (some 20 years his junior), contradicts the above myth with elements of her husband's autobiography, which was presented to John after his father's death. The tale successfully recreates life in turn of the century Liverpool—complete with its various teas, toddies, and famous Scouse soup—and probes Freddie's troubled youth (ironically, he also lost his father at six), exploits at sea (most probably exaggerated), and romance with Julia Lennon (John's giddy, sarcastic mom). Surprisingly coherent and engaging early on, *Daddy Come Home* reveals some seam-splits midway as the author can't get any of her facts straight regarding John's musical career.

Pang, May and Edwards, Henry. *John Lennon: The Lost Weekend*. New York: S.P.I. Books (division of Shapolsky Publishers, Inc.), 1992. 344 pages. One 34-page black-and-white photo insert.

Pang fell in love with John Lennon during their 18-month "lost weekend" together, amidst John's split with Yoko. Pang has a very different story to tell than the one offered to the press by John and Yoko: She says John romanced her at Yoko's bidding—and the ex-Beatle dumped her when "Mother" wanted him back. Mentally and emotionally manipulated and abused by the couple (in many instances, physically by a drunken Lennon), Pang had some beautiful moments as well and was a witness to the last recordings John made prior to his five-year hiatus from the recording studio. Pang has great reason to despise Yoko (for making her a full-time geisha) and even John (for his inability to make decisions), but she doesn't take full advantage and make this an all-out diatribe. First published by Warner Books as *Loving John*.

Seaman, Frederic. *John Lennon: Living on Borrowed Time*. London: Xanadu Publications, 1991. 262 pages. Three glossy eight-page black-and-white photo inserts. Index.

It's very difficult to judge this book. Seaman, Lennon's assistant in the last year of his life, was the man accused of having held in his possession John Lennon's journal—a priceless item, which either he stole outright or "borrowed" so he could hand it over to Julian Lennon, the rightful owner. In any event, Seaman is not a trustworthy fellow—his sole supporter is sleazemonger Albert Goldman—and he clearly has an axe to grind against the Lennons. Fans will not want to know about John's bald patch or how Yoko controlled him "in a viselike grip." "This is fairly trashy stuff..."—*Booklist*.

Shotton, Pete and Schaffner, Nicholas. *John Lennon: In My Life*. New York: Stein and Day, 1983. 208 pages. Approximately 60 black-and-white photographs throughout. Index.

Who was John Lennon's best childhood friend? Stuart Sutcliffe? Paul McCartney? Wrong twice. Pete Shotton, ex-skiffler in The Quarry Men and later Apple director, holds that honor. With an assist from the talents of Schaffner, Shotton tells of a young Lennon who loved wordplay and practical jokes, hated sports, and could publicly ejaculate nine times to the sight of a naked sunbather. Shotton is too good of a friend to tell the full extent of Lennon's cruelty—and that is a plus for a book of this kind. Enjoyable, even though the chapters on the boys' youth pass too briefly.

PICTORIALS

Fawcett, Anthony. *John Lennon: One Day at a Time: A Personal Biography*. New York: Grove Press, 1976. 191 pages. Approximately 200 black-and-white photographs, covering every page. Chronology. Discography.

The late 1960's-early 70's was a highly creative, energetic period for John Lennon: he organized public art exhibitions, sketched erotic lithographs of his wife, hosted bed-ins for peace, and recorded some of his most personal music. This was also a traumatic time, as The Beatles collapsed, he and Yoko went through primal scream therapy, and the media had a field day portraying the couple as the bores of the century. Fawcett, who briefly worked for the Lennons, blends into the scenery as he demonstrates several, but not all, creative sides of the artist. Upbeat.

Giuliano, Geoffrey and Giuliano, Brenda. Introduction by Charles Lennon. *The Illustrated John Lennon*. London: Sunburst Books, 1993. 96 pages. Approximately 100 color and black-and-white photographs, covering every page. A John and Yoko Conversation 1989[sic]. A Lennon Chronology.

One of three Beatles pictorials from the Giulianos and Sunburst Books (see Harrison and McCartney), this rendering of the Lennon story is cheap and full of mistakes. Introduced by John Lennon's uncle, Charles Lennon—who gushes about Geoffrey Giuliano's work (most likely without having seen the more controversial passages)—the book sputters along through John's Beatles years and solo career, with a photo emphasis on the early 1970's. All of the way through, errors creep in: Ringo's fill-in drummer, Jimmy Nichol, is identified as Billy Nichols; photos of John cavorting with May Pang circa mid-1970's are opposite a page recounting reaction to his death several years later; and a slapped on conversation with John and Yoko is dated 1989—nine years after Lennon's death! As the Rutles said, let it rot.

Gruen, Bob. Text by Bob Gruen and Stanley Mieses. Foreword by Yoko Ono. *Listen to These Pictures: Photographs of John Lennon*. New York: William Morrow and Company, 1985. 212 pages. 135 black-and-white photographs, covering every page.

Gruen was fortunate enough to have been accepted into John and Yoko's inner circle, and captured key events and moments in their lives throughout the 1970's. Some of these photos, such as John holding up the peace sign at the Statue of Liberty and another one in which he poses coolly in his cut-off New York City t-shirt, are postcard classics and have become the visual images of Lennon as soloist and cult hero. There are also some fine shots of John performing and recording. Gruen goes out of his way to avoid making it seem like he is "cashing in" on his old friends; Lennon's death is not even mentioned in the book.

Hoffmann, Dezo. Written by Jopling, Norman. *The Faces of John Lennon*. New York: McGraw-Hill, 1986. 166 pages. 157 black-and-white photographs, covering every page.

Implicitly, these are publicity photos of John as a Beatle, hence they are not very intimate. In fact, they seem to be leftovers from

Hoffmann's *With the Beatles* (see Beatles, Pictorials). We should be grateful Hoffmann was there to record these moments: John is smiling, cute, intellectual, etc., all of the positive characteristics the public wants to see, even though it's not quite the full picture. The captions "...are, unfortunately, all positioned at the back of the book"—*Publishers Weekly*.

Norman, Philip. *Days in the Life: John Lennon Remembered*. London: Random Century Limited, 1990. 120 pages. Approximately 115 color and black-and-white photographs, covering almost every page.

Norman's photo tribute to Lennon contains some fine color and a few little treats in black-and-white: young Lennon standing outside Dovedale Primary school in Liverpool and the cover of Lennon's art and poetry notebook (on which he wrote his own funny blurb reviews). The book sorely lacks photos from the late 1970's. There's no need to suffer through Norman's indulgent introduction, in which he tells of his entrance into Beatledom and how he came about writing his brilliant biography, *Shout!* (see Beatles, Biographies). "The anecdotal text...doesn't offer much new information"—*Booklist*.

Ono, Yoko. *John Lennon: Summer of 1980*. New York: Perigee (Putnam Publishing Group), 1983. 112 pages. 104 black-and-white photographs, covering every page. *Double Fantasy* Lyrics.

The summer of 1980 marked John Lennon's return to the recording studio with Yoko. These black-and-white shots depict a cool, consummate, confident artist who finally seems relaxed with himself as he returns to the fold. The pictures are by eight photographers, including several lovemaking shots captured by Allan Tannenbaum. An intimate and teensy slice of the pie.

Robertson, John. *Lennon 1940-1980*. London: Omnibus Press (division of Book Sales Limited), 1995. 128 pages. Approximately 200 color and black-and-white photographs, covering nearly every page.

Day-by-day "journey through John Lennon's life and times in words and pictures." The calendar is set in four columns (without any running heads for guidance), and photos that are often screened behind the text. The book has intermittent success in its focus (mixing recording information with personal events) and occasionally struggles to get a meaning across. Optional for Lennon fans, who will be pleased to see updates through "Free as a Bird."

Saimuru, Nishi F. *The John Lennon Family Album.* San Francisco: Chronicle Books, 1990. 162 pages. Approximately 150 color photographs. (First published in Tokyo, Japan in 1982 by Kadokawa Shoten as *John Renon Kazoku Seikatsu.*)

Opening with "A Love Letter from John and Yoko to People Who Ask Us What, When and Why," this loving photo collection shows us the Lennons' travels and day-to-day events from spring 1977 to the summer of 1979. We are treated to the warm, human side of John Lennon, as he enjoys life's pleasures with son Sean and wife Yoko: sledding, going to the circus, swimming, celebrating birthdays, exploring Japan, etc. Teenage Julian shows up and shares in the fun. "A collection of fine intimate color photographs..."—*Reference and Research Book News.*

Solt, Andrew and Egan, Sam. Foreword by Yoko Ono. Preface by David L. Wolper. *Imagine: John Lennon.* New York: Macmillan, 1988. 256 pages. Approximately 250 color and black-and-white photographs, covering every page. Chronology. Discography.

The companion piece to Solt's 1988 film of the same name, with marvelous, rare shots of every phase of Lennon's life and career. Even the familiar photos of the boys in Germany have been reproduced larger and in better focus than elsewhere. John's quotes also appear throughout, most of which convey either positive or philosophical messages. A beautifully done trip through memory lane, closing with—what else? The lyrics to "Imagine." One visual distraction: The word "foreword" is incorrectly spelled "forword" throughout. "A classic volume..."—*Booklist.*

QUIZBOOKS AND QUOTEBOOKS

Miles. *John Lennon: In His Own Words.* London: Omnibus Press (division of Book Sales Limited), 1994. 128 pages. Approximately 100 black-and-white photographs throughout.

First published in 1980, this often-seen quotebook has been reissued many times over the years. The photos are inferior and grainy; more recent Omnibus Press quotebooks have done a better job in selection and printing. Since Lennon was incontrovertibly the most outspoken and politically-minded Beatle, a quotebook on him is more than viable. Unfortunately, this is arranged chronologically, so readers have to dig for Lennon's remarks on specific topics. It's especially hard to find a quote on Vietnam, for example, although there are passages on his famous bed-in. Bennahum's volume on all four Beatles is much better (see Beatles: Quizbooks and Quotebooks). Fans are advised to find Lennon's *Rolling Stone* interviews or read Lennon's books.

RELATED WORKS

Keen, Linda. *John Lennon in Heaven: Crossing the Borders of Being.* Ashland, OR: Pan Publishing, 1994. 296 pages.

Imagine: You can expand your mind into another dimension and meet John Lennon in heaven on the other side. John chomps his gum, talks about the power of intuition, his love for Yoko, and other topics. Insipid and contrived.

Long, Jeff (editor). *Search for Liberation.* Los Angeles: The Bhaktivedanta Book Trust, 1981. 70 pages.

A transcript of dialogues between A.C. Bhaktivedanta, Swami Prabhupada, and the unlikeliest of subjects, John Lennon. The Beatle had several philosophical and theological conversations with the swamis, in which he asked questions about God, mantras, finding a guru, and reincarnation. George Harrison and Yoko also appear in various sessions. A leftover from The Beatles' India mecca in the late 1960's, and not that relevant considering the fact that shortly after the conversations Lennon determined it was all malarkey.

Richmond, Len and Noguera, Gary. *The Gay Liberation Book.* San Francisco: Ramparts Press, 1973. 208 pages. Approximately 25 black-and-white photographs throughout.

Classic collection of essays, cartoons, and photographs celebrating gay liberation and pride in the early 1970's. Among the notable contributors are Allen Ginsberg, Gore Vidal, William Burroughs—and John Lennon. His contribution? A Lennonesque doodle and a limerick.

One of the first works of its kind, and still relevant in the 1990's.

Young, Paul. *The Lennon Factor*. New York: Stein and Day, 1972. Unpaginated (about 118 pages).

Poetry from Young, with references throughout to The Beatles and John Lennon. The multitudinous literary namedropping (Kurt Vonnegut and Henry Miller) and political jibing ("hello milhous") do not help set this above the giddy scribblings of a high school student.

WRITTEN WORKS

Lennon, John. Illustrated by Lancaster-Poh, Lynn and Reitzle, Tilman. *Imagine*. New York: Carol Publishing Group, 1990. 14 pages. Original art throughout.

A children's book reprinting the lyrics to John's most famous anthem. Images of kites, balloons, nature, etc. abound. A boyish fellow with glasses, looking very much like John, makes an appearance here and there. Colorful and to the point.

Lennon, John. *Imagine: A Celebration of John Lennon*. New York: Penguin Studio, 1996. Unpaginated (approximately 48 pages). 50 black-and-white photographs, covering every page.

The complete words to John Lennon's "Imagine," alternating with photos of the artist making music and celebrating life with Yoko. A simple and effective package suitable for kids and adults (although the former would prefer Lancaster-Poh's art, see *Imagine* above), with pretty cloud designs appearing throughout.

Lennon, John. Foreword by Paul McCartney. *In His Own Write & A Spaniard in the Works*. New York: New American Library, 1967. 176 pages. Approximately 75 original black-and-white sketches and drawings throughout.

These two works were originally published a year apart, in 1964 and 1965 respectively, and have been reissued in various forms over the years. Lennon actually won the Foyle's Literary Prize for these brief, nonsensical tales. Paul's foreword asks the question: "Is he deep?" The Thurberesque prose and verse are still fresh and funny after all of these years, though I have heard some readers say they don't get the puns and have a hard time deciphering some of Lennon's intentional distortions of the English language. My favorite pieces: "Good Dog Nigel," "No Flies on Frank," and "The Fat Growth on Eric Hearble." "He writes like a Beatle possessed...inspired nonsense"—*The New York Times Book Review*.

Lennon, John. Edited by Horzogenrath, Wulf and Hanson, Dorothee. Foreword by Yoko Ono. *John Lennon: Drawings, Performances, Films*. No city: Cantz, no date. 228 pages. Approximately 200 original black-and-white drawings, lithographs, and watercolors throughout; approximately 50 black-and-white photographs throughout. Bibliographic Notes. Selected Bibliography.

A tribute to the visual aspects of John Lennon's career, including, for the first time in one volume, a wide range of Lennon's watercolors, drawings, and lithographs. Thus it demonstrates Lennon was more than just a whimsical doodler: from drawings drafted in his childhood (a few of which were included in the original *Walls and Bridges* album cover art) to works completed 1968-1979 (many of which are self-portraits and visions of New York City life) to experimentations with Japanese Sumi ink (one wonderful section features a cute Japanese dictionary, which Lennon illustrated in 1971) and, of course, highly erotic art (nude studies of Yoko plus various representations of John and Yoko copulating). If one isn't completely absorbed in Lennon's art, the book offers additional chunky sections on his political activism, live performances, album concepts, films, and more. Definitive proof of Lennon's multi-faceted talents and creative interests.

Lennon, John. Afterword by Yoko Ono. *Skywriting by Word of Mouth and Other Writings, Including the Ballad of John and Yoko*. New York, Harper & Row, 1986. 200 pages. Several Lennon drawings and sketches throughout.

More than twenty years went by between publication of Lennon's work *A Spaniard in the Works* and this posthumous collection of gibberish, stories, and assorted artwork. The early chapters from John's notebooks (titled "The Ballad of John and Yoko") are disjointed and express his miscellaneous upset over whatever was going on at the time of writing—the public's prejudices against Yoko, his deportation problems, and so on. Then the *Skywriting* section begins and the text takes off. Even nonfans will howl with laughter over Lennon's undeniable gift for wordplay (chapters entitled "Lucy in the Sky with Diabetics," "A Complete Change of Pacemaker," etc.). The sketches do not cover every page as in his earlier works, but those present are still effective. Despite his small body of work, Lennon was rock's greatest literary humorist.

Lennon, John. *A Spaniard in the Works*.

See: *In His Own Write & A Spaniard in the Works*.

Tynan, Kenneth. *Oh! Calcutta*. New York: Grove Press, 1979. 192 pages. Approximately 75 black-and-white photographs throughout.

Kenneth Tynan conceived this outrageous late 1960's nudie sexploitation musical comedy, which features uncredited skits by John Lennon, Sam Shepard, Edna O'Brien, Jules Feiffer, Dan Greenberg, and several other notables. Something of a camp period piece, this one obviously needs to be experienced *live*, not read. The disrobing, intermingling bodies à la Matisse, rock avant-gardism, and Velvet Underground deviancy (wife-swapping) have now become legendary. Now, which piece is from John Lennon? Extensive research and consultations with experts have yielded no conclusive evidence. Based on Lennon's sense of humor, my vote is for the side-splitting "Four in Hand" sequence about a group of guys who meet regularly to jerk off together. The show is still kinky, hilarious, and thought-provoking.

YOUNG ADULT

Concord, Bruce W. Introduction by Leeza Gibbons. *John Lennon* New York: Chelsea House Publishers, 1994. 128 pages. Approximately 40 black-and-white photographs throughout. Discography. Further Readings. Chronology. Index.

Part of Chelsea House's "Pop Culture Legends" series, with emphasis on John Lennon's status as cultural icon. Concord, like many other writers, first introduces Lennon as a Beatle. In a succinct, inviting tone, Concord then backtracks to the artist's past, bringing to

life his early friendships, his mother's death, The Beatles' trips to Germany, his legendary recordings, and his involvement in various political and social movements. "For present-day teenagers with little knowledge of Lennon and the Beatles..."—*Goldmine*.

Lennon, John. *Imagine*:

See: Written Works.

Santrey, Laurence. Illustrated by Beier, Ellen. *John Lennon: Young Rock Star*. Mahwah: Troll Associates, 1990. 48 pages. 23 original pencil drawings.

A children's story that details several episodes in John Lennon's childhood. The tale addresses some of the harsher realities, such as when Lennon had to choose between living with his mother and father. However, the author fibs about Lennon's academic prowess and evades the fact that he was a troublemaker. Beier's art is unsatisfactory; the face simply does not look very much like a young John Lennon. Not recommended.

OTHER TITLES OF INTEREST

Baird, Julia. *In His Own Youth, In My Words*. No city: River Women Press, 1985.

Bradman, Tony. *John Lennon*. London: Hamish Hamilton, 1986.
School Library Journal *commented: "Bradman occasionally succumbs to the use of irony in describing Lennon's life and death, but he generally maintains a matter-of-fact tone in this brief biography."*

Buskin, Richard. *John Lennon: Life and Legend*. New York: Outlet Book Company, 1991.

Carpozi, George. *John Lennon: Death of a Dream*. No city: Manor Books, 1980.

Concord, Bruce W. *John Lennon*. New York: Chelsea House, 1994.

Garbarini, Vic. *Strawberry Fields Forever*. New York: Bantam, no date.

Hamilton, Sue. *The Killing of a Rock Star*. Minneapolis, MN: Abdo & Daughters, 1989.

Heatley, Michael. *Immortal John Lennon*. Stamford, CT: Longmeadow, 1992.

Huyette, Marica. *John Lennon: A Real Live Fairy Tale*. No city: Hidden Studio, 1976.

King, L.R.E. *Unfinished Music, No. 1: An Unauthorized Companion to the Lost Lennon Tapes*. No city: Storyteller Productions, 1990.

King, L.R.E. *Unfinished Music, No. 2: An Unauthorized Companion to Year Two of the Lost Lennon Tapes*. No city: Storyteller Productions, 1992.

Leen, Jason. *Peace at Last: The After-Death Experiences of John Lennon*. No city: Illumination Arts, 1989.

Leigh, Vanora. *John Lennon*. New York: Franklin Watts, 1986.
School Library Journal *commented: "...surface fluff."*

Lennon, Cynthia. *A Twist of Lennon*. New York: Avon, 1986.

Lennon, John. *Ai: Japan Through John's Lennon's Eyes: A Personal Sketchbook*. San Francisco: Viz Communications, 1992.

Lennon, John. *John Lennon's Japanese Lesson*. San Francisco: Viz Communications, no date.

Lennon, John; Kennedy, Adrienne; and Spinetti, Victor. *In His Own Write: The Lennon Play*. New York: Simon & Schuster, 1972.
Actor Victor Spinetti, the only non-Beatle to act in The Beatles films A Hard Day's Night, Help!, *and* The Magical Mystery Tour, *co-adapted (with Adrienne Kennedy) John Lennon's two books* In His Own Write *and* A Spaniard in the Works *as this stage play.*

Martins, Tadeu Gonzega. *John Lennon*. No city: Sintese Books, 1982.

McCabe, Peter. *John Lennon: For the Record*. New York: Bantam, 1984.

Noebel, David A. *The Legacy of John Lennon: Charming or Harming a Nation?*. No city: Nelson, Thomas, 1982.

Ono, Yoko. *The Last Lennon Tapes*. New York: Dell, 1983.

Ruhlmann, William. *John Lennon*. New York: Smithmark (Penguin USA), 1993.

Tremlett, George. *The John Lennon Story*. London: Futura, 1976.

Wenner, Jann. *John Lennon Remembers*. New York: Penguin, 1980.

JULIAN LENNON

(See also Lennon, John)

YOUNG ADULT

Flesch, Yolande. *Julian Lennon*. Philadelphia, PA: Running Press, 1985. 76 pages. 70 black-and-white photographs throughout.

Cheesy pictorial on Julian Lennon that doesn't go any further than the obvious. Everyone knows that Julian never received the attention that his father, John, later gave to his younger son, Sean. And everyone knows the difficulty Julian faced having to live up to comparisons with his father. The book does not investigate Julian's alcohol dependency or insecurities with women. The captions are certainly not helpful to the young fan; in one shot young Julian is photographed with the entourage from the film *Rock 'n' Roll Circus*, but John Entwistle, Keith Moon, and Eric Clapton are not even identified.

OTHER TITLES OF INTEREST

Bego, Mark. *Julian Lennon*. New York: St. Martin's Press, 1986.

Green, Carl and Sanford, William R. *Julian Lennon*. New York: Macmillan, 1986.

Lulow, Kalia. *Julian Lennon*. New York: Ballantine, 1985.

Mabery, D.L. *Julian Lennon*. Minneapolis, MN: Lerner Publications, 1986.

Martin, Nancy. *John Lennon and Julian Lennon*. New York: Avon, 1986.

ANNIE LENNOX

See Eurythmics, The.

LES PAUL

BIOGRAPHIES

Shaughnessy, Mary Alice. *Les Paul: An American Original*. New York: William Morrow & Company, Inc.,1993. 348 pages. Four eight-page black-and-white photo inserts. Source Notes. Bibliography. Selected Discography. Index.

Les Paul, born Lester William Polfuss (a name only film director Preston Sturges could have created), was a pioneer of the electric guitar, both as inventor and virtuoso. While steadily employed in radio work with the likes of Bing Crosby, he developed a unique style of solo playing that to this day makes guitar aces such as Jimmy Page and Eddie Van Halen salivate. Mary Shaughnessy had access to Paul for a while, but he withdrew from the project when he discovered she was prying too much into his rocky marriage with Mary Ford. No matter, it's "...a rock- music-lover's delight"—*Kirkus*.

HUEY LEWIS AND THE NEWS

FANZINES AND FAN CLUBS

Newsline II. P.O. Box 99, Payson, UT 84651.

This fan club publishes a 20-page quarterly newsletter of the same name, with reproductions of black-and-white photos, news flashes, contests, "Ask the Band" (questions from club members answered by Huey Lewis and the News or their press office), interviews, reviews of shows by fans, tour itineraries, and more. The cost of membership is $10 by check or money order in the U.S. and $12.50 everywhere else.

PICTORIALS

Byrd, Jay. *Huey Lewis and the News.* Wauwatosa: Robus Books, 1985. 32 pages (unpaginated). Approximately 20 color and 30 black-and-white photographs throughout.

Dumb promotional book with a slender chronological format (one or two paragraphs per year). The heart of rock and roll just had a coronary.

OTHER TITLES OF INTEREST
Draper, Rob. *Huey Lewis & the News.* New York: Ballantine, 1985.

JERRY LEE LEWIS

BIOGRAPHIES

Tosches, Nick. *Hellfire: The Jerry Lee Lewis Story.* New York: Dell Publishing Co., Inc., 1982. 276 pages. Approximately 50 full-page black-and-white photographs throughout. Index.

Aping the tone of a preacher from Lewis' childhood church, the Assembly of God, Nick Tosches takes us through the saucy moments in the performer's life, from his childhood thievery to the IRS auctioning of his possessions due to tax fraud in the early 1980's. We already know of the vitriol in "the Killer's" (Lewis' high school nickname) blood and need not be reminded of it at every turn. As the pages ramble on, the quotes become fewer, the tales staler—and you're left feeling like you've read a very bad treatment for a screenplay. Let it burn you know where.

CRITICAL/ANALYTICAL COMMENTARY

Guterman, Jimmy. *Rockin' My Life Away: Listening to Jerry Lee Lewis.* Nashville: Rutledge Hill Press, 1991. 224 pages. Approximately 75 black-and-white photographs throughout. The Records: A Sensitive Collection. Index.

Author Jimmy Guterman minces the 1989 film *Great Balls of Fire!* and decries that the world should take a closer look at Lewis' music and a myopic view of his controversial personal life. Guterman investigates Lewis's roots and influences—Al Jolson, Jimmie Rodgers, and Hank Williams—and, more than other volumes, explores how Lewis assimilated the musical styles of contemporaries Presley, Perkins, Domino, and Berry. As for Lewis today, Guterman assures us the legend is capable of coming back and that, in his late 50's as of publication, he still looks better than Elvis did 30 years ago. A fan's care package with only a sliver of real critical meat, but it provides some understanding of the method behind the madness.

FANZINES AND FAN CLUBS

Jerry Lee Lewis International Fan Club. Wim de Boer, Jan Hendrikxstraat 22, NL-5684 XJ Best, Holland.

International fan club that publishes *Fire-Ball Mail*, a 20-page pamphlet with a glossy cover. The bimonthly publication includes black-and-white photographs, commemorative events, Lewis' concert itinerary, reprinted newspaper articles, essays about Lewis, notes on 1950's rock stars, occasional reviews, and more. The cost of membership is $15 in the U.S., Canada, Japan, and Australia; and £9 in the U.K.

LEWIS FRIENDS AND FAMILY

Lewis, Myra and Silver, Murray. *Great Balls of Fire: The Uncensored Story of Jerry Lee Lewis.* New York: Quill (division of William Morrow, Inc.), 1982. 320 pages. Three eight-page black-and-white photo inserts. Index.

Myra Lewis, Jerry Lee's cousin and third wife at the tender age of thirteen, receives coauthorship on this biography, which was adapted to the 1989 film of the same name. The book is executed in third person, not first, which leads one to believe that Myra took little part in the actual writing. While her voice is not present, her firsthand insights are highly valuable: We feel the confusion of her rape (by a neighbor *before* she was wed to Lewis) and her personal humiliation by the British press in the late 1950's at being a child bride. Fans of Jerry Lee will love the early tales of his rabble-rousing with cousin Jimmy Lee Swaggart. The book ends with the couple's divorce in 1970 and leaves you wanting more. Written with aplomb.

PICTORIALS

Cain, Robert. *Whole Lotta Shakin' Goin' On*. New York: The Dial Press, 1981. 148 pages. Over 100-black-and-white photographs scattered throughout. Discography.

A well-intentioned but jumbled tribute. The author never really made the decision over whether this is a bio, a pictorial, a collection of interviews, or a history of early rock and roll. Some chapters provide biography of Lewis with supportive quotes from friends, relatives, and Lewis himself; other chapters include random history of Sun records, a film career summary, and lengthy interviews with those who knew Lewis. The book falls short in nearly all of these areas, and doesn't address the performer's personal feelings about his controversial private life, e.g., his marriage to his thirteen-year-old cousin and the death of his three-year-old child, Steve Allen (yes, named after the comedian).

Palmer, Robert. *Jerry Lee Lewis Rocks!*. New York: Delilah Books, 1981. 128 pages. Approximately 100 black-and-white photos, covering every page.

About as subtle as a bang on a honky-tonk piano, *Jerry Lewis Rocks!* dares to be dangerous, with four-letter words in the chapter titles and interpretations of Lewis' lyrics that might make members of Motley Crue blush. The photos reveal the chaotic world of Lewis: performing with wavy blonde hair flopping in disarray; and smooching his child-bride. Palmer's claim that "Whole Lot of Shakin' Going On" is one of the most "profound" songs of all-time is laughable, especially since his case rests on the premise that the song is about sex in a barn. He even reprints the lyrics to that song incorrectly. Much shakin' about nothing.

GORDON LIGHTFOOT

CRITICAL/ANALYTICAL COMMENTARY

Fetherling, Douglas. *Some Day Soon: Essays on Canadian Songwriters*. Kingston, Ontario (Quarry Press), 1991. 176 pages. Approximately 20 black-and-white photographs throughout. Selected Discography.

Profiles of five internationally acclaimed artists, all of whom spawned from the northern end of the North American continent: Gordon Lightfoot, Leonard Cohen, Joni Mitchell, Robbie Robertson, and Neil Young. These composers were selected based on whether "conscious Canadianism" appeared in their work. Not all of the pages preach Canadian patriotic liturgy, however. Fetherling has remarkable skill in defining each artist's respective areas: the "soothing" tones of Lightfoot; the "dark romanticism" of Cohen; the folk artist as "diarist" in Mitchell; the "historical sensibility" and "religiosity" of Robertson; and the uncompromising "primitive" sound of Young. Masterfully written, though unfortunately not indexed.

WRITTEN WORKS

Lightfoot, Gordon (lyrics) and Delessert, Etienne (illustrations). *The Pony Man*. New York: Harper's Magazine Press, 1972. Unpaginated (approximately 32 pages). Approximately 20 original watercolors throughout.

Wonderful children's story from Lightfoot's song and beautifully illustrated by Etienne Delessert. The Pony Man takes the children on a magical journey "inside the moon" where the "streets are paved with chocolate" and "there's chewing gum for everyone." Sounds good to me! Fun for kids eight and younger and certainly worth a glance for Lightfoot's fans.

YOUNG ADULT

Gabiou, Alfrieda. *Gordon Lightfoot*. New York: Quick Fox (division of Music Sales Corporation), 1979. 128 pages. Approximately 50 black-and-white photographs throughout. Discography.

The singer from Orilla, Ontario, Canada had a sizeable following in North America in the

1970's, and this book is a strong reminder that Lightfoot was around in the 1960's as well—playing folk festivals and covering the classic Dylan ditties. At the height of his popularity, Lightfoot released some noteworthy (though musically redundant) albums (e.g., *Sundown*) and was onstage with Dylan for the Rolling Thunder Revue. This book, which shows Lightfoot to be a sensitive and dedicated artist, is objectively written, presenting both positive and critical assessments of his work. Optional for younger fans.

Lightfoot, Gordon (lyrics) and Delessert, Etienne (illustrations). *The Pony Man.*

See: Written Works.

OTHER TITLES OF INTEREST
Lightfoot, Gordon. *I Wish You Grand Spaces.* Boulder, CO: Blue Mountain, 1977.

LITTLE RICHARD

BIOGRAPHIES

White, Charles. Foreword by Paul McCartney. *The Life and Times of Little Richard: Quasar of Rock.* New York: Pocket Books (division of Simon & Schuster), 1984. 300 pages. Two 16-page black-and-white photo inserts. Testimonials. The Little Richard Chronicles: Recording Sessions; Discography/Filmography. Index.

An oral biography that is partially copyrighted in Little Richard's original name (Richard Wayne Penniman) and dedicated to the rocker's mom (Leva Mae Penniman). The anecdotes, told by Richard and associates (e.g., Bumps Blackwell, the man who recorded him at Specialty Records), are occasionally funny, predominately lewd, and dubiously truthful. How can one believe that back in the late 1950's Little Richard shared his buxom girlfriend with clean-cut Buddy Holly just moments prior to a concert? With Little Richard, one never knows for sure. Richard is outspoken about his homosexuality (which in his case seems more about self-love) and his forays into evangelism. Irresistibly smutty.

DISCOGRAPHIES, RECORDING GUIDES, AND COLLECTIBLES

Garodkin, John. *Little Richard: King of Rock and Roll.* Copenhagen, Denmark: 11975. 71 pages. Approximately 50 black-and-white photographs throughout.

A publication of the Danish Rock `N' Roll Society, this cheap vanity press book contains a chronology, a recording sessions listing, an alphabetical list, chart information, and more. The bulk of the book consists of the recording sessions, which are alphabetical by studio and only include (in chart form) dates for U.S., U.K., and Denmark. Shoddy.

OTHER TITLES OF INTEREST
Cohen, Nik. *WopBopaLooBopLopBamBoom.* London: Paladin, 1972.

LOVIN' SPOONFUL

TITLES OF INTEREST
Sebastian, John. Illustrated by Williams, Garth. *J.B.'s Harmonica.* New York: Harcourt Brace Jovanovich, 1993.
Children's story by the ex-member of Lovin' Spoonful. Booklist commented: "...a genial story with a satisfying conclusion that addresses an unusual part of growing up."

LYDIA LUNCH

(See also X)

Lunch, Lydia. Illustrated by Hoffman, Kristian. *Incriminating Evidence.* San Francisco: Last Gasp, 1992. 184 pages. Approximately 50 original pen-and-ink drawings throughout; approximately ten black-and-white photographs throughout.

With its cover image of a dismembered female hand holding a knife—and a naked female on the back pulling a trigger on a gun—the reader immediately knows we are not in for a Mickey Spillane-type mystery, as the title might suggest. Instead, what we have are Lunch's miscellaneous paranoid ramblings about sadomasochism, rape, violence, death, etc., many of which we must assume stem from her real-life experiences. In one harrowing passage, she hitches a ride with a psycopath who forces her at gunpoint to lick his car's tires. In an even worse scenario, "Daddy Dearest," she recounts—in all capital letters—how her father had raped and sodomized her as a little child. This work is an extreme case of catharsis as ragged pop culture; not for the weak-at-heart or the pure-of-soul.

LORETTA LYNN

AUTOBIOGRAPHY

Lynn, Loretta with Vecsey, George. *Loretta Lynn: Coal Miner's Daughter*. Chicago: Henry Regnery Company, 1976. 204 pages. One glossy 16-page black-and-white photo insert.

Born in Butcher Holler, Kentucky, Loretta Lynn was, in fact, a coal miner's daughter, as her classic song of that name has long told us. What people don't know—unless they happened to have read this book or seen the 1980 film adaptation, which garnered actress Sissy Spacek an Academy Award—is that she married before her fourteenth birthday to a fellow named Doo (short for Doolittle) and mothered four children by the time she was eighteen. The beautiful country legend tells of her slow rise from a life of squalor to her string of country hits (e.g., "Honky Tonk Woman"), friendships with other performers (Patsy Cline), and taste in music (a surprising fondness for soul music). A monster best seller, told with humor and candor.

DISCOGRAPHIES, RECORDING GUIDES, AND COLLECTIBLES

Zwisohn, Lawrence J. *Loretta Lynn's World of Music*. Los Angles: Palm Tree Library, 1980. 114 pages. Approximately 20 black-and-white photographs throughout. Index of Song Titles. Recording Log.

Vanity Press discography that opens with a dull interview with Teddy Wilburn (of The Wilburn Brothers), which is followed by a horrendous chronological rundown of Lynn's work. The text blindingly incorporates both narrative and lists, which makes it difficult for anyone to cull serious information. The list of Lynn's songwriting credits is somewhat stronger, although it barely goes up to 1975.

Only for those needing everything on the artist.

FANZINES AND FAN CLUBS

The Loretta Lynn Swap Shop. c/o Lenny Mattison/Andy Comer, 87 Hong Kong Road, Parish, NY 13131.

Established in 1991, this fan club offers members four newsletters per year, a color 8x10 photo, a membership certificate, a fact sheet, and an album discography. The 12-page stapled newsletter contains photocopies of black-and-white photos, news on Loretta Lynn (and other country stars), reprinted newspaper articles, collectibles, and more. Membership dues are $10 U.S.; $12 Canada; and $15 elsewhere. Payable by check or money order to Lenny Mattison or Andy Comer.

YOUNG ADULT

Krishef, Robert F. *Loretta Lynn*. Minneapolis, MN: Lerner Publications, 1978. 64 pages. Approximately 32 black-and-white photographs throughout. Recordings of Loretta Lynn. Index.

Part of Lerner's Country Music Library, this installment on Loretta Lynn traces her life from her poverty-ridden childhood (what country star *didn't* have a poverty-ridden childhood?) to her "Cinderella" story and phenomenal commercial success. (At the time this book came out she was MCA's biggest-selling artist.) An excellent, though dated, starting point for fans 10 or younger.

LYNYRD SKYNYRD

FANZINES AND FAN CLUBS

Lynyrd Skynyrd Fan Club. P.O. Box 120855, Nashville, TN 37212.

Fan club that offers members a t-shirt, an 8x10 glossy black-and-white photo, a chronology packet, a band itinerary, and merchandise listings. Publishes a glossy four-page newsletter, *The Rebel Report*, which contains black-and-white photographs and provides news on Lynyrd Skynyrd and related musicians. The cost of membership is $20 U.S.; $22 Canada;

and $25 everywhere else (payable in U.S. currency only).

MADONNA

BIOGRAPHIES

Andersen, Christopher. *Madonna Unauthorized.* New York: Simon & Schuster, 1991. 352 pages. One 32-page glossy black-and-white photo insert. Sources and Chapter Notes. Index.

Far more comprehensive than Thompson's unauthorized waste of time (see below), this book at least delivers the smut. Andersen tells in lurid detail about how Madonna first learned to insert a tampon; how she showed off her red panties during cheerleading practice; and how she lost her virginity at 15 to a fellow named Russell Long (ahem). Is any or all of this true? When it comes to Madonna, no one is likely to care. The photo spread is a direct complement, including her topless shot with pussycat on lap, a close-up of Sean Penn spitting out a wad, and bosomy stills from Madonna's various videos. Despite its failure to include the obligatory discography/videography/filmography, *Madonna Unauthorized* is fairly complete in terms of events à la *National Enquirer.* "...Andersen's is definitely the first choice"—*Booklist.*

Bego, Mark. *Madonna!.* New York: Pinnacle Books, 1985. 190 pages. One 16-page black-and-white photo insert. Madonna's Discography/Videography/Filmography.

"She's gorgeous! She's gutsy! She's great!..." There's even more hype on the front cover copy, but I suspect readers get the idea. Bego, a rock writer with plentiful credits, knew a hot commodity like Madonna circa 1985 would do well in mass market. An advantage he had over other writers is his October 1984 interview with the star. Other interviews (e.g., dance club owner Mark Kamins) crop up as well. The usual cheese.

King, Norman. *Madonna: The Book.* New York: William Morrow and Company, 1991. 256 pages. Two eight-page black-and-white photo inserts. Index.

Down-to-earth study of Madonna, which downplays her sex-crazed image and highlights lesser-known aspects of her life to at least attempt to give her a margin of complexity. Her mother died when she was slightly older than six and, when her father remarried, she had a difficult time adjusting to her new step-mother and siblings. In describing the race between *Playboy* and *Penthouse* to see which porno magazine would print Madonna's nude photos first, the author casts Madonna in the highly original role of victim. While not nearly as eye-opening as other treatments—and entirely lacking in discography, videography, and filmography—this is among the more level-headed Madonna bios. "Steamy life of Madonna, who comes off as worse and better than you might expect"—*Kirkus.*

Thompson, Douglas. *Madonna Revealed: The Unauthorized Biography.* New York: Birch Lane Press (Carol Publishing Group), 1991. 180 pages. Two glossy black-and-white photo inserts. Notes.

Choppy Madonna tale that attempts to be racy through its title, chapter headings (e.g., "Sexual Beginnings"), and back cover copy boasts ("gives all the clues necessary to inform Madonna watchers"). Not only does this atrociously written book fail to provide anything substantive about its star, it also shirks basic details such as her appearance in the film *A Certain Sacrifice.* Unrevealing, uninformed, and unexciting.

CRITICAL/ANALYTICAL COMMENTARY

Frank, Lisa and Smith, Paul. *Madonnarama: Essays on Sex and Popular Culture.* Pittsburgh, PA: Clei Press, 1993. 192 pages.

Amidst the media huff about Madonna's book *Sex* (see Written Works, below) comes this collection of pieces on Madonna's influence on American sexual politics. Many of the works are actually discursive bits of poetry, journal entries, and interviews. A piece by Cathy Che is typeset in blinding capital letters and lapses into a write-up on notable Asian women. Thomas Allen Harris's work "Phallic Momma Sell My Pussy for a Dolar"[sic] is a strange mind jaunt about "a black frekete queen." An idiosyncratic compendium and not nearly as entertaining as Sexton's work (see next page).

Schwichtenberg, Cathy (editor). *The Madonna Connection: Representational Politics, Subcultural Identities, and Cultural Theory.* Boulder, CO: Westview Press, Inc., 1993. 336 pages. Approximately 30 black-and-white photographs throughout. Index.

Collection of scholarly works on Madonna, subdivided into sections on her ability to break racial, sexual, feminist, and celebrity barriers. These thirteen scholarly works deal with her role as pop icon and how she has managed to relate to so many diverse groups—and cause such hatred among others. Opening the book is a fine piece from Laurie Schulze, Anne Barton White, and Jane D. Brown, in which the writers assail why so many people despise Madonna for appealing "to the lowest common denominator." Other contributions come from Cindy Patton, Ann Kaplan, David Tetzlaff, and Schwichtenberg herself. Stimulating, although it's doubtful fans would choose this over one of the color pictorials (see below) or even Sexton's slightly less stuffy work (see below). "These forays are highly entertaining..." —*London Times.*

Sexton, Adam (Editor). *Desperately Seeking Madonna: In Search of the Meaning of the World's Most Famous Woman.* New York: Dell Publishing (division of Bantam Doubleday Dell), 1993. 294 pages. 10 black-and-white photos and comic strips throughout. Madonna Videography, Discography, Filmography.

Where else can you find writings from the likes of Dave Marsh, Russell Baker, Vincent Canby, Sandra Bernhard, and Liz Smith all in one place—and deliberating on Madonna? In this chunky compendium, Sexton has collected a wealth of album and film reviews, satire, comic strips, lists (including a David Letterman "Top Ten List"), and general commentary that ranges from the supportive to the downright vicious. "...readers who view Madonna as a remarkable cultural icon will relish this collection's breadth and diversity of opinion"— *Booklist.*

DICTIONARIES AND ENCYCLOPEDIAS

Rettenmund, Matthew. *Encyclopedia Madonnica.* New York: St. Martin's Press, 1995. 216 pages. Approximately 150 black-and-white photographs throughout; one glossy eight-page color insert. Appendix 1: The Madonna U.S. Discography. Appendix 2: Videography. Appendix 3: Filmography. Appendix 4: Directography. Appendix 5: A Selected U.S. Bibliography.

Faltering A to Z covering "everything you ever wanted to know about Madonna," with entries on her songs and music, as well as larger and more frequent headings on random issues, subjects, and terms. There is no rhyme or reason to the criteria for entry inclusion, and thus trivial topics (e.g., "dates" and "love letters"), which could have been worked into larger headings (such as "lovers"), waste the reader's time entirely. Meanwhile, notable figures in her life, such as George Harrison (*Shanghai Surprise* producer) and Dick Clark (on whose show, "American Bandstand," Madonna appeared), are slighted. As for content, Madonna herself could have written more intelligent copy. (The opening for "lawsuits": "They increase exponentially with wealth.") The author should have checked out other music encyclopedias before embarking on this one.

FANZINES AND FAN CLUBS

Everybody: A Pro-Fan Madonna Zine. 3100 S. 208th St. #A-304, Seattle, WA 98198.

Started in 1991, this 30-page stapled packet features creative submissions from fans, photocopies of black-and-white photographs, drawings, cartoons, news, letters, lists, and more. Subscribers receive six issues per year, plus newsletters, a member card, and the opportunity to enter various contests. The cost of subscription is $20; each zine may be purchased separately for $3.

In Touch With Madonna. Rua da Sede, Lote 462-A Bairro da Fraternidade, 2685 Sao Joao da Talha, Portugal.

Portuguese Madonna fanzine founded in 1991. The bimonthly, 28-page stapled packet contains black-and-white photographs and articles predominately written in Portuguese. Also prints two-to-four page supplemental newsletters between issues. Write for pricing information.

Italian Madonna Fan Club. c/o C. Battisti, 74023, Grottaglie, Italy.

Founded in 1986, this Italian fan club organizes trips to see Madonna live, supports Madonna impersonator Ivana Cerdelli and the group Blue Eyes, and sponsors festivals of collectibles. The club publishes *Like a Virgin*, a 48-page booklet in Italian with a color cover and many glossy black-and-white photographs. In between issues, the club publishes *Madonna Press*, a four-page newsletter with reproductions of black-and-white photographs throughout and news updates. Write for cost of membership.

Like a Faggot!: For Fans of Madonna and Sodomy. Matthew Rettenmund, P.O. Box 149, Old Chelsea Station, New York, NY 10113-0149.

Begun in 1992, this sixteen-page, double-sided fanzine consists of collages of Madonna spanning every phase of her career. Emphasizes gay erotica, with stories written out in longhand and containing topics such as masturbation and oral sex. The cost is $6 per issue (published infrequently), payable by check or money order to Matthew Rettenmund.

Madonna Mania. Attn: Gavin Coe, 3 Beaumont Vale, Haverhill, Suffolk CB9 8QG England.

First started in 1991, this fanzine is currently published twice annually. The 32-page stapled packet includes photocopies of black-and-white photographs, letters, news and rumors, "The Girlie Show" (poetry), collectibles, reprinted interviews, bootlegs, books, occasional Madonna comics, and more. The cost of a two-year subscription (four issues) is £11.20 America and Canada; £9 U.K.; and £10 elsewhere in Europe. Payable in pounds sterling only.

MADONNAMANIA

Rosenzweig, Ilene. *The I Hate Madonna Handbook.* New York: St. Martin's Press, 1994. 112 pages. Approximately 50 black-and-white photographs and drawings throughout.

Whether you love Madonna, hate her or—if this is possible—have no opinion whatsoever about her—this book is still a trip. Full of wry commentary, gags, games, and profiles of people who knew Madonna at one time or another, this is probably the sort of humor one would eyeball in the store and giggle about with friends—but be too embarrassed to purchase. Rosenzweig presents hilarious icons to illustrate how Madonna used and abused her various contacts: whips (stepped on); dollar sign (cashed in on the victim's misfortune);

skidmarks (collision left career on skids); etc. The quizzes are lots of fun as well. "Question: What inspires Madonna to follow a strict vegetarian lifestyle? Answer: Belief that `vegetarians are paler.'"

Turner, Kay (editor). *I Dream of Madonna: Women's Dreams of the Goddess of Pop.* San Francisco: Collins Publishers (division of HarperCollins), 1993. 128 pages. 128 color and black-and-white drawings, art reproductions, photos, and graphics.

Kay Turner, a Ph.D. in folklore studies, has assembled 50 or so "dreams of Madonna" from women around the world ages 13-61. These show Madonna as a spiritual healer, a figure of feminine power (policewoman), a comforting friend and, let's not forget, sexual liberator (lesbian lover). The art and designs surrounding the dream tales are first-rate (many were actually done by the author), and some of the passages do have a resoundingly sensual feel. Madonna swooners will pounce on it, though probably for reasons quite different from the psychoanalytical ones the editor has in mind. "Lustily conceived like a Dada art object..." —*Publishers Weekly.*

PICTORIALS

Cahill, Marie. *Madonna.* London: Omnibus Press (division of Book Sales Limited), 1991. 96 pages. Approximately 150 color and black-and-white photographs, covering every page. Index. Discography. Comes with a pull-out poster.

Madonna, again doing her thing for the camera, delivers few surprises. Chapters (if you can call them such) are divided by Madonna's albums, films, and tours. Only long-term fans will be able to sort through the same slutty shots for the millionth time. The one glimmer of genuine sexiness is in the section on the film *Dick Tracy* which, admit it or not, will have men looking twice.

Gulick, Rebecca. *Madonna: Portrait of a Material Girl.* Philadelphia: Courage Press (imprint of Running Press), 1993. 72 pages. Approximately 80 color and black-and-white photographs throughout. Discography, Films, Tours, Plays, Books. Index.

Madonna in the 1990's looks very much as she did in the 1980's, although now she has several more films and a major stage role (*Speed the Plow*) to her credit (or discredit, as the case may be). Madonna sucks lollipop. Madonna shows us her jewelry. Madonna flaunts her cleavage. Next!

James, David. *Madonna: Her Complete Story: An Unauthorized Biography*. Lincolnwood: Publications International Limited, 1991. 80 pages. 75 color photographs covering every page.

Here's a novel idea: How about an unauthorized biography of Madonna with more space devoted to photos than information? The pictures are colorful and glitzy, but nothing we haven't seen a million times before. The subject's hair is done in countless ways throughout the book; if you own a ladies salon and need a book full of head samples, this one is for you.

Lagerfeld, Karl. *Madonna, Superstar: Photographs*. New York: W.W. Norton, 1988. 96 pages. Approximately 100 color and black-and-white photographs, covering every page. Discography.

Chronological, pint-sized photo book with some text from Lagerfeld. See Madonna sit yoga-style; see Madonna writhe; see Madonna strut; see Madonna tease; see Madonna flex. Don't buy it: You've seen it all before.

McKenzie, Michael. *Madonna: The Early Days: 65 Classic Photographs of Madonna and Friends*. No city: Worldwide Televideo Enterprises, 1993. 96 pages. Approximately 65 color tinted black-and-white photographs throughout.

This book is completely mistitled: The photos, outside of three previously seen shots (one of which seems to be from the resurfaced film *A Certain Sacrifice*), are *not* "early" by any sense of the word. Where is her high school photo? Where are pictures of her earliest performances? Almost all of the other books listed herein contain more photos of her pre-stardom days. The publishers attempt to red herring the shortcomings by covering over the pictures with bluish tints and by filling the blank spaces with rancid graphic art. Blech.

No author. *Madonna*. New York: New American Library, 1985. Unpaginated (approximately 32 pages). Approximately 40 color and 25 black-and-white photographs, covering very page.

Ridiculous magazine that pretends to have the goods on Madonna, this is really a lame excuse to hype the star's "secret movie," *A Certain Sacrifice*, in which she appeared at the age of 19. The photos are way out-of-focus, and too much attention is paid to other Live Aid acts in the better part of the final pages. Immaterial.

No author. Foreword by Madonna. *Madonna: The Girlie Show*. No city: Callaway Editions, Inc., 1994. Unpaginated (approximately 48 pages). Approximately 40 full-page or two-page color photographs, covering every page. Comes with a three-song CD.

Oversized document of Madonna's 1993 world tour. This is much of what you'd expect: Madonna in costume, Madonna partially out of costume, Madonna with no costume. Why buy an oversized, costly hardcover girlie show book when it's a quarter in Times Square for the real thing?

Randall, Lee. *The Madonna Scrapbook*. New York: Carol Publishing Group, 1992. 226 pages. Over four hundred black-and-white photographs throughout; two eight-page glossy color inserts.

One of the better Madonna pictorials, this one opting more toward paraphernalia and memorabilia items (dolls, t-shirts, watches, etc.). The color inserts don't do justice to the Madonna mystique, mostly consisting of her face on the covers of major magazines; while several of the black-and-white photos are rare and capture Madonna in unusual settings (e.g., discos), too many pages are full of text without any illustrative matter. The first color insert contains a handful of never-before-published photos of Madonna's first live performance in New York City, in 1980; neither the exact date nor the club is identified in any of these. If you're into Madonna kitsch, you'll probably need this scrapbook to call your own.

Voller, Debbi. *Madonna: The Illustrated Biography*. London: Omnibus (division of Book Sales Limited), 1990. 104 pages. Approximately 125 color and black-and-white illustrations. Complete Madonna U.K. Discography.

Lots of flash and only a touch of trash in this pictorial, which was no doubt intended for young fans. The photos are the focus here, and they're so-so. The text itself is plausible and not excessively pandering; in fact, only Madonna's *negative* notices for her performance in the play *Speed the Plow* are addressed. The U.K.-only Discography won't be of much help to U.S. collectors or fans. Average.

Voller, Debbi. *Madonna: The Style Book.* London: Omnibus Press (division of Book Sales Limited), 1992. 96 pages. Approximately 125 color and black-and-white photographs, covering every page.

Learn the secrets of what makes this sex goddess tick: How does she handle her image? How does she put on make-up? Why does she dress the way she does? You don't need the answers to any of the questions, but this book provides them for you anyway, with plenty of full-page Madonna shots and images of her influences (Monroe, Garbo, Dietrich, etc.). And on the lips? "Coat lips with foundatoion[sic] and line with a pencil that is the same shade as your lipstick; just lining the center bottom lip and top arch will do." Read further, and you too can make a million overnight!

QUIZBOOKS AND QUOTEBOOKS

St. Michael, Mick *Madonna: In Her Own Words.* London: Omnibus Press (division of Book Sales Limited), 1990. 96 pages. Approximately 100 black-and-white photographs, covering every page.

There's something to offend just about everyone's tastes in this trivial quote/photo book. Then again, this is par for the course for Madonna, who was quoted as saying, "Crucifixes are sexy because there's a naked man on them." Quotes by and about Madonna are divided into chapters called "Growing Up," "Making It," "Men," "Music," "Stage," "Movies," etc., plus two chapters including her remarks on other celebrities and what they had to say about her (both of which could at some point be expanded to fill a ten-volume set). The editors truly goofed by not naming a chapter "sex," which is really the point of it all. For diehards.

WRITTEN WORKS

Madonna. *Sex.* New York: Warner Books, 1992. Unpaginated (approximately 192 pages). Approximately 200 color and black-and-white,

full-page photographs, covering every page. Comes with a CD.

Wrapped in a shiny silver bag as if it contained food for an Apollo mission, Madonna's best seller was evidently inspired (in name only) by Mae West's play. The oversized book is bound with a metal spine and silver metallic covers in what seems to be an effort to simulate a metal bondage fantasy. Next to Madonna's throwaway poetry ("I Like My Pussy") are photographs of Madonna masturbating, receiving and/or giving oral pleasure, and dressing in leather and S&M outfits. Unarguably, Madonna has a sexy figure, but her attempts at being risqué are sleazy, forced, and overtly posed. In other words, more dare than truth, more trash than camp. Given all the wrappers this package comes with, the one glaring omission is one containing a condom. Rumors have it that approximately half of the books purchased were returned to stores not because of content but because buyers complained the bindings were weak and fell apart.

YOUNG ADULT

Claro, Nicole. Introduction by Leeza Gibbons. *Madonna.* New York: Chelsea House Publishers, 1994. 128 pages. Approximately 50 black-and-white photographs throughout. Appendix: Filmography; Discography; Home Videos. Further Reading. Index.

Part of Chelsea House's "Pop Culture Legends" series, which strives to summarize the artist's life and career and at the same time place him or her into the context of society as a whole. The writing is of an unusually high quality, but not so dense that young readers won't be able to follow it. Issues such as Madonna's sexual proclivities (her alleged lesbian affair with comedienne Sandra Bernhard) are treated with finesse and taste. Recommended for fans in the 8-12-year-old range.

Greenberg, Keith Elliot. *Madonna.* Minneapolis: Lerner Publications Company, 1986. 40 pages. A dozen color and black-and-white illustrations throughout. Glossy paper stock.

Nicely done biography of Madonna for the young fan. Controversies such as the suggestive content of the song and video "Like a Virgin" are smoothly treated and balanced with more wholesome Madonna statements— crosses, floppy bow-ties, her love of authors such as William Faulkner and Ernest Hemingway, etc. "Fans will appreciate...the many glossy full-color and black-and-white photographs..."—*Booklist*.

OTHER TITLES OF INTEREST

Bego, Mark. *Madonna: Blonde Ambition*. New York: Crown, 1992.

Black, Susan. *Madonna: Live!* London: Omnibus Press (division of Book Sales Limited), 1987.

Guralnick, Rebecca. *Madonna*. No city: Courage, 1993.

Kamin, Philip. *Madonna*. Milwaukee, WI: Hal Leonard, 1985.

Kelleher, Ed and Vidal, Hariette. *Madonna*. No city: Dorchester, 1987.

Matthews, Gordon. *Madonna*. New York: Simon & Schuster, 1985.

School Library Journal *commented: "...brief but not entirely superficial..."*

McKenzie, David. *Madonna: Lucky Star*. New York: Contemporary, 1985.

Riley, Tim. *Madonna Illustrated: Madonna in the 90's*. New York: Hyperion, 1992.

Starbooks, Sharon. *Madonna, Spirit and Flesh*. New York: NAL, 1985.

YNGWIE MALMSTEEN

FANZINES AND FAN CLUBS

Malmsteen's Militia. P.O. Box 5032, Tallahassee, FL 32301.

Fan club for Malmsteen music lovers that delivers to members: two black-and-white 8x10 photos; a letter from Yngwie himself; an imprinted guitar pick; stickers; and materials comprising a biography, discography, and videography. Members can also receive the eight-page quarterly newsletter *Dragon's Fire*, which contains quotes from and interviews with Malmsteen, tour and CD updates, contest information, Internet chat, and more. The cost of membership is $15 in the U.S. and $20 elsewhere. Yngwie rulz!

THE MAMAS AND THE PAPAS

AUTOBIOGRAPHIES

Phillips, John with Jerome, Jim. *Papa John: An Autobiography*. New York: Doubleday & Company, 1986. 444 pages. One 32-page black-and-white photo insert. Index.

The famous Papa who was nailed by the FBI for drug possession and trafficking bares his soul in this heavily detailed autobiography. Phillips began as a folkie in the early 1960's, but by 1967 he was tripping among the best of them and helping to create a timeless sound and harmony rivalled only by The Beatles and The Byrds. As a result of (or despite) a perpetual high on acid and speed, Phillips also wrote many of The Mamas and the Papas classic songs—and helped conceive the Monterey Pop Festival. Phillips tells all about his open relationship with pop sex goddess Michelle Phillips and his plagued marriage to Gen Waite, which resulted in fires, car accidents, and all-out clashes with buddy Mick Jagger. A searing set-the-record-straight book in which "glamor is tempered with grimness"—*Library Journal*.

Phillips, Michelle. *California Dreamin': The True Story of the Mamas and the Papas*. New York: Warner, 1986. 178 pages. One glossy 16-page black-and-white photo insert.

The fetching ex-Mama delivers her story of the 1960's, which makes for a more upbeat alternative to her ex-husband's work (see above). Phillips quickly points out how young, naïve, and carefree she was when she first met John Phillips, who was married at the time with two children. John divorced his first wife to marry Michelle, but the two never lived a married couple's life; their relationship was full of infidelities (including Michelle's tryst with another man the day President Kennedy was shot) and tensions that rocked the group itself. According to Michelle, she had the hots for Denny (Doherty), who was lusted after by Cass (Elliott), who was seduced by...no one. "...for her [Phillips], it was a beautiful time of good vibrations"—*Library Journal*.

MANFRED MANN

Russo, Greg. *Mannerisms: The Five Phases of Manfred Mann*. Floral Park, NY: Crossfire Publications, 1995. 278 pages. Approximately 150 black-and-white photographs of album covers. Discography. Sessionography.

Few bands have ever undergone as many personnel changes as the durable Manfred Mann. To some people's surprise, there really *is* a Manfred Mann in the group, who was actually born Manfred Lefcowitz in South Africa. With a cast of musicians led by vocalist Paul Jones—Mann, Tony Roberts (not the actor), Mike Vickers, Mike McGuinness, and Mike Hugg—the group recorded one of the all-time great songs of leering male lust, "Do Wah Diddy." With members coming and going (bassist Jack Bruce was in for a spell before moving on to Cream; he was replaced for a few years by artist and Beatles' buddy Klaus Voorman) and forming their own groups (Rogers went solo, while McGuinness established McGuinness Flint), the group restructured as The Manfred Mann's Earth Band and struck big with their version of Springsteen's "Blinded by the Light." This book, named after Mann's early album (a pun on *The Five Faces of Manfred Mann*), is an uneven, if generous, mix of biography and discography.

MARILLION

TITLES OF INTEREST
Clerk, Carol. *Marillion: In Words and Pictures*. London: Omnibus Press (division of Book Sales Limited, 1985.

MARKY MARK (AND THE FUNKY BUNCH)

BIOGRAPHIES

Reisfeld, Randi. *Marky Mark and the Funky Bunch*. New York: Avon Books, 1992. 152 pages.

Eighty black-and-white photographs. Facts on File (personal data). Discography/Videography.

Did you know Marky Mark was in Nynuk, the first formation of New Kids on the Block with his brother, Donnie Wahlberg? Apparently, Mark didn't like the syrupy ballad direction the group was taking and went out on his own to find rap music. "The baby of the family" (as one chapter refers to him) is a baby in more than one sense: You just wish somebody's mother would come along and tell him to adjust his underwear. This book, full of beefcake photos of Mark's crotch-grabbing, hammy sneers, and conceited displays of his biceps, is not likely to please parents of young fans and is a complete turn-off for rap-haters. Hey, at least Jim Morrison wore leather.

WRITTEN WORKS

Mark, Marky and Goldsmith, Lynn. *Marky Mark*. New York: HarperCollins, 1992. Unpaginated (approximately 144 pages). Approximately 150 color and black-and-white illustrations, covering every page.

Classless, obnoxious, and utterly revolting collection of color shots and quotes from the king of self-love himself. Mark has the gumption to dedicate the book to his dick, which, thankfully, we never see. However, his multi-colored boxers are everywhere and—hold your gagging until this review is over—so are his barren chest (with an arrow pointing to a third nipple!), his tattoo, and his flying spit as he brushes his teeth. Sexy, half-naked female models and groupies fawn over him—and hopefully were heavily paid. Enough said.

OTHER TITLES OF INTEREST
Danwick, Chad. *Marky Mark: Who's Hot!*. New York: Dell, 1992.

BOB MARLEY (AND THE WAILERS)

BIOGRAPHIES

Davis, Stephen. *Bob Marley*. Garden City, NY: Doubleday & Company, Inc., 1985. 276 pages. Two eight-page glossy photo inserts. Bibliography. Index.

Stephen Davis, whose other works include *Reggae Bloodlines* and *Hammer of the Gods* (see

Led Zeppelin, Biographies), tackles the legend of Bob Marley with believable authority. From the parish of St. Ann's in Jamaica to The Wailers' first recording test (that very nearly went bust) to Marley's untimely death due to cancer, Davis fills this biography with crisp insights into the artist's genius and outlook. White's book (see below) contains far greater details of Jamaican history and reggae culture; this book is a worthwhile alternative for those who want a more digestible read.

White, Timothy. *Catch a Fire: The Life of Bob Marley*. New York: Holt, Rinehart and Winston, 1983. 380 pages. Three eight-page black-and-white photo inserts. Discography. Bibliography. Index.

Author Timothy White draws on his extensive interviews with Bob Marley, his family, fellow musicians, and record industry personnel for this penetrating and revealing investigation into the artist's life and into the culture of reggae. Much of the book consists of White's in-depth telling of the socio-economic and political history of Jamaica, plus his fascinating account of the spiritual and folkloric traditions that shaped Marley's vision. Highly recommended for fans who dig the reggae beat, but do not fully understand the complexities of Marley's powerful message. Revised in 1989.

GENERAL REFERENCE

No author. *Bibliography: Bob Marley*. Kingston, Jamaica: National Library of Jamaica, 1985. 24 pages.

Simple informational lists citing books and articles on Jamaica's most lauded performer. Assembled by the National Library of Jamaica as part of their "Occasional Bibliography" series, this pamphlet is essential for those doing Marley research. Of special relevance are works cited from Kingston's *Daily Gleaner*.

MARLEY FRIENDS AND FAMILY

Taylor, Don. *Marley and Me*. New York Barricade Books, 1995. 256 pages. Two glossy black-and-white photo inserts. Selected Discography.

Marley's manager, Jamaican Don Taylor, is a powerful and enigmatic figure in world music. The man who also worked with legends such as Marvin Gaye, Sam Cooke, and Martha

Reeves tells all about his often discordant relationship with Marley. According to Taylor, the performer was a violent and hypocritical man—a paranoid, gun-toting, wifebeating philanderer on one hand and a serious musician committed to human rights issues on the other. Taylor is no less blunt when reporting Marley's chaotic financial and contractual matters or the ugly battles that ensued over his estate. Clearly, this is only one side of the story—and one that's worth listening to, with the proviso that Marley isn't around to voice his.

PICTORIALS

Boot, Adrian and Salewicz, Chris. Introduction by Rita Marley. *Bob Marley: Songs of Freedom*. London: Bloomsbury Publishing, Inc., 1995. 288 pages. Approximately 400 color and black-and-white illustrations, covering every page. Bibliography. Index.

Exciting photo tribute to Marley, his heritage, The Wailers and reggae in general. With cooperation from Executive Editor Rita Marley, Bob's widow, the book takes the reader on a delightful journey through the sights and peoples of Jamaica—with breezy observations for tourists and Jamaicans alike—followed by an eyeful of illustrative material on the music scene, The Wailers (several pages on Peter Tosh), Marley and family, and much more. Photographs by author Adrian Boot, Dennis Morris, Vicky Fox, Arthur Gorson, Stephanie Nash, and others deserve lavish praise. "Visually it's a definitive volume for collectors..."—*People*.

Bronson, Marsha. *Bob Marley*. Watford, Herts (England): Exley Publications, 1993. 64 pages. Approximately 60 color and black-and-white illustrations, covering every page. Important Dates. Glossary. Index.

Slightly more than just a promotional book, *Bob Marley* also covers the social, political, and religious upheavals taking place in Jamaica in the 1960's and 70's, as well as the history and background of reggae. Marsha Bronson provides an easy-to-follow description of the Rastafari religion, but comes up very shy in terms of Marley's musical contributions. All in all, this installment in Exley Publications' "World's Greatest Composers" series is a handy reference for students of reggae and its most revered leader.

Lazell, Barry. *Marley: 1945-1991*. London: Hamlyn (Reed Consumer Group), 1994. 80 pages. Over 1,100 color and black-and-white photographs throughout. Selective Discography.

Slender photo book on Marley that is probably not worthwhile for those who own Boot's work (see above). For those who don't, the raw elements are all here, neatly presented, from Marley's home town of Trench Town, Jamaica; to the foundation of The Wailers; to a chapter on jamming; to violence; and more. Photographs by the likes of Annie Leibovitz makes this a cut-above other quickie pictorials.

Morris, Dennis. *Bob Marley: Rebel with a Cause*. London: Epoch Productions, Limited, 1986. Unpaginated (approximately 48 pages). Approximately 40 color and black-and-white photographs, covering every page.

Oversized photo book that contains full-page color and black-and-white photos of Marley, all accentuating his face and highly emotional expressions. The text consists of quotes from Marley, as well as traces of lyrics to a few songs. Recommended only for those who truly worship Marley's physical image.

Talamon, Bruce W. (photos) and Steffens, Roger (text). Foreword by Timothy White. *Bob Marley: Spirit Dancer*. New York: W.W. Norton & Company, 1994. 128 pages. Approximately 80 glossy full-page black-and-white photographs throughout.

Talamon was fortunate to have had full photographic access to Marley, and took advantage of the opportunity on several occasions during the years 1978-80. Following lengthy essays by Marley biographer White (see Biographies, above) and Steffens, we see Talamon's superb black-and-white work: He captures the nuances and deep spirituality expressed through Marley's stage movements. Marley looks pensively off into space in a few shots and kicks up a soccer ball in a couple of others. A fitting tribute to a consummate artist. "At its core are the exceptional black and white pictures..."—*People*.

Welch, Chris. *Bob Marley*. Miami, FL: MBS, 1996. 120 pages. Approximately 75 color and black-and-white photographs throughout. Appendix 1. Appendix 2. Discography. Index.

Promotional CD-format book designed with attractive Jamaican borders on every page. The package contains quite a bit considering the low dollar value: solid history of reggae and Marley's influences; details on the legendary recordings; a chapter on the assassination attempt on his life; and a wealth of reference material in the back (including U.S. and U.K. data). The photos are rare, to boot. This nicely designed and illustrated book is priced just right at $7.99.

Whitney, Malika Lee and Hussey, Vermott. Foreword by Rita Marley. *Bob Marley: Reggae King of the World*. San Francisco: Pomegranate Artbooks, 1994. 208 pages. Approximately 300 color and black-and-white photographs, covering every page.

With over vibrant 300 photos, a foreword by Marley's widow, and interviews with key insiders, where can a book on Bob Marley by Jamaican reggae authorities go wrong? This one does—and in too many ways to list them all. Precious details of Marley's life are completely ignored or neglected, including the 1976 assassination attempt on his life (one measly paragraph) and his losing seven-month battle against cancer. A discography is buried somewhere in the middle, as are valuable tour maps and album capsules. No way mon. First published in 1984 by New American Library.

QUIZBOOKS AND QUOTEBOOKS

McCann, Ian. *Bob Marley: In His Own Words*. London: Omnibus Press (division of Book Sales Limited), 1993. 96 pages. Approximately 100 black-and-white photographs, covering every page.

Marley's philosophy, compacted down to paragraph-length quotes (which is longer than average for an Omnibus book). Marley's reflections on his early days, reggae, music, politics, Rasta, business, women, stardom, illness, etc. are all here for posterity. Author Ian McCann is on target when he writes that the "thrust of Marley's thought remains piercing." The man on violence: "Me don't want fight no guy with guns. Me musn't fight for my rights, my rights come to me...." This quotebook packs a lot in a tight space; its most obvious shortcoming, however, is in the skimpy section on women. An excellent starting point for those just learning about Marley's vision.

YOUNG ADULT

May, Chris. Illustrated by Parkin, Trevor. *Bob Marley*. London: Hamish Hamilton, 1985. 60 pages. Approximately 40 pen-and-ink drawings throughout.

Chris May, former editor of *Black Music* magazine, has written a respectable biography of Marley for young fans. May does an admirable job bringing readers directly into the story so they can immediately relate to events such as the Marley family's move from Rhoden Hall to Kingston. Parkin's line drawings are precise and feature images of Jamaican streets, as well as calamitous moments, such as Marley's collapse while on tour. "Consider buying as a starter volume..."—*School Library Journal*.

OTHER TITLES OF INTEREST
Goldman, Vivien. *Bob Marley: Soul Rebel: Natural Mystic*. New York: St. Martin's, 1981.
Green, Jonathon. *Bob Marley & the Wailers*. No city: Wise, 1977.

MARTHA REEVES AND THE VANDELLAS

AUTOBIOGRAPHY

Reeves, Martha and Bego, Mark. *Dancing in the Street: Confessions of a Motown Diva*. New York: Hyperion, 1994. 190 pages. Two glossy eight-page black-and-white photo inserts. Discography. Index.

Moving with her family from Alabama to Detroit, Michigan (where else?), Martha Reeves rose from being a gullible high school graduate and musical contest singer to the A&R secretary at Motown (an amusing fluke landing), and then backup singer to Marvin Gaye. Nurtured by Berry Gordy, she and the other Vandellas (whose personnel changed on a few occasions) became national hitmakers rivaled only by The Supremes. Enlightening on several accounts, particularly in reference to the group's evolution and interaction among the various Motown singing groups of the early 1960's. Reeves, who looks marvelous these days, "...emerges as a stoic and likable survivor"—*Publishers Weekly*.

RICHARD MARX

PICTORIALS

No author. *Richard Marx: In Person*. Port Chester, NY: Cherry Lane, 1990. Unpaginated (approximately 32 pages). Approximately 40 color and black-and-white photographs, covering every page. Comes with a full-color poster.

"The ultimate fan book" contains photos, feature articles, and the complete lyrics to Marx's *Repeat Offender* album. A glossy pamphlet that milks a few bucks out of fans.

JOHN MAYALL (JOHN MAYALL'S BLUESBREAKERS)

(See also Clapton, Eric)

TITLES OF INTEREST
Newman, Richard. *John Mayall: Bluesbreaker*. Chessington, Surrey (England): Castle Communications, 1995.

CURTIS MAYFIELD

See Impressions, The.

MICHAEL (MIKE) MCCARTNEY

(See also McCartney, Paul)

WRITTEN WORKS

McCartney, Mike. *The Macs: Mike McCartney's Family Album*. New York: Delilah Communications (Putnam), 1981. Unpaginated (approximately 180). Approximately 150 black-and-white photographs throughout.

A member of the Liverpool band Scaffold—and to his misfortune, primarily known in the U.S. as the younger brother of Paul McCartney—Mike McCartney (in the 1960's known as Mike McGear) produced this nostalgic photographic history of his family, The Beatles' rise, and his own musical career. McCartney has many enticing stories to tell about his mother (who died when he was a child), father (who enjoyed sticking his tongue out in public), more famous older brother (who always got the girls and the gold records), and even other musicians, such as Jimi Hendrix (who contributed lead guitar to a McGear album), but his writing here is hamfisted. McCartney's never-before-seen photos (several of which, we must assume, he took himself) are the book's focal point and saving grace.

McCartney, Mike. Introduction by Willy Russell. *Mike McCartney's Merseyside*. Manchester, England: Cornerhouse Publications, 1992. 72 pages. Approximately 72 color and black-and-white photographs, covering every page.

A photo tribute—also known as *MMM...*—to the proud docking port of Liverpool by the ex-member of Scaffold. There are exquisite shots of the city from a distance through odd angles, as well as steeples, buses, gardens, and various friendly faces. Even Paul McCartney's musician, Hamish Stuart, turns up with a smile. Classy—and very clean.

McCartney, Michael. *Remember: The Recollections and Photographs of Michael McCartney*. London: Merehurst Limited, 1992. 144 pages. Approximately 125 glossy black-and-white and 10 color photographs, covering every page.

To some degree, a continuation of McCartney's earlier work (see above), this vivid collection still contains a few early family pictures, but mainly the focus is on the youthful Beatles. What's most intriguing is the sheer volume of never-before-seen photographs and the amount of attention Michael devoted to his famous brother. (When The Beatles first appeared on British television, Michael actually photographed the tube's screen.) This one reads a thousand times better than Michael's previous book; one memorable caption describes Lennon and McCartney's synergistic relationship as they composed "I Saw Her Standing There" with guitars in hand. Michael McCartney's recurring images of Paul's head (envisioned as wallpaper!) foreshadow the *With the Beatles* (*Meet the Beatles*, U.S.) album cover. Fab.

OTHER TITLES OF INTEREST
McCartney, Mike. Foreword by David Puttnam. *Mike Mac's White and Blacks*. New York: Viking Penguin, 1987.
Publishers Weekly *commented: "As Puttnam observes, these snapshots make this book `a very special time machine.'"*

PAUL MCCARTNEY (AND WINGS)

(See also Beatles, The; McCartney, Mike)

BIOGRAPHIES

Benson, Ross. *Paul McCartney: Behind the Myth*. London: Victor Gollancz Limited, 1993. 290 pages. Eight glossy two-page black-and-white photo inserts. Bibliography. Index.

Benson had some access to McCartney, but not nearly enough to warrant a full-fledged biography. He grants valuable book space to tabloid biographers Peter Brown and Albert Goldman, when he should have been seeking out musicians, such as Wings guitarist Laurence Juber (who isn't even mentioned) and Apple discovery, singer Mary Hopkin, for firsthand source material. Although Benson doesn't shred the McCartney myth to pieces, he doesn't analyze it with any depth either. We are also left without any sense of McCartney's activities in human issues, ranging from rain forests to animal rights.

Flippo, Chet. *Yesterday: The Unauthorized Biography of Paul McCartney*. New York: Doubleday (division of Bantam Doubleday Dell), 1988. 400 pages. One glossy 16-page black-and-white photo insert. Discography. Index of Names.

Essentially a biography of The Beatles, with the usual disappointing encapsulation of McCartney's solo career and a Beatles tour date agenda sandwiched in the middle. Why omit the solo tours when it's supposedly a book on McCartney himself? You'll be hard-pressed, however, to find another biography mentioning Paul's circumcision or one that suggests that George Harrison was The Beatles' most proficient guitarist. The author's writing is occasionally foppy, and often he phrases sentences as if he was a participant in the events being reported (which he obviously wasn't). Fair.

Giuliano, Geoffrey. Introduction by Denny Laine. *Blackbird: The Life and Times of Paul McCartney*. New York: Dutton (division of New American Library), 1991. One glossy 16-page black-and-white photo insert. Afterword by Steve Holly. Paul McCartney Family Tree. Diary of Events. An Interview with Paul McCartney. A Conversation with Denny Laine. Band History. Discographies. Bibliography. Index.

Giuliano should have titled this work *Black Bull*; his McCartney is more of a procreating Zeus than a harmless fowl. According to Giuliano, there are more than a few little German Paulies out there. But what's the author's fixation on the "dark" motif anyway? (See Giuliano's *Dark Horse*, Harrison, George: Biographies.) The author brown-noses his connections with two members of Wings (Laine wrote the foreword and drummer Steve Holly contributed the afterword), and pathetically swoons over Laine's voluptuous ex-wife, Jo Jo. Once again, Yoko is held responsible for all of the evils in the world. A "...vapid gusher..."—*Kirkus*.

Salewicz, Chris. *McCartney: The Definitive Biography*. New York: St. Martin's Press, 1986. 264 pages. Four eight-page glossy black-and-white photo inserts. Bibliography. Index.

Paul McCartney was only 14 when his mother died from breast cancer, a little-known fact that is brought to the forefront of Salewicz's biography. The author suggests that McCartney's loss contributed to the bond he shared with John Lennon (whose mother died one year later). While this is an original angle—and Salewicz has a talent for describing the McCartney persona (clean-cut, wholesome, charming, perfectionist, etc.)—he tries too hard to boost McCartney by deflating the erstwhile Lennon. The early years contain some good details but omit a few important ones, such as the fact that McCartney was turned down as a choir boy. "The book closes with skimpy coverage of Paul's post-Beatles career"—*Library Journal*.

Tremlett, George. *The Paul McCartney Story*. London: Futura Publications, 1975. 192 pages. One glossy 16-page photo insert. Appendix: The Paul McCartney Chronology.

Tremlett's Paul McCartney is a cautious, shrewd musician/businessman who knows exactly what he wants and sticks to it. As his case in point, Tremlett cites McCartney's marriage to Linda, which even at the time of this book's publication in 1975 was the longest lasting of all Beatle marriages. The troubling aspect of this dated work is that the author accepts almost all previous hype written about The Beatles, and adds virtually nothing to the scholarship on McCartney's development as a composer. Nearly a third of the book consists of a day-by-day chronology, which only goes up to the end of 1974.

DISCOGRAPHIES, RECORDING GUIDES, AND COLLECTIBLES

Gross, Edward. *Paul McCartney: 20 Years on His Own*. Las Vegas: Pioneer Books, Inc., 1990. 112 pages. Approximately 50 black-and-white photographs. The McCartney Bootlegs by Mark Wallgreen[sic].

An album-by-album retrospective of McCartney's solo career, beginning with *McCartney* in 1970 and ending with *Flowers in the Dirt* in 1989. The author presents a good case for judging McCartney's solo work based on its own merits and not in comparison with Beatles material. However, he reflects excessively on what the other ex-Beatles were doing at the time of each McCartney release, which seems contrary to this goal. "Mark Wallgreen" is credited for the reviews in the bootleg section, but this must be an error. Could it be Mark *Wallgren*, author of *The Beatles on Record*?

FANZINES AND FAN CLUBS

Club Sandwich. P.O. Box 110, Westcliff, Essex SS0 8NW England.

Fan club devoted exclusively to the Mighty Mac (and Mrs. Mac) that provides members with a McCartney chronology packet, band biographies, glossy color and black-and-white photographs, postcards of Linda McCartney's photographs, color posters, and lots of other goodies. Also offers merchandising such as calendars, t-shirts, music folios, books, sweatshirts, and more. The club publishes a fanzine that is copyright by MPL Communications and is written and edited by Mark Lewisohn. The 16-page, oversized foldover magazine contains rare color and black-and-white photographs, updates on McCartney's recordings and live performances, books, revisitations of old McCartney events, books, Linda's recipes, Write Away (question and answer), and many other tidbits. Write for pricing information.

FILM

No author. *Paul McCartney's Give My Regards to Broad Street*. London: Pavilion Books, Limited, 1984. 128 pages. Over 200 color and black-and-white photographs, covering every page.

The catalog for McCartney's 1984 flop film with stills, outtakes, song lyrics (Beatles, Wings, and McCartney solo), and scene summaries. This print companion does nothing to assist the film's shortcomings. Co-stars Bryan Brown, Sir Ralph Richardson, and Tracey Ullman look almost as bewildered about what's going on as Paul and Linda. Only Ringo Starr's loveable face and good cheer prevent this from being as wretched as Bee Gees' book tributes following the *Sgt. Pepper's Lonely Hearts Club Band* film. No more movies Paul, please!

INTERVIEWS

Gambaccini, Paul. *Paul McCartney: In His Own Words*. New York/London: Flash Books (division of Music Sales), 1976. 112 pages. Approximately 80 black-and-white illustrations. The Singles of Paul McCartney. The Albums of Paul McCartney.

This rings like a quotebook, but it isn't. The heavily illustrated work consists primarily of interviews with McCartney conducted in 1973 and 1975. Sections are divided thematically and have evidently been heavily edited. If you're a fan of the *Band on the Run* and *Venus and Mars* LPs, you're in luck because there is some good detail here (e.g., Cream drummer Ginger Baker contributed the classic "Ho, hey, ho" in "Picasso's Last Words"). Otherwise, pretty standard stuff.

PICTORIALS

Giuliano, Geoffrey and Giuliano, Brenda. *The Illustrated Paul McCartney*. Secaucus, N.J.: Chartwell Books (division of Books Sales Limited), 1993. 96 pages. 117 color and black-and-white illustrations throughout.

Hackneyed bargain book from Beatles' biographer Geoffrey Giuliano and his wife, Brenda Giuliano. You know the authors have major ego problems when their faces appear more prominently in the printed end paper than the subject of the book itself! Photos from all periods of Paul's musical career and family life are jumbled together with the Giulianos' cockily

written text. The cover image of a rather chubby-faced Paul could have been selected with better care. Hastily concocted. "...there is really very little, if anything, new offered here. Except for some new errors..."—*Goldmine*.

Jasper, Tony. *Paul McCartney and Wings*. Secaucus: Chartwell Books, Inc. (division of Book Sales Limited), 1977. 94 pages. Over 100 color and black-and-white illustrations, covering every page. Discography.

Would you believe it's been over a decade and a half since Wings' last record? Only three or so years after this book was published, the group disbanded without much fanfare in the wake of McCartney's Japan drug bust and renewed solo career. Author Tony Jasper adds insult to injury here by focusing more attention on The Beatles, their break-up, and the potential for a reunion than on Wings' Lane, McCulloch, and English. Aside from one rare shot of Paul sharing a toast with his brother Mike (McGear) McCartney, the photos are exactly what one might expect.

Mendelsohn, John. *Paul McCartney: A Biography in Words and Pictures*. No city: Sire Books (Chappell Music Company), 1977. 54 pages. 60 black-and-white photos scattered throughout. Paul McCartney Appendix (Solo Discography).

Judge this book for yourself, based on the following excerpt: "In Chapter Six, I'm going to attempt to merit the staggeringly generous advance-against royalties this volume's publishers has little recourse but to award me before I would so much as touch typewriter to paper by getting a grip on myself long enough to say something insightful and provocative about Paul McCartney as both a songwriter and person." Yes, the entire book is an ungrammatical run-on sentence—and the photos are rather stodgy as well. Avast, belay!

TOURBOOKS

Gelly, David. Photographs by Sykes, Homer. Introduction by Paul McCartney. *The Facts about a Pop Group Featuring Wings*. London: G. Whizzard Publications Limited, 1976. 54 pages. Approximately 50 black-and-white and 10 color illustrations throughout. Glossary of Pop Music Terms. Paul McCartney & Wings Rooming List.

Background examination, presumably for young readers, of what it takes to get a rock tour off the ground. Focusing on Paul McCartney & Wings—who lent their cooperation to the project—this book profiles the band members (at the time, Paul, Linda, Denny Laine, Jimmy McCulloch, and Joe English), roadies, equipment, rehearsing, sound, security, and more. Though primitive by today's standards, it's still an educational tour through the basic components of preparing a stage show.

WRITTEN WORKS

McCartney, Linda. *Linda McCartney's Home Cooking: Quick, Easy and Economical Vegetarian Dishes for Today*. New York: Arcade Publishing (Little, Brown and Company), 1989. 170 pages. Approximately 75 color and black-and-white illustrations throughout.

The photographer, musician, and mother of several children tackles yet another personal passion: cooking. With this, her first cookbook, McCartney hoped to spread the word of vegetarianism and animal rights; judging by how quickly this book left the shelves, she must have been successful. McCartney provides information about nutrition and how to use fruits, vegetables, grains, and legumes before moving on to the recipes, which range from gnocchi to a spaghetti omelette. A strong introduction for those embarking on the vegetarian path.

McCartney, Linda. *Linda McCartney's Sixties*. Boston: Little, Brown and Company, 1992. 176 pages. Approximately 200 black-and-white and color photographs, covering every page.

Even if you don't like Linda McCartney as a musician or for the fact that she stole Paul McCartney away from bachelordom all those years ago, there's a good chance you'll still love this book. As John Lennon once pointed out, Linda has a keen eye for the moment: Brian Jones reclining with a yawn; Jim Morrison caressing a microphone; Keith Moon's puffing cheeks as he thrashes his drums; Frank Zappa with child; and, of course, The Beatles in their final months together. Linda's anecdotes about the various artists are punchy and effective. Highly recommended. "Perhaps McCartney's photos are most impressive for capturing the youth and vitality of their era"—*Booklist*.

McCartney, Linda. *Linda McCartney's Sun Prints*. London: Barrie & Jenkins, 1988. 75 original color and black-and-white photographs, covering every page.

Neither a cookbook nor a collection of rock snapshots, this is purely an art for art's sake catalog of Linda McCartney's photos, which were inspired by W. Fox Talbot—developer of the sun printing technique. If you are interested in photography or nineteenth century printing, these might pique your interest. The lovely blue or brown-tinted works are of various subjects, both inert and active: horses ("Shadow Jumping"), fruit ("Still Life"), children ("Monkey Boy"), etc. Beautiful work that was displayed in dozens of galleries all over the world, culminating with a major exhibition at the Royal Photographic Society in Bath in 1987.

McCartney, Linda. *Linda's Kitchen: Simple and Inspiring Recipes for Meatless Meals*. New York: Little, Brown and Company, 1995. 192 pages. Approximately 75 color photographs throughout. Nutrition for Vegetarians.

McCartney's second cookbook includes 200 vegetarian recipes, many of which Linda herself states she incorporates into her own family's meals. From soup (the staple, lentil) and main courses (vegetarian hotch-potch), to pasta, rice and potatoes, this book has a tasty and attractive selection of options for any palate. The illustrations are generally good, if a tad too much on the orange side. For a wider audience than yuppie veggie rockers.

McCartney, Linda. *Linda's Pictures: A Collection of Photographs*. New York: Knopf, 1976. 148 pages. Approximately 125 color and black-and-white photographs, covering every page.

Say what you will about Linda McCartney's musical ability (and most have), but no one can deny her keen, masterful eye as a photographer of rock's elite. Her snapshots, collected here for the first time, are among the best ever taken of The Rolling Stones, Jimi Hendrix, Janis Joplin, The Beach Boys, Cream, Grace Slick, and many others. And let's not forget her memorable portraits of John and Yoko, George, Ringo, and hubby Paul. The final quarter consists primarily of Paul and kids frolicking about the McCartney farm estate in the early 1970's. Essential for lovers of 1960's classic rock. Paul, by the way, receives title page credit as "reviewer" of the photos.

McCartney, Paul. Photographs by McCartney, Linda. *Paul McCartney: Composer/Artist*. New York: Simon & Schuster, 1981. 272 pages. Approximately 50 original pen-and-ink drawings throughout.

Songbook containing chords and lyrics to 50 McCartney compositions, and featuring many Beatles and Wings tunes. Included here because the book features original drawings by McCartney himself. Most of these are childish doodles of goonish faces that have little to do with the music or the artist's life. The project would have been better suited to a more elaborately designed lyric book with additional drawings and photos—and minus the chords. Fans desperately seeking this out will be disappointed.

YOUNG ADULT

Gelfand, M. Howard. *Paul McCartney*. Mankato, MN: Creative Education, 1983. 32 pages. 10 black-and-white photographs throughout.

Part of the "Rock 'n Pop Stars" series, this entry on McCartney is among the worst. The facts provided are skimpy (his mother's death isn't even mentioned) and virtually every line wreaks from trumped-up misinformation. Listen to what the man said: Stay clear.

OTHER TITLES OF INTEREST

Grove, Martin A. *Paul McCartney: Beatle with Wings*. No city: Manor, 1978.

Hamilton, Alan. *Paul McCartney*. London: Trafalgar Square, 1983.

Hipgnosis. *Hands Across the Water: Wings Tour the U.S.A.*. London: Reed Books, 1978.

Ocean, Humphrey. Preface by Paul McCartney. *The Ocean View*. London: Plexus, 1983.

Schwartz, Francie. *Body Count*. No city: Straight Arrow, c.1969.
Schwartz kisses-and-tells about her summer affair with Paul McCartney.

Welch, Chris. *McCartney: The Definitive Biography*. London: Proteus, 1980.

M.C. HAMMER

BIOGRAPHIES

Hildebrand, Lee. *Hammertime*. New York: Avon, 1992. 168 pages. One eight-page black and white photo insert. Discography (U.S. only).

Mass-market paperback without the usual hype and gossip. In fact, Hammer has been dissed by other rappers on account of his clean-cut image (staying away from drugs, avoiding the groupie scene, etc.). As a child, Hammer (then Stanley Burrell) was batboy for the Oakland A's baseball team, where he befriended Vida Blue, Reggie Jackson, and manager Charlie Finley. His nickname came from his striking resemblance to slugger Hammering Hank Aaron. A respectable attempt at showing why M.C. Hammer is an ideal role model for the 1990's.

PICTORIALS

Dessau, Bruce. Introduction by M.C. Hammer. *M.C. Hammer: U Can't Touch This*. London: Boxtree, 1991. 96 pages. Over 100 color photographs, covering nearly every page.

Written with full cooperation of M.C. Hammer, his band, and his entourage, this book sports some fine color performance shots of Hammer on tour in the early 1990's. In the poses, Hammer certainly has more class and charisma than several of his rivals, namely Marky Mark. Hammer also seems to have a congenial attitude to his fans and a certain way with kids. The book falls short on surprises—unless one can get excited about seeing Tom Jones with Hammer's luscious female singers—and doesn't include song lists or concert dates. U can touch it.

YOUNG ADULT

Krulik, Nancy E. *M.C. Hammer and Vanilla Ice: The Hip-Hop Never Stops*. London: Scholastic Publications Limited, 1991. 76 pages. One glossy eight-page color insert.

"High-powered" effort on two of the world's leading rappers, Hammer and Vanilla Ice. Divided in two sections, the book provides enthusiastic biographies of each artist, ending with a "quickie quiz." A decent way to introduce very young fans of either rapper to the merits of the other star.

Saylor-Merchant, Linda. *Hammer 2 Legit 2 Quit*. New York: Dillon Press, 1992. 64 pages. Approximately 12 color photographs throughout. Discography.

Dazzling biography of Hammer for fans 12 and younger. Author Linda Saylor-Merchant provides a solid background of rap and then traces back to Hammer's batboy days and early love of James Brown (with whom he is captured burning up the stage). Some top-notch photos round out this worthwhile, colorful volume.

OTHER TITLES OF INTEREST
Peeples, Jerome. *Hammer: What's Hot*. New York: Dell, 1992.

MEATLOAF

Robertson, Sandy. *Meatloaf*. London: Omnibus Press (division of Book Sales Limited), 1981.

MEGADETH

FANZINES AND FAN CLUBS

Megadeth CyberArmy P.O. Box 883488, San Francisco, CA 94188.

Megadeth fan club offering members access to priority tickets, the CyberArmy hotline, special contests, and exclusive merchandise. New members also receive a package containing a membership card, a band biography and discography, a souvenir color photo, and subscription to the newsletter, which contains concert information, album release dates, interviews, photos, and more. The cost of membership is $19 U.S.; $25 elsewhere.

JOHN (COUGAR) MELLENCAMP

BIOGRAPHIES

Torgoff, Martin. *American Fool: The Roots and Improbable Rise of John Cougar Mellencamp*. New York: St. Martin's Press, 1986. 226 pages. Approximately 100 black-and-white photographs throughout; one eight-page color insert.

Mellencamp may be an "American Fool" as the title (taken from the LP of the same name) indicates, but he is having the last laugh. The rebellious youth from Seymour, Indiana was discovered by Tony DeVries (who also nurtured

David Bowie), and was shaped into a pop star —with the all-too-bubblegum pseudonym "Cougar." The singer fought this image for years, until he was able to break free and develop his own successful "all-American smart-ass" persona. Despite an inconsistent editing job (in the first half of the book curse words are printed, but in the second they are bleeped out) and the omission of a discography, this book has enough beefcake photos for the female fans and just enough smut for the guys.

FANZINES AND FAN CLUBS

The John Mellencamp Official International Fan Club. P.O. Box 679, Branford, CT 06405.

Members receive an 8x10 photo, a Mellencamp biography, a membership card, and more. *Minutes to Memories*, a 20-page stapled packet, contains reproductions of black-and-white photographs, reprinted newspaper and magazine articles, news updates, crossword puzzles, letters from members, and more. The cost of membership per year is $22 U.S. and Canada; $28 elsewhere.

YOUNG ADULT

Fissinger, Laura. *John Cougar*. Mankato, MN: Creative Education, 1983. 32 pages. Approximately 20 black-and-white photographs throughout.

Part of Creative Education's "Rock 'n Pop Stars" series, this installment on John Cougar (yes, he was then still known by his pop star name) is less than satisfactory. One isn't liable to learn much about a singer from lines such as "John had a good time in high school." Oversimplified and not very attractive.

OTHER TITLES OF INTEREST
Harshfield, David. *Manchild for Real: The Life and Lyrics of John Cougar Mellencamp*. New York: Vantage, 1986.
Holmes, Tim. *John Cougar Mellencamp*. New York: Ballantine, 1985.

MENUDO

TITLES OF INTEREST
Greenburg, Keith. *Menudo*. New York: Pocket, 1983.
Molina, Maria. *Menudo*. New York: Simon & Schuster, 1984.

METALLICA

BIOGRAPHIES

Crocker, Chris. *Metallica: The Frayed Ends of Metal*. New York: St. Martin's Press, 1993. 226 pages. 50 full-page black-and-white photographs throughout. Discography. Videography.

Chris Crocker tackles Metallica's history and numerous contradictions with remarkable skill. In addition to telling of the group's diverse influences, which range from The Kinks to Judas Priest, he points out that Metallica is one of the few politically correct headbanging bands around, promoting AIDS-awareness at the Freddie Mercury tribute in 1992. And did you know Metallica has members with the first name James and Kirk? "This is a refreshing story of hard work, determination, and talent succeeding on its own terms.... Recommended"—*Library Journal*.

PICTORIALS

Doughton, K.J. *Metallica Unbound*. New York: Warner Books, 1993. 176 pages. Approximately 180 color and black-and-white photographs, covering every page. A Complete Metallic Discography.

The cover of this photo book is slickly designed in glossy jet black with chrome color type in the title. The interior photographs are somewhat stringently boxed color and black-and-white photographs that betray the band's image. Aren't these guys supposed to be free-wheeling and dangerous? Doughton's writing about the band is generic, even when reporting on Metallica's wild parties and pulsating shows. Putterford's pictorial (see below) is somewhat more appropriate.

Hotten, John. *Metallica*. Miami, FL: MBS, 1994. 120 pages. Approximately 75 color and black-and-white photographs throughout. Discography. Chronology. Index.

CD-format book covering all aspects of Metallica's career. This nicely designed and illustrated book is priced just right at around $7.99.

No author. *Metallica In Person*. Port Chester, NY: Cherry Lane, 1990. Unpaginated (approximately 32 pages). Approximately 40 color and black-and-white photographs, covering every page. Comes with a full-color pull-out poster.

Lots of hype on the kings of metal, but nothing on the order of hard information. The pictures, surprisingly, lack the live action of the cover. Any color metal mag would serve this purpose.

Putterford, Mark and Russell, Xavier. *Metallica: A Visual Documentary*. London: Omnibus Press (division of Book Sales Limited), 1992. 80 pages. Approximately 150 color and black-and-white photographs, covering nearly every page. Discography.

Atypical "visual documentary" from Omnibus Press, as this one is not in a day-by-day format. Authors Putterford and Russell chart the metal group's course from their garage band days through their controversial performance at the Freddie Mercury Tribute—at which they played their own tunes, not Queen songs (or anything remotely related to the event). Klunky text mixed with some raucous head-flailing color and black-and-white shots.

Wall, Mick and Dome, Malcolm. *The Complete Guide to the Music of Metallica*. London: Omnibus Press (division of Book Sales Limited), 1995. 88 pages. Approximately 80 color and black-and-white photographs throughout.

CD-format book covering all aspects of Metallica's career. Overlaps with Hotten's CD-format book (see above), but each offers something of different appeal: this has more photos, the other more informational back sections.

QUIZBOOKS AND QUOTEBOOKS

Putterford, Mark. *Metallica: In Their Own Words*. London: Omnibus Press (division of Book Sales Limited), 1994. 96 pages. Approximately 100 black-and-white photographs, covering every page.

What does this metal band have to say that's worth hearing? Not much, at least judging by this quotebook. In Mark Putterford's collection, Metallica mostly speaks about each other and their albums; there is hardly anything relevant to specific issues or even to the general topic of rock and roll itself. The "in the beginning" section tells the reader nothing about these guys, nor does the one on influences. In one full statement, Lars Ulrich comments, "I was truly obsessed by the New Wave of British Heavy Metal." Headbangers can put the headphones on and turn the volume up when looking at this book.

TOURBOOKS

Putterford, Mark. *Metallica Live* London: Omnibus Press (division of Book Sales Limited), 1994. 32 pages. Approximately 35 color photographs, covering every page. Discography. Comes with a pull-out color poster.

Color photo book capturing Metallica in places unidentified. Putterford's contribution only seems to be a 5,000-word essay, which reads like a laundry list of the band's turnovers, not like an eyewitness account of the group on the road. The photos themselves are not captioned, but large type non-sequitors run throughout: "Social comment? Political protests? Polystyrene pillars or pantomime productions"?" Buy a metal mag instead.

OTHER TITLES OF INTEREST
Harrigan, Brian. *Encyclopedia Metallica*. London: Omnibus Press (division of Book Sales Limited), 1990.

McSquare, Eddie. *Metallica: Whiplash*. London: Omnibus Press (division of Book Sales Limited), 1990.

MIAMI SOUND MACHINE

See Estefan, Gloria.

GEORGE MICHAEL

See Wham!

BETTE MIDLER

BIOGRAPHIES

Baker, Robb. *Bette Midler*. New York: Popular Library, 1975. 190 pages. One eight-page black-and-white photo insert.

Long before Midler was a screen and stage star, she was queen of the gay baths and somewhat of a cult diva. Who would think the Divine Miss M had enough of a following way back when to deserve a mass-market tribute biography? In any event, this is a sleazy treatment by any standards. The photos are unflattering; even her ardent fans might toss their cookies. Not recommended.

Collins, Ace. *Bette Midler*. New York: St. Martin's Press, 1989. 166 pages. One eight-page black-and-white photo insert. Movies, Broadway, Albums, Singles.

Sketchy Midler bio that actually offers less than Baker's terrible *Bette Midler* (above), which was published fourteen years earlier! If you're a fan of Midler's music, you'll be especially disappointed; there is nothing on her musical influence and barely anything in regard to her first starring role in *The Rose*. However, there is good coverage of her friendship with Barry Manilow. Enough said! Contains "...only superficial insight into Midler's motives..."—*Booklist*.

Spada, James. *The Divine Bette Midler*. New York: Macmillan Publishing Company, 1984. 214 pages. Approximately 140 black-and-white photographs, covering nearly every page.

Decent pictorial biography that offers far more for readers than either work listed above. Spada shows how a young Midler, raised in the most unlikely place—Hawaii—dreamt of being a star like Debra Paget, but instead faced the realities of being an overweight, unattractive Jewish girl in a tough neighborhood. Fans can learn that the real "chesty" in her family was her father, Fred, a powerful guy who evidently ran the house like a tyrant. Spada's work will be appreciated by fans, even though the photos don't match up to the color images in Midler's work (see Written Works, below).

RELATED WORKS

Fleischer, Lenore. *The Rose.*

See: Joplin, Janis: Related Works.

WRITTEN WORKS

Midler, Bette. *A View from a Broad.* Photographs by Sean Russell. New York: Simon and Schuster, 1980. 160 pages. Over 100 color illustrations throughout.

Divine Miss M takes the reader along for the ride on her first world tour (the "monumental shlep") that included places such as England, France, Germany, and Australia. Her offbeat presence and cleavage are everywhere: Remember when she dressed as a mermaid and in a giant hotdog suit? The accompanying writings and captions are full of non sequiturs ("Hath not a mermaid eyes? Hath she not ears?") and bizarre observations (German "...women's faces had a set, mannequin-like attitude, very Helmut Newton"). Her "band application" form is quite clever, including questions such as "Do you take drugs?," "Can you arrange for your own supply?," "Can you arrange for mine?" and the punch line: "Have you been able to read this application by yourself?" Funny stuff.

OTHER TITLES OF INTEREST
Bego, Mark. *Bette Midler: Outrageously Divine.* New York: NAL, 1987.
Mair, George. *Bette: An Intimate Biography.* New York: Citadel (Carol Publishing Group), 1996.

JONI MITCHELL

(See also Lightfoot, Gordon: Critical/Analytical Commentary)

PICTORIALS

Fleischer, Lenore. *Joni Mitchell: Her Life, Her Loves, Her Music.* New York: Flash Books (division of Music Sales Corporation), 1976. 80 pages. Approximately 75 black-and-white photographs, covering nearly every page.

The "Magic Princess" of the late-1960's and early 70's is the subject of this outdated book for fans. Encased by a lovely head portrait of Mitchell on the front cover and a sensual, sidestroking image on the back—not to mention the diverse and generally flattering mix of ethereal shots inside—the book tells a concise and readable version of her story. The "loves" in the subtitle is highly misleading, since author Lenore Fleischer mostly tells us how "private" the star is; we only get some details of her relationship with Graham Nash and innuendos on Stephen Stills, Neil Young, Leonard Cohen, and Warren Beatty (who would doubt that one?). Despite its years, *Joni Mitchell* still has its moments.

OTHER TITLES OF INTEREST
Mitchell, Joni. *Both Sides Now.* New York: Scholastic, 1992.
School Library Journal *commented: "The tale of love between two cutesy caterpillars is trite and uninspired."*
Mitchell, Joni. *The Circle Game.* New York: Scholastic, 1993.

THE MONKEES

AUTOBIOGRAPHY

Dolenz, Micky with Bego, Mark. *I'm a Believer: My Life of Monkees, Music, and Madness.* New York: Hyperion, 1993. 217 pages. Two glossy eight-page black-and-white photo inserts. Discography. Index.

Monkeeman Dolenz has no pretensions about his musical ability or what his television group stood for. The son of actor George Dolenz and a noted child star (the title character of television's "Circus Boy"), Dolenz would much rather lavish praise on genuine musicians (e.g., The Beatles) and his more naturally gifted bandmates (Nesmith and Tork). Yet Dolenz was the man who sang lead on many of The Monkees' greatest hits, and he was the force that brought the group back together for their successful mid-1980's reunions. As the book ends, Dolenz gives up trying to curb Davy Jones' prissy temper and washes his hands of the band altogether (although this has changed since publication). Dolenz tells his story through various screenplay scenarios that either produce outloud laughter or a roll of the eyes. Fans of Dolenz's campy persona will go bananas; others may be put off by the book's excessive errors and oversights.

DISCOGRAPHIES, RECORDING GUIDES, AND COLLECTIBLES

Reilly, Edward; McManus, Maggie; and Chadwick, William. *The Monkees —A Manufactured Image: The Ultimate Guide to Monkee Memories and Memorabilia.* Ann Arbor, MI: Pierian Press, 1987. 308 pages. Hundreds of glossy black-and-white photos throughout. Song and Album Title Index; Index to People, Place and Things; Record Number Index; Date Index.

A fabulous guide for the "serious" Monkees buff, containing: a complete day-by-day chronology; listings of The Monkees work on film and on record; a photo inventory of memorabilia; and much more. The photos—of the band members, girlfriends, groupies, spouses, musicians, and actors (e.g., Jack Nicholson)— are rare and well selected; the text is smoothly written and informative (pointing out that The Beatles, notably George Harrison, were among their staunch supporters). The indexes listed above will be of excellent use to researchers.

FANZINES AND FAN CLUBS

Head of the Monkees Fan Club. Teresa Jones, 262 Baltimore Avenue, Baltimore, MD 21222.

Fan club founded in 1986 that provides members with a photograph, a club pencil, fact sheets, a membership card, a certificate, and four issues of *Head of the Monkees* newsletter. The 36-page stapled packet contains photocopies of black-and-white photographs, news briefs, reprinted newspaper articles, updates on all four individual Monkees, excerpts from TV and film scripts featuring any of the solo Monkees, CD releases, puzzles, and more. The club also sponsors an annual contest and sends each member a birthday card and a special Christmas present. The cost of membership is $10 U.S. and Canada; $13 elsewhere. The cost per newsletter is $2.50.

Monkee Business Fanzine. Att. Maggie McManus, 2770 South Broad Street, Trenton, NJ 08160.

Quarterly fanzine devoted exclusively to The Monkees. The 36-page, stapled packet contains: updates on The Monkees live appearances; news; profiles of inner circle people; record, TV and book reviews; black-and-white photographs; pen pals; question-and-answer; essay-length articles from subscribers; classi-fieds; and more. The cost of subscription is $12 U.S.; $13 Canada; and $17 overseas. Payable by checks or money orders, in U.S. funds only.

PICTORIALS

Baker, Glenn A.; with Tom Czarnota and Peter Hogan. *Monkeemania: The True Story of the Monkees.* New York: St. Martin's Press, 1986. 144 pages. Approximately 150 black-and-white photos throughout. Discography.

Somewhat dated photo book of The Monkees, with an ugly yellow cover and many murky interior black-and-white reproductions of photographs. Baker et. al. provide a decent history of the band—from its inspiration in The Beatles' films to the now-famous auditions, which included a candidate named Stephen Stills—but the stories have all been heard before and the photos don't do justice. Fans probably have this already, so why bother? Doesn't compare to Jones' work (see Written Works, below).

Finn, Ed and Bone, T. *The Monkees Scrapbook.* San Francisco, CA: Last Gasp of San Francisco, 1986. 62 pages. Approximately 50 black-and-white photographs throughout. Monkees 20th Anniversary Tribute.

Amateurish collection of photos and data on The Monkees, with scattered spreads on discography, bibliography, trivia, episode songs, and separate profiles of each Monkee. Junky stuff and way too dated.

Lefcowitz, Eric. *The Monkees Tale.* San Francisco: Last Gasp, 1985. 104 pages. Approximately 75 black-and-white glossy photos throughout. Monkees Filmography. Monkees Discography.

This "fun" group, as characterized by author Lefcowitz, was TV's first "test tube baby"— created by masterminds Bob Rafaelson and Bert Schneider to capitalize on The Beatles' movie success. In effect, The Monkees were taking over the slack left when The Beatles stopped touring in 1966. Lefcowitz has a knowledgeable and objective view of The Monkees' place in music history, recognizing their synthetic origins and silly pop image, but also demonstrating that the foursome rose above it all and created some damn good music. Lefcowitz throws in many enjoyable quotes, including Jimi Hendrix's view of their music ("Dishwater!") and Dolenz's description of how he made the leap from guitar to drums ("Well, it's not brain surgery, is it?"). The book closes with excellent chapters focusing on the individual Monkees on their own.

Russo, Joe. *The Monkees Photo Album.* Saddle Brook, NJ: SM Enterprises, 1987. 40 pages. Approximately 40 color and black-and-white photographs, covering every page.

See Monkee as a baby. See Monkee scratch his head. See Monkee play guitar (or at least pretend). This unspectacular color vanity press book contains many gooey period photographs (from the TV show and the film *Head*), balanced with more recent shots from the band's mid-1980's tours. (For one show, at least, Michael Nesmith did join in.) Schlocky stuff, all culled from Russo's private collection, that's all in the spirit of mindless fun. To order, write Joe Russo at P.O. Box 917, Saddle Brook, NJ 07663-0917 ($12, payable to Joe Russo).

WRITTEN WORKS

Jones, Davy and Green, Alan. Foreword by Don Kirchner. *Mutant Monkees Meet the Masters of the Multimedia Manipulation Machine.* Selingsgrove: Click! Publishing, 1992. Approximately 200 color photos and computer graphics throughout. 176 pages.

There are no deep reflections on the group here—only a brilliantly colorful collage of shots from Monkee Jones himself, as well as original color computer graphics by Thirty-Two Macintosh, Artists with Really Warped Minds. Cheekily taking credit as "the world's first video band" and "the world's first rap group," Jones tells The Monkees' wacky story through color photos, designs, and many images of real monkeys! Amidst the chaos, Jones reflects on the taping of the first shows (he identifies the four as "two actors and two musicians," meaning Tork and Nesmith as the latter and he and Dolenz as the former) and throws in many quotes from the past and present. The book integrates photos from the 1960's with more recent ones—equally featuring all four Monkees (no grudges here!)—and the results are imaginative and entertaining. One of the most vibrant and original works included in this Guide: highly recommended.

OTHER TITLES OF INTEREST
Puerzer, Ellen L. *The Ultimate Monkees Trivia Book.* No city: Puerzer Publishing, 1987.

BILL MONROE

(See also Waters, Muddy: Biographies)

TITLES OF INTEREST
Rosenberg, Neil. *Bill Monroe & His Blue Grass Boys: An Illustrated Discography.* No city: Country Music Foundation, 1974.

THE MOODY BLUES

FANZINES AND FAN CLUBS

The Friends of Michael Pinder. P.O. Box 6078, Auburn, CA 95604.

Fan club devoted exclusively to ex-Moody Blues musician Mike Pinder. The club offers biographical information about Pinder, a membership card, an 8x10 color autographed photo, an exclusive pin, a sticker, members club only offers, and subscription to the quarterly newsletter. *Have You Heard?*, an eight-page glossy news packet, contains some color, black-and-white photographs, occasional articles from Mike Pinder, and his wife, Tara Pinder, lengthy articles on Mike's personal and professional life, interviews with Mike, raffles, and more. The cost of membership is $20 U.S.; $25 elsewhere.

Higher & Higher: The Moody Blues Magazine. P.O. Box 829, Geneva FL, 32732.

Quarterly, high-quality Moody Blues magazine that includes anywhere from 32-48 pages and many black-and-white and color photographs. Issues contain profiles of past and members of the band, Moody News, interviews, concert updates, television appearances, recording information, videos, classifieds, and potpourri. The cost is $9.50 per issue and $37 per year; in Canada, $41 per year; elsewhere, $49 per year.

The Moody Blues Fan Club. 53055 High Street, Cobham Surrey KT11 3DP England.

Fan club that provides members with: a membership card; a black-and-white photograph of The Moody Blues; a personal information sheet on each musician; a Moody Blues biography; a list of Moody Blues albums and videos; merchandising; and subscription to the club's publication. The 20-page magazine features original color art on the cover, and includes color photographs throughout, updates on group and solo activities, reviews, letters, tour schedules, pen pals, and more. The cost of annual membership is £15 U.S. and Canada; £10 U.K.; and £12 elsewhere in Europe.

GARY MOORE

See Thin Lizzy.

VAN MORRISON

BIOGRAPHIES

Rogan, Johnny. *Van Morrison: A Portrait of the Artist*. London: Elm Tree Books, 1984. 192 pages. One glossy eight-page black-and-white photo insert. Discography. Notes.

Densely written but informative biography of Morrison, intended by its author to show that rock artists of lesser stature than The Beatles and Elvis still deserve some scholarship. Born in Belfast, Ireland, the son of a blues junkie (not in the druggie connotation), Morrison was a poetic child who resisted formal musical training (but received it anyway on the saxophone) and taught himself how to play guitar. By 14 he was in a band, The Monarchs, who actually recorded an album in Germany. With the group Them, Morrison discovered his songwriting aptitude, but his legendary moodiness, band financial disputes, and a succession of studio musicians thrust upon them by the record company caused Them to split. As a soloist, Morrison has developed into a visionary poet who combines sophisticated elements of blues and jazz with a rhythm and infectious melody worthy of any top-flight rocker. A notable, if dry, addition to Morrison literature.

York, Ritchie. *Van Morrison: Into the Music*. New York: Futura Publications Limited, 1975. 190 pages. Three glossy four-page black-and-white photo inserts. Van Morrison Discography. (First published in Great Britain in 1975 by Charisma Books Limited.)

"The first biography of Van Morrison" (research hasn't exposed anything earlier), this grungy-looking publication doesn't penetrate Van the Man's wall of silence, but it does begin to open up discussion of his art. With lyrics to a number of Morrison's songs ("Astral Weeks," "Sweet Thing," "Ballerina," etc.), this book has a slight edge over Rogan's work (see above). However, most fans will want something more recent than both titles. For those needing critical and popular reaction to Van Morrison's work up through the mid-1970's, this book will not be a disappointment.

FANZINES AND FAN CLUBS

Wavelength: The Van Morrison Newsletter. P.O. Box 80 Winsford Cheshire CW7 4ES England.

Started in 1995, this is a quarterly magazine covering Morrison's activities (such as live performances), and articles based around his work and influences. The cost of subscription is $32 U.S.; £15 U.K.; and £20 elsewhere in Europe.

PICTORIALS

Turner, Steve. *Van Morrison: Too Late To Stop Now*. New York: Viking (Viking Penguin USA, Inc.), 1993. 192 pages. Approximately 200 color and black-and-white photographs, covering every page. Discography. Selected Bibliography. (Published simultaneously in Great Britain in 1993 by Bloomsbury Publishing Limited.)

A magnificent pictorial/biography/critical analysis of Van the Man, the singer/songwriter who to many has become the spiritual center of modern rock and roll. Turner provides an extensive overview of Morrison's life and career, and essentially confirms his image as a shy, sensitive recluse and consummate artist who blends the best of folk, jazz, rhythm and blues, and rock and roll into a sound distinctly his own. The illustrations range from shots of Van Morrison's estranged homeland (Belfast, Ireland) to several photos of his bands (first The Monarchs and, subsequently, the legendary Them) and solo. Many of the photo contact sheets are reprinted, as are original music line-ups and concert posters. Morrison is looking rather baldish and paunchy in the most recent photos, but we can forgive him; he never claimed to be Mick Jagger. "It's refreshing to see Turner's admiration tempered with a bit of clear-eyed neutrality"—*Select*.

OTHER TITLES OF INTEREST

Copple, Cynthia (editor). *Van Morrison: Reliable Sources.* No city: Caledonia Productions, 1973.

DeWitt, Howard A. *Van Morrison: The Mystic's Magic.* No city: Horizon, 1983.

MORRISSEY

See Smiths, The.

MOTLEY CRUE

PICTORIALS

Simmons, Sylvie and Dome, Malcolm. *Lude[sic], Crude and Rude: The Story of Motley Crue.* Chessington, Surrey (England): Castle Communications, 1994. 160 pages. Approximately 150 glossy full-page or two-page color and black-and-white photographs, covering nearly every page. Appendix A: Album Discography.

The metal dudes with a touch of Kiss, Alice Cooper, and Boy George (yes, Boy George) are lifted to new heights of greatness in this full-blown magazine. Pages switch from pure text on black backgrounds to graphic designs on text (some, such as Da Vinci's human anatomy are overused) and splashy two-page spreads. The results are glossy and powerful to look at, but difficult to read. Simmons and Dome's collaboration is uneven; some sentences are over-simplified, while others include language perhaps over the heads of teen metal fans (words such as "portentous"). An even greater number of sentences are purely awkward ("Which is where Vince Neil punches out Guns N' Roses guitarist Izzy Stradlin"). Fans, if you don't know already: Lude is spelled lewd!

OTHER TITLES OF INTEREST

Dwight, Billy. *Motley Crue.* New York: Ballantine, 1986.

McSquare, Eddie. *Motley Crue.* London: Book Sales Limited, 1990.

MOTORHEAD

DISCOGRAPHIES, RECORDING GUIDES, AND COLLECTIBLES

Burridge, Alan with Stevenson, Mick. Introduction by Lemmy. *The Illustrated Collector's Guide to Motorhead.* Burlington, Ontario (Canada): Collector's Guide Publishing, 1994. 204 pages. Approximately 100 reproductions of album covers and posters throughout.

Motorhead, consisting of Phil Taylor, Lemmy, and Brian Robertson, has somehow survived for nearly two decades, despite changing musical trends and their own self-hype as "the Worst Band in the World." This book contains all you need to know about collecting their releases, including 7" singles, EPs, LPs, bootlegs, box sets, CDs, and more. The authors toss in a bare bones family tree/history of the band, along with a list of concerts. The illustrations capturing Motorhead are poorly reproduced, but since these guys aren't exactly from the Cary Grant school of aesthetics, this may be a blessing in disguise. Except for the fascinating tidbit that Motorhead released an *Anthology Vol. 1* ten years ahead of The Beatles, this book will not exactly light up your gray cells.

OTHER TITLES OF INTEREST

Dadomo, Giovanni. *Motorhead.* London: Omnibus Press (division of Book Sales Limited), 1981.

No author. *Motorhead: Born to Lose, Live to Win.* Manchester, England: Babylon, 1981.

MOTT THE HOOPLE

WRITTEN WORKS

Hunter, Ian. *Ian Hunter: Reflections of a Rock Star.* New York: Flash Books (division of Music Sales), 1976. 104 pages. Approximately 75 black-and-white photographs throughout.

A day-by-day diary of life on the road from rocker Ian Hunter, the former lead man of Mott the Hoople, spanning November 1972-December 24, 1972. If you love rock and roll—and especially if you enjoy Hoople's recording of "All the Young Dudes"—you'll love this tale of early 1970's glamour and excess, as Hunter et. al. go from airplanes to hotels to stadiums, and pop pills, mingle with groupies, and wolf down quick meals. Hunter's comments on artists such as David Bowie and Marc Bolan are saucy and energetic. Raucous, uncensored, and at times incomprehensible, this wacked-out joy ride suffers from poor-quality photos.

HOLLY NEAR

TITLES OF INTEREST
Near, Holly with Richardson, Dirk. *Fire in the Rain...Singer in the Storm: Holly Near: An Autobiography*. New York: William Morrow & Company, 1990.
The actress and singer's autobiography.

RICKY NELSON

BIOGRAPHIES

Bashe, Philip. *Teenage Idol: The Complete Biography of Rick Nelson*. New York: Hyperion, 1992. 312 pages. One 14-page glossy black-and-white photo insert. Discography. Bibliography. Index.

Just acing out Selvin's biography (see below), Bashe's work delves slightly deeper into the Nelson myth and provides ample justification for Nelson's being reexamined as a performer with a "valiant determination to remain a vital, contemporary artist." In Nelson's case, addictions to prostitutes and cocaine humanize the synthesized child TV star, and convert him back to the true rock and roller he longed to be. In effect, he was a normal American teen rebelling against his manipulative, overbearing 1950's TV and real-life dad (Ozzie). Bashe refutes claims that Nelson's freebasing cocaine caused his fatal plane crash. "Fluidly told and thoroughly documented..."—*Kirkus*.

Selvin, Joel. *Ricky Nelson: Idol for a Generation*. Chicago: Contemporary Books, 1990. 332 pages. Two 16-page glossy black-and-white photos. Discography. Bibliography. Index.

Selvin's bio is a fine effort in its own right, and somewhat more plaintive about Nelson's memory than Bashe's (above). A broke, deeply in debt has-been at the time of his death,

Nelson was forced to travel to local family outings to make a buck. There are plenty of anecdotes herein not found in Bashe's, particularly regarding the star's TV and film career. In one, John Wayne presents him with a three hundred pound bag of steer manure for his birthday. This book also boasts an additional photo insert. Fans of the sock hop will want both books.

WILLIE NELSON

AUTOBIOGRAPHY

Nelson, Willie with Shrake, Bud. *Willie: An Autobiography*. New York: Simon & Schuster, 1988. 420 pages. One insert containing 72 black-white photographs. Index.

A down-to-earth story from "the outlaw" of country music himself. Willie's fans will love it, particularly his passages on "breathing properly" and his descriptions of what it's like to take the stage in front of 100,000 people. The book abounds in his mischievous humor, as in the top three items from his list of "the 60 great lies on the road": "(1) Your booking is definite. (2) Your check is in the mail. (3) I promise not to come in your mouth." Nearly every chapter begins with lyrics from a Nelson song. The text is supplemented with oral history from those in Nelson's inner circle: Mildred Wilcox, his cousin; Zeke Vernon, a longtime friend; Tom Gresham, music promoter; and several others. Yet it's Nelson's voice, as usual, that stands out from the crowd. As *The New York Times* said: "Willie Nelson in print is a lot like Willie Nelson in concert—a captivating experience."

BIOGRAPHIES

Scobey, Lola. *Willie Nelson: Country Outlaw*. New York: Kensington, 1982. 414 pages.

Cleverly written biography of the country music renegade, which crosscuts background information on the history of country music (The Carter Family, Jimmy Rodgers, et. al) with the birth and early years of the titular hero. Scobey smugly asserts that Nelson's legend was evident at the age of seven when, long before he even met a city babe, he was writing songs about unfaithful women. Nelson's influences, which included Bob Wills, Hank

Williams, and many others, are well documented, as are his early recordings, his string of failed marriages, his various entrepreneurial dealings, and his forays into religion. A relaxed, non-insider's account that is unfortunately not supplemented with photos. Most fans would opt for Nelson's autobiography (see above).

PICTORIALS

Allen, Bob. *Waylon & Willie: The Full Story in Words and Pictures of Waylon Jennings and Willie Nelson*. New York: Quick Fox (division of Music Sales), 1979. 128 pages. Approximately 100 black-and-white photographs throughout. Willie Nelson: Discography. Waylon Jennings: Discography.

A dual portrait of the country music heroes, who are dubbed "Butch and Sundance." While it goes without saying that both artists deserve volumes unto themselves, the pairing does bring to the surface several fascinating commonalities between Willie and Waylon, aside from the obvious, (re: country music): they were both Depression-era children who worked in the cotton fields; they both played bass for other artists before they went solo; they both went through messy divorces; and they both brought their charisma to the silver screen. *Waylon & Willie* is as old as a country trail, but it's worth a look if you're passing through town.

OTHER TITLES OF INTEREST
Bane, Michael. *Willie: A Biography of Willie Nelson*. New York: Dell, 1984.

Nelson, Susie. *Heart Worn Memories: A Daughter's Personal Biography of Willie Nelson*. No city: Eakin Publications, 1987.
Library Journal *commented: "To research this biography, the author interviewed family, friends, and country music cohorts of her famous father, Willie Nelson.... For diehard fans."*

NEW EDITION

PICTORIALS

George, Nelson. *Cool It Now: The Authorized Biography of New Edition*. Chicago: Contemporary Books, 1986. 128 pages. Approximately 84 black-and-white photographs throughout; two glossy four-page color inserts. Discography/Videography.

Ricky, Ronnie, Ralph, Michael, and Bobby hailed from Roxbury, a slum suburb of Boston. The boys, inspired by the Jackson 5 (Michael Jackson in particular), struck big with pop hits "Candy Girl" and "A Little Bit of Love (Is All It Takes)" and branched out to touring and video. Bobby Brown separated from his mates on good terms to carve out a solo career in his true calling: hip hop and funk. Features a wealth of upbeat photos, trivia quizzes, and tidbits about the performers. "...George manages to capture some of the excitement..."— *Publishers Weekly*.

NEW KIDS ON THE BLOCK

PICTORIALS

Nance, Scott. *New Kids on the Block*. Las Vegas, NV: Pioneer Books, 1990. 96 pages. Approximately 50 black-and-white photographs throughout. Appendix.

"The first serious book about their music/their lives/their dreams" is nothing more than a fanzine with the usual oversensationalized copy. Separate chapters covering Donnie Wahlberg, Danny Wood, the Knights (Jordan and Jonathan), Joe McIntyre, and the group's coming together amount to a PR jumble, hammering home that these boys love breaking dancing if it's for a politically correct cause. Fails to provide the insights of McGibbon's work (see New Kids Friends and Family, below).

YOUNG ADULT

Clifford, Mike. *New Kids on the Block*. New York: Mallard Press (division of BDD Promotional Book Company), 1990. Unpaginated (approximately 32 pages). Color photos on every page. Staying in Touch.

Promo book that no doubt served its purpose at the time of release. In various high-quality photos, the boys pose on stage and in fields to show off their cheeky good looks, muscular frames, and funky threads. In the tradition of The Jackson 5, The Brady Bunch, and Donny & Marie, the pseudo-camp of New Kids on the Block will live on and no doubt find its way into a CD boxed set. School-age girls may still shriek with glee at Donnie Wahlberg's smug indifference.

Greenberg, Keith Elliot. *New Kids on the Block*. Minneapolis, MN: Lerner Publications, 1991. 48 pages. Approximately 40 black-and-white and ten color photographs throughout.

Glossy study of the popular quintet, with a separate chapter on each member and various follow-up sections praising their meteoric rise and chart successes. The color pages have a school notebook cover feel, which may actually be appreciated by young fans. The book ends with details on the New Kids' cartoon TV show and plans for a feature film—which evidently never transpired. An inoffensive starting point for fans six to eight. "...tells the boys' story in competent if adulatory fashion" —*Booklist*.

Matthews, Jill. *The Lives and Loves of New Kids on the Block*. New York: Pocket Books, 1990. 154 pages. One 16-page glossy black-and-white photo insert. Handy Addresses. New Kids Lingo. New Kids Discography. New Kids Videography.

Fanzinelike assortment of facts on the boys from Boston. There's a chapter on each of the kids (Jonathan and Jordan Knight share a chapter), and lots of stuff about how cute they are. Vital statistics are provided, as are their likes and dislikes. Several rumors are disproved (none of the kids smoke), though many of these seem to be intended to make them appear clean-cut for public relations purposes. The page on lingo, which consists of only seven words, is stupid; even in 1990 kids could figure out what "dude," "dis," and "homeboy" mean. As for the music: "...don't look for insight and analysis"—*School Library Journal*.

NEW KIDS FRIENDS AND FAMILY

McGibbon, Robin. *New Kids on the Block: The Whole Story*. London: Self-published, 1990. 120 pages. One glossy 32-page color photo insert.

A biography of New Kids on the Block, as reported by those who knew them—including teachers, friends, neighbors, etc.— as they climbed toward fame. Author (and publisher) Robin McGibbon actually takes their quotes and incorporates them into some sort of narrative, hence the "friends" angle is merely a

hook. Compared with other books on the lads, this one holds up better than most, containing a good color insert (with exception to one shot in which Joey McIntyre's eyes are red from a flashbulb) and emphasizing the group's love of their Boston roots. "Neither the British flavor of McGibbon's style nor the fact that he qualifies terms for readers (e.g., American football) is disruptive to the text's lively flow"—*Booklist*.

OTHER TITLES OF INTEREST
Catalano, Grace. *New Kids on the Block*. New York: Bantam, 1989.
  Booklist *commented: "cursory and adulatory...."*
Goldsmith, Lynn. *New Kids on the Block*. New York: Rizzoli, 1990.
  Booklist *commented: "...there's Goldsmith's lavish coffee-table edition featuring her original photographs and the words of the New Kids themselves."*
Krulik, Nancy. *On the Road with the New Kids on the Block*. New York: Scholastic, 1990.
McEvoy, Seth or Yockey, Paul. *New Kids Series*. New York: Pocket, various years.
  In the early 1990's, Pocket published several of McEvoy's and Yockey's respective young adult stories featuring New Kids on the Block. Some of McEvoy's titles include: Backstage Surprise (1990); and Between Brothers, Block Party, New Kids on the Block: Workin' Out, On Stage, and On Tour (all 1991). Yockey's books include: Peace Out (1990); and Where's Joe? (1991).
New Kids on the Block. *Our Story: New Kids on the Block*. New York: Bantam, 1990.
Raso, Anne. *New Kids on the Block Scrapbook*. No city: Modern Publishing, 1990.
Sinclair, Charlotte. *New Kids on the Block*. No city: Outlet Book Company, 1990.

NEW ORDER

See Joy Division.

OLIVIA NEWTON-JOHN

DISCOGRAPHIES, RECORDING GUIDES, AND COLLECTIBLES

Branson-Trent, Gregory. *Olivia: More Than Physical: A Collector's Guide*. Burlington, Ontario (Canada): Collector's Guide Publishing, 1994. 152 pages. Approximately 125 black-and-white photographs throughout.

Author Gregory Branson-Trent corners the market on Newton-John's releases, which span the 1970's, 80's and (what there is of) the 90's. The album listings provide song names, singles, chart positions, and record company names. These are supplemented with quotes, reviews (positive and negative), the author's commentary and, on virtually every opposite page, black-and-white photographs. The sections in the back cite her concerts, radio shows, picture disks, singles, television/video appearances, and magazines. An extended fanzine.

FANZINES AND FAN CLUBS

Belgian Olivia Newton-John Fan Club. Attn. Kristin van de Wijer, Zonneboslaan 82, 1950 Kraainem, Belgium.

Belgian fan club founded in 1978 that offers a membership card, t-shirts, photos, posters, LPs, singles, CDs, calendars, and other collectibles. Also publishes a bimonthly 20-page booklet that contains black-and-white illustrations and very little English. The cost of membership is $35 U.S. (payable international money order only via registered letter).

Olivia: Dutch Olivia Newton-John Fan Club. Karekiethof 20, 6005 JM Weert England.

Dutch Olivia Newton-John Fan Club founded circa 1991. The club publishes a bimonthly four-page newsletter in Dutch that is translated separately in English as an insert. Each issue contains news, interviews, competitions, special offers, black-and-white photos, and more. The cost of membership is $23 per year U.S.; $20 Europe.

OTHER TITLES OF INTEREST
Jacobs, Linda. *Olivia Newton-John.* Sunshine Supergirl. St. Paul, MN: EMC, 1975.
Morse, Ann. *Olivia Newton-John.* Mankato, MN: Creative Education, 1976.
Newton-John, Olivia. *A Pig Tale.* New York: Simon & Schuster, 1993.
Ruff, Peter. *Olivia Newton-John.* New York: Quick Fox (Putnam), 1979.

THE NEW YORK DOLLS

PICTORIALS

Morrissey, Steven. *New York Dolls.* Todmorden, England: Babylon Books, 1995. Unpaginated (approximately 48 pages). Approximately 50 photocopies of black-and-white photographs throughout. The New York Dolls Discography.

Long before Steven Morrissey was Morrissey, the frontman for The Smiths, he was president of The New York Dolls Fan Club and their staunch supporter. In 1981 he first published this book, which has been updated (very slightly) in the 1990's—with no visible further participation from Morrissey himself. More of a curio fanzine than anything else, with reprinted newspaper articles, a slapdash year-by-year chronology, and some discographical information in the back. This relic fails to show how The Dolls connected glitter rock with pre-punk, and certainly shortchanges their influence on 1980's New Wave. David Johansen fans will want this book to see him in glitter rock garb; Morrissey fans will want it for the novelty of his name on the title page.

NINE INCH NAILS

PICTORIALS

Dean, Jeremy. *Nine Inch Nails.* Miami, FL: MBS, 1995. 120 pages. Approximately 75 color and black-and-white photographs throughout. Discography. Chronology. Index.

CD-format book covering all aspects of Nine Inch Nails' career. This nicely designed and illustrated book is priced just right—around $7.99.

Remington, Tuck. *Nine Inch Nails.* London: Omnibus Press (division of Book Sales Limited), 1995. 48 pages. Approximately 50 glossy color and black-and-white photographs throughout. Discography.

Hands down (please!), Nine Inch Nails are the filthiest rock band in existence. Or at least that's how they're portrayed on the cover of this book, which depicts singer Trent Reznor at

Woodstock 1994 caked in mud and mustering some kind of vocal with his lips mushed against a microphone. One must wonder if even the groupies were saying no to him that day. Some colorful images still don't make this any better than a magazine article. Sloppy seconds.

NIRVANA

(See also Hole)

BIOGRAPHIES

Azerrad, Michael. *Come As You Are: The Story of Nirvana*. New York: Doubleday (division of Bantam Doubleday Dell), 1994. 358 Approximately 125 black-and-white and color photographs throughout. Discography.

First published in 1993, this biography was unsubtly updated "with a new final chapter" in 1994 to summarize the events just before and after Kurt Cobain's suicide. Azerrad, a contributing editor to *Rolling Stone*, has produced a comprehensive and highly readable study of the band from Aberdeen, Washington who turned the music scene inside-out in the early 1990's. He throws in a lot of superfluous detail—such as scientific detail on turtles—but thankfully this is far more than a cut-and-paste job of quotes. It might be said, in fact, that the 1993 edition of this book set the precedent for the wave of Nirvana books that followed. Amidst misspelling the author's last name, *AP* commented: "And *Come As You Are* by Michael Azzerad[sic]...Ah, that old chestnut."

Sandford, Christopher. *Kurt Cobain*. London: Victor Gollancz, 1995. 292 pages. Two glossy eight-page black-and-white photo inserts. Appendix I: Chronology. Appendix II: Discography. Sources and Chapter Notes. Index.

The comparisons between Cobain and other figures flow freely throughout this uneven biography. Cobain is hailed as having the songwriting abilities of a John Lennon; the Seattle legend/status of a Jimi Hendrix; and the "joyous derangement of a Dylan," whatever that means. Author Christopher Sandford goes as far as comparing Cobain to Jesus Christ, whose pain and suffering was also displayed for the world to see. Thus Sandford portrays many aspects of this complex figure, but doesn't

bring us any closer to the real man. Interviews with friends, family, lovers, etc. fail to add anything new to what's already out there. Fans will find this book boorish.

Thompson, Dave. *Never Fade Away: The Kurt Cobain Story*. New York: St. Martin's Paperbacks, 1994. 172 pages. One 16-page black-and-white photo insert. Crisis Hotlines.

Kurt Cobain died at 27 in April, 1994 and, as expected, the know-nothing tribute biographies continue to multiply on the rock and roll shelves. What's next—his published poetry? In the rush to pop out this little number, the publishers didn't even obtain photos of the title subject. Fifteen out of the 16 pages in the insert are of mourners sobbing over Cobain's loss. According to Thompson, Cobain's cocaine addiction and suicide were the product of "neglect," which tied into his longtime psychological trauma over his parents' divorce. Nice try, Sigmund. The Crisis Hotlines section in the back is obviously the publisher's lame attempt at preventing lawsuits against the publisher from families of teenage suicide victims.

DEATH OF COBAIN

Black, Suzi. *Nirvana Tribute*. London: Omnibus Press (division of Book Sales Limited), 1994. 48 pages. Approximately 50 color and black-and-white photographs, covering every page.

Although labeled a tribute to Nirvana, the emphasis is clearly on eulogizing Kurt Cobain. Sporting some charismatic color and black-and-white photographs, this book primarily recounts the sensationalized events leading up to and concluding with Cobain's death. The author supplies a thumbnail sketch of his life and career, straddling the fence about whether his overall influence on kids has been positive or negative. Only for diehards. "The author can't even get Kurt's birthdate right..."—*Vox*.

PICTORIALS

Arnold, Gina. *Route 666: On the Road to Nirvana*. New York: St. Martin's Press, 1993. 228 pages. Approximately 150 black-and-white photographs, reproductions of album covers and concert programs.

Gina Arnold, a freelance rock writer and former NCAA champion swimmer, explains how Nirvana's album *Nevermind* justifies everything the punkers were trying to say back in the 1970's. Arnold has disdain for commercial performers such as Mariah Carey, Def Leppard, and Bruce Springsteen, among others, all of whom she feels are out to make a buck and ultimately end up playing Muzak for conservative fogeys. Suburbia, the middle-class, chauvinism, and music in general are also on the receiving end of some bashing. Although only peripherally concerned here with Nirvana as a band, Arnold does speak about her friendship with Courtney Love and provide her own personal vibes about concerts and festivals. Iconoclastic dogma that is often funny and revelatory. "...*Route 666* buzzes like the music it celebrates"—*Goldmine*.

Editors of *Rolling Stone*. *Cobain*. Boston and New York: Little, Brown and Company, 1994. 144 pages. Approximately 150 color and black-and-white photographs and graphics, covering every page. Discography.

Commemoration of the life and work of Kurt Cobain, containing more than 25 pieces culled from *Rolling Stone* magazine. Generously illustrated with upbeat photos of Kurt—bonding with his child, playing with a kitten, and rocking on stage—this book is also teeming with full-page quotes from other musicians (e.g., Mark Lanegan of Screaming Trees, Michael Stipe of R.E.M., and Mac MacCaughan of Superchunk) remarking on his death. The type is as chaotic as Cobain's life, ranging from the miniscule print in the essays to the oversized, overlapping characters in the quotes. The pieces by heavyweights Michael Azerrad, Greil Marcus, David Fricke, Ann Powers, et. al. are not to be missed. Fans that *don't* own this book should be punished (but nothing *too* violent).

Haus, Paul. *Nirvana*. Miami, FL: MBS, 1995. 120 pages. Approximately 75 color and black-and-white photographs throughout. Discography. Chronology. Index.

CD-format book covering all aspects of Nirvana's career. This nicely designed and illustrated book is priced just right at around $7.99.

Morrell, Brad. *Nirvana and the Sound of Seattle*. London: Omnibus Press (division of Book Sales Limited), 1993. 96 pages. Approximately 100 color and black-and-white photographs, covering nearly every page. Seattle and Sub Pop Chronology. Nirvana Discography. Major Releases by Related Bands.

This photo book broadens its scope to not only feature Nirvana, but also other top Seattle rock acts, such as Pearl Jam. Published prior to Kurt Cobain's death—which is a blessing in disguise—the book is thus able to concentrate on the group's outlook and traditions, which coincide with other local acts generally tossed under the heading "alternative." Morrell can't resist focusing on the relationship between Cobain and Courtney Love, and even goes as far as suggesting the two have punk attitudes but with a twist of Lennon/Ono social consciousness. An above-average investigation into how Seattle became the rock stronghold of the early 1990's.

No author. *Nirvana In Utero: The Pachyderm Sessions*. London: Vinyl Experience, no date. Unpaginated (approximately 48 pages). Approximately 50 glossy black-and-white and color photographs throughout.

Photos of Nirvana taken during the recording of the album *In Utero*. Boasts some fine shots of the group immersed in musical concentration, but literally nothing else. Attractive, hollow package.

No author. *Nirvana Tear-Out Photo Book*. London: Oliver Books, 1993. Unpaginated (approximately 48 pages). 20 color and black-and-white photographs throughout.

Both live and posed shots of Cobain and company. Not much spiritual nirvana here, unless you're in your early teens.

Wall, Mick and Dome, Malcolm. *Nirvana: The Legacy*. London: Omnibus Press (division of Book Sales Limited), 1996. 96 pages. Approximately 115 glossy black-and-white and color photographs throughout. Selective Discography.

The pictorials on Nirvana keep on coming. This one tries to highlight the band's overall influence on world music, with obvious reflections on Cobain's death. More of a glossy magazine than a book, this work does contain many rare and deeply personal photos. The material dealing with the "legacy" aspect is merely a summary of song and album positions, Hole's progress as a band, and Courtney Love's attempts to pick up the pieces since 1994. Only buy it for the photos.

Wilson, Susan. *Nirvana: Nevermind*. London: Omnibus Press (division of Book Sales Limited), 1995. 80 pages. Approximately 80 color and black-and-white photographs, covering every page. Discography.

Yet another Omnibus Press tribute to Nirvana, something of a déjà vu to Black's work (see Death of Cobain, above), which was even more of an obvious cash-in on Cobain's death. This time, the ironic message is on the front and back cover: Cobain is seen holding his breath underwater (simulating drowning), while on the back he holds his son, a vivid reminder of his hypocrisy in having taken his life. Wilson's writing is shamefully sparse—even for a picture book—with very little history of the Seattle scene. As the title goes, never mind!

OTHER TITLES OF INTEREST

Bego, Mark. *Kurt Cobain: In Search of Nirvana*. No city: Sure Sellers, 1994.

Collins, Britt. *Nirvana: Flower Sniffin', Kitty Pettin', Baby Kissin' Corporate Rock Whores*. New York: Hyperion, 1993.

Coolidge, Clark. *For Kurt Cobain*. New York: Small Press, 1995.

Harrison, Hank. *Kurt Cobain, Beyond Nirvana: The Legacy of Kurt Cobain*. Los Altos, CA: Archives, 1996.
Author Harrison is Courtney Love's father, and therefore was Kurt Cobain's father-in-law.

Sprague, David. *Teen Spirit: The Stories Behind Every Nirvana Song*. New York: Fireside (Simon & Schuster), 1996.

THE NOLANS

BIOGRAPHIES

Treasurer, Kim. *In the Mood for Stardom: The Nolans*. New York: Hippocrene Books, Inc., 1982. 128 pages. Approximately 100 black-and-white photographs throughout. Discography. (First published in 1982 in the U.K. by Midas Books.)

The Nolans were six real-life siblings—five singing girls, plus a drummer younger brother—who originated from Dublin, Ireland and moved to Blackpool, England. Emulating the Von Trapps (celebrated in the musical *The Sound of Music*), the girls shot to fame in England in the 1970's with songs such as "Don't Make Waves." The group never made

the U.S. Top Forty charts, but then again, we did have the Osmonds. A well-intended, though immeasurably dated biography, with glowing photos for that special angelic effect.

TED NUGENT

PICTORIALS

Holland, Robert. *The Legendary Ted Nugent*. London: Omnibus Press/Savoy Editions, 1982. 96 pages. Approximately 100 black-and-white photographs and pen-and-ink drawings, covering every page, Discography.

Macho, ultra-violent photos from a politically incorrect era, accompanied by amateurish and equally offensive pen-and-ink drawings. Nugent poses after having shot Santa, holds a doll to his crotch, threatens to maim and stuff various animals, and thrusts his guitar out like a machete—all for what? Nugent's splits, fist-raising, and wide-mouthed grins are grossly infantile, even compared with today's noncon-formist groups. Representations of sado-masochism and other depraved acts detract attention from his guitar playing. And Nugent's answer to his critics? "Well, fuck them right in the eye." Bottom of the barrel.

GARY NUMAN

PICTORIALS

Coleman, Ray. *Gary Numan: The Authorised Biography*. London: Sidgwick & Jackson, 1982. 128 pages. Approximately 100 black-and-white photographs throughout. Discography. Index.

One of the original stars of synthesizer rock in the late 1970's, Gary Numan was a rebellious child who was tossed out of grade school for bad behavior. With his naughty attitude and tortured expressions, he had all the makings of a would-be rock star. Unfortunately, without any knack for guitar playing, it took him several years to find his niche with the electronic sounds of synthesizer rock, which suitably fit his brooding appearance. Author Coleman resoundingly defends Numan against critics who branded him a Bowie clone and, in fact, he's so convincing one might think he's attained legend status (which he hasn't). For those willing to admit they've grooved to "Cars."

OTHER TITLES OF INTEREST

Vermorel, Fred. *Numan by Computer.* London: Omnibus Press (division of Book Sales Limited), 1981.

OASIS

PICTORIALS

Lester, Paul. *Oasis: The Illustrated Story.* London: Hamlyn (Reed Consumer Books), 1995. 80 pages. Approximately 80 glossy color and black-and-white photographs throughout.

Text and photos about Oasis culled from the pages of *Melody Maker* magazine. The usual cut-and-paste quotebook, with the added benefit of this being the first book out on the band. The photo spreads are attractive, but the biographical data doesn't add up to much. If you've been keeping up with your issues of *Melody Maker*, you don't need this book.

PHIL OCHS

BIOGRAPHIES

Eliot, Marc. *Death of a Rebel: Phil Ochs and a Small Circle of Friends.* Garden City: Anchor Press (Doubleday), 1979. 320 pages. Approximately 100 black-and-white photographs throughout. Discography. Index.

Part Brando, Dean, Presley, and Dylan, Ochs was a folk protest singer/songwriter in the 1960's who committed suicide in 1976. Marc Eliot plowed through the Ochs' family archives and conducted numerous interviews with those who knew the man. Most engaging are the descriptions of the Greenwich Village folk clubs circa 1963—the Gaslight, Gerde's Folk City, Cafe Wha, etc. Some of Ochs' early politics are rather baffling (he was a fan of *both* Kennedy and Castro) and he was a major egotist. In one memorable passage, he accidentally swallowed a contact lens and, refusing to perform with his glasses on, forced himself to

regurgitate the lens. Recommended for Ochs cultists and anyone interested in the 1960's folk/rock scene.

HAZEL O'CONNOR

AUTOBIOGRAPHY

O'Connor, Hazel. *Hazel O'Connor: Uncovered Plus.* London: Proteus, 1981. 128 pages. 12 color illustrations and 75 black-and-white photographs throughout. Discography.

Britisher O'Connor seems to have much in common with Bette Midler—she sings, she's appeared in films, and she loves to manipulate her persona. More than once in this memoir does she seem out to get attention through her outrageous posings and wardrobe. Yet O'Connor uncovers a good deal more about herself than her wigs, hair dyes, and shapely figure (one nude photo): she writes candidly about her rape in Marrakesh; her so-called "porno" career; her career-making role in *Breaking Glass*; her thoughts on drugs; and her bout with malaria. Worth a look.

SINÉAD O'CONNOR

BIOGRAPHIES

Guterman, Jimmy. *Sinéad: Her Life and Music.* New York: Warner Books, 1991. One 16-page black-and-white photo insert and approximately 10 black-and-white photographs throughout. Discography. Selected Videography.

Born to a broken Irish Catholic home (her parents separated but wouldn't divorce), O'Connor attended Catholic reform school and joined the band Ton Ton Macoute before she set out on her own. Through the lyrics of her music and the shaving of her head, she gained a reputation as a controversial political and social activist. At the time this book came out, O'Connor only had two albums on the market, hence there really isn't much substance to her story. One may be inclined to agree with her own observation about her personal life: "I'm the most boring person in the world." Strictly for fans.

OTHER TITLES OF INTEREST

Hayes, Dermott. *Sinéad O'Connor: So Different*. London: Omnibus (division of Book Sales Limited), 1991.

YOKO ONO

(See also Lennon, John)

BIOGRAPHIES

Hopkins, Jerry. *Yoko Ono*. New York: Macmillan, 1986. 272 pages. One eight-page glossy black-and-white photo insert. Index.

Few people are more despised than Yoko Ono. After all, wasn't she a crackpot artist? A shrill vocalist? The Dragon Lady who broke up The Beatles? Ignorant stereotypes and clichés aside, Ono remains one of the century's most complex figures: she was a descendant of Japanese shoguns; a key figure in the peace and women's liberation movements; and, whether directly or indirectly, an influence on several New Wave groups in the 1980's. This unauthorized bio is rather sketchily written, but is "an even-handed account" (*Library Journal*). There are numerous passages depicting Ono as manipulative and dominating; yet there are also moments of compassion, when the critics mercilessly lambasted her without attempting to understand her work. Ultimately, however, the book fails to bring us closer to the artist herself. The last chapter, with nowhere else to go, discusses the entourage of Lennon-related books released after his death. There is no discography or bibliography, and no photos of Yoko prior to 1965.

WRITTEN WORKS

Ono, Yoko with Haskell, Barbara and Hanhardt, John G. *Yoko Ono: Arias and Objects*. Salt Lake City, UT: Peregrine Smith Books, 1991. 140 pages. 120 black-and-white and color illustrations throughout.

More than anything else, Yoko Ono might best be regarded as a raw performance artist. Her songwriting and vocal abilities take a backseat to her avant-garde art pieces and contributions to stage, film, and video. Her work may seem ludicrous and downright daft to some, but there is both humor and ingenuity in *Object in Three Parts* (a diaphragm, an outstretched condom, and the pill each placed on a separate slab) and *Play It by Trust* (an ivory chess board with all white pieces on both sides). Ono's simplistic messages—peace, antiracism, antisexism, and love of the human body—are meaningfully conveyed in nearly every work. Her lyrics and album cover art, placed toward the back, detract from the book's overall artistic vision. All we are saying is: Give Ono a chance.

OTHER TITLES OF INTEREST

Ono, Yoko. *The Bronze Age*. No city: Cranbrook Academy of Art, 1989.

Ono, Yoko. *Grapefruit*. New York: Simon & Schuster, 1969.

Ono, Yoko. *Instruction Paintings*. New York: Weatherhill, 1995.

ROY ORBISON

BIOGRAPHIES

Amburn, Ellis. *Dark Star: The Roy Orbison Story*. New York: Carol Publishing Group, 1990. 284 pages. Two glossy eight-page black-and-white photo inserts. Notes. Bibliography. Discography. Index.

Roy Orbison, the "dark star," was initially an ugly duckling from Wink, Texas. Growing up, Orbison was unattractive (bad skin, squinty eyes, floppy ears, a mop of hair), unathletic, and embarrassingly shy of girls. Orbison was determined to overcome his appearance by hiding behind a cool, sunglasses-coated image and his much-envied voice. (Elvis was among his fans.) Like other rock stars of his era, he had a penchant for young girls (he married a fourteen-year-old) and suffered his share of tragedies (the death of his wife and two children). Amburn's revealing, though occasionally derogatory, portrait is a "...well-researched account of the singer's life..."—*Booklist*.

Clayson, Alan. *Only the Lonely: Roy Orbison's Life and Legacy*. New York: St. Martin's Press, New York, 1989. 260 pages. Two glossy eight-page black-and-white photo inserts. Discography. Index. (First published in Great Britain in 1989 by Sidgwick & Jackson under the title *Only the Lonely: The Life and Artistic Legacy of Roy Orbison*.)

The first major biography of Orbison comes from British music critic and biographer

Clayson, which should not be surprising given Orbison's large following in Great Britain. (Orbison made several tours across the Great Pond, including one historic stint headlining for the fledgling Beatles.) Amburn's *Dark Star* (see above), released one year later, covers much greater ground, particularly in reference to the early years. Clayson's work should not be ignored, however, as his focus on Orbison's musical legacy and influence is compelling. He also has an uncanny flair for words: He describes the Orbison family as resembling "a cageful of ruminating hamsters."

FANZINES AND FAN CLUBS

In Dreams: Roy Orbison Magazine. Attn. Burt Kaufman, 484 Lake Park #80, Oakland, CA 94610.

"A tribute to Roy Orbison & the rock & roll era," this quarterly 30-86-page magazine focuses on legends of the late 1950's and early 60's, predominately Orbison, but also others, such as Johnny Cash, Elvis Presley, Del Shannon, Jackie Wilson, and Sam Cooke. The magazine features black-and-white photographs, news, articles from subscribers, interviews, reviews, collectibles, tapes, videos, and more. Subscribers also receive an Orbison color poster, a button, and a few other extras. The cost of subscription is $18; $25 elsewhere. Payable in U.S. cash, check, or money order only.

TONY ORLANDO AND DAWN

TITLES OF INTEREST
Morse, Ann. *Tony Orlando.* Mankato, MN: Creative Education, 1978.

OZZY OSBOURNE

TITLES OF INTEREST
Bushell, Garry; Wall, Mick; and Rhea, Stephen. *Ozzy Osbourne: Diary of a Madman.* London: Omnibus Press (division of Book Sales Limited), 1990.
Vare, Ethlie. *Ozzy Osbourne.* New York: Ballantine, 1986.

THE OSMONDS

BIOGRAPHIES

Daly, Marsha. *The Osmonds: A Family Biography.* New York: St. Martin's Press, 1983. 136 pages. One eight-page black-and-white photo insert. Appendix: Vital Statistics.

Semi-intelligent biography of the Osmond family up through the early 1980's. Daly puts a different spin on her subjects, opting to focus on "their share of sorrow, heartache, and bad times," instead of the usual glitz and goody-goody froth. In the first chapter, much coverage is devoted to Virl and Tom—the two hearing-impaired, never-seen brothers—while later chapters divulge the pain caused by tabloid innuendos and false rumors spread about the prim and proper Mormon clan. As Donny and Marie's popularity started to wane, the duo continued to fight (with limited success) to establish their own names and find clean, family-oriented vehicles for their talents. Average.

Dunn, Paul H. Foreword by Ronald J. Clark. *The Osmonds: The Official Story of the Osmond Family.* New York: Doubleday, 1975. 246. Approximately 75 black-and-white photographs throughout.

What makes this book "the official story of the Osmond family"? The author explains: "I have seen them perform, and I have many times been in their home." To do what, one must wonder. Dunn doesn't even begin to address what this family is really like behind closed doors. Surely *someone* in that family used a four-letter word once or started a major food fight. Full of forced media hype and little substance; as anticipated, more placid than a night with The Waltons.

TOURBOOKS

Roeder, Lynn and Lisa. *On Tour with Donny & Marie and the Osmonds.* New York: Grosset & Dunlap, 1977. 220 pages. Two eight-page black-and-white photo inserts.

A major case of the cutes plagues this 1977 tourbook. Written by two 16-year-old girls who followed The Osmond clan along for a few concert dates in Pennsylvania, it is a dreary testament to The Osmonds' squeaky-clean reputation. One particularly nauseating moment involves The Osmond clan picking corn out of their teeth at dinnertime, to the apparent gigglish delight of those present. And as for the authors' tearful farewell to The Osmonds— no, readers can probably pass on that one.

YOUNG ADULT

Hudson, James A. *With the Osmonds: Special Arrow Edition of The Osmond Brothers*. New York: Scholastic Book Services, 1972. 80 pages. 25 black-and-white photographs throughout.

Fanzine-like bio for the young Osmond fan (are there any left?). A quarter of a century since its publication and still nauseating; do you really care to remember The Osmonds skating on "The Andy Williams Show"? Nearly every sentence ends with an exclamation point and every photo is too dark. Here's an exclamation: Stay away!

McMillan, Constance Van. *Donny and Marie Osmond: Breaking All the Rules*. St. Paul, MN: EMC Corporation, 1977. 40 pages. Approximately 30 black-and-white photographs throughout.

Part of the "Superstars: So Young, So Far" series, this joke of a book is hopelessly unhip and off-target; it's no wonder people question the tastes of the mid-to-late 1970's. At the time this book came out, Donny and Marie were still a hot commodity on television, and their family still had an unparalleled reputation for wholesome values. So, what rules did these siblings break? Well, saints preserve us, Donny wore purple socks every day as a gag. Abounds in inadvertent hilarity.

OTHER TITLES OF INTEREST
Delaney & Lacey. *The Osmonds*. Mankato, MN: Creative Education, 1975.
Eldred, Patricia. *Donny & Marie*. Mankato, MN: Creative Education, 1978.
Gregory, James. *At Last...Donny!*. Manchester, England: World Distributors, 1973.
Gregory, James. *Donny and the Osmonds Backstage*. Manchester, England: World Distributors, 1973.
No author. *The Fantastic Osmonds*. London: Daily Mirror Books, 1972.
Osmond, Marie. *Marie Osmond's Guide to Beauty, Health & Style*. New York: Simon & Schuster, 1980.

Osmond, Olive D. *Mother Osmond's Favorite Recipes*. No city: Knowledge Unlimited, 1990.

JOHN OTWAY

TITLES OF INTEREST
Otway, John. *John Otway: Cor Baby, That's Really Me!*. London: Omnibus Press (division of Book Sales Limited), 1990.

PANTERA

FANZINES AND FAN CLUBS

Pantera Hot Wire. P.O. Box 884554, Dept. PN-54 San Francisco, CA 94188.

Pantera fan club offering members access to tour packages, merchandising, and contests. Members also receive a newsletter including interviews, photos, and behind-the-scenes details of the band. The cost of membership is $16 U.S.; $22 elsewhere.

GRAM PARSONS

(See also Byrds, The)

PICTORIALS

Fong-Torres, Ben. *Hickory Wind: The Life and Times of Gram Parsons*. New York: Pocket Books (Simon & Schuster), 1991. 236 pages. One glossy eight-page black-and-white photo insert. Discography. Bibliography. Index.

A comprehensive biography of the original country rocker, Gram Parsons, whose work and friendship had touched Elvis Costello, Emmylou Harris, Keith Richards, and many others. Born Cecil Connor in Waycross, Georgia, Parsons came from a broken family, his genetic father having committed suicide when he was 13. A fixation on Elvis Presley led to his becoming a guitarist; years later, he was a member of The International Submarine Band, The Byrds, and The Flying Burrito Brothers. Parsons died at 26 in 1973 under extremely odd circumstances and, even after his death, mysterious events continued to occur. Among the many vivid anecdotes recounted here, author Ben Fong-Torres tells how road manager Phil Kaufman (who at one time had been Charles Manson's cellmate) unsuccessfully attempted to burn Parson's corpse in order to prevent the musician's stepfather from burying him in New Orleans. A richly detailed study of a country rocker who at least deserves to be named among rock's elite casualties. "Fong-Torres drops music-biz names and reports on the colorful 1960's and 70's fast lane with finesse"—*Publishers Weekly*.

Griffin, Sid. *Gram Parsons: A Music Biography*. Pasadena, CA: Sierra Records & Books, 1985. 192 pages. Approximately 200 black-and-white photographs, covering nearly every page. Selected Discography. Reference List.

Gram Parsons, who founded The Flying Burrito Brothers and briefly put a little country into The Byrds, was a proud southerner who had a musical career that stretched back to 1959. This retrospective, which includes a number of photos, interviews, and essays, shows many aspects of his professional life, including his collaborations with Emmylou Harris (who is interviewed here in-depth). The wealth of photos only partially overcomes the fact that we never really get to know Parsons or find out any inside information about his death. (Author Sid Griffin only mentions that it was due to heart failure, and that it had been upstaged in the press by Jim Croce's passing the following day.) Will be enjoyed by those already familiar with Parsons and his work.

DOLLY PARTON

AUTOBIOGRAPHY

Parton, Dolly. *Dolly: My Life and Other Unfinished Business*. New York: HarperCollins, 1994. 332 pages. One glossy 32-page photo insert. Discography.

Just a good ole' country gal from "back in the hollers at the foothills at the Great Smoky Mountains of East Tennessee," Dolly Parton was one of 12 kids from a poor sharecropping family. A pubescent appearance on "The Grand Ole Opry" led to her prodigious country/pop songwriting and singing career, with some excursions into films (e.g., *Nine to Five*, 1980;

Steel Magnolias, 1989). In her autobiography, Dolly's at her best when she does her outspoken, naughty-girl shtick, and at her worst when she pitches her cosmetic and lingerie lines and describes her own extensive cosmetic surgeries. The photos consist of too many vain shots of her awards, statues, and Dolly-clone "little fans."

FANZINES AND FAN CLUBS

The Dollywood Ambassadors. The Dollywood Foundation, 1020 Dollywood Lane, Pigeon Forge, TN 37863-4101.

Non-profit fan club established by Parton under the auspices of The Dollywood Foundation, a charitable organization directly involved with educational programs for children in the Smoky Mountain, TN community (where the star was born). *The Foundation Gazette* is the Foundation's official newsletter, containing information on Dollywood Entertainment Park, Dolly news, merchandise, pen pal information, and more. The cost is $20 in the U.S. and $30 abroad.

PICTORIALS

Caraeff, Ed (photographs) and Amdur, Richard (text). *Dolly: Close Up/Up Close*. New York: Delilah (distributed by Putnam Publishing Group), 1983. Unpaginated (approximately 96 pages). 75 color and black-and-white photographs throughout.

Unsatisfactory photo book of Dolly with too much tinkering done in some places and not enough in others. Dolly is photographed in a variety of poses, costumes, wigs, etc. and the results don't match up with the standard *People* magazine cover. Many of the photos are introspective black-and-white, which doesn't suit the subject. The color shots are screened and or tinted, and occasionally Dolly is set against a background of clouds and other surrealistic or period images; none of these come off successfully. Dolly deserves better.

James, Otis. *Dolly Parton: A Personal Portrait*. New York: Quick Fox (division of Music Sales Corporation), 1978. 96 pages. Approximately 100 black-and-white photographs, covering nearly every page. Discography.

"Her music, her life, her style," all captured in one anachronistic volume. James' writing is purple and absurd: "Her [Parton's] face is round and dimpled, and framed in a platinum blonde wig that looks like a glinting light of a clear blue morning by a high-speed camera." The photo selection is somewhat unusual, especially in terms of the pairing of Parton with stars such as Mick Jagger, John Belushi, and Lily Tomlin. (Parton has the same smile in all of them.) Not nearly personal enough.

WRITTEN WORKS

Parton, Dolly. Illustrations by Sutton, Judith. *Coat of Many Colors*. New York: HarperCollins, 1994. 32 pages. Thirty-two original color paintings throughout.

In Parton's children's story based on the hit song, an unnamed little girl must face the jeering of her schoolmates when she wears a colorful coat her mother sewed together with rags. Ostensibly, Parton is facing her own childhood poverty and attempting to pass on her wisdom to youngsters: riches come in many forms. While Parton's intentions are admirable and sweet, the book short-cuts the tear-jerking emotions a girl experiences when she is embarrassed by peers. Sutton's paintings, framed by cute patchwork designs, effectively depict subdued country settings.

YOUNG ADULT

Keely, Scott. *Dolly Parton*. Mankato, MN: Creative Education, 1979. 32 pages. Approximately 12 black-and-white photographs throughout.

Part of the "Rock n' Pop Stars" series from Creative Education, this entry is slightly better than the others. Keely smartly focuses on Parton's song "Coat of Many Colors," which clearly is an important theme in the artist's life and work (see Written Works, above). The photos are not flattering, however, and that—coupled with the fact that this book predates Parton's film career—make the work obsolete.

Krishef, Robert K. *Dolly Parton*. Minneapolis: Lerner Publications Company, 1980. 72 pages. 50 black-and-white photographs throughout. Recordings of Dolly Parton. Index.

Part of "The Country Music Library Series," this book for the young fan begins with a trite analogy between a young, poverty-stricken Dolly and Cinderella. Once the book gets

underway, however, the presentation improves; Dolly is linked with the country tradition and placed in perspective with other pop/country performers, such as Emmylou Harris and Linda Ronstadt. The book predates quite a few Dolly classics—and her entire film career.

Saunders, Susan. Illustrations by Pate, Rodney. *Dolly Parton: Country Goin' to Town*. New York: Puffin Books (Viking Penguin), 1985. 58 pages. Approximately 30 pencil drawings.

Part of the "women of our time" series from Puffin, this breezy book for kids eight to ten reads like a character sketch. Saunders drops many cute details about what Parton was like as a child—how she winked, how she put mercurochrome on her lips (to simulate lipstick), and how she dreamed of stardom. Parton is an ideal subject for this overtly sweet treatment, which is adroitly handled by the author. The only disappointment is in Pate's drawings, which never come close to capturing Parton's beauty. "Pleasing fare..."—*Booklist*.

THE PARTRIDGE FAMILY

(See also Cowsills, The)

AUTOBIOGRAPHIES

Cassidy, David with Deffa, Chip. *C'Mon, Get Happy: Fear and Loathing on the Partridge Family Bus*. New York: Warner Books, 1994. 242 pages. One glossy 16-page color and black-and-white photo insert.

Teen idol David Cassidy had it all in the early 1970's: gold records, groupies galore, and gobs of cash. When a female fan was crushed to death at a stadium concert in 1974, he suffered a breakdown and virtually vanished from the limelight. Cassidy lived through substance abuses and failed marriages to survive as good-looking as ever in the 1990's (though with shorter hair) and making occasional cable television and theatrical appearances. This tell-all autobiography failed to make the splash it should have, but perhaps that's because it's only written in one note. Seemingly against his will, Cassidy drags his story along through an endless stream of steamy sexual encounters (including with Partridge co-star Susan Dey) that are an undeniable hook, but a very shallow one at best. A male fantasy gone awry.

Jones, Shirley and Ingels, Marty with Herskowitz, Mickey. *Shirley & Marty: An Unlikely Love Story.* New York: William Morrow & Company, Inc., 1990. 336 pages. Three 16-page black-and-white photo inserts. Index.

After a long and rocky marriage to actor Jack Cassidy that ended in separation, Shirley Jones was comforted by the unlikeliest of would-be lovers, neurotic comedian Marty Ingels—the one-time star of the TV show "I'm Dickens, He's Fenster." Jack Cassidy's good looks and charms cast a shadow of doubt on Shirley and Marty's relationship, until Cassidy died tragically in a fire; Ingels, the lovable loser finally got the girl, but seemingly at the cost of a man he and everyone else respected. What does all of this have to do with Shirley's role in "The Partridge Family"? Not much—only a half dozen pages are devoted to the series—but those interested in Jones' early start in Rodgers and Hammerstein musicals will be entranced.

FANZINES AND FAN CLUBS

Friends of the Cassidys. c/o Cheryl Corwin, 2601 E. Ocean Blvd. #404, Long Beach, CA 90803-2503.

An extension of the *Friends of Shaun Cassidy* club, which is no longer in existence. Contains news on all of the Cassidys, including Shaun, David, Patrick, Ryan, and Shirley (Jones). Members receive a monthly newsletter, a membership roster, and a current year calendar. The illustrated 12-page reprints newspaper clips and prints fan letters and editorials. Dues are $12 plus 12 self-addressed stamped envelopes (two stamps); Canada $15.50 per year and 12 self-addressed stamped envelopes; and overseas, $19 and 12 self-addressed stamped envelopes. U.S. currency only.

International David Cassidy Fan Club. c/o Katy Leuty, The Old Post House, The Street, Litlington, Polegate, East Sussex, United Kingdom.

Also known as DCAS and the David Cassidy Appreciation Society, this non-profit club claims authorization from Cassidy, who serves as "Honorary President." Members receive a recent color photo of David and an eight-page newsletter, published bimonthly, which lists Cassidy news, reprints clippings and photos, holds competitions, and more. The cost of full membership is £14.50 plus six large self-addressed stamped envelopes outside the U.K.; £8 plus six large self-addressed stamped envelopes in the U.K.

Just David: International David Cassidy Fan Club. North America/South America: Barbara Pazmino, 979 E. 42nd Street, Brooklyn, N.Y. 11210. Europe and Asia: Tina Funk, Bueltbek 20, 22962 Siek, Germany.

Begun in 1974, this international club claims to have support from David Cassidy as well as his manager, associates, and family. The club provides members with two oversized posters, a special single release of "The Last Kiss," and a badge. Publishes five illustrated 20-page fanzines per year, containing updates on David's professional career and citing recent appearances and media mentions of Cassidy, his family, and The Partridge Family. The text is in German and English. Also offers merchandising such as videos, t-shirts, etc. The cost of membership is $15 in the U.S.; Australia and Asia $20; and Great Britain £10.

The Shirley Jones Fan Club. Martina Schade, President, 2295 Maple Road, York, PA 17404.

Fan club approved and supported by Shirley Jones herself (who is honorary president). Members receive: an 8x10, autographed color photo; two 4x6 color photos; a bio/fact sheet; and a membership card. Members also receive *Shirley's World*, a quarterly 26-page stapled packet that contains a letter from Shirley herself, photocopies of photos, questions answered by Shirley, updates on Shirley and family, reprinted newspaper articles, upcoming news, Shirley's tour schedule, and more. The cost of membership is $13 U.S.; $16 Canada and Mexico; $20 everywhere else. Payable in U.S. dollars only (personal check in U.S.).

GENERAL REFERENCE

Green, Joey. Foreword by Shirley Jones. *The Partridge Family Album: The Official Get Happy Guide to America's Grooviest Television Family.* New York: HarperCollins, 1994. 332 pages. Approximately 150 photographs throughout. Fan Clubs Index.

The ultimate in Partridgemania, magically boosted by the support of the entire cast, producers, songwriters—and even Columbia Pictures for use of the partridge logos and song lyric copyrights. Shirley Jones provides the foreword, while the other stars lend chunky quotes reflecting on the show's popularity and on the characters themselves. Green overdoes things somewhat in his introduction (referring to the show's "genius"), but he goes on to reconstruct a superlative history of the show's phenomenon, including both negative and positive press. The core of the book delves into a complete show-by-show listing (96 episodes), with partridge icons for ratings and impressive details about guest stars. Other filler material includes campy lists (e.g., all of Danny's get-rich schemes), a very funny *Mad* magazine spoof ("The Putrid Family"), pop quizzes, and their records (both group and solo). An absolute treasure for those stuck in the era. One complaint: Why isn't there an update on whatever happened to four-year-old child singer Ricky Stevens?

OTHER TITLES OF INTEREST

Avalone, Michael; Fairman, Paul; Crume, Vic; Stanton, Vance; Hays, Lee; and Fenton, Edward. *The Partridge Family.* New York: Curtis Books, 1970-1974.
We have Joey Green (see General Reference, above) to thank for cataloguing this series of 17 mystery books featuring the characters from the popular show. For specific titles written by the above authors, see pp. 278-279 of his work.

Cassidy, David. *David in Europe: Exclusive: David's Own Story In His Own Words.* London: Daily Mirror, 1973.

Gregory, James. *The David Cassidy Story.* Manchester, England: World Distributors, 1973.

No author. *David Cassidy Annual 1974.* Manchester, England: World Distributors, 1973.

No author. *The David Cassidy Story.* New York: Reese Publishing Company, 1971.

No author. *9 Lives of David Cassidy.* New York: *Spec Magazine,* 1972.

PAUL REVERE AND THE RAIDERS

TITLES OF INTEREST

Doege, Claudia M. *Paul Revere and the Raiders: History Repeats Itself!* No city: Dial Press, 1985.

PEARL JAM

BIOGRAPHIES

Wall, Mick. *Pearl Jam.* London: Sidgwick & Jackson, 1994. 176 pages. One glossy eight-page black-and-white photo insert. Chart of the Seattle Scene. Pearl Jam: The Complete Discography.

Rock journalist Mick Wall came out of the starting gate first in the race to get out a Pearl Jam biography. (Morrell's work, below, was the first pictorial.) Wall is more thorough than the photo book writers in setting the Seattle scene circa the mid-1980's, from which Pearl Jam evolved. He investigates the guitar virtuosity of Seattle-born Jimi Hendrix, then knowledge-ably traces it to the gap-bridging metal of northerners Kiss and to the first unofficial grunge band, The Melvins. It takes nearly 67 pages to get a solitary word in about Edward Louis Severson, a young man who pumped gas nights and surfed when his shift ended; later, of course, he became known as Eddie Vedder. Some fans may not have the patience to wade through Wall's eight line sentences, but then again, this isn't a biography of Philip Norman exhaustiveness (see Beatles, Biographies). Researchers will be thankful for the neatly-presented Seattle band genealogy chart in the back and the discography.

FANZINES AND FAN CLUBS

Release: An International Fanzine for Pearl Jam Fans. 410 A Gilbert Street, Bryan, TX 77801-3407.

Illustrated, 46-page Pearl Jam fanzine pub-lished twice a year. Offers recent Pearl Jam arti-cles culled from newspapers and rock mags, complete play-by-play of the band's live per-formances, interviews with the musicians, song lyrics, information on bootlegs, and more. The cost in the U.S. and Canada is $24 for four issues (two years); in Europe, $40.

PICTORIALS

Blake, Mark. *Pearl Jam.* Miami, FL: MBS, 1994. 120 pages. Approximately 75 color and black-and-white photographs throughout. Discography. Chronology. Index.

CD-format book covering all aspects of Pearl Jam's career. This nicely designed and illustrated book is priced just right at around $7.99.

Jones, Allan. *Pearl Jam: The Illustrated Story*. London: Reed Consumer Books (Hamlyn), 1994. 80 pages. Over 100 black-and-white and color photographs covering every page.

"I wasn't Jimi Hendrix," Eddie Vedder once said, "It just seemed like it was easier and more direct to scream in somebody's face." To no one's surprise, Vedder had a pain-filled childhood that culminated with his being told the identity of his real father—who shortly thereafter died of multiple sclerosis. The angry young man, originally from Evanston, IL, became the vocal cords of Pearl Jam, the band that would blow away rivals such as Stone Temple Pilots, R.E.M., and Nirvana. While there's more meat here than in Morrell's book (below), it's still only slightly more than you'd find in a CD booklet. Worth a scan for the pictures and to read Vedder's verbal lashing against Paul Simon—ouch!

Morrell, Brad. *Pearl Jam: An Illustrated Biography*. London: Oliver Books, 1993. Unpaginated (approximately 48 pages). Approximately 50 color and black-and-white photographs, covering every page. Pearl Jam Discography.

Shorthanded account of the world's top grunge band that shamefully abuses the word "biography." The photos, which are nothing spectacular, serve as the obvious focal point. The copy consists of cut out type, which appears to have been randomly glued to the pages. Overtaken by Wall's work (see Biographies, above).

No author. *Pearl Jam: Tear-Out Photo Book*. London: Omnibus Press (division of Book Sales Limited), 1993. Unpaginated (approximately 48 pages). Approximately 20 color photographs throughout.

Ask yourself one serious question: What do you suspect Pearl Jam would think of the concept of a tear-out book? Then make your own decision about whether or not to purchase this title. For what it's worth, one can speculate that Eddie Vedder might say that a tear-out book isn't different from any other bound publication.

TOURBOOKS

Lorenzo, Joey. *Live Pearl Jam*. London: Omnibus Press (division of Book Sales Limited), 1994. Unpaginated (approximately 32 pages). Approximately 40 color and black-and-white photographs throughout. Comes with a pull-out full-color poster.

Pearl Jam on stage in the early 1990's playing in front of various crowds in the U.S. and Europe. The accompanying 5,000-word essay barely covers enough for a magazine article. Only for young fans whose parents won't let them go out to the shows.

CARL PERKINS

AUTOBIOGRAPHY

Perkins, Carl and McGee, David. *Go, Cat, Go! The Life and Times of Carl Perkins*. New York: Hyperion, 1996. 440 pages. Two glossy 16-page black-and-white photo inserts. Discography. Bibliography. Notes. Index.

Although not a household name like other 1950's legends—Presley, Berry, and Holly, for example—Perkins was one of rock's true pioneers, blending hillbilly music with fast-paced guitar rock and roll. Perkins, best known for his classic "Blue Suede Shoes," influenced The Beatles to such extent that their LPs contained more covers of his songs than any other outside artist: "Honey Don't," "Act Naturally," "Matchbox," and "Everybody's Trying to Be My Baby." Written in third person through McGee's pen, this well-detailed life story takes readers from Perkins' sharecropping family in Lake County, TN; to his early Grand Ole Opry influences; to his days at Sun Studios mingling with Johnny Cash and Elvis Presley. Unlike many of his contemporaries, Perkins seems to have led a clean, unblemished life, although he still had his share of tragedies (the suicide of his brother, Clayton). Readers expecting to hear Perkins' voice in the prose may be disappointed; everyone else will be thoroughly satisfied by this incredibly detailed work.

OTHER TITLES OF INTEREST
Perkins, Carl. *A Disciple in Blue Suede Shoes*. Grand Rapids, MI: Zondervan, 1978.

PET SHOP BOYS

FANZINES AND FAN CLUBS

Pet Shop Boys Club. P.O. Box 102, Stanmore, Middlesex HA7 2PY England.

Club devoted exclusively to The Pet Shop Boys that offers members a full-color poster, two color photographs and three issues of *Literally* fanzine. The 24-page glossy magazine includes black-and-white photographs, interviews with Neil Tennant and Chris Lowe, and various merchandising. The cost of membership is $26 U.S. (payable cash only); £10 U.K.; and £11.50 elsewhere in Europe.

TOURBOOKS

Heath, Chris. Introduction by Neil Tennant and Chris Lowe. *Pet Shop Boys, Literally.* London: Penguin Books, 1991. 340 pages. Two glossy eight-page black-and-white photo inserts.

The two boys from Newcastle (Neil Tennant) and Blackpool (Chris Lowe), England are the subject of this detailed, authorized diary of the group's 1989 tour of Britain and the Far East. After years of refusing to perform live, the princes of "dance-floor twelve-inch remixes" packed up some dancers, a jazz saxophonist, and the all-important button for digital/electronic music programming and hit the road. Journalist Chris Heath unobtrusively asks the boys questions along the way, only pausing for a brief observation or informed opinion. Tennant and Lowe are portrayed as likable, if occasionally hypocritical, sad sacks who complain about concert sponsorship, but still wear Adidas sneakers provided by that company. "Recommended only for die-hard Pet Shop Boys fans"—*Choice.*

Heath, Chris and Smith, Pennie. Foreword by Neil Tennant and Chris Lowe. *Pet Shop Boys Versus America.* Miami, FL: MBS, 1994. 250 pages. Approximately 150 full-page black-and-white photographs throughout. (First published in Great Britain in 1993 by Viking.)

A British overview of The Pet Shop Boys' interaction in the U.S. for their 1991 tour, which encompassed 14 cities on the North American continent. So what was the controversy? If America survived The Beatles, The Stones, and

The Sex Pistols, what was the problem with The Pet Shop Boys? Not much—this is really a simple travelog that is heavy on backstage and hotel room banter. Heath's earlier work (see above) had slightly more pizzazz.

TOM PETTY (AND THE HEARTBREAKERS)

FANZINES AND FAN CLUBS

Makin' Some Noise. Amanda Saladine, 69 Crofthill Road, Slough, SL2 1HG, England.

Thirty five-page, illustrated booklet spanning the history of Petty and the Heartbreakers. Includes discographical information, articles on recent recordings, readers' comments, tour information, classifieds, crosswords, and more. Write for subscription information.

OTHER TITLES OF INTEREST
Kaye, Annene. *Tom Petty and the Heartbreakers.* New York: Ballantine, no date.

(THE) PINK FLOYD

BIOGRAPHIES

Schaffner, Nicholas. *Saucerful of Secrets: The Pink Floyd Odyssey.* New York: Harmony Books (division of Crown), 1991. 348 pages. Two glossy eight-page black-and-white photo inserts. Selected Discography. A Collection of Great Set Lists. End Notes.

Rock has probably never seen a stranger amalgam of imagery than in the work of Pink Floyd (or *The* Pink Floyd, as they were originally known): pigs, cows, sheep, walls, outer space, money, babies, war, axes, dead fathers, and so on. Schaffner makes a strong case that the lingering vibes of ex-Floyd Syd Barrett has somehow overshadowed the band and its imagery—even years after he left the group because of his erratic behavior. He also links Pink Floyd's technical wizardry to The Beatles' influence (both bands recorded at Abbey Road studios; and among Floyd's engineers were Alan Parsons and Norman Smith, both of whom had worked on Beatles' recordings). We may never understand the full intricacies of Pink Floyd and their laser spectacles, but this engaging book takes us as close as we are going to get.

Watkinson, Mike and Anderson, Pete. *Crazy Diamond: Syd Barrett & the Dawn of Pink Floyd*. London: Omnibus Press (division of Book Sales Limited), 1991. 168 pages. One glossy eight-page black-and-white photo insert. Appendix 1: Where Are They Now? Appendix 2: Discography.

One of the founding members of Pink Floyd and the undisputed creative leader of the band's psychedelic sound in 1967-68, Syd Barrett lost his mind rather quickly in the larger scheme of rock and roll. Was it LSD that caused his mania (often described as paranoia and/or schizophrenia)? Or was it the pressures of a rock band? In any event, when Barrett left Pink Floyd he actually released two highly influential solo albums and then retreated from the music scene altogether, spending some periods in a sanitorium. So what is Syd Barrett up to in the 1990's? These authors don't really tell us; the end chapters focus more on Pink Floyd's activities in the 1980's and don't even touch on the 1990's. The definitive bio remains to be written—if at all possible, with Barrett's input.

CHRONOLOGIES

Miles and Mabbett, Andy. *Pink Floyd: A Visual Documentary*. London: Omnibus Press (division of Book Sales Limited), 1988. Unpaginated (approximately 128 pages). Approximately 175 color and black-and-white photographs, covering every page. Appendix (discography).

Day-by-day diary of events related to Pink Floyd—reprinted numerous times since 1980—and including live performances, releases, radio appearances, and related events (the death of Peter Watts, their former manager). The listings are supplemented with lengthy quotes and an eyeful of spectacular color and black-and-white photographs. Concisely displaying the evolution of a band that had just reached its 21st anniversary, this book has its limitations, but is nonetheless a good starting point for fans who don't mind the generic flavor.

FANZINES AND FAN CLUBS

Brain Damage: The International Pink Floyd Magazine. P.O. Box 109, Westmont, IL 60559.

Twenty-eight-page magazine with a glossy cover bearing high-quality (usually erotic) art. Includes: color and black-and-white photographs; exclusive interviews; reports on past and present band members (Syd Barrett, for example); CD, book, and video reviews; questions from fans (answered by "Uncle Custard"); discographical data; past concert listings; bootlegs; collectibles; classifieds; and much more. For more information on the magazine and Pink Floyd news, call the Brain Damage Hotline at (708) 545-7131 in the U.S. and (0891) 299-734 in the U.K; note that neither is a free call. The cost of six issues is $28 in the U.S., Canada and Mexico. (Call the latter hotline number for U.K. prices.) Individual copies at newsstands: $4.95 U.S.; $5.95 Canada; and £2.99 U.K.

Czech & Slovak Pink Floyd Fan Club. Attn: Pavel Simek, Pizenska 25, CZ-37004 Ceske Budejovice, Czech Republic.

Eastern European fan club that publishes *eclipse 7*, a 20-page stapled booklet issued approximately ten times per year that contains photocopies of black-and-white photographs, plus articles exclusively in Czech. Write for subscription information.

Interstellar Overdrive. c/o Nino Gatti, via Caroli 75 72015 Fasano (BR) Italy.

Italian Pink Floyd fanzine published three times a year with a slight leaning toward collectors. The 16-page booklet is entirely in Italian, but the zine offers a special finding service (books, CDs, records, videos, etc.). Write for pricing information.

Pink Collectors Floydzine. c/o Durgante Alberto, Borge Treviso 120 31033 Castelfranco V.to, TV-Italy.

Italian fanzine founded circa 1993. The 26-page fanzine is Italian-only and features a color cover, photocopies of black-and-white photographs, interviews, reviews, rarities, and numerous ads. The cost of six issues is $32 U.S.; £20 Europe.

Pulse & Spirit: Pink Floyd und Roger Waters Magazin. Attn.: Werner Haider, Tegetthoffstrasse 13, A - 4840 Vocklabruck, Austria.

Austrian magazine, with little English, devoted to Pink Floyd and Roger Waters. The 24-page magazine has a color cover, black-and-white photographs throughout, exclusive interviews, collectibles, and more. Write for pricing information.

REG: The International Roger Waters Fan Club. 214 Lake Ct., Aptos, CA 95003.

Non-profit international fan club that claims sponsorship from Mark Fenwick, Roger Waters' manager. This fan-based club provides members with a club card and three-four newsletters per year. The 30-page newsletter, known as *REG: The International Roger Waters Fan Club Newsletter*, is a stapled packet that includes news about the band, tour information, letters, photocopies of black-and-white photos, reproduced interviews with Waters, trivia tidbits, want-ads, fanzines, and addresses of collectors. And what is "REG"? To put it simply: REG was the name of a caricature dog in 1984-85 Pink Floyd tour programs, as designed by artist Gerald Scarfe. (As poetic license, Scarfe had altered the abbreviated "Rog" from "Roger Waters" to "Reg.") The cost of membership is $20 in the U.S. and $25 abroad. (U.S. currency preferred.)

Us and Them. c/o Cassulo Luciano, Via Righi N5 15100 Alessandria Italy.

Fanzine that invites submissions from fans, both in terms of articles and photos. *Us and Them* includes photographs, record reviews, fans' personal experiences, correspondence, record classifieds, and more. Subscribers also receive a photo per issue and occasional stickers. The cost of four issues is 40 Italian liras in the U.S.; 20 Italian liras in Europe.

GENERAL REFERENCE

MacDonald, Bruno (editor). *Pink Floyd: Through the Eyes of...the Band, Its Fans, Friends and Foes.* London: Sidgwick and Jackson, 1996. 348 pages. Index.

Presented like a biography, this unusual book is actually an uncoordinated mix of reference materials on Pink Floyd organized thematically: welcome to the machine, art & architecture, cracking up, etc. The book reprints some excellent essays, reviews, and interviews from predominately British journalists such as Mick Farren and Miles, but this is only part of the package: There's also a meaty A to Z section in the back that mostly lists songs. Unfortunately, the descriptions and commentary on Pink Floyd's tunes are rigorous to read and fail to get to the point. Without any photos, this one is just another brick in the wall.

PICTORIALS

No author. *Pink Floyd: The Wall: Christie's Animation Art Auction.* London: Christie's, 1990. 66 pages. Approximately 120 color animation stills, covering nearly every page.

Exhibition catalog from a 1990 auction at Christie's, featuring works created by Pink Floyd friend and animator Gerald Scarfe for the film *Pink Floyd—The Wall*. Roger Waters' moody lyrics occasionally appear throughout, but the focus is clearly on selling the art (prices are included), which may well be a shock cure to those who are scared at the sight of blood. Monsters, bloody crosses, carnivorous plants, marching hammers, etc.—it's all visually stunning, but ghastly; you'd need to have strange tastes to hang these above the sofa. A nice collectible for Floyd fans, although there is very little of Waters in here.

No author. *Pink Floyd Tear-Out Book.* London: Oliver Books, 1993. Unpaginated (approximately 48 pages). Approximately 20 color and black-and-white photographs throughout.

Oliver Books released a slew of these tear-out books in 1993 (see, for example, Pearl Jam: Pictorials). This one on Pink Floyd has a freaky cover image of a snarling pig—but not much else going for it. Only for kids in their early teens.

Rich, Jason. *Pink Floyd.* Miami, FL: MBS, 1994. 120 pages. Approximately 75 color and black-and-white photographs throughout. Discography. Chronology. Index.

CD-format book covering all aspects of Pink Floyd's career. This nicely designed and illustrated book is priced just right at approximately $7.99.

Welch, Chris. *Pink Floyd: Learning to Fly*. Chessington, Surrey (England), Castle Communications, 1994. 160 pages. Approximately 200 color and black-and-white illustrations, covering every page.

Glossy, overloaded magazine that traces the entire history of Pink Floyd from its psychedelic origins in the late 1960's to the band's 1994 "Division Bell" tour. One striking fact about this book is that while the cover image is blurry and out-of focus (or poorly printed), the inside shots are first-rate. The designs and headings are very attractive as well, although without any indexing it's difficult for readers to find their way around the group's various tours and albums. *The Wall* double-LP ends up buried in an unfortunately titled section "Punk Floyd," and is only represented with one out-take from the film. One might do better catching the Floyd laser show.

WRITTEN WORKS

Waters, Roger. *The Wall*. New York: Avon Books (Hearst Corporation), 1982. Unpaginated (approximately 128 pages). Approximately 100 color stills from the film.

Companion to the 1982 hit film and album *Pink Floyd—The Wall*, this is a faithful document of both. Roger Waters' grim lyrics accompany each still, none of which is captioned (or identified to name actors). All of Floyd's classic tracks used in the film are here, however, from "Comfortably Numb" to "Waiting for the Worms." You'll have a hard time following the story and imagery, but undeniably there was (and still is) a cult following for certain scenes (such as the kids being dropped in the meat grinder). So who said Syd Barrett was the only crazy one in Pink Floyd? Fans, eat up.

OTHER TITLES OF INTEREST
Dallas, Karl. *Pink Floyd*. New York: Shapolsky Publishers, 1988.
Mason. *Pink Floyd*. New York: Simon & Schuster, 1995.
Miles. *Another Brick*. London: Omnibus Press (division of Book Sales Limited), 1984.
Miles. *Pink Floyd: An Illustrated Discography*. New York: Quick Fox (Putnam), 1981.
Ruhlmann, William. *Pink Floyd*. New York: Smithmark (Penguin U.S.A.), 1993.
Sanders, Rick. *The Pink Floyd*. London: Futura, 1976.

THE POGUES

WRITTEN WORKS

MacGowan, Shane. Illustrated by Hewitt, John and Pyke, Steve. Foreword by Sean O'Hagan. *Poguetry: The Lyrics of Shane MacGowan*. London: Faber and Faber, 1989. 96 pages. Approximately 50 photographs and 50 original drawings throughout.

Thirty-two original compositions by the Pogues' composer and vocalist, Shane MacGowan. These murky and macabre works reveal the author's Irish roots and punk attitudes, covering subjects such as death, aging, drinking, and the sea. Tunes such as "Lullaby of London" and "Fiesta" may sound optimistic, but even these are depressing. Steve Pyke's photos and John Hewitt's squiggly, dotted drawings appropriately complement the material. Enjoyable in a perverse sort of way, this book is, as foreword writer Sean O'Hagan says, "Poguetry in motion."

OTHER TITLES OF INTEREST
Scanlon, Ann. *Pogues: The Lose Decade*. London: Omnibus Press (division of Book Sales Limited), 1990.

THE POLICE

(See also Sting)

CHRONOLOGIES

Miles. *The Police: A Visual Documentary*. London: Omnibus Press (division of Book Sales, Limited), 1981. Unpaginated (approximately 128 pages). Approximately 150 color and black-and-white photographs throughout. The Records/Singles.

Heavily illustrated day-by-day account of The Police, beefed up with biographies of the band members and lengthy quotes. Most of the information on the daily events covers recording and release dates and TV and concert appearances. The photo captions are indistinguishable from the text itself, and some of the photo choices are questionable. An example of the latter is an uncaptioned photo of Mick Jagger looking at a magazine; on the back, not facing The Rolling Stone, is a barely visible snippet of the words "The Police." A lewd shot of Cherry Vanilla (with Sting looking back) is well off the subject. A marginal find for fans.

PICTORIALS

Goldsmith, Lynn. *The Police*. New York: St. Martin's Press, 1983. Unpaginated. Approximately 75 black-and-white photographs, on every page.

Half a promotional book of Sting photos, while the other is of Sting with Stewart Copeland and Andy Summers. There are few concert and recording shots, and even less in the way of group personality. The author/photographer provided literary aphorisms rather than captions. A genuine blunder.

Kamin, Philip and Goddard, Peter. *The Police Chronicles*. Toronto, Ontario (Canada): Musson (division of General Publishing Co., Limited), 1984. 128 pages. Approximately 150 color and black-and-white photographs, covering every page.

Coverage of "one concert near the end of a tour" (we're never sure which one—or even which year—although it's safe to assume c.1984) from the Kamin/Goddard team. Goddard's writing is so confusing we are never certain where we are either; the only two cities mentioned are Sydney, Australia and Champaign, Illinois, so take your pick. Suddenly, somewhere in the middle of the book, the story flashes back to The Police's early albums and career. Chaotic, although Kamin's camera does capture the orange stage lights shining down on Sting.

Quatrochi, Danny (photographer). Introduction by Sting. Captions by the Police. *Police Confidential*. New York: Beech Tree Books, 1986. 128 pages. 12 pages of glossy color; over 100 black-and-white glossy photos throughout. Comes with a poster of the cover.

Aqua green is the prevailing motif here. This background design peculiarity can be forgiven by fans because the photos are intimate and only focus on the three band members themselves; there are no shots of groupies and no stadiums full of screaming women. Yes, there is plenty of Sting: licking the sharp end of a long knife, inhaling from a humidifier to clear his lungs before a show and—only to make

non-fans nauseous—recording in his underwear. Sting's introduction is humorous, though predictably smug. The captions, written by the band and printed from their original handwriting, could have been a little more detailed. Strictly for Sting and Police fans.

POLICE FRIENDS AND FAMILY

Copeland, Ian. *Wild Thing: The Backstage, on the Road, in the Studio, off the Charts Memoirs of Ian Copeland*. New York: Simon & Schuster, 1995. 364 pages. One glossy, 16-page black-and-white photo inserts. Index.

Although lesser-known to the general public than his brother, Police drummer Stewart, Ian Copeland has had an equally impressive and fascinating career on the business side of music. As a child, he traveled the globe with his father, a CIA agent, and later earned several honors serving in Vietnam. With musical ambition but limited musical talent (part of one of his fingers had been amputated), he pursued agenting instead. Copeland's company, FBI, developed a client list that reads like a who's who in the music business: Adam Ant, The B-52s, The Bangles, Morrissey, The Ramones, and of, of course, The Police. (A full list appears before the Index.) While not containing the "gratuitous sex and violence" the book cheekily promises, this autobiography is of strong interest to Police fans and to those interested in the workings of the music business.

OTHER TITLES OF INTEREST
Nikart, Ray. *Sting & the Police*. New York: Ballantine, 1984.
Woolf, Rosetta. *Message in a Bottle*. London: Virgin Books, 1981.

IGGY POP

PICTORIALS

Nilsen, Per. and Sherman, Dorothy. *The Wild One: The True Story of Iggy Pop*. London: Omnibus Press (division of Book Sales Limited), 1988. 128 pages. Approximately 150 black-and-white photographs, covering every page. Appendix.

James Newell Osterberg Jr. was born in Muskegon, Michigan of Danish/Norwegian/

Irish/English descent. He lived in a trailer park with his parents, which he felt gave him a stigmatic reputation in his stuffy school. The formerly good student became Iggy Pop the rebel: a professional drummer (few are aware that he had backed numerous live Motown acts, such as The Four Tops), a Hawaiian guitarist with the bizarre group The Stooges, and ultimately a solo punk singer. Pop's entourage of friends and colleagues (political activist John Sinclair, Velvet Underground singer/junkie Nico, and David Bowie, among others) are quite a unique crew; the tales of raucous live performances, orgies, drug parties, and all-around wild antics make for juicy reading—and build up to the disquieting closing chapters showing how much Pop has mellowed. The back material includes tour dates, discography, filmography (did you catch Pop in *The Color of Money*?), and more. Fans will go wild for at least the first three quarters of the book.

WRITTEN WORKS

Pop, Iggy. Foreword by Andy Warhol. *I Need More: The Stooges and Other Stories.* New York: Karz-Cohl Publishing, 1982. 128 pages. Approximately 100 black-and-white photographs throughout. Discography.

Wacko punkster Iggy Pop abuses the English language with this collection of anecdotal stories about his life and career. In "First Fuck," Pop recalls the first time he went all the way with a woman. Twenty years old, slightly stoned, and exhausted from cleaning his feces off his terrace (yes, that's how he tells it), young Iggy first resisted the woman's seductions because she was mother of a child and he didn't want "sloppy seconds." Pop barely consummated the act, only to run away afterward in disgust and get hit by a car. The extent of exaggeration in this and other stories involving people such as his ex-wife ("a Jewish girl from Shaker Heights"), roadies, etc.—and the fact that few sentences are grammatically correct—probably won't matter to fans: It's 100 percent Iggy, which means it's irresistibly crappy. For those few who haven't seen Iggy's phallus, turn to page 79.

OTHER TITLES OF INTEREST
West, Mike. *The Lives & Crimes of Iggy Pop.* No city: Babylon, 1987.

ELVIS PRESLEY

BIOGRAPHIES

Clayton, Rose and Heard, Dick. *Elvis Up Close: In the Words of Those Who Knew Him Best.* Atlanta: Turner Publishing, 1994. 406 pages. Two glossy 16-page black-and-white photo inserts. Those Who Knew Him Best. Index.

"Those who knew Elvis best" reconstruct his saga through lengthy, meticulously edited quotes. Many of the speakers who had already written their own books—including Billy Stanley, Sonny West, Larry Geller, Marian Cocke, and Joe Esposito (see Elvis Family and Friends, below, for each)—also contribute to the story here. Some girlfriends participated in the interviews (Linda Thomson), while others (Joyce Bova) did not. Elvis' medical practitioners (Dr. George Nichopoulos) theorize about his condition at the time of his death, with interesting results. Much less sex-oriented than other Elvis publications, the book is "...full of thoughtful commentary..."—*Publishers Weekly*

Goldman, Albert. *Elvis.* New York: McGraw-Hill, 1981. 598 pages. One glossy 16-page black-and-white photo insert. Index.

This is the Elvis of gross excess, who ate his way into oblivion, was addicted to prescription drugs (Dilautid, Demerol, and speed), and in his last years couldn't control his sexual appetite or his bowels. Goldman's intent from the beginning was to portray the King as a power hungry (and just hungry hungry) sexual deviant who enjoyed watching his Memphis Mafia have sex with women through two-way windows and relished playing knock-down roller derby games with Amazonian females. Goldman leaps to all-new heights of cesspool tabloid as he ponders whether Elvis was a homosexual. The lack of any source material except for West and Hebler's almost equally offensive *Elvis—What Happened* (see below) allows one to easily dismiss the claims herein.

Guralnick, Peter. *Last Train to Memphis: The Rise of Elvis Presley.* New York: Little, Brown and Company, 1994. 560 pages. Approximately 20 full-page black-and-white photographs as chapter openers. Notes. Bibliography. Index.

A penetrating retelling of Elvis' rise—without

the hype, gossip, and tabloid filth. Guralnick faithfully examines what the shy mama's boy was like growing up in Memphis, a guitar strapped on his back and a dream of getting on The Grand Ole Opry in his heart. The year-long build-up of his relationship with Sam Phillips of Sun Records is mesmerizing, and the effect his mother's death had on him (by book's end) is haunting. An admirable, objective glimpse into the King's early development. Stay tuned for a sequel. "...a triumph of biographical art..."—*The New York Times*.

Hopkins, Jerry. *Elvis: The Final Years*. New York: Berkley, 1983. One eight-page black-and-white photo insert.

One of the earlier tell-all books on Elvis, somewhat gentler than Goldman's (see above), but still not close to a puff-piece. Elvis parades around airports with a gun, condemns left wingers and drug abusers, was kept on a short leash by Colonel Tom Parker and his father, Vernon, and, it almost goes without saying, had no control over his desires for food and sex. While Hopkins claims to have interviewed Colonel Parker, Elvis' girlfriend Ginger Alden, nurse Marian Cocke, and others, there isn't a list of sources or even a bibliography to indicate who said what. Tawdry innuendos without the evidence.

Hutchins, Chris and Thomson, Peter. *Elvis Meets the Beatles: The Untold Story of Their Untold Lives*. London: Smyth Gryphon Limited, 1994. 248 pages. Two glossy eight-page black-and-white photo inserts.

The much-anticipated meeting between Elvis and The Beatles in 1965 lasted for about three hours and began as something of a letdown. According to more credible reports, The Beatles were so in awe of Elvis they were tongue-tied for the early part of the evening. It wasn't until a late night jam session (with Elvis on bass) that things loosened up. The authors of this book couldn't care less about the realities behind the artists' interaction on that occasion; instead, this absurd book is about gossipy hearsay, such as whether Elvis informed to the FBI about John Lennon's radical political and social affiliations. Don't say I didn't warn you.

CHRONOLOGIES

Cotten, Lee. *All Shook Up: Elvis Day by Day: 1954-1977*. New York: Pierian Press, 1985. 580 pages. Approximately 250 black-and-white photographs throughout. Appendixes: A Discussion of Elvis' Place in the Memphis Music Scene Prior to July, 1954; The Sun Records Sessions; A Chronological List of Elvis' Appearances, 1954-1977; Billboard Memphis Country and Western Singles Charts; Billboard Singles Charts; Billboard Album Charts; Billboard EP Charts; Variety's "Top Grossing Films" Charts. Bibliography. Index.

"1935. January 8. Shortly after 11:30 a.m. in the house at 306 Old Saltillo Road, Elvis Aaron Presley was born." And so begins this day-by-day study of the King's life, which ends with Christmas Day, 1977. Each listing indicates the date and the day of the week—a rarity in a book of this kind—as well as specific times of events, locations, and little-known tidbits. Some of the appendix material is overkill (why shove in the "discussion"?), but the chart information is of some value. A "superbly crafted reference volume" (*Choice*) that has been blown out of the water by Pierce's more up-to-date chronology (see below). Typeset on finger-pleasing glossy paper.

Pierce, Patricia Jobe. *The Ultimate Elvis: Day by Day*. New York: Simon & Schuster, 1994. 560 pages. Approximately 200 black-and-white photographs throughout. Bibliography. Index.

A monster reference work, two thirds of which consists of chronology up through 1993, and the final third of which contains all sorts of miscellany. Excessive is the operative word here. Take one entry in the chronology: "June 3-6—Some members of the Memphis Mafia suggested to Elvis that he appear at the Newport Jazz Festival in Rhode Island, but the idea was rejected." The other sections include lists of Elvis vital stats, women in his life (and not just lovers), a Mafia who's who, movie data, studio musicians, employees, discography, and even participants in football games! "...an astonishing compendium of factoids"—*Publishers Weekly*.

CRITICAL/ANALYTICAL COMMENTARY

Matthew-Walker, Robert. *Elvis Presley: A Study in Music*. London: Omnibus Press (division of Book Sales Limited), 1979. 154 pages. One glossy twelve-page black-and-white photo insert. Appendix 1: Filmography. Appendix II: Select Bibliography. Appendix III: Select Discography. Index.

This is one of the few works to focus specifically on Elvis' music itself, and it's a shame that it isn't more substantive. The book consists of one third biography, one third musical commentary, and one third appendix material and back matter. The meat of the book, Part Two, takes readers through all of Elvis' recordings and, in one-to-three paragraphs, pinpoints the highlights of each song. Almost all of the comments lavish praise on Elvis, most noticeably in cases where the material wasn't exactly up to snuff. Treads in shallow water.

Quain, Kevin. Foreword by Mojo Nixon. *The Elvis Reader: Texts and Sources on the King of Rock 'N' Roll*. New York: St. Martin's Press, 1992. 344 pages. Reference Section: Cast of Characters; Locations; Selected Listening List; Elvis Goes to Hollywood; Selected Viewing List; Filmography; Documentaries; Television Specials; The Literary Elvis; Bibliography; Index.

A collection of reading material on Elvis in the following formats: short stories, essays, interviews, articles, reviews, and extracts from biographies. Pieces are divided by sections entitled: the Musical Elvis; the Mythical Elvis; the Southern Elvis; the Physical Elvis; the Mortal Elvis; and the Metaphysical Elvis. Lo and behold, this work includes three bilious contributions by Albert Goldman, which are countered by more reliable work from the likes of Lester Bangs, Roy Blount, Nick Tosches, and Stanley Booth. Some reference material is provided in the back, but the coverage is skimpy. "Quain's assortment of texts and sources is broad and serious..."—*Booklist*.

Tharpe, Jac L. (Editor). *Elvis: Images and Fancies*. Jackson, MI: University Press of Mississippi, 1979. 180 pages. One 19-page black-and-white photo insert.

A collection of essays that deliberate on Elvis' audience, voice, and social significance. Pieces by Linda Ray Pratt, Van K. Brock, and Bill Malone probe Elvis' importance to the South; essays by Patsy G. Hammontree and Stephen Tucker investigate the reasons for his mass-appeal and public perception; and works by Jeannie Deen and Gay McRae go inside the minds of those who idolize the King. Outmoded by later works that examine the impact of Presley's death.

DEATH OF ELVIS

Brewer-Giorgio, Gail. Foreword by Raymond Moody, Jr., M.D. and Detective Monte W. Nicholson. *The Elvis Files: Was His Death Faked?*. New York: Shapolsky Publishers, Inc., 1990. 276 pages. Approximately 50 black-and-white photographs throughout. A Selected Elvis Bibliography.

Follow-up to Brewer-Giorgio's *Is Elvis Alive* (see below), this book provides more substance in the way of documents and description, but in no way convinces that the King is out there living, breathing, and stuffing himself with fried chicken. Brewer-Giorgio repeatedly asserts that Elvis was sighted by "very credible" people, yet none of those mentioned here fit that description. She also cites two national surveys that state "between 84 and 86 percent of American people" think Elvis is alive. Who conducted this survey and when? The photos of Elvis sightings could not possibly appear to be more doctored (lurking behind Jesse Jackson and Muhammad Ali!). The real howler comes at the end when the author points a finger at Presley insider Joe Esposito because he accidentally referred to Elvis in the present tense, "proving" he must know his friend is still alive. For those who think Elvis is alive: Get a life!

Brewer-Giorgio, Gail. *Is Elvis Alive?*. New York and Los Angeles: Tudor Publishing Company, 1988. 220 pages. Reprinted letters and documents. Comes with "The Elvis Tape."

Here it is, the story that's sweeping the world—the incredible Elvis tape! Did Elvis hoax his own death? I can safely say that, having suffered through this dreadful book and listened to this onerous tape, the only hoaxers here are the author and her publisher. It may or may not be Elvis on the tape but, even if so, there is not a shred of evidence to support that it was recorded post-August 16, 1977. Brewer-Giorgio is simply attempting to boost profits of her novel *Orion* (about a rock star who fakes his own death). Hunk a' hunk of burning bunk!

Eicher, Peter. *The Elvis Sightings*. New York: Avon, 1993. 216 pages. One eight-page black-and-white photo insert.

Author Peter Eicher (if it's his real name) sorts through the details of Elvis' life (and death), with the intent of proving the King faked his demise. Sure, Elvis planned it all out, but every now and then, as a whim, shows up at a bowling alley so a tabloid photographer can snap him out-of-focus and blurry. A fifth-hand description of how Elvis' body "sweated" during the funeral ceremony is as unchilling as a book of this kind can get. Try not to catch this book in your sight.

Gregory, Neal and Janice. *When Elvis Died*. Washington, D.C.: Communications Press, Inc., 1980. 290 pages. One glossy eight-page black-and-white photo insert. Selected Newspaper Editorials. Sources and Notes. Bibliography. Index.

A blow-by-blow account of reactions to Elvis' death, with emphasis on the media. The first chapter reenacts the confusion Memphis newspapers were faced with when attempting to confirm initial rumors. Subsequent chapters deal with disc jockey tributes, television reportage, the world's reaction, posthumous film biographies, etc. Amidst the hubbub of the funeral, soulman James Brown affirms that, although few black people showed up, the King had a black following: "You think a black girl could run up and kiss Elvis?" An important work, despite a drab photo insert.

Marcus, Greil. *Dead Elvis: A Chronicle of a Cultural Obsession*. New York: Doubleday (division of Bantam Doubleday Dell), 1991. 240 pages. 50 black-and-white photographs and color illustrations. Citations. Index.

This rather strange assemblage of writings is intended to form a sort of sociology behind the King's influence after his death. Marcus provides a spoof scenario of a 1950's rock movie (with Elvis, Gene Vincent, Fats Domino, et. al.), critiques of various Elvis books, and lots of off-putting imagery, ranging from Elvis as Hitler to Elvis as hamburger meat. This complex and often cryptic study does not give us tangible conclusions, but is "...a graphically as well as intellectually stimulating foray into the farthest reaches of Elvisdom"—*Kirkus*.

Parker, John. *Elvis: The Secret Files*. London: Anaya Publishers, Limited, 1993. 272 pages. Two glossy, eight-page black-and-white photo inserts. Index.

Like Fenton Bresler, who had investigated John Lennon's death (see Lennon, John: Death of Lennon), Parker received a huge collection of documents from FBI files (courtesy of the Freedom of Information Act), which he claims support his theory that Elvis was killed by the Mafia (the Italian, not the Memphis) and the U.S. government covered it up. Parker never fully explains why either side would have such great interest in an overweight rock star well past his prime—and whose views were so conservative he made a publicity stunt of shaking Nixon's hand—and has no proof that any shady events transpired on the night of Presley's death. Not even up to *Hard Copy* standards. "...an implausible foul-play theory..."—*Publishers Weekly*.

Thompson II, Charles C. and Cole, James P. *The Death of Elvis: What Really Happened*. New York: Delacorte Press (Bantam Doubleday Dell), 1991. 408 pages. Three glossy eight-page black-and-white photo inserts. Bibliography. Index.

Thompson, who first brought forth his theories on the TV show "20/20," delves through what he considers to be a mass of cover-ups and botched autopsy reports to produce this study of Elvis' death. Four things the book proves for certain: (1) The King is, in fact, dead (2) He did not commit suicide (3) Addictions to prescription drugs led to his downfall and (4) Neither the CIA, the FBI, nor the Mafia (Memphis or Italian) had anything to do with it. As for any greater specifics, the controversies and discrepancies continue unabated, with arguments and defenses on both sides of the medical/legal battle still garnering media attention. Now that all of that is settled, go read Guralnick's biography instead (see above). "As Charlie Brown...would say, `Auggh!'"—*Booklist*.

DICTIONARIES AND ENCYCLOPEDIAS

Farren, Mick. *The Hitchhiker's Guide to Elvis*. Burlington, Ontario (Canada): Collector's Guide Publishing, 1994. 180 pages. Approximately 100 black-and-white photographs throughout.

Feeble-minded A to Z of Elvis data that really only has the cool title going for it. Here you'll find entries on "peanut butter and jelly sandwich" and "bubblegum," but nothing on Elvis' songs or records—though some scattershot coverage of books and movies. Not only are there more omissions than inclusions, but some non-present figures—including Elvis' lover Joyce Bova, his half-brother David Stanley, and his cousin Earl Greenwood, to name a few—are so obvious it's hard to grasp what author Mick Farren had in mind. He did, however, fill in the letter "Q" with one entry—for QVC network! Take a hike.

Stanley, David E. with Coffey, Frank. Foreword by Lamar Fike. *The Elvis Encyclopedia: The Complete and Definitive Reference Book on the King of Rock and Roll*. Santa Monica, CA: General Publishing Group Inc., 1994. 288 pages. Over 300 color and black-and-white photographs, covering every page. Trivia Quiz. Index.

Magnificently illustrated reference on everything related to Presley, boasting a whopping 300-plus color and black-and-white photos and documents—many of which can genuinely be considered "never-before-seen." Stanley, Elvis' step-brother, and New York writer Coffey, have amassed a wealth of details in sections covering day-by-day events, brief biographies on inner-circle people, movies, and discography. While not nearly as up-to-the-minute as Pierce's work (see Chronologies), it has quite a bit more flavor and visual candy. Sidebar boxes by David Stanley and Lamar Fike recount lesser and controversial issues surrounding the King, such as death threats, meeting Led Zeppelin, drug abuse, and more. Presley fanatics should grab this and sandwich it between Guralnick's book (see Biographies) and Pierce's chronology.

Worth, Fred L. and Temerius, Steve D. *All About Elvis: The King of Rock and Roll from A to Z*. New York: Bantam, 1981. 416 pages. Bibliography.

Despite the title, this book actually does belong under reference, as is evidenced by the more revealing subtitle. The entries contain solid information on songs, records, people pertaining to Elvis (ranging from The Beatles to Colonel Parker), places (with addresses for many), Elvis films, and so on. Excellent for quick reference and solving those seemingly unanswerable questions about the King. (Under the entry for "black belt," not only does it tell you that Elvis made it to the eighth level, it also names all of the films in which he uses karate.)

DISCOGRAPHIES, RECORDING GUIDES, AND COLLECTIBLES

Aros, Andrew. *Elvis: His Films & Recordings*. Diamond Bar, CA: Applause Publications, 1980. 65 pages.

Yet another vanity press discography of the King, this time containing an oversimplified discography, films (director, screenwriter, cast, year, and studio: no songs), album discography, and a bibliography. The closing sections comprise cast and song indexes. Poor.

Banney, Howard F. Photographs by Weitz, Charles. *Return to Sender: The First Complete Discography of Elvis Tribute and Novelty Records, 1956-1986*. Ann Arbor, MI: Pierian Press, 1987. 320 pages. Approximately 200 black-and-white reproductions of album covers. Personal Name Index. Song and Album Title Index. Record Numbers.

A collector's guide to seven-inch and twelve-inch records that pay tribute to Elvis; mention his name; include excerpts of his recordings; parody his music or image; and cover his songs in his style. One section *not* included is one listing songs in which another vocalist is simply paying vocal homage to Elvis (à la Paul McCartney and Wings' "Name and Address"). An offbeat slice of Presleyana, concisely and neatly laid out on the pages.

Barry, Ron. *All American Elvis: The Elvis Presley American Discography*. Philipsburg, N.J.: Spectator Service, 1976. 220 pages. 75 black-and-white photographs throughout.

Why would a researcher or fan want a book of only U.S. releases? There is no table of contents, so you have to fend for yourself while searching the various sections: singles; gold standard series records; extended play albums; LPs; movie songs; chronology; and songs A to Z. The book ends with three pages of trite phrases and advice for the collector. Unprofessionally done.

Bartell, Pauline. *Everything Elvis*. Dallas, TX: Taylor Publishing Company, 1995. 174 pages. Approximately 75 black-and-white photographs throughout. Bibliography.

"Your ultimate sourcebook to the memorabilia, souvenirs, and collectibles of the King!," this book not only tells you *what* to get, but who has it and how to order it. Most of the book consists of Elvis paraphernalia distributors and suppliers, with information such as address, phone, fax, specialties, and more. The introductory information on developing your collection and recognizing authenticity is somewhat limited. Recommended only as a starter's directory of sources.

Buskin, Richard. *Elvis Memories and Memorabilia.* London: Salamander Books, 1995. 96 pages. Approximately 150 color and black-and-white photographs, covering every page.

The usual schlocky stuff—poster art, dolls, medallions, keychains, etc.—all in color and supplemented with retreaded history. Some attractive items are assembled here, but it's nothing on the level of similar works listed above and below. As there is no indexing or pricing information, this one is strictly for browsing.

Carr, Roy and Farren, Mick. *Elvis Presley: The Illustrated Record.* New York: Harmony Books (division of Crown), 1982. 192 pages. Over 400 color and black-and-white photographs, covering every page. RCA Gold Standard Series. Spoken Word Records. Bootlegs. Mail Order Records. U.K. Discography.

Oversized record guide that is, quite simply, a lot of fun to flip through. Loaded with both color and black-and-white photos, images, cutouts, graphics, album covers, and more, you can see Elvis on the cover of *TV Guide,* cavorting with Ann-Margret, hamming it up in Vegas and, well, just being Elvis. The pictures overwhelm you throughout—and actually dwarf the discographical information, which is printed rather small. Carr provides critical assessments of each album (with song titles, release dates, label, and catalog numbers), but no running times. Dated but bouncy.

Cotten, Lee. *The Elvis Catalog: Memorabilia, Icons and Collectibles Celebrating the King of Rock 'n' Roll.* Garden City, NY: Doubleday & Company, 1987. 256 pages. Over 500 black-and-white photographs, covering every page; approximately 24 pages of color throughout. Licensed Manufacturers.

Brace yourself: Elvis lipstick; Elvis bubblegum wrappers; Elvis dog tag jewelry. But not everything hypes the King—an original "I Hate Elvis" pin was valued at $20 (in 1987), a full five bucks more than "I Like Elvis." Then

again, it's the rarity of the items that generally guides the value of a collectible, not the sentiment. The collectibles included here are captioned with a one-paragraph description and a commercial value, if in mint condition. The book is virtually useless because it doesn't have any indexing or other reference points. "...lots of librarians will be, justifiably, all shook up" —*Booklist*

Cotten, Lee and DeWitt, Howard. *Jailhouse Rock: The Bootleg Records of Elvis Presley 1970-1983.* Ann Arbor, MI: The Pierian Press, 1983. 368 pages. Approximately 150 black-and-white reproductions of album covers.

A virtual clone of Charles Reinhart's *You Can't Do That!* (see Beatles, Discographies, Recording Guides, and Collectibles) but on Elvis Presley bootlegs. This aptly titled book is yet another prize for collectors and Presley buffs from the people at Pierian Press (aka Popular Culture Ink). After presenting a cogent explanation of bootlegging and a handy glossary of terms (that probably would have been better situated in the back), the book tackles all Elvis Presley LPs, singles, special releases, cassettes, super 8 films, and videotapes that were pirated between 1970 and 1983. The authors provide useful data ranging from bootleg packager to year and distributor address, as well as commentary on packaging, content highlights, and consumer summary (is it a rip-off or not?). The song and record indexes are mixed throughout the book—a baffling editorial decision. Otherwise, an exciting option for collectors looking for material bootlegged during the aforementioned years.

Hawkins, Martin and Escott, Colin. *Elvis: The Illustrated Discography.* London: Omnibus Press (division of Book Sales Limited), 1981. 96 pages. Approximately 60 black-and-white photographs throughout. Selected Bibliography.

First published in 1974 as *The Elvis Session File: 20 Years of Elvis,* this book lists Presley's session dates, albums, singles, EPs, movies, bootlegs, and some tidbits about roots. Many other books listed herein (notably those by Pierian Press) delve deeper into the sessions, resurrecting names of players from all recordings. Too slim to be of any significance.

Jorgenson, Ernst; Rasmussen, Eric; and Mikkelsen, Johnny. Foreword by Lee Cotten. *Reconsider Baby: The Definitive Elvis Presley Sessionography 1954-1977*. Ann Arbor, MI: Pierian Press, 1986. 308 pages. Approximately 75 glossy black-and-white photographs throughout. Discography. Bootlegs. Glossary of Technical Terms. Appendix: Additions to the Sessionography. Index to Songs and Album Titles, Index to People, Places, and Things.

Revised edition of a 1984 work, this was updated by three Danes who are a veritable warehouse of information on the King. They chronologically identify each Presley recording session, followed by song titles, participating musicians, and additional notes. The authors also throw in catalog numbers, engineer names, session hours, and even reproductions of session sheets. Not for the layperson or the fan wanting stories about the sessions, but for the Presleyfile who takes this information very seriously. Pierian Press adds its usual high standard reference sections in the back.

No author. *All the King's Things: The Ultimate Elvis Memorabilia Book*. San Francisco, CA: Bluewood Books, 1993. 32 pages. Approximately 20 one- and two-page color photo spreads, covering every page.

Aesthetically pleasing but brainless promotional book of Elvis miscellany, culled from the collection of one Robin Rosaaen, a dedicated (or shall we simply say fanatical?) fan who owns thousands of pieces of Elvis bric-a-brac. The items are thrown together on display in categories such as Elvis' bedroom, Hawaii, jewelry box, the kitchen, etc.; dates, prices, and history are not provided. The only guiding force through the book is that readers are encouraged to "find Elvis' hidden treasures." This game concept could have been better developed, so readers could have had at least a little bit more of a challenge. Not worthy of royalty.

Osborne, Jerry. *Official Price Guide to Elvis Presley Records and Memorabilia*. New York: House of Collectibles (Random House), 1994. 432 pages. Approximately 300 black-and-white photos and reproductions of records and sleeves.

First published circa 1980 and revised almost every other year since (with paperback and mass market editions released simultaneously by different publishers), this congested catalog for the very dedicated collector goes as far as

advising readers on how to insure a record collection, and dubiously provides warnings against other "defective" recording guides. The book is divided into too many sections to list here, but, suffice it to say, it covers all singles, LPs, EPs, eight-tracks, cassettes, and CDs up through 1993. Listings include catalog number, price, warnings about recording and graphic quality, song lists, etc. Also included are song variations, novelty recordings, cover versions, and more. Buried in the back is a chronology, a guide to non-recorded memorabilia, and a directory of buyers and sellers. A useful, down-and-dirty bible for collectors that, unfortunately, is not indexed in any way.

Peters, Richard. *Elvis: The Music Lives On: The Recording Sessions 1954-1976*. London: Pop Universal/Souvenir Press, 1992. 144 pages. Approximately 100 black-and-white photographs throughout.

A slightly misleading title, in that only the final portion of the book details Presley's recordings one-by-one. The preceding chapters provide a history of Elvis' singing career, from his days at Sun studios to his many album soundtracks. Fans will probably gloss over the text and concentrate on the behind-the-scenes studio photographs, in which Elvis is seen on drums, piano, and guitar (although it's never fully established how much of his instrumentation—vocals aside—actually appears on record). The book would have had significant value if the section on studio sessions had been expanded to include lengthier descriptions, and if it had contained a song index. Written with the cooperation of the Official Elvis Presley Fan Club of Great Britain.

Tunzi, Joseph A. *The First Elvis Video Price and Reference Guide*. Chicago, IL: J.A.T. Enterprises, 1988. 192 pages. Approximately 75 black-and-white photographs throughout.

One of the only Elvis books exclusively devoted to video, this work abounds in typos—which doesn't exactly instill one's confidence in the pricing information. Tunzi introduces, in no particular order, movie prints, videos, CDs, promotional tapes, foreign discs, and more. But this is superficial in terms of both the volume of collectibles and the depth of information about them. A teensy slice of the pie.

ELVIS FRIENDS AND FAMILY

Adler, David and Andrews, Ernest. *Elvis My Dad: The Unauthorized Biography of Lisa Marie Presley*. New York: St. Martin's Press, 1990. 180 pages. One eight-page black-and-white photo insert.

Lisa Marie Presley may have had a turbulent upbringing—from her parents' rocky marriage to her legendary father's death in 1977—but she seems to have inflicted most of her woes on herself. A high school dropout, a former drug-addict, a member of L. Ron Hubbard's Scientology cult, and an unwed mother at 20, she has failed to make a name for herself—except as Elvis' daughter and as every parent's Drew Barrymore nightmare. Based entirely on other trashy books and predating the Presley/Jackson so-called marriage, *Elvis My Dad* only furthers Lisa Marie's reputation as a spoiled brat who doesn't have a tangible personality.

Bova, Joyce. As told to Nowels, William Conrad. *Don't Ask Forever: My Love Affair with Elvis*. New York: Pinnacle Books (Kensington Publishing Corp.), 1994. 432 pages. One 16-page black-and-white photo insert.

Bova, a Congressional aide who bore more than a slight resemblance to Priscilla Presley, had a long affair with Elvis, which was based completely on his terms. She followed him on tour, pacified his ego, made love to him at his whim, swallowed pills at his command—and claims to have aborted his child. Those who dream of living the Elvis courtesan fantasy might want to give this a try at bedside. To her credit, "Bova was no pubescent groupie"—*The New York Times*.

Cocke, Marian J. *I Called Him Babe: Elvis Presley's Nurse Remembers*. Memphis: Memphis State University Press, 1979. 160 pages. One 11-page black-and-white photo insert.

From the back cover photo and insert pics one can envision nurse Marian Cocke as a sweet old lady and, if this is really the case, it's no wonder Elvis had affection for her. Like many other small town folks with whom he crossed paths, Elvis gave his private nurse just a few trinkets over the years—a golden cross, a mink coat, and a gorgeous Grand Prix automobile—and he was ever-so-polite to her, in typical Elvis fashion. No doubt there was a mother fix-

ation here. In any event, Cocke has no story to tell: no revelations, no emotional moments, and no gossip either. In fact, the author doesn't even reveal that Elvis was admitted to Baptist Memorial Hospital (where they first met in 1975) for drug rehab. Somehow, I just don't see Elvis with the nickname "Babe."

Crumbaker, Marge with Tucker, Gabe. *Up and Down with Elvis Presley*. New York: G.P. Putnam's Sons, 1981. 256 pages. Approximately 50 black-and-white photographs throughout.

Gabe Tucker, a Nashville publicist, was the man who first suggested the name Elvis Presley to Tom Parker. He and Marge Crumbaker tread on the familiar path of Elvis' story, but they manage to fill in some fuzzy spots regarding business dealings, such as contract negotiations and Presley's relationship with RCA records. Throughout the book, however, are sleazy tales of Elvis' cruelty, such as when he had an old Memphis flame strip for him—and then turned her over to the Memphis Mafia to provide sexual favors. Pointless, and don't be fooled by the non sequitur title.

de Barbin, Lucy and Matera, Dary. Foreword by Charles Hamilton. *Are You Lonesome Tonight?*. New York: Charter, 1988. 326 pages. Bibliography. One 16-page black-and-white photo insert.

The memoirs of Lucy de Barbin, the dancer who claimed Elvis was the father of her daughter, Desiree. The book was a controversial best seller, as reviewers were divided as to the truth to the tale. The book relies heavily on the testimony of Charles Hamilton, a handwriting expert who verifies the accuracy of the letters Elvis wrote to de Barbin. Hamilton's foreword is a strange puff piece on a love poem Elvis presumably wrote to his lover: "Seen only by the eyes of my love, you're my life...." Whether the account described in this book is true or false (this reviewer has grave doubts), the personal details of de Barbin's life are fragmented and often read like a syrupy romance novel. (She was forced to marry a man at eleven?) Even tabloid Elvis fans could probably pass.

Dundy, Elaine. *Elvis and Gladys*. New York: Macmillan Publishing Company, 1985. 352 pages. Two glossy eight-page black-and-white photo inserts.

Author Elaine Dundy tackles what was perhaps the most famous mother/son relationship in entertainment history. Gladys Presley, whose lineage goes back to Native American roots, was a happy-go-lucky child who enjoyed dancing and sports, despite insurmountable poverty that forced her to work in the fields eight months out of the year. In a moment of "uncontrollable passion," the teenager wed Vernon Presley and endured years of even worse indigence—which was emotionally exacerbated by the death of Elvis' twin brother at birth and Vernon's three-year prison term. Dundy's research into Gladys Presley's genealogy is a critical slice of Elvis history, although her constant allusions to Captain Marvel Jr. (Elvis' favorite comic book hero) grow tiresome. "...entertaining reading..."—*Choice*.

Edwards, Michael. *Priscilla, Elvis and Me*. New York: St. Martin's Press, 1988. 280 pages. Two eight-page glossy black-and-white photo inserts.

More correctly, this should be titled *Priscilla, Lisa Marie and Me*; Elvis has little to do with this carnal tale. Edwards, formerly a top male model, insists he always loved Priscilla during their seven-year affair, but he's confusing love with lust. Both Edwards and Priscilla Presley were guilty of numerous infidelities and seemingly have no control of their hormones. Shortly after his relationship with Priscilla "matured," Edwards actually set his eyes on 13-year-old Lisa Marie! Tripe of the worst kind. "It's hard to believe that someone could be so hard up for money as to write this book"—*Booklist*.

Esposito, Joe and Oumano, Elena. *Good Rockin' Tonight: Twenty Years on the Road and on the Town with Elvis*. New York: Simon & Schuster, 1994. 272 pages. One 16-page glossy black-and-white photo insert. Index.

Joe Esposito, the don of the Memphis Mafia, befriended Elvis while they were in the Army stationed in Germany. The pair shared the best of times via touch football games and, after the two completed their duty, Elvis kept Esposito on as road manager—not a position to be taken lightly. After all, serving dozens of women to the King on a silver platter and maneuvering them around so they don't sniff each other out can be arduous labor. Elvis' sizzling affairs are well documented in this book, but fans might want to pick at it to get a flavor for what Elvis was like on a night out with the boys: jamming

the blues and tossing friendly karate kicks. "...Esposito and his co-writer maintain a spirited, affable tone throughout"—*Goldmine*.

Geller, Larry; Spector, Joel; with Romanowski, Patricia. *If I Can Dream: Elvis' Own Story*. New York: Simon & Schuster, 1989. 336 pages. One 12-page glossy black-and-white photo insert. Appendix: Elvis Books.

An oddball assortment of Elvis moments based on the diaries kept by Larry Geller, Elvis' hairdresser, personal confidante, and spiritual adviser. Geller gives this compendium the ridiculous pretense of being verbatim testimony from the King himself, in response to the trash-biographies from others in the Memphis Mafia. He treats religious and philosophical issues on the same level of importance as Elvis' fetish with women's feet. And please—avoid the spiritual "Elvis books" in the back; after all, what did they do for Elvis? "Presley fans will be gratified by the confirmation that the King was a fine fellow; detractors will discover little new fodder here"—*Publishers Weekly*.

Greenwood, Earl and Tracy, Kathleen. *The Boy Who Would Be King: An Intimate Portrait of Elvis Presley by His Cousin*. New York: Dutton (division of Penguin Books USA), 1990. 310 pages. Two eight-page glossy black-and-white photo inserts.

Earl Greenwood was Elvis' second cousin, childhood friend, and, later on, his press agent. Greenwood starts out with good intentions, especially in his tales of the King as a child frustrated by his mother's alcoholism, his father's imprisonment, and the family's state of poverty. Suddenly, Greenwood falls into the same trap as the smut-mongers he criticizes, and his emphasis turns towards Elvis' filmed orgies with the "good, simple, pure" women he used to respect. A "sensationalized, dull portrait"—*Publishers Weekly*.

Jenkins, Mary. As told to Pease, Beth. *Memories Beyond Graceland Gates*. Buena Park, CA: West Coast Publishing, 1989. 110 pages. Approximately 100 color and black-and-white photographs throughout.

We've heard from Presley's maid (see Rooks and Gutter, below), his nurse (see Cocke, above), and his hairdresser (see Geller, above), so why not his cook? Mary Jenkins is such a warm, kind individual, she eschewed publishers' offers for a tell-all book, when all she truly wanted was to "share all the beautiful, loving memories" with the public. Thus, accompanied by a number of her own personal photos (many of which are out of focus), she tells about her first meeting with the King and Queen (Priscilla), their generosity (donating a car to her, among many other things), the Presleys' married life, holidays, and so on. Only once does she report that Elvis lost his temper but, according to the story, he rectifies this with what seems to be a weepy, sincere apology. A very sweet book with some truly endearing photos of young Lisa Marie and a few recipes in the back.

Nash, Alanna with Smith, Billy; Lacker, Marty; and Fike, Lamar. *Elvis Aaron Presley: Reflections from the Memphis Mafia.* New York, HarperCollins, 1995. 796 pages. One glossy 16-page black-and-white photo insert. Index.

Billy Smith was Elvis' first cousin; Marty Lacker was the best man at Elvis' wedding; and Lamar Fike was part of Elvis' touring crew, as well as an army companion. This Memphis Mafia triumvirate shoots the breeze about Elvis' career, family, sex life, marriage, and just about everything else under the sun. Sometimes the speakers chat directly amongst each other and even disagree about a point or two; in other passages, the interviews seem to have been conducted at different times and strung together later. While several myths are debunked (namely assertions by writers such as Albert Goldman), these three support the claims that Elvis was a porno voyeur, the King of foreplay, and loved white panties on girls (which we are reminded of ad nauseam). While it's difficult to separate myth from reality, faulty memory from fact, and bias in either direction, the myriad reflections herein will have enormous appeal to Elvis gossip lovers.

Presley, Dee; Presley, Billy; Presley, Rick; Presley, David. As told to Torgoff, Martin. *Elvis, We Love You Tender.* New York: Delacorte Press, (Bantam Doubleday Dell), 1979. 396 pages. Two glossy 32-page black-and-white photo inserts. Index.

A family affair, as it were: The story of how the Presley and Stanley clans became one, and told by the latter's matriarch and her three sons. The text switches back and forth between Dee's romance with soldier Bill Stanley and that of Vernon and Gladys. When Gladys dies,

Vernon crosses paths with the blue-eyed Dee, and the two have an affair that culminates in the Stanleys' divorce (their marriage was on the rocks anyway) and the union of the Presleys. Some of the details on the Stanleys are a bit tedious, although things pick up when the families merge. Fans may just as well dig this up rather than waste time on later separate volumes by Billy and Rick (see below for both).

Presley, Priscilla Beaulieu with Harmon, Sandra. *Elvis and Me.* New York: G.P. Putnam's Sons, 1985. 216 pages. Three glossy eight-page black-and-white photo inserts.

Priscilla Beaulieu was a fourteen-year-old Air Force brat when she first met Elvis during his Army stint in Germany. The two developed a painfully slow, but nonetheless charged courtship that led to marriage, the birth of their daughter Lisa Marie and, ultimately, divorce. Partially out of genuine sincerity and warmth for her late ex-husband—and also to pander to the hordes of Elvis manics—Priscilla Presley creates a highly flattering and endearing portrait of the man who controlled her every move for a good portion of her early life. Not exactly for the *Ms.* magazine crowd.

Rooks, Nancy and Gutter, Mae. *The Maid, the Man, and the Fans: Elvis Is the Man.* New York: Vantage Press, 1984. 51 pages. Three black-and-white photographs throughout.

Three brief essays on Presley, the first of which—by Gutter—attempts to show how the man reflected his Memphis roots. The second, also by Gutter, is a fan's appreciation of Elvis; a housewife with three children, Gutter tells of her involvement with the Oklahoma Fans for Elvis fan club and of her emotional trip to Graceland. The final section, by Graceland maid Nancy Rooks, clears up myths about Elvis (he didn't wear diapers!) and supports others, such as that he was a ladies' man and was hooked on prescription drugs. These two women seem to be exceedingly nice, but it's clear they have no idea what they are doing with this book. Unnecessary.

Stanley, Billy with Erikson, George. *Elvis, My Brother.* New York: St. Martin's Press, 1989. 296 pages. Two eight-page glossy black-and-white photo inserts. Index.

Billy Stanley, Elvis' stepbrother through Vernon Presley's marriage to Dee Stanley, lived the dream of many young males of his time: lots of cars, sports, and loose women. When reality set in, Stanley's emulation of his famous older brother led to addictions and detoxification at a drug clinic. Stanley also played the part of helpless flunky, being cuckolded by his stepbrother (and never really standing up to him about it). His tale has some profound moments of Elvis up-close, but the parts on Stanley himself are numbing. Who cares about how he french kissed for the first time? "Not an essential purchase, except in those communities where most of the residents get up each day hoping to run into the King down at the A & P"—*Booklist*.

Stanley, Rick with Harold, Paul. *Caught in a Trap*. Dallas: Word Publishing, 1992. 232 pages. One glossy 16-page black-and-white photo insert. Appendixes.

After books from Elvis' cousins, the entire family (including stepbrothers Billy and Rick), an ex-wife, plentiful lovers, and a horde of Memphis Mafiosos, what is left for stepbrother Rick Stanley to say on his own? Not much but, for what it's worth, this book is less sensational than Billy Stanley's memoir (see above). Stanley emphasizes the happy times of growing up at Graceland, from learning boxing from members of the Memphis Mafia to selling his brother's autographs in school at high profit. Stanley retreads details of Presley's overuse of prescription drugs (which by now is probably a boiler-plate created by publishers), but he does stick to more puritanical aspects of Elvis' relations with women (perhaps a result of his becoming a Christian). A lengthy question-answer section is among the book's stronger suits. "...this book is poorly written"—*Bookstore Journal*.

Sumner, J.D. with Terrell, Bob. *Elvis: His Love for Gospel and J.D. Sumner*. Nashville, TN: WCI Publishing, 1991. 106 pages. One glossy 16-page black-and-white photo insert.

J.D. Sumner, a member of the gospel group The Stamps, tells of his encounters with rock royalty. Presley was so taken by Sumner and company that he hired them as his back-up group for his 1971 tour. According to a letter from Jack Soden, executive director at Graceland, the record on Presley's turntable on the day of his death was by The Stamps. Co-writer Bob Terrell doesn't lend any visible assistance in repairing Sumner's grammatically

incorrect prose (starting a sentence "Too, I never let any other people run my business....") and the stories herein lack spark. Not really an insider's story.

Taylor, Jr., William J. *Elvis in the Army: The King of Rock `n' Roll As Seen by an Officer Who Served With Him*. Novado, CA: Presidio, 1995. 170 pages. One 16-page black-and-white photo insert.

Did Elvis, as John Lennon asserted, die when he went into the Army? Retired Colonel William J. Taylor Jr. doesn't think so. For seven months between 1958-59, Taylor—then "Lootenet" Taylor—was Presley's superior officer and a guiding figure through some difficult training routines in the 32nd Tank Battalion stationed in Germany. Presley was never given special treatment, nor did he ever ask for it; he proved himself a fit soldier the hard way and became part of the battalion's "team." Taylor only sees Presley as one of the boys, well mannered and always doing what he was told—which fits in with Lennon's observation: Rockers *never* do what they're told. A well-intentioned snoozer.

Vallenga, Dirk with Farren, Mick. *Elvis and the Colonel*. New York: Dell Publishing (division of Bantam Doubleday Dell Publishing Group), 1988. 372 pages. One 16-page glossy black-and-white photo insert. Discography. Index.

This should have been titled *The Colonel and Elvis*, as he is the primary focus of this work. Colonel Tom Parker, Elvis' manager, was a 20th century P.T. Barnum. The authors' research about his life is impressive, taking us all of the way back to Holland, where Parker was born Andreas van Kujik. Parker snuck into the States and never actually became an American citizen; he worked in carnivals and in other oddball professions before becoming involved with country performers and "hawking" Elvis Presley and his image. After that, there really is not much here of interest about this selfish man. "More sad and tawdry than sensational..."—*Booklist*.

West, Red; West, Sonny; and Hebler, Dave. As told to Dunleavy, Steve. *Elvis—What Happened?*. New York: Ballantine, 1977. 332 pages.

The ultimate story of betrayal and irony, this book comes from Elvis' three bodyguards and writer Steve Dunleavy. Red West, who knew

Elvis longer than anyone else in the Memphis Mafia, collaborated with his cousin Sonny and Dave Hebler when the latter two were fired by Vernon Presley (the King's dad). The trio allegedly sought to "help" Elvis clean up his act by reporting on the star's drug addictions, sexual deviances, and violent tendencies; apparently, it didn't serve as much of a remedy, since Elvis died fifteen days after publication (and then book sales *really* skyrocketed). Mean-spirited, gossipy, and not for a minute as chummy as the authors would have you believe.

FANZINES AND FAN CLUBS

Elvis Business: The High Tech Newsletter. P.O. Box 668, Mt. Prospect, IL 60056.

Fan club that offers members a membership card, a bumper sticker, and a newsletter bearing the club's name. The eight-page, stapled packet contains: photographs; news; interviews with musicians (such as pianist Tony Brown) who worked with Elvis; information on music technology; merchandising; books; CDs; videos; and more. For a free sample back issue, send a $3 check or money order.

Elvis International Forum. P.O. Box 3373, Thousand Oaks, CA 91359.

Founded circa 1986, this quarterly magazine has a color cover and contains photos, contributions from Presley insiders, news from Graceland, memorabilia, and more. Also offers for sale two collector's books, *Elvis 15th Anniversary* and *Elvis 60th Birthday*. The cost of annual subscription is $19.95 (or $17.95 for gift orders); anywhere outside the U.S. add $10 to both prices.

Elvis Monthly. HRC Editorial Services, 6 Empire Road, Leicester LE3 5HE England.

An "organ of the Elvis Presley Organization of Great Britain & the Commonwealth," this hand-size magazine consists of about 48 pages. The booklet features a color cover, glossy black-and-white photographs, memorabilia, record and CD reviews, letters, pen pals, and more. Each issue costs $3 U.S.; £1.60 U.K. Write for subscription information.

Elvis Presley Fan Club. P.O. Box 4, Leicester LE3 5HY England.

British Presley fan club that provides members with a quarterly magazine, intermittently published newsletters, a membership card, and a CD or cassette. The club sponsors conventions, trips, and parties. *The Official Elvis Presley Fan Club Magazine*, a 52-page four-color magazine, features a color cover, color photographs, essays on periods in Elvis' career, interviews with celebrities (e.g., Cliff Richard), performances, movies, pen pals, reviews, and more. The cost of membership is £10 Europe; $30 North America; and £20 elsewhere.

The Elvis Presley Fan Club of the Capital District. 392 Rynex Corners Rd., Schenectady, NY 12306.

Non-profit fan club formed in 1978 with the goal of spreading the name, music, and legacy of Elvis Presley. The club's activities include occasional meetings, an annual "Our Memories of Elvis" party and various fundraising events. Members receive a membership card and an eight-page newsletter, published six times per year, containing member news, reprinted newspaper articles, and various records and collectibles. The cost of membership is $15 per year in the U.S. and Canada; $20 everywhere else. Payable in U.S currency by check.

Elvis Presley Fan Club of Victoria. Attn. Wayne Hawthorne, P.O. Box 82, Elsternwick, Victoria 3185, Australia.

Founded circa 1963, this durable club claims to be the oldest and largest Presley fan organization in Australia. Publishes a 20-page, stapled newsletter, *Accent on Elvis*, which reports on club dances, books, records, auctions, and merchandising. Also contains photocopies of black-and-white photos, news, pen pals, and more. The cost of membership is $15 in U.S.; $10 in Australia.

Elvis World. Bill E. Burk, Box 16792, Memphis, TN 38186.

This quarterly fanzine was founded a decade ago by Burk, a genuine Memphis man. The glossy, 16-page booklet includes black-and-white photographs, news on Presley-related events, Memphis activities, CD releases, books, merchandising, and much more. The cost of subscription is $15 U.S.; $20 elsewhere.

Elvis Worldwide Fan Club. 3081 Sunrise Memphis, TN 38127.

Club formed to keep members up-to-date on Memphis and Graceland news. Publishes a newsletter and supports charities such as The Special Olympics and The Elvis Presley Trauma Center. The cost of membership is $20 per year (U.S. funds only).

If I Can Dream: Elvis Fan Club of Massachusetts. Marsha Hammond, 4 Solar Road, Billerica, MA 01821-3430.

Fan club that supports many local charities, as well as the Elvis Presley Memorial Trauma Center in Memphis, TN. The membership package consists of a picture of Elvis, an Elvis button, and a membership card. The club also embarks on numerous trips and activities. A quarterly 28-page newsletter provides news, writing by members, photocopies of photographs, reflections on Elvis, interviews, contests, book reviews, advertising, and more. The cost of membership is $15 U.S.; $20 everywhere else.

In a New York Minute: Ronnie McDowell Fan Club. 38 Lynn Road, Averill Park, NY 12018.

Fan club devoted to Elvis imitator Ronnie McDowell that provides members with four newsletters, a photograph, a biography, a discography, latest concert schedules, and merchandise lists. The cost of membership is $12 per year.

It's Elvis Time. Attn. Peter Haan, Postbus 27015, 3003 LA, Rotterdam, Holland, Netherlands.

A 58-page Dutch magazine with a glossy, color-tinted cover that contains many black-and-white photographs. Includes CD reviews, reprinted articles, feature articles, classifieds, and more. Prints very little English. Write for pricing information.

Presley-ites Fan Club. Kathy Ferguson, 6010 18th Street, Zephyrhills, FL 33540.

Fan club involved in raising money for various charities and finding ways of spreading the glory of Elvis (such as petitioning the president to establish an "Elvis Presley Day of Recognition"). The club kit includes a membership badge and an audiotape containing four interviews. Members also receive an eight-page newsletter featuring announcements from members, stories about the King, games, reprinted clippings, and more. The cost of membership in the U.S. is $10 per year plus ten self-addressed stamped legal-size envelopes; overseas and Canada $20 plus stamped envelopes. Make checks or money orders payable to Kathy Ferguson.

Tender Loving Elvis Fan Club. Attn.: Tina Grimes, 898 Sunday Street, Defiance, OH 43512.

This fan club began in 1993 as an outgrowth of the *Elvis Press* newsletter, which began in 1991 and still continues. Proceeds from the club go to two charities: Elvis Presley Memorial Trauma Center (in Memphis, TN) and the Path Center (in Defiance OH). *Elvis Press*, the four-page newsletter, contains: reproductions of black-and-white photographs; Elvis world news; updates on Lisa Marie, Priscilla, and Graceland; and more. The cost of six issues of *Elvis Press* is $6; membership to the club, which includes the full newsletter subscription and a membership kit, is $8 in the U.S. The cost everywhere else for full membership is $12.

True Fans for Elvis Fan Club. 62 Lowell Street, South Portland, ME 04106.

Founded in 1977, this non-profit club strives to keep Elvis' memory alive and help out worthwhile causes. The club holds an annual dinner to commemorate the King's performance on May 24, 1977 at the Augusta Civic Center (Maine). Members receive four newsletters and a deluxe membership card. The 50-page stapled newsletter includes birthday wishes, letters from "true fans," numerous stories from members, reprinted newspaper articles, puzzles, fundraising activities, merchandising, books, poetry, and more. The cost of membership is $15 per year in the U.S.; $23 overseas. Payable in U.S. currency by check or money order.

The United Elvis Presley Society. Pijlstraat 15, 2070 Zwyndrecht, Antwerp, Belgium.

Founded in 1961, this long-lived club began under the name "International Elvis Presley Fan Club," but assumed the present title in 1986. The club donates money to medical charities and publishes an illustrated 42-page booklet, *Elvis Quarterly*, which is primarily in French. Write for subscription information.

FILM

Lichter, Paul. *Elvis in Hollywood*. New York: Simon & Schuster, 1975. 188 pages. Approximately 200 black-and-white and color photographs throughout. Movie music.

Presley's movie career, as catalogued by maven Paul Lichter. After a brief chapter on the King's early years and rise to fame, Lichter provides the cast, credits, and synopsis for each of his 34 movies (including the two documentaries of his early 1970's performances), but not running times or much in the way of tidbits. Better stills have been reproduced elsewhere, and the color promotional posters do not pop off the page as they should. The section "The Lazy Years" (ironically including 19 films, the largest in the book) is somewhat suggestive of this title as well.

McClafferty, Gerry. *Elvis Presley in Hollywood: Celluloid Sell-Out*. London: Robert Hale, 1989. 240 pages. Approximately 100 black-and-white photographs throughout. A Complete Filmography. Index.

The book title is intended to be ironic; while it's true Elvis did "sell-out" in terms of the quality of his films, he didn't deserve to have his reputation as an actor and movie personality so soiled. In fact, as director Don Siegel (*Flaming Star*, which starred Elvis) once pointed out, Elvis was something of a laughing-stock in the film world. Author Gerry McClafferty goes through each Presley film, highlighting the highs (and mostly lows) of Presley's checkered film career. While the photos consist of strong stills, they aren't oversized or color as in other works. Critics may want to give this read, let out all of their uncontrollable giggles, and then take a closer work at Elvis' celluloid magic.

Zmijewsky, Steven and Zmijewsky, Boris. *Elvis: The Films and Career of Elvis Presley*. Secaucus, NJ: Citadel Press, 1976. 224 pages. Approximately 250 black-and-white photographs, covering every page. The Elvis Presley Discography of Million Sellers.

Another photo retrospective of Elvis in Hollywood, and actually an improvement over Lichter's book (see above). Opening with 100 pages of biography—the usual data on his mother, Army service, etc.—the book encapsulates the credits, cast, and songs for all of the

King's "classics," with a two-to-four paragraph synopsis for each. This book includes weightier credits, release dates, running times, and quotes than Lichter's—and the photos, while not color, are sexier. (Check out shots of Ann-Margret, Judy Tyler, Dolores Hart, et al., and especially one in which Elvis and Tuesday Weld hold a shooting hose!) Written while Elvis was still alive, and with the authors' bizarre hope that he return to movies.

GENERAL REFERENCE

DeWitt, Howard A. *Elvis: The Sun Years: The Story of Elvis Presley in the Fifties*. Ann Arbor, MI: Popular Culture Inc. (Pierian Press), 1993. 364 pages. Approximately 150 black-and-white photographs throughout. Appendix 1: Early Elvis Presley Concerts & Reviews, 1953-1955. Appendix 2: Elvis Top Ten Memphis Nightclubs. Appendix 3: Elvis Sun Sessions and Other Early Recordings. Appendix 4: Other Presley Records from the Sun Records Era. Appendix 5: The Sun Label's Influence on Elvis Presley. Appendix 6: Musicians Influencing Elvis' Sun Years. Appendix 7: Sun-Era Elvis Bootleg 45s, EPs and Albums. Appendix 8: Jerry Osborne's Elvis Presley Recording. Appendix 9: The Sun Records Era: A History of Authenticity. Bibliographic Essay. Sources. Index.

Monster guide to Presley's hot early years at Sun Records, and part of the "Rock & Roll Reference" series from Pierian Press. A combination of history, biography, discography, and general commentary, this book investigates Elvis' roots, musical influences, his guiding forces, and how he honed his style in the studio and on stage. An excellent volume that fills many holes in Presleyana research.

Hammontree, Patsy Guy. *Elvis Presley: A Bio-Bibliography* Westport, CT: Greenwood, 1985. 302 pages. Five-page black-and-white photo insert. Chronology. Filmography. Discography. Index.

Hammontree, an assistant Professor of English at the University of Tennessee at the time of writing, has presented a comprehensive academic study on Elvis, nearly a third of which consists of biography. An interesting chapter on "interviews" points out that Elvis never really experienced an in-depth interview in which he had to face difficult questions. In the passage preceding her bibliography,

Hammontree explores the motives and sources for Goldman's tabloid biography (see above), with some startling conclusions. Marred by typos and poor syntax, this bio-bibliography is substandard in comparison to Pierian Press publications, but is engaging nonetheless.

Lichter, Paul. *The Boy Who Dared to Rock: The Definitive Elvis.* Garden City, NY: Dolphin Books (Doubleday and Company), 1978. 304 pages. Approximately 400 black-and-white photographs, covering nearly every page; four glossy four-page color photo inserts.

"Renowned Elvisologist" (or at least that's what Geraldo Rivera called him) Paul Lichter tries to cover all bases of his subject: biography; live Presley; recording sessions; discography; and films. Either due to ignorance, neglect, or to wheedle the Presley estate, Lichter overlooks crucial turning points in the Presley story (his father's prison term, for example)—omissions that leave the reader questioning his authoritativeness. Later works have delved much deeper.

Nash, Bruce and Zullo, Allan; with McGran, John. *Amazing But True Elvis Facts.* Kansas City, MO: Andrews and McMeel, 1995. 152 pages. Approximately 50 line drawings throughout.

Offbeat tidbits on Elvis, by no means intended as comprehensive. Learn all-about Elvis' butt-pinching chimp, Scatter; discover how Elvis was named special deputy in Shelby County, Tennessee; and find out how he once gave a young Lisa Marie look-alike a diamond medallion cross. So-so; the stories don't produce any belly laughs.

No author. Introduction by Glenn A. Baker. *The Elvis Album.* Sydney, Australia: Weldon Publishing, 1991. 240 pages. Approximately 250 black-and-white photographs throughout; approximately 50 glossy full-page photographs throughout. Films. Singles.

A massive amalgam of excerpts from books, newspapers, magazines, and other printed material. The clippings tell the chronological story of Elvis, from a few pages culled from Dundy's book (see Elvis Friends and Family) that explore everything from Elvis' birth to articles that feature interviews with those who claimed to know Presley, reviews of his performances, news items (coverage of his wedding), his death, and much more. If you are looking

for that rare Elvis clipping—such as one comparing Elvis' LP sales vs. those of Bing Crosby—this is a fine place to look, even though this book is not indexed. More expansive than Rijff's work (see below).

Rijff, Ger. *Long Lonely Highway: A 1950's Elvis Scrapbook.* Ann Arbor, MI: Pierian Press, Inc., 1988. 200 pages. Approximately 200 black-and-white photographs throughout. Index to People, Places & Things. Index to Dates. (First published in 1985 in Holland, under the title *Elvis Presley: Long Lonely Highway*, by Tutti Frutti Publications.)

Valuable, if not pretty, collection of rare clippings and snapshots spanning 1950-1958—Presley's formative years—and starting with a profile of Dewey Phillips, the disc jockey who first put Elvis on the air in 1954. Sandwiched between the newspaper articles and photos are nifty playbills and advertisements (one with Slim Whitman as top billing over Elvis, whose first name is misspelled!). A fine document of Presley's early career.

Sauers, Wendy. *Elvis Presley: A Complete Reference.* Jefferson, NC: McFarland & Company, 1984. 194 pages. Six photographs in the front of the book. Bibliography. Books, The New York Times, Periodicals. Index.

Thumbnail reference source sketchily prepared by Sauers that includes a (very) selected chronology, concert dates, films, records, (with labels, catalog numbers, and chart positions), memorabilia, documents (such as Elvis' will), and substantial bibliographies. The introductory biography is shoddily written and researched, while the other sections lack cohesiveness.

Whistler, John A. *Elvis Presley Reference Guide and Discography.* Metuchen, NJ: The Scarecrow Press, Inc. 1981. 260 pages. Sony Title Index. General Index.

A combination reader's guide and recording guide, with far more emphasis on the former. The first sections cover books and newspaper clippings on Elvis, while the discography follows. All titles in the book bibliography are listed alphabetically by author name, whereas articles are organized by both title and subject in the periodical index—which is incredibly confusing. An irritating assemblage.

KING OF KINGS

Canada, Lena. *To Elvis, With Love*. New York: Everest House, 1978. 178 pages.

A strange tale based on author Lena Canada's real experiences tending to a woman named Karen who had cerebral palsy and an Elvis fixation. The author cared for Karen and tried to coax language and expression out of her, but with only limited results. This soapy memoir might have made interesting TV drama fare.

Harrison, Ted. *Elvis People: The Cult of the King*. London: Fount Paperbacks (HarperCollins), 1992. 188 pages.

Author Ted Harrison describes Elvis as "the first prophet of the electronic age." With so much available hyperbole, why go for a label that's too easily up for debate? (Any earlier crooners such as Bing Crosby and Frank Sinatra could be labeled as "the first.") In any event, like many authors before and since, Harrison defines the Elvis gospel and points out the direction for people to follow if they want to pray to him. Hokey stuff, from the semblance of stained glass on the cover depicting Elvis with wings, to ludicrous passages that compare Elvis to Jesus. Wasn't Jesus slightly more slender than Elvis at the time of death?

Hazen, Cindy and Freeman, Mike. *The Best of Elvis: Recollections of a Great Humanitarian* . New York: Pinnacle Books (Windsor Publishing Corp.), 1994. 216 pages. One 42-page black-and-white photo insert. Bibliography.

Dime-store tribute to the King that tries to paint him as a Boy Scout who "read the Bible" to many of his love conquests. Chronicled throughout are various tales of Elvis' gift-giving, special awards he received, and charity events he attended. Superfluous and cheesy; the photo insert is the book's only saving grace.

Ludwig, Louie. *The Gospel of Elvis: The Testament and Apocrypha of the Greater Themes of the King*. Arlington, TX: The Summit Publishing Group, 1994. 180 pages. Bibliography.

Gimmicky humor book that pokes fun at the "Elvis as religion" cult. Ludwig goes after the King and rock and roll itself, creating his own biblical passages and providing his own satiri-

cal commentary in the margins. Among the many analogous characters are: Brother, aka Buddy Holly; the Virgin, aka Priscilla Presley; and the Comb, aka Ricky Nelson. Whether you think Ludwig's mock-parables are funny is a question of taste; this reviewer thinks it should have been handled with a much lighter touch, and with a structure more parallel to the Bible.

Moody, Jr., M.D., Raymond. *Elvis After Life: Unusual Psychic Experiences Surrounding the Death of a Superstar*. Atlanta: Peachtree, 1987. 160 pages.

One can be relieved that the title and subtitle do not accurately reflect the content of this book. Dr. Moody (whose medical specialty is not actually revealed) is an Elvis fan but not a maniac, and he does not assert that the stories detailed herein represent genuine psychic phenomena. Instead, he suggests that they relate to the power Elvis had on our psyches while he was a living human being. The tales largely concern fans' dreams of Elvis' passing shortly before his real death and ghostly appearances he made in the years that followed. Unlikely to produce the intended spine-tingling effects.

Panta, Ilona. *Elvis Presley: King of Kings*. Hicksville, NY: Exposition Press, 1979. 248 pages.

Laughable drivel from a self-professed visionary. Panta, a former milk-processor from Eastern Hungary, spouts that Elvis wasn't just the "king of rock and roll," but the "king of kings" whose birthplace in Tupelo, Mississippi is holy. Yeah, right. Not only does she claim to have predicted Elvis' death (she says she wrote warnings to him on several occasions), she also takes credit for having predicted World War II! Rock bottom.

Stearn, Jess. *Elvis: His Spiritual Journey*. Norfolk, VA: The Donning Company, 1982. 254 pages. One glossy eight-page black-and-white photo insert.

Jess Stearn, author of various books on yoga and psychic phenomena, probes the spiritual side of Elvis—and his "new-age teacher," hairdresser Larry Geller. In fact, Geller had asked Stearn to write the book and made himself available to the writer for interviews. Instead of elucidating Presley's religious outlook and beliefs, the book only shows how confused he was—sexually dominating women while at the same time placing them on a virginal pedestal.

According to Stearn, Presley would embark on sexual rampages but then feel a spark of religion and abstain from sex for intolerable periods to purify himself. The end-all seems to be that God had little to do with all of this: Elvis just missed his mommy.

Strausbaugh, John. *E: Reflections on the Birth of the Elvis Faith*. New York: Blast Books, 1995. 224 pages. Approximately 50 black-and-white photographs throughout.

An investigation into the origins and path of "Elvism"—no, not the religion of elves, but that of Elvis Presley. Author John Strausbaugh sees the King as a pagan God to millions of people for various reasons, namely that his followers pray to him, shrines are created in his honor, "scriptures" exist, impersonators constitute his "priestly caste," and his legion of followers form an order of nuns. Someone should explain to Strausbaugh the difference between a cult phenomenon and an actual religion. An interesting topic not handled in scholarly fashion.

West, Joe. *Elvis: His Most Intimate Secrets*. Boca Raton, FL: Globe Communications, 1993. 64 pages.

Pocket-sized tabloid item no doubt available at your local supermarket. Sections include brief write-ups on: Elvis the actor; the animal lover; his family; girlfriends and lovers; Colonel Tom; and so on. For 89 cents how can you go wrong?

Wiegert, Sue. *Elvis for the Good Times*. Los Angeles, CA: Blue Hawaiians for Elvis, 1978. 178 pages. One three-page black-and-white photo insert.

A collection of random thoughts and reflections by Presley's fans, assembled by Wiegert shortly after the star's death. Self-published by the Blue Hawaiians for Elvis Fan Club, this typed (not typeset) book includes a medical report from nurse Carole Neely and various writings by Wiegert and others, but all of their affectionate words are hard to read—and even more difficult to swallow.

MEMPHIS AND TUPELO

Barth, Jack. *Roadside Elvis: The Complete State-by-State Travel Guide for Elvis Presley Fans*. Chicago: Contemporary Books, 1991. 184 pages. Approximately 70 black-and-white

photographs throughout. Elvis Fan Clubs; Official "Elvis Day" Map; Bibliography; How to Lobby for the Elvis Stamp; Index.

Okay, why *not* a travel guide on all Elvis-related places? At least the author harshly renounces all Elvis sightings: "Elvis is dead, dead, dead," Jack Barth writes in his introduction. However quirky, this book does present quite a bit of information for those who plan to do the complete Elvis mecca. In the state-by-state listings you can find Elvis museums, where Elvis performed, where family members worked, where films were set, and quite a bit more. If you're really hard up for locales, there are hospitals, shopping malls, and even an "Elvis Around the World" section. Take along on your trip to Graceland.

Urquhart, Sharon Colette. *Placing Elvis: A Tour Guide to the Kingdom*. New Orleans, LA: Paper Chase Press, 1994. 112 pages. Approximately 60 black-and-white photographs and maps. Sources. Index.

A road map to Elvis-related sites that also trails through the histories of Tupelo and Memphis. Better as a travel guide than as a true reference, *Placing Elvis* is handier than Barth's work for those planning a trip only through those two cities. Places as obscure as Riley's Jewelers (which once housed Dr. Hunt, the attending physician at Elvis' birth) and the Presley hotel (where Elvis had his senior prom) are of curio interest. A serious, quick source for place information, neatly presented and easy-to-use. Casual Presley fans may want something more selective.

Winegardner, Mark. *Elvis Presley Boulevard: From Sea to Shining Sea Almost*. New York: Atlantic Monthly Press, 1987. 224 pages.

Winegardner reports on his no-frills travels across several states in the U.S. Presley fans will skip over to his visit to Graceland, where he took a tour and purchased an Elvis ashtray. Winegardner points out the tear on Elvis' pool table (not caused by the King, of course), the trophy room, and his motorcycles, and even shares his experiences walking through Presley's private plane, *The Lisa Marie*. "It's a journey as intriguing as Steinbeck's..." —*Booklist*.

PICTORIALS

Barker, Kent and Pritikin, Karin. *The King and I: A Little Gallery of Elvis Impersonators*. San Francisco: Chronicle Books, 1992. 96 pages. Approximately 60 black-and-white photographs throughout.

One of the many reasons people are sick to death of Elvis: his imitators. These proud (or none-too-proud, as the case may be) phonies sing, shake, twist, and snarl—but they're not by a longshot close facsimiles of the original; if you get right down to it, there are some pretty ugly dudes in here. Andy Kaufman was far more convincing with his Elvis shtick. Presley and Rodgers and Hammerstein (note the title) just turned in their graves.

Curtin, Jim. Assisted by Ginter, Renata. *Elvis and the Stars*. Wayne, PA: Morgin Press, Inc., 1993. 144 pages. Approximately 150 black-and-white photographs, covering every page.

Curtin, who claims to own 25,000 Presley photographs, has compiled a collection of shots of the King with other musicians and actors. Elvis is spotted with Bill Haley, the Dorsey Brothers, Liberace, Brenda Lee (at 13), Juliet Prowse, Barbara Eden, and many others. For Elvis fans on a star kick.

Doll, Susan. *Elvis: A Tribute to His Life*. Lincolnwood: Publications International, 1989. 256 pages. Approximately 500 color and black-and-white illustrations, covering nearly every page. Films and Singles. Index.

A tome almost as large as the Ten Commandments, this ten-pounder contains the usual biographical details and photos, but with additional rare photographs of Graceland's interior, various monuments and tourist sites, and up-close shots from Presley's funeral. The off-white matted background on every page is dull and does little to emphasize the text or art. Full of clichés and few knock 'em dead pictures, Doll's book takes up way too much shelf space to make it worthwhile.

Doll, Susan. *Elvis: Portrait of the King*. Lincolnwood: Publications International, 1995. 240 pages. Approximately 400 color and black-and-white photographs throughout.

Amply illustrated pictorial of the King, with biographical chapters on his childhood, rise to fame, Army stint, movie career, live performances, and death. Elvis, the cool, dangerous dude from the mid-to-late-1950's, is once again lost amidst pop trivializing. End sections include a feature on Elvis imitators (uh-huh!) and influence in the 1990's—but who cares? On the positive side, author Susan Doll does avoid addressing Lisa Marie's fiasco with Michael Jackson.

Giuliano, Geoffrey; Giuliano, Brenda; and Black, Deborah Lynn. *The Illustrated Elvis Presley*. Edison, NJ: Chartwell Books (division of Book Sales, Inc.), 1994. 96 pages. Approximately 80 color and black-and-white illustrations throughout.

Pictorial biography of the King by the husband-and-wife Giuliano team and some help from Deborah Lynn Black. Unlike the Giulianos' other collaborations, we do not have to suffer through Geoffrey's hyperactive writing voice and an unrelated introduction from Ginger Baker (see Stewart, Rod: Biographies). The photos in this book are attractive and largely half or full-page, but the three authors don't touch on anything that hasn't been handled before. Yes, it's just another illustrated Elvis book.

Glade, Emory. *Elvis: A Golden Tribute*, Wauwatosa, WI: Robus, 1984. Unpaginated (approximately 32 pages). Approximately 40 glossy color and black-and-white photograph throughout.

Magazine-format book with photo spreads on some—but not all—of the high points of Elvis' life and career. Promotional fluff, all of which you've seen before.

Harbinson, W.A. *Elvis Presley: An Illustrated Biography*. London: Michael Joseph Limited, 1975. 160 pages. Approximately 175 black-and-white photographs, covering every page.

Pre-mortem pictorial biography of Elvis that starts and ends with some very poor language. For example, here's a description of young Elvis: "He is here amongst them and he goes quite unnoticed. He is normal. A growing lad. But that's not to say that's he's ignored." Some decent photos are wasted alongside Harbinger's robotic, flavorless, and uninformative prose. In some ways, this is more painful to read than West, et. al.'s book (see Elvis Friends and Family, above).

Harper, Betty. Foreword by Bill E. Burk. *Suddenly and Gently: Visions of Elvis through the Art of Betty Harper.* New York: St. Martin's Press, 1987. Unpaginated. Approximately 50 full-page original drawings in pencil.

In these delicately penciled studies by Betty Harper, the King's eyes tend to be the focal point. He is dreamily pensive in many of the drawings; his eyes tend to be either closed or he just gazes into nothingness. While this works successfully in a couple of pieces, most of the images depict him as too innocent and too pretty. Where's that sneer we all love (and/or hate)? Harper's poetry, written in calligraphy alongside some of the art, oozes sap.

Hirshberg, Charles and the Editors of *Life. Elvis: A Celebration in Pictures.* New York: Warner, 1995. 128 pages. Approximately 150 glossy black-and-white and 12 glossy color photographs, covering every page.

From the producers of *Life* magazine comes this glossy picture study of Elvis. The photos trace his roots from childhood, to classic performance shots, to his Army years, to fans mourning his loss. The emphasis is slightly on the early years, with some limited coverage of Vegas and his plump 1970's appearance. No need to feel embarrassed displaying this one—the camp is kept to a minimum.

Kilgore, Al (art); **Fitzgerald, Jim** (text). *Elvis: The Paper Doll Book.* New York: St. Martin's Press, 1982. Unpaginated (approximately 32 pages). Approximately 30 color cutouts and 30 black-and-white photographs, covering every page.

Elvis in swim trunks! Elvis in cotton undies! Elvis in costume for "The Steve Allen Show"! Elvis in military garb! This old chestnut is exactly what you'd expect—and lots of cheesy fun for kids and adults. The drawings for some of the movie costumes (*Charro*, for example) are funnier without Elvis' head stuck on. Hard to resist—even a decade and a half later.

Kricun, Morrie E. and **Kricun, Virginia M.** *Elvis 1956 Reflections.* Wayne, PA: Morgin Press, 1991. 182 pages. 115 glossy full-page black-and-white photographs throughout. Chronology. Concerts and Performances. Discography. Filmography. Newspapers and Periodicals. Bibliography.

Gorgeous, oversized collection of photographs,

all from Presley's magical year: 1956. This is Elvis doing common activities, albeit with a few too many on the following subjects: reading a magazine; talking on the phone; playing a phonograph; and looking ever-so-cool in jeans. The back sections are exhaustive only in relation to the year 1956. Fans who fell in love with Elvis four decades ago may do so again looking at this book.

Krogh, Egil "Bud." *The Day Elvis Met Nixon.* Bellevue, WA: Pejama Press, 1994. 62 pages. Approximately 50 black-and-white photographs and documents throughout.

The meeting between Elvis and President Nixon back on December 21, 1970 has become part of American lore. Despite their radically different personalities, the men shared one thing in common: the social view that, literally speaking, the country was going to pot. Deputy Counsel Egil Krogh was present on that strange day, and here recalls how he had set up the meeting, "auditioned" Elvis, and then became eyewitness to the King's discussion with President Nixon. While the photos of various letters and the pair mingling are nothing spectacular, a few pieces of dialog are good for a chuckle (Elvis bragging about his badge collection). The sad story of two important men both out of sync with the rest of the world.

Leviton, Jay B. and **Rijff, Ger.** Introduction by Kurt Loder. *Elvis Close-Up: Rare, Intimate, Unpublished Photographs of Elvis Presley in 1956.* London: Century Hutchinson Limited, 1988. 136 pages. Approximately 120 black-and-white photographs, covering every page.

In the summer of 1956, photographer Jay Leviton was asked by *Collier's* magazine to photograph Presley and his band during their tour of the South. Little did Leviton realize he had lucked upon a fan craze that would shake the nation—and that he would be there to capture it in progress. Leviton rose to the occasion and snapped the boy who would be King in hotel rooms, diners, theater entrances, mingling with girls and, of course, performing on stage. An excellent collection of pictures honing in on a crucial moment in Presley's career; unfortunately, however, the publishers didn't splurge for glossy paper, and the results don't match the potential.

Marsh, Dave. *Elvis*. The New York Times Book Co., 1982. 246 pages. Approximately 200 tinted black-and-white photographs and 50 color illustrations throughout. Discography. Filmography. Bibliography.

Oversized photo book packaged by *Rolling Stone*. The photos, slightly tinted for a hint of simulated color, consist of the usual screaming women, gyrating performance shots, Army pictures, etc., but thankfully few film stills and Vegas appearances. Marsh does solid justice to the King's elusive myth—and in a coffee table format somehow finds a comfortable fit for commentary on controversial issues, such as whether or not the Presley family was "white trash." One eight-page Elvis headshot spread has enough sex appeal to make even today's female teens go gaga. Still a classic.

No author. *Elvis: A Tribute to the King of Rock N' Roll*. London: IPC Magazines, 1977. 62 pages. Approximately 100 color and black-and-white illustrations, covering every page. The Facts Behind the Legend.

Flimsy British magazine celebrating the King just after his passing. The color emphasis is clearly on Presley's films. For collectors who need everything.

No author. *Elvis Tear-Out Photo Book*. London: Oliver Books, 1994. Unpaginated (approximately 48 pages). 20 color and black-and-white photographs throughout.

Twenty pictures of Elvis, with more of a leaning toward black-and-white. All but four shots are exclusively of Elvis, either performing or posing for publicity shots. Unnecessary is a tremendous understatement.

No author. *Graceland: The Living Legacy of Elvis Presley*. San Francisco: Collins Publishers (division of HarperCollins), 1993. 256 pages. Approximately 400 color and black-and-white photographs, covering every page. Index. Gold & Platinum Certifications.

The Bible for those interested in the decorating tastes of nouveau riche rock stars. Graceland, the erstwhile King's residence, had special significance to Presley and to his parents, Gladys and Vernon. This book, through introductory text by Chet Flippo, expands on previously known history and then takes readers on a room-by-room tour of the house, which makes

the Kennedys look impoverished. We enter the dining room, which features Elvis' favorite "blue, white, and gold" scheme; the music room, which is yellow and boasts a shiny black Story and Clark piano; the bizarre jungle room, which actually has carpeting on the ceiling; and many other oddities. If one needs only one book on this landmark house, this is clearly the one to choose.

Roberts, Dave. *Elvis Presley*. Miami, FL: MBS, 1994. 120 pages. Approximately 75 color and black-and-white photographs throughout. Discography. Chronology. Index.

CD-format book covering all aspects of Presley's life and career. This nicely designed and illustrated book is priced just right at around $7.99.

Roberty, John. *The Complete Guide to the Music of Elvis Presley*. London: Omnibus Press (division of Book Sales Limited), 1994. 118 pages. Approximately 100 color and black-and-white photographs throughout.

CD-format book covering all aspects of Presley's life and career. Overlaps with Roberts' CD-format book (see above), but each offers something of different appeal: This has more photos, the other more informational back sections.

Scherman, Rowland. *Elvis is Everywhere*. New York: Clarkson N. Potter (member of the Crown Publishing Group), 1991. 80 pages. Approximately 70 black-and-white photographs, covering every page.

Professional photographer Scherman takes several fresh approaches in shooting Presleyana: the photos are grainy black-and-white; many of the images contain subtle pieces of Elvis hiding in backgrounds; and Elvis in the flesh is not included. Thus you can see Elvis on the cover of a tabloid rag being read by a comfortable beachgoer, his likeness on playing cards, or as a shrunken head on the end of long stick being waved in a parade. Moody, effective kitsch.

Schröer, Andreas. *Private Presley: The Missing Years—Elvis in Germany*. New York: William Morrow and Company, Inc., 1993. 160 pages. Approximately 375 black-and-white and color illustrations, covering every page. Comes with a CD. (First published in Great Britain in 1993 by Boxtree Limited.)

Was Elvis really "missing" during his two-year Army stint from 1958-60? Hardly. With the Colonel's assistance, his tour of duty was a three-ring media circus; photographers and reporters surrounded him, from his departure to Germany to his return with Priscilla Beaulieu. In these lively period photographs, you can see Elvis as a PR man of astonishing good cheer: kissing young girls; visiting the less fortunate; donating blood; and posing as he demonstrates his newfound Army skills. The book provides detailed captions and photos of numerous Elvis artifacts ranging from an autographed pen to his BMW. You can't beat the free CD, which contains seven rare cuts and brief interviews with Elvis.

Stern, Jane and Stern, Michael. *Elvis World*. New York: Alfred A Knopf, 1987. 216 pages. Approximately 250 color and black-and-white photographs, covering every page.

A revitalizing look into the impact of Elvis, published with Graceland's cooperation, that contains a heaping of coverage on Elvis' early appearances, movies, and much more. The book unfolds with a four-page foldout spread of Graceland, with ample kitsch behind the pearly gates. This is followed by some magnificent dynamic shots of Elvis performing, snarling, strutting through a crowd, and looking as tantalizing as ever. Amidst the array of glowing color shots that almost blind the eye—from a neon-lit Graceland to rare family photos of Elvis with Priscilla and baby Lisa Marie—are recipes, factoids, quotes, and much more. This excellent mish-mosh of kingly relics restores the faith that Elvis Presley was, and will always represent, a rock and roll threat. "...a potpourri of Elvis trivia with plenty of pix to document the phenomenon."—*Booklist*.

Taylor, Roger G. *Elvis in Art*. New York: St. Martin's Press, 1987. Unpaginated (approximately 128 pages). Approximately 100 color and black-and-white paintings, drawings and lithographs throughout.

These hundred or so portraits of Elvis were collected from record sleeves, billboards, magazine covers, greeting cards, gallery art, and other sources. The artists include Andy Warhol, Gunter Blum, Stanislaw Fernandez, Leroy Marsh, George Underwood, and a host of others. Each illustration is accompanied by a quote or two from a prominent actor, musician, or critic; these tend to be flattering to the King, although a couple—e.g., from Jackie Gleason and Johnny Rotten—actually do some flattening. Contains lots of colorful images for Elvis fans and a couple of stinging satires for humbugs.

Torgoff, Martin (Editor). *The Complete Elvis*. New York: Delilah Communications Limited, 1982. 256 pages. Approximately 75 black-and-white photographs throughout; two 32-page color inserts. Bibliography.

Incomplete though *The Complete Elvis* may be, it is still a bunch of fun as an early 1980's photo-factbook. Forget the incongruous essays (contributed by journalist Stanley Booth, among others) and the dated A to Z section—just lean back, relax, and flip through the photos and graphic designs for your quick amusement. How could you resist the still from the film *Tickle Me* in which Elvis frets over lifting Julie Adams' derriere into a convertible?

White, Wayne (illustrations) and Pearlman, Jill. *Elvis for Beginners*. London: Unwin Paperbacks, 1986. Unpaginated (approximately 172 pages). Approximately 200 pen-and-ink drawings and black-and-white photographs, covering every page. Elvis Testimonials. Bibliography.

A cartoon history of Elvis focusing on the roots of rock in the South and key events in the singer's life. The drawings and text are jaunty and somewhat all over the place; they are not visually attractive, funny, or all that informative. A page on Pat Boone is denigrating, and the trivializing of major events (rock and roll deaths) inappropriate. Beginners: You're better off playing the records.

QUIZBOOKS AND QUOTEBOOKS

Choron, Sandra (Sandy) and Oskam, Bob. *Elvis!: The Last Word*. New York: Citadel (Carol), 1991. 108 pages. Approximately twenty black-and-white photos throughout. Index.

The sell line reads: "The 328 Best (and Worst) Things Anyone Ever Said About `The King.'" The number 328 does seem to be pulled out of the air. But the thematic arrangement of quotes (e.g., "Memphis Train," "Suspicious Minds," "Love Me Tender," "A Jury of His Peers,"

"Elvis Inc.") and variety of speakers (e.g., Roy Orbison, Richard Nixon, John Lennon) make for a rather tasty skim. Although the book is not intended for substantive value—neither years nor sources were provided for quotes—you can have some fun comparing and contrasting quotes from the same figures. To be specific, Frank Sinatra said both of the following: "His kind of music is deplorable, a rancid smelling aphrodisiac," and "There have been many accolades uttered about his talent and performances over the years, all of which I agree with wholeheartedly. I shall miss him dearly as a friend."

Davis, Arthur. *Elvis Presley: Quote Unquote*. New York: Crescent Books, 1995. 80 pages. Approximately 50 black-and-white photographs throughout.

Bland promotional book that once again trudges through the Elvis story via quotes and photos. There is little here one hasn't seen before, but a few quotes are well chosen. For example, after Elvis' death, Colonel Parker was quoted as saying: "Nothing has changed. This won't change anything. We must immediately make sure that outsiders cannot exploit the name of Elvis Presley." For Presley beginners only.

Farren, Mick and Marchbank, Pierce. *Elvis: In His Own Words*. London: Omnibus Press (division of Book Sales Limited), 1994. 126 pages. Approximately 150 black-and-white photographs, covering every page.

First published in 1977, this throwaway quotebook deceives, with its picture-perfect cover image of Elvis (albeit his face is smattered with Hollywood make-up). It seems very few of the quotes or photos have been updated since the first edition, so there aren't any sections covering the 1980's and 90's, such as "Elvis is Alive" hoaxes. All of the images are dark and blurry, and many of them have been poorly grouped together. The quotes don't reveal very much at all. Elvis on actresses as dates: "Well, they're just like everybody else." Thanks, El!

Higgins, Patrick. *Before Elvis There Was Nothing*. New York: Carroll & Graf, 1994. 128 pages. Approximately 70 glossy black-and-white photographs, on every other page.

The title comes from words spoken by John Lennon, and has appeared in numerous other sources. Each page of this book bears one solo quote opposite a classic black-and-white photo (mostly from the mid-to-late 1950's). The quotes can be seen elsewhere with too much frequency; in fact, a handful of them are in Choron's earlier collection (see above). Attractive but derivative.

Rovin, Jeff. *The World According to Elvis: Quotes from the King*. New York: HarperPaperbacks (HarperCollins), 1992. 140 pages.

CD-size quotebook from pop culture writer Jeff Rovin. There isn't much here to marvel at, as there are only two or three quotes on a page, but Rovin knows a good Presley line when he sees one: "Anything that don't frighten the children is in good taste as far as I'm concerned." The quotes aren't dated or sourced. An affordable gift item not intended to be comprehensive.

RELATED WORKS

Adler, David. *The Life and Cuisine of Elvis Presley*. New York: Crown, 1993. 160 pages. Approximately 100 black-and-white photographs throughout. Index.

Author David Adler at least consulted with top authorities when preparing this collection of sumptuous recipes fit for a king: Pauline Nicholson, Elvis' cook; Bill Stanley, his stepbrother; and Marian Cocke, his nurse. Throw in a few recipes from the Army Quartermaster Corps. and you have quite a buffet. From Tupelo specialties to Army mess gruel, this book will either tempt your taste buds or make you become a vegetarian very fast. If you dare, try the barbecued pork chops or the crepes suzette (in the "Vegas Cuisine" section!). Not nearly as attractive as McKeon's work (see below), but more in-depth on the various cuisines. "...the book's bound to entertain a good many people who may or may not want to raise new tastes to their lips."—*Publishers Weekly*.

Bleasdale, Alan. *Are You Lonesome Tonight?*. London and Boston: Faber and Faber, 1985. 96 pages.

A play about Elvis Presley's final days. Rest assured, this isn't a pretty picture—Elvis stuffs himself with pills and a ton of greasy food (in the character's exact words: "four portions of hashed browns, coupla pound of bacon, a lot of that gravy, two of sauerkraut, some crowder peas and a whole stack of fried tomatoes—oh an' five or six eggs."). Funny, touching, and tragic—with appearances from Vernon, Gladys, the Colonel, and Priscilla, but no Memphis Mafia—this play showcased the talents of Martin Shaw as older Presley and Simon Bowman as younger Presley. Fans would prefer something more upbeat.

Bourgeau, Art. *The Elvis Murders*. New York: Charter, 1986. 216 pages.

A fictional murder mystery concerning a murderous plot to kill the King—who actually did not die in 1977. Pulp writing that might please some fans as fast reading, though plainly the premise is contrived and the details a bit lacking. One wonders, for example, why the first description of the King does not remark about his physical appearance. (Is he a blimp? Is his hair gray? Does he still have that legendary sneer?) Instead we are given a truly corny description of what Elvis' mouth tastes like when given mouth-to-mouth resuscitation: "cigarettes, beer, and hurt." Yuck!

Butler, Brenda Arlene. *Are You Hungry Tonight? Elvis' Favorite Recipes*. New York: Gramercy Books, 1992. 66 pages. Approximately 75 color and black-and-white photographs throughout.

Yet another Elvis Presley cookbook, except that this one opts for color rather than comprehensiveness. So how do we know *these* are authentic Elvis favorites when other authors claim to have done the same? We don't—which means you may be eating all of this high-cholesterol slop for nothing. Adler's book (see above) at least had the advantage of detailed research with some of the King's family and friends. If you're desperately in need of recipes for franks or fried chicken, it's doubtful you'd turn to this book. Soup's on!

Charters, Samuel. *Elvis Presley Calls His Mother After the Ed Sullivan Show*. Minneapolis, MN: Coffee House Press, 1992. 104 pages.

A novel told through the device of a monologue phone call from Elvis to his mother, Gladys, after his legendary performance on "The Ed Sullivan Show." The narrative begins with Elvis' alarm at discovering that he had only been filmed from the waist up—a concern he brings up repeatedly. Elvis' words are full of

innocence, energy, and wonder as he explores how his presence affects women, how he copes with the press, and how he tries to understand why everyone thinks his act is so dirty. This is one long, expensive phone call, but one can get through it in a sitting. "An affectionate but shapeless character sketch..."—*Kirkus*.

Ebersole, Lucinda and Peabody, Richard (editors). *Mondo Elvis: A Collection of Stories and Poems About Elvis*. New York: St. Martin's Press, 1994. 228 pages.

From the editors of *Mondo Barbie* comes this similar treatment on Elvis. The book culls 30 or so stories and poems by writers such as Mark Childress, Samuel Charters, Greil Marcus, Mark Winegardner, Elizabeth Nash, Janice Eidus, and Nick Cave, all having something to do with Elvis' influence or image. Many of the works (e.g., Marcus and Winegardner) have previously been included in other books. Not nearly as exciting as Sloan and Pierce's work (see below), this book—printed on freaky blue paper!—will nevertheless rope in many Presleyfiles. "...raggedly uneven..."—*The New York Times Book Review*.

McCray, Patrick. *Elvis Shrugged*. San Diego, CA: Revolutionary Comics, 1993. 112 pages. Approximately 500 pen-and-ink cartoon panels, covering every page.

Hilarious three-issue comic book miniseries about Elvis, who never died—or even went to Vegas—but was substituted by a clone, while the real King circled the globe as "Reuben Sandwich" and learned about the meaning of life. Our heroine, Madonna, finds the herculean Presley and falls madly in lust with him. As Elvis attempts to save the world from over-commercialism and general bad music, he reels in other performers—John Lennon, Roy Orbison, Frank Zappa, etc.—to fake their deaths and help his cause. The drawings are lots of fun. This work is actually a parody of Ayn Rand's novel *Atlas Shrugged*.

McKeon, Elizabeth. Foreword by Wayne Newton. *Elvis in Hollywood: Recipes Fit for a King*. Nashville, TN: Rutledge Hill Press, 1994. 237 pages. Approximately 100 black-and-white photographs throughout. Index.

"A cookbook and a memory book" that integrates 250 recipes Elvis ate while in Hollywood (or else served to others) with photos and some 115 anecdotes. This binder-bound book will tell you how to make Sloppy Joe, stuffed chicken, ham and green beans, apple crisp— and let's not forget fried chicken, the King's staple. Needless to say, only the "before" photos of Elvis are included, not the "after." Suck in your arteries and enjoy, if your doctor allows it.

Panter, Gary. *Invasion of the Elvis Zombies*. New York: Raw Books and Graphics, 1984. Unpaginated (approximately 32 pages). Approximately 50 pen-and-ink and charcoal drawings or graphics, covering every page. Comes with a flex-disc.

Hardcover comic book full of ugly monsters and creatures, supplemented by Panter's bizarre poetry. Kind of repulsive, but interesting in light of Greil Marcus's work (see Death of Elvis, above). The flexi-disc contains Panter's own recording, "Precambrian Bath."

Sloan, Kay and Pierce, Constance. *Elvis Rising: Stories on the King*. New York: Avon, 1993. 262 pages.

Sixteen tales of Elvis by several contemporary fiction writers, including T. Coraghessan Boyle, W.P. Kinsella, Samuel Charters, Julie Hecht, Rebecca Adams, and others. Most of the stories deal with the psychology of how and why individuals get sucked into Elvismania. Boyle's semi-erotic "All Shook Up" concerns a high school guidance counselor who has an affair with the lover of an Elvis impersonator; Kinsella's humorous "Elvis Bound" tells of a ballplayer who can't accept that his wife's orgasms are the result of an Elvis poster on the wall; and Julie Hecht's nostalgic "I Want You I Need You I Love You" examines our need to sustain the larger-than-life qualities of our heroes. Although first published in various magazines, the stories fit together to produce uniform, though lightweight, entertainment.

TOURBOOKS

Cotten, Lee. *Did Elvis Sing in Your Hometown?*. Sacramento, CA: High Sierra Books, 1995. 258 pages. Approximately 100 black-and-white photographs and copies of show programs throughout. Index by City.

A meticulous chronology of Elvis' live performances, with details of virtually every time he opened his mouth in front of an audience to hit

a note. The book includes some peripheral information, including background sidebars on musicians (Scotty Moore), venues (Reo Palm Isle), and clarifying myths (was Elvis dumped by the New Frontier Hotel in Las Vegas?). Fans may want to check out the index first (which is state-by-state), to locate various cities, including Little Rock, AK; Carlsbad, NM; and North Tonawanda, NY. A valuable, although not too pretty, view of Elvis' stage career.

YOUNG ADULT

Love, Robert. *Elvis Presley*. New York, London, Toronto, Sydney: Franklin Watts, 1986. 128 pages. 25 black-and-white photographs throughout. Getting to Know Elvis (books, films). Index.

Part of the "impact biography" series, this one on the King discusses the glitter and successes alongside the failures and excesses. Author Love tactfully presents controversial issues to a young audience: the conflict of "black music" being accepted as sung by a white performer; and Presley's drug addictions and weight problems. The book refuses to pander to the blind fan crowd; both negative and positive criticism are given space. "Fans will enjoy the great variety of photographs spanning Presley's life in this sane and welcome book"— *Library Journal*.

OTHER TITLES OF INTEREST
Adair, Joseph. *The Immortal Elvis Presley*. Stamford, CT: Longmeadow, 1992.

Alico, Stella H. *Elvis Presley-The Beatles*. No city: Pendulum, 1979.

American Graphic Systems Inc. *I Am Elvis*. New York: Pocket, 1991.

Aros, Andrew A. *Elvis Presley: His Films, His Music*. No city: Applause, 1980.

Bartel, Pauline. *Reel Elvis!*. No city: Taylor Publishing, no date.

Bauman, Kathleen. *On Stage with Elvis Presley*. Mankato, MN: Creative Education, 1975.

Booth, Stanley. *Elvis Presley's Graceland*. New York: Aperture, 1986.

Bowser, James. *Starring Elvis*. New York: Dell, 1977.

Brown, Hal A. *In Search of Elvis: A Fact-Filled Seek and Find Adventure*. No city: Summit, 1992.

Burke, Bill E. *Elvis: A Thirty Year Chronicle*. No city: Osborne Enterprises, 1985.

Burke, Bill E. *Elvis Memories: Press Between the Pages*. No city: Propwash, 1993.

Burke, Bill E. *Elvis Through My Eyes*. No city: Shelby, 1987.

Carson, Lucas. *Elvis Presley.* No city: Taco, 1989.

Clayson, Alan and Leigh, Spencer. *Aspects of Elvis.* London: Sidgwick & Jackson, 1995.
The Beat Goes On *commented: "A collection of essays by thirty-five of the country's leading music writers illustrating many different aspects of the King...."*

Cogan, Arlene and Goodman, Charles. *Elvis, This One's for You.* Chessington, Surrey (England): Castle Communications, 1985.

Consumer Guide Staff. *Elvis: The Younger Years.* New York: NAL, 1989.

Consumer Guide Staff. *Films of Elvis Presley.* New York: Smithmark, 1991.

Cranor, Rosalind. *Elvis Collectibles 2nd Edition.* No city: Overmountain Press, 1987.

Curtin, Jim. *Candids of the King: Rare Photographs of Elvis Presley.* New York: Little, Brown, 1993.
Publishers Weekly *commented: "More than 400 illustrations capture the private Presley from almost every conceivable angle."*

DeMarco, Gordon. *Elvis in Aspic.* Portland, OR: West Coast Crime, 1993.

Doll, Susan. *The Films of Elvis Presley.* No city: Publications International, 1993.

Esposito, Joe. *Elvis: A Legendary Performance.* Chicago, IL: JAT Publishing, 1990.
Esposito was the number one man in Presley's Memphis Mafia.

Eversz, Robert M. *Shooting Elvis.* New York: Grove, 1996.

Flinn, Mary C. *Elvis in Oz: New Stories and Poems from the Hollins Creative Writing Program.* Charlottesville, VA: University Press of Virginia, 1992.

Fortas, Alan. *Elvis: From Memphis to Hollywood: Memories from My Eleven Years with Elvis Presley.* Ann Arbor, MI: Popular Culture, Inc., 1992.

Gelfand, Craig and Blocker-Krantz, Lynn. *In Search of the King.* New York: Putnam, 1992.

Gentry, Tony. *Elvis Presley.* New York: Chelsea, 1994.

Gibson, R. and Shaw, S. *Elvis.* New York: McGraw-Hill, 1987.

Gilmore, Brian. *Elvis Presley Is Alive and Well and Living in Harlem.* No city: Third World Press, 1992.

Goldman, Albert. *Elvis: The Last 24 Hours.* New York: St. Martin's Press, 1991.

Gordon, Robert. *The King on the Road: Elvis Live on Tour.* New York: St. Martin's, 1996.

Greenwood, Earl. *Elvis Top Secret: The Untold Story of Presley's Secret FBI Files* New York: NAL, 1991.
Greenwood was an Army buddy of Elvis.

Gripe, Maria. *Elvis & His Friends.* New York: Delacorte, 1976.

Gripe, Maria. *Elvis & His Secret.* New York: Dell, 1979.

Grizzard, Lewis. *Elvis Is Dead and I Don't Feel So Good Myself.* No city: Peachtree, 1984.

Haining, Peter. *Elvis in Private.* New York: St. Martin's, 1987.

Haining, Peter. *Elvis Presley Scrapbooks, 1955-1965.* No city: Trans-Atlantic, 1991.

Hallum, Boen. *Elvis the King.* No city: self-published, 1987.

Hanna, David. *Lonely Star at the Top.* No city: Dorchester, 1977.

Harmer, Jeremy. *Elvis.* White Plains, NY: Longman, 1982.

Harms, Valerie. *Tryin' to Get to You: The Story of Elvis Presley.* New York: Macmillan, 1979.

Harper, Betty. *Elvis: Newly Discovered Drawings of Elvis Presley.* New York: Bantam, 1979.

Hegner, Mary. *Do You Remember Elvis?.* No city: Tech Data, 1980.

Henderson, William M. *Stark Raving Elvis.* New York: Fireside (Simon & Schuster), 1987.

Hill, Wanda J. *Elvis: Face to Face, 1985.* No city: Lonestarr, 1985.

Hill, Wanda J. *Elvis: We Remember, 1978.* No city: Lonestarr, 1985.

Hill, Wanda J. *We Remember Elvis.* No city: Palo Verdes, 1978.

Hodge, Charlie. *Me N' Elvis.* Chessington, Surrey (England): Castle Communications, 1984.
Former rhythm guitarist Charlie Hodge was Elvis' close friend and aide.

James, Antony. *Presley: Entertainer of the Century.* No city: Dorchester, 1976.

Jenkins, Mary. *Elvis the Way I Knew Him.* No city: Riverpark, 1984.
Mary Jenkins was Elvis' cook at Graceland.

Jones, Ira. *Soldier Boy Elvis.* No city: Propwash, 1992.

Krohn, Katherine. *Elvis Presley: The King.* St. Paul, MN: Lerner, 1993.

Lacker, Marty; Lacker, Patsy; and Smith, Leslie. *Elvis: Portrait of a Friend.* New York: Bantam, 1980.
Marty Lacker was a close personal friend of Elvis in the 1960's, and was co-best man (with Joe Esposito) at his wedding.

Latham, Caroline and Sakol, Jeannie. *E Is For Elvis: An A to Z Guide to the King of Rock and Roll.* New York: NAL, 1991.

Leigh, Vanora. *Elvis Presley.* New York: Franklin Watts, 1986.
School Library Journal *commented: "...surface fluff."*

Lichter, Paul. *Elvis All My Best.* No city: Jesse Books, 1989.

Lichter, Paul. *Elvis Behind Closed Doors.* No city: Jesse Books, 1987.

Lichter, Paul. *Elvis Memories.* No city: Jesse Books, 1985.

Lichter, Paul. *Elvis Rebel Heart.* No city: Jesse Books, 1992.

Maliay, Jack D. *Elvis: The Messiah?* No city: TCB, 1993.

Mann, May. *Elvis & the Colonel*. New York: Sterling, 1975.

Mann, May. *Elvis, Why Don't They Leave You Alone?*. New York: NAL, 1982.

Mann, Richard. *Elvis Presley*. No city: TSELF, no date.

Marino, Jan. *The Day Elvis Came to Town*. New York: Avon, 1993.
Publishers Weekly commented: "a nostalgic glimpse of The King's era...."

Marling, Karal Ann. *Graceland: Going Home With Elvis*. Cambridge, MA: Harvard University Press, 1996.

Moore, W. Kent. *Elvis Quiz Book: What Do You Want to Know About the King of Rock and Roll*. New York: Contemporary, 1991.

Nash, Bruce M. *The Elvis Presley Quiz Book*. New York: Warner Books, 1978.

Nelson, Pete. *King: When Elvis Rocked the World*. London: Proteus, 1985.

No author. *Elvis: His Life and Music*. No city: Friedman/Fairfax, 1994.

Olmetti, Bob and McCasland. Sue. *Elvis Now/Ours Forever*. No city: self-published, 1984.

Osborne, Jerry. *Elvis, Like Any Other Soldier*. No city: Osborne & Browne, 1989.

Parish, James R. *Elvis Presley Scrapbook*. New York: Ballantine, 1975.

Parker, Ed. *Inside Elvis*. No city: Rampart House, 1978.

Peters, Richard. *Elvis: The Golden Anniversary Tribute*. No city: Salem, 1985.

Pierson, Jean. *Elvis: The Living Legend*. No city: Carlton Press, 1983.

Pond, Steve. *Elvis in Hollywood*. New York: NAL, 1990.

Presley, Vester and Rooks, Nancy. *Presley Family Cookbook*. No city: Wimmer Brothers, 1980.
Vester Presley was Elvis Presley's uncle through marriage.

Pritchett, Nash L. *One Flower While I Live: Elvis As I Remember Him*. No city: Shelby House, 1987.
Minister Nashval Lorene Pritchett was Elvis' aunt (his father's sister).

Putnam, Stan P. *Momento[sic], Souvenir, Keepsake and Collector's Kit on the Life and Music of Elvis Presley*. No city: Research Improvement Institute, no date.

Putnam, Stan P. *Newfound Facts and Memorabilia on Elvis Presley*. No city: Research Improvement Institute, 1987.

Rijff, Ger J. *Elvis Fire in the Sun*. No city: Atomium Books, 1991.

Rijff, Ger J. *Elvis, the Cool King*. No city: Atomium Books, 1991.

Rosenbaum, Helen. *The Elvis Presley Trivia Quiz Book*. New York: NAL, 1978.

Roy, Samuel. *Elvis: Prophet of Power*. No city: Branden, 1985.

Rubel, David. *Elvis Presley: The Rise of Rock and Roll*. New York: Houghton Mifflin, 1992.

Sammon, Paul. *The King Is Dead*. New York: Delta, no date.

Schuster, Hal. *The Magic Lives on: The Films of Elvis Presley*. No city: Movie Publishers, Inc., 1989.

Shauer, Sean. *Elvis: Photographing the King*. No city: Timur, 1981.

Shauer, Sean. *Elvis' Portrait Portfolio*. No city: Timur, 1983.

Shauer, Sean. *The Life of Elvis Presley*. No city: Timur, 1984.

Shauer, Sean. *Our Memories of Elvis*. No city: Timur, 1984.

Smith, Gene. *Elvis' Man Friday*. Nashville, TN: Light of Day, 1994.

Stanley, David. *Life with Elvis*. No city: Baker Book, 1986.
David Stanley was one of Elvis Presley's stepbrothers.

Staten, Vince. *The Real Elvis: Good Old Boy*. No city: Media Centures, 1978.

Stearn, Jess and Geller, Larry. *The Truth About Elvis*. No city: Jove, 1980.
Larry Geller was Elvis' hairdresser and unofficial spiritual guru.

Tanner, Isabelle. *Elvis: A Guide to My Soul*. No city: Elisabelle International, 1993.

Taylor, John A. *Forever Elvis*. New York: Smithmark, 1993.

Taylor, Paula. *Elvis Presley*. Mankato, MN: Creative Education, 1974.

Tunzi, Joseph A. *Elvis, Encore Performance*. Chicago, IL: JAT Publishing, 1990.

Tunzi, Joseph A. *Elvis, Encore Performance Two: In the Garden*. Chicago, IL: JAT Publishing, 1993.

Tunzi, Joseph A. *Elvis Highway 51 South Memphis Tennessee*. Chicago, IL: JAT Publishing, no date.

Tunzi, Joseph A. *Elvis Sessions, The Recorded Music of Elvis Aaron Presley 1953-1977*. Chicago, IL: JAT Publishing, no date.

Tunzi, Joseph A. *Elvis Sessions II: The Recorded Music of Elvis Aaron Presley 1953-1977*. Chicago, IL: JAT Publishing, 1996.

Tunzi, Joseph A. *Elvis '69: the Return*. Chicago, IL: JAT Publishing, 1991.

Tunzi, Joseph A. *Elvis '70: Bringing Him Back*. Chicago, IL: JAT Publishing, 1994.

Tunzi, Joseph A. *Elvis '73: Hawaiian Spirit*. Chicago, IL: JAT Publishing, 1992.

Tunzi, Joseph A. *Elvis '74: Enter the Dragon*. Chicago, IL: JAT Publishing, 1996.

Tunzi, Joseph A. *Elvis Standing Room Only*. Chicago, IL: JAT Publishing, 1994.

Tunzi, Joseph A. *Elvis the Lost Photographs*. Chicago, IL: JAT Publishing, no date.

Westmoreland, Kathy. *Elvis & Kathy*. No city: Glendale, 1987.
Westmoreland was a singer who sporadically toured with Elvis from 1970-1977.

Whitmer, Ph.D., Robert. *The Inner Elvis*. New York: Hyperion, 1996.

Wombacher, Marty. *Elvis Presley Is a Wormfeast*. No city: POP, 1991.

Wootten, Richard. *Elvis*. New York: Random House, 1985.
School Library Journal *commented: "No new information here...."*

Worth, Fred L. and Temerius, Steve. *Elvis: A Golden Tribute*. No city: Outlet, 1992.

Yancey, Becky and Linedecker, Cliff. *My Life with Elvis*. New York: Warner, 1978.
Becky Yancey worked for Elvis from the early 1960's to the mid-1970's.

THE PRETENDERS

TITLES OF INTEREST

Salewicz, Chris. *Pretenders*. London: Proteus, no date.

Wrenn, Mike. *The Pretenders with Hyndesight*. London: Omnibus Press (division of Book Sales Limited), 1990.

PRINCE

BIOGRAPHIES

Feldman, Jim. *Prince*. New York: Ballantine Books, 1984. 148 pages. One glossy 16-page black-and-white photo insert. Appendixes: Genealogy; Prince Projects; Quiz; Discography; Videography; Fan Club Information.

One of Ballantine's better mass-market pop biographies from the early 1980's (Cyndi Lauper, Duran Duran, etc.), this book doesn't exactly live up to its billing as "everything you need to know about..." but it does offer more than most other early 1980's books herein. Jim Feldman writes on a level more suited to a high school than middle level audience, and draws some interesting comparisons between the Prince phenomenon and those of other 1984 megastars, such as Bruce Springsteen and Michael Jackson. Whether fans would opt for

the greater detail here over the glossy color in other works is a matter of taste.

Ivory, Steven. *Prince*. New York: Perigee (Putnam), 1984. 176 pages. Two 16-page black-and-white photo inserts. Discography.

Trite overdramatization of Prince's life and rise to success. Compared to the main character of *A Star Is Born*, Prince is described as having been a "pleasant child" who disliked his strict stepfather and at a later point ran off to live with his real father (which didn't work out too well either). Music, it seems, was Prince's escape from the drudging reality around him. The copy is not all that informative, and it doesn't begin to compete with the sexy photos in the inserts.

Hill, Dave. *Prince: A Pop Life*. New York: Harmony Books (Crown), 1989. 242 pages. 20 black-and-white photographs throughout; eight-page glossy black-and-white and color photo insert. Bibliography. Discography. Index.

Lacking any real access to the proper music industry moguls, British journalist Dave Hill gamely attempts to trace Prince's career. Hill doesn't have the prerequisite funk attitude, and his feeble attempts to be hip (using phrases like, "perfectly awesome video") will make you cringe. However, he does have a strong sense of Prince's roots (Little Richard, Jimi Hendrix, Sly Stone, et. al.) and piercing insight into the suggestive lyrics in his hits. If you're looking for dry commentary on the musical Napoleon's songs, check this out; if you want to know about Prince's personal life, find other sources to complement this one. Young fans: don't bother.

FANZINES AND FAN CLUBS

Uptown: The Magazine for Prince Fans and Collectors. Editorial offices: P.O. Box 87 S-590 62 Linghem, Sweden. For U.S. orders: P.O. Box 43, Cuyahoga Falls, Ohio 44222.

Quarterly, 32-page Prince magazine with a glossy, color front and back, and glossy black-and-white photographs inside. Each issue focuses on a different aspect of the artist, including posters, discography, funk roots, comprehensive concert-by-concert reports, and more. Issues also report on news, CD releases, books, videos, interactive products, and more. The cost of five issues (members receive an additional special magazine) is $40 in the U.S., Canada and Great Britain; write for pricing in other countries. The cost per issue is $5.95 U.S. and $6.95 Canada.

PICTORIALS

Brown, Geoff. *The Complete Guide to the Music of Prince*. London: Omnibus Press (division of Book Sales Limited), 1995. 130 pages. Approximately 115 color and black-and-white photographs throughout. Bibliography. Index.

CD-format book covering all aspects of Prince's life and career. Overlaps with Ewing's CD-format book (see below), but each offers something of different appeal: This has more photos, the other more informational back sections.

Ewing, Jon. *Prince*. Miami, FL: MBS, 1994. 120 pages. Approximately 75 color and black-and-white photographs throughout. Discography. Chronology. Index.

CD-format book covering all aspects of Prince's life and career. This nicely designed and illustrated book is priced just right at around $7.99.

Nilsen, Per. *Prince: A Documentary*. London: Omnibus Press (division of Book Sales Limited), 1993. 160 pages. Approximately 225 black-and-white photographs, covering every page. Appendix: Discography.

A day-by-day account of the artist known (on-and-off) as Prince, beginning with his birth on June 7, 1958. It's a shame to see a well-illustrated book on this artist not contain any color—especially purple!—but fans won't mind the compensatory images of Prince's hometown (Minneapolis, MN) and some early childhood photos of young Roger Nelson sporting an early 1970's afro. Club and recording dates are duly noted, as are many other various appearances and details. The Appendix contains not only a discography, but also films, videos, concerts, bootlegs, and more. More accessible than Hill's book (see Biographies above).

Olmeca. *Prince*. New York: Proteus Books, 1984. 32 pages. Approximately 30 color and black-and-white photographs throughout. A Chronology of Singles in America.

Another photo book that attempts to cash-in on Prince's *Purple Rain* fame. Paisley flower patterns border each right-hand page, while many other pages feature a scripted P insignia over the text. The book contains some interesting details on early business dealings—notably with American Artists—but you won't be satisfied with coverage of his sexy persona or the musical commentary. For a photo of Prince sniffing his underarm, turn to page 23.

YOUNG ADULT

Mabery, D.L. *Prince*. Minneapolis, MN: Lerner Publications, 1985. 40 pages. Approximately 35 color and black-and-white photographs throughout.

Glossy book for kids with some excellent shots of the Purple One performing, and a few images of friends (Andre Anderson, a childhood pal). Mabery accentuates Prince's shyness, diverse musical talents, and dress affectations, but neatly avoids any pitfalls about the star's blatant sexuality and vanity (as it were). A good start for children 8-12. "The text is in large print and simply written, with vocabulary most young readers will understand"— *School Library Journal*.

Matthews, Gordon. *Prince*. New York: Wanderer Books (Simon & Schuster), 1985. 64 pages. Approximately 50 black-and-white photographs throughout. Discography.

Junky hype book that doesn't begin to pierce Prince's enigma. Author Gordon Matthews plays up Prince's diverse talents, but fails to support his work with a steady biography. Corny phraseology abounds: "He had a purple car, a purple coat, a purple motorcycle. He might as well have a purple movie [*Purple Rain*], too!" There's something else that's noticeably purple here: Matthews' prose. Fans desperate for material on Prince would do better to find something in a larger format and with color.

OTHER TITLES OF INTEREST
Williams, Jeanette. *Prince*. No city: Carlton Press, 1981.

PUBLIC ENEMY

TITLES OF INTEREST
Chuck D. and Public Enemy. *Public Enemy*. New York: Thunder's Mouth Press, 1994.

PUBLIC IMAGE LTD.

(See also Sex Pistols, The)

TITLES OF INTEREST

Heylin, Clinton. *Public Image Ltd.: Rise and Fall.* London: Omnibus Press (division of Book Sales Limited), no date.

SUZI QUATRO

TITLES OF INTEREST

Mander, Margaret. *Suzi Quatro.* London: Futura, 1976.

QUEEN

BIOGRAPHIES

Gunn, Jacky and Jenkins, Jim. Introduction by Brian May. *Queen: As It Began.* New York: Hyperion, 1992. 292 pages. Two glossy eight-page black-and-white photo inserts; one glossy eight-page color insert. Discography.

Hyperion did an exemplary job producing this nicely designed authorized biography, the cover of which is stamped with the band's official emblem (consisting of the musicians' astrological signs). One would wish the authors had done better on their end, however. The book is crammed with details about these four highly intelligent men (e.g., Roger Taylor, for one, was very nearly a dentist!), but it is sorely lacking description of the band's process in the recording studio and of events behind closed doors. Mercury's death of AIDS in November, 1991 is only treated for three pages in the last chapter, serving as the authors' attempt to tell history as events became publicly known. While we don't necessarily need every stone turned in regard to Mercury's private life, at least we expect some reflections on his last days from those who knew him best. "...the authors include *everything*, burying fascinating anecdotes..."—*Publishers Weekly*.

Hodkinson, Mark. *Queen: The Early Years.* London: Omnibus Press (division of Book Sales Limited), 1995. 208 pages. One glossy 12-page black-and-white photo insert.

Author Mark Hodkinson contests that the dirt and grimy gossip of a band is never nearly as interesting as the facts about the musicians' early years. In the case of Freddie Mercury, Hodkinson has a poor case; while his early years in Zanzibar are of major interest, the public has an even greater fascination with his carefree lifestyle, which was integral to his showmanship. Hodkinson is somewhat confused, therefore, as he fills this book with details about the Oadby Library in Leicester, England (who is going to care?) and the Cathedral of Truro, located in the city in which Roger Taylor was born. The final chapter ends with the release of "Bohemian Rhapsody," the point at which most fans would expect the story to begin. Only for hardcore devotees.

Jackson, Laura. *Queen & I: The Brian May Story.* Miami Springs, FL: MBS, 1994. 216 pages. Two glossy eight-page black-and-white photo inserts. Discography. Index. (First published in Great Britain in 1994 by Smith Gryphon Limited.)

After the death of rock legend Freddie Mercury in 1991, Queen guitarist Brian May carried the band's torch by heading back to the studio and touching up a batch of unreleased tracks containing Mercury's vocals. Although May is clearly the subject of this aptly titled work, it's difficult to get past the looming presence of the more charismatic Mercury (both are on the cover). Yet writer Laura Jackson proves that May's story is worth telling, from how the young prodigy carved his own guitar, to his movie soundtracks (*Highlander*), to his successful solo career (the *Back to the Light* LP). Essential for bona fide Queen fans.

Rider, Stephen. *Queen: These Are the Best Days of Our Lives.* Chessington, Surrey (England): Castle Communications, 1993. 248 pages. One glossy eight-page color insert.

"The essential Queen biography" was first published in 1991 and was slightly amended in 1993 to update events through Freddie Mercury's death. This book is better written than Gunn and Jenkins' bio (see above), with less cluttered prose on their backgrounds and more detail on the band's eccentricities (e.g., the famous nude bicycle race with 50 naked women). Unfortunately, it also falls well short of being definitive. The color insert, featuring several stunning up-close poses, doesn't include any portraits of Queen as lads. There is no discography—a major setback for fans who need to check on the completeness of their CD collections.

Sky, Rick. *The Show Must Go On: The Life of Freddie Mercury.* New York: Citadel (Carol Publishing Group), 1994. 202 pages. Two glossy eight-page black-and-white photo inserts. Chronology.

First published in 1992 by HarperCollins, this uninformed outsider's account misses the mark chronicling Mercury's brilliant life and career. Sky doesn't dig nearly deep enough into Mercury's flamboyant lifestyle and virtually neglects his long relationship with Jim Hutton (see Mercury Friends and Family, below). He does, however, overplay the role of ex-lover Mary Austin and his friendship with former singer/drummer Dave Clark. Not comprehensive.

CHRONOLOGIES

Dean, Ken. *Queen: The New Visual Documentary.* London: Omnibus Press (division of Book Sales Limited), 1991. 128 pages. Approximately 250 black-and-white photographs, covering every page; 12 pages of color. Discography.

Book-bound magazine, first published in 1986, that traces the group's career from 1970-1991. As it doesn't contain much detail on the musicians' backgrounds (only the basic data is in the introduction) and no photos prior to 1970, the book will only have limited value for researchers. The photos take up quite a bit of space—up to five shots on a page—and somehow quotes and anecdotes are also shoved in. The book's cover claim that it features "the life and times of Freddie Mercury" is false; this is an even treatment of the band, with an add-on section reporting Mercury's death in the back. Optional.

DEATH OF MERCURY

Evans, David and Minns, David. *More of the Real Life...Freddie Mercury.* London: Britannia Press Publishing, 1992. 192 pages.

Freddie Mercury's friends pay detailed tribute to the singer. These firsthand reflections from school chums, colleagues, confidants, and his staff are sincere and lengthy, generally filling up a page. Among those represented are: jewelry designer Ann Ortoman; Mercury's roadie,

Peter Hince; his physician, Gordon Atkinson; and singer Billy Squier. A non-saccharine, affectionate tip-of-the-hat that hasn't received much distribution in the United States.

No author. *The Freddie Mercury Tribute: Concert for AIDS Awareness.* Woodford Green, Essex (England): International Music Publications Limited, 1993. 96 pages. Approximately 110 color photographs, covering every page. Tribute Concert Song List.

When Freddie Mercury died of AIDS on November 24, 1991, the world mourned the loss of a true rock legend. Several months later, on April 20, 1992, 72,000 people gathered at Wembley Stadium to see a star-studded live festival tribute to Mercury. This color scrapbook documents the festival with excellent shots of diverse performers such as Metallica, Bob Geldof, Spinal Tap, Guns N' Roses, Elizabeth Taylor (yes, Elizabeth Taylor), Roger Daltrey, Ian Hunter, David Bowie, Elton John, Liza Minnelli, and many others. This book only has two photos of Mercury himself and contains very little commentary. One also wonders why the concert organizers didn't invite more black performers. Proceeds from the book went to promote AIDS charities worldwide.

MERCURY FRIENDS AND FAMILY

Hutton, Jim with Wapshott, Tim. Foreword by Peter Freestone. *Mercury and Me.* New York: Boulevard Books (Berkley Publishing Group), 1996. 244 pages. One 16-page black-and-white photo insert. (First published in Great Britain in 1994 by Bloomsbury Publishing.)

An affectionate memoir from Jim Hutton, Freddie Mercury's best friend and lover from 1983 to Mercury's death from AIDS in 1991. Hutton claims he didn't know who Mercury was when they met and wasn't even attracted to him on first glance—or the second either. Freddie was persistent, however, and his efforts paid off; the two ultimately became involved in a highly charged, emotional relationship and were virtually inseparable. Hutton describes his years with Freddie with candor, creating a vivid image of what Freddie was like backstage and out fashion shopping. Hutton also conveys the heartache of Mercury's final days, which is the stuff of a TV weeper; true fans won't be able to resist it.

PICTORIALS

Hogan, Peter K. *The Complete Guide to the Music of Queen*. London: Omnibus Press (division of Book Sales Limited), 1994. 136 pages. Approximately 115 color and black-and-white photographs throughout. Discography.

CD-format book covering all aspects of Queen's career. Overlaps with St. Michael's CD-format book (see below), but each offers something of different appeal: This has more photos, the other more informational back sections.

St. Michael, Mick. *Queen*. Miami, FL: MBS, 1994. 120 pages. Approximately 75 color and black-and-white photographs throughout. Discography. Chronology. Index.

CD-format book covering all aspects of Queen's career. This nicely designed and illustrated book is priced just right at around $7.99.

QUIZBOOKS AND QUOTEBOOKS

St. Michael, Mick. *Queen: In Their Own Words*. London: Omnibus Press (division of Book Sales Limited), 1992. 112 pages. Approximately 100 photographs throughout.

Quotes by and about the dinosaur rock band, heavily illustrated with performance shots. Sections cover their early days, the music, albums (each seems to be covered), competition, fame, etc. There are a good many quotes from Roger Taylor, Freddie Mercury, and Brian May, but significantly fewer from John Deacon—which is probably fine. The book treats Mercury with special dignity, incorporating quotes from him personally ("The reason we're successful, darling? My overall charisma, of course") and the band on him (Roger: "Freddie's just his natural self: just a poof, really"). Closing with excerpted quotes from "The Freddie Mercury Tribute" in 1992, this book offers some fun and fond memories for fans.

TOURBOOKS

Brooks, Greg. Foreword by Bob Harris. *Queen Live: A Concert Documentary*. London: Omnibus Press (division of Book Sales Limited), 1995. 176 pages. Approximately 250 color and black-and-white photographs, covering every page. Discography. Bootlegs. Statistics.

An excellent catalog of concert performances, complete with venues, songs played, descriptions of the shows, and many worthwhile stories. If you're a fan of Queen's live act, you'll want this book over Dean's work (see Chronologies, above), as the tales herein are meatier and the observations more informed. Brooks, an avid collector of Queen memorabilia, was evidently in attendance at a number of these shows, or at least when he wasn't, he knew where to find reliable reviews and quotes. With ample color throughout and substantial discographical information in the back, this is perhaps the best available document of Queen's 704 live performances.

YOUNG ADULT

Davis, Judith. *Queen: An Illustrated Biography*. London: Proteus, 1981. 96 pages. Approximately 40 black-and-white photographs; one four-page color insert. Discography.

A joke of a biography that won't even please the youngest child who can mouth the four words "we are the champions." Mistakes abound (*A Day at the Races* is titled *Away at the Races*) and, color insert aside, the photo selection is terrible. The book throws in a ridiculous quiz but fails to recount any of the band's history pre-1968, omitting crucial details such as that Mercury was born in Zanzibar. Distributed in the U.S. by the Scribner Book Companies, Inc.

OTHER TITLES OF INTEREST
Lowe, Jacque. *Queen's Greatest Pix*. London: Quartet, 1981.
Pryce, Larry. *Queen*. London: Star Books, 1976.
Tremlett, George. *The Queen Story*. London: Futura, 1978.
West, Mike. *Queen: The First Ten Years*. London: Omnibus Press (division of Book Sales Limited), 1981.

QUEEN LATIFAH

TITLES OF INTEREST
Peeples, Freda. *Queen Latifah*. New York: Dell, 1992.

QUIET RIOT

PICTORIALS

Gett, Steve. *Quiet Riot: The "Official" Biography*. Port Chester, NY: Cherry Lane, 1985. 48 pages. Approximately 50 color and black-and-white illustrations, covering nearly every page.

Magazine history of the band, with major emphasis on their activities in the early 1980's. The book is thoroughly dissatisfying, unless you are a teen looking for more clips for your wall. There is precious little on guitar legend Randy Rhoads (who left the band to play with Ozzy Osbourne), failing to include even one photo of him. Fans will be further dismayed that the final pages end with question-and-answer interviews instead of a discography. Like the name of the Quiet Riot album: condition critical.

RAINBOW

TITLES OF INTEREST
Makowski, Peter. *Rainbow*. London: Omnibus Press (division of Book Sales Limited), 1981.

BONNIE RAITT

BIOGRAPHIES

Bego, Mark. Foreword by Joan Baez. *Bonnie Raitt: Just in the Nick of Time*. New York: Birch Lane (Carol Publishing Group), 1995. 248 pages. One glossy eight-page black-and-white photo insert; one glossy eight-page color insert. Discography. Source Notes. Index.

Pop biographer Bego goes after yet another celebrity, this time singer/composer/guitarist Bonnie Raitt. Born in Burbank, California to Scottish lineage, Raitt is the daughter of Quaker musical star John Raitt (*Oklahoma!*, among others). Raitt's love of the blues led to her career as a singer who uniquely blended rock, pop, folk, blues, country, and soul into her own sound. In the 1970's she garnered some respect in the music industry—she worked with notable producers Paul Rothchild

and Don Was—but it wasn't until after her recovery from alcohol addiction and the release of her album *Nick of Time* that she became a national sensation. Even Joan Baez's glowing foreword doesn't do full justice to Raitt's stature as rock's veteran queen. For a change, Bego's hype meshes with the subject.

THE RAMONES

BIOGRAPHIES

Bessman, Jim. *Ramones: An American Band*. New York: St. Martin's Press, 1993. 202 pages. Approximately 75 black-and-white photographs throughout. Tour Schedule. Discography. Index.

This biography's sleek black cover and elegant silver type belie the work's mischievous intent; if one looks carefully at the cover's graphic design of an American eagle, it is clear that the creature is holding a baseball bat and is spouting The Ramones theme "Hey Ho/Let's Go." One would expect nothing less from a work telling the history of the punk middle-class boys from Queens, New York, who have managed to outlast their contemporaries. Although he had The Ramones' cooperation on this book, Bessman lacks the skill to successfully convince readers that The Ramones are remotely comparable to The Beatles. (Moppish hair aside, there couldn't be two bands any further apart.) His giddy attempts to recreate The Ramones' lingo gets on your nerves after a while, unless you're a heartened fan. "Gabba gabba hey!"—*Booklist*.

OTHER TITLES OF INTEREST
Miles. *Ramones*. London: Omnibus Press (division of Book Sales Limited), 1981.

THE RASPBERRIES

TITLES OF INTEREST
Beckers, Patrick. *The Eric Carmen Story*. Naastricht, Netherlands: ECB Productions, 1995.
Sharp, Ken. *Overnight Sensation: The Story of the Raspberries*. No city: Power Pop Press, 1995.

RATT

PICTORIALS

Gett, Steve. *Ratt: Renegade Angels*. Port Chester, NY: Cherry Lane, 1985. 48 pages. Approximately 75 color and black-and-white photographs throughout.

Steve Gett, one of Great Britain's top heavy metal authorities, slapped together this colorful photo book of Ratt in action back in the mid-1980's. This high-kicking quintet sold ten million copies of their first LP *Out of the Cellar*, but hadn't done much else at the time of press. Gett has merely recycled quotes from magazines and newspapers, and doesn't waste any space filling in details such as dates of birth. The pages have been splotched with red, black, blue, or yellow dots, which seems to be an intentional device to dissuade fans from actually reading the text. This book's main purpose: tear-sheets for teenagers' walls (but please don't use a library copy!).

OTHER TITLES OF INTEREST
DeCordobes, Dominique. *Ratt*. New York: Ballantine, 1986.

OTIS REDDING

BIOGRAPHIES

Schiesel, Jane. *The Otis Redding Story*. Garden City, NY: Doubleday & Company, Inc., 1973. 144 pages.

The lone biography of legendary performer Otis Redding is, unfortunately, a quarter of a century old. Still, it's unknown how much is left to be uncovered about this artist who died in a plane crash in 1967 and was posthumously inducted into the Rock and Roll Hall of Fame in 1989. A fan of gospel rockers like Little Richard, Georgia-born Redding was having a fantastic year in 1967 until his death: his music had crossed over to an integrated audience; he was a smash at the Monterey Pop Festival; and he had an international hit with "(Sittin' on the) Dock of the Bay." In dire need of an update—and next time with photos.

THE RED HOT CHILI PEPPERS

BIOGRAPHIES

Thompson, Dave. *The Red Hot Chili Peppers*. New York: St. Martin's Press, 1993. 276 pages. One eight-page glossy color photo insert; approximately 20 black-and-white photographs throughout. Discography.

What's the first thing a fan does when opening a book on his or her favorite band? Turn to the photos, of course. In the color insert in this book about "the high priests of hip hysteria," The Peppers are positioned across a two-page spread stark naked (tattoos excluded) in the "descent of man" pose. Very scary stuff. Thompson's prose also has the mindset to intimidate his readers, comparing The Peppers to the "bad" acts of rock's past, namely The Rolling Stones. But then things settle down (slightly), as he tells of the band's roots (Fairfax High School in Hollywood), Anthony Kiedis' strange upbringing (sharing a woman with his dad when the former was only 12), and his friendship with an unlikely fellow, Sonny Bono. Full of unnecessary, overconfident boasts (that Pearl Jam would not have existed if not for the Peppers), this book has enough testosterone to fill a packed stadium. A must for fans who enjoy the band's dangerous image. The British title, *The Red Hot Chili Peppers: True Men Don't Kill Coyotes* (Virgin, 1993) is better, but that edition doesn't contain color.

PICTORIALS

Harvey, Spike. *Red Hot Chili Peppers*. London: Omnibus Press (division of Book Sales Limited), 1995. Unpaginated (approximately 72 pages). Approximately 80 color and black-and-white photographs, covering every page.

If pictures tell more than words, this book is an epic. The Chilies are more naked than dressed in this colorful menagerie, but when they *are* clothed, the items are enough to make Boy George blush: drag, rabbinical outfits, tube socks on their penises (displayed on stage and in the crosswalk in front of *Abbey Road* Studios!), wearing flaming construction helmets and, overall, appealing to the lowest form of puerile. The "Let's Make a Deal" game show never saw such creative fashion.

Watts, Chris. *Red Hot Chili Peppers: Sugar and Spice*. Chessington, Surrey (England): Castle Communications, 1994. 144 pages. Approximately 80 color and black-and-white photographs throughout.

After bashing Woodstock II, author Chris Watts tells the history of the Red Hot Chili Peppers, beginning with the end of the California punk movement. The entire book consists of one line sentences and paragraphs that hype the band's outrageousness; what it comes down to, though, is that Watts thinks any Chili Pepper quote incorporating the word "cock" must be revelatory. The photos are on about the same level as those in Harvey's work (see above), although in that case at least the author (and publisher) were savvy enough to know to keep the author's pen off the page. Spice without substance.

LOU REED

(See also Velvet Underground, The)

BIOGRAPHIES

Bockris, Victor. *Transformer: The Lou Reed Story*. New York: Simon & Schuster, 1995. 446 pages. One glossy 16-page black-and-white photo insert. Source Notes. Bibliography. Index.

Bockris goes right for the balls, as it were, in this biography of Lou Reed. Starting right off with Reed's electric shock therapy in Creedmore State Psychiatric Hospital—his parents' ignorant attempt to "cure" his homosexuality—Bockris elucidates this pivotal moment in his life better than any other writer up to present. The author not only demonstrates how this trauma shaped his life, but also how it possibly fostered the very attributes that would make him the most changeable rock genius of his time, rivaled only by David Bowie. The tracing of Reed's life from suburban nerd to punkster in The Velvet Underground to solo visionary and iconoclast is handled with skill and finesse. "The degree of detail is exhaustive..."—*The New York Times*.

Doggett, Peter. *Lou Reed: Growing Up in Public*. London: Omnibus Press (division of Book Sales Limited), 1992. 189 pages. One glossy eight-page black-and-white photo insert. Discography.

Doggett, editor of *Record Collector* magazine, sets his aspirations high by trying to unmask Reed and show how he made a Houdini-like transformation "from sexual outlaw to contented husband" (albeit with second wife). Reed's drug addictions are more than public knowledge; they have come to represent the method behind his madness, and one can never tell whether his songs were a result of the drugs or vice versa. This book moves at a snail's pace through Reed's life story and lacks the pizzazz of Bockris' more thorough work (see above). Optional.

QUIZBOOKS AND QUOTEBOOKS

Wrenn, Michael with Marks, Glen. *Lou Reed: Between the Lines*. London: Plexus, 1993. 144 pages. Approximately 150 black-and-white photographs, covering nearly every page.

Quotebook on Lou Reed—before, during, and after The Velvet Underground—accentuated with black-and-white photographs, album art, newspaper clips, and more. Unlike the Omnibus Press quotebooks, this work is straightforward chronological, rather than divided by subject. Reed is quoted on his religion ("Of course I'm Jewish, aren't all the best people"), electric shock therapy ("They put the thing down your throat so you don't swallow your tongue, and they put electrodes on your head"), songwriting ("People don't deserve good lyrics because they never listen to them these days"), and other topics. Although the quotes do not have sources and are not dated, they are well selected and not cluttered. Enjoyable.

WRITTEN WORKS

Reed, Lou. *Between Thought and Expression: Selected Lyrics of Lou Reed*. New York: Hyperion, 1991. 182 pages.

The lyrics to Reed's songs are highly imaginative and often disturbing visions of tortured sexuality, life in the city, and drug experimentation. Transcribed here are some of his most influential recordings with The Velvet Underground and solo (e.g., "Heroin," "Sweet Jane," and "Walk on the Wild Side"), as well as his conversations with Vaclav Havel and Hubert Delby. Reed seems to have had at least some involvement with the preparation of the manuscript, as his brief comments appear in small italics below many of the works. Brace yourself for the horror of "The Gift," the sardonic irony of "I Wanna Be Black," and the blunt humor of the three-line "Ferryboat Bill." "[Reed is] one of rock's most literary writers, adept at detailed observation and flavorful dialogue"—*Los Angeles Times*.

OTHER TITLES OF INTEREST

No author. *Loud Reed: Rock and Roll Animal*. Manchester, England: Babylon, 1979.

R.E.M.

ATHENS, GA

Brown, Rodger Lyle. *Party Out of Bounds: The B-52's, R.E.M., and the Kids Who Rocked Athens, Georgia*. New York: Plume (division of Penguin), 1991. 222 pages. One eight-page glossy black-and-white photo insert.

At one time only known for its cotton farms, Athens, Georgia became "a Liverpool of the South" in the 1980's—a fertile farming ground for New Wave talent. The B-52s (here B-52's), R.E.M., The Fans, Pylon, and Method Actors headlined the clubs during the period and countered the no-purpose violence of punksters such as The Sex Pistols with a polite, almost feminine, pop culture. Reported almost completely in the passive tense, Brown's book never does go out of bounds, unless one considers an occasional dragfest an earthshaker. Optional for fans of the aforementioned bands.

BIOGRAPHIES

Bowler, Dave and Dray, Bryan. *R.E.M.: From Chronic Town to Monster*. New York: Citadel (Carol Publishing Group), 1995. 208 pages. One glossy eight-page color and black-and-white photo insert. Discography. Sources. (First published in Great Britain in 1995 by Boxtree as *R.E.M. Documental*.)

This very basic bio is intended strictly for fans, although it's by no means a hype job. British in terms of style and content, the book contains a U.K.-only discography and only limited information on U.S. tours. Compared to other works, this is especially weak on the Athens, Georgia musical scene. On the whole, however,

many young fans might prefer the book's overall lack of pretense. Older fans might feel slightly insulted by the babyish questions that introduce many paragraphs (e.g., "Why the drums?" regarding Bill Berry). Light reading.

CRITICAL/ANALYTICAL STUDIES

Editors of *Rolling Stone*. Foreword by Holly George-Warren. Introduction by Anthony DeCurtis. *R.E.M.: The Rolling Stone Files: The Ultimate Compendium of Interviews, Articles, Facts and Opinions*. New York: Hyperion, 1995. 196 pages. Discography. Videography.

Non-illustrated collection of interviews, narrative pieces, reviews, and performance reviews on R.E.M.. The articles span the years 1982—a piece by Andrew Slater about a new band from Athens, Georgia named R.E.M. that "doesn't play New Wave"—to a 1994 question-and-answer between Anthony DeCurtis and Michael Stipe. Among the other journalists represented are Jimmy Guterman, Michael Azerrad, and David Fricke—but even into the 1990's no women are featured. An otherwise excellent reference volume for fans and biographers.

GENERAL REFERENCE

Gray, Marcus. *It Crawled From the South: An R.E.M. Companion*. New York: Da Capo Press, 1993. 350 pages. One glossy 32-page black-and-white photo insert. (First published in the U.K. in 1992 by Guinness Publishing Limited.)

Neither a comprehensive biography nor a standard band discography, *It Crawled from the South* contains random elements of both formats in eighteen incoherently assembled chapters. Gray evidently has enough knowledge of the band to have ventured in either direction, but he seems determined to arrange his book cryptically, like the messages in R.E.M.'s lyrics. Thus, he begins with an effective summarization of the musicians' backgrounds, followed by chapters on their recorded material, songwriting achievements, demos, tours, etc., followed by broader material on the band's significance and the Athens scene. Fans who have the patience to deal with the author's often trying organization will find insightful information in dribbles and spurts.

PICTORIALS

Fletcher, Tony. *Remarks: The Story of R.E.M.*. New York: Bantam, 1990. 128 pages. 50 black-and-white and 12 color photographs throughout. Discography. (First published in Great Britain in 1990 by Omnibus Press.)

"The first full biography of the American band of the nineties" suffers in comparison to the later work by Greer (see below), which is more recent, contains more color, and is published in a larger trim size. The photos are smaller and are framed by black borders; the essence of the band is never really captured. While this work is slightly British, Fletcher has an admirably detached tone (not fully accepting the "Michael Stipe as visionary poet" theory) and a good knowledge of R.E.M.'s punk influences (e.g., The Sex Pistols). Optional.

Greer, Jim. Photographs by Levine, Laura. *R.E.M.: Behind the Mask*. Boston: Little, Brown and Company, 1992. 140 pages. 125 color and black-and-white illustrations throughout. Discography, Tours and Guest Appearances.

An appealing retrospective of R.E.M., the band that revolutionized "college rock." Greer, a Senior Editor at *Spin* magazine as of publication, occasionally writes too conversationally and leans towards a critical assessment when it's not really necessary. He also relies heavily on his interviews with one band member, Peter Buck. A sidebar on other Athens, Georgia bands lends some historical perspective. Teenagers take note: The book ends with a ballot in favor of the "Motor Voter Bill" (allowing kids to register when they get their driver's licenses). Recommended.

Harrington, David. *R.E.M.*. Miami, FL: MBS, 1994. 120 pages. Approximately 75 color and black-and-white photographs throughout. Discography. Chronology. Index.

CD-format book covering all aspects of R.E.M.'s career. This nicely designed and illustrated book is priced just right at around $7.99.

Hogan, Peter. *The Complete Guide to the Music of R.E.M.*. London: Omnibus Press (division of Book Sales Limited), 1995. 114 pages. Approximately 100 color and black-and-white photographs throughout.

CD-format book covering all aspects of R.E.M.'s career. Overlaps with Harrington's CD-format book (see above), but each offers something of different appeal: This has more photos, the other more informational back sections.

QUIZBOOKS AND QUOTEBOOKS

Sullivan, Denise. *Talk About the Passion: R.E.M.: An Oral History*. Lancaster, PA: Underwood-Miller, 1994. 200 pages. Approximately 50 black-and-white photographs throughout. Discography.

Quotebook arranged chronologically or, more specifically, by R.E.M.'s albums. After an opening section on beginnings, insiders are quoted at length about various topics related to the band. Among those featured are Danny Beard (co-owner of Wax n' Facts Records in Atlanta), Kurt Cobain (who had made plans to record with Stipe, but committed suicide before the collaboration came to fruition), Geoff Gans (art director), and dozens of others—except for the band itself. Some interesting observations here and there, but fans would want more information directly related to R.E.M., both in terms of photos and their voices.

OTHER TITLES OF INTEREST
Weidner, Annette. *R.E.M.* No city: VIP, 1993.

REO SPEEDWAGON

YOUNG ADULT

Peterson, Paul. *REO Speedwagon*. Mankato, MN: Creative Education, 1983. 32 pages. Approximately six black-and-white photographs throughout.

Part of the "Rock 'n Pop Stars" series from Creative Education, this is one of the better informed installments, sporting details on the group's formation at Southern Illinois University in Carbondale, early tours, hit albums (notably *Hi Infidelity*), and the band's knack for catchy melodies. If there are any fans 8-12 left with an interest in this late 1970's-early 80's group, this book will serve.

CLIFF RICHARD (AND THE SHADOWS)

AUTOBIOGRAPHY

Richard, Cliff with Latham, Bill. *Which One's Cliff?: The Autobiography of Cliff Richard.* London: Hodder and Stoughton, 1977. 192 pages. Approximately 100 black-and-white photographs throughout; one glossy four-page color insert. Cliff Richard Discography.

The "English Elvis" tells his life story through writer Bill Latham. Richard, born Harry Webb, grew up in semi-luxury in India, where his father was manager of a catering firm. When the family returned to England, his mother and sister became Jehovah's Witnesses, while young Cliff fell into Elvis and later Christianity, producing light rock and appearing in a number of forgettable films. Despite some occasional injections of humor, Richard is a rather dreary storyteller, and his tale lacks cohesion. Fans into Richard's theology and brand of pop will need to own a copy, but others can live without it.

BIOGRAPHIES

Doncaster, Patrick and Jasper, Tony. *Cliff.* London: Sidgwick & Jackson, 1982. 240 pages. Approximately 100 black-and-white photographs throughout. Facts. Index.

Written with Richard's cooperation, this very British biography (it's impossible to have it any other way) begins with a dry history of rock and roll—with a distinctly white orientation. (Haley and Presley are mentioned, but the words rhythm and blues do not appear, nor do the names Domino, Berry, et. al.). With many of Richard's details already covered in his autobiography (see above), the book's main value lies in the photos of young, handsome Cliff—almost all of which are from the late 1950's and early 60's—and the extensive data in the back (under "Facts"), which includes, in no particular order, Christian activities, discography, fan clubs, TV and radio appearances, and more. Optional.

Tremlett, George. *The Cliff Richard Story.* London: Futura Publications, 1975. 156 pages. One glossy 16-page black-and-white photo insert. Cliff Richard Chronology.

Dated mass-market biography of Richard, one third of which is taken up by the chronology. Over the years, rock writer Tremlett interviewed Richard and friends, such as Olivia Newton-John, but this is by no means a comprehensive work. The "Vicar of Pop" (a title Tremlett despises) is afforded only a generic outline of events, with little in the way of analytical commentary or his influence. Many of Tremlett's sentences ramble on without a point to be found. Look elsewhere.

Turner, Steve. *Cliff Richard: The Biography.* Oxford, England: Lion Publishing, 1993. 384 pages. Two glossy black-and-white photo inserts. Sources. Where Are They Now? Discography. Memorabilia. Family Trees. Index.

Author Steve Turner, who helped research a BBC documentary called "Cliff," delivers this thorough biography of the performer. Although Turner knows little about the world of rock biography (he complements Albert Goldman's trashy works on Elvis Presley and John Lennon, simply because the author cites excessive source material), he handles his subject well, and avoids too much overlap with Richard's autobiography (see above). In fact, Turner had Richard's blessing on this project, which enabled him to amass countless first-hand interviews with insiders. If you want to know personal details such as what Richards eats for breakfast or why he chose to wear pink socks 30 years ago, read this scrupulously detailed book.

Winter, David. *New Singer, New Song: The Cliff Richard Story.* Waco, TX: Waco Books, 1968. 154 pages. 24 full-page glossy black-and-white photographs throughout.

Cliff Richard, born Harry Webb from Cheshunt County, England, would ultimately tally more number ones hits in England than The Beatles in a career spanning nearly five decades. At the time of this book's publication, Richard had already conquered both the recording and film industries and seemed to be involved in some deep soul searching, first with the Jehovah's

Witnesses and later with Billy Graham and Catholicism. This book had Richard's cooperation—it's even co-copyrighted in his name—yet it fails to hold any interest a quarter of a century and change later.

FANZINES AND FAN CLUBS

Cliff Richard & the Shadows Fan Club France. Attn: Bernard Broche, 10 rue Edouard Rouviere 38450 VIF France.

Founded in 1990, this fan club is associated with the International Cliff Richard Movement (see below). Publishes a bimonthly 20-page fanzine, which is half French and English. Offers for sale records, CDs, videos, and books, and holds an annual meeting for all members.

Cliff Richard Fan Club of Belgium. Att. Marleen Suykerbuyk, Korte Damstraat 15, 9180 Moerbeke-Waas, Belgium.

Fan club begun in 1981 affiliated with The International Cliff Richard Movement (see below), which offers members *Dynamite International* newsletter (from the ICRM), as well as its own original fanzine, *Green Light.* The bimonthly 16-page magazine, available in Dutch or French, features a glossy cover, news on latest recordings and tours, and more. The club also holds a meeting once a year for collectors.

Cliff Richard Fan Club of Birmingham. 1 Aldis Road, Walsall West Midlands WS2 9AY England.

Fan club affiliated with The International Cliff Richard Movement (see below) that offers members *Dynamite International* newsletter (from the ICRM), *Hot Shot* magazine, and a membership card. *Hot Shot* is a 28-page booklet with a color cover that contains black-and-white photographs, meeting notices, collectibles, charity information, pet care advertisements (Richard is an animal lover), and more. The cost of membership is £8; for £10, members receive an intermediary publication, *Urgent Information,* which reports the latest-breaking news.

Cliff Richard Fan Club of Denmark. Attn: Jytte Mathiasen, Ostergarden 7, 1, th 2635 Ishoj Denmark.

Begun circa 1993-94, this club is affiliated with The International Cliff Richard Movement (see below) and offers members *Dynamite International* newsletter (from the ICRM). Write for other club activities.

Cliff Richard Fan Club of Isle of Wight. 5 Park Road Kings Town Estate Brading Sandown IW PO36 OHU England.

Fan club affiliated with The International Cliff Richard Movement (see below), which offers members *Dynamite International* newsletter (from the ICRM), as well as its own extra news sheets, a membership card and photographs. Offers some merchandising. The cost of membership is £5 per year, plus self-addressed stamped envelopes.

Cliff Richard Fan Club of Lincolnshire/East Yorkshire. c/o Julie Leighton, 3 Folkingham Road, Billingborough, Lincolnshire NG34 ONT England.

Fan club affiliated with The International Cliff Richard Movement (see below) that offers members *Dynamite International* newsletter (from the ICRM), a club button, and a 12-page booklet containing photocopies of black-and-white photos, radio appearances, news, letters from members, contests, and more. The club sponsors trips and charity events, and offers members merchandising such as t-shirts, pens, pencils, desk pads, diaries, posters, and more.

Cliff Richard Fan Club of Manchester. 4 Dowlish Avenue, Cheadle Hulme, Stockport, Greater Manchester SK8 6SF England.

Fan club affiliated with The International Cliff Richard Movement (see below) that offers members *Dynamite International* newsletter (from the ICRM) and its own publication, *Simply Cliff.* The 18-page booklet includes black-and-white photographs, reprinted newspaper articles, letters, merchandising, notices about club events, and more. The club is heavily involved in fundraising, holding events such as raffles and concerts to raise money for hospitals and other charities.

Cliff Richard Fan Club of Middx & Bucks. 11, Southview Downley, High Wycombe Bucks HP 13 5UL England.

Fan club affiliated with The International Cliff Richard Movement (see below) that offers members *Dynamite International* newsletter (from the ICRM) and prints its own fanzine for the Middx (Middlesex) and Bucks area. The six-page brochure updates fans on local events and get-togethers and offers merchandising such as badges, writing paper, photos, t-shirts, and more.

Cliff Richard Movement of New Zealand. Attn. Mrs. Katrina Richards, 29 Cotton Street St. Johns Auckland 6 New Zealand.

Fan club affiliated with The International Cliff Richard Movement (see below) that offers members *Dynamite International* newsletter (from the ICRM) and prints its own fanzine for New Zealand. The central focus of the club is its fundraising activities with the Tear Fund (The Evangelical Alliance Relief Fund) and various hospitals and wildlife parks. *Small Corners*, a glossy 36-page magazine, includes black-and-white photographs, news updates, Cliff's sports activities, news releases, advertisements for various charities, merchandise for sale, and more. Club members also receive *CustardyCapers* (see Related Works, below), badges, pens, stationery, and many other goodies.

Cliff Richard Fan Club of Sweden. c/o Knutson, Tyringegatan 3 SE-252 76 Helingsborg Sweden.

Fan club affiliated with The International Cliff Richard Movement (see below) that offers four fanzines and occasional separate newsletters per year.

The International Cliff Richard Movement. ICRM, P.O. Box 2BQ, London W1A 2BQ England.

This organization, actually based in Amsterdam, is the mother body uniting Cliff Richard clubs all around the globe, including 25 in Great Britain alone. The club, also known as ICRM, publishes *Dynamite International*, a four-page bimonthly mailing that cites Cliff Richard fan club meeting houses all around the world; it also chronicles Richard's recent public appearances, performances, books, records, videos, and more. Write to the British address above for more information. Note that the club generally does not permit its various affiliated clubs around the world to allow in members outside its own country (hence pricing information was not released by the clubs above).

PICTORIALS

Jasper, Tony. *Silver Cliff: A 25-Year Journal 1958-1983.* London: Sidgwick & Jackson, 1983. 136 pages. Approximately 150 black-and-white photographs throughout, covering every page; one four-page color insert. U.K. Recorded Releases.

Photo tribute to the enduring legend of Cliff Richard. Each four-to-six page chapter covers a year or two in the artist's fantastic career, from his early TV appearances (on "Oh Boy!") to film performances (dancing up a storm in *The Young Ones*), to mixing it up with other stars (Olivia Newton-John), and much more. Accessible for an American audience—if there is one—although those requiring discographical information would do better with Jasper's previous work with Patrick Doncaster (see Biographies, above).

RELATED WORKS

No author. *CustardyCapers from Christchurch: Cliff Richard Recipe Book.* St. Johns Auckland, New Zealand: Cliff Richard Movement of New Zealand, no date. Unpaginated (approximately 128 pages). Approximately 100 line drawings and 35 black-and-white photographs throughout.

Cookbook assembled by the Cliff Richard Movement of New Zealand (see Fanzines and Fan Clubs, above) and featuring recipes from fans all around the world. If your taste buds start to see the light, give "Chicken a la Pope" a try; if your family wants a spiked treat after a holiday meal, "Christmas Cake" might be right for your festive table. Some ethnic delicacies, such as tabbouleh (parsley salad), are also included. The drawings are cute and the glossy paper may help repel some of those troublesome kitchen splatterings.

OTHER TITLES OF INTEREST

Ferrier, Bob. *Cliff Around the Clock.* London: Daily Mirror, 1964.

Ferrier, Bob. *The Wonderful World of Cliff Richard.* London: R. Davies, 1964.

Geddes, George Thomson. *Foot Tapping: The Shadows 1958-1978.* Glasgow, Scotland: George Thomson Geddes, 1978.

Geddes, George Thomson. *The Shadows: A History and Discography.* Glasgow, Scotland: George Thomson Geddes, 1981.

Harris, Jet and Ellis, Royston. *Driftin' With Cliff Richard: The Inside Story of What Really Happens on Tour.* London: Charles Buchan's Publications, 1959.

Lewry, Peter and Goodall, Nigel. *Cliff Richard: The Complete Recording Sessions.* New York: Sterling, 1992.

Richard, Cliff. *Cliff In His Own Words.* W. H. Allen, 1981.

Richard, Cliff. *Happy Christmas from Cliff.* London: Hodder and Stoughton, 1980.

Richard, Cliff. *It's Great to Be Young.* London: World Distributors, 1961.

Richard, Cliff. *Me and My Shadows.* London: Daily Mirror, 1963.

Richard, Cliff. *Questions: Cliff Answering Reader and Fan Queries.* London: Hodder and Stoughton, 1970.

Richard, Cliff. *The Way I See It.* London: Hodder and Stoughton, 1970.

Richard, Cliff. *The Way I See It Now.* London: Hodder and Stoughton, 1973.

The Shadows. *The Shadows by Themselves.* London: Consul Books, 1961.

The Shadows. *The Story of the Shadows: An Autobiography.* London: Elm Tree Books, 1983.

Sutter, Jack. *Cliff, the Baron of Beat.* London: Valex, 1960.

KEITH RICHARDS

(See also Rolling Stones, The)

BIOGRAPHIES

Bockris, Victor. *Keith Richards: The Biography.* New York: Poseidon Press (Simon & Schuster, Inc.), 1992. 416 pages. Approximately 50 black-and-white photographs throughout. Bibliography. Index.

To the general public he's the image of Satan and the symbol of 1960's drug decadence; to rock fans he's the guitar legend who perfected the rock guitar lick; and to those who know him he's a shy, sensitive artist in dire need of collaborators to make his art successful. Bockris' retelling of The Stones' story through Keith's point of view is fresh, funny, and objective. He successfully incorporates many quotes from Richards' friends, relatives, and fellow musicians excerpted (not footnoted, though) from interviews he conducted over the years. The power-plays and shared sexual intercourse among band members (Richards, Jagger, and

Jones) and their respective women (Anita Pallenberg, Linda Keith, Marianne Faithfull, Bianca Jagger, etc.) make for nonstop reading. "...a solid, straight-ahead look at The Rolling Stones' none-too straight musical genius." —*Rolling Stone.*

Booth, Stanley. *Keith: Standing in the Shadows.* New York: St. Martin's Press, 1995. 212 pages. Approximately 20 full-page black-and-white photographs throughout.

Trailing in the dust of Bockris' fine oral biography (see above), Booth makes an effort to show new angles of Keith Richards: as a ball boy for tennis matches; as a choir boy; and as a deprived post-war child sucking on scant candy rations. These fascinating, rarely investigated early images, introduced by quotes taken from the author's various interviews with Richards, are dismissed all too quickly in Booth's I-don't-give-a-damn prose. Richards' art school days, blues influences, The Stones' rise through the clubs, and classic album collaborations receive such short attention, one wonders what Booth had in mind here—except possibly to reinstate midway how he personally fit into The Rolling Stones' history. Supplemented with grainy, and generally terrible photos.

PICTORIALS

Charone, Barbara. *Keith Richards: Life as a Rolling Stone.* Garden City, New York: Doubleday, 1982. 198 pages. Approximately 100 black-and-white photographs throughout. Discography.

Oversized photo history of Keith Richards' life and career, with surprisingly substantial coverage of the Jagger/Richards partnership and (though Jagger probably wouldn't care to admit it) competition. The book also contains a wacked-out section on Richards' family life with Anita Pallenberg and their son Marlon, who had a fixation on the horror film *Murders in the Rue Morgue.* Not without its moments of hilarity, but randomly pulled together and hopelessly entrenched in 1981, which at this point leaves the reader a decade and a half behind in concert performances.

QUIZBOOKS AND QUOTEBOOKS

St. Michael, Mick. *Keith Richards: In His Own Words*. London: Omnibus Press (division of Book Sales Limited), 1994. 96 pages. Approximately 100 black-and-white photographs, covering every page.

Keith Richards is quoted on a variety of topics, from his longtime mates, The Stones, to growing old. On Mick Jagger: "The only thing Mick and I disagree about is the band, the music, and what we do." On Brian Jones: "As far as I know Brian Jones never wrote a single finished song in his life...." On Charlie Watts: "It's Charlie Watts' band—without him...we wouldn't have a group." Despite the guitarist's image as a spooky figure, one will be amazed by Richards' humor, generosity, and objectivity when remarking on other artists. All in all, a respectable compilation.

LIONEL RICHIE

BIOGRAPHIES

Plutzik, Roberta. *Lionel Richie*. New York: Dell Publishing Co., 1985. 192 pages. One 16-page black-and-white photo insert. Lionel Richie Awards & Nominations. Lionel Richie Discography.

Mass-market biography of the longtime star. Richie had unusual exposure to racial harmony during his youth in the 1950's and 60's, as he was born and raised in Tuskegee, Alabama, the site of the famous Tuskegee Institute—which had been founded by Booker T. Washington and drew professors and scholars of all races. In fact, it was in Tuskegee, only one half mile from Richie's home, that George Washington Carver revolutionized the peanut. Richie's solid upbringing (his father was a career Army man, his mother a teacher) no doubt had an influence on how he became one of the few stars not ruined by drugs and controversy. A basic, accessible book on the man who hit his stride with The Commodores and then struck gold as a soloist with "Hello" and "All Night Long."

PICTORIALS

Nathan, David. Introduction by Dionne Warwick. *Lionel Richie: An Illustrated Biography*. New York: McGraw-Hill, 1985. 128 pages. Approximately 75 black-and-white photographs throughout; two eight-page color inserts. Lionel Richie Discography.

Superficial photo tribute to Richie, with many photos spanning the early days of The Commodores to Richie's high-flying solo career in the 1980's. As expected, the text hurries through his childhood; five pages into chapter one, he's already fallen in love with his future wife, Brenda, joined The Commodores, and secured a recording contract. The author's writing is on a simplistic level perhaps more suitable for younger fans. A laundry list of events better handled in Plutzik's work (see Biographies, above).

YOUNG ADULT

Koenig, Teresa. *Lionel Richie*. Mankato, MN: Crestwood House, 1986. 32 pages. Approximately 30 color and black-and-white illustrations throughout.

Part of Crestwood House's "Center Stage" series, this five-chapter book is a decent introduction to the star for young fans. Koenig reports the basics about Richie, from his childhood in Tuskegee, Alabama, to his success in the Commodores (unfortunately, the group photo is circa 1981, not the 1970's), to his devotion to his wife, Brenda, to his friendships in the music industry (Diana Ross), and more. Parents who still believe in the message of "We Are the World" will want to share this with their kids.

SMOKEY ROBINSON (AND THE MIRACLES)

AUTOBIOGRAPHY

Robinson, Smokey with Ritz, David. *Smokey: Inside My Life*. London: Headline Publishing, 1989. 292 pages. Two glossy 16-page black-and-white photo inserts. Records. Selected Songs of Smokey Robinson. Index.

Smokey Robinson may not have lived the tragic life of his pal Marvin Gaye (whom he nicknamed "Dad"), but he faced his own demons in his rise and fall from the top. Illicit affairs (one with a Playboy bunny), cocaine addictions, and the death of his friend Gaye contributed to Robinson's divorce from his wife and co-Miracle Claudette, and very nearly the end of his own life. Robinson was fortunate enough to have many friends in the business—including Aretha Franklin, Diana Ross, and Berry Gordy—who have helped him persevere. Robinson is revealed as a sensitive and honest artist, but this book suffers from too many one-sentence paragraphs and excessive flattery of people in the industry who are known to have raging egos. "Collaborator Ritz faithfully preserves Robinson's vigorous streettalk narrative style."—*Publishers Weekly*. Published in the U.S. in 1989 by McGraw-Hill.

FANZINES AND FAN CLUBS

The Smokey Robinson and The Miracles Fan Club Newsletter. 8 Hillside Road, Narragansett, RI 02882-2821.

Quarterly non-profit publication founded in 1994 by Miracle (and Smokey's ex-wife) Claudette Robinson. A dozen pages celebrate the legacy of Smokey Robinson and the rest of The Miracles (Ron White, Bobby Rogers, Pete Moore, and Claudette Robinson) and Motown with itineraries, spotlights, photos, games (crossword puzzles), classifieds, and more. The cost is $11.20 for four issues in the U.S. and $15 (or £10) in Great Britain.

JIMMIE RODGERS

BIOGRAPHIES

Paris, Mike and Comber, Chris. *Jimmie the Kid: The Life of Jimmie Rodgers.* London: Eddison Press, Ltd., 1977. 212 pages. One hundred black-and-white photographs throughout. Jimmie Rodgers Discography. Tribute Recordings. Notes. Index.

Excellent retrospective on Jimmie the Kid Rodgers' life and career, tracing his roots from the cotton country of Mississippi, to the musician's years as a railman, to his formation of the Jimmie Rodgers Entertainers, and to his untimely death at 35 due to tuberculosis. Rodgers' influence on contemporary country and rock is often overlooked, but this book contains penetrating descriptions of his

method and an overwhelming assortment of rare photographs. The highlights are shots dating back to the 1920's that depict Jimmie touring with a medicine show. Valuable, though dated.

Porterfield, Nolan. *Jimmie Rodgers: The Life and Times of America's Blue Yodeler.* Chicago: University of Illinois Press, 1979. 460 pages. Approximately 35 black-and-white photographs throughout. Sources and Acknowledgments. The Recordings of Jimmie Rodgers. Appendix I: The Blue Yodels of Jimmie Rodgers. Appendix II: Jimmie Rodgers's Personal Appearances. Index.

Massive biography of the country pioneer that begins with the author's perky descriptions of his own travels down South. In scholarly but not overly rigorous prose, author Nolan Porterfield avoids the clichés of Rodgers' rise to folk hero status, building substantially on volumes that preceded it (see Paris, above). While not a popular account—the footnotes take up more book space than the photos—it will be enjoyed by country fans and anyone interested in music from the first quarter of the 20th century.

YOUNG ADULT

Krishef, Robert K. *Jimmie Rodgers.* Minneapolis, MN: Lerner Publications, Company, 1978. 64 pages. Approximately 40 black-and-white photographs throughout. Recordings of Jimmie Rodgers. Index.

Part of Lerner Publications' Music Library, this informative and lively book introduces the "singing Brakeman" to fans 8-12. Krishef points out Rodgers' influence on Johnny Cash, Merle Haggard, and Elvis Presley, and shows how cool it is to yodel while playing guitar. Nicely handled.

OTHER TITLES OF INTEREST
Rodgers, Carrie. *My Husband Jimmie Rodgers.* No city: Country Music Foundation Press, 1975. *Written by Jimmie Rodgers' widow, Carrie.*

TOMMY ROE

FANZINES AND FAN CLUBS

Tommy Roe International Fan Club. P.O. Box 813, Owatonna, MN 55060-0813.

Fan club devoted to performer Tommy Roe that offers a complete membership package: an album-collectors item (a special gift from Tommy); an updated discography; a membership card; a biography and fact sheet; and an autographed, black-and-white 8x10 photo. The club's quarterly newsletter is a ten-page stapled packet that includes news, classifieds, games, photocopies of black-and-white photographs, merchandising, and a tour itinerary. The cost of membership is $12 in the U.S.; $14 in Canada; and $17 overseas.

KENNY ROGERS

FANZINES AND FAN CLUBS

Kenny Rogers International Fan Club. P.O. Box 24240, Nashville, TN 37202-4240.

Fan club that offers merchandising, books, CDs, videos, and a newsletter published three times per year. Provides information on Rogers' concert schedule. Enrollment is $12 in the U.S.; $14 elsewhere.

PICTORIALS

Hume, Martha. Photographs by Reggero, John. *Kenny Rogers: Gambler, Dreamer, Lover.* New York: Plume (New American Library), 1980. 160 pages. Approximately 100 black-and-white photographs throughout; one eight-page glossy color photo insert. Discography.

While today most people think of Kenny Rogers as a country star, he began his career as a stand-up bassist for the jazz group The Bobby Doyle Trio, after which he joined a pop/psychedelic/country group, First Edition. As a soloist in the 1970's, he racked up country hits (e.g., the staple "The Gambler"), some of which had crossover pop appeal. Hume and Reggero's treatment throws lots of PR tumbleweed into the story, making Rogers' four mar-

riages seem like harmless, quick conquests and his stints with LSD like less than Clinton's with pot.

WRITTEN WORKS

Rogers, Kenny. Foreword by Yousuf Karsh. *Kenny Rogers' America.* Boston: Little, Brown and Company, 1986. 120 pages. Approximately 110 black-and-white photographs throughout.

Kenny Rogers: singer, songwriter, actor—and photographer? Okay, he's not exactly Richard Avedon with a lens. Rogers' landscape photography and portraits are dark and not all that breathtaking, but his subjects are of interest to for those keen on Americana: horses, ranchers, mountains, sheep, etc. Fans will enjoy Rogers' many notes that accompany the photos, especially when he points out a peacock or a bank robber. Optional.

Rogers, Kenny and Epand, Len. *Making It With Music: Kenny Rogers' Guide to the Music Business.* New York: Harper & Row, 1978. 224 pages. Approximately 30 black-and-white photographs throughout. Appendix I: A Union Performance Contract Form. Appendix II: A Sample Publishing Contract for One or Several Songs. Appendix III: An Extract of Terms for a Typical New Artist's Record Contract. Appendix IV: An Extract from a Performance Contract Rider. Index.

Country and popular performer Rogers spreads his vast knowledge on to those seeking fame and glory in the more than occasionally cruel music industry. Although published in 1978, this work still holds up nearly two decades later. On the musical end, Rogers and Epand explain how to form a band, develop a musical style, recover from mistakes, etc. More substantial sections inform musicians on how to: make themselves known (finding booking agencies, managing investors); protect themselves before making any deals (copyrighting, negotiating, etc.); handle fame (clauses to watch out for); build on success (touring, road life, media, etc.); and avoid the pitfalls of fame (e.g., groupies). A practical self-help guide for the starting out rock player—it's unlikely professionals would humble themselves enough to seek this out—with helpful documents as appendixes.

THE ROLLING STONES

(See also Faithfull, Marianne; Jagger, Mick; Richards, Keith)

AUTOBIOGRAPHIES

The Rolling Stones. As told to Goodman, Pete. *Our Own Story*. London: Beat Publications, 1964. 188 pages. Two 16-page black-and-white photo inserts; approximately 20 black-and-white pen-and-ink drawings throughout.

The Stones so-called "official" account was written just as the boys were licking their wounds from their first miserable tour of the United States. The quintet was so offended by the press jeerings and Dean Martin's on-camera insults that they nearly packed up and went home. Pete Goodman, the obvious force behind this book, attempts to present The Stones as serious, thoughtful musicians, and succeeds only in making them seem wimpy. One for the time-capsule. Reissued by Bantam in 1970.

Wyman, Bill with Coleman, Ray. *Stone Alone: The Story of a Rock `N' Roll Band*. New York: Viking Penguin, 1990. 594 pages. Four eight-page glossy black-and-white photo inserts. Appendix 1 (Letter of Agreement between Allen Klein and the Rolling Stones). Appendix 2 (1964-1969: Records, Awards, Film and Television, Radio). Index.

The only true Stone autobiography is an epic history of the band from its origins through to Brian Jones' death. Wyman, the self-professed "orderly" Stone, has sifted through his diaries and has produced an amazingly cohesive, though occasionally repetitive, rendering of The Stones' evolution. He also briefly lashes out against his mates: Jagger for placing his solo career as a higher priority than The Stones; and Richards for his heroin addiction in the mid-1970's. Charlie Watts ("easy-going"), Mick Taylor ("a great, inspired guitarist"), and Ron Wood ("the peacemaker") are given more flattering portrayals. Wyman's theory that Brian Jones may have been an epileptic is a fascinating concept, but it's doubtful it caused his death. No doubt a sequel is in the works, spanning the 1970's and 80's: Get ready to pounce. "Essential for all Stones fans and libraries"—*Library Journal*.

BIOGRAPHIES

Booth, Stanley. *Dance with the Devil: The Rolling Stones and Their Times*. New York: Random House, 1984. 540 pages.

"Astonishing," raved *The Los Angeles Reader*, "...part oral history and part midnight diary in a world where midnight goes on forever." On this level, agreed. This 1960's bio of The Stones from circa 1963 up through the ill-fated Altamont concert is eerie to say the least. But Booth's reminiscences—given stamp of approval from five Stones—are full of inadvertent blunders—perhaps a result of being too close to the drug happenings of the time. Chapters flip-flop back and forth through the 1960's, sometimes forgetting to alert the reader to what year we are in. George Harrison leaves a party twice, although he only enters once. Fans will revel in the mood of the period, which is well captured here. Released in paperback in 1985 as *The True Adventures of the Rolling Stones*.

Dowley, Tim. *The Rolling Stones*. New York: Hippocrene Books, Inc., 1983. 156 pages. One glossy eight-page black-and-white photo insert. Discographies: U.S. and U.K. Filmography. Bibliography. (First published in Great Britain in 1983 by Midas Books.)

A thumbnail sketch on the band, with only 102 pages of text devoted to history. The key missing ingredient is reportage on The Rolling Stones' flamboyant lifestyles; it would seem an absolute must, especially given that the author begins by calling his subjects "sexy macho nasties." Some of the author's "musical analysis" is uninformed and over-generalized: "Gimme Shelter," for example, is described as merely "a rework of `Under My Thumb.'" Ashamedly tame.

Hotchner, A.E. *Blown Away*. New York: Fireside (Simon & Schuster), 1990. 352 pages. One glossy 16-page black-and-white photo insert. References.

"A no-holds barred portrait of The Rolling Stones and the sixties told by the voices of the generation," this oral biography contains reminiscences from founding Stones Ian Stewart and Dick Taylor, Stones' manager Andrew Oldham, two key Stones' women (Anita Pallenberg and Marianne Faithfull), and several other eyewitnesses, except the current

Stones. Hotchner's work lacks the detail of Wyman's autobiography or the brooding tension of Stanley Booth's book (see both, above), and in many ways has been superseded by the raucousness of Marianne Faithfull's autobiography (see Faithfull, Marianne). Still, this will have you turning pages, as when Pallenberg recounts how Brian Jones beat her mercilessly and when the late Ian Stewart lets loose a verbal tirade against The Beatles. "...of mild interest to diehard Stones fans"—*Library Journal*.

Jackson, Laura. *Golden Stone: The Untold Life and Tragic Death of Brian Jones*. New York: St. Martin's Press, 1992. 242 pages. One glossy 16-page black-and-white photo insert. Index. (First published in Great Britain in 1992 by Smith Gryphon Limited.)

Well over two decades have passed since Brian Jones' drowning, and the mysteries surrounding his life and demise continue to perplex rock fans. Laura Jackson clearly wants to shed positive light on Jones' legacy: that he was The Stones' true blues force, their founding leader, their most gifted and versatile musical talent, and, in the early days, their charismatic icon. The one thing Jones could not do—either through lack of confidence or the overpowering egos of the combined Jagger/Richards team—was write songs, and that contributed to his downfall. Jackson unsuccessfully tries to garner sympathy for a man who failed to stand up to his peers and then blubbered to the women he had severely abused. The book sheds no new light on Jones' death, although we do get an update on what happened to two of his illegitimate sons (both blonde with the same name, Julian, although they had different mothers!).

Norman, Philip. *Symphony for the Devil: The Rolling Stones Story*. New York: Linden Press/Simon & Schuster (division of Simon & Schuster, Inc.), 1989. 416 pages. One 16-page black-and-white photo insert. Index.

Equally as verbose as Norman's earlier *Shout!* (see Beatles: Biographies), this is a painstakingly precise history of The Stones's early career. Norman is right on target in characterizing the band members: Jagger, on the one hand, is the "ideal student" and on the other a purveyor of devilish blues; Brian Jones (unaffectionately dubbed "Mr. Shampoo") comes off as a brilliant but prissy egomaniac, the one most likely to knock up your daughter; and Keith

Richards, the icon who has an incredible knack for whipping out guitar licks, but his head is in such a void he can't for the life of him grasp why "Satisfaction" is a classic. A monumental work that only suffers from its lack of depth (only 50 pages) on the years subsequent to the Altamont concert.

Tremlett, George. *The Rolling Stones*. New York: Warner Books, 1975. 176 pages. One 16-page black-and-white photo insert. Appendix 1 (Chronology). Appendixes II-IV (Decca press releases).

A dated and generally incompetent account of The Stones that stupidly begins with a write-up on Alexis Korner ("the catalyst who brought The Stones together"), rather than focusing on the band itself. The author is more concerned with Brian Jones' fixation on buying buses than the group's early blues influences and inner-dynamics. Only 123 pages are devoted to biography, the rest to appendix material. A turkey.

CHRONOLOGIES

Bonanno, Massimo. *The Rolling Stones Chronicle: The First Thirty Years*. New York: Henry Holt and Company, 1990. 226 pages. Approximately 350 black-and-white photographs, covering every page.

A highly illustrated chronology of events, beginning in 1960-61 and concluding with the end of 1989. There is no introductory material, so it's difficult to grasp the author's rationale for inclusion of events. The book also fails to provide indexing—song and album lists would have been the minimal effort required—hence song searching is problematic. Browsing fans will be able to hold on through the wealth of sexy photos and the decadent quotes interspersed in the day-by-day listings. "Heck, if you're of a certain age or less, you'll have a very hard time not eyeballing it half to death yourself!"—*Booklist*.

Miles. *The Rolling Stones: A Visual Documentary*. London: Omnibus Press (division of Book Sales Limited), 1994. 158 pages. Approximately 200 color and black-and-white photographs, covering every page.

The Rolling Stones, day-by-day, starting in 1960—the actual famed meeting between Jagger and Richards, during which they first discussed music. Quarter-page bios of each member precede the chronology, filling in bare details, such as birthdates, educational backgrounds, etc. Each citation in the main part of the book lists either a recording, a release date, or a public appearance, so there isn't anything by way of anecdotal information, save for a quote here and there. The photos are of a high-level, however, visually demonstrating how the group's dynamic shifted from Jones to Jagger over the years. Serious competition for Bonanno's work (see above), this book is more recent but not as minutely detailed.

CRITICAL/ANALYTICAL COMMENTARY

No author. *The Rolling Stones* No city: Straight Arrow, Publishers, 1975. 96 pages. Approximately 60 full-page color and black-and-white photographs throughout. Discography.

Essays and interviews on The Rolling Stones culled from *Rolling Stone* magazine between 1968-1975. Authors include the *Rolling Stone* regulars, such as John Landau, Ralph J. Gleason, Greil Marcus, Robert Greenfield, and Vincent McGarry; Rita Rea provided the discography; and photographic contributions—which are nothing one hasn't seen by now—were made by David Bailey, Annie Leibovitz, Terry O'Neill, et. al. Greenfield's chat with Keith Richards stands the test of time; the guitarist opens up on the blues, Brian Jones, The Stones' image, and more. Otherwise, too dated for contemporary use.

DEATH OF JONES

Giuliano, Geoffrey. *Paint It Black: The Murder of Brian Jones.* London: Virgin, 1994. 256 pages. One glossy eight-page black-and-white photo insert. Discography. Filmography and Sources. The Official Sources.

Geoffrey Schlock—err Sherlock, that is—Giuliano comes to the rescue decades later to solve the mystery of Brian Jones' death. Does he have the answer? And does he tell us if Oswald was a single assassin? Once again fixated on the dark motif (see Giuliano's books on Paul McCartney and George Harrison, for two examples) in the title, Giuliano relies heavily on Laura Jackson's *Golden Stone* (see Biographies, above) for most of his information and doesn't fulfill the expectation of providing the "exclusive eyewitness confession"

promised on the back cover. Rawlings' work (below) soundly defeats this rip-off.

Rawlings, Terry. *Who Killed Christopher Robin? The Truth About the Murder of Brian Jones.* London: Boxtree, 1994. 228 pages. Two glossy eight-page black-and-white photo inserts. Appendix (documents).

Yet another investigation into the death of Brian Jones, this one emerging almost simultaneous with Giuliano's book. Author Rawlings, whose only credit is that he was a post-boy at Decca Records (no kidding) starts out with what seems to be another bland, uninformative biography of the dead Stone. Things pick up immeasurably, however, when Rawlings describes his recent discussions with one Tom Keylock, who points a finger at Jones' childhood friend, Frank Thorogood. According to Keylock (who was there on that ill-fated day), Thorogood had argued with Jones several times over an unpaid debt; tempers raged while the two were in the pool, and Thorogood plunged Jones up and down several times in the water until the musician drowned. Keylock, who signed an official statement to this effect reprinted in the back of this book, claims Thorogood confessed to him on his deathbed in 1993. A poorly written investigation that may, finally, fill in a few pieces to the puzzle—if one can believe Keylock.

DICTIONARIES AND ENCYCLOPEDIAS

Weiner, Sue and Howard, Lisa. *The Rolling Stones A to Z.* New York: Grove Press, Inc., 1983. 150 pages. Over 200 black-and-white photographs, covering every page.

Follow-up to Weiner's *Beatles A to Z* (see Beatles: Dictionaries and Encyclopedias). Appropriately, emendations in entry headings were made to suit The Stones' peculiarities. For example, there is one main heading for "arrests" that contains 20 subheadings for each bust location (including one in Liverpool!). A lot of gossip is provided (the entry on Jimi Hendrix confirms that he swept Marianne Faithfull away from Jagger for at least one night), which also befits the subject. This is a solid reference, though the information is crammed into a tight 150 pages and certain vital entries are lacking in meaty biographical text. Charlie Watts is relegated to a fact sheet done in 1964 and four quotes.

DISCOGRAPHIES, RECORDING GUIDES, AND COLLECTIBLES

Aeppli, Felix. *Heart of Stone: The Definitive Rolling Stones Discography, 1962-1983*. Ann Arbor, MI: Pierian Press, 1985. 536 pages. Approximately 90 black-and-white photographs throughout. Indexes.

Similar in scope and format to other Pierian Press discographies (see Beatles: Castleman/Podrazik and Fenick), this book has ample coverage of both group and solo releases and bootlegs, with studio, television, radio, film, and live recordings all mixed together. The formatting allows for a vast amount of headings (entry number, recording date, songs recorded, song title formats, recording location, producer, composer, release information, bootleg information, and session musicians), but you have to have the patience —if not necessarily the intelligence—of a rocket scientist to wade though it. Indexes include chart positions, side players, media appearances, film songs, songs only on bootleg, all officially released songs, alternate versions, and a complete listing of all records. "The first comprehensive...Stones discography in print"—*Library Journal*.

Elliott, Martin. *The Rolling Stones Complete Recording Sessions: From the Early Chart Toppers to the Infamous Rarities—January 1963 to November 1989*. London: Blandford (an imprint of Cassell), 1990. 224 pages. Sessions in Date Order. Discography: U.S. and U.K. Song Title Index. Songwriters' Index.

Rather dry synopsis of The Stones' career, minus general history (day-by-day events) and without any illustrative matter. Instead, the text contains several sections, each spanning a period of one to five years, with numbered entries on all of The Stones' known recordings at the time of press (October 1989). Each song listing includes recording date, location and name of recording studio, availability on albums, chart positions (if released as a single), and a bare-bones, one paragraph description of the track's genesis. The word "bootlegs" appears for many tracks, but titles are not identified. Collectors would want a lot more information about alternate releases, special discs, etc.; Stones' fanatics would want some pictures; and rock connoisseurs would want more description of the actual recording process.

Giuliano, Geoffrey. Foreword by Andrew Loog Oldham. Afterword by Ginger Baker. *Not Fade Away: The Rolling Stones Collection*. Limpsfield, Surrey (England): Dragon's World, 1993. 256 pages. Approximately 500 color and black-and-white photos of records, CDs, posters, clippings, merchandising, publications, etc. Discography. Index.

Self-proclaimed "Beatle man" Giuliano, who authored several Fab Four books, admits that he's always dug The Stones because they "had balls" and were "slightly dangerous." In his collection of memorabilia and collectibles, Giuliano certainly puts his money where his mouth is. This astounding compendium contains high-quality reproductions of rare album covers, releases, publications, etc., and in doing so splashes a blinding amount of color on each page. Giuliano elaborates on some, but not all, of the images in brief captions; prices and catalog information are not included. The index will only guide readers to names of people, songs, and records, not to specific merchandising. A treasure-chest of beautiful items, marred by Giuliano's now-habitual self-propagandizing (inclusion of his childishly rendered pastel, "She's Like a Rainbow"). So what does Ginger Baker have to do with The Rolling Stones? Distributed in the U.S. in 1993 by Studio Books as *The Rolling Stones Album: 30 Years of Music and Memorabilia*.

FANZINES AND FAN CLUBS

Beggar's Banquet. P.O. Box 6152, New York, NY 10128.

Illustrated newsletter published monthly by Stones' insider Bill German. Provides complete monthly updates of the band's group and solo projects and tours; lots of current photos. Occasional contests and listings of Stones collectibles for sale. The cost is $20 for 12 issues.

FILM

Randolph, Mike. Introduction by Michael Lindsay-Hogg. *The Rolling Stones' Rock and Roll Circus*. London: Faber and Faber Limited, 1991. Unpaginated (approximately 114). Approximately 75 full-page black-and-white photographs throughout.

A photo companion to the 1968 television film *The Rolling Stones' Rock and Roll Circus*, which might be considered very belated for 1991, except that the show was not released as of publication. (In 1996 it became available as a video and on a soundtrack CD.) Hence, for Stones fans, this book is essential: Where else can you find Ian Anderson (of the budding Jethro Tull), The Who, John Lennon (with Mitch Mitchell, Keith Richards, and Eric Clapton), Marianne Faithfull, and the Rolling Stones all on the same bill? Director Lindsay-Hogg's introduction is the book's only insight into the events that transpired before, during, and after the event. How many people are aware that Steve Winwood was originally going to appear but pulled out? Or that Paul McCartney was chosen before John Lennon (but said he was unavailable)? Highly worthwhile.

GENERAL REFERENCE

Dimmick, Mary Laverne. *The Rolling Stones: An Annotated Bibliography*. Pittsburgh, PA: University of Pittsburgh Press, 1979. 160 pages. Chronology. Author Index. Periodical Index.

First published in 1972, this was the first study of Rolling Stones' literature in newspapers, books, magazines, and periodicals. Sections are arranged chronologically and contain brief overviews of each period; the publications themselves are not numbered in any particular order. The author has provided brief personal insights into each work's slant and potential usefulness. Not nearly as comprehensive as MacPhail's *Yesterday's Papers* (see below).

MacPhail, Jessica. Foreword by Tom Schultheiss. *Yesterday's Papers: The Rolling Stones in Print 1963-1984*. Ann Arbor, MI: Pierian Press, 1986. 216 pages. Approximately 30 black-and-white reproductions of publication covers. Author Index. Title Index. Subject Index. Date Index. Publications Index.

Unattractive but informative compendium of reading lists for The Rolling Stones' connoisseur. Sections include: books (author, title, publisher, city, date, number of pages, illustrated or not); chapters and parts of books; magazine articles; newspaper articles; periodical issues; and more. The indexes are guaranteed to have what you're looking for (at least up through 1984), but it'll take you a while to find it because headings are not distinguished in any way. In addition, none of the lists includes descriptive text, so you may end up searching

for articles that are ultimately useless for your purpose. As a general starting point, however, "This labor of love should be in the collections of libraries..."—*Choice*.

PICTORIALS

Barnard, Stephen. Foreword by Bill Wyman. *Street Fighting Years*. London: Studio Editions, 1993. 176 pages. Approximately 150 color and black-and-white photos, covering nearly every page. Discography.

According to foreword writer (and ex-Stones bassist) Wyman, these "are pictures that show The Stones in their entirety." While that is not nearly the case—there aren't any childhood portraits or shots of stadium-filled crowds—much pleasure can be derived from browsing through this oversized volume. The Stones captured here are artists musically, socially, and theatrically—not the slovenly misfits many come to expect. Even traditionally trampy-looking Jerry Hall has a touch of class. Highly recommended coffee table fare (if your furniture can support it!).

Cahill, Marie. *Rolling Stones: A Pictorial History*. New York: Mallard Press, 1990. 112 pages. Approximately 100 color and black-and-white photographs, covering every page. The Albums of the Rolling Stones.

Towering promotional book on The Stones, predictably highlighting the visual and downplaying the facts. Many photos are full-page—which, in essence, is a foot and a half—and that may be more than enough to draw in fans. The pink cover sort of takes the balls out of rock's most enduring band.

Carr, Roy. *The Rolling Stones: An Illustrated Record*. New York: Harmony (division of Crown), 1976. 120 pages. Approximately 200 color and black-and-white illustrations, covering every page. Filmography. U.S. Discography. Bootlegs. Extracurricular Activities. Tours.

Spurious collection of photos and miscellany on The Stones, with four to six pages on each year up through 1976 (the *Black and Blue* LP). Not up to Harmony's later standards for photo retrospectives: the photos are slapped on the pages; the writing is devoid of insight; and the color is unevenly distributed. The cover is simply ghastly: seven black-and-white shots of individual Stones, two of which—Ron Wood and Mick Taylor—appear to have been from high school yearbooks!

Carter, David. *The Rolling Stones*. New York: Crescent Books (distributed by Outlet Book Company, division of Random House), 1992. 80 pages. 37 color and 62 black-and-white illustrations. Discography. Index.

This one tries for a balanced history of the band, with coverage of every phase of the group's career up through the *Steel Wheels* LP and tour. The book doesn't present anything new, however, and has the general look and feel of a promotional piece. Some of the color is on the orange side and has a faded appearance; the jacket design is dull. If you're looking for yet another picture of Bianca Jagger's cleavage, turn to page 57.

Dalton, David. *Rolling Stones*. London and New York: AMSCO Music Publishing Company, 1972. 352 pages. Approximately 200 black-and-white photographs throughout; approximately 10 pages of color throughout. Discography.

Ancient gathering of miscellaneous photos and articles on The Stones, with chronologies, interviews, song lyrics, and essays from Dalton, Greil Marcus, Lester Bangs, Stephen Farber, and others. A highly uneven combination of materials. Dalton fared better with his later project (see below).

Dalton, David. *The Rolling Stones: The First Twenty Years*. New York: Knopf, 1981. 192 pages. Approximately 125 black-and-white and 75 color illustrations, covering every page. Sessionography.

Unusual photo collection and Stones retrospective, with first-rate contributions from Dalton, Kenneth Anger, Stanley Booth, Lisa Robinson, Victor Bockris, and several others. Tom Beach and James Karnbach compiled the comprehensive and readable sessionography (that goes up to 1981), while the book itself is smattered with ample stage blueprints, newspaper clips, graphic art, and grainy photos. Highlights include odes to Brian Jones (Jim Morrison's poem, as well as quotes from Pete Townshend, George Harrison, and Charlie Watts) and two fanzine inserts (*Teen Fax and Pix* and *Midnite Rambler*). Biting and offbeat.

Goodall, Nigel. *Jump Up: The Rise of the Rolling Stones*. Chessington, Surrey (England): Castle Communications, 1995. 114 pages. Approximately 100 black-and-white photographs throughout; two glossy eight-page color inserts. Appendix A: Chronology. Appendix B: U.K. Album Discography 1963-1973.

Attractive but vapid photo-biography of The Stones' early years. What Goodall seems to forget in terms of photo and text emphasis is that Brian Jones had been the creative and charismatic leader of the band during its formative years. This book also contains very little on the Altamont Festival, which was a major turning point for the band. Boasts some nice pictures, but not really necessary.

Hector, James. *The Complete Guide to the Music of the Rolling Stones*. London: Omnibus Press (division of Book Sales Limited), 1995. 168 pages. Approximately 130 color and black-and-white photographs throughout.

CD-format book covering all aspects of The Rolling Stones' career. Overlaps with Welch's CD-format book (see below), but each offers something of different appeal: This has more photos, the other more informational back sections.

Jasper, Tony. *The Rolling Stones*. London: Octopus, 1976. 92 pages. Approximately 125 color and black-and-white illustrations, covering every page. A to Z of Personalities. Discography.

Lackadaisical rendering of The Stones' history, loaded with mistakes, typos (music critic Robert Christgau's name is misspelled), and overgeneralizations. Other problems abound: The chronology is poorly designed and sketchily prepared, while the photo montages are an eyesore. Don't bother to look at the A to Z of personalities; the entry for Jimi Hendrix reports that the guitarist was "admired by Mick Jagger," yet omits the essential detail that Brian Jones was among his staunch supporters. A mess.

Mankowitz, Gered. Introduction by Andrew Loog Oldham. *Satisfaction: The Rolling Stones 1965-1967*. 104 pages. 150 black-and-white photographs, covering every page; six pages of color at front and back.

Mankowitz's photos are an unusual slice of The Stones' history: the mid-1960's, after their bluesy start and on the verge of their psyche-delic period. The band is captured in perfor-mance, recording, and messing about back-stage. Mankowitz holds the distinction of hav-ing taken two pictures of Keith Richards when he received an electric shock on stage in Sacramento. Paul McCartney and Marianne Faithfull are the only additional celebs present. Generally good stuff.

No author. *The Rolling Stones Tear-Out Photo Book*. London: Oliver Books, 1993. Unpaginated (approximately 64 pages). Approximately 20 color photographs throughout.

Photo book consisting of full-page tear-sheets of The Stones, almost exclusively from the 1960's. Feel free to tear away—there's not much here worth collecting.

Norman, Philip. *The Life and Good Times of the Rolling Stones*. New York: Harmony Books (division of Crown), 1989. 128 pages (over-sized). Over 100 color and black-and-white photographs, covering nearly every page.

The Stones photographed here are the naughty boy rockers of the 1960's. The 1970's and 80's are pared down to a photo montage and a news clip about Bill Wyman's sex scandal. Most of the photos are full page, and some spread over to a second. The obligatory shots of girlfriends, wives, roadies, managers, and stadium-filled crowds are here, though for some reason, it's Brian Jones' dufus puss that sticks out in nearly every photograph. While Philip Norman's introduction is on the snotty side and his captions are light on information, the book is nicely designed and makes for good browsing.

Palmer, Robert. *The Rolling Stones*. New York: Doubleday, 1983. 256 pages. Approximately 200 black-and-white photographs, covering every page; 12 pages of color.

Magnificent oversized pictorial biography, the third in The Rolling Stone Press' acclaimed series (following, as expected, The Beatles and Elvis). Gracing the pages are photo contribu-tions from notables such as Annie Leibovitz, Michael Cooper, Ethan Russell, and Gered Mankowitz, among others, who have provided some of the world's best known Stones' pho-tographs. While the book is a little bit short in representing the group's formative years, the illustrative material of the late 1960's more

than compensates. One photo of Keith Richards underneath a "Drug Free America" sign is a real hoot. Dated and without any discographical information, but a treat for fans nonetheless, complete with graffiti endpaper.

Pascall, Jeremy. *The Rolling Stones*. London and New York: The Hamlyn Publishing Group, 1977. 96 pages. Approximately 70 black-and-white and color illustrations throughout. Film by Film. The Stones Hits.

Inferior photo retrospective in which The Stones look more like prancing zombies than legendary rockers. Pascall's prose is less than riveting, and his film-by-film analysis and pseudo-discography will have knowledgeable fans laughing out loud. Rubbish.

Southern, Terry (text); Cooper, Michael (photo-graphs); and Richardson, Perry (origination). Foreword by Keith Richards. *The Early Stones: Legendary Photographs of a Band in the Making 1963-1973*. New York: Hyperion, 1992. 174 pages. Approximately 200 black-and-white photographs, covering every page.

How could any fan of The Rolling Stones turn down at least a look at a book that boasts a foreword by Keith Richards? In the text itself, Richards, along with Marianne Faithfull and Anita Pallenberg, participate in a question/answer format with satirical writer Southern (author of the book *Candy* and the film's screenplay) as they reflect on the photos in front of them. The results are gritty and remarkable; it's a treat to glance through pages (see The Rolling Stones stoned at Stonehenge!) or to read Richards' various comments on drug busts ("The arresting officers—complete with file—took away all our incense and left most of the drugs."). Recommended.

Welch, Chris. *The Rolling Stones*. Miami, FL: MBS, 1995. 120 pages. Approximately 75 color and black-and-white photographs throughout. Discography. Chronology. Index.

CD-format book covering all aspects of The Rolling Stones' career. This nicely designed and illustrated book is priced just right at around $7.99.

QUIZBOOKS AND QUOTEBOOKS

Dalton, David and Farren, Mick. *Rolling Stones: In Their Own Words*. London: Omnibus Press (division of Book Sales Limited), 1994. 144 pages. Approximately 125 black-and-white photographs throughout.

First published in 1980, this collection of Stones' quotes has been reprinted and revised many times since then. The boys speak out on various topics, including: performance; drugs; sex and violence; music; etc. As in many of the books in this series from Omnibus, the photos are smudged and too dark. Several of the quotes themselves are well selected, however. Jagger: "I don't go out with housewives." Most of the remarks are from Jagger or Richards, but occasionally Watts lets loose a zinger: "We're a terrible band, really. But we are the *oldest*. That's some sort of distinction, isn't it?" Fair.

RELATED WORKS

Littlejohn, David. *The Man Who Killed Mick Jagger*. Boston and Toronto: Little, Brown and Company, 1977. 246 pages.

Novel of only remote interest to Stones' fans, this is the story of Henry Harrington, a college student who hates his restrictive suburban middle-class life. Harrison finds sanctuary and frenzy at a Rolling Stones concert and imagines he's "free," like Mr. Lips himself. Blah.

TOURBOOKS

Elman, Richard. *Uptight with the Stones*. New York: Charles Scribner's Sons, 1973. 120 pages. 21 black-and-white photographs throughout.

In 1972 novelist Elman stood backstage with The Stones for several concerts in Texas. This lengthy essay follows the band plus the usual mess of roadies, groupies, drug dealers, and security people, with a much-needed comedic boost from guest writers Truman Capote and Terry Southern. Elman defeats his purpose by insulting his subjects instead of reporting about them. The interior photos and cover (which does not have an illustration) leave much to be desired.

Flippo, Chet. *On the Road with the Rolling Stones: 20 Years of Lipstick, Handcuffs and Chemicals.*

Garden City, NY: Doubleday. 1985. 178 pages. Appendix I: The Rolling Stones Tour History. Appendix II: The Royal Canadian Mounted Police Report.

Without the assistance of photographic material, Flippo attempts to characterize The Stones' traveling circus through America between 1975-79. Flippo immediately contradicts his book's subtitle by stating this is not intended as a gratuitous tale of sex, drugs, and scandal; however, several racy passages and the police report in Appendix II indicate that is precisely what's on his mind. The author rambles on about The Stones' antics in San Antonio, Kansas City, Canada, and elsewhere with little rhyme or reason. "Better rounded and more richly detailed accounts are Stanley Booth's *Dance with the Devil* and Robert Greenfield's *S.T.P.*"—*Library Journal*.

Greenfield, Robert. *S.T.P.: A Journey Through America with the Rolling Stones*. New York: E.P. Dutton & Co., 1974. 338 pages. One glossy 16-page black-and-white photo insert.

Rolling Stone writer Greenfield went on the road with The Stones in 1974, joining them for what was known as the S.T.P. Tour. (The initials stand for, among a few lurid suggestions, Stones Touring Party.) Greenfield relays memorable impressions of peripheral players such as disc jockey Wolfman Jack, Chip Monck (production manager), Bill Graham (promoter), and Truman Capote (writer), but it's his details of the freak shows and crazed groupies that will hold your attention. For fanciers of The Stones' bawdy underbelly.

Kamin, Philip and Goddard, Peter. *The Rolling Stones: The Last Tour*. New York: Beaufort Books, 1982. 128 pages. Approximately 150 black-and-white photographs, covering every page.

How final was The Stones 1981-82 tour? Not very—and we can be sure that the 1994-95 Voodoo Lounge tour won't be their last either. Do we need this book to remind us that we were hoodwinked way back when? The gimmickry is everywhere—from Jagger's U.S./U.K. cape to his shirtless prances and flying splits. While the authors were thoughtful enough to provide cities under the photos, they weren't the least bit generous in terms of song lists.

Kamin, Philip (photographs) and Karnbach, James (text). *The Rolling Stones on Tour in Europe.* New York: Beaufort Books, 1983. 128 pages. Over 90 color and 75 black-and-white illustrations, covering every page.

A follow-up to the Kamin and Goddard collaboration (see above), but this time with a better selection of photos and more balanced text from videographer Karnbach. Most of the pictures are close-up and you can get a wide range of emotions from Jagger and company, as opposed to the usual early 1980's preening. The book closes with a Ron Wood interview and a list of songs performed on the tour.

No author. *Rolling Stones Stripped: A Trip Through the Voodoo Lounge Tour 1994-95.* London: Omnibus Press (division of Book Sales Limited), 1995. 80 pages. Approximately 100 color illustrations, covering every page.

Raucous visual documentation of The Stones' 1994-95 Voodoo Lounge Tour, and further evidence that these boys can still rock. Full of hype regarding both the *Voodoo Lounge* and *Stripped* CDs and accompanying singles, this book is really nothing more than a concert program, albeit with some very erotic stage poses of Jagger with one of his stage dancers/singers. The photographs were primarily taken by Gunnar Skibsholt and Dave Hogan. Only for those who have just caught The Stones for the first time.

Southern, Terry (text); and Leibovitz, Annie and Sykes, Christopher (photos). Foreword by Mick Jagger. *The Rolling Stones on Tour.* London: Dragon's Dream, 1978. 144 pages. Approximately 150 black-and-white and 50 color illustrations, covering every page.

Humorist and screenwriter Southern (*Candy*), along with photographers Annie Leibovitz and Christopher Sykes, tagged along with The Rolling Stones for their 1975 tour and produced this offbeat photo collection. Behind the scenes, Richards poses under moose antlers, while Jagger shows off his knee and armpit. On stage, the stadiums throb to The Stones' beat and an enormous phallus. One might say things really got out of hand when keyboardist Billy Preston brushed up against Jagger and simulated coital positions. An exercise in rock frivolity, well captured by the three collaborators.

WRITTEN WORKS

No author. *The Rolling Stones Complete Works.* Amsterdam: Thomas rap publishers[sic] Limited, no date. 120 pages. Titles.

Lyrics to over 100 original Stones songs, all of which were composed up through 1970. Includes classics ranging from "Little by Little" to "Dead Flowers" with an obvious absence of design and illustrative matter. Unnecessary.

Watts, Charlie. *Ode to a High-Flying Bird.* London: Beat Publications, 1965. 32 pages. Approximately 25 original color illustrations.

A picture-book "compiled by one Charlie to a late and great Charlie" that was originally published in 1965 and since has been sporadically seen in various CD booklets. The Stones' skinsman—who was not a contributing vocalist or composer—distinguishes himself outside of rock and roll through this children's story tribute to jazz great Charles Christopher "Yardbird Bird" Parker. Watts tells how Bird (drawn as an actual fowl) whistled to his own tune—thereby "flying higher" than the others—until people finally caught on. A cute, unpretentious ode to cool.

Wood, Ron with German, Bill. *Ron Wood: The Works.* New York: Harper & Row, 1987. 122 pages. Approximately 120 original sketches, watercolors and paintings throughout; approximately 10 black-and-white photographs throughout.

All the while Ron Wood was rocking out with The Jeff Beck Group, The Faces, and (continuing at present) The Rolling Stones, he was mischievously capturing his colleagues on paper and canvas, and somehow finding time to raise a happy family (with four kids). In this timeless catalog of his art, Woody provides some biographical data, but it's really his work and comments on other celebrities that are of greatest interest. Wood executed some fine headshot portraits of, among others, Bo Diddley, Jimi Hendrix, Groucho Marx (who said to him: "I"d give up every dollar I earned if I could just get an erection"), Boy George, Keith Moon, and, of course, Mick Jagger and Keith Richards. Funny and intimate.

YOUNG ADULT

Watts, Charlie. *Ode to a High-Flying Bird.* See: Written Works.

OTHER TITLES OF INTEREST

Aftel, Mandy. *Death of a Rolling Stone: The Brian Jones Story.* New York: Delilah (Putnam), 1982.

Benson, Joe, *Uncle Joe's Record Guide: The Rolling Stones.* No city: Benson J. Unlimited, 1987.

Coral, Gus. *The Rolling Stones: Black and White Blues.* No city: Turner, 1995.

Eisen, Richard. *Altamont: Death of Innocence in the Woodstock Nation.* New York: Avon, 1970.

Farren, Mick. *Rolling Stones 76.* No city: Second Foundation, 1976.

Fitzgerald, Nicholas. *Brian Jones: The Inside Story of the Original Rolling Stone* New York: Putnam, 1985.

Library Journal *commented: "...his [Jones'] notorious abuse of women and drugs is glossed over."*

Flippo, Chet. *It's Only Rock N' Roll: My on the Road Adventures With the Rolling Stones.* New York: St. Martin's, 1989.

Fricke, David. *Rolling Stones: Images of the World Tour 1990.* New York: Simon & Schuster, 1991.

Hall, Jerry and Hemphill, Christopher. *Jerry Hall's Tall Tales.* New York: Pocket, 1985.

Hinckley, David. *The Rolling Stones: Black & White Blues, 1963.* Atlanta, GA: Turner Publishing, 1995.

Hoffmann, Dezo. *The Rolling Stones: The Early Years.* New York: McGraw-Hill, 1985.

Heinlein, Robert A. *The Rolling Stones.* New York: Ballantine, 1985.

Marchbank, Pierce and Miles, Barry. *The Rolling Stones File.* London: Omnibus Press (division of Book Sales Limited), 1976.

Markle, Gil. *Rehearsal: The Rolling Stones at Longview Farm.* Self-published, 1981.

Martin, Lisa. *The Rolling Stones in Concert.* No city: Colour Library International, 1982.

Miles. *Rolling Stones: An Illustrated Discography.* London: Omnibus, 1980.

Porter, William S. *Rolling Stones.* No city: Reprint Services, 1993.

Quill, Greg. *The Rolling Stones Anniversary Tour.* No city: Kamin & Howell, 1989.

Rosenbaum, Helen. *The Rolling Stones Trivia Quiz.* New York: NAL, 1979.

Ruhlmann, William. *Rolling Stones.* New York: Smithmark (Penguin USA), 1993.

Sanchez, Tony. *Up and Down with the Rolling Stones.* New York: NAL, 1980

Stewart, Alan. *Time Is on My Side: The Rolling Stones Day-by-Day 1962-1984.* Ann Arbor, MI: Popular Culture Ink, 1994.

ROLLINS BAND

RELATED WORKS

Cole, Joe. *Planet Joe.* Los Angeles, CA: 2.13.61, 1992. 140 pages.

The late Joe Cole was Henry Rollins' best friend. He was murdered by two thieves, who also tried to take Rollins' life (but missed and fled). Like his buddy, Cole also kept a journal and took notes on the various Black Flag and Rollins Band tours and activities. Of appeal to Rollins' fans.

Overton, R.K. *Letters to Rollins.* Los Angeles, CA: 2.13.61, 1995. Unpaginated (approximately 72 pages). Approximately 20 black-and-white photographs throughout.

A collection of letters to Rollins, as assembled by friend R.K. Overton. One woman writes to him complaining that Rollins once remarked in *Thrasher* magazine that roller blading "knee pads are for pussies." As a result, her son refuses to wear them! Some letters are true non sequiturs (one correspondent seems to be playing the game Battleship with Rollins), while many are from kids. Not handled with enough wit or explanation.

WRITTEN WORKS

Rollins, Henry. *Art to Choke Hearts & Pissing in the Gene Pool.* Los Angeles, CA: 2.13.61, 1992. 256 pages.

Two works collected in one: *Art to Choke Hearts* and *Pissing in the Gene Pool.* This collection is full of Rollins' usual odes to rats, roaches, and death, all building up to the fact that life sucks. Generation X never had it so depressing. One can't tell the difference between this book or the others listed herein by Rollins (except *Get in the Van,* see below), but here and there a sexually-charged passage will perk up your interest. As usual for 2.13.61, the book features excellent cover art (front by Peter Cunis and back by Mark Mothersbaugh).

Rollins, Henry. *Bang!.* Los Angeles, CA: 2.13.61, 1990. 144 pages.

More avant-garde poetry by Rollins that is essentially divided into two sections: verse

("Knife Street") and four-line stanzas ("1000 Days to Die"). The latter is by far the more creative and effective, succeeding at establishing pointed messages or images. The expressionistic cover art by Peter Cunis is wonderfully ghastly.

Rollins, Henry. *Black Coffee Blues*. Los Angeles, CA: 2.13.61, 1992. 124 pages.

More penned gripes from musician and publisher Henry Rollins. Fortunately, this one isn't exclusively in verse (except at the end); instead, the passages are paragraph-length observations that won't do much for the average reader: "He fights a lot. He gets his ass kicked a lot. Two reasons for this: he fights when he is drunk and he isn't all that good." Likewise for this book.

Rollins, Henry. *Get in the Van: On the Road with Black Flag*. Los Angeles, CA: 2.13.61, 1994. 256 pages. Approximately 125 black-and-white photographs throughout. Black Flag Lineups/Tour Dates.

A member of Black Flag for six years (1981-86), Henry Rollins later formed his own Rollins Band and even created 2.13.61 Publications—a vanity press that publishes books on poetry and music (see above and below for Rollins' other titles as author). This book traces back to his days as Black Flag's vocalist, relying heavily on his journal entries from that period. Supplemented by many magnificent performance shots of the band, Rollins evidently harbors a great deal of resentment against his former bandmates, the critics, and even fans. Being spat on, cursed at, and beaten up by screaming crowds may seem like fun to some, but this is a frightful document of hell on the road. Featuring 2.13.61's high standards for book production values and some raucous tales of behind-the-scenes escapades, this terrific book eclipses many other rock diaries.

Rollins, Henry. *High Adventures in the Great Outdoors*. Los Angeles, CA: 2.13.61, 1992. 140 pages.

Originally, three books in one: *2.13.61* (now the name of Rollins' press), *End to End*, and *Polio Flesh*. As usual for Rollins, this book contains conjoined and untitled poetry, prose, and observations. Many of the lines are more like lyrical throwaways than real poetry. Lots of backstage blow-jobs and druggies, but not much real sense. Strictly for fans.

Rollins, Henry. *Now Watch Him Die*. Los Angeles, CA: 2.13.61, 1993. 188 pages. Band Dates. Spoken dates.

The prolific Rollins is at it again with more visions of death and destruction. Hasn't this guy ever been to Disneyland? The book is actually divided into two parts: "Now Watch Him Die" (poetry) and "Cities" (journal entries). The latter is of far greater interest, containing one-paragraph descriptions of his travels around Europe.

Rollins, Henry. *One from None*. Los Angeles, CA: 2.13.61, 1993. 144 pages.

A two-part book that includes Rollins' collected poetry from 1987 (after *Get in the Van* ends; see above) and the author's interview with Robert Fleischer. The poetry delves into Rollins' self-mutilation fantasies and general thoughts on feces and urine, while the interview concentrates more on the state of society, reality, women, and censorship. Digestible in small doses.

Rollins, Henry. *See a Grown Man Cry*. Los Angeles, CA: 2.13.61, 1992. 192 pages.

More stream-of-consciousness style from the lead man of the Rollins Band. The moody green cover and Peter Cunis' expressionistic painting of a sinister face are brilliant. As for Rollins' poetry—that depends on your point of view. Reading this, one might think Rollins had survived a nuclear war rather than a few tours with a rock band. Same old same old.

OTHER TITLES OF INTEREST
Rollins, Henry. *Eye Scream*. Los Angeles, CA: 2.13.61, 1996.

THE RONETTES

(See also Spector, Phil)

AUTOBIOGRAPHY

Spector, Ronnie with Waldron, Vince. Foreword by Cher. Introduction by Billy Joel. *Be My Baby: How I Survived Mascara, Miniskirts and Madness or My Life as a Fabulous Ronette*. New York: Harmony Books (division of Crown), 1990. 318 pages. Ronnie's Hot 101: A Ronnie Spector Discography. Index.

The lead-singing Ronette tells her incredible life story, notably details of her professional and personal relationship with producer Phil Spector. After a hasty rundown of her family lineage, Ms. Spector introduces Phil as the dominating, eccentric, and passionate figure who helped her find her voice in classic hits such as "Be My Baby." After the couple's romance blossomed, Phil became a reclusive pop Citizen Kane and imprisoned his wife in his mansion, subjecting her to all kinds of psychological torment. Ronnie escaped, but not without the scars of alcoholism, lost child custody battles, and a faded singing career. Fortunately, she has started life over with a new husband and family. Her reflections are juicy and enjoyable, particularly when she describes seduction attempts by John Lennon and David Bowie. "...a cut above the standard self-serving, bonkers-and-back autobiography." —*Publishers Weekly*.

LINDA RONSTADT

BIOGRAPHIES

Bego, Mark. *Linda Ronstadt: It's So Easy!*. Austin: Eakin Press, 1990. 212 pages. Approximately 50 full-page black-and-white photographs throughout. Discography. Bibliography.

An unauthorized biography that shows off Ronstadt's talents in rock, jazz, country, opera, and Broadway tunes. The author rattles off the singer's numerous relations with politicians, musicians, and actors without much flair, but is successful at pointing out her outstanding contributions as background vocalist, e.g., on Neil Young's "Heart of Gold" and on Paul Simon's *Graceland* LP. Some fans will nitpick at inconsistencies, such as that the back cover reports she has 16 gold records, while the author cites 17 in the introduction. Bego's study is a highly readable synthesis of second-hand source material, but "rarely does he [the author] attempt to probe beneath the surface of Ronstadt's California cool."—*Publishers Weekly*.

PICTORIALS

Berman, Connie. *Linda Ronstadt: An Illustrated Biography*. London: Proteus Books, 1980. 118 pages. Approximately 60 black-and-white and six color photographs throughout. Linda Ronstadt Discography.

"An intimate biography of the queen of country rock" that marginally improves upon Moore's photo book (see below) for solid details and falls behind Bego's book (see Biographies, above) in the tabloid areas. Berman has earnest intentions, but her sentences are either full of gushy hyperbole or clumsy generalizations ("The Stone Poneys became mildly successful in a kind of tepid way that many rock groups do."). Ronstadt wears a ridiculous Boy Scout uniform in what seems to be half of the photographs, and there aren't nearly enough color shots to compensate. Slight.

Moore, Mary Ellen. *The Linda Ronstadt Scrapbook: An Illustrated Biography*. New York: Sunrise Press (division of Grosset & Dunlap), 1978. 122 pages. Over 100 black-and-white photographs throughout.

While not much of a scrapbook—there isn't anything here in the way of collector's items, childhood photos, letters, documents, etc.—this is a passable collection of photos of Ronstadt during the prime of her commercial success. The author and publisher selected a better-than-average mix of illustrative material, showing off Ronstadt's personable sweetness in a variety of semi-sexy performance shots and posed close-up photos. Country singer/occasional Ronstadt collaborator Emmylou Harris is captured in a couple of alluring pictures. Non-reading material for Ronstadt-worshippers.

YOUNG ADULT

Clarke, Vivian. *Linda Ronstadt*. New York: Flash Books (division of Music Sales Corporation), 1978. 72 pages. Approximately 40 black-and-white photographs throughout. Discography.

The cover image of Ronstadt dressed in a Dodgers' windbreaker and singing "The Star-Spangled Banner" at the third game of the 1977 World Series is not exactly going to make this a hot item today. The author covers the basics, though, making mention of Ronstadt's Mexican/German lineage, her early recordings with The Stone Poneys, and even spicing things up with her admittance that she'd love to seduce a priest. Ronstadt is cute enough to hold her own in photos that are extremely dark and grainy.

Fissinger, Laura. *Linda Ronstadt*. Mankato, MN: Creative Education, 1983. 12 black-and-white photographs throughout.

Part of the "Rock 'n Pop Stars" series from Creative Education, this book misses an excellent opportunity. *Linda Ronstadt* lacks so many crucial details on the singer, even the youngest, most uneducated fan has reason to complain. Where are details on her lineage? What about the diversity of her talents? What about her *songs*? Full of sloppy typos, this outdated title is best kept hidden.

OTHER TITLES OF INTEREST

Amdur, Richard. *Linda Ronstadt: Mexican-American Singer*. New York: Chelsea, 1994.

DIANA ROSS

(See also Supremes, The)

AUTOBIOGRAPHY

Ross, Diana. *Secrets of a Sparrow: Memoirs*. New York: Villard Books, 1993. 304 pages. Approximately 200 photos, including: one eight-page glossy color insert; two glossy black-and-white photo inserts; and black-and-white photographs throughout. Lifeline: Music, Music, and More Music (Chronology).

This highly illustrated summation of Ross' life and career is haphazardly organized, but does provide an enormous wealth of history through the singer's point of view: her relations with Berry Gordy and Motown; her respect for, and conflicts with, Mary Wilson and Florence Ballard of the Supremes; and her genuine love of singing and performing. The author's writing voice is sweet—but also flighty, repetitive, and not based in reality (everything seems to be either "magical" or in a "dream"). Someone didn't take care to salvage some of her real goofs (on her Central Park concert: "I was in a wet dream"). Although Ross is alluring in the plethora of photos spanning all phases of her life, she "...comes across as painfully self-absorbed and shallow."—*Goldmine*.

BIOGRAPHIES

Haskins, James. *I'm Gonna Make You Love Me: The Story of Diana Ross*. New York: Dell, 1980.

186 pages. One eight-page black-and-white photo insert. Discography.

Mass-market biography primarily intended for teenage readers, but also palatable for older fans. Haskins deserves a lot of credit for seeing the true Ross—a glamorous performer who is buried in her own image and is desperate for attention. Haskins details her cool, levelheaded rise from the slums of Detroit and even handles issues such as The Supremes' pivotal role during the civil unrest of the 1960's. Dated, but useful for information up to the end of the 1970's. "It's refreshing to read a biography—particularly of a rock star—that is not only well written but presents a clear view of the subject's background."—*School Library Journal*.

Taraborrelli, J. Randy. *Call Her Miss Ross: The Unauthorized Biography of Diana Ross*. New York: Ballantine Books, 1989. 568 pages. One 32-page black-and-white photo insert. Notes and Sources. Bibliography. Diana Ross Discography. Index.

Taraborrelli's thorny biography doesn't allow any of the characters in this show biz bio to come out smelling like a rose. Ex-Supreme Mary Wilson is accused of intentionally omitting details from her autobiography (see The Supremes, Autobiography), such as that Ross had given her a loan and once unsuccessfully tried to give Florence Ballard a financial boost. To no one's surprise, Berry Gordy is cast as a ruthless, sex-hungry megalomaniac intent on obliterating everyone in his path. Ross resembles Berry in more ways than anyone cares to admit, manipulating her boss to ignite her solo career and chewing up and spitting out a roster of lovers that includes Gordy, Ryan O'Neal, and Gene Simmons. This controversial best seller is quite a contrast to Ross' autobiography. "Enough is enough!"—*Library Journal*.

FANZINES AND FAN CLUBS

Reach Out International: Celebrating the Music That Is Diana Ross. Subscription Department, P.O. Box 4562, Portland, OR 97208.

Diana Ross fan club authorized by the star herself, and covering her careers as both soloist and Supreme. Publishes a quarterly fanzine of the same name consisting of 24 to 32 pages (and double for special issues) and containing many color and black-and-white photos. The publication also features recent interviews, puzzles, classifieds, song lyrics, and more. The cost of membership in the U.S. is $23 per year; in Canada, $39.50; and in Europe, $29.

PICTORIALS

Brown, Geoff. *Diana Ross:*. London: Sidgwick & Jackson, 1981. 144 pages. Approximately 160 black-and-white photographs throughout; one eight-page color insert. Discography. Index.

Affectionate photo tribute to the enduring star, with biographical text charting Ross' career from the early 1960's to the 1978 film *The Wiz.* The photos of Ross' glitzy stage act—with and without The Supremes—are good, if not spectacular, but Brown's writing is convoluted. Interestingly, among the film scripts Ross turned down was one called *The Bodyguard,* which would have paired her with Ryan O'Neal, and was made years later with Whitney Houston and Kevin Costner. Author Brown wrote here that the idea for that film "...sounds particularly awful." Optional for fans.

Pitts, Jr., Leonard. Introduction by Cher. *Reach Out: The Diana Ross Story.* Cresskill, NJ: Sharon Starbook, 1983. 96 pages. Approximately 100 black-and-white photographs and graphics, covering every page.

Hopelessly bad pictorial of Diana Ross that somehow manages to incorporate every picture of the star in existence that has her eyes closed. The most interesting thing about this mess is Cher's very catty introduction, in which she flares her claws at Ross: "I first met Ross in 1965. I couldn't stand the broad." One of the worst.

YOUNG ADULT

Eldred, Patricia Mulrooney (text). *Diana Ross.* Mankato, MN: Creative Education, 1975. 32 pages. Approximately 20 watercolors throughout.

Colorful entry in the "Rock 'n Pop Stars" series, with art from John Keely, that tells Ross' story from her childhood in the slums of Detroit. One page of a teeming garbage can with an oversized carcass of a rat and a roach will either gross out young readers or draw them in. The coverage of the film *Lady Sings the Blues* is very strong, no doubt because it was new at the time. Optional for fans.

Haskins, James. Illustrated by Spence, Jim. *Diana Ross: Star Supreme.* New York: Viking, 1985. 58 pages. Approximately 20 pencil drawings throughout.

Part of the "Women of Our Time" series, this charming book tells the bare aspects of Ross' rise to success, detailing how she struggled to keep her dignity as a poor child in Detroit, Michigan and dreamed of stardom. A good portion of the work is ground in Ross' childhood and teenage years, which should prove inspiring to youngsters with ambitions in music. The Supremes' legend is given short attention, especially in regard to the glossed-over break-up. (It doesn't mention how Mary Wilson kept the group going, sans soloist Ross.) With Jim Spence's attractive drawings, however, this fluffy tale will be enjoyed by Ross' fans.

OTHER TITLES OF INTEREST

Holiday, Billie with Dufty, William. *Lady Sings the Blues.* London: Abacus, 1975.
Holiday's autobiography, which was later adapted to the film starring Diana Ross.

DAVID LEE ROTH

See Van Halen.

ROXY MUSIC

CRITICAL/ANALYTICAL COMMENTARY

Tamm, Eric. *Brian Eno: The Music and the Vertical Color of Sound.* Boston and London: Faber and Faber, 1989. 228 pages. Notes. Glossary. Bibliography. Discography. Other Music Cited.

The artist who began his career as synthesizer player for Roxy Music became legendary for his ability to fuse classical patterns with rock. His productions with U2 (*Joshua Tree*) and work with David Bowie and Robert Fripp have made him a highly sought-after producer and collaborator. This academic treatise first defines Eno's place in music, identifying his audience and exploring the images he uses. The second part deals with his music from progressive rock, to his ambient works, to his numerous collaborations. "This is a most puzzling book..."—*Choice.*

WRITTEN WORKS

Eno, Brian; Mills, Russell; and Poynor, Rick (commentaries). *More Dark Than Shark*. London: Faber and Faber Limited, 1986. 144 pages. Approximately 75 original color watercolors and 75 black-and-white drawings and graphics throughout. Biographical Notes: Brian Eno. Biographical Notes: Russell Mills.

Complex mix of watercolors, graphics, and sketches from artist Russell Mills, based on the music and lyrics to Brian Eno's equally as challenging recordings. Opening chapters by Rick Poynor contain musical, literary, and poetic commentaries, supplemented with assorted diagrams and notes that will no doubt make the layperson's head spin. Eno's lyrics are printed very small on the page and end up lost; Mill's works are culled from his notebooks, and many of them have an intentionally incomplete look. This exercise in surrealism is perhaps too technical for most people's tastes but is a "...visually beautiful document"— *Library Journal*.

OTHER TITLES OF INTEREST
Rogan, Johnny. *Roxy Music: Style With Substance: Roxy's First Ten Years*. London: Star Books, 1982.

THE RUNAWAYS

(See also Jett, Joan)

TITLES OF INTEREST
Currie, Cherie and Schusterman, Neal. *Neon Angel: The Cherie Currie Story*. No city: Price Stern Sloan, 1989.
Publishers Weekly *commented: "Currie lets readers know that drug abuse destroyed her family, her career, and almost her life... This turbulent, frightening story sends mature readers a potent warning against drugs."*

RUN-DMC

BIOGRAPHIES

Adler, B. *Tougher Than Leather: The Authorized Biography of Run-DMC*. New York: New American Library, 1987. 192 pages. One 16-page black-and-white photo insert.

Run-DMC, the "kings of rap," were originally three kids from Hollis (Queens), New York: Joseph Simmons (Run), Darryl McDaniels (DMC), and Jason Mizell (Jam Master Jay). The group's anti-gang, anti-apartheid, anti-promiscuity, and anti-drug stands—as well as support from rockers such as Lou Reed—have garnered this trio an enormous amount of respect in and out of the rap community. Throughout B. Adler's authorized work are Run-DMC's funny and socially relevant rhymes. The book's informativeness is countered by its lack of a discography and videography. Worth a read for rappers and non-rappers alike.

RUSH

FANZINES AND FAN CLUBS

A Show of Fans: A Rush Fanzine for and by Rush Fans. 5411 E. State St., Suite #309, Rockford, IL 61108.

A 28-page, glossy stapled magazine for fans of Rush. Contains all-new photos and original artwork, interviews with band members, tour information, articles by fans, announcements, classifieds, and more. The cost of a four-issue subscription is $15 in the U.S.; $20 everywhere else. The cost per issue is $5.

PICTORIALS

Banasiewicz, Bill. *Rush: Visions: The Official Biography*. London: Omnibus Press (division of Book Sales Limited), 1988. 96 pages. Approximately 80 black-and-white and color illustrations throughout. Rush Discography (U.K.).

Pictorial history of the Canadian power trio that still holds up, despite the fact that the original 1988 edition is still in print and hasn't been revised for the 1990's. Author Bill Banasiewicz had some involvement from singer/bassist Geddy Lee and his wife, Nancy, and much of their cooperation comes across through the wealth of intimate photographs and original quotes that appear throughout. Banasiewicz is on target depicting Rush as a continuance of the hard rock threesome tradition begun by Cream and The Hendrix Experience. The book devotes some attention to the band's innovative instrumentation

(Geddy Lee's Fender Precision), but fans could find out a lot more from articles in *Musician, Bass,* and *Modern Drummer,* in which Lee, Peart, and Alex Lifeson have been profiled.

OTHER TITLES OF INTEREST

Harrigan, Brian. *Rush.* London: Omnibus Press (division of Book Sales Limited), 1981.

SADE

BIOGRAPHIES

Bego, Mark. *Sade!.* Toronto and New York: PaperJacks, 1986. 114 pages. One eight-page black-and-white photo insert. Discography. Videography. Filmography. Chronology. Sources.

These one hundred-plus pages do not constitute much more than a PR piece on the mid-1980's star best known for her hit "Smooth Operator" and for her silky presence, replete with braided hair down her back. Born Helen Folasade (hence her stage name) Adu in Nigeria, Sade was influenced more by 1940's crooners such as Billie Holiday and Frank Sinatra than by pop or rock singers; for understandable reasons, she prefers not to be typecast as an artist limited to that time frame. The usual noncritical pop fluff and magazine quotes, which will please fans immensely.

SANTANA

FANZINES AND FAN CLUBS

Santana International Fan Club. P.O. Box 88163, San Francisco, CA 94188-1630.

Club that offers members a merchandise catalog, advance notice of concerts, a 12-20 page quarterly newsletter, and fun items such as guitar picks and souvenir stamps. The cost of a lifetime membership is $25.

ERIC VON SCHMIDT

WRITTEN WORKS

von Schmidt, Eric and Rooney, Jim. *Baby Let Me Follow You Down: The Illustrated Story of the Cambridge Folk Years.* Garden City: Anchor Press (Doubleday), 1979. 320 pages. Approximately 300 black-and-white photographs, covering nearly every page.

Outstanding period piece capturing the personalities and flavor of the Boston/Cambridge folk community in the late 1950's and early 60's. Bursting with shots of young musicians before the psychedelic era, menu covers, programs, and calendars, this book is also an oral history that is full of quotes from those who were there (and some of whom may still be): Manny Greenhill, Richard and Mimi Fariña, John Sebastian, Joan Baez, and Bonnie Raitt. Falling short in several areas—there is no discography, who's who, or index, and we'd love to know what these musicians are doing today—*Baby Let Me Follow You Down* is wonderful, nevertheless; you can actually hear the guitars, ukeleles, and banjos twanging in your head. Follow.

THE SEARCHERS

FANZINES AND FAN CLUBS

Mike Pender's Searchers Fan Club. 14 Goldfields Close, Greetland, Halifax, West York's, England HX4 8LD.

Fan club dedicated to the Liverpool band, with some involvement from Mike Pender. Offers tapes, CDs, and photos, as well as a 20-page newsletter with reproductions of black-and-white photographs, concert information, fans' reviews, special notes on British 1960's bands, and more. The cost of a one-year membership is £12 in the U.S.; £7 in the U.K.; and £12 elsewhere in Europe.

PETE SEEGER

(See also Weavers, The)

BIOGRAPHIES

Dunaway, David. *How Can I Keep from Singing?*. New York: McGraw-Hill, 1981. 386 pages. One nine-page black-and-white photo insert. Notes. Bibliography. Discography. Index.

A fully-sourced biography of the legendary folk star, written with some cooperation from Seeger and about 50 insiders. Dunaway portrays this multi-talented artist as a stalwart patriot who battled the Ku Klux Klan, segregation, the FBI, and just about everyone else who threatened personal or civil liberties. Despite his slight stature and nice guy image, Seeger strikes the reader immediately as a feisty and fearless soldier of peace. While other books deal at length with Seeger's substantial musical legacy, this biography shows other aspects of his life, such as his long marriage to his Japanese American wife, Toshi (who handles much of his business affairs). Exhaustive but not intimidating.

WRITTEN WORKS

Seeger, Pete (text) and Hays, Michael (illustrations). *Abiyoyo*. New York: MacMillan Publishing Company, 1986. Unpaginated (approximately 48 pages). Approximately 48 color paintings, covering every page.

Based on a South African lullaby and folk story, this beautiful children's book regales readers with the tale of a father who has a magic wand that makes things disappear and a son who plays the ukelele. The two are declared a public nuisance and are thrown out of town. When an ugly giant name Abiyoyo arrives, the father and son come to the rescue. Seeger mixes up his dialects throughout the story, but on the whole this is so entertaining one can overlook such gripes. "Seeger combines his sense of humor and drama to turn disturbing events into high-spirited fun..." —*School Library Journal*.

Seeger, Pete and Reisner, Bob. *Carry It On: A History in Song and Picture of the Working Men and Women of America*. New York: Simon & Schuster, 1985. 256 pages. Approximately 75

black-and-white photographs throughout. Index of Songs.

The first of Seeger's books exploring the American free spirit (see *Everybody Says Freedom*, below), this work chronicles the history of American labor. Beginning with farmers in the 18th century, Seeger and Reisner tell how Americans sweated and toiled on the land to survive, to feed their families, and to establish lives for their offspring. The working people of this country also faced poverty, unemployment, harsh weather conditions, and all kinds of misery—yet had that spark and determination necessary to carry on. A multitude of songs appear throughout, as do photos and other documents. A gritty, rewarding, educational experience that should be welcomed by teachers of social science and humanities classes.

Seeger, Pete and Reisner, Bob. *Everybody Says Freedom: A History of the Civil Rights Movement in Songs and Pictures*. New York: W.W. Norton & Company, 1989. 266 pages. Approximately 75 black-and-white photographs throughout. More Reading, Listening, Looking, and Doing. Notes.

As anyone remotely familiar with musical history should know, Pete Seeger has long been involved in political causes and in defending human rights. Seeger collaborates with Reisner to tackle America's history of segregation and the people who fought it, starting with the 1955 Montgomery bus boycott. Through lyrics and music to Seeger's songs, profiles of the most important figures in African-American history (such as Rosa Parks), and firsthand testimony of many people present at marches and sit-ins, Seeger and Reisner have created one of the best narratives of non-violent resistance ever catalogued. Highly recommended, particularly in light of the 1995 Million Man March.

Seeger, Pete and Seeger, Charles. Illustrated by Jagr, Miloslav. *The Foolish Frog*. New York: Macmillan Publishing Co., 1973. Unpaginated (approximately 42 pages). Approximately 42 original watercolors, covering every page.

Generally enjoyable book adaptation of Pete Seeger's song, accompanied by lush cartoon-like watercolors and some musical notes. The humorous story involves a farmer who has a tune, but no lyrics; finally, inspired by a klutzy frog, he writes some words and the town rejoices. Kids will love the bouncy illustrations and the action they depict, but may be heart-broken by the downer ending. Parents will have to figure out the moral and explain it to their kids.

Seeger, Pete. Edited by Schwartz, Jo Metcalf. *The Incompleat Folksinger*. New York: Simon & Schuster, 1972. 596 pages. Approximately 100 black-and-white photographs throughout.

Published after the dusk of the folk-rock movement of the 1960's, this compendium traces the evolution of folk from the early pioneers (Lead Belly) to folk heroes (Woody Guthrie) to international artists, instruments, and trends. With photos, chord progressions, lyrics, book recommendations, excerpts from folk magazines (*Sing Out!*), and even advice on how to play folk guitar and write songs, this book can hardly be called "incompleat." Another admirable work from this modest star. "...an enduring account of the folk song revival"—*Booklist*.

Seeger, Pete. *Where Have All the Flowers Gone: A Singer's Stories, Songs, Seeds, Robberies*. Bethlehem, PA: Sing Out!, 1993. 288 pages. Approximately 100 black-and-white photographs throughout.

Not really an autobiography—although it does contain quite a bit of personal detail—this valuable work primarily consists of lyrics and music to Seeger's 200 some-odd songs, supplemented with the famed folk singer's unaffected reflections. In essence, Seeger tries to tell his life story through these songs—a highly original concept that works successfully all the way through. Whether discussing politics, Jewish history, Marlene Dietrich, The Byrds, or Bob Dylan, Seeger soaks up diverse culture and presents it with originality, appreciation, and respect. Young musicians will want this exceptional book to marvel at Seeger's simple but brilliant chord progressions; fans would want it for too many reasons to mention. This book will have you tapping your feet in no time.

YOUNG ADULT

Seeger, Pete (text) and Hays, Michael (illustrations). *Abiyoyo*.

See: Written Works.

SELENA

BIOGRAPHIES

Patoski, Joe Nick. *Selena: Como la Flor*. Boston and New York: Little, Brown and Company, 1996. 296 pages. One glossy eight-page color and black-and-white photo insert. Notes. Discography.

A celebration of Selena that literally frames her beautiful countenance on the cover and borders it with cheery flowers. The subtitle, "Como la Flor," also accentuates the positive, referring to her hit song (meaning "like a flower"). Yet life was never easy for the bubbly singing star. Born in Lake Jackson, Texas to Mexican parents, Selena grew up in a town where there were few Mexican Americans; but through her tightly-knit musical family, she developed her own unique style and sang live at a very early age. Author Joe Patoski doesn't have any real insider's knowledge, but he tells her story well, especially when observing the pressures young Selena faced as a star on the road. Highly readable.

Ruiz, Geraldo. *Selena: The Last Song*. New York: El Diario Books, 1995. 256 pages. One 16-page black-and-white photo insert.

Mass-market approach to Selena's life, hyping her story with the words "love, cash, fame...murder." At least it can be said that proceeds from the book go to the Selena Foundation, created by Selina's family to help educate future Tejano stars. The book is actually two-sided, with an English section heading one way and the Spanish the other—which leaves only 128 pages of story per section. Selena's father assesses that: "this is not our family's version of Selena's story, but it is in our opinion a fair compilation of the many published articles about Selena...." Printed in large type for kids, this is a largely superficial work of value only to fans who want everything. The Spanish title is *Selena: La Ultima Cancion*.

DEATH OF SELENA

Novas, Himilce and Silva, Rosemary. *Remembering Selena: A Tribute in Words and Pictures*. New York: St. Martin's Press, 1995. 116 pages. Approximately 72-black-and-white photographs throughout; one glossy eight-page photo insert.

On March 31, 1995, a 23-year-old beautiful singer named Selena Quintanilla Pérez was gunned down by the president of her authorized fan club, former nurse Yolanda Saldivar. The world will never know to what heights Selena might have reached had she lived: But one certainty is that we are now deprived of a lovely and gifted young star. This tribute biography contains text in both English and Spanish, and is filled with many photos that capture Selena's exquisite beauty and charisma. While this book doesn't tell you much about her music or where to find her recordings, it does succeed at creating a new pop music martyr. Note: This edition was published prior to the conclusion of Saldivar's trial.

OTHER TITLES OF INTEREST

Arrarás, Maria Celeste. *Selena's Secret: The Revealing Story Behind Her Tragic Death*. New York: Fireside (Simon & Schuster), 1996.

THE SEX PISTOLS

AUTOBIOGRAPHIES

Lydon, John with Zimmerman, Keith and Kent. *Rotten: No Irish, No Black, No Dogs*. New York: St. Martin's Press, 1994. 329 pages. 23 black-and-white photographs throughout. Cast of Characters.

John Lydon, best known as Johnny Rotten, was the outspoken leader of The Sex Pistols. Iconoclastic, pugnacious, tenacious, and generally proud of his repulsiveness, Lydon speaks out against virtually everyone and everything: drugs, sex, rock and roll, his friends, his enemies, violence, non-violence, and most of all, The Sex Pistols' image and punk itself. The only topic Lydon doesn't seem to have an opinion on is his own schizophrenia, which is revealed in his scattered, self-contradicting prose. Lydon's father, Pretender Chrissie Hynde, guitarist Steve Jones, and many others contribute lengthy quotes to this chaotic oral

autobiography, but whatever messages they are trying to transmit are lost in the slapped together paragraphs. As Lydon himself warns the reader: "Enjoy or die."

Matlock, Glen with Silverton, Peter. *I Was a Teenage Sex Pistol*. Boston/London: Faber and Faber, 1990. 180 pages. 12 black-and-white photos throughout.

Concise biography from Pistol bassist Matlock (a former artist and sex shop clerk, among other occupations) who claims he was thrown out of the group because he said he liked The Beatles. Matlock was the only member of the band who actually took the music seriously, although Johnny Rotten's opinion is that he was trying to turn the group into The Bay City Rollers. Matlock's axe to grind is that he was the right player in the wrong band. True fans of The Pistols will no doubt want this book so they can burn it. "...one wonders why he bothered to write about it [the band]..."—*Library Journal*.

BIOGRAPHIES

Savage, Jon. *England's Dreaming: Anarchy, Sex Pistols, Punk Rock and Beyond*. New York: St. Martin's Press, 1992. 604 pages. Approximately 75 black-and-white illustrations throughout; one glossy color and black-and-white photo insert. Discography. Index. (First published in Great Britain by Faber and Faber.)

The granddaddy of all books on The Sex Pistols and a superb tracing of the origins of punk music, this is a dense and scholarly book not suited for The Pistols' fan looking for a joy ride. The scene is set in 1971 in London's King's Road, where Malcolm McLaren and Vivienne Westwood first meet, sharing one thing in common: hatred of hippies (which they dubbed "hippos"). The two sought to revert back to the no-bullshit Teddy Boys street gang image and, when McLaren met Steve Jones—who first had the idea of putting a band together—The Sex Pistols were formed in an attempt to prove that chaos and violence could be raised to an art form. Savage's detailed descriptions of the Pistols' stage performances, Sid Vicious and Johnny Rotten's blistery personalities, and the climax of Nancy Spungen's death are all riveting. "Scholarship with spunk."—*Rolling Stone*.

Vermorel, Fred and Vermorel, Judy. *Sex Pistols: The Inside Story.* London: W.H. Allen & Co. (A Star Book), 1981. 288 pages. One eight-page black-and-white photo insert.

A juicy paperback on the rise and fall of the classic punk band, complete with excerpts from interviews, letters, clippings, and even lyrics, such as their anthem "Anarchy." The review from the *New Musical Express* says it all: "Sheer revelatory potency...stands in a category rare in the rock `n' roll sweepstakes...the indepth biography."

CRITICAL/ANALYTICAL COMMENTARY

Marcus, Greil. *Lipstick Traces: A Secret History of the Twentieth Century.* Cambridge, MA: Harvard University Press, 1989. 496 pages. Approximately 75 black-and-white graphics throughout. Index.

This analysis and social history of anarchic forms in pop culture is almost always uttered in the same breadth as Savage's work (see Biographies, above). Marcus' stream of consciousness-style commentary is especially apropos of the subject: why punk—The Sex Pistols in particular—had such an impact. Marcus challenges the reader on every page with diversions into Dadaism, the influence of other icons (Elvis Presley and Michael Jackson), and other less pop references that will fly over many readers' heads. An intellectual tribute to the movement that paved the way for a band to slip the words "fuck you" on TV. "Timely, brilliant and often revelatory...."— *Boston Phoenix.*

CHRONOLOGIES

Wood, Lee. *Sex Pistols: Day by Day.* New York: Omnibus Press (division of Book Sales Limited), 1988. Unpaginated (approximately 96 pages). Approximately 100 black-and-white photos throughout.

According to the book cover, this is "the most accurate account of their history ever published." While this is certainly not the case, fans will still want a copy of this offbeat compilation of facts and tales of destruction. The offbeat design and typewriter-like typeface is more than appropriate to the subject. As for its being a day-by-day of the group—not quite. The book only goes year-by-year (not breaking it down any further), mostly covering the years between 1974-1978.

PICTORIALS

Morris, Dennis. *Never Mind the Bullocks: A Photographic Record of the Sex Pistols.* London: Omnibus Press (division of Book Sales Limited), 1991. Unpaginated (approximately 96 pages). Approximately 80 full-page, glossy black-and-white photographs throughout; 16-pages of color throughout.

One hundred percent punk, as captured by Virgin Records' frequent photographer, Dennis Morris. At the time these shots were taken, the group had been banned from playing in Great Britain; needless to say, that didn't stop them from one final tour. The group spontaneously continued on, playing clubs and universities unannounced and generally raising hell. Morris was on hand to capture for posterity the frenzied punk characters, who look like fist-waving zombies. The black-and-white photographs are incredible, but the color pages detract from the overall effect; John Lydon's spastic faces make him look more like AC/DC's Angus Young than a leathery punk rabble-rouser. Never mind: Bullocks will love it.

Reid, Jamie. *Up They Rise: The Incomplete Works of Jamie Reid.* London: Faber and Faber, 1987. 144 pages. Approximately 150 collages, clippings, and assorted artwork.

Jamie Reid, the man responsible for much of The Sex Pistols imagery, presents his miscellaneous pieces of art and graphics. Born and raised in Croydon, Reid was greatly influenced by Jackson Pollock and studied at the same school as Ray Davies and Malcolm McLaren. Reid integrates elements of his life story, fused with his influential artistic visions of violence, chaos, and destruction. Many of these pieces were part of the album art for The Pistols' *Anarchy in the U.K.* album. Reid's cut-out letters, montages, photos, designs, and slogans ("Sex Pistols fuck forever") are of peripheral interest to Pistols' fans. "Reid's startling color combinations are sadly absent from this black-and-white book"—*Publishers Weekly.*

Stevenson, Ray. *Sex Pistols File*. London: Omnibus Press (division of Book Sales Limited), 1980. Unpaginated (approximately 72 pages). Approximately 125 black-and-white photographs, covering every page. Chronology.

Manic collection of newspaper articles on The Sex Pistols, a good portion of which seem to report that the band was—well, banned. Some of the headlines are still shocking and perverse: "Terrorize *Your* Fans the Sex Pistols Way," "Sex Pistols Give EMI Chief a Four-Letter Reply," and "Pistols: New Label, New Row." Mavens who don't have their own scrapbooks would want a copy; those who do may still want this in order to see various band members nude and/or cleaning toilets. An updated edition was released in 1991.

QUIZBOOKS AND QUOTEBOOKS

Thomas, Dave. *Johnny Rotten: In His Own Words*. London: Omnibus Press (division of Book Sales Limited), 1988. 96 pages. Approximately 100 black-and-white photos, covering nearly every page.

Designed in a discordant manner Rotten should appreciate (but obviously won't), this book of excerpts gets to the core of the man's views on life ("Turn the other cheek too often and you get a razor through it") and on music ("I grabbed rock n' roll by the testicles"). The quotes will supply ample laughs and reflections for both Pistol junkies and daring browsers.

Burchill, Julie and Parsons, Tony. *The Boy Who Looked at Johnny: The Obituary of Rock and Roll*. Boston and London: Faber and Faber, 1987. 96 pages. Two ten-page black-and-white photo inserts.

First published in 1978, this whiny, offensive book was intended to signal the end of rock and roll and welcome punk as the new king. Including more anti-hippie, Woodstock-was-a-fake pronouncements than anyone can tolerate, this book is a period piece that just doesn't hold up in its revised form. Badly written and full of irrelevancies and digressions.

SEX PISTOLS FRIENDS AND FAMILY

No author. *Impresario: Malcolm McLaren and the British New Wave*. Cambridge, MA: The Mit Press, no date (c.1988). 80 pages. Approx-

imately 50 black-and-white photographs throughout. Chronology.

Catalog assembled by the New Museum of Contemporary Art, which had sponsored this unusual exhibition on Malcolm McLaren in 1988. For those who don't know, McLaren had begun his career as an artist (he went to three art colleges) and was heavily involved in the fashion, films, and poster and album art of his bands, most prominently The Sex Pistols. This glossy pamphlet, which features brief contributions from Paul Taylor, Jon Savage, Dan Graham —and even a chronology by McLaren himself —are full of excellent quotes, anecdotes, and history. Of peripheral interest to Pistols' fans.

Spungen, Deborah. *And I Don't Want to Live This Life*. New York: Fawcett, 1983. 436 pages. One eight-page black-and-white photo insert.

First published in 1983 and revised in 1994 with a new introduction, this is the story of Deborah Spungen, mother of Nancy, who was brutally murdered by Sid Vicious on October 12, 1978 at twenty years of age. Spungen conveys the emotions of what it was like to experience such a shock, and conducts a therapy session of sorts exploring how she overcame the agony of having her life reduced to a tabloid headline. To no one's surprise, her daughter was an emotionally disturbed child, and things only worsened as she became a teenage heroin addict. As for Deborah herself, after years of helpless suffering and feeling victimized by the press, she went back to school, received a Master's degree, and founded the Anti-Violence Partnership of Philadelphia. "Honest and moving..."—*Washington Post*.

TOURBOOKS

Monk, Noel E. and Guterman, Jimmy. *12 Days on the Road: The Sex Pistols and America*. New York: William Morrow and Company, 1990. 240 pages. Two eight-page black-and-white photo inserts.

A history of the group's controversial 1979 tour of the American South, which included an assortment of groupies and numerous assaults on hotel staffs. The authors interviewed junkies, bus drivers, reporters, and anyone else caught in the hoopla. Many of the photos are out of focus—although this may have been intentional. The text itself provides the band's activities day-by-day and hour-by-hour, which is amazing in the sense that anyone could possibly keep up with the antics. An epilogue concisely lists what the main players were up to as of 1990. If America could survive the tour, readers could survive a read through this book.

OTHER TITLES OF INTEREST

Bateson, Keith and Parker, Alan. *Sid Vicious: Sid's Way*. London: Omnibus Press (division of Book Sales Limited), 1991.

Beverley, Anne and Marchbank, Pearce. *The Sid Vicious Family Album*. London: Virgin, 1980.

Bromberg, Craig. *The Wicked Ways of Malcolm McLaren*. New York: HarperCollins, 1989.
Booklist *commented: "Bromberg has no idea how to reconstruct trendy 1970's Britspeak, but he has a great subject and no shortage of spleen-venting interview sources."*

Cox, Alex and Wool, Abe. *Sid and Nancy: Love Kills*. New York: Faber & Faber, 1986.
The screenplay for the 1986 film, Sid and Nancy, which was also directed by Cox. Booklist *commented: "...the script seizes on the ghastly romanticism of the pair's sordid relationship and treats them as if they were Romeo and Juliet reconceived by Edgar Allan Poe and William Burroughs."*

Walsh, Gavin. *God Save the Sex Pistols: A Collector's Guide to the Priests of Punk*. East Haven, CT: Inbook, 1995.

CARLY SIMON

FANZINES AND FAN CLUBS

The Official Carly Simon International Fan Club. P.O. Box 679, Branford, CT 06405.

Members receive 8x10 photos, a personal bio, news updates, and more. The club's illustrated four-page newsletter contains a lengthy introductory letter from Simon herself, in which she talks about her works in progress. The cost of membership is $22 per year in the U.S. and Canada; $28 elsewhere.

WRITTEN WORKS

Simon, Carly and Datz, Margot (illustrator). *Amy the Dancing Bear*. New York: Doubleday (division of Bantam Doubleday Dell), 1989. Unpaginated (approximately 32 pages). Approximately 32 original color drawings, covering every page.

Lovely, violet-hewn children's book by the Simon/Datz team (the print debut for both

artists). Amy is told by her mother that it's time to sleep, but the gleeful dancing bear has other plans. A warm and cuddly night-time read to be told to children four and under. "Datz's paintings swarm with color, action, good humor and detail..."—*Publishers Weekly*.

YOUNG ADULT

Morse, Charles and Morse, Ann. *Carly Simon*. Mankato, MN: Creative Education, 1975. 32 pages. Approximately 12 original watercolors throughout.

Attractive book for fans 8-12 that is, unfortunately, two decades out of date. Dick Brude's pastel watercolors are lovely, albeit derivative of familiar album cover art. The text takes readers through the *Hotcakes* album and emphasizes the romantic aspects of Simon's lyrics. Despite many missing details (why is Warren Beatty not included in the list of those possibly ridiculed in "You're So Vain"?), this book has some qualities youngsters will appreciate.

Simon, Carly and Datz, Margot (illustrator). *Amy the Dancing Bear*.

See: Written Works.

OTHER TITLES OF INTEREST

Simon, Carly. *The Boy of the Bells*. New York: Doubleday, 1990.
School Library Journal *commented: "...a well-meaning book, but hardly the stuff of which classics are made."*

Simon, Carly. *Fisherman's Song: A Romantic Story for All Ages*. New York: Doubleday, 1991.
School Library Journal *commented: "An illustrated song about unrequited love that holds little appeal for children."*

Simon, Carly. *The Nighttime Chauffeur*. New York: Doubleday, 1993.

Simon, Carly; Simon, Peter; and Simon, Richard. *Carly Simon Complete*. New York: Knopf, 1975.

PAUL SIMON

(See also Simon and Garfunkel)

BIOGRAPHIES

Humphries, Patrick. *Paul Simon: Still Crazy After All These Years*. New York: Doubleday (division of Bantam Doubleday Dell), 1988. 164 pages. One eight-page glossy black-and-white photo insert. Discography. Bibliography. (First published in Great Britain in 1988 as *Boy in the Bubble* by Sidgwick & Jackson.)

A highly readable yet overtly critical biography of the composer and musician. Humphries has a distinctively British point of view, which adds significantly to the book's value; there is a substantial chapter on Simon's English sojourn in the mid-1960's. Most of the rock criticism is on target, but there are a few zingers here and there that may upset rock fans: The Byrds are tossed aside as a Beatles clone and "an otherwise unremarkable band"; Simon's song "I Am a Rock" is written off as "one of his weakest ever songs"; and the author smashes Iron Butterfly's "In-A-Gadda-Da-Vida." Is nothing sacred? Otherwise, "This book is crammed full of information..."—*Booklist*.

OTHER TITLES OF INTEREST

Marsh, Dave. *Paul Simon.* New York: Quick Fox (Putnam), 1978.

Simon, Paul. *At the Zoo.* New York: Doubleday, 1991.

School Library Journal *commented: "Simon's musical romp through the zoo has been transformed into a picture book for young children."*

SIMON AND GARFUNKEL

(See also Simon, Paul)

BIOGRAPHIES

Morella, Joseph and Barey, Patricia. *Simon and Garfunkel: Old Friends.* New York: Birch Lane Press Limited (division of Carol Publishing Group), 1991. 262 pages. One eight-page glossy black-and-white photo insert. Discography.

"A dual biography" of two singers who are, the authors claim, "inseparable halves of the same whole." These childhood friends lived within three blocks of each other in Kew Gardens, Queens, and early on, shared affinities for baseball and rock music. According to the authors, Garfunkel never forgave Simon for beginning a solo career only shortly after their original teaming as Tom and Jerry; Simon never forgave Garfunkel for being taller than he is and for receiving more praise for his singing voice. While it does not present all that

much new information, *Old Friends* does capture the full flavor of the Simon and Garfunkel musical partnership and friendship. *Kirkus* felt that it was marred by "...the questionable slighting of Simon's far more critically acclaimed solo career."

CRITICAL/ANALYTICAL COMMENTARY

Matthew-Walker, Robert. *Simon and Garfunkel.* New York: Hippocrene, 1984. 166 pages. One four-page glossy black-and-white photo insert. Discography. Filmography. Bibliography. Index of Song Titles. Index of Persons. (First published in 1984 by the Baton Press Limited, Southborough, Tunbridge Wells, England.)

Faulty study of the singing dynamic duo, with only 14 pages devoted to biography and influence. The errors are too many to repeat, but here are two blunders: James Taylor is written as "James Tyler"; and Queens College is frequently referred to as "Queens University." The remainder of the chapters break down the recordings by period and contain stilted criticism on each album (collaborative and solo). The book makes no attempt to relate Simon and Garfunkel to the emotions and trends of the 1960's, and fails to cut into even the first layer of meaning behind their work.

PICTORIALS

Cohen, Mitchell S. Edited by Greg Shaw. *Simon & Garfunkel: A Biography in Words and Pictures.* No city: Chappell Music Company (Sire Books), 1977. 56 pages. Approximately 65 black-and-white photographs throughout. Simon & Garfunkel Appendix (duo and solo discography).

Shoddy presentation all around: the photos are dull and poorly arranged; the text is full of errors (a caption for Simon and Garfunkel's early incarnation as Tom and Jerry is dated 1968, when clearly it should be 1958); and the production is so poor that on some pages you can actually see the lines indicating where the repro cut off. Bottom drawer.

Humphries, Patrick. *Bookends: The Simon and Garfunkel Story.* London and New York: Proteus Publishing Co., Inc., 1982. 128 pages. Approximately 75 black-and-white photographs throughout; approximately eight pages of color in the middle. Discography.

More of a tribute than a biography, this generously illustrated book provides only the bare details about how Simon and Garfunkel rose to fame and split for solo careers. At least Humphries treats the two from a rock tradition—as opposed to the "adult contemporary" mold (which really doesn't have a tradition). This attractive but dated work contains ample buddy pictures of Simon and Garfunkel and some fun details on the background of *The Graduate*. (Apparently, Simon hated Charles Webb's book, calling it "bad Salinger.") With an emphasis on the duo's contemporaries, this book might be worth it for long-term fans who happen to be collectors.

WRITTEN WORKS

Garfunkel, Art. *Still Water: Prose Poems*. New York: E.P. Dutton, 1989. 120 pages. Map of Travels.

This collection conveys some of Art Garfunkel's innermost thoughts during his travels spanning 1983-1988. Each section opens with a brief self-interview. Some of the poetry and verses reflect on his girlfriend's suicide and the Nicholas Roeg film *Bad Timing...A Sensual Obsession*, in which Garfunkel starred. Garfunkel's language is often saccharine and uninvolving. Awkward lines like "Her lips were wet with tea" are not likely to make Garfunkel required reading in literature classes. For fans only.

NINA SIMONE

AUTOBIOGRAPHY

Simone, Nina. *I Put a Spell on You: The Autobiography of Nina Simone*. New York: Penguin Books, 1991. 182 pages. Two glossy eight-page black-and-white photo inserts. Discography. Index. (First published in Great Britain in 1991 by Ebury Press.)

The brilliant, classically trained singer from Tryon, North Carolina tells her story in this wonderful biography. Simone recalls racial injustices and segregation present in her hometown during her childhood and which evidently left an indelible mark on her psyche. After some influential crossover success in jazz, pop, R&B, and blues (tunes she covered, such as "I

Put a Spell on You" and "Don't Let Me Be Misunderstood," were recorded by Creedence Clearwater Revival and The Animals, respectively), she became involved with the black power movement and fell out of the music spotlight. Simone gains the reader's attention immediately and holds them in rapture for the duration.

SIMPLE MINDS

TITLES OF INTEREST

Boz, Alfred. *Simple Minds: The Race Is the Prize*. New York: Putnam, 1986.

Thomas, Dave. *Simple Minds: Glittering Prize*. London: Omnibus Press (division of Book Sales Limited), 1985.

Wrenn, Mike. *Simple Minds: A Visual Documentary*. London: Omnibus Press (division of Book Sales Limited), 1990.

JOHN SINCLAIR

WRITTEN WORKS

Sinclair, John. *Guitar Army: Street Writings/Prison Writings*. No city: World Publishing Company, 1972. 366 pages. Approximately 150 black-and-white photographs throughout. Rainbow Reading & Listening List.

John Sinclair, manager of MC5 (dubbed "the rock and roll guerrillas"), was one of the in-your-face radicals of the late 1960's and 70's. Sinclair was sentenced to a stiff 9 1/2-10-year prison sentence for possession of two joints; thanks to these writings—and the support of luminaries such as John and Yoko, Allen Ginsberg, Jerry Rubin, and many others—Sinclair was released after 29 months. Sinclair's basic premise in these street and prison writings is that rock and roll could lead to revolution; it seems, however, that he didn't think that just singing about it (as in The Beatles' "Revolution") would do it. Contains some fascinating documents and photographs from the era, as well as history of radical groups such as the White Panther Party (which became the Rainbow Party). Freda Peeple!

SIOUXSIE AND THE BANSHEES

TITLES OF INTEREST

Johns, Brian. *Entranced: The Siouxsie and the Banshees Story.* London: Omnibus Press (division of Book Sales Limited), 1990.

Stevenson, Ray. *Siouxsie and the Banshees: Photo Book.* London: Omnibus Press (division of Book Sales Limited), 1990.

SKID ROW

FANZINES AND FAN CLUBS

Skid Row: Chain Gang. P.O. Box 884464, San Francisco, CA 94188.

Skid Row fan club that offers members access to concert tickets, album and tour information, the Chain Gang hotline, special contests, and more. Members also receive subscription to the newsletter, which contains concerts, single and video releases, interviews, and more. The cost of membership is $19 U.S.; $24 elsewhere.

THE SMALL FACES

(See also Stewart, Rod)

PICTORIALS

Hewitt, Paolo. Foreword by Kenney Jones. *Small Faces: The Young Mods' Forgotten Story.* London: Acid Jazz, 1995. 160 pages. Approximately 175 black-and-white photographs, covering every page; two glossy 16-page color inserts. Discography.

Before Rod Stewart and before The Faces there were The Small Faces: Steve Marriott, Jimmy Winston, Ronnie Lane, and Kenney Jones. Though these guys literally were small (all under five foot six), their music helped launch the Mod movement in the U.K. and continues to influence bands such as Oasis and Blur in the 1990's. This splendid book bursts with rare black-and-white photographs of the band in their heyday and tops it all off with two generous color inserts. Author Paolo Hewitt explores how such a major group not only unraveled (Marriott left in 1968 to form Humble Pie; he

died in a fire in 1991), but how they've all but been forgotten in the annals of rock history. A stylish book that should be welcomed by fans of U.K. rock.

SMASHING PUMPKINS

PICTORIALS

No author. *Smashing Pumpkins Tear-Out Photo Book.* London: Oliver Books, 1994. Unpaginated (approximately 48 pages). Approximately 50 color and black-and-white photographs throughout.

For younger fans, here is a book of rip-out photos of Smashing Pumpkins. Some of the photos repeat those in Wise's book (see below), so it's certainly not worth getting both.

Stapleton, Jim. *Smashing Pumpkins.* Miami, FL: MBS, 1995. 120 pages. Approximately 75 color and black-and-white photographs throughout. Discography. Chronology. Index.

CD-format book covering all aspects of Smashing Pumpkins' career, although if predates all of the band's 1996 turmoil (e.g., their drummer's heroin addiction). This nicely designed and illustrated book is priced just right at around $7.99.

Wise, Nick. *Smashing Pumpkins.* London: Omnibus Press (division of Book Sales Limited), 1994. Unpaginated (approximately 48 pages). Approximately 50 color and black-and-white photographs throughout. U.K. Discography.

Omnibus Press didn't waste any time putting out a photo book on this Chicago-based band. More of a magazine than a book, with little in the way of biographical detail. Some photos will catch your eye, but you don't get much of a sense of the group's personality. For browsing only.

PATTI SMITH

PICTORIALS

No author. *Patti Smith: High on Rebellion*. Manchester, England: Babylon Books, c.1979. 54 pages. Approximately 60 black-and-white photographs, covering every page. Selected Articles. Interviews and Discography.

A disciple of French poet Rimbaud, Smith was by no means an ordinary child from suburban New Jersey. A chronic bout with tuberculosis left her with an emaciated frame and odd visions fixed in her mind from her hallucinatory state. With the no-bullshit attitude of Dylan and the macabre outrageousness of Jim Morrison, Smith created music and poetry that some cite as the start of the New York punk scene. This trashy book without an author fails to supply the most basic biographical details about Smith (such as that she was born in Chicago), but does contain several kinky photos, excerpts from various collections of poetry, magazine interviews, and song lyrics. Despite the inherent sleaziness of Smith's masturbatory poses, she is also beautiful, daring, and poetic in a way that puts Madonna to shame. Fans will need a copy of this rarity.

WRITTEN WORKS

Shepard, Sam. Introduction by Michael McClure. *Sam Shepard: Mad Dog Blues and Other Plays*. New York: Winter House Limited, 1972. 160 pages. Approximately 20 black-and-white photographs throughout.

Collection of four early plays by Shepard (the title, *Cowboy Mouth*, *The Rock Garden*, and *Cowboys #2*). Included here because *Cowboy Mouth* was coauthored by Patti Smith in 1971; the pair starred in a production of the show that same year. Depressing, as you'd expect from this combination, with some very loud rock and roll thrown in the middle. Smith closes this volume with a poem of sorts ("Sam Shepard: 9 Random Years").

Smith, Patti. *Babel*. New York: G.P. Putnam's Sons, 1978. 208 pages. Approximately 35 black-and-white photographs throughout.

First published in 1974, this book consists of verse, free-form poetry, prose, and other miscellaneous writings by Smith. The volume contains many tributes to her idol, Rimbaud, but also to other artistic visionaries, such as Georgia O'Keefe. Her main fortés, drugs and sex, continue to pervade her work. An absolute must for Smith's core audience, although not recommended for young readers.

Smith, Patti. *The Coral Sea*. New York: W.W. Norton & Company, 1996. 72 pages. Approximately 12 black-and-white photographs throughout.

A spiritual journey through the vision of photographer Robert Mapplethorpe, Smith's long-time friend and colleague—she had modeled for him early in her career and the two collaborated on a film—who died in 1989 of complications due to AIDS. Through elegant chunks of prose poetry, Smith chronicles the voyages of an individual venturing to see the Southern Cross, while at the same time battling a life-threatening illness. Mapplethorpe's works appear throughout and make a fine complement to Smith's dreamy, allegorical pieces. Nicely done.

Smith, Patti. *Early Work: 1970-1979*. New York: W.W. Norton and Company, 1994. 180 pages. Approximately 30 black-and-white photographs throughout.

A greatest hits of Smith's poetry, uniting *Babel*, *Seventh Heaven*, *The Night* (see above and below), and other miscellaneous pieces. Readers wanting a retrospective of all of her works from the 1970's would do best to obtain this work, since the type and design are better here and, for a change, Smith actually opens with an introductory note called "to the reader." Don't miss "Dog Dream," a reflection of animals as they relate to Bob Dylan and his work.

Smith, Patti and Verlaine, Tom. *The Night*. London: Aloes Books, 1976. Approximately 20 pages.

Pamphlet containing works composed by both Patti Smith and Tom Verlaine. According to the back page, Smith wrote the odd numbered stanzas, while Verlaine then wrote the even ones. The lines don't necessarily match, and one easily distinguishes Smith's titillating language. Not nearly as interesting as Smith's other works.

Smith, Patti. *Seventh Heaven*. Philadelphia, PA: Telegraph Books (Folcroft Press), 1971. 48 pages.

Pocket collection of poetry written during the early stages of Smith's career. Smith reflects on her favorite subjects—sex, death, and drugs— with equal alacrity. One brief work, "marianne faithfull," immediately peaks a reader's interest, but it seems to be just a random quote from Faithfull herself about her leap from convent school to popping sleeping pills. Otherwise essential.

OTHER TITLES OF INTEREST

Muir. *Patti Smith: High on Rebellion*. Manchester, England: Babylon, 1980.

Roach, Dusty. *Patti Smith: Rock & Roll Madonna*. No And Books, 1979.

Smith, Patti. *Ha! Ha! Houdini*. No city: Gotham Book Mart, 1973.

Smith, Patti. *Witt: A Book of Poems*. No city: Gotham Book Mart, 1973.

THE SMITHEREENS

FANZINES AND FAN CLUBS

The Smithereens Fan Club. P.O. Box 35226, Richmond, VA 23235.

Founded in 1995, this club publishes *'Reen Thoughts*, a quarterly, glossy newsletter. The six-eight pages of *'Reen Thoughts* consist of black-and-white photographs, news updates, tour schedules, articles on bass guitar, new releases, collectibles, and more. The cost of membership is $5 in the U.S.; $6 Canada; and $8 everywhere else.

OTHER TITLES OF INTEREST

Battin, B.W. *Smithereens*. New York: Fawcett, 1987.

THE SMITHS

(See also New York Dolls, The: Pictorials)

BIOGRAPHIES

Bret, David. *Morrissey: Landscapes of the Mind*. London: Robson Books, 1994. 194 pages. One glossy 12-page black-and-white photo insert. Appendix I: Discography. Appendix II: Etchings. Index.

Stoic biography of The Smiths' former frontman, who stirs the souls of what Morrissey himself describes as "very big men." Steven Patrick Morrissey was born in Manchester, England. Influenced by James Dean and Oscar Wilde—and drawn to rock by Nico (of The Velvet Underground) and The New York Dolls—he teamed with John Martin Maher (later, of course, John Marr) and the two followed a "sanitized" course to fame, completely free of the usual rock vices, such as drugs, alcohol, sex, meat, and anything else any past star has deemed as an essential part of life. This book isn't nearly as detailed as Rogan's work (see below).

Rogan, Johnny. *Morrissey & Marr: The Severed Alliance*. London: Omnibus Press (division of Book Sales Limited), 1993. 358 pages. Two glossy eight-page black-and-white photo inserts. Discography. Index.

A controversial dual biography of the founding Smiths, this book wowed critics but inflamed Morrissey, who publicly announced he wanted to see the author die painfully in a hotel fire. To add gasoline to the flames, Rogan writes that he intends to generate *two additional* volumes on these figures, each separately treating Marr and Morrissey's solo careers. (Instead, however, he subsequently issued a day-by-day treatment; see Pictorials, below.) Well-written but somewhat dense, this book meticulously chronicles Morrissey's Irish Catholic roots and runs down a seemingly unending list of every teacher he ever had. By the time Marr enters the picture, casual readers may already be asleep. The more faithful will agree with *Melody Maker's* assertion that "it's a bloody marvellous book."

CHRONOLOGIES

Rogan, Johnny. *The Smiths: The Visual Documentary*. London: Omnibus Press (division of Book Sales Limited), 1994. 176 pages. Approximately 150 black-and-white photographs, covering every page; one glossy 16-page color insert. Discography.

Continuing from his earlier study of The Smiths (see Biographies, above), author Johnny Rogan is evidently still alive, despite persistent threats from Morrissey. More recently, Morrissey specified his preference for Rogan to die by having the Almighty himself send a squad of German shepherds to tear him apart.

It can safely be said there is little here for Morrissey to bitch about. In fact, this book presents more documentation on the band than any other work to date, with minute birthdates and events stemming back to the birth of Morrissey's grandfather in 1901. The early pages contain some marvelous family photos of Morrissey and Marr, while the book ends with a comprehensive discography. The major shortcoming is that it doesn't detail any of Morrissey's solo efforts, but perhaps—just to spite Morrissey—Rogan is still planning separate books on Morrissey and Marr as soloists. Morrissey will no doubt be waiting for him at the first book signing.

PICTORIALS

Middles, Mick. *The Smiths: The Complete Story.* London: Omnibus Press (division of Book Sales Limited), 1988. 128 pages. Approximately 125 black-and-white photographs, covering nearly every page; eight pages of color throughout. Discography.

First published in 1985 and revised in 1988 to reflect the band's 1987 break-up, this intelligent book reconstructs what made The Smiths tick, why they never fell into the easy path of video fashion, and how rifts formed between Morrissey and Johnny Marr that lead to the split. Middles sprinkles magazine quotes throughout the text, but also injects his own analytical commentary: *"The Smiths* [album] wasn't the masterpiece it could have been." In effect, this is a slightly more expanded version of Robertson's book (see Quizbooks and Quotebooks, below), with the bonus of color. If one had to choose between the two, this is the better option.

Rogan, Johnny. *The Complete Guide to the Music of the Smiths & Morrissey/Marr.* London: Omnibus Press (division of Book Sales Limited), 1995. 120 pages. Approximately 100 color and black-and-white photographs throughout. Index.

CD-format book covering all aspects of The Smiths' career, as well as Morrissey and Marr solo. This nicely designed and illustrated book is priced just right at around $7.99.

Slee, Jo. *Peepholism: Into the Art of Morrissey.* London: Sidgwick & Jackson, 1994. 168 pages. Approximately 200 color and black-and-white photographs, covering every page. Discography.

Attractive, album cover-shaped book divided into two parts: The Smiths and Morrissey as soloist. The author makes it clear that Morrissey not only reflects his genius in his lyrics, but also in his expressive cover art, stage poses, and publicity shots. Vastly more suitable for the coffee table than other Morrissey works listed herein, this book also contains greater insight into what went into the artist's recordings. Essential for those who want more than just a peep into the full range of Morrissey's talents.

QUIZBOOKS AND QUOTEBOOKS

Robertson, John. *Morrissey: In His Own Words.* London: Omnibus Press (division of Book Sales Limited), 1988. 96 pages. Approximately 100 black-and-white photographs, covering nearly every page.

Morrissey, dubbed a "contradiction" by Robertson, isn't that different from other pop stars: he's reclusive but loves (and needs) crowds and the public spotlight; and he does enjoy his enigmatic image. In typical Omnibus Press fashion, Morrissey is quoted on a variety of subjects, such as sex ("I've always found it [sex] particularly unenjoyable"), fans ("Communication with an audience is not anything you can buy"), his heroes ("Oscar Wilde and James Dean were the only two companions I had as a distraught teenager"), and, of course, his music and The Smith's split. Almost all of the quotes are circa 1983-84. A diverse, thought-provoking collection, with a fair range of up-close headshots and performance photos.

West, Mike. Photographs by Cummins, Kevin. *The Smiths in Quotes.* Woodford Green, Essex (England): IMP, 1985. 48 pages. Approximately 25 black-and-white and color illustrations throughout.

Average quotebook on The Smiths, with quotes alphabetized by subject ranging from adolescence to videos. While not as comprehensive as Robertson's work (see above), the photos are cleaner and this one does include a complete list of 50 or so Morrissey heroes (such as The Kinks and Fabian). Good for a laugh here and there ("I've never known a marriage that was happy"), but far from comprehensive.

SMITHMANIA

Gallagher, Tom; Campbell, Michael; Gillies, Murdo. Foreword by John Peel. *The Smiths: All Men Have Secrets*. London: Virgin, 1995. 256 pages. Discography.

An international collection of fan reflections on one of the most beloved bands of the 1980's. Most of the statements are only a paragraph or two, but in compact form convey to the reader why The Smiths' songs (or Morrissey and Marr as icons) had such an influence on the speakers. Not all of the stories are positive. One English fan: "I was punched in the face while listening to *The Queen Is Dead* on a bus." The stories also come from other places around the globe, such as the U.S.: "This song ("How Soon Is Now?") always articulated my seemingly endless wait for a lover or even a boyfriend." Strictly for those who would buy a Smiths' fanzine.

TOURBOOKS

Sterling, Linder. Introduction by Michael Bracewell. *Morrissey Shot*. London: Secker & Warburg, 1992. 140 pages. Approximately 150 black-and-white photographs, covering every page.

A record of Morrissey's 1991 solo "Kill Uncle" tour, which smashed a number of box-office records in America, Europe, and Japan. Photographer Sterling, a longtime Morrissey friend, recreates the fanfare of Morrissey's stage spectacular, with some intentionally fuzzy headshots and introspective photos balancing out the images of rioting fans. One picture of Morrisseys' bare chest covered with sand is particularly creative. This superb collection should still hold tremendous interest for fans.

SOFT CELL

BIOGRAPHIES

Reed, Jeremy. *Marc Almond: The Last Star*. London and San Francisco: Creation Books, 1995. 182 pages. Approximately 50 black-and-white photographs throughout. Discography.

Marc Almond, the former lead singer of Soft Cell, and now solo poet and torch singer, is the subject of this analytical biography. Author Jeremy Reed cites a universe of influence on Almond, from French poet Baudelaire to entertainer Judy Garland, and the results depend on one's affinity for gender-bending pop. Fans of Soft Cell or any of Almond's subsequent bands—Marc and the Mambas, Marc and the Willing Sinners, and Marc Almond with La Mangia—will have a grand time with this handsome volume.

FANZINES AND FAN CLUBS

Vaudeville & Burlesque: The Official Marc Almond Fan Club. P.O. Box 4RX, London W1A 4RX England.

Marc Almond fan club that provides members with a presentation folder, a numbered membership card, a special edition color photo, a color postcard, and four newsletters each year. *Fantastic Star*, the club's glossy 16-page newsletter, opens up like a map and contains black-and-white photographs, concert updates, interviews, pen pals, questions and answers, Marc Almond merchandising (badges, t-shirts, cassettes, records, etc.), and more. The cost of membership is $13.50 in U.S.; £10 U.K.; and £11 elsewhere in Europe.

SONIC YOUTH

BIOGRAPHIES

Foege, Alec. Foreword by Thurston Moore. *Confusion Is Next: The Sonic Youth Story*. New York: St. Martin's Press, 1994. 276 pages. 32-page black-and-white photo insert. Discography.

Apparently trying to prove that the titular theory is correct, the confusion begins right way when one opens this book up and finds the 32-page insert in the beginning, not in the expected center. This authorized biography (singer Thurston Moore contributes the foreword) succeeds best at examining how Sonic Youth bridged the gap between punk, No Wave, and alternative, having been too young for the first two and too old to fit the bill for the third. Foege has a valid point, which is that Sonic Youth stands as a supergroup in the alternative music world, predating Nirvana in terms of iconoclastic vision. Required reading for listeners of alternative music. "You will not read a better recounting of the New York art scene in the post-punk '70's."—*Alternative Press*.

SONNY AND CHER

(See also Cher)

AUTOBIOGRAPHY

Bono, Sonny. *And the Beat Goes On* New York: Pocket Books, 1991. 274 pages. One glossy 16-page black-and-white photo insert.

Bono seems to review history on a cheerful, nostalgic note, an unsurprising fact given his change to a career in politics. Bono would prefer to characterize himself as a loveable, sensitive oaf, which is quite a contradiction to the "Svengali" image most Cher biographers care to depict. As a child, Bono was likely to be the kid who broke a glass window while peeking at a neighborhood girl undressing. Bono can't offset his label as a predictable, overachieving bore—and a conservative one at that. It's no wonder Cher later became insatiable in her quest for the stud factor with the likes of Gregg Allman. And the beat goes zzzzzzzzz....

OTHER TITLES OF INTEREST
Braun, Thomas. *Sonny & Cher*. Mankato, MN: Creative Education, 1978.

SOUNDGARDEN

BIOGRAPHIES

Nickson, Chris. *Soundgarden: New Metal Crown*. New York: St. Martin's Press Griffin, 1995. Approximately 12 black-and-white photographs throughout. 228 pages. Discography. Chronology.

One of the few Seattle bands *not* associated with grunge, Soundgarden combines the sounds of 1970's metal, hard rock, and punk into its own, distinctive brand of thrash rock. The group—whose present members include singer Chris Cornell, drummer Matt Cameron, guitarist Kim Thayill, and bassist Ben Shepherd—took its name from Douglas Hollis' wind sculpture *A Sound Garden*; such pretensions aside, the musicians seem to have their

egos in check, despite triple platinum albums, Grammy awards, and prize-winning videos. This book, therefore, isn't the usual tale of torn-up hotel rooms and groupie orgies. Author Nickson comes through for fans with a well-researched history of Soundgarden, which in the early chapters encompasses all of hard rock. The photos are the only major disappointment, buried as quarter page shots rather than highlighted as a glossy insert.

FANZINES AND FAN CLUBS

Soundgarden Fan Club. P.O. Box 61275, Seattle, WA 98121.

Fan club that offers both "mailing list" and "fan club" packages. The former offers members information on merchandise and touring ($2), while the latter provides the same plus photos, guitar picks, posters, stickers, and more ($8 one-time fee U.S.; $10 one-time fee everywhere else). The club also supplies question-and-answer with the band, profiles of each member, a general biography, and a discography.

PICTORIALS

Ewing, Jon. *Soundgarden*. Miami, FL: MBS, 1996. 120 pages. Approximately 75 color and black-and-white photographs throughout. Discography. Chronology. Index.

CD-format book covering all aspects of Soundgarden's career. This nicely designed and illustrated book is priced just right at around $7.99.

SPANDAU BALLET

PICTORIALS

Travis, John. *Spandau Ballet*. London: Sidgwick & Jackson, 1986. 64 pages. Approximately 65 color photographs, covering every page.

The dedicated followers of early 1980's fashion are the subject of this trendy pop pictorial. Photographer Armando Gallo captures the boys—Gary Kemp, Anthony Hadley, Martin Kemp, Steve Norman, and John Keeble—live, with expected results. There's nothing exceptional to be gained here, except that Spandau

Ballet hailed from North England, was first known as The Angel Boys and became known as Spandau Ballet when a friend caught the name in graffiti on a toilet wall. (In actuality, the term derives from the section of Berlin known as Spandau, which was the site of Rudolph Hess' imprisonment. Coincidentally, it's also the name of a ballet.) All style, little substance.

THE SPANIELS

BIOGRAPHIES

Carter, Richard G. *Goodnight, Sweetheart, Goodnight*. Sicklerville, NJ: August Press, 1994. 212 pages. Discography.

One of the major doo-wop singing groups of the 1950's, The Spaniels consisted of James ("Pookie") Hudson, Gerald Gregory, Willie C. Jackson, Opal Courtney, Jr., and Ernest Warren. The group made some strides with songs later covered by The Beatles ("Baby It's You" and an early rarity, "Red Sails in the Sunset"), but were never quite a chart success. It's difficult to read a book with so many "doos" on a page, but fans of this early group will be immensely pleased to see it—though disappointed that there aren't any photos.

THE SPECIALS

BIOGRAPHIES

Williams, Paul. *You're Wondering Now: A History of the Specials*. Dunoon, Argyll (Scotland): S.T. Publishing, 1995. 128 pages. Approximately 30 black-and-white photographs throughout. Specials Discography.

What most people in the U.S. are probably wondering is *who* were The Specials? Originally from Coventry, England, this quintet was one of the leaders of the two-tone movement, which also included Madness, The Beat, The Selecter, and a few others. The group brought their own form of ska music to the fore, and through the 1981 hit "Ghost Town" sent a message to the British people about poverty and racial tension. After only a two-year flourish, the group folded and moved on

to other bands. A well-written book that will be considered special by the group's remaining followers.

PHIL SPECTOR

(See also Ronettes, The)

BIOGRAPHIES

Ribowsky, Mark. *He's a Rebel: The Truth About Phil Spector*. New York: Dutton, 1989. 342 pages. One glossy 16-page black-and-white photo insert. Phil Spector Discography. Index.

Berry Gordy aside, what producer's life story is really all that interesting to tell? Phil Spector's, of course. The man with the "Napoleon complex" was a Jewish kid from the Bronx who entered the music world between the eras of Elvis and The Beatles. His explosive Wall of Sound technique changed the face of rock and roll, while his groups—The Teddy Bears, The Crystals, The Ronettes, The Righteous Brothers, and even the solo Beatles—topped the charts in the 1960's and 70's. Spector retired from music after he produced legendary music for The Ramones and Leonard Cohen. This book is strong on defining Spector's music, but somewhat weak on his private life. Fans of his records will need this in conjunction with Ronnie Spector's autobiography to gain a wider picture.

CRITICAL/ANALYTICAL COMMENTARY

Williams, Richard. *Out of His Head: The Sound of Phil Spector*. New York: E.P. Dutton & Co., 1972. 206 pages. Approximately 30 black-and-white photographs throughout. Appendix 1: Phil Spector Discography. Appendix 2: Where Are They Now? Appendix 3: Songs. Index.

Published in 1972, during which time Spector was still actively producing the solo efforts of John Lennon and George Harrison, this book shows how Spector first made his impact on records by The Teddy Bears, The Ronettes, and The Crystals. Later, The Righteous Brothers, Tina Turner, and many others would benefit from his studio mastery and Wall of Sound. Author Richard Williams presents a fair defense of Spector's much-maligned work on The Beatles' *Let It Be* album, pointing out that the album did sell millions and earned a Grammy (which Paul McCartney accepted, even though he claimed he hated Spector's work). Very basic commentary for the layperson that will hold the reader's interest, although in Spector's case it's difficult to separate his madness from his music.

DISCOGRAPHIES, RECORDING GUIDES, AND COLLECTIBLES

Fitzpatrick, John J. and Fogerty, James E. *Collecting Phil Spector: The Man, the Legend, and the Music.* St. Paul, MN: Spectacle Press, 1991. 128 pages. Approximately 50 black-and-white photographs throughout; one glossy eight-page color insert. Index.

Connoisseur's guide to producing legend Phil Spector, which celebrates his work starting from his early days with composers Leiber and Stoller and his formation of Philles Records, where he first developed his Wall of Sound. With The Crystals and The Ronettes, Spector was christened a genius by those who listened to the music, but a tyrant by those who worked with him. Spector adapted to musical changes that accompanied the British invasion, and worked with Tina Turner, The Righteous Brothers, and three solo Beatles (George, John, and Ringo). Authors Fitzpatrick and Fogerty rush through Spector's 1970's work, but some may forgive the shortcoming because it's followed by an insert of album covers. Not complete, but worthwhile.

SPINAL TAP

FANZINES AND FAN CLUBS

This Is the Spinal Tap Zine. Attn. Chip Rowe, P.O. Box 11967, Chicago, IL 60611-0967.

"An A to Z guide to one of England's loudest bands" is a 76-page booklet containing brief alphabetical entries on all things related to Spinal Tap, plus sections on sources, trivia, a timeline, and more. This teeters on the edge of seriousness and humor, but anyone who loved the film will want a copy. Costs about $3.50.

RICK SPRINGFIELD

FANZINES AND FAN CLUBS

Rick's Loyal Supporters. c/o Vivian Acinelli, 4530 E. Four Ridge Rd. Imperial, MO 63052.

Established in 1989 and claiming authorization from Rick Springfield and his management team, this fan club provides members with four issues of its newsletter, a club folder, a membership card, a biography, a discography, a filmography, photos of Rick, pen pal listings, and more. The 32-page, stapled newsletter carries the same title as the club and contains black-and-white photographs, "Ask Rick," news, letters from members, poetry from members, items for sale, and more. The cost of membership is $15 in the U.S.; $17 in Canada and Mexico; and $20 everywhere else.

YOUNG ADULT

Gillanti, Simone. *Rick Springfield.* New York: Wanderer Books (Simon & Schuster), 1984. 64 pages. Approximately 32 black-and-white photographs throughout. Facts and Figures.

In the early 1980's, Rick Springfield had a hit with "Jessie's Girl," won a couple of awards, and starred on the television soap "General Hospital." In the 1990's, Springfield is already buried deeply in the "Whatever happened to..." file. This infantile kiddie book is a stretch even at 64 pages. Did you know that Rick sometimes gets song ideas from his dreams?

BRUCE SPRINGSTEEN (AND THE E STREET BAND)

BIOGRAPHIES

Eliot, Marc. With the participation of Mike Appel. *Down Thunder Road: The Making of Bruce Springsteen.* New York: Simon & Schuster, Inc., 1992. 384 pages. One eight-page glossy black-and-white photo insert. Appendix A: Documents. Appendix B: The Lawsuit Letters. Sources and Notes. Index.

Posing as an autobiography of Bruce during

his rise to fame, this is really a "set the record" straight book for Mike Appel—Springsteen's first manager and the man accused of ripping him off. Appel opened up his files and provided most of the firsthand quotes and testimony provided in Eliot's work; quotes from the "opposition"—including Jon Landau, Dave Marsh (author of two Springsteen bios listed below) and Springsteen himself—are reprinted from magazines and books. That hardly sounds like fair journalism. The author is quick to point out that Springsteen wouldn't exist if not for Appel, but doesn't have a definitive answer to why the musician's greatest commercial success and monetary gains came after he terminated his relationship with Appel. "Libraries shouldn't buy it..."—*Booklist*.

Marsh, Dave. *Glory Days: Bruce Springsteen in the 1980's*. New York: Thunder's Mouth Press, 1996. 476 pages. Three glossy 16-page black-and-white photo inserts.

Marsh follows up his earlier *Born to Run: The Bruce Springsteen Story* (see Pictorials, below) with this study of Springsteen in the 1980's. For the Boss, this was a decade of stadium-packed concerts, European tours, and mega-selling albums (most notably, *Born in the U.S.A.*). Springsteen in the Reagan-era was a gritty, conservative, hard-working rock-and-roller who made political statements without sacrificing his integrity. Non-gossipy, insightful, and intelligent, this overview won't reveal who Springsteen slept with, but it will tell you some of the books he read (e.g., *History of the United States* by Henry Steele Commager and Allen Nevins). A superb reminder of the era, with three generous glossy photo inserts. "Marsh is a good, smart rock commentator." —*Booklist*.

Meyer, Marianne. *Bruce Springsteen*. New York: Ballantine, 1984. 180 pages. Eight-page glossy black-and-white photo insert. Appendixes: Discography, Videography, Fanzine Information.

This is more or less "a brief history of the Boss." Meyer writes succinctly, and this is because she doesn't have much new to say about Springsteen's style or his albums. She devotes little attention to his private life, relations with other musicians, etc. and we don't get any sense of the real man. How many other books depict him as a drug-free, working-class rocker from Asbury Park? Readers are left feeling there must be more. The "Encore" chapter,

which contains very brief bios on members of The E Street Band, should probably have been expanded and incorporated into the narrative.

FANZINES AND FAN CLUBS

Backstreets. P.O. Box 51225, Seattle, WA 98115.

Begun in 1980, this 66-page glossy magazine has a four-color cover with a design not unlike *Entertainment Weekly*. The interior contains high-quality black-and-white photographs, reviews, concert coverage, reminiscences, interviews, upcoming releases, news, classifieds, collectibles, and more. Write for information about their special 24-hour Backstreets Hotline. A separate division called Backstreets Records publishes a mail order catalog listing official and unofficial releases. (Write to Box 51219, same address as above.) The cost of subscription is $18 per year (three or four issues) in the U.S. and Canada; $25 elsewhere (payable U.S. funds only).

PICTORIALS

Cross, Charles R. and the editors of *Backstreets*. *Backstreets: Springsteen: The Man and His Music*. New York: Harmony Books (division of Crown Publishers, Inc.), 1989. 220 pages. Approximately 150 color and black-and-white photographs throughout. Springsteen Collectibles. Springsteen Studio Sessions. Springsteen's Performances. Resources and Photo Credits.

Photo book and miscellany from the editors of *Backstreets* (see Fanzines and Fan Clubs, above). The text consists of sections on Springsteen's roots (the Jersey Shore), interviews with Springsteen and various band members (e.g., Little Steven Van Zandt, Clarence Clemons, Nils Lofgren, and Vini Lopez), articles from fans, and recording information. The book is a magnificently designed array of color and black-and-white photographs, all printed on glossy paper stock; this one does justice to Springsteen's image as an American icon, but affords nothing in the way of criticism or early biography. "Unabashed adulation adorns this tribute to Bruce Springsteen."—*Booklist*.

Gambaccini, Peter. *Bruce Springsteen*. New York: Quick Fox (division of Music Sales, Inc.), 1979. 128 pages. 60 black-and-white photographs throughout. Discography.

This photo book/biography covers the early years up through 1978 and the *Darkness at the Edge of Town* LP. Not much in the way of information here (a good deal of the text relies on magazine commentary), and the photos are way too dark. The discography only lists four LPs. For those in dire need of a book with photos exclusively of a boyishly young and gritty Bruce Springsteen.

Halbersberg, Elianne. *The Boss: Bruce Springsteen.* Cresskill: Sharon Starbook Publications, Inc., 1984. 96 pages. Approximately 100 black-and-white photographs throughout. Discography and Extras.

A tag-along to the release of Springsteen's *Born in the U.S.A., Bruce Springsteen* covers the basics but suffers in comparison to later pictorials because of the author's admitted lack of contacts to Springsteen and his inner circle. The author compensates somewhat by her enthusiasm and coverage of subjects ranging from lawsuits to bootlegs to a couple of chapters on The E Street Band. The photos are standard.

Hilburn, Robert. Art direction by Howard Klein. *Springsteen.* New York: Scribner's, 1985. "A Rolling Stone Press Book." 256 pages. 200 black-and-white, duotone, and color illustrations.

Above-average mid-1980's pictorial from music critic Hilburn. The photos are blown-up and full of typical Boss poses; in one you can see the sweat literally fly off his shoulders and chest. (How is *that* for a recommendation to female fans?) The book could have gone further: there is a significantly greater number of black-and-white and duotone shots than color; and the book does not contain any kind of discography, bibliography, or index. Otherwise, "This is a solid, informative book that will please fans..."—*Publishers Weekly.*

Humphries, Patrick and Hunt, Chris. *Bruce Springsteen: Blinded by the Light.* New York: Owl Books (Henry Holt and Company, Inc.), 1985. 176 pages. Over 250 black-and-white photographs throughout. Career Milestones; Springsteen Songbook; Bootlegs; World Discography; Covers; E Street Band Discography.

Two books in one: the first half, by Humphries, is a general biography of Springsteen and his career; the second, by Hunt, is a comprehen-

sive chronology and recording history. In addition to containing countless photos of albums, magazine covers, and concert posters, the book also boasts a rare photo of 17-year-old Springsteen in his early band The Castiles, and another one of him as a mischievous hippie, circa 1970. Those interested in Springsteen's international releases and bootlegs will find the second half of this work essential. "A thorough compilation of Springsteen facts and comments." —*Library Journal.*

Kamin, Philip (photographs) and Goddard, Peter (text). *Springsteen Live.* New York: Beaufort Books, 1984. Unpaginated. Approximately 150 color and black-and-white photographs throughout.

These superior photos were taken from Springsteen's 1978, 1981, and 1984 tours and show the performer in every imaginable pose amidst a number of creative designs. Goddard's firsthand text is printed vertically on the pages, in five columns and often is interrupted by ten-plus pages of photos; the publishers evidently didn't think fans would be *reading* this one.

Lynch, Kate. *Bruce Springsteen: No Surrender.* London: Bobcat Books (division of Book Sales Limited), 1986. 126 pages. Approximately 100 color and black-and-white photographs throughout. Discography.

An odd mix of hype, photos, and commentary on Springsteen, published when *Born in the USA* was just past its infancy. Using the hook of the song "No Surrender" for this book's title, author Kate Lynch shows how those two words have always been part of Springsteen's philosophy, even as a teenager: "...in the face of a lot of misunderstandings and outright antagonism," she writes, "[he] has remained true to himself and the music." A so-so effort that lacks the prerequisite Jersey attitude.

Marsh, Dave. *Born to Run: The Bruce Springsteen Story.* New York: Doubleday/Dolphin, 1979. 176 pages. Approximately 150 black-and-white photographs throughout. The Songs. The Shows.

Marsh, like John Landau, felt rock history was right in front of his eyes when he first witnessed Springsteen in action. It's no wonder, then, that this book was among the earliest and (at the time) best of all Springsteen photo-biographies. This work has a high emphasis on photos, and many of these early shots retain Springsteen's youthful vitality. Marsh captures the spirit of Springsteen's early performances, drawing elaborate comparisons with legendary acts of the 1960's and 70's. As with most of Marsh's writings on the Boss, he sticks to the music and evades smutty details of his personal life. Recommended in concordance with more recent sources. Marsh followed up with *Glory Days* (see Biographies, above). This book was revised by Thunder's Mouth Press in 1996.

Slaughter, Mike. *Bruce Springsteen: An American Classic*. Port Chester, NY: Cherry Lane, 1984. 32 pages. Approximately 32 color and black-and-white photographs, covering every page. Albums.

Mr. America is captured during the glory days of his *Born in the USA* album. His other releases—*Greetings from Asbury Park, Darkness on the Edge of Town*, et. al.—are all in black-and-white and are thus buried amidst the hype about Bruce turning pop. Overtly red, white, and blue (go Reagan!), this promotional book may have helped sell a few extra records, but it's really a bill of goods.

Yopp, Chuck and Fenton, Donna. *Greetings from Asbury Park, NJ: A Look at the Local Scene*. Asbury Park, NJ: Greetings, 1983. 300 pages. Approximately 300 black-and-white photographs throughout.

Self-published photo-journal of Springsteen's hometown, Freehold, New Jersey, and nearby sites. Subjects include Springsteen's grammar and high schools (shamefully, neither is identified), the myriad houses he lived in (spanning Freehold, Ocean Township, West End, Holmdel, and other places), night clubs, beaches, and other Bruce haunts. The bulk of the book consists of photos of Springsteen on the local club scene 1977-1983, with all venues cited and performances dated. A great idea wasted: Why isn't a Jersey map thrown in? And why isn't there commentary about what Bruce means to his hometown?

QUIZBOOKS AND QUOTEBOOKS

Duffy, John. *Bruce Springsteen: In His Own Words*. London: Omnibus Press (division of Book Sales Limited), 1993. 96 pages. Approximately 100 black-and-white photographs, covering every page.

Bruce's life and work sketched out through quotes by and about the artist. Springsteen on his home state: "New Jersey's a dumpy joint. I mean it's okay, but every place is a dump." On influences: "I play Buddy Holly every night before I go on, that keeps me honest." The photos, in particular the reproductions of early performance shots, are a surprising treat. While not striving to be all-encompassing, this Omnibus Press publication may provide fans with some light entertainment.

Higgins, Heather and Laiderman, Beth. *Bruce! The Ultimate Springsteen Quiz Book*. New York: M. Evans & Company, Inc., 1985. 96 pages. 40 black-and-white photographs throughout.

This quizbook contains 200 laughably easy questions and answers. Example: "What is Bruce's ethnic heritage? a) American Indian b) Jewish c) Italian d) German." (The answer, of course, is c) Italian, but this is not even fully accurate; he's really Irish-Italian, since his father is Irish and his mother Italian.) The answers are mixed in with the questions (on the backs of pages), which can cause a lot of confusion. Sorry, *not* the ultimate.

Mayer, Deborah. *Prove It All Night!: The Bruce Springsteen Trivia Book*. New Haven: Mustang Publishing, 1987. 96 pages. Approximately 20 black-and-white scattered photographs throughout.

The title of this trivia book is cleverly from the Springsteen song of the same name. The questions, which vary in difficulty, are loosely divided by theme (e.g., growing up, unreleased songs, the band) and include straight question-and-answer, match-ups, fill in the blanks, word searches, and bonus questions ("Though cars and driving figure prominently in Bruce's lyrics, he sings about only two gas stations. Name them."). The questions and format make this best suited for young fans in the 12-15 age range.

WRITTEN WORKS

Weinberg, Max with Santelli, Robert. *The Big Beat: Conversations with Rock's Great Drummers*. Chicago: Contemporary Books, Inc. 1984. 198 pages. Approximately 50 full-page photographs throughout. Index.

Springsteen's E Street Band drummer interviewed 14 rock drummers, all with distinct and influential styles: Johnny Bee, Dino Danelli, Levon Helm, Roger Hawkins, "Pretty" Purdie, Hal Blaine, Earl Palmer, Russ Kunkel, D.J. Fontana, Dave Clark, Kenney Jones, Charlie Watts, Jim Keltner, and Ringo Starr. Watts (who talks jazz) and Starr ("*Abbey Road* was tom-tom madness") conversations are best, showing that excellent timing and a laid-back style can make all the difference in a band. In his segment, "Pretty" Purdie makes the preposterous claim that he drummed on 21 Beatles songs (a fact which has been disproved in many sources, most prominently Lewisohn's *The Beatles Recording Sessions*). An inspirational read for drummers. (This book was also published in paperback by Billboard Books in 1984, but is since out of print.)

YOUNG ADULT

Koenig, Teresa. Edited by Howard Schroeder, Ph.D. *Bruce Springsteen: Center Stage*. Mankato: Crestwood House, 1986. 32 pages. 15 color and black-and-white illustrations throughout.

The Boss "center stage"—and in 7,500 words or less. The photos are nothing to speak of, and the text makes no specific reference to any of Springsteen's songs. Even a five-year-old expects more.

OTHER TITLES OF INTEREST

Bain, Geri and Leather, Michael. *Picture Life of Bruce Springsteen*. New York: Franklin Watts, 1986.

Elliott, Brad. *Wild and Innocent: The Recordings of Bruce Springsteen, 1972-1985*. Ann Arbor, MI: Popular Culture Ink, 1994.

Frankl, Ron. *Bruce Springsteen*. New York: Chelsea, 1994.

Greenberg, Keith. *Bruce Springsteen*. St. Paul, MN: Lerner, 1986.
   School Library Journal *commented: "Greenberg looks at Springsteen's career and music, while blandly avoiding any comment that might be taken as critical."*

Leibowitz, Howard. *Bruce Springsteen*. New York: Ballantine, 1984.

MacInnis, Craig. *Bruce Springsteen: Here & Now*. Hauppauge, NY: Barron's, 1988.

Major, Kevin. *Dear Bruce Springsteen*. New York: Dell, 1988.
   Novel about a kid named Terry who conveys his life story via letters to Bruce Springsteen. Booklist commented: "Readers will find this a spirited, realistic piece of writing...."

Monroe, Marty. *Springsteen Born in the U.S.A.*. Milwaukee, WI: Hal Leonard, 1984

Tuszynski, Carole. *Bruce Springsteen: Our Reasons to Believe*. No city: Carole, 1986.

Zadra, Dan. *Bruce Springsteen*. Mankato, MN: Creative Education, 1983.

BILLY SQUIER

TITLES OF INTEREST

Atkinson, Terry and Cerf, Martin. *Billy Squier: An Illustrated History*. Port Chester, NY: Cherry Lane, 1983.

RINGO STARR

(See also Beatles, The)

BIOGRAPHIES

Clayson, Alan. *Ringo Starr: Straight Man or Joker?*. New York: Paragon House, 1992. 292 pages. One eight-page black-and-white photo insert. Index. (First published in 1991 in Great Britain by Sidgwick & Jackson.)

Poor Ringo. Even in his lone biography he gets the short end of the stick (forgive the drumming pun). He's cast here as "the working class Beatle" of limited skills as a drummer, singer, composer, and actor—and yet with that indefinable spark that has made him worthy of his success. Ringo fans would prefer less criticism and more on his drumming: his conflict over being forced by his mother to change from left to right-handed; his so-called "funny fills"; his infamous head waving while playing; and his influence on drummers such as Max Weinberg, Phil Collins, and Levon Helm. Ringo's drum solo on *Abbey Road* is given little attention, as are his exceptional performances on songs such as "She Loves You," "I Me Mine," and "She Said, She Said." Clayson is, however, quite strong in deflating several myths. Ringo did not originate the expression "a hard day's night"; and, contrary to ludicrous gossip, he confirms that Ringo was the drummer on The Beatles' albums. "A poignant portrait of an ordinary man cast in an extraordinary role—and just barely surviving." —*Kirkus*.

YOUNG ADULT

Awdry, Rev. W and Heinemann, William (artist). *A Cow on the Line and Other Thomas the Tank Engine Stories* New York: Random House, 1992. 32 pages. Approximately 32 color illustrations, covering every page. Comes with a cassette narrated by Ringo Starr.

The immeasurably cute tales of Thomas the Tank Engine, as written by Awdry, illustrated by Heinemann, and narrated on tape by Ringo (who played Mr. Conductor on the "Shining Time Station" TV show, featuring Thomas). This volume for kids four and younger contains "Double Trouble," "A Cow on the Line," "Old Iron," and "Percy Takes the Plunge." Each tape runs 10-12 minutes on each side. All aboard! (And no, it's not the Yellow Submarine or the Magical Mystery Tour....)

Awdry, Rev. W and Heinemann, William (artist). *Trouble for Thomas and Other Stories.* New York: Random House, 1992. 32 pages. Approximately 32 color illustrations, covering every page. Comes with a cassette narrated by Ringo Starr.

Contains "Trouble for Thomas," Thomas Saves the Day," "Thomas Goes Fishing," and "Terence the Tractor." See *A Cow on the Line and Other Thomas the Tank Engine Stories* for more details.

Awdry, Rev. W and Heinemann, William (artist). *Diesel's Devious Deed.* New York: Random House, 1992. 32 pages. Approximately 32 color illustrations, covering every page. Comes with a cassette narrated by Ringo Starr.

Contains "Pop Goes the Weasel," "Diesel's Devious Deed," "A Close Shave for Duck," and "Woolly Bear." See *A Cow on the Line and Other Thomas the Tank Engine Stories* for more details.

Awdry, Rev. W and Heinemann, William (artist). *Thomas Gets Tricked.* New York: Random House, 1992. 32 pages. Approximately 32 color illustrations, covering every page. Comes with a cassette narrated by Ringo Starr.

Contains "Thomas Gets Tricked," "Come Out, Henry," "Henry to the Rescue," and "A Big Day for Thomas." See *A Cow on the Line and Other Thomas the Tank Engine Stories* for more details.

OTHER TITLES OF INTEREST
Starr, Ringo. *Ringo's Photo Album.* No city: Jamie Publishers, 1964.

STATUS QUO

TITLES OF INTEREST
Hibbert, Tom. *Status Quo.* London: Omnibus Press (division of Book Sales Limited), 1981.
Shearlaw, John. *Status Quo: The Authorized Biography.* London: Sidgwick & Jackson, 1982.

TOMMY STEELE

TITLES OF INTEREST
Kennedy, John. *Tommy Steele.* London: Transworld, 1959.
Kennedy, John. *Tommy Steele: The Facts About a Teenage Idol and an Inside Picture of Show Business.* London: Souvenir, 1958.
Tatham, Dick. *The Wonderful Tommy Steele Picture Story Album.* London: Record Mirror, 1957.

STEELY DAN

BIOGRAPHIES

Sweet, Brian. *Steely Dan: Reelin' in the Years.* London: Omnibus Press (division of Book Sales Limited), 1994. 216 pages. One glossy 12-page black-and-white photo insert. Discography.

The first and only biography of the elusive Steely Dan, the group that has kept such a low profile, despite its 50 million in record sales spanning three decades. Steely Dan was all but ignored by the critics, but this is no doubt because the band rarely interviewed, never toured—and, a few session musicians aside, had only two mainstays: Walter Becker and Donald Fagen. This British biography, printed in miniscule type, is worth the eyestrain to discover little-known facts about Fagen's Jersey, Jewish upbringing and to read about Becker and Fagen's early days in the 1960's trying to peddle hits at the famous Brill building. An excellent survey of rock's jazzy introverts.

RELATED WORKS

Burroughs, William S. *Naked Lunch*. New York: Grove Press, 1990. 224 pages.

This William S. Burroughs novel was first published in 1959 and is reputedly the inspiration for the band name Steely Dan. The savagely humorous satire concerns a drug addict's pharmaceutical and sexual exploits as he travels the globe. Readers will have to search a while to discover that Steely Dan refers to a dildo! Lusty and wild all of these years later. Fans who enjoy this also should go directly to Jim Carroll's *The Basketball Diaries* (see Carroll, Jim: Written Works).

STEPPENWOLF (JOHN KAY & STEPPENWOLF)

AUTOBIOGRAPHY

Kay, John and Einarson, John. *Magic Carpet Ride: The Autobiography of John Kay and Steppenwolf*. Kingston, Ontario (Canada): Quarry Press Rocks!, 1994. 372 pages. Approximately 75 black-and-white photographs throughout. Discography.

Compelling autobiography from John Kay, the rocker who symbolized the rebellious heavy metal thunder of late 1960's hard rock and roll. Ironically, Kay's shades and biker leather image are just a front—he couldn't ride a motorcycle even if he wanted to because he is legally blind (hence the sunglasses). Contrary to popular belief, Kay isn't southern or even from California, having been born in Germany in 1944 near the end of the war. He and his mother made an incredible three-day escape across the Iron Curtain, ending up in Toronto. A true rock and roll rebel, Kay still believes in the messages of the group's staple songs—"Born to Be Wild," "Magic Carpet Ride," "The Pusher," and "Don't Step on the Grass, Sam"—and he will always be fondly recalled by bikers, hippies, and Vietnam Vets. Full of excellent photos from the psychedelic period and oral documentation from witnesses, this work demands serious attention.

FANZINES AND FAN CLUBS

The Wolfpack: Official Fan Club of John Kay and Steppenwolf. P.O. Box 271496, Nashville, TN 37227-1495.

Fan club authorized by John Kay, the leader of Steppenwolf, that provides members with: a newsletter subscription; a bumper sticker; a glossy, 8x10 color autographed band photo (yes, original signatures); a membership card; a letter from John Kay; merchandise mail order forms; a Steppenwolf family tree; a discography; and more. *Howl*, the eight-page pamphlet, is published seasonally and offers band updates, tour schedules, registration information for "Wolf Fest" (annual Steppenwolf festival in Nashville, which features John Kay's active participation), announcements, and more. To no one's surprise, the club's Editor is Charlie Wolf. The cost of membership is $10 per year in the U.S.; $15 everywhere else. (Payable in U.S. funds only.)

OTHER TITLES OF INTEREST
Hesse, Hermann. *Steppenwolf*. Cutchogue, NY: Buccaneer Books, 1983.
First published in 1927, this novel inspired the name of the rock band.

SHAKIN' STEVENS

TITLES OF INTEREST
Barrett, Paul with Haywood, Hilary. *Shakin' Stevens*. London: Star Books, 1983.
Leese, Martyn. *Shakin' Stevens*. London: Prize Books, 1981.

AL STEWART

FANZINES AND FAN CLUBS

Al Stewart Chronicles. Attn. Kim Dyer, 4656 Wilcox Road Holt, MI 48842.

Quarterly publication devoted exclusively to Al Stewart's career, past and present. The 12-page, stapled packet includes reprinted interviews with Stewart, inserts on CD availability, reproduced black-and-white photographs, updates on musicians Stewart has worked with (Laurence Juber, Peter White, etc.), other fanzines, and more. The cost of subscription is

$8 U.S.; $8.50 Canada; and $11 overseas. Payable in U.S. funds only.

ROD STEWART (AND THE FACES)

(See also Small Faces, The)

BIOGRAPHIES

Ewbank, Tim and Hildred, Stafford. *Rod Stewart: A Biography*. London: Headline Book Publishing, 1994. 264 pages. One eight-page black-and-white photo insert. Discography.

First published in 1991, this unremarkable biography omits a slightly important detail— Rod's birthdate—but quickly recovers and moves his story along, from his love of British football, to his early romantic conquests, to his beatnik period, to his Mod phase and long, successful career in pop music. The book stoically reports on Rod's evolvement from invisible player on records with Long John Baldry to his breakthrough as frontman for The Faces. Aside from a few requisite references to Rod's many "leggy blondes," this biography lacks the punch needed for a book on the hyperactive star. While far from perfect, Giuliano's work (see below) more closely fits the bill.

Giuliano, Geoffrey. Foreword by Ginger Baker. *Rod Stewart: Vagabond Heart*. London: New English Library (division of Hodder and Stoughton), 1993. 262 pages. Two glossy eight-page black-and-white photo inserts. Rod Stewart Discography. Index.

Author Geoffrey Giuliano seems to enjoy the inherent lustiness of his subject. In only the first few pages, he unleashes a sizable portion of trashy exposition about Rod's belligerent ex-wives, various children, love of tall blonde models, drinking, infidelities, and more—all of which seems to snidely imply that his most recent marital conquest, Rachel Hunter, may ultimately end up on the heap as well. Giuliano then teeters the other side of the fence—that Rod is an artist of Dylanesque stature—but that is a ridiculous comparison given Dylan's indifference to chart success compared with Rod's need for commercial hits. Despite several other tenuous comparisons (Stewart with Robert Plant), this is a far more accessible and juicy rendering of events than other biographies listed herein.

Pidgeon, John. *Rod Stewart and the Changing Faces*. London: Panther, 1976. 144 pages. One glossy eight-page black-and-white photo insert. Faces Family Tree. Discography. Notes.

The only all-out biography of The Faces— Kenney Jones, Ron Wood, Ian McLagan, Rod Stewart, and Jetsu Yamuchi—and their relation to bands such as Humble Pie, Free, and The Yardbirds. The early incarnation of the band, The Small Faces (Steve Marriott, Jimmy Winston, Ronnie Lane, Kenney Jones, and Ian McLagan), were rivaled only by The Who in terms of Mod influence. More than anything else, this book serves to show how Stewart flitted from band to band until The Faces finally clicked with *Every Picture Tells a Story* and Stewart became a sensation; the problem emerged, however, that the band couldn't take the "Rod Stewart and the Faces" label. Sorely dated, but still offers some nuggets for the band's followers.

Tremlett, George. *The Rod Stewart Story*. London: Futura Publications, 1976. 144 pages. One glossy 16-page black-and-white photo insert. Appendix One: The Rod Stewart Chronology. Appendix Two: Press Releases.

Bubblegum mass-market biography of the 1970's superstar who has "seen too many late nights, smoked too many cigarettes, and put away too much booze," sounding more like an aging prostitute than a rock star. Fans who want to know about Rod's early ambitions to be a football player and about his then-sizzling affair with Britt Ekland might want to take a peek, but otherwise, this doesn't hold up. Those interested in a book written during Stewart's early years would do better with Pidgeon's work (see above).

CHRONOLOGIES

Gray, John. *Rod Stewart: The Visual Documentary*. London: Omnibus Press (division of Book Sales Limited), 1992. 96 pages. Approximately 125 black-and-white photographs, covering every page. Complete U.K. Discography.

Glossy day-by-day chronology of events in the life of Rod Stewart. With its cherry red cover, it's doubtful this will appeal to fans of Rod as early 1970's rocker as much as it will those who have an adult contemporary slant. The book itself catalogs nearly every occurrence in Rod's life, starting with autumn 1963, when he joined his first band, The Buckinghams. It might have been better to include some childhood events in the listing for easy access, but some of that basic information can be found in the introduction. The photos are quirky and fun, and are supplemented with a number of terrific quotes. In two memorable blurbs, Rod and Jeff Beck recall the former's early bouts with stage fright. Better than average entry in the "visual documentary" series.

PICTORIALS

Burton, Peter. *Rod Stewart: A Life on the Town.* London: New English Library, 1977. 120 pages. Approximately 150 color and black-and-white photographs, covering every page.

While slightly better than other pictorials of the late 1970's, this is still not nearly as glamorous as coffee table books on The Beatles, The Rolling Stones, or Elvis. This "authorised" biography reveals Stewart to be nothing more than a second-rate, pampered Mick Jagger—idolized because of his vanity, love of fashion, and overall self-gratifying decadence. Throughout the book are some excellent photos of Rod's early bands—Steampacket (with Long John Baldry), The Jeff Beck Group, and The Faces—and Rod as solo act. Part Two of the book consists of a four-page discography (solo first, followed by his earlier bands), while Part Three features lyrics to all his solo efforts, with matching reproductions of album covers. Hardly worth the effort.

Cromelin, Richard. *Rod Stewart: A Biography in Words & Pictures.* No city: Sire Books (Chappell & Co., Inc.), 1976. 56 pages. Approximately 30 black-and-white photographs throughout. Appendix: Rod Stewart and the Faces on Record.

A poorly executed study of Stewart when he was still semi-fresh out of The Faces. A typo on nearly every page, a stilted sentence in nearly every paragraph, and some plain lousy photos. Don't miss Britt Ekland sucking Rod's finger on p. 31.

Jasper, Tony. *Rod Stewart.* Secaucus: Chartwell Books, Inc. (division of Book Sales Limited), 1977. 96 pages. Over 100 color and black-and-white illustrations, covering every page. Rod's Career Calendar.

Funky collection of pictures that has the benefit of just preceding Rod's disco kick. The rare

early Faces photos in the first half are soiled by awful cutouts and drab montages in the second. Rod's musicians are given reasonable space throughout; one photo of Kenney Jones will make you do a double-take, as he looks like the spitting image of John Lennon circa 1965. The career calendar fails to serve as a genuine discography.

TOURBOOKS

Nelson, Paul and Bangs, Lester. *Rod Stewart: 1977-78.* New York: Delilah Books, 1981. 160 pages. Approximately 80 black-and-white photographs throughout.

Bangs and Nelson went on the road with Stewart in 1977-78 and, with some exposure to the singer, produced this oily, fragmented document. Hounded in court (and the press) by his wounded ex, Britt Ekland, Rod managed to keep a smug grin on his face and churn out his callous, studly sayings: "Take twenty Valiums and have a stomach pump and that's the end of it." Middle chapters reflect back on his early years, with unsatisfactory results. Nearly every photo of Rod has him flinging open his shirt or dipping over a slinky, leggy babe; the appeal is a faded disco memory. The story closes with Rod marrying Alana Hamilton in 1979, another pre-Rachel Hunter fling, and Rod's battles against the punk movement. Nonsense.

STING

(See also Police, The)

BIOGRAPHIES

Sellers, Robert. *Sting: A Biography.* London: Omnibus Press (division of Book Sales Limited), 1989. 126 pages. Two eight-page glossy black-and-white photo inserts. Discography.

Sketchy biography of Sting that barely provides the basics: he was born in Newcastle-on-Tyne; underwent a harsh Catholic background; had a first career as a schoolteacher; and played in various jazz bands until he joined The Police. Where are the specifics? It's not mentioned, for example, how and why he made the gutsy career move from teaching to music. The book also fails to shed any light on The Police's break-up. His love-life is only mentioned in passing. The passages about recordings and films are uncritical to the point of inaccuracy. (*Dune*, one of cinema's all-time biggest lemons, is called a "creditable achievement.") The glossy photos are the book's only saving grace.

PICTORIALS

Gett, Steve. *Sting*. Port Chester, NY: Cherry Lane Books, 1985. 48 pages. Approximately 60 color and black-and-white illustrations, covering every page.

A photo history of Sting's life and career, published just as the artist embarked on his solo career. This lightweight book has a fair amount of color and captures some of the star's moody charisma, but only adds gloss to the literature. Flimsy.

OTHER TITLES OF INTEREST
Cohen, Barney. *Every Breath He Takes*. New York: Berkley, 1989.

STONE TEMPLE PILOTS

PICTORIALS

Gittins, Ian. *Stone Temple Pilots*. Miami, FL: MBS, 1994. 120 pages. Approximately 75 color and black-and-white photographs throughout. Discography. Chronology. Index.

CD-format book covering all aspects of Stone Temple Pilots' career. This nicely designed and illustrated book is priced just right at around $7.99.

Wall, Mick and Dome, Malcolm. *Stone Temple Pilots*. London: Omnibus Press (division of Book Sales Limited), 1995. Unpaginated (approximately 64 pages). Approximately 75 color and black-and-white photographs, covering every page. Discography.

Colorful, non-critical portrait of the San Diego-based band accused of jumping on the Seattle bandwagon. While the images are powerful and packed with movement, the text doesn't do that much to help their case and distinguish them from their competitors. The standard cut-and-and-paste copy, with little more than you'll find in the average rock magazine. However, you do find out that an early group name was Shirley Temple's Pussy. (At least the initials stayed the same!)

SUEDE

PICTORIALS

Membery, York. *Suede: The Illustrated Biography*. London: Omnibus Press (division of Book Sales Limited), 1993. Unpaginated (approximately 48 pages). Approximately 50 color and black-and-white photographs, covering every page. Suede Discography.

Introductory pictorial biography of the up-and-coming British band Suede. More here about looks, sexuality, and drug use than music. Strictly for fans.

SUICIDE

WRITTEN WORKS

Vega, Alan. *Cripple Nation*. Los Angeles: 2.13.61, 1994. Unpaginated (approximately 80 pages). Approximately 12 pencil drawings and handwritten lyric sheets throughout.

Vega, the lead singer of Suicide who has now gone solo, contributes some of his poetry amidst some bizarre black-and-white or gray video photography backdrops provided by Ric Ocasek of The Cars. (Vega himself actually seems to have supplied the front and back cover video enhancements.) Each poetic work consists of lines that are really primitive one-to-five word shouts. Neither here nor there, but fans of the artist may be able to empathize and find meaning.

DONNA SUMMER

BIOGRAPHIES

Haskins, Jim and Stifle, J M. *Donna Summer: An Unauthorized Biography*. Boston and Toronto: Little, Brown and Company, 1983. 142 pages. One six-page black-and-white photo insert. Discography. Index.

Born in Boston, Massachusetts, LaDonna Andrea Gaines was part of a strong churchgoing family. While in her teens, as she dreamed of becoming a singing star, she joined the church choir; later, she became a rock fan and listened to The Velvet Underground and Janis Joplin. Among her first big breaks was the landing of a part in a touring company of *Hair*. Non-fans of the woman who would become Donna Summer, the 1970's disco queen, may be surprised by some of the aforementioned details. Despite the negative vibes many people have toward disco, they can't deny Summers' place as an innovator of one of popular music's most commercial sounds. James Haskins and J M (no periods in the initials) Stifle don't overdo their enthusiasm for the subject, making this an objective and pleasant read.

FANZINES AND FAN CLUBS

The Donna Summer Fan Club. P.O. Box 40965, Redford, MI 48240.

Fan club providing concert information, recording and release dates, promotional items of interest, and a quarterly newsletter. The cost of membership is $7 U.S.; $8 Canada; and $10 Mexico.

The Endless Summer: The European Fan Club of Donna Summer. 160, rue Oberkampf 75011 Paris, France.

Fan club that publishes a quarterly newsletter, available in French and English. The eight-page, unbound packet includes photocopies of black-and-white photographs, discography/videography/filmography, latest news, remember yesterdays (flashbacks), and more. Write for subscription information.

SUPERTRAMP

PICTORIALS

Melhuish, Martin. Abbott, Kandice and Hutchinson, Reed (photographers). *The Supertramp Book*. London: Omnibus Press (division of Book Sales Limited), 1986. 193 pages. Approximately 200 color and black-and-white photographs throughout.

At the time this book was written, Roger Hodgson had left Supertramp to pursue a solo career, while Supertramp continued on, releas-

ing the *Brother Where You Bound?* LP. Author Martin Melhuish briefly examines the British pop scene and then moves into the history of Supertramp's formation, which began with Rick Davies joining The Lonely Ones, who later became known as The Joint. Davies met Hodgson at an audition and formed the group Daddy, renamed Daddy Long Legs, and ultimately titled Supertramp after R.H. Davies' book (see Related Works, below). The band first drew attention because of its controversial *Indelibly Stamped* album sleeve, which displayed a topless, tattooed woman. This endlessly fascinating book is full of reproductions of Supertramp's album art, wacky stage performances, and many studio shots. An almost flawless tribute, shortchanged by its lack of a discography.

RELATED WORKS

Davies, W.H. Preface by George Bernard Shaw. *The Autobiography of a Supertramp*. London: A.C. Fifield, 1908. 302 pages.

The autobiography of W.H. Davies, penned close to the turn-of-the century and prefaced by playwright George Bernard Shaw. Davies recalls life as a child growing up with siblings and falling head-over-heels in love with books. Later, he heads to the U.S. where he meets Brum, a professional tramp whose favorite method of travel is stowing away on trains. The pair discover a passion for visiting prisons, where they have a grand old time comparing the conditions of each. Eccentric and funny—and, if you haven't already guessed, the inspiration for the name of the group Supertramp.

THE SUPREMES

(See also Ross, Diana)

AUTOBIOGRAPHIES

Wilson, Mary with Romanowski, Patricia and Juilliard, Ahrgus. *Dreamgirl: My Life as a Supreme*. New York: St. Martin's Press, 1986. 292 pages. Four glossy eight-page black-and-white photo inserts. Appendix 1: A Supremes Itinerary. Appendix II: Supremes Discography. Index.

Mary Wilson's first autobiographical best seller guides us through The Supremes' career up through 1970, and ends with a lengthy epilogue summarizing events of 1975 leading up to Florence Ballard's tragic death due to a heart attack in 1976. Motown fans won't want to pass up Wilson's unflattering (and somewhat catty) portrayal of her former partner, Diana Ross. The Sparrow, it seems, was a microphone hog, a boyfriend stealer, the teacher's pet (Berry Gordy's, that is), and a jealous bitch. Wilson unleashes her worst attacks when blaming Ross for Motown's snubs of The Supremes as she sought to claim the spotlight for herself. Florence Ballard, on the other hand, is more of a tragic figure, never having fully recovered from an early rape and the pressures of stardom. Highlighted by four glamorous photo inserts.

Wilson, Mary with Romanowski, Patricia. *Supreme Faith: Someday We'll Be Together.* New York: HarperCollins, 1990. 304 pages. One glossy 16-page black-and-white photo insert. Discography. People Who have Worked With the Supremes Over the Years.

From 1970 to 1979, Mary Wilson struggled to prove that The Supremes could churn out the hits minus lead singer Diana Ross and the support of Motown. Working with a string of replacements—including Debbie Sharpe, Cindy Birdsong, Susaye Green, Scherrie Payne, and Jean Terrell—she recorded several semihits and performed around the world with general success. Her solo career has not met with commercial reward, but Wilson optimistically continues on. Several of the incidents surrounding her love/hate relationship with Diana Ross are repeats from her prior autobiography (see *Dreamgirl*, above), but the details of her failed marriage and battles to maintain the rights to The Supremes' name are fresh. An optional addition for music library collections.

BIOGRAPHIES

Ruuth, Marianne. *Triumph and Tragedy: The True Story of the Supremes.* Los Angeles: Holloway House, 1986. 226 pages. One 10-page black-and-white photo insert. Appendix: Discography.

It's easy to call this biography "a true story"—there's nothing here that's remotely controversial or uncovered elsewhere. The author even goes as far as supplying parenthetical notes assuring the reader her facts are accurate (e.g., how The Primettes, an early version of The

Supremes, were formed); yet nowhere in these sections does she provide clues to her sources. This is what we are given as Diana Ross' reaction to Florence Ballard's death: "She was deeply sad." Thanks for the enlightenment!

SUPREMES FRIENDS AND FAMILY

Turner, Tony with Aria, Barbara. *All That Glittered: My Life With the Supremes.* New York: Dutton (Penguin Group), 1990. 308 pages. Two eight-page glossy black-and-white photo inserts. Index.

Tony Turner was part of The Supremes' family when he was just a tyke of 12, and served as their "mascot and gopher." Overwhelmed by the group's glamour, money, and fame, Turner raced around with them on their various tours and appearances, always being certain to do as Berry Gordy instructed and keep up with his schoolwork. Turner, who had been brought into the inner circle by Florence Ballard, was caught in the middle of the ladies' bitchy behavior and power struggles, which ended with the former quitting the group (or, as has never been made certain, getting tossed out and blacklisted by Gordy). Turner stayed in contact with Ballard until her tragic death in 1976, but doesn't have all that much to report about Ross, Wilson, or himself into the 1980's. "...a sometimes appealing, occasionally tedious story..."—*Publishers Weekly.*

OTHER TITLES OF INTEREST
Wilson, Randall. *Forever Faithfull: A Study of Florence Ballard of the Supremes.* No city: Renaissance Sound, 1987.

SWINGING BLUE JEANS

FANZINES AND FAN CLUBS

Swinging Blue Jeans Information Service. c/o Tina Barnett, 237 Magpie Close, Hoe Lane, Enfield, Middlesex EN1 4JG England.

Service that provides up-to-date reportage on Swinging Blue Jeans' performances, new releases, TV/radio appearances, and more. Updates are sent to members once a month; send 12 SASEs (self-addressed stamped envelopes).

TAKE THAT

PICTORIALS

St. Michael, Mick. *Take That: Talk Back*. London: Omnibus Press (division of Book Sales Limited), 1994. Unpaginated (approximately 48 pages). Approximately 50 color and black-and-white photographs throughout. Comes with a pull-out poster.

If you aren't a girl between the ages of 10 and 14, stay far away from this teen hunk book. Gary, Howard, Jason, Mark, and Robbie no doubt will stir the souls of many pubescent maidens, but they don't look much like musicians. The Hardy Boys mixed with Menudo mixed with 90210...you get the idea.

THE TALKING HEADS

BIOGRAPHIES

Davis, Jerome. *Talking Heads*. New York: Vintage Books, 1986. 146 pages. One eight-page black-and-white photo insert. Discography.

Part of Vintage's *Musician* magazine series, this is a critical account of the life, times, and music of the Talking Heads, from their start as The Artistics (or "Autistics," as some critics then called them). This series attempted to highlight the achievements and talents of the respective bands, rather than gossip. A generally objective and successful biography mixed with analytical commentary, although somewhat outdated and now out of print.

Howell, John. Photographs by Fitzgerald, F-Stop. *David Byrne*. New York: Thunder's Mouth Press, 1992. 160 pages. Approximately 100 black-and-white photographs throughout. Filmography, Discography, and Bibliography.

This self-proclaimed "cutting edge" biography, part of the American Originals Series, contains an interview with the title subject, as well as a few photos taken by Byrne. The book covers much the same ground as other titles on the artist, but with interesting forays into subjects such as mythology and photography, and featuring excerpts from Byrne's diary penned

during his North and South American Tour. None too deep. "...the book risks the charges of superficiality and triviality."—*Goldmine*.

FILM

Byrne, David. Photographs by Eggleston, William. *True Stories*. New York: Penguin, 1986. 192 pages. Approximately 175 color illustrations throughout.

Companion to the 1986 film, this glossy photo book contains the complete shooting script and a detailed introduction from Byrne, in which he describes how the project came about—as ideas he had culled from tabloids. This intriguing collection contains many of the original articles that inspired Byrne but, as the artist admits in a closing note, he made up quite a few of the incidents and people himself. A must for Byrne's fans, but hard to grasp for those who haven't seen the film (which is available on video). "A very attractive, very hip 8x10 inch paperback."—*Booklist*.

PICTORIALS

Gans, David. *Talking Heads: The Band & Their Music*. New York: Avon, 1985. 160 pages. Approximately 75 black-and-white glossy photos throughout. Discography. Sources.

A complete and intelligent treatment of Byrne and his Heads from their 1977 debut in the New York New Wave Underground to the *Little Creatures* LP. Interspersed throughout the text are extracts from interviews with Byrne and the other Heads. Some might disagree with the author's opening statement that The Heads are "the sixties vision of the band of the eighties," but in spite of this slant, the book is nevertheless valuable for fans.

Reese, Krista. *The Name of This Book Is the Talking Heads*. London/New York: Proteus, 1982. 132 pages. Approximately 125 black-and-white and color photographs, covering nearly every page. Discography.

A photo history of the group from the early days to stardom and creative differences. Ample text and descriptions of tours are provided, and there is an illustration on nearly every page. Good for browsing, but short on hard facts and details. One might do better with Gans' book (see above).

WRITTEN WORKS

Byrne, David. *Strange Ritual*. San Francisco, CA: Chronicle Books, 1996. Unpaginated (approximately 128 pages). Approximately 125 original color photographs throughout.

David Byrne: an artist of many talents. In this vibrant collection, he displays his versatility as a photographer. The themes here are ethnic diversity, inner spirituality, commercialism, and the overall strangeness of being. Many of the works are non sequitur montages, while the more effective images—such as a collection of multicolored Buddhas—make compelling statements about how God comes in all forms and colors. Byrne's one-line comments tend to get lost on the bottoms of the pages—which is probably a good thing, since more emphasis might have spoiled the subtleties of the works themselves. Bursts with creativity and originality.

Cohen, Lynne; with Byrne, David; Ewing, William; and Mellor, David. Foreword by David Byrne. *Occupied Territory*. New York: Aperture, 1987. Unpaginated (approximately 96 pages). Approximately 100 black-and-white photographs, covering every page.

A collection of photographs by renowned photographer Lynne Cohen. Her works—of a jet simulator, tennis courts, park benches, offices, etc.—are all taken of her actual *re-creations* of such objects and places. Byrne's contribution is a two-page essay in which he writes, "These pictures are a nice antidote to the glut of sloppy art recently." One has to be at Cohen's exhibit to get it.

Olinsky, Frank and the Talking Heads. Introduction by David Byrne. *What the Songs Look Like*. New York: Harper and Row, 1987. 128 pages. Approximately 115 black-and-white and color illustrations throughout.

Inspired by Alan Aldridge's *The Beatles Illustrated Lyrics* (see Beatles, Pictorials), this attractive and colorful book combines artwork from a variety of sources against text from Olinsky and The Talking Heads themselves. A miraculous visual accomplishment, though the writing is amateurish and often embarrassing, as demonstrated in the following excerpt from "The Big Country": "GOO GOO GA GA GA, GOO GOO GA GA GA." Gag.

OTHER TITLES OF INTEREST
Byrne, David. *Stay Up Late*. New York: Viking Children's, 1987.

THE TEARDROP EXPLODES

See Echo and the Bunnymen.

TEARS FOR FEARS

OTHER TITLES OF INTEREST
Hall, Will. *Tears for Fears...Tears from the Big Chair*. Milwaukee, WI: Hal Leonard, 1986.
Kamin, Philip. *Tears for Fears*. Milwaukee, WI: Hal Leonard, 1985.

TOMMY TEDESCO

AUTOBIOGRAPHY

Tedesco, Tommy. *Tommy Tedesco: Confessions of a Guitar Player*. Fullerton, CA: Centerstream Publishing, 1993. 104 pages. Approximately 75 black-and-white photographs throughout.

One of the most recorded and revered of all studio guitarists, Tommy Tedesco has had a long career in the music industry, spanning TV, session work, movies, and live performances. He played guitar on episodes of "The Waltons," for the film soundtrack to *Naked Gun 2 1/2*, and on The Beach Boys' "Good Vibrations." Tedesco tells his life story from Niagara Falls to California, describing his early days during the Big Band era. This sloppily assembled volume tacks on some self-propagandizing articles in the back and an ill-prepared question-and-answer dialog with the author. Tedesco fared much better with his instructional book (see Written Works, below).

WRITTEN WORKS

Tedesco, Tommy. Foreword by Shelley Manne. *For Guitar Players Only: Short Cuts in Technique, Sight Reading and Studio Playing*. Westlake Village, CA: Dale Zdenek Publications (division of Lyndale Corporation), 1979. 116 pages. Musical Index.

Notable jazz and rock guitarist Tommy Tedesco—known for his work with The Beach Boys, Wayne Newton, The Supremes, and many others—divulges his secrets of guitar playing. His advice is cogent and valuable: "Don't be overbearing and cocky [to other players] "; "If you are practicing reading and get tired, stop and take a rest"; "Don't make fun of any style"; etc. His instructions on picking, scales, sight reading, and working as a studio player are immensely practical. As the subtitle says: for serious pickers only.

THE TEMPTATIONS

AUTOBIOGRAPHY

Williams, Otis with Romanowski, Patricia. *Temptations*. New York: Fireside (Simon and Schuster), 1989. 240 pages. Two glossy eight-page black-and-white photo inserts. Temptations Singles Discography. Temptations Album Discography. Top 10 Otis'isms.

The founder of The Temptations tells his story with the help of veteran writer Romanowski. Williams was born to a 16-year-old unwed mother in Texarkana; the family's move to Detroit proved to be a relief for the child, who had faced some racism in the South. Williams met up with the right man at the right time— Berry Gordy—and also had the benefit of learning the ropes from the likes of Smokey Robinson, who wrote and produced some of The Temptations' best known hits (e.g., "My Girl"). Williams tells of his affairs with singers Florence Ballard and Patti LaBelle, as well as inner squabbles in his group that led to the ousting of singers Elbridge Bryant and Eddie Kendricks, but the stories lack necessary tension and build-up; we never get to know any of his partners up-close. "...Williams writes as a man who is proud of having kept it [the group] alive for so long."—*Publishers Weekly*.

10,000 MANIACS

PICTORIALS

No author. *10,000 Maniacs*. London: Omnibus Press (division of Book Sales Limited), 1990.

33 pages. Approximately 35 black-and-white and 20 color tinted illustrations throughout. Discography.

Unfolding like a map of Jamestown, New York—from whence 10,000 Maniacs came—this vaguely constructed compilation of pictures and text (in various typefaces and sizes) is a New Wave album unto itself. The book, copyright in the band's name, is crammed with photos of them playing live—and just playing around in general. It also contains a unique group history, background on the *Secrets of the I Ching* LP, and even some postcards stuck in the middle. The discography also lists two songbooks and the band's video. Middling.

THEM

See Morrison, Van.

THIN LIZZY

BIOGRAPHIES

Putterford, Mark. *Philip Lynott: The Rocker*. Chessington, Surrey (England): Castle Communications, 1994. 308 pages. One glossy 16-page color and black-and-white photo insert.

"The story of a cowboy's life" is yet another tale of a rock casualty. Born in Dublin, Ireland, Philip Lynott—whose first band was The Black Eagles—fronted Thin Lizzy for years, and became one of the true guitar heroes of the 1980's—if not the best known black player since Hendrix. At 36 years of age, however, Lynott died for reasons related to his chronic heroin addiction. Putterford's book contains some good firsthand quotes and much detail on Thin Lizzy's interaction with bands such as Queen (with whom Lynott feuded), but there isn't all that much real storytelling here. The chapter titled "A Little Black Boy" is sure to offend P.C. readers. "*The Rocker* was obviously written with a real love for Lynott..."—*Vox*.

PICTORIALS

Welch, Chris. *Gary Moore*. London: Bobcat Books (division of Book Sales, Limited), 1986. 48 pages. Approximately 65 black-and-white and color illustrations, covering every page. Selective Discography.

Moore, the guitar hero who was inspired by the likes of Jeff Beck and Eric Clapton, was born in Belfast, Ireland. After years of flunking out with Skid Row and his own band, Moore met up with Phil Lynott of Thin Lizzy and the group had stellar success in the mid-1970's with songs such as "Whisky in the Jar." Once he had a following, Moore went out on his own, producing albums with The Greg Lake Band and The Gary Moore Band. Some dynamic guitar photos are barely supported with information about Moore's personal life and career. Less, not Moore.

OTHER TITLES OF INTEREST

Lynott, Phil. *A [The] Collected Works of Philip Lynott*. London: Chappell, 1978.

THOMPSON TWINS

PICTORIALS

Hizer, Bruno. *Thompson Twins*. New York and London: Proteus Publishing Company, 1984. 32 pages. Approximately 40 color and black-and-white photographs, covering every page. Discography.

Giddy, ultra-pop rendering of the Thompson Twins' rise. The book should have been subtitled "ode to hair gel," since that's the most unified fashion statement here. It's a weird circumstance when a group has nearly 30 singles and only four albums, but the Thompson Twins were that kind of band. More aesthetic than Rouse's work (see below), but even less informative.

Rouse, Rose. *The Thompson Twins: An Odd Couple*. Wauwatosa, WI: Robus Books, 1985. 128 pages. Approximately 100 black-and-white photographs throughout; two eight-page color inserts. Discography. Index.

This is a case where the publisher seems to have been trying too hard with too little. After a beautiful rose cover image, the opening pages present several grainy black-and-white images that are simply horrific. Despite the book's many black-and-white photographs and two color inserts, what catches the eye are the visually unpleasant line drawings, predominately of the Thompson Twins' three heads (yes, the "twins" were a threesome) and a globe with uncertain meaning. Rose Rouse tries her best to provide history of the Sheffield, England music scene, while at the same time supplying quotes from those who knew the trio as kids, questions-and-answers, and more. A mixed bag.

QUIZBOOKS AND QUOTEBOOKS

No author. *Thompson Twins: In Their Own Words*. London: Omnibus Press, 1984. Unpaginated (approximately 32 pages). Approximately 40 color photographs, covering every page. Comes with full-color poster.

Pictures and quotes (printed rather small) on the group, with nothing in the way of biography or career highlights. The only revelation comes from musician (and now former band member) Joe Leeway, who is quoted saying, "We're more a bunch of misfits who happen to work well together." Will not exactly make you long for the 1980's.

THREE DOG NIGHT

AUTOBIOGRAPHY

Greenspoon, Jimmy with Bego, Mark. *One Is the Loneliest Number: On the Road and Behind the Scenes with the Legendary Rock Band Three Dog Night*. New York: Pharos Books, 1991. 322 pages. One 16-page black-and-white photo insert. Discography.

Jimmy Greenspoon, keyboardist of Three Dog Night, was a 20-year drug and alcohol addict who barely survived to tell his story. Greenspoon had quite a reputation for his cocaine habits, and it wasn't until one near-death experience (he was actually without a heartbeat for a minute) that he managed to turn his life around. Greenspoon's mother, part-Cherokee actress Mary Thompson, was a player at Mack Sennett and Hal Roach Studios and appeared in both silent and talkie films. Young Greenspoon developed a taste for drugs, sex, and rock and roll, learning early on that each of the three fed on the other two. These tales of all-night drug and sex orgies, musical jams, stadium-filled tours, and legendary recording sessions are recommended for those interested in this popular band from the late 1960's and early 70's; others may see Greenspoon as too much of a side player and not worth the angst.

THREE DOG NIGHT FRIENDS AND FAMILY

Cohen, Joel with Payne, Harold. *Three Dog Night and Me.* Los Angeles: Open Horizons, 1971. 184 pages. Approximately 50 black-and-white photographs throughout.

Joel Cohen, Three Dog Night's former road manager, conveys the behind-the-scenes intrigues of the group during its first year in existence. Cohen's observations of life on the road with Three Dog Night are intriguing; he is on target whether describing what the guys ate in the dressing room or how they interacted with their female fans. A dozen pages into the book, Cohen traces back to the childhoods of Danny Hutton, Cory Wells, and Chuck Negron, which includes some cute boyish shots (Wells on a pony) and details of Hutton's early days touring with Sonny and Cher. Impossibly dated and failing to include much-needed chapter titles for direction, this is off-the-beaten-track for most people, but indispensible for fans.

TINY TIM

BIOGRAPHIES

Stein, Harry. *Tiny Tim.* Chicago, IL: Playboy Press, 1976. 244 pages. One glossy eight-page black-and-white photo insert.

Would any rock compendium be complete without a reference to Tiny Tim? This very strange performer, who played ukelele, sang "Tip Toe Through the Tulips," and recorded cover versions of Beatles songs, somehow managed to garner attention as a pop culture figure. According to author Harry Stein, all of Tiny's eccentricities are true: he showers four times a day in his private bathroom; he will not eat in front of other people; and he has a genuine fear of people. This is a well-written but trivial book only suited to those who have

fond memories of Tiny's wedding to Miss Vicki on "The Tonight Show."

PETE TOWNSHEND

(See also Who, The)

WRITTEN WORKS

Townshend, Pete. *Horse's Neck.* New York: Harper & Row, 1986. 140 pages.

The poems and prose collected here, written between 1979 and 1985, might take Townshend fans by surprise. While some of the works contain reflections of childhood (à la *Tommy*), there is nothing of the rebelliousness or anger characteristic of the composer's classic songs and album concepts. The only vague reference to The Who is in a description of a disco ("flashing trash lamps" from "Goodbye Sister Disco"). This should not in any way hinder the vicarious pleasure some might get from reading these bizarre allegorical pieces. "Champagne on the Terraces" tells of alcoholism and lost love; "Winston" is a short story about a party coincidentally taking place one year after the anniversary of John Lennon's assassination; and "Laguna, Valentine's Day 1982" consummates the odd sexual imagery of horses that pervades the other passages. (Townshend has no doubt seen the play *Equus.*) "...intriguing experimental writing packed with vivid imagery"—*Library Journal.*

Townshend, Pete. *The Who's Tommy.* New York: Pantheon, 1993. 176 pages. Approximately 200 color and black-and-white photographs throughout. Comes with a CD.

At once thrilling and magnificent, this companion to Townshend's smash-hit stage musical is boosted by a first-rate history of the work by Ira Robins, the complete playscript (with lyrics), and numerous stage and behind-the-scenes photos. Not nearly as collage-like or as busy as Barnes and Townshend's document of the Ken Russell film (see Who, The: Written Works), this book is superior in every other way, especially attractiveness. The back of the book contains a history of the rock musical by Frank Rich and a piece on what went into the production by Rita D. Jacobs. The CD includes the single "I Believe My Own Eyes." If fans could only choose one Who book it would be a toss-up between this and Marsh's work (see Who, The: Biographies); fortunately, one doesn't have to make that decision.

TRAFFIC

See: Winwood, Steve.

T.REX

See: Bolan, Marc.

THE TROGGS

FANZINES AND FAN CLUBS

Trogg Times. c/o Jacqueline Ryan, 56 Waite Davies Road, Lee, London SE12 OND England.

A 24-page pamphlet containing reprints of newspaper articles, photocopies of black-and-white photos, "Trogglodynamite" (news), "Gig Guide" (concert information), reviews, collectibles and more. Published four times a year. The cost is $20 in the U.S.; £6 in the U.K.; and £9.50 elsewhere in Europe.

TINA TURNER

AUTOBIOGRAPHY

Turner, Tina with Loder, Kurt. *I, Tina: My Life Story*. New York: Avon, 1986. 268 pages. One 16-page black-and-white photo insert. Appendix A: Cast of Characters. Appendix B: Tina Turner's Greatest Hits.

This likable book mixes explanatory matter (probably by Loder) with quotes from musicians, friends, relatives, and, of course, Tina herself. *I, Tina* seems to intentionally avoid divulging Tina's personal feelings toward sex, rock and roll, songs, influence, fame, etc. However, we do get a shocking sense of the extent of torture she underwent at the hands (and shoes) of her deranged ex-husband and

producer, Ike. Tina Turner's stamina shines through: Somehow she kept drug and alcohol-free throughout her years of suffering. The story ends rather abruptly with her triumphant *Private Dancer* LP and the film *Mad Max: Beyond Thunderdome*; we are not told about whatever became of Ike (arrests for drug arrests and telephone fraud). Adapted to the hit 1993 film *What's Love Got to Do With It*. "...high-powered, sexy, honest..."—*Library Journal*.

BIOGRAPHIES

Ivory, Steven. *Tina!*. New York: Perigee (The Putnam Publishing Company), 1985. 192 pages. One 16-page black-and-white photo insert. Discography.

Mass-market biography of Turner that highlights her incredible comeback in the early 1980's and Grammy victory. Ivory enjoys showing how Turner had a mesmerizing effect on male stars. Gregory Peck, of all people, was so taken by her at the Grammys that he asked her to accompany him to the Oscars. (She turned him down.) Ivory tells Turner's story well, though cursorily, and confronts Ike and Tina's stormy relationship head-on. Reliable only up to the mid-1980's.

Mills, Bart. *Tina*. London: New English Library, 1985. 128 pages. One glossy eight-page black-and-white photo insert. Selected Discography. Filmography.

British mass-market book with a sizzling, sweaty image of Tina on the cover and not much else to its credit. Uninformed and underwritten, this book doesn't skim the surface of the abuse Turner suffered at the hand of Ike, limiting it down to four words: "So Ike hit her." Author Bart Mills also glosses over her spiritual side, relying heavily on magazine copy. Easily replaced by Tina's autobiography (see above).

FANZINES AND FAN CLUBS

Simply the Best: Tina Turner Fan Club. Att. Mark Lairmore, 4566 S. Park Avenue, Springfield, MO 65810.

Founded in 1990, this fan club issues a newsletter four times a year covering the latest news about the star, including releases, performances, appearances, and more. All members of the club are invited to the annual Tina Turner Day in her hometown, Nutbush, Tennessee. The cost of membership is $8 for one year.

PICTORIALS

Welch, Chris. *The Tina Turner Experience*. London: Virgin, 1994. 224 pages. Approximately 75 black-and-white photographs throughout; one glossy eight-page black-and-white photo insert. Discography.

Basic biography of Tina Turner that was first published in 1986 as *Take You Higher: The Tina Turner Experience* (W.H. Allen). The book is truly odd in that it updates her performances in 1993, but doesn't mention her autobiography or the subsequent hit movie. Amidst some fine black-and-white photos and a terrific color insert (although it is hard to go wrong photographing Tina Turner) is the author's rendering of her story, from her childhood, to her meeting Ike Turner in a St. Louis club, to their partnership, years on the road, her work with Phil Spector, and late 1980's comeback. Sparsely detailed, although fans will have trouble resisting it.

Wynn, Ron. *Tina: The Tina Turner Story*. New York: Macmillan Publishing Company, 1985. 158 pages. Approximately 100 black-and-white photographs throughout; one glossy eight-page black-and-white photo insert. Discography.

Photo tribute to Tina that seems written for a young audience. Tina shakes, rattles, shimmies, and rolls through these hundred or so photos that make one want to flip on one of her videos. Wynn's prose dodges around meaning, and he quotes extensively from Dave Marsh, which leaves readers realizing he doesn't have all that much to say. Turner deserves an all-out, expensive glossy color photo book; until that comes along, the most devout fans will have to settle for this imperfect work. "Worth acquiring only for the photos..."—*Library Journal*.

YOUNG ADULT

Koenig, Teresa. Edited by Shroeder, Dr. Howard. *Tina Turner*. Mankato: Crestwood House, 1986. 32 pages. Approximately 12 color and black-and-white photographs throughout.

An affectionate contribution to Crestwood's "Center Stage" series. Koenig's writing is lucid and candid: Ike's abuse of Tina is cleverly mentioned and then sidestepped. She treats the star as just an ordinary gal who happens to have a lot of charisma on stage. However, only one of the photos shows Turner before her shaggy hair days, which is a serious loss to those fans who don't know what she looked like in the 1960's.

OTHER TITLES OF INTEREST
Busnar, Gene. *The Picture Life of Tina Turner*. New York: Franklin Watts, 1987.
Fissinger, Laura. *Tina Turner*. New York: Ballantine, 1985.
Kamin, Philip *Tina Turner*. Milwaukee, WI: Hal Leonard, 1985.
Mabery, D.L. *Tina Turner*. Minneapolis, MN: Lerner, 1986.

TWISTED SISTER

WRITTEN WORKS

Snider, Dee and Bashe, Philip. *Dee Snider's Teenage Survival Guide*. New York: Dolphin (Doubleday & Company, Inc.), 1987. 260 pages. Bibliography.

Otherwise known as *How to Be a Legend in Your Own Lunchtime*, this is a congenial common-sense advice-column from Twisted Sister's lead singer, Dee Snider. All of the basic teen problems are covered here—coping with drugs, alcohol, sex, skin problems, siblings, parents, school, etc. Snider's underlying theme is teenage self-confidence and being happy with what you've got. He himself proclaims to have been a major nerd while growing up in Baldwin, New York and look at him now (or back then)—he's financially successful, he's rocking and rolling, he has a family, and he's drug free. The hair and makeup aside, even my grandmother would see him as a suitable role model. The writing is authoritative and is enlivened by Snider's colorful and witty interjections. ("Don't thank me—I'm being paid," he writes in his introduction.) "Snider touches on most of the major concerns of today's teenagers, and his personal memories are refreshingly unaffected."—*Booklist*.

OTHER TITLES OF INTEREST
Goldstein, Toby. *Twisted Sister*. New York: Ballantine, 1986.

2 LIVE CREW

WRITTEN WORKS

Campbell, Luther & Miller, John R. *As Nasty As They Wanna Be: The Uncensored Story of Luther Campbell of the 2 Live Crew*. Fort Lee, NJ: Barricade Books, 1992. 244 pages. One eight-page glossy black-and-white photo insert.

In 1990, 2 Live Crew's song "As Nasty As They Wanna Be" was put on trial in Florida court for obscenity. Luther Campbell, the group's star, battled the charges, won the first round, and released this book documenting the fiasco. After Campbell briefly tells about his rebellious childhood in Miami Beach, Florida and how he single-handedly turned himself into the "King of Dirty Rap" (a history that buries the other members of 2 Live Crew), co-author John R. Miller plunges into a vulgar chapter about a sex-crazed groupie who does just about anything to please her musicians. Subsequent chapters contain court transcriptions and, for some quick thrills, lyrics to several songs. Objectively speaking, grade school kids could write comparable dirty song lyrics—and with funnier results. For the bathroom walls.

U2

BIOGRAPHIES

Carter, Alan. *Outside is America: U2 in the U.S.*. Boston and London: Faber and Faber, 1992. 248 pages. Two eight-page glossy black-and-white photo inserts. Appendix 1: The Peace Museum. Appendix 2: Amnesty International. Appendix 3: American Discography and Videography. Appendix 4: American U2 Fanzine List Sources.

A comprehensive study of the circumstances under which U2 began to make its claim to fame in the United States, beginning in the 1980's. Despite starting out as a warm-up band act in small clubs, U2 rose to the top of the music scene in more ways than one can fathom. Alan Carter, a Boston radio music commentator, has a unique DJ's perspective on U2, and does an excellent job tracing how the polit-

ically and socially active Irish band made it in the U.S. While not a tourbook per sé, this is nonetheless valuable for those interested in the development of U2 as a live act.

Dunphy, Eamon. *Unforgettable Fire: The Definitive Biography of U2*. New York: Warner, 1987. 320 pages. Two glossy 16-page black-and-white photo inserts. (First published in Great Britain in 1987 by Viking Penguin.)

Early British biography of U2 that claims to have had some measure of involvement with Bono and company. This isn't a Bono-only tell-all, however; separate chapters are devoted to the backgrounds of Adam Clayton, Larry Mullen Jr., and Edge (Dave Evan) as well, and all seem to be elaborately detailed. The book succeeds best in showing how the group came to mesh over the years, blossoming in the wake of punk's decline. The final chapter is by John Waters, who deciphers the question: "Is U2 as big as The Beatles?" *Publishers Weekly* groaned that the author "...focuses too much on the band members and not enough on their musical message." Fans looking for the former will not be disappointed; others may want to give *U2: The Rolling Stone Files* (see Critical/Analytical Commentary, below) a try.

Seal, Richard. *U2: The Story So Far*. London: Britannia Press Publishing, 1993. 128 pages. One four-page glossy black-and-white photo insert. British Discography. British Videos. Other U2 Contributions. Rarities. Witticisms.

Static, Euro-centric biography of U2. This book lacks the detail and background supplied in the other biographies listed herein, and also suffers by way of illustrative material. Author Richard Seal's sentences ramble on and don't seem to lead anywhere. The 30 pages of back material only cover British releases, although on the positive side he does annotate his lists of rarities with estimated value and explanation. The two closing pages of Bono's witticisms are a bad joke: "If I start talking about drugs I'm going to have to have every custom official up my bum every time I come into the country." John Lennon he isn't.

CRITICAL/ANALYTICAL COMMENTARY

Bowler, Dave and Dray, Bryan. *U2: A Conspiracy of Hope*. London: Sidgwick & Jackson, 1993. 326 pages. One glossy eight-page black-and-white photo insert. U2 Discography. Sources. Index.

A well-intended, but ultimately snobby and affected interpretation of U2's overall importance. Borrowing the pretentious title from Amnesty International, Bowler and Dray take the opportunity to investigate whether or not it is feasible for a rock group to be involved in political and social causes. The authors convey some biographical detail—how U2 evolved from a garage band doing covers of Bay City Rollers tunes to an internationally celebrated success—but the primary message is that U2 is a tight quartet of patriots fighting for human liberty. The writers' over-pontificating about the hedonism of the Reagan era and MTV will get on your nerves midway. Dreary.

Editors of *Rolling Stone*. Foreword by Elysa Gardner. *U2: The Rolling Stone Files*. New York: Hyperion, 1994. 226 pages. Discography. Videography.

"The ultimate compendium of interviews, articles, facts & opinions" amasses dozens of *Rolling Stone* articles and miscellany on U2 spanning 1981-1993. Among the in-depth interviews, reviews, and news stories are James Henke's "U2: Here Come the Next Big Thing," David Fricke's "Caravan for Human Rights," and Jimmy Guterman's "Performance Review" (of the September 14, 1987 Giants Stadium concert). Among the other contributors are Kurt Loder, Jon Pareles, Steve Pond, and Debra Rae Cohen. Appearing throughout is useful chart information spanning the aforementioned 12 years, including top 100 albums and singles. Essential for anyone researching "the band of the 80's."

Flanagan, Bill. *U2: At the End of the World*. New York: Delacorte (Bantam Doubleday Dell), 1995. 536 pages. One glossy 16-page black-and-white photo insert. Index.

Lengthy critical overview of U2's career, utilizing the band's excitement over the falling of the Berlin Wall. Author Bill Flanagan observes how the critics maligned U2 for coming off as egotistical and self-indulgent in the film *Rattle and Hum*, a situation he says Bono brought upon himself. Flanagan attempts to create a whole picture of how Bono composes songs, rehearses with the group, and stages a show, yet these summaries—mixed with stories about the band's involvement in human rights

issues—stray so far off course on so many occasions we're never really sure what he's aiming at. Other works are better unified.

FILM

Williams, Peter and Turner, Steven. *U2: Rattle and Hum: The Official Book of the U2 Movie*. London: Pyramid Books (Octopus Publishing Company), 1988. 96 pages. Approximately 125 color and black-and-white photographs throughout. Discography.

Companion to the film *Rattle and Hum*, with photographs of the band on the road in Dublin and across the United States. Throughout the book are lyrics to songs performed on the tour ("Helter Skelter") and many photos of the band onstage, but really it's not much different from any other pictorial history. The distinction is that a few pages are devoted to the film and concert crew—who, though they obviously deserve credit, aren't very interesting. The book contains a fair blend of black-and-white and color images and some fine attention to Bono's influences, such as John Lennon and B.B. King, but this treatment is mostly "ho" and "hum."

IRELAND

Prendergast, Mark J. *The Isle of Noises*. New York: St. Martin's, 1987. 316 pages. 145 black-and-white illustrations throughout. Selective Index. (First published in Ireland by The O'Brien Press Limited.)

Prendergast, a black rock journalist of Irish and North African descent, reflects on the unique heritage and tradition of Irish popular music. While few Irish bands made the big time in the 1960's (notably, The King Bees and Them), the 1970's brought forth Thin Lizzy (featuring Phil Lynott) and The Boomtown Rats (with Bob Geldof); the 1980's saw U2 climb to the top of the music world; and the 1990's have Sinéad O'Connor. Prendergast sifts through a tremendous amount of history and information, but is not dull for a minute. He voices as much enthusiasm for Celtic sounds as he does American rhythm and blues, and sheds light on heretofore neglected Irish groups. Highly recommended.

PICTORIALS

Fallon, BP. *U2: Faraway So Close*. London: Virgin, 1995. Unpaginated (approximately 128 pages). Approximately 200 color and black-and-white photographs, covering every page.

BP (yes, with no periods) Fallon, teaming with designer Steve Averill (who designed all of U2's album sleeves up to that time), has produced the wildest, most exhilarating tribute to U2 yet produced. Unlike other works that focus only on glossy shots of Bono, this book highlights Adam Clayton, Larry Mullen Jr., and Edge with equal flair. From the backstreets of Dublin to the band in studio, this hectic document combines swirling designs, fabulous rare photographs, and many quotes from Bono and other players. Several pages boast the genius of photographer Annie Leibovitz. With the style of the best fanzine—and more value for the money with anecdotes involving the likes of Eddie Vedder and Keith Richards—this excellent pictorial should be kept on or close to the coffee table. "It really rankles to recommend a U2 book, but *Faraway So Close* actually goes way beyond U2."—*Alternative Press*.

Goodman, Sam. *U2: Burning Desire: The Complete U2 Story*. Chessington, England: Castle Communications, Inc., 1993. 224 pages. Approximately 150 black-and-white and color illustrations throughout. Discography.

A magnificent design, hundreds of dynamic photos and numerous moody motif graphics don't classify this as "the complete story" of the band. Readers are advised to ignore the superficial fanzine copy and scan the excellent images explicitly of U2—sans fans, roadies, wives, and groupies. The photos, mostly taken during concert performances, have been neatly cropped and are set against black backgrounds. Bono appears as a cool, hip rocker throughout.

Graham, Bill. *The Complete Guide to the Music of U2*. London: Omnibus Press (division of Book Sales Limited), 1995. 118 pages. Approximately 100 color and black-and-white photographs throughout.

CD-format book covering all aspects of U2's career. Overlaps with Taylor's CD-format book (see below), but each offers something of different appeal: This has more photos, the other more informational back sections.

Graham, Bill. Photographs by Brocklebank, Patrick; Mahon, James; and McGuinness, Hugo. *U2: The Early Days*. New York: Dell Publishing (division of Bantam Doubleday Dell Publishing Group, Inc.), 1989. 96 pages. Approximately 100 black-and-white photographs, covering every page. (First published in Great Britain in 1989 by Octopus Publishing Group.)

The teenagers captured here in black-and-white are dressed in leather and aspire to conquer the world—or at least get their first recording contract. These photos of U2 in their Irish homeland up through the release of their first LP, *Boy*, are certainly of historic value, but they don't reveal enough personality and expression to show why U2 had so much appeal later on. Only in a few shots does Bono have an intriguing, Morrison-like smirk and stage presence. Graham's text assumes the reader has expert knowledge about Ireland's post-punk rock scene. Ardent fans and biographers will find *The Early Days* essential; others will want something more expansive.

No author. *U2 Tear-Out Photo Book*. London: Oliver, 1993. Unpaginated (approximately 48 pages). Approximately 20 color and black-and-white photographs throughout.

This tear-out book might serve for young fans, especially females. A few of stylish shots of Bono are worthy of wall display, as are one or two group shots, notably those in black-and-white. Kids, have a blast.

Parkyn, Geoff. *U2: Touch the Flame: An Illustrated Documentary*. London: Omnibus (division of Book Sales Limited), 1987. 96 pages. 125 black-and-white and color illustrations, covering every page. Discography. Video Catalog. Gig Listing.

Generously illustrated early retrospective of the group, published at the same time as the release of *The Joshua Tree* LP. Most of the biographical details are conveyed in quotes lifted from unidentified media sources. The book contains chapters devoted to the band's 1980's festival appearances (Live Aid), which now only seems to point out the scarcity of such events in the 1990's. The chronologies in the margins are informative, but uneven in focus. "...boasts a marvelous collection of rare photographs..."—*Booklist*.

Scott, Tony. *U2 4 the People*. Port Chester, NY: Cherry Lane Books, 1985. 64 pages. Approximately 50 black-and-white photographs throughout; one glossy 16-page black-and-white photo insert.

Glossy mid-1980's photos book that is an instant reminder of how far these guys have come. At this point, the band hadn't yet released their masterpiece *The Joshua Tree* and Bono could still pass for a rebellious teen. The color insert contains some primitive performance shots, but fans would probably prefer Graham's work on the early years (see above).

Taylor, Mark. *U2*. Miami, FL: MBS, 1995. 120 pages. Approximately 75 color and black-and-white photographs throughout. Discography. Chronology. Index.

CD-format book covering all aspects of U2's career. This nicely designed and illustrated book is priced just right at around $7.99.

QUIZBOOKS AND QUOTEBOOKS

Charlesworth, Chris. *Bono: In His Own Words*. London: Omnibus Press (division of Book Sales Limited), 1989. 96 pages. 60 black-and-white photographs throughout.

One of the better "in his own words" presentations from Omnibus Press. Quotes are arranged within the following subject areas: the band; the albums; the shows; beginnings; the creed (a very oblique reference to who knows what). Through these snippets—which typically range from one line to three paragraphs—we gain some general insight into Bono's enigma and his thoughts on Ireland, fellow band members, rock icons, peacework, and other subjects. Like John Lennon (a musician Bono admires for his ability to express emotions through music), he is particularly biting on religion: "I think the church is a big problem."

TOURBOOKS

Parra, Pimm Jal de la. *U2 Live: A Concert Documentary*. London: Omnibus Press (division of Book Sales Limited), 1994. 176 pages. Approximately 170 black-and-white photographs, covering every page; one 16-page color insert. Discography.

A visual record of U2's 1,000 or so concerts, performed between 1976 and 1994. Parra is no stranger to U2 as a live act, having attended 47 shows in 11 countries. This book relies heavily on other works, but provides the needed information so neatly and concisely one can hardly complain. Parra identifies the date, city, venue, and attendance for every performance (where known), and presents a lively one-to-four paragraph description of the show. For several performances, Parra cites the support band name and the set list. Many people will be surprised by tidbits such as that U2 opened with "Gloria" for nearly two years. A solid reference for researchers that can be enjoyed by fans.

OTHER TITLES OF INTEREST
Brandt, Winston. *U2*. New York: Ballantine, 1985.
Negativland. *Fair Use: The Story of the Letter U & the Numeral 2*. Concord, CA: Seeland, 1995. *Book accompanying Negativland's CD that sifts through their battle with U2 over trademark and copyright infringement.*
Thomas, Dave. *Stories for Boys*. London: Omnibus Press (division of Book Sales Limited), 1990.
Waters, John. *Race of Angels: The Genesis of U2*. London: Fourth Estate, 1984.

RITCHIE VALENS

BIOGRAPHIES

Mendheim, Beverly. *Ritchie Valens: The First Latino Rocker*. 160 pages. Tempe: Bilingual Press/ Editorial Bilingue, 1987. Three eight-page black-and-white photo inserts. Bibliography. Discography.

Ritchie Valens was the first commercially recognized Latino rock and roller, but perhaps the last of the major 1950's hitmakers to be the subject of a life study. Beverly Mendheim is a fan of Valens' neglected compositions, and her analyses of them are the strength of this work. Having interviewed several people who worked with Valens (e.g., manager Bob Keane), Mendheim provides a few genuine surprises, such as that Valens was not fluent in Spanish. While it's hard to ignore the misspelling of Greil Marcus' name and several other errors, this book should serve until a genuine comprehensive biography surfaces. "She [Mendheim] concludes with an amateurish debunking, but appreciative prerelease review of the movie [*La Bamba*]."—*Booklist*.

LUTHER VANDROSS

FANZINES AND FAN CLUBS

The Luther Vandross Official International Fan Club.
P.O. Box 679, Branford, CT 06405.

Members of this club receive 8x10 photos (one color, the rest black-and-white), a biography, a membership card, merchandise offers, news updates, and more. The cost per year is $22 U.S. and Canada; $28 elsewhere.

VAN HALEN

FANZINES AND FAN CLUBS

The Inside: The International Van Halen Magazine.
784 N. 114 St. Suite 200, Omaha, NB 68154.

Quarterly, thirty-two-page glossy magazine with a color cover and never-before-published color and black-and-white photographs throughout. Includes letters from subscribers, reprinted interviews with various band members, flashback essays, updates on personal events for members, chart information, merchandising (t-shirts), and more. Subscribers also receive a band biography, two promotional photos, access to a tourline, bonus issues, and more. The cost per issue at newsstands is $4.95 U.S. and $5.95 Canada. The cost of subscription is $19.95 U.S (write for prices elsewhere).

PICTORIALS

Craven, Michelle. *Van Halen.* London and New York: Proteus Publishing Co., 1984. 32 pages. Approximately 40 color and black-and-white photographs, covering every page.

Grotesque photo book, consisting 75 percent of David Lee Roth's high kicks and bare chested poses. There is some detail on Eddie Van Halen, but next to nothing on Alex Van Halen and Michael Anthony. The cover image features Roth in mid-air with eyes closed and a bandage on his nose! Hideously designed and low on information, this book is an unfortunate reminder of the days when hard rock meant that men could wear leopard leotards.

Dome, Malcolm. *Van Halen: Excess All Areas.* Chessington, Surrey (England): Castle Communications, 1994. 144 pages. Approximately 75 color and black-and-white photographs throughout. Discography.

Some fine color photography is wasted in this uproariously bad story of the band. Ridiculous statements are on every page, including that without David Lee Roth "Van Halen were left with just musical talent." Is that intended as praise to the Sammy Hagar/Van Halen line-up or as an insult to Roth? The author's musical analyses are almost as dimwitted as his phraseology: "Brilliantly conceived and executed, it ["And the Cradle Will Rock"] actually sees Dave [Roth] sounding rather like Jimmy Durante, rather than a rock god. But it works, oh boy does it work." Back to the cradle.

Kamin, Philip and Goddard, Peter. *Van Halen.* New York: Beaufort Books, 1984. 128 pages. Approximately 125 color and black-and-white photographs, covering every page.

One of the better early photo books on the first incarnation of Van Halen—but that's not saying much. These obnoxious American dudes stomp, jump, hump, squat, leg-kick, pirouette, and fawn over themselves in well over a hundred photographs, each one making you think Roth in particular could have learned a thing or two from Martha Graham. (Although how many other guys can touch a knee to an ear while standing?) For fans of early 1980's *Creem* magazine.

No author. *The Van Halen Scrapbook.* Cresskill: Sharon Starbooks, 1984. 64 pages. Approximately 50 black-and-white photographs throughout; 14 pages of color.

"A collection of facts, photos, and interviews" that will only hold your attention if you're a fan of the original Halen lineup and need a pinup of Roth on your wall to annoy your folks. Laziness abounds here; the article on Alex Van Halen is a reprint of a shoddy *Tiger Beat* interview. Jump—out of the way.

Sherlaw, John. *Van Halen: Jumpin' for the Dollar.* Port Chester, NY: Cherry Lane, 1984. 96 pages. Approximately 100 black-and-white illustrations, covering nearly every page; six pages of color throughout.

Slipshod mix of factoids, photos, history, and quotes on the band that David Lee Roth once pompously claimed created the soundtrack of the 1980's (which they didn't; only U2 can perhaps lay claim to that role). Poorly written with information cribbed from then-prevalent metal mags, this book seems pleased with its shortcomings: "Within their own strictly defined parameters and their own self-created legend (of which this slim volume is merely an outline), Van Halen are as happy as pigs in shit."

YOUNG ADULT

Considine, J.D. *Van Halen!*. New York: Quill (division of William Morrow & Co.), 1985. 160 pages. Over 100 black-and-white photographs throughout. Appendix: Guitar Techniques. Discography.

Considine is honest about Van Halen's attributes and limitations, defining the group as a hard-edged rock band that doesn't use gimmickry, doesn't have a message, and whose members don't present themselves as visionaries à la Bob Dylan. These are guys who like to have fun, deafen your ears, and fight authority (teachers, parents, bosses, etc.) in a way with which any pimply air-guitar playing teen can relate. The guitar techniques in the back may be appreciated by young Eddie Van Halen worshippers. Optional for pre-Sammy Hagar fans.

Hedges, Dan. *Eddie Van Halen*. New York: Vintage (division of Random House), 1986. 140 pages. One 12-page black-and-white photo insert. Discography.

Part of the Vintage/*Musician* series, this installment is more of a homage to the guitar hero myth than it is the story of Eddie Van Halen. The book misses its mark by attempting to suck up to both the fan who plays air guitar in front of a mirror and the serious musician who wants to know the master's tricks of the trade. The author often sounds like a grandpappy talking about legends of the Old West, beginning sentences with verbal expressions such as "Problem was" and "Mind you." Enthusiastic, if nothing else.

Kaye, Annene. *Van Halen*. New York: Julian Messner (division of Simon & Schuster, Inc.), 1985. 64 pages. Approximately 40 black-and-white photographs scattered throughout. Fun Facts. Discography.

Miscellany of facts for the young fan that is

unavoidably dated, since David Lee Roth was the group's singer at press time. Still, the book does contain coverage of Eddie Van Halen and separate chapters on drummer Alex Van Halen, and bassist Michael Anthony. The author has limited knowledge of musical equipment and lingo. (The best she can say is that "Alex is serious about his drumming.") "Fun Facts" details "vital" things such as each musician's height, weight, nickname, and dog's name.

OTHER TITLES OF INTEREST

Kamin, Philip. *David Lee Roth*. Milwaukee, WI: Hal Leonard, 1985.

Kasbah, Mimi. *David Lee Roth: What a Guy*. New York: Ballantine, 1986.

Matthews, Gordon. *Van Halen*. New York: Ballantine, 1984.

VANILLA ICE

BIOGRAPHIES

Bego, Mark. *Ice Ice Ice*. New York: Dell (Bantam Doubleday Dell), 1991. 104 pages. One glossy 16-page black-and-white photo insert. The Vanilla Ice Discography. (Also known as *To the Extreme: Vanilla Ice Story*.)

With hits such as "Ice Ice Baby" and "Play That Funky Music," Vanilla Ice has become the top white rapper in the business—with mean moody stares and a dance act that makes Marky Mark look like Pee Wee Herman. Pop biographer Bego doesn't quite have the knack for rap jive, but it's not anything a young reader would notice. Born in Miami and raised in Carrolton Texas, Ice in his younger days was a competitive motocross racer and even a gang member. His activities in gangs led to his nearly being stabbed to death in a street clash. At the time of press, Bego was unable to find out details such as Ice's real name, which leads one to believe there isn't much more here than one can find in a *People* magazine article. Cold Cold Cold.

YOUNG ADULT

Krulik, Nancy E. *M.C. Hammer and Vanilla Ice*. See: M.C. Hammer.

OTHER TITLES OF INTEREST

Teitlebaum, Mike. *Vanilla Ice Poster Book*. No city: Kidsbooks, 1991.

Vanilla Ice. *Ice by Ice*. New York: Avon, 1991.

STEVIE RAY VAUGHAN

BIOGRAPHIES

Patoski, Joe Nick and Crawford, Bill. *Stevie Ray Vaughan: Caught in the Crossfire*. Boston and New York: Little, Brown and Company, 1993. 314 pages. Two eight-page black-and-white photo inserts. Notes. Discography. Collectors Tapeography. Index.

Leigh's book (see Pictorials, below) places Vaughan at the highest level of rock demigods; this title enriches readers with the story of a Texan who played one hell of a guitar (as did his idol, elder brother Jimmie). Patoski and Crawford have a good ear for dialect and scene-setting and, in fact, regale the reader with novelesque description. Their characterization of homely young Vaughan is poignant: "Stevie was all legs and arms, had a scrawny physique and a face dominated by a mashed nose, never mind the smile that revealed tiny teeth and small gums." While far less visually appealing than Leigh's book, this highly perceptive work demands a full read from cover to cover. "...this burrito supreme is a meaty read indeed."—*Creem*.

FANZINES AND FAN CLUBS

Stevie Ray Vaughan Fan Club. Attn. Lee Hopkins, P.O. Box 800353, Dallas, TX 75380.

Formed in early 1993, this club provides members with: a bulletin board for collectors to buy, sell or trade memorabilia; a discography, videography, and bibliography; notice of memorial concerts and events; support of Stevie Ray Vaughan charities; a quarterly newsletter containing interviews with people who knew Stevie Ray; a directory of club members; tours of Austin and Dallas sights; blues record reviews; and more. The cost of membership is $8 U.S.; $12 Canada and Mexico; and $16 elsewhere.

PICTORIALS

Leigh, Keri. Foreword by B.B. King. Introduction by Buddy Guy. *Stevie Ray: Soul to Soul*. Dallas, TX: Taylor Publishing Company, 1993. 186 pages. Approximately 125 black-and-white and color photographs throughout. Bibliography. Index.

Originally begun as a joint venture with Vaughan—who had artistic control over the project—this ended up being Keri Leigh's sole work after Vaughan's passing. Leigh determinedly tries to show this is a labor of love and not a hatchet job, but the supportive introductory messages from King *and* Guy speak for themselves. This glossy, illustrated biography creates a powerful overview of Vaughan's friendships and influences, elucidating just how beloved and respected the guitarist was among his contemporaries. As with many rockers who died, Vaughan also claimed to have visited his own funeral two days before his death. A reverent tribute.

SUZANNE VEGA

TITLES OF INTEREST

Vega, Suzanne. *Bullet in Flight*. London: Omnibus Press (division of Book Sales Limited), 1990.

THE VELVET UNDERGROUND

(See also Reed, Lou)

BIOGRAPHIES

Witts, Richard. *Nico: The Life & Lies of an Icon*. London: Virgin Books, 1993. 334 pages. One glossy eight-page black-and-white photo insert. Discography and Filmography. Index.

Nico, whose name conveniently unscrambles to spell "icon," is portrayed here as a chronic liar—or game player, deceiver, storyteller. On the other hand, author Richard Witts considers her a survivor, rather than a rock casualty. (She died in a mysterious biking accident, not directly attributed to heroin.) This magnificent, spectral figure, who drifted through a Fellini film, sang with The Velvet Underground, befriended Andy Warhol and bedded down both Jim Morrison and Brian Jones, influenced figures in folk, rock, and punk, but her presence only seems to have left smokescreens. Witts briefly knew the singer and delivers an exhaustive and revealing account of Nico's incredible life and legend, filling in all the non-junkie elements not in Young's work (see Velvet Underground Friends and Family, below). Highly recommended, especially if you've seen the film *Nico: Icon*.

GENERAL REFERENCE

Kostek, M.C. *The Velvet Underground Handbook.* London: Black Spring Press, 1992. 224 pages. Approximately 20 black-and-white photographs throughout. Appendices: I. A History of the First Album. II. Song Order. III. Bootlegs. IV. Post Velvet Underground Solo Discographies.

A total reference on The Velvet Underground, encompassing discography, cover songs, films, books, articles, and more. Author M.C. Kostek also provides a brief overview of the band and a timeline, which puts all of the members in perspective, both before and after the band's split. Listings for singles and EPs contain a wealth of information, such as catalog number, release date, running time, musicians (with instruments played), producer, cover artists, and notes about chart placement. The only sore point concerns whether release dates are U.S., U.K., or both. Otherwise, a highly intelligent and broad reference work that will prove useful for researchers and collectors alike.

PICTORIALS

Bockris, Victor and Melanga, Gerard. Introduction by Sterling Morrison. *Uptight[sic]: The Velvet Underground Story.* New York: Morrow, 1985. 128 pages. Approximately 150 black-and-white photographs, covering nearly every page. Discography. (First published in Great Britain in 1983 by Omnibus Press.)

The title comes from *Andy Warhol, Up-Tight*, a multimedia rock show in the mid-1960's that included the likes of The Velvet Underground, Paul Morrissey—and even the coauthor of this book, Gerard Melanga. Melanga and coauthor Bockris have spliced quotes from The Velvet Underground—predominately Sterling Morrison—and others, with filler text that brings the reader right into the happenings. You can even find out how The Beatles' man-

ager Brian Epstein almost managed The Velvet Underground. Lots of priceless photos throughout—especially of the famous Boston Tea Party—though a few too many good ones are hidden in the margins. Far from perfect, but thoroughly cool.

Clapton, Diana. *Lou Reed and the Velvet Underground.* London: Bobcat Books (division of Book Sales Limited), 1987. 128 pages. Approximately 75 black-and-white photographs throughout; eight pages of color. Discography. (First published in England in 1982 by Proteus Books.)

Whether you'll like Diana Clapton's photo-history of The Velvet Underground depends on whether you're looking for something on the band or one on Lou Reed with the band as supporting cast. This book is evidently the latter, devoting more than half of its pages to Lou's solo efforts. The organization is chronological by album release and the tone largely uncritical. Nico's enchanting face only appears in a couple of photos, so we're left suffering through Lou Reed glitter-rock shots—several with blonde hair and one in which he resembles Bowie as a drag queen—until we find a few in which the artist looks like the hip punkster the intellectual art and music world came to adore.

Shore, Stephen (photographs) and Tillman, Lynne (text). *The Velvet Years: The Warhol Factory 1965-67.* New York: Thunder's Mouth Press, 1996. 176 pages. Approximately 200 glossy black-and-white photographs throughout. Index.

Stunning collection of photos that brings us inside Andy Warhol's Factory on East 47th Street, where he fostered the talents of filmmakers, artists, photographers, and musicians. Shore's photos are incredible, depicting a surprisingly youthful view of The Velvet Underground members, who are cleaner and more subdued than one might imagine. Amidst reminiscences recounted by Lynne Tillman, there are black-and-white shots of Nico, John Cale, Sterling Morrison, and Lou Reed, as well as others in the Factory such as Warhol, Billy Name, Ultra Violet, and Ingrid Superstar. "...enigmatic, posed but casual portraits"—*New York Times*.

West, Mike. *The Velvet Underground and Lou Reed*. Manchester, England: Babylon Books, 1982. Unpaginated (approximately 64 pages). Approximately 50 black-and-white photographs throughout. Discography.

Amateurish, schlocky patchwork of data and photos on The Velvet Underground, devoting as much to discography and random newspaper articles as it does to actual biography. The book was first published as a special edition (publisher unknown), and it's uncertain why it was revised when it covers Lou Reed's solo career so sparsely. The photos are redundancies from several other sources. Not recommended.

QUIZBOOKS AND QUOTEBOOKS

Thomson, Dave. *Beyond the Velvet Underground*. London: Omnibus Press (division of Book Sales Limited), 1989. 96 pages. Approximately 75 black-and-white photographs throughout.

This book should have been part of Omnibus Press' "in their words" series. In other words, it's really a quotebook with sections on each musician and some very odd topics. The photos of Nico are disappointing, but her quotes are memorable: "...they [The Velvet Underground] wanted to get rid of me because I had more attention in the press..." For casual readers only.

RELATED WORKS

Leigh, Michael. Introduction by Louis Berg, M.D. *The Velvet Underground*. New York: Macfadden-Bartell Corporation, 1963. 176 pages.

A shocking, groundbreaking work when it was published in the early 1960's, this book was determined to show that even "normal," everyday people expressed their hidden lusts and alleged perversions. Full of orgies, wife-swapping, and other naughty stuff, this book may or may not have inspired the name of the famed group The Velvet Underground; in any event, at the very least it helped coin the term which became popular enough for use. Followed by an equally as lusty sequel (see below).

Leigh, Michael. Introduction by Louis Berg, M.D. *The Velvet Underground Revisited*. New York:

Macfadden-Bartell Corporation, 1968. 176 pages.

Sequel to Leigh's work from five years earlier (see above), which continues to report the kinky behind-the-scenes goings-on in America. This raunchy study is very tame by today's standards, detailing various acts of "furtive fornication" such as bondage, flagellation, pornography, and, of course, wife-swapping. Full of wacked-out case studies and letters (women, ducks, and vibrating bells: you get the picture) that may or may not have been made up by the author.

VELVET UNDERGROUND FRIENDS AND FAMILY

Young, James. *Nico: The End*. Woodstock: The Overlook Press, 1992. 208 pages. One glossy 16-page black-and-white photo insert. Nico Discography.

Nico began her career as Germany's leading fashion model, a blonde icy beauty. Her magnetic presence caught the eye of Federico Fellini (she appeared in *La Dolce Vita*), Andy Warhol, and Jim Morrison (The Doors' "The End" became one of her staples as a soloist). After her brief success as The Velvet Underground's chanteuse, she fell into a life of heroin and methadone, living from one shot to the next and drudging from one horrendous performance to another. Author James Young was Nico's keyboardist during her final tours and witnessed the decay of rock's grand duchess up close. A distasteful but "...well written black comedy."—*The New York Times Book Review*.

OTHER TITLES OF INTEREST

Trevena, Nigel. *Lou Reed & the Velvets*. Falmouth, Cornwall (England): Bantam, 1973.

Woronov, Mary. *Swimming Underground: My Years in the Warhol Factory*. No city: Journey Editions, 1996.
The story of Mary Woronov, singer, dancer, and active participant in the activities taking place in Andy Warhol's Factory. The New York Times Book Review *commented: "This Factory alumna offers few insights into the famous-for-being famous people around her."*

Zak. *The Velvet Underground Companion*. New York: Schirmer Books, 1997.

GENE VINCENT

BIOGRAPHIES

Hagarty, Britt. *The Day the World Turned Blue.* Vancouver, British Columbia (Canada): Talonbooks, 1983. 262 pages. Approximately 50 black-and-white photographs throughout.

The only complete biography of this early, dangerous rock and roller, *The Day the World Turned Blue* is an unsensationalized portrait of the man who pretty much experienced firsthand the life of Marlon Brando's character from *The Wild One*. Perhaps more than any other 1950's rocker, he lived and breathed his unique style: greasy wild hair, biker's leather, and a reputation for drinking rivaled only by Jim Morrison (who later became his guzzling partner). Author Britt Hagarty tells of Vincent's delinquent childhood, Navy stint, and traumatic accident in which a car ran a red light and permanently injured his right leg. Despite the trauma and subsequent osteomyelitis, Vincent became one of rock's true icons with "Be-Bop-a-Lula." Vincent's chart success didn't spill over to the 1960's, but he never sold out like Elvis and died with his image intact. This work is not exhaustive, but will serve until something more expansive comes along. "...rekindles the fire of a tortured rock legend..."—*Publishers Weekly*.

DISCOGRAPHIES, RECORDING GUIDES, AND COLLECTIBLES

Henderson, Derek. *Gene Vincent: A Discography.* Southampton, Hants (England): Spent Brother Productions, 1992. 50 pages. Five black-and-white photographs throughout.

British vanity press discography listing sessions, live recordings, singles, EPs, LPs, and CDs. Coverage includes both U.S. and U.K. releases, but the book itself looks like it was published in the 1970's when it was actually issued in 1992. Author Derek Henderson lists labels, catalog numbers and musician line-ups, yet provides very little annotation; even composers are not identified. A flawed eyesore that will have to serve, since it's the only work of its kind available.

BOBBY VINTON

FANZINES AND FAN CLUBS

The Bobby Vinton International Fan Club. 153 Washington Street, Mt. Vernon, NY 10550-3541.

In existence since 1962, this durable club offers a membership card, a button, glossy black-and-white snapshots of Vinton, a biographical pamphlet, a brief newsletter, a packet of news clippings, and a letter from the man himself. The cost of membership is $6 plus seven stamps.

OTHER TITLES OF INTEREST
Vinton, Bobby with Burger, Robert E. *The Polish Prince.* New York: M. Evans, 1978.

TOM WAITS

BIOGRAPHIES

Humphries, Patrick. *Small Change: A Life of Tom Waits.* New York: St. Martin's Press, 1990. 144 pages. Two eight-page black-and-white photo inserts. Discography. (First published in 1990 in England by Omnibus Press.)

The first biography of singer, composer, and actor Tom Waits. Influenced by Jack Kerouac and the Beat Generation, Waits spent much of his life on the road in the 1960's, and it was only in the middle of the decade he took on various jobs ranging from dishwasher to fireman. Turning to music by the early 1970's, Waits' career paralleled that of Bruce Springsteen; while the Boss plays to larger audiences (except for a few unannounced Jersey time-outs) and sells more records, Waits' lyrical treatment of hoboes, vagrants, and rebels has proven more authentic. An insightful and direct biography, unfortunately marred by bold typeface.

THE WALKER BROTHERS

BIOGRAPHIES

Watkinson, Mike and Anderson, Pete. *Scott Walker: A Deep Shade of Blue.* London: Virgin, 1994. 288 pages. One glossy eight-page black-and-white photo insert. Discography. Sources. Index.

The first and only biography of Scott Walker (formerly Engel), the lead singer of The Walker Brothers. Who were The Walker Brothers, you ask? An American comprised band that actually formed in England, The Walker Brothers had hits in the 1960's with "Make It Easy on Yourself" and "The Sun Ain't Gonna Shine Anymore." Although something of a sensation in the U.K., the band never quite captured the U.S. and ended up fading into oblivion, outside of a 1975 reunion and some solo projects from Scott Walker himself. According to the authors, the Walkers influenced a range of artists such as Marc Almond and Bono, but it's doubtful that will make a difference to American book buyers. Further narrowing the appeal is its emphasis on Scott Walker, as opposed to the original band. Only for those with special interest in The Walker Brothers.

DIONNE WARWICK

FANZINES AND FAN CLUBS

Dionne Warwick Fan Club. P.O. Box 343, Wind Gap, PA 18091.

Operating since 1985, this fan club claims authorization by Dionne Warwick herself. The kit includes a membership card, a biography packet, Warwick's recipes, a discography sheet, Warwick's charity list, a bumper sticker, and a glossy 8x10 black-and-white photograph. Also offers a stapled 14-page newsletter reporting on her musical and professional ventures, from CD releases to her perfume. It also includes reprints of newspaper articles, concert itineraries, classifieds, articles from members, and more. The cost of membership is $20 per year ($10 for renewal), payable by check or money order; $22 everywhere else.

MUDDY WATERS

BIOGRAPHIES

Rooney, James. *Bossmen: Bill Monroe and Muddy Waters.* New York: Da Capo, 1991. 160 pages. 50 black-and-white photographs throughout.

Dual biography of Bill Monroe and Muddy Waters that compares and contrasts their roots, influences, and musical careers. First published in 1970, this enriching book shows how these fine musicians hailed from rural backgrounds and shared a love of music. (For Monroe, the leaning was toward bluegrass and country; for Waters, it was urban blues.) Beginning with a concise discography of each (that should have been expanded and placed at the end of the book), Rooney conveys to the reader both men's stories through their own words and a wealth of period photographs. A book that truly shows how great music can transcend racial and ethnic differences.

THE WEAVERS

(See also Seeger, Pete)

BIOGRAPHIES

Willens, Doris. *Lonesome Traveler: The Life of Lee Hays.* New York: W.W. Norton, 1988. 282 pages. Approximately 25 black-and-white photographs throughout. Notes. Index.

Searing biography of Lee Hays, one of the powerful voices of The Weavers, along with Pete Seeger, Ronnie Gilbert, and Fred Hillerman. (Seeger left the group in 1958 for a solo career.) What many people don't realize is that Hays cowrote "If I Had a Hammer" with Seeger, and that he and The Weavers were the forerunners of the politically active folkies of the 1960's. The Weavers became a government target and were blacklisted, which seriously hindered their recording and performance success. Hays, who hailed from various towns in Arkansas, is a crucial if not overlooked figure in 20th century music and this book—unfortunately sans discography—does justice to his legend. "Fans...of the Weavers will keenly appreciate Willens' effort"—*Booklist.*

WHAM!

AUTOBIOGRAPHY

Michael, George and Parsons, Tony. *George Michael Factfile*. London and New York: Penguin Books, 1992. Unpaginated (approximately 128 pages). Approximately 100 color and black-and-white photographs, covering every page.

Comprised of transcriptions of conversations with George Michael, this book is a highly illustrated oral work, beefed-up with quotes from friends, colleagues, and collaborator Tony Parsons. The photos of Michael—which look like color prints, not real glossies—range from Boy George effeminate to David Bowie androgynous to Tom Selleck ultra-macho, and the text hedges equally as much regarding Michael's sexual leaning. If anything, this only retreads material available just about anywhere, such as how he was influenced by Elton John and what it took to leave Wham! for solo fame. Low on facts.

BIOGRAPHIES

Dessau, Bruce. *George Michael: The Making of a Superstar*. London: Sidgwick & Jackson Limited, 1991. 244 pages. One glossy eight-page black-and-white photo insert. Discography.

Biography that tracks George Michael's life as a soloist after the split from Wham! Far more informative than Michael's own work (see Autobiography, above), this at least fills in the blanks of Michael's childhood—how young Georgios Kyriacos Panayiotou, son of a Greek restaurateur, befriended Andrew Ridgeley, and the two formed the mega-successful pop band Wham! Dessau then moves on to Michael's solo career and how he attempted to transcend his pretty boy image and appeal to those who actually listen to music. Fans will complete the book still perplexed about Michael's sexual orientation.

Rogan, Johnny. *Wham! Confidential: The Death of a Supergroup*. London: Omnibus Press (division of Book Sales Limited), 1987. 162 pages. One glossy eight-page black-and-white photo insert.

Why did Wham! split? What rifts formed between the dynamic duo of George Michael and Andrew Ridgeley? For starters—asserts Rogan—the pair, who had originally enjoyed playing the game with the press, was suddenly constantly hounded by them and couldn't keep up with the pressure. Ridgeley, in particular, seemed determined to goad the tabloids with his erratic social behavior, which only dragged Michael's name in. According to Rogan, Wham!'s management knew a split was inevitable two years before it actually occurred and began to make arrangements. Controversies such as the band's involvement with South Africa did not help matters, nor did general financial disputes (which, it seems, every pop band must endure). Rogan thinks certain controversies about Wham! are juicier than they really are, but Wham! or George Michael fans would want to give this a read.

OTHER TITLES OF INTEREST

Crocker, Chris. *Wham!* New York: Simon & Schuster, 1985.
     School Library Journal *commented: "All major information comes from secondary sources (uncited)."*
Fredericks, Darlene. *Wham!*. New York: Ballantine, 1985.
Goodall, Nigel. *George Michael: In His Own Words*. London: Omnibus Press (division of Book Sales Limited), 1995.
Kamin, Philip. *Wham!*. Milwaukee, WI: Hal Leonard, 1985.

WHITESNAKE

TITLES OF INTEREST
Hibbert, Tom. *Whitesnake*. London: Omnibus Press (division of Book Sales Limited), 1981.

WHITE ZOMBIE

FANZINES AND FAN CLUBS

Psychoholics Anonymous. P.O. Box 885343, Dept. New, San Francisco, CA 94188.

White Zombie fan club offering members access to priority tickets, travel packages, and exclusive merchandise. Members also receive an 8x10 color photo of the band, a bumper sticker, an embroidered patch, a membership card, and subscription to the club's magazine, which contains photos and White Zombie news. The cost of membership is $20 U.S.; $25 elsewhere.

THE WHO

(See also Townshend, Pete)

BIOGRAPHIES

Butler, Dougal with Trengrove, Chris and Lawrence, Peter. *Full Moon: The Amazing Rock and Roll Life of the Late Keith Moon*. New York: William Morrow and Company, Inc., 1981. 272 pages. Glossary.

Previously published under the more apt title *Moon the Loon*, this wacky bio celebrates the excesses, charms, and brilliance of Keith Moon, rock and roll's pre-eminent drummer until his death in 1978. Written in a chaotic style befitting its subject, the book goes off on many tangents yet never fails to satisfy with its tales of drugs, sex, and raunchy Monty Pythonesque humor. One of the best bits: a manic drum solo featuring Moon, Ringo Starr, and Jim Keltner—with John Lennon as the audience! The glossary is helpful for those who don't know what terms such as "beef torpedo" (male organ) and "scrubber" (an unattractive female).

Marsh, Dave. *Before I Get Old: The Story of the Who*. New York: St. Martin's Press, 1983. 546 pages. Three glossy 16-page black-and-white photo inserts. Selected Bibliography. Index.

A truly comprehensive biography of The Who, from their youth to international stardom. The author, lauded rock writer Dave Marsh, makes clear that "however critical *Before I Get Old* may be of The Who, there is no way to deny the best music that the band created...." Roger Daltrey has made statements indicating that the book was based entirely on interviews with Townshend and that the old boy—at the time a compulsive liar and addicted to drugs—had exaggerated a few bits. (Specifically, Townshend claimed Daltrey and Entwistle wanted to kick Keith Moon out of the group at one point because he was no longer up to snuff; Daltrey has stated this is not true at all.) You can decide who's right for yourself. The bibliography (called "selective") and index are thorough, and the writing is crisp and lively. A must for mod, rocker, and everyone else in between.

Waterman, Ivan. *Keith Moon: The Life and Death of a Rock Legend*. London: Arrow Books, 1979. 142 pages. Two black-and-white photo inserts.

One of the more sympathetic looks at The Who's phenomenal drummer who guzzled himself into oblivion at thirty-two. Among his friends was actor Oliver Reed who said: "He was a great clown. He mirrored all the madness in the world today." Interestingly, the book notes that Moon was greatly influenced by the Marx Brothers—notably the way Chico played piano (as well as the quartet's obvious destructiveness). Not as entertaining as Butler's *Full Moon* (listed above), this will still satisfy the eager Moon buff.

GENERAL REFERENCE

Wolter, Stephen and Kimber, Karen. *The Who in Print: An Annotated Bibliography 1965-1990*. Jefferson, NC: McFarland & Company, Inc., 1992. 156 pages. Discographies. Index.

Assemblage of data on Who literature, encompassing books, articles, reviews, and special sections on Pete Townshend. While there hasn't been nearly as much literature on The Who as on The Beatles or The Rolling Stones, the fact that all works have been gathered in one place does make researching easy. The entries within each section are chronological, containing general publication data and a very brief description of every work. Decently handled, although the stage version of *Tommy* (and its companion book, see Townshend, Pete: Written Works) makes this seem dated. "...highly recommended..."—*Choice*.

PICTORIALS

Barnes, Richard. *The Who: Maximum R&B*. New York: St. Martin's Press, 1982. 168 pages. Approximately 200 color and black-and-white photos, covering every page. Discography. Comes with a flexidisc.

A remarkable photo compilation of Who miscellany from the band's early days as The Detours through the release of the *Face Dances* LP and related tours. Reportedly done "in full cooperation" with the group—but since when did they ever cooperate on anything? Highly recommended for its assortment of visual material: rare childhood photos and school report cards, ancient concert posters, album cover outtakes (Daltrey's infamous bath of baked beans for the *Who Sell Out* sleeve), clippings, and much more. Keith Moon is in fine form here: dressed in drag, posing nude, kicking up his drums, etc. The text is in tiny print and in three columns, so those aging rockers with poor vision might need to purchase a magnifying glass.

Charlesworth, Chris. *The Complete Guide to the Music of the Who*. London: Omnibus Press (division of Book Sales Limited), 1995. 136 pages. Approximately 125 color and black-and-white photographs throughout.

CD-format book covering all aspects of The Who's career. This nicely designed and illustrated book is priced just right at around $7.99.

Herman, Gary. *The Who*. London: Studio Vista Limited, 1971. 112 pages. Approximately 100 black-and-white photos throughout. Discography. Appendix: Interviews with Roger Daltrey and John Entwistle.

Small format British publication drawing mostly on the early years of the group. Interesting to note that British publications such as this one tend to spell Entwistle's name "Entwhistle." The photos are of passable quality, although the writing is a bit too analytical. Who fans can pass.

Welch, Chris. *The Who: Teenage Wasteland*. London: Castle Communications, 1995. 126 pages. Approximately 80 glossy black-and-white photographs throughout. The Who Discography.

It's good to see an all-new photo book on The Who in the 1990's—especially one that emphasizes the group's early years. Welch's book is exclusively in black-and-white and includes only one photo of Kenney Jones. The rest depicts the hyperactive, rebellious Mod group of the 1960's, with Moon thrashing away on his drums and Townshend skipping in the air better than anyone else of the era. Welch lacks the ability to drive home a good anecdote (one in which Keith Moon drives a limo into a pool could have been much more thrilling), but he gets the information across. The photos, which were selected with a keen visual eye, have been reproduced on fine quality paper. Still, those expecting childhood photos of the original foursome or a picture of The Who at Woodstock will be disappointed. Undeniably appealing, though flawed.

QUIZBOOKS AND QUOTEBOOKS

Clarke, Steve. Designed by Neville, Perry. *The Who: In Their Own Words*. New York: Delilah/Putnam, 1979. 132 pages. Black-and-white photographs throughout.

Organized chronologically, this highly browsable but fluffed-up book consists of photos and miscellaneous quotes taken out of context from band members. Typically, the excerpts are funny and unpredictable: Roger Daltrey—"We got discovered by a Jewish door handle manufacturer. He decided he wanted to waste some money on a pop group"; Pete Townshend—"Electric guitar hurts my ears"; John Entwistle—"Keith was the hardest drummer in the world to play with"; Keith Moon—"I was always considered management material." Average.

TOURBOOKS

Kamin, Philip and Goddard, Peter. *The Who: The Farewell Tour*. New York: Beaufort Books, 1983. 128 pages. Approximately 100 glossy color and black-and-white photos throughout.

Stunning shots taken during The Who's tour of America in 1982. The paper quality is excellent, as is the interior design. The photos cover the group both on stage and off, and succeed at capturing the flavor of each event; one word captions identify the cities in which the photos were taken. The look (minus Keith Moon) is perhaps too polished for fans of The Who's late 1960's and early 70's bad boys image, but the book is still a treat for collectors.

Stein, Jeff and Johnston, Chris. *The Who*. New York: Stein and Day, 1979. Unpaginated (approximately 128 pages). Approximately 100 black-and-white photographs throughout.

A collection of black-and-white photos from three U.S. tours in the early 1970's (no concerts are actually dated or identified). Stein, who receives author credit, directed The Who's film *The Kids Are Alright*. The photos are okay, but there are no captions and no complementary text. In fact, the creators might have done well to at least supply page numbers. Not recommended. First published in 1973.

WRITTEN WORKS

Barnes, Richard and Townshend, Pete. *The Story of Tommy*. Twickenham, Middlesex (England): Eel Pie, 1977. 128 pages. Approximately 200 color stills, covering every page.

The companion to the 1975 Ken Russell film *Tommy*, this book is arranged in interview format through Townshend himself, who discusses how he created the original story and what his original words and images signify. Interesting in light of the musical adaptation (see Townshend, Pete: Written Works), this book contains song lyrics, elaborate sketches of how Townshend mapped out his characters' development, handwritten notes, and more. The photos almost make one think the film is better than it really is. Who can resist the bean and mud covered Ann-Margret as the mother, the sultry magnetism of Tina Turner as the Acid Queen, or the jovial perversion of Keith Moon as wicked Uncle Ernie? This book's value shot up only when the musical hit the stage.

No author. *A Decade of The Who*. London: Fabulous Music Limited, 1977. 238 pages. Approximately 100 black-and-white and color illustrations throughout. Discography.

The decade referred to is 1965-1975—The Who's early period through *The Who by Numbers* LP. The book itself contains lyrics with guitar chords, plus quotes from the group and original art and photos. Recommended only because it's one of few books of this kind available on The Who.

YOUNG ADULT

Deegan, Michael P. *The Who*. MN: Creative Education, 1983. 32 pages. 10 black-and-white full page photos.

Part of the "Rock 'n Pop Stars Series," this book for young readers was written during Kenney Jones' stint on drums in the early 1980's. For those rockers 10 and younger who like the song "You Better You Bet."

McKnight, Connor and Silver, Caroline. *The Who...Through the Eyes of Pete Townshend*. New York: Scholastic Book Services, 1974. 116 pages. Approximately 30 black-and-white photographs throughout.

Mid-1970's book on The Who for young readers, with emphasis on the group's sensational live performances of *Tommy* in opera houses, such as the Metropolitan Opera House in New York City. Authors McKnight and Silver shed some light on The Who's history, providing separate sections on each Who band member, but clearly Townshend is the selling point. The most problematic aspect of this work is that the authors' insist this is an "up close" look at Townshend, which it isn't; there is no evidence Townshend was interviewed or consulted. Thus phrases such as "Pete is charming to meet and talk to" don't make much sense. Superficial.

OTHER TITLES OF INTEREST

Ashley, Brian and Monnery, Steve. *Who's Who? A Who Retrospective*. London: New English Library, 1978.

Charlesworth, Chris. *The Who: The Illustrated Biography*. London: Omnibus Press (division of Book Sales Limited), 1982.

Davis, John. *A Decade of the Who: An Authorized History in Music, Paintings, Word and Photographs*. London: Elm Tree Books, 1977.

Fletcher, Alan. *Quadrophenia*. London: Corgi, 1979. *Novelization of The Who's 1979 film.*

Hanel, Ed. *The Who: An Illustrated Discography*. London: Omnibus Press (division of Book Sales Limited), 1981.

Swenson, John. *The Who*. London: Star Books, 1981.

Tremlett, George. *The Who*. London: Futura, 1975.

HANK WILLIAMS

BIOGRAPHIES

Caress, Jay. *Hank Williams: Country Music's Tragic King*. New York: Stein and Day, 1979. 256 pages. One 16-page black-and-white photo insert. Discography. Index.

Decent, though now dated, study of the musician. Caress is actually very strong chronicling Williams' rise to fame in the Grand Ole Opry and summarizing his brief career as a would-be bronc rider. (He quit when he suffered a back injury that would bother him the rest of his short life.) Caress also finds some sport following Williams' years on the road in the Alabama circuit, fightin', drinkin', cussin', and general hellraising. This book has quite a bit of action for casual readers, but most would be better off opting for Escott or Flippo's respective works (see below).

Escott, Colin; with Merritt, George and MacEwen, William. *Hank Williams: The Biography*. Boston and New York: Little, Brown and Company, 1994. 308 pages. Two glossy eight-page black-and-white photo inserts. Sources. Discography. Index.

In the world of popular myth—especially when it comes to musicians who have become popular myths—it always helps to live fast, die young, and drink heartily along the way as Williams did. The three able writers (Escott, Merritt, and MacEwen) set about the task of revisiting such a legend, trying to uncover the mystery of how the 29-year-old country performer really did die. Despite the fact that Williams' corpse was spotted with needle marks and that he had a welt on his head, no real investigation was ever made to determine whether the cause of death was drug overdose, suicide, or even murder. The prose is occasionally hard-edged compared to Flippo's work (see below), but scholars and country lovers will want this book for its painstaking research.

Flippo, Chet. *Your Cheatin' Heart: A Biography of Hank Williams*. New York: Simon & Schuster, 1981. 256 pages. One glossy 16-page black-and-white photo insert. Index.

According to writer Chet Flippo, Hank Williams "was the first country singer and songwriter whose songs consistently crossed over to the pop music audience." Born to a poor family in Mount Olive West, Alabama, Williams (born "Hiram Hank" but misspelled "Hiriam" on the birth certificate) was abandoned by his father at seven and left in poverty-stricken squalor with his gargantuan mother. Williams learned to reach his soul through his local Baptist church and was taught guitar by a black street singer named Tee-tot. Flippo's storytelling is highly digestible for fans, although other works have dug deeper.

Williams, Roger. *Sing a Sad Song: The Life of Hank Williams* Chicago: University of Illinois Press, 1981. 320 pages. Discography. Index.

The second edition of this academic treatise on country star Hank Williams. Without any illustrations, it's doubtful this book will have contemporary interest—especially with the availability of Escott et. al.'s work (see above). Still, Williams provides an excellent history of the Grand Ole Opry and a meaty discography, assembled by Bob Pinson. Only for those performing in-depth research.

GENERAL REFERENCE

Koon, George William. *Hank Williams: A Bio-Bibliography*. Westport, CT: Greenwood Press, 1983. 180 pages. Approximately 10 black-and-white photographs throughout. Appendix I: Chronology. Appendix II: Discography. Index.

A handy reference for the country music academician, this book is divided into four parts: biography; song analysis; interviews; and bibliographic material. The biography section is dry but serviceable, supplying excellent details on the aftermath of Hank's death—especially its effect on the Williams family. The song evaluation section separates myth and its influence on Williams' art. The interviews section is a bit of a disappointment, including only three: Hank and his wife Audrey; Bob Pinson (head of acquisitions at the Country Music Foundation Library in Nashville); and musicians Jerry Rivers and Don Helms. The bibliographic material, discography, and index are among the best reference sections prepared on the artist to date. Recommended for scholars.

PICTORIALS

Moore, Thurston. *Hank Williams: The Legend*. Denver, CO: Heather Enterprises, 1972. 64 pages. Approximately 50 black-and-white photographs throughout. Discography.

Strange paperback compendium of essays by contributors such as Bill C. Malone, Irene Williams Smith (Hank's sister), John Stephen Doherty, and others. The photos, presumably taken in black-and-white, have been reproduced in a brown tint and are very unappealing. This ill-assembled package also features some of Williams' letters and lyrics, as well as newspaper clips—and even recipes. While the shrimp jambalaya looks delicious, it sticks out amidst the reference material. Not recommended for either hard research or for browsing.

WILLIAMS FRIENDS AND FAMILY

Williams, Lycrecia and Vinicur, Dale. *Still in Love With You: The Story of Hank Williams*. Nashville, TN: Rutledge Hill Press, 1989. 204 pages. Two glossy 16-page black-and-white photo inserts.

The memoir of Lycrecia Williams, the daughter of country legend Hank Williams and Audrey Williams. Hank was not actually her blood father, who had abandoned the family and she never even met. Despite Williams' many character flaws and the fact that he died when his daughter was very young, Lycrecia always considered him her real "Daddy." In this book she attempts to set the record straight about her mother (frequently depicted as a "bitch") and how her father's problems with alcohol impacted on the family. Guaranteed to have some emotional significance to fans.

WRITTEN WORKS

Williams, Sr., Hank. Cusic, Don (editor). *Hank Williams: The Complete Lyrics*. New York: St. Martin's Press, 1993. 152 pages.

Accessible collection of lyrics to 139 of Williams' songs, although not nearly all-inclusive. The tunes are alphabetized, but there isn't a table of contents or an index in the back identifying titles. The songs are not annotated, but editor Cusic provides some marginal insights in the introduction. From "I Can't Get You Off My Mind" to "Your Cheatin' Heart," these are the original classics and they still retain their vitality, emotion, and flavor. Not illustrated. "...Cusic's essay is clumsy and error-ridden..."—*Country Music*.

WINGS

See McCartney, Paul.

STEVE WINWOOD

BIOGRAPHIES

Welch, Chris with Winwood, Steve. *Steve Winwood: Roll With It*. New York: Perigee (division of Putnam), 1989. 168 pages. Two eight-page black-and-white photo inserts. Discography. (First published in England in 1989 as *Winwood: Keep on Running* by Omnibus Press.)

Don't be misled by the coauthor attribution to Winwood: This is not an autobiography. With Winwood's approval over the manuscript, noted U.K. rock writer Chris Welch attempts to get the facts straight and occasionally defend the artist's position on various issues. For one

thing, Winwood was born in Handworth Nursing Home, not in a friend's house, as has been frequently reported; the relevance of this fact is never explored. And this holds true for a number of other interesting issues brought forth, ranging from Winwood's rage at his songs being used in TV commercials to his brother Muff Winwood's retirement from recording. (He had been bassist with Steve in The Spencer Davis Group). Worthwhile for fans, but hopelessly superficial. The U.K. edition has a far better jacket, and the photo insert pages are glossy.

OTHER TITLES OF INTEREST

Clayson, Alan. *Back in the High Life: A Biography of Steve Winwood*. London: Sidgwick & Jackson, 1988.

WIRE

INTERVIEWS

Eden, Kevin S. *Wire...Everybody Loves a History*. Wembley, Middlesex (England): SAF, 1991. 192 pages. Approximately 75 black-and-white photographs throughout. Discography. Gigography.

Wire was among the wave of bands unleashed in the wake of the mid-1970's English punk explosion. Yet the group eschews titles and music movements, preferring not to be categorized; instead, they've moved to other kinds of entertainment, such as performance art and audio-visual presentations. This book is neither a biography nor a pictorial, but a series of conversations among the musicians themselves. Of peripheral interest to those studying the links between punk and New Wave.

STEVIE WONDER

BIOGRAPHIES

Elsner, Constanze. *Stevie Wonder*. New York: Popular Library (CBS Publications), 1977. 366 pages. One glossy 16-page black-and-white photo insert. Discography. Index.

Choppily written but serviceable mass-market biography of the famed musician. When it comes to Wonder, it's easy to believe the apocryphal; author Constanze Elsner takes some of these stories at face value. On the plus side, she inserts a good deal about his influences (The Dixie Hummingbirds, Mary Wells, and Sam Cooke) and his early singing days at his Baptist church. Non-tabloid fare.

Fox-Cumming. *Stevie Wonder*. London: Mandabrook Books, 1977. 128 pages. Stevie Wonder's Career Highlights. Stevie Wonder Discography.

Way off-track British biography of Wonder that insipidly begins with an astrological study of Wonder's sign, Taurus the Bull. Who the hell cares? This mass-market publication sponsored by the *Daily Mirror Pop club* doesn't contain any photos and has a U.K.-only discography. The text on the front and back covers has actually been cut off, so one can hardly even decipher what the book is about. Don't bother trying.

Peisch, Jeffrey. *Stevie Wonder*. New York: Ballantine Books, 1984. 152 pages. One glossy 16-page black-and-white photo insert. Appendixes: Discography. Videography. Fan Club Information.

Proclaiming to include "everything you need to know about Stevie Wonder," this is an ultrapop biography for teenage fans. The volume not only doesn't live up to its billing—other books are far more detailed and comprehensive—it also has a fairly ridiculous illustrative insert (keyboards stretched across two pages). Given the time period of this book, the early 1980's, it's understandable that it highlights Wonder's duets with Paul McCartney ("Ebony and Ivory")—but is anyone interested now? Breezy and superficial.

PICTORIALS

Haskins, James with Benson, Kathleen. *The Stevie Wonder Scrapbook*. London: Cassell, 1978. 160 pages. Approximately 125 black-and-white photographs throughout. Books. Articles.

Late 1970's photo book that contains some excellent early shots: young Stevie with a cute puppy, performing, riding on a bicycle, holding his child, etc. Haskins proficiently shows that not only was Wonder an incomparably versatile musician as a child, but a highly literate speaker and knowledgeable musical technician as well. A fine, though dated, visual study

that shouldn't be missed—if only to see Wonder tweaking Bobby Darin's nose!

Swenson, John. *Stevie Wonder*. London: Plexus, 1986. 160 pages. Approximately 125 black-and-white photographs throughout. Discography.

Molded and protected by Motown since he was a child, Stevie Wonder continues to have an elusive story. Motown kept him under close watch and prevented details of his youth from leaking out to the press. Speculation abounds, even today, as to how he lost his sight. Author John Swenson conveys Wonder's explanation, that as a baby he was kept in an incubator too long, which exposed him to too much oxygen; the result was a dislocated nerve in one eye and a cataract in the other. Amazing confidence, balance, and heightened other senses enabled the legally blind Wonder to do just about all of the sports and activities of other kids—and become one of the most famous performers of all time. This is a good introductory biography, highlighting Wonder's charitable involvements as well as his longtime associations with Marvin Gaye and Diana Ross. "...a short but remarkably comprehensive biography..."—*Booklist*.

YOUNG ADULT

Edwards, Audrey and Wohl, Gary. *The Picture Life of Stevie Wonder*. New York and London: Franklin Watts, 1977. Unpaginated (approximately 32 pages). Approximately 20 black-and-white photographs throughout.

Sparsely detailed biography of Wonder intended for children eight and younger. The text—only one or two paragraphs per page—tells very little about Wonder's life and music, and even exaggerates a few claims (e.g., that white people didn't listen to his music at all until his 1972 tour with The Rolling Stones). Some good photos of Wonder playing a multitude of instruments fail to compensate.

Hasegawa, Sam. *Stevie Wonder*. Mankato, MN: Creative Education, 1975. 32 pages. Approximately eight original watercolors throughout.

Decent entry in the "Rock 'n Pop Stars" series from Creative Education, with lively prose focusing on Wonder's performances with The Rolling Stones in 1972 and how, despite his great fame and wealth, he has remained a humble and gentle guy. Far superior to Edwards' work (see above), with imaginative art by Dick Brude. Sadly, over two decades out-of-date.

Jacobs, Linda. *Stevie Wonder: Sunshine in the Shadow*. St. Paul, MN: EMC Corporation, 1976. 40 pages. Approximately 30 black-and-white photographs throughout.

Part of EMC's "Men Behind the Bright Lights" series of the 1970's, this nicely titled entry unfortunately repeats the same information as other volumes listed herein. The book only slightly discusses his original compositions and a fragment more about his live performances. Too old and too recycled to be of use today.

Ruuth, Marianne. *Stevie Wonder*. Los Angeles: Holloway House Publishing Co., 1980. 96 pages. One eight-page black-and-white photo insert.

Enthusiastic, if erratic telling of the Stevie Wonder story up through the end of the 1970's. Ruuth begins the tale with the star's 1973 car crash, which caused Wonder to fall into a four-day coma—and became yet another miracle in his life, in the sense that not only did he recover, but he would go on to record some of the best music of his career. The writing could have used a stronger editorial hand, but young fans may still derive some pleasure from the positive emphasis of this work.

OTHER TITLES OF INTEREST

Green, Carl and Sanford, William R. *Stevie Wonder*. New York: Macmillan, 1986.

Haskins, James. *The Story of Stevie Wonder*. New York: Dell, 1979.

Pitts, Jr., Leonard. *Mr. Wonderful: The Stevie Wonder Story*. No city: Sharon Starbook, no date.

Taylor, Rick. *Stevie Wonder: The Illustrated Discography*. London: Omnibus Press (division of Book Sales Limited), 1990.

X

WRITTEN WORKS

Cervenka, Exene. *Virtual Unreality*. Los Angeles: 2.13.61 Publications, 1993. Unpaginated (approximately 128 pages).

Avant-garde, bizarre collection of scribblings by Cervenka, the poetess and lead singer of X. Cervenka's cryptic handwriting is not the only problem here; the untitled pieces do not convey any consistent meaning, unless one is on a freaky hallucinogenic drug. Fans drawn in by Cervenka's name, the attractive cover, and the book's cool title may be disappointed.

Cervenka, Exene (text) and Jarecke, Kenneth (photography). Introduction by John Hockenberry. *Just Another War*. Joliet, MO: Bedrock Press, 1992. Unpaginated (approximately 128 pages). 54 black-and-white photographs throughout.

Images of the Persian Gulf War, as captured by photographer Kenneth Jarecke. Opposite each work, in thick black scrawl, are Exene Cervenka's reflections on conflict—which are clearly from an armchair view back home. In fact, most of Cervenka's words reflect the discord between reality and television reportage and the bizarre unity of death and entertainment. Some of Cervenka's writing is hard to decipher, and the chaos doesn't really match the poised artistic nature of Jarecke's photos.

Lunch, Lydia and Cervenka, Exene. *Adulterer's Anonymous*. New York: Grove Press, 1982. 110 pages.

The combined efforts of Lydia Lunch (formerly of Teenage Jesus and Eight-Eyed Spy) and Exene Cervenka (X's lyricist and lead singer) make for a racy and unsettling read. If readers can get past the alternating typefaces (helvetica for Cervenka and times roman capital letters for Lunch), some might find the raw, sexually tinged passages titillating. Do not be fooled into thinking any of the work comes close to the imagery of Patti Smith or Lou Reed.

PICTORIALS

Fitzgerald, F-Stop (editor) and Morris, Chris. *Beyond and Back: The Story of X*. San Francisco: Last Gasp, 1983. 64 pages. Approximately 65 black-and-white photographs and graphics, covering every page. X Discography.

The only major band named after a letter of the alphabet (or, depending on one's perspective, the rating for porno flicks), this pictorial tells the story of the American punk band that fused 1950's and 60's rock and roll, the blues, and even beat poetry into its own unique sound.

The book includes a smattering of quotes from X members, critics, strange graphic patterns, and limited biographical data. The background on Cervenka is limited to one paragraph in which she discusses her move from St. Petersburg to Los Angeles; there aren't even very many photos of her here. Most of the other text concerns X's live performances, which will not be enough to satisfy fans.

XTC

BIOGRAPHIES

Twomey, Chris. *XTC: Chalkhills and Children: The Definitive Biography*. London: Omnibus Press (division of Book Sales Limited), 1992. 188 pages. One glossy eight-page black-and-white photo insert. Complete XTC Discography.

Published with cooperation from XTC band members Andy Partridge, Colin Moulding, and Dave Gregory, this is an excellent study of a band that has survived changing trends in the music industry during its 15-year career. Author Chris Twomey cites 1982 as the climactic moment in the band's development, as it was at this point that Andy Partridge quit touring because he couldn't handle the pressure. Aside from the group's durability, there isn't that much here to catch the attention of an American readership: XTC doesn't tour and their songs rarely chart. Still, for those with interest, this book does exist.

THE YARDBIRDS

(see also Clapton, Eric; Led Zeppelin)

AUTOBIOGRAPHY

Platt, John; Dreja, Chris; McCarty, Jim. *Yardbirds*. London: Sidgwick & Jackson, undated. 160 pages. Approximately 125 black-and-white photographs throughout. Yardbirds Tree. Discography. Index.

The Yardbirds were one of the most influential blues-based blues bands of the 1960's, and several members would go on to even greater fame as guitar legends in the 1970's: Jimmy

Page, Eric Clapton, and Jeff Beck. None of those three—nor singer Keith Relf (who died from electric shock while practicing guitar at home)—had anything to do with this volume, but lesser founding members Chris Dreja (rhythm guitar and later bass) and Jim McCarty (drums) did (although it's hard to tell what specifically). These guys at least have a wonderful sense of humor, opening the book up with a 1966 ad The Yardbirds did for talcum powder! Yet Dreja and McCarty's personalities do not appear anywhere in the book, and the authors' assertion that The Yardbirds follow The Beatles and The Stones in terms of overall importance (what about The Who? The Kinks?) can be debated into the next millennium. Set your sights low and you might derive some pleasure from this book.

YES

PICTORIALS

Hedges, Dan. *Yes: The Authorised Biography*. London: Sidgwick & Jackson, 1981. 146 pages. Approximately 150 black-and-white photographs, covering nearly every page; one eight-page color photo insert. Discography.

Above-average photo-biography of Yes that traces the musicians' careers up through 1980. Prepared with the band's cooperation, the book goes back to their origins in Accrington, England and provides some background data on members Jon Anderson, Peter Banks, Chris Squire, Bill Butford, Tony Kaye, Steve Howe, and a few other players. The book has some eye-catching photos of the musicians as youngsters and in their early bands (e.g., Tony Kaye in The Federals). While Yes could never compete with harder rocking contemporaries such as Led Zeppelin, the group's brand of synthesizer rock was a central part of the sound of the 1970's. Author Dan Hedges, the band's personal publicist for three years, has created a book with high, if dated, appeal to Yes fans. The album cover art of birds soaring is reminiscent of Yes album art.

QUIZBOOKS AND QUOTEBOOKS

Morse, Tim. *Yes Stories: Yes In Their Own Words*. New York: St. Martin's Press, 1996. One glossy eight-page color insert; approximately 20 black-and-white photographs throughout. 162 pages. A Select Discography. Sources. Fan Publications.

Yes tells their own story—at least through quotes culled by Tim Morse. St. Martin's Press has taken the "in his/their own words" theme from Omnibus Press and have expanded on it, with several unique features: a more attractive design; a color insert; a discography; and, for this type of work, high-quality photos. The quotes are arranged by time periods and phases of Yes' career, from their beginnings, to their albums and to life on the road. These guys aren't the funniest musicians in the world (Rick Wakeman on the *Union* LP: "I call it the Onion album because every time I hear it, it brings tears to my eyes"), but fans will appreciate most of the selections here.

OTHER TITLES OF INTEREST
Howe, Steve and Bacon, Tony. *The Steve Howe Guitar Collection*. No city: Miller Freeman, 1993.
Wooding, Dan. *Rick Wakeman: The Caped Crusader*. St. Albans: Panther, 1979.

NEIL YOUNG

(See also Crosby, Stills, Nash and Young; Lightfoot, Gordon: Critical/Analytical Commentary)

BIOGRAPHIES

Downing, David. *A Dreamer of Pictures: Neil Young: The Man and His Music*. New York: Da Capo, 1994. 248 pages. Two glossy eight-page color and black-and-white photo inserts. Discography. Index. (First published in Great Britain in 1994 by Bloomsbury Publishing Limited.)

British biography of the Canadian singer that unemotionally takes readers through his childhood tragedies: nearly drowning (he was rescued by child radio actress Beryl Braithwaite), polio, and his parents' divorce—to his long and eventful musical career. The glossy color inserts feature some worthwhile shots of Young in his various bands, although nothing from his childhood. This book isn't as well-detailed on the early Canadian years as Einarson's work (see below), but Downing is much stronger on Young's mixed messages about militarism, economics, and human rights issues. He has also uncovered some previously unreported facts about Zeke, Young's son who has cerebral palsy. A decent option for enthusiasts.

Einarson, John. *Neil Young: Don't Be Denied*. Kingston, Ontario (Canada): Quarry Press, Inc., 1992. 224 pages. Approximately 50 black-and-white photographs throughout.

Biographer John Einarson takes what seems to be a limited subject—Neil Young in his formative years in Canada—and turns it into an impressive study of the development of a brilliant artist. With the help of Young himself, Einarson recreates the painful split between Young's parents, his bout with polio, his experiences with his first musical instrument (a plastic ukelele), and a good deal of detail on the Winnipeg music scene in the early 1960's. Surprisingly, despite the aforementioned conflicts and his public image as something of a downer, Young is depicted as a "happy-go-lucky child"—well liked and always chewing gum. A fine portrait of the artist as a young man.

CHRONOLOGIES

Robertson, John. *Neil Young: The Visual Documentary*. London: Omnibus Press (division of Book Sales Limited), 1994. 160 pages. Approximately 200 black-and-white photographs throughout; two glossy 16-page black-and-white photo inserts. Discography.

Highly illustrated day-by-day account of Neil Young, with details starting in 1940 with his parents' marriage and ending in 1991 with his Grammy nominations. While not as colorful or as richly detailed as Heatley's work (see Pictorials, below), it does contain important bits of information ranging from the final Buffalo Springfield performance (May 5, 1968) to Young's more recent dates with Bob Dylan. A valuable book that is marred by a cluttered design for the discography. Those who would enjoy this book should also take a look at Rogan's "visual documentary" on Crosby, Stills, Nash and Young (see Chronologies).

CRITICAL/ANALYTICAL COMMENTARY

Editors of *Rolling Stone*. Introduction by Holly George-Warren. *Neil Young: The Rolling Stone Files*. New York: Hyperion, 1994. 308 pages. Discography. Selective Videography.

"The ultimate compendium of interviews, articles, facts, and opinions" is an exhaustive retrospective of materials culled from *Rolling Stone* magazine over the last three decades. Fans, critics, and researchers will all get a kick out of reading original reviews of Buffalo Springfield, Crosby, Stills, Nash and Young, and Crazy Horse. In one very early album review, Young is described as "a very capable and original guitarist." Yet this work also contains profiles, interviews, and random notes contributed by rock's elite literati, including Ben Fong-Torres, Greil Marcus, Dave Marsh, Stephen Holden, David Fricke, and many other predominately male *Rolling Stone* regulars. Articles on drug busts, concert performances, and even film/video are of major historical significance. Highly recommended, in spite of the goofy, cartoonish cover design.

Jenkins, Alan (editor). *Neil Young and Broken Arrow: On a Journey Through the Past*. Wales, U.K.: Neil Young Appreciation Society, 1994. 296 pages. One glossy 20-page black-and-white photo insert. Discography. Set Lists. Cover Versions.

Publication of the Neil Young Appreciation Society in Wales (see Fanzines and Fan Clubs, below), this work essentially culls articles from the club's fanzine, *Broken Arrow*. Without breathing in to make room for an introduction, the book starts right off with Mark Lyons' description of Neil Young being quite drunk for a Miami Beach performance. Other pieces address Young's role as a guitar hero (influenced by Jimi Hendrix), the formation of Buffalo Springfield, the Canadian influence on his work, and other interesting topics. This work contains some fine contributions by notable authors such as John Bauldie and John Einarson. This book is to be savored by connoisseurs and experts of Neil Young's development and legacy; those less familiar with Young's career will need to start off with something more basic and build up to this.

DISCOGRAPHIES, RECORDING GUIDES, AND COLLECTIBLES

Fisson, Bruno and Jenkins, Alan. *Neil Young: A Complete Illustrated Bootleg Discography*. Wales, U.K.: Neil Young Appreciation Society, no date. 272 pages. Approximately 300 black-and-white reproductions of albums and sleeves. Checklist.

Published by the Neil Young Appreciation Society (see Fanzines and Fan Clubs, below), this easy-to-use guide features accessible information on illicit records spanning all phases of Neil Young's career. The authors list year and country of release for each bootleg, followed by straightforward headings for label, cover description, vinyl reference, song line-up, and occasional source citations. Nearly every bootleg is represented by a photo. A well-researched guide for the collector that unfortunately doesn't rate sound or performance, and doesn't identify running times or other characteristics of the songs themselves.

FANZINES AND FAN CLUBS

Neil Young Appreciation Society. 2A LLYNFI Street Bridgend Mid Glamorgan CF31 1SY WALES, United Kingdom.

Also known by its abbreviated name, *NYAS*, this international fan club publishes *Broken Arrow*, a glossy, 80-page booklet, and offers members two exhaustive, illustrated publications: *Neil Young and Broken Arrow: On a Journey Through the Past* (see Critical/Analytical Commentary, above); and *Neil Young: A Complete Illustrated Bootleg Discography* (See Discographies, Recording Guides, and Collectibles, above). *Broken Arrow*, which is published quarterly, contains black-and-white photos, news, reviews, interviews, song transcriptions, information on related artists (Bob Dylan, Pearl Jam, etc.), classifieds, and more. The cost of membership is $22 in the U.S.; £10 in the U.K.; and $12.50 elsewhere in Europe.

PICTORIALS

Dufrechou, Carole. *Neil Young*. New York and London: Quick Fox, 1978. 126 pages. Approximately 75 black-and-white photographs throughout. Discography.

Frightful-looking photo-biography of Neil Young, presumably intended for younger readers. In the early pages, there's a hideous picture of Young's face covered with some kind of cake glop (which drips down from his nostril). The photos of Buffalo Springfield and Crosby, Stills, Nash and Young have only slightly greater aesthetic content in that they are either too dark or too faded. The text is full of unnecessary hype about Young's legendary status and doesn't provide anything on his childhood. Go with any other book on Young and related artists.

Heatley, Michael. *Neil Young: His Life and Music.* London: Hamlyn (an imprint of Reed Consumer Books), 1994. 192 pages. Over 200 color and black-and-white photographs, covering every page.

"The spiritual godfather of grunge" is the subject of this solid photo-retrospective. Born in Toronto just after World War II, Young was the son of a navy man. He suffered from polio as a child (many rock stars, it seems, experienced physical or emotional traumas as children) and became involved with music early on. Heatley chronicles the "first" supergroup, Buffalo Springfield, which initially modeled itself on The Beatles (although Springfield turned out to be a quintet), but trivia nuts will be more impressed with photos of Young in pre-Springfield groups, The Squires, and The Shadows. The albums are spread throughout the book—as opposed to a standard discography—which will be detrimental to those doing serious research. This is an excellent collection of photos, however, boasting a tremendous selection of 1960's poster and album art and featuring various Neil Young hairdos: messy long hair, messy short hair, messy with sideburns, messy with beard, and just plain messy.

RELATED WORKS

Clark, Tom. *Neil Young.* No city (Canada): The Coach House Press, 1971. 32 pages.

Mawkish vanity press publication from poet Clark (who is not Canadian). There's a line or two of poetry per page and, if you look hard enough, you'll find distinct lyrics cribbed from Young's songs. Young's legal people couldn't have been too thrilled with this bend of fair use doctrine. As Jon Lovitz would say on his animated show "The Critic": It stinks!

OTHER TITLES OF INTEREST
Dufrechou, Carole. *Neil Young.* New York: Putnam, 1978.
Rogan, Johnny. *Neil Young: Hear We Are in the Years.* London: Proteus, no date.

PAUL YOUNG

PICTORIALS

Johnson, Gary. *Paul Young.* New York and London: Proteus Publishing Company, 1984. 32 pages. Approximately 40 color and black-and-white photographs, covering every page. Discography.

Pictorial bio of the man the back cover copy describes as "one of the finest white soul singers Britain has produced." Young began as the singer of The Tips, which seems to have been a general flop; his follow-up band, The Royal Family, had a few hits in the U.K. in the early 1980's. This book has very limited appeal for an American audience, and it's possible many Brits would be just as turned off. Young comes across as an even more bland version of Cliff Richard.

OTHER TITLES OF INTEREST
Kamin, Philip. *Paul Young.* Milwaukee, WI: Hal Leonard, 1985.
Merill, John. *Paul Young.* London: Omnibus Press (division of Book Sales Limited), 1990.

FRANK ZAPPA

(See also GTO's, The)

AUTOBIOGRAPHY

Zappa, Frank with Occhiogrosso, Peter. *The Real Frank Zappa Book.* New York: Poseidon Press (division of Simon & Schuster, Inc.), 1989. 352 pages. Approximately 50 black-and-white photographs and pen-and-ink drawings throughout.

Zappa—iconoclast, satirist, absurdist, and musician—admits he has no conception of how to write an autobiography, and thus we are treated to this often freaky assemblage of reminiscences, musical reflections, and political commentary. Zappa is funniest when putting an end to ludicrous myths (e.g., his having eaten shit on stage), recounting his childhood experiences (experimenting with mercury), and telling anecdotes about celebrities (how he nearly got into a brawl with John Wayne). The last chapters on censorship, politics, religion, and marriage are crucial to knowing the man's philosophy. No discography provided. "Biting, cogent social commentary very much of the sometimes profane and scatological sort that Lenny Bruce might be making if he were still alive..."—*Booklist Upfront.*

BIOGRAPHIES

Gray, Michael. *Mother! The Frank Zappa Story.* London: Plexus, 1994. 256 pages. Two glossy 16-page black-and-white photo inserts. Dizcography[sic]. Indexz[sic].

Rushed out in view of Zappa's death, this readable book seems determined to show that Frank Zappa was not a frivolous, freaky, flash-in-the-pan, but a highly capable musician, a workaholic, a clean-cut Stalinist, and a stalwart perfectionist (especially with other musicians). Michael Gray also gives Zappa ample credit for maintaining his marriage over three decades (although he did have a previous wife). In terms of musical criticism, Gray didn't do nearly enough homework to satisfy most Zappafiles. For his description of Zappa's *Sometime in New York City* recording with John Lennon he only says the results were "largely hideous," without discussing how the project came about (or Zappa's superior remix of the same material). Casual fans might be serviced by this book, but Watson's work (see Critical/Analytical Commentary, below) is much better.

Walley, David. *No Commercial Potential: The Saga of Frank Zappa: Then and Now.* New York: E.P. Dutton, 1980. 184 pages. Approximately 25 black-and-white photographs throughout. Album Chronology, Singles, Bibliography.

First published in 1977 and revised in 1980, this oversimplified biography of Zappa has long been replaced by Gray's work (see above) and Watson's (see below). Walley doesn't give the story much of a chance to unfold; he throws in random passages and quotes that don't really fit together, while his prose just rambles. Amidst the details of the Zappa family travels, we never get a complete sense of Zappa's rise to prominence. No potential.

CHRONOLOGIES

Miles. *Zappa: A Visual Documentary.* London: Omnibus Press (division of Book Sales Limited), 1993. 112 pages. Approximately 125 color and black-and-white photographs, covering every page.

Unlike several other "visual documentaries" from Omnibus Press, this one at least begins the chronology with the artist's birth on December 12, 1940. Miles' introduction is only one page, however, and doesn't even pretend to put Zappa into any kind of perspective. Since this book contains many quotes and quite a few color photos, it is probably a better purchase than Miles' "in his own words" quotebook (see Quizbooks and Quotebooks, below). Still, most people would want at least *some* commentary and explanation to accompany the listings, which Miles doesn't supply. For fans not patient enough to read Watson's work (see Critical/Analytical Commentary, below).

CRITICAL/ANALYTICAL COMMENTARY

Watson, Ben. *Frank Zappa: The Negative Dialectics of Poodle Play.* New York: St. Martin's Griffin, 1996. 622 pages. Appendix: Discography. Index. (First published in Great Britain in 1995 by Quartet Books Limited.)

Absolute proof that Zappa was not just a rock and jazz satirist and musical innovator. Watson, a self-professed "Zappologist," asserts that the man was a brilliant manipulator of words (on the same level as Joyce) and a philosopher extraordinaire who firmly believed that knowledge is the best enemy to oppression. Watson coasts through Zappa's early years in Baltimore, Maryland, incorporating the artist's love of R&B (but surprising dislike of Elvis Presley) and other influences, such as Bob Dylan, part Cherokee lumberjack/comedian Lord Buckley, and Captain Beefheart. Watson also makes many astute observations on music packaging, imaging, and commercialism. A penetrating sociological and psychological evaluation, "this is the ultimate book for serious Zappa fans." —*Publishers Weekly.*

PICTORIALS

Chevalier, Dominique. *Viva! Zappa.* New York: St.

Martin's Press, 1986. 128 pages. Approximately one hundred black-and-white and ten color photographs throughout. Zappa Archives (bibliography, discography). (First published in Paris, France in 1985 by Editions Calmann-Levy.)

This French production shoots for the zany, absurd side of Zappa; in this respect, the photos succeed, but the writing does not. Chevalier covers the basic Zappa history with little flair and fanfare. Passages on friends, drugs, sex, video, recording techniques, etc. are more fully covered in other books, notably Zappa's autobiography (see above). The photos are dynamic, however, and capture the man in his various moods and facial contortions. A few Zappa articles are reprinted in the back for some much-needed zip. The design is clumsily done; in some cases, the text is dangerously close to being cut off at the bottom of the page. Optional for Zappa fans.

QUIZBOOKS AND QUOTEBOOKS

Miles. *Frank Zappa: In His Own Words*. London: Omnibus Press (division of Book Sales Limited), 1993. 96 pages. Approximately 100 black-and-white photographs throughout.

This Omnibus Press quotebook opens with a cheating fanzine questionnaire from 1966, but then moves on to his Baltimore childhood and years in San Diego. Zappa is quoted on sections divided into the story, Mothers of Invention, on the road, at home, and politics, with further subsections in each. The passages on drugs mostly concern Zappa's sociological explanation for why people take them (and he didn't). Given the complexity of Zappa's philosophies, interested parties would do far better to find a copy of Watson's work (see Critical/Analytical Commentary, above).

ZAPPA FRIENDS AND FAMILY

Lennon, Nigey. *Being Frank: My Time with Frank Zappa*. Los Angeles: California Classics Books, 1995. 154 pages. Approximately 50 black-and-white photographs and drawings throughout. Selective Discography and Notes.

Composer and musician Nigey Lennon (captured on the back cover sitting on a toilet seat!) provides her impressions of Zappa during their twenty-plus years of friendship. The two first met when, as a young Zappa fan, Lennon

dashed off a letter to her idol—and he actually responded. Lennon is more than a tad nutty—reflecting at length on the size of Zappa's schnozz—but that may be what endeared Zappa to her in the first place. Way too much about Lennon's negligible (and unfamiliar) recording career and not enough about Zappa.

OTHER TITLES OF INTEREST

Kostelanetz, Andre. *The Frank Zappa Companion*. New York: Schirmer Books, 1997.

No author. *The Lives and Times of Zappa and the Mothers*. Manchester, England: Babylon, 1979.

Obermanns, Nobbi. *Get Zapped: Zappalog: The First Step to Zappology*. Bremen, Germany: Dwarf Nebula Publications, 1981.

Zappa, Frank and Zappa, Moon. *The Official Valley Girl Coloring Book*. No city: Price Stern Sloan, 1982.

ZZ TOP

BIOGRAPHIES

Blayney, David. *Sharp Dressed Men: ZZ Top Behind the Scenes from Blues to Boogie to Beards*. New York: Hyperion, 1994. 240 pages. Two glossy eight-page black-and-white photo inserts. The ZZ Top Roadie Roster. Index.

Author David Blayney was a high school chum of Billy Gibbons and later became ZZ Top's roadie and all-around "galley slave" for their tours between 1969-1984. Blayney's writing and research skills aren't exactly top drawer, but one can envision him holding his own in backstage brawls with competing bands' roadies. He also bore witness to some incredible rock events, since in the early days ZZ Top opened for or shared the bill with legendary acts such as Janis Joplin, Jimi Hendrix, The Allman Brothers, and Ten Years After. While the book contains more information on the early years than Thomas' work (see Pictorials, below) and some gritty backstage anecdotes, it shortchanges the band's studio work (only discussed at length in the closing chapter), videos, and love-lives. Generally fun for fans—until they are informed by Blayney that Frank Beard's skin-playing was replaced by a drum machine on the *Eliminator* LP.

FANZINES AND FAN CLUBS

ZZ Top International Fan Club. P.O. Box 19744, Houston, TX 77224-9744.

Fan club offering a wide range of items, including memorabilia, merchandising (t-shirts, caps, key chains, etc.) plus a quarterly 12-page newspaper, *Top Newzz*. The *Newzz* contains color photos, group history, discography, interviews, classifieds (e.g., cool cars), pen pal info., and more. A yearly membership in the U.S. and Canada is $15; $20 overseas. Renewals are $10 in North America and $15 elsewhere.

PICTORIALS

Frost, Deborah. *ZZ Top: Bad and Worldwide.* New York: Collier (Macmillan), 1985. 120 pages. Approximately 125 black-and-white photographs throughout; one glossy eight-page black-and-white photo insert.

This "Rolling Stone Press" book is geared toward young fans who like to see ZZ full-page, captured with their shades, demonstrating their snazzy guitars, and leaning on some hip roadsters. The band that at one time went on the road with live rattlesnakes and steer as part of its act, look like a mess of fun in this book, although there is very little information on the musicians themselves; we only learn that Dusty Hill was a loner as a child. The discography is pretty shabby as well. For kids seeking a harmless thrill.

Thomas, David. *Elimination: The `ZZ Top' Story.* London: Omnibus Press (division of Book Sales Limited), 1985. 96 pages. Approximately 50 black-and-white and 16 color photographs throughout. Discographies.

"That li'l ol' boogie band from Texas" receives breezy treatment in this ride on the ZZ Express. The book design bears some traces of Texas flavor—e.g., chapter openings of a car progressively zooming further down a highway and running heads of a ZZ Top license plate—but this concept could have been taken further. Stories of the band's saxophone lessons, video escapades, and fascination with cars and guitars abound, though ultimately we'd like to know at least some pre-stardom facts—most importantly what the bearded blues dudes were like in high school.

OTHER TITLES OF INTEREST
Draper, Robert. *ZZ Top.* New York: Ballantine, 1984.
Kamin, Philip. *ZZ Top.* Milwaukee, WI: Hal Leonard, 1984.
Nance, Scott. *Recycling the Blues.* No city: Movie Publisher Services, 1991.

AUTHOR INDEX

TITLE INDEX

BillboardBooks

THANK YOU FOR BUYING A BILLBOARD BOOK.
IF YOU ENJOYED THIS TITLE, YOU MIGHT WANT
TO CHECK OUT OTHER BOOKS IN OUR CATALOG.

THE BILLBOARD BOOK OF
AMERICAN SINGING GROUPS:
A History, 1940-1990 *by Jay Warner*
The definitive history of pop vocal groups, from the doo wop of Dion and the Belmonts, to the Motown hits of the Supremes, to the surf sound of The Beach Boys, to the country rock of Crosby, Stills and Nash. More than 350 classic acts spanning five decades are profiled here, with fascinating information about each group's career, key members, and musical impact as well as extensive discographies and rare photos. A one-of-a-kind reference for vocal group fans and record collectors alike. 544 pages. 80 photos. Paperback. $21.95. 0-8230-8264-4.

THE BILLBOARD BOOK OF
NUMBER ONE ALBUMS:
The Inside Story Behind Pop Music's
Blockbuster Records *by Craig Rosen*
A behind-the-scenes look at the people and stories involved in the enormously popular records that achieved Number One album status in the Billboard charts. Inside information on over 400 albums that have topped the chart since 1956, plus new interviews with hundreds of superstar record artists as well as a wealth of trivia statistics and other facts. 448 pages. 425 photos. Paperback. $21.95. 0-8230-7586-9.

THE BILLBOARD BOOK OF NUMBER ONE
HITS,Third Edition, Revised and Enlarged
by Fred Bronson
The inside story behind the top of the charts. An indispensable listing of every single to appear in the top spot on the Billboard Hot 100 chart from 1955 through 1991, along with anecdotes, interviews, and chart data. 848 pages. 800 photos. Paperback. $21.95. 0-8230-8298-7.

THE BILLBOARD BOOK OF TOP 40
ALBUMS,Third Edition, Revised and Enlarged
by Joel Whitburn
The complete guide to every Top 40 album from 1955 to 1994. Comprehensive information on the most successful rock, jazz, comedy, country, classical, Christmas, Broadway, and film soundtrack albums ever to reach the top of the Billboard charts. Includes chart positions, number of weeks on the chart, and label and catalog number for every album listed. 416 pages. 150 photos. Paperback. $21.95. 0-8230-7631-8.

THE BILLBOARD BOOK OF
TOP 40 COUNTRY HITS:
Country Music's Hottest Records,
1944 to the Present *by Joel Whitburn*
From the classic recordings of Hank Williams and Bob Wills, to enduring artists Patsy Cline and Tammy Wynette, to today's young superstars Garth Brooks and Shania Twain, the rich history of country music is documented in this comprehensive compilation of Billboard's Country Singles charts. Provides exhaustive data on every record to score at least one Top 40 hit. 562 pages. 96 photos. Paperback. $21.95. 0-8230-8289-X.

THE BILLBOARD BOOK OF TOP 40 HITS,
Sixth Edition, Revised and Enlarged
by Joel Whitburn

A perennial favorite, listing every single to reach the Top 40 of Billboard's weekly Hot 100 charts since 1955. Includes new chart data and expanded biographical information and trivia on artists listed. 800 pages. 300 photos. Paperback. $21.95
0-8230-7632-6.

THE BILLBOARD BOOK OF ONE-HIT WONDERS, Second Edition, Revised and Expanded
by Wayne Jancik

A one-of-a-kind rock and roll reference guide that charts the flip side of the pop music story. Uncovers the fascinating circumstances surrounding the rise to fame—and occasional rapid return to obscurity—of performers who had only one hit in Billboard's Top 40 charts. Contains over 100 new entries and a wealth of data and entertaining information that just can't be found elsewhere. A must for pop music fans and record collectors. 512 pages. 235 photos. Paperback. $21.95. 0-8230-7622-9.

THE BILLBOARD GUIDE TO HOME RECORDING,
Second Edition, Revised
and Updated *by Ray Baragary*

The complete do-it-yourself reference to recording techniques and equipment options. Provides a step-by-step approach to producing high-quality tapes, demos, and CDs in a home studio. Includes information on recorders, mixers, microphones, and signal processors; recording basic tracks and overdubbing; expanding the home studio with MIDI; the development of General MIDI standards; and the use of computers in sequencing. 272 pages. 97 illustrations. Paperback. $19.95. 0-8230-8300-4.

THE BILLBOARD GUIDE TO MUSIC
PUBLICITY, Revised Edition
by Jim Pettigrew, Jr.

A clear-headed reference providing career-minded musicians and their representatives with key information about such vital activities as getting media exposure, preparing effective publicity materials, and developing short-term and long-range publicity. New to the revised edition is coverage of desktop publishing, compact disks, basic copy-editing tips, and a recommended reading list. 176 pages. 16 illustrations. Paperback. $18.95. 0-8230-7626-1.

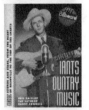

BILLBOARD'S HOTTEST HOT 100 HITS,
Revised and Enlarged Edition *by Fred Bronson*

The ultimate music trivia book. An illustrated compendium of 40 years of Billboard's chart data broken down into 175 categories, including artists, writers, producers, and record labels. Plus, a definitive list of the Top 5000 hits from 1955 through 1995. 512 pages. 250 photos. Paperback. $21.95. 0-8230-7646-6.

BLACK & WHITE BLUES:
Photographs by Marc Norberg,
edited by B. Martin Pedersen

From Graphis Publications, portraits of 60 of the finest blues musicians of all time, accompanied by the artist's personal statement about the blues. A CD-ROM disc is packaged with the hardcover edition. 192 pages. 60 photos. Hardcover (with CD): $69.95. 0-8230-6471-9. Paperback: $45.95. 0-8230-6480-8.

GIANTS OF COUNTRY MUSIC
Classic Sounds and Stars, from the Heart of Nashville to the Top of the Charts
by Neil Haislop, Tad Lathrop, and Harry Sumrall

An inside view of country's biggest names, drawing upon dozens of never-before-published interviews with such stars as Garth Brooks, Mary Chapin Carpenter, and Willie Nelson. Each entry focuses of the artist's career in detail and explains how their work has fit into the surrounding musical landscape. 288 pages. 100 photos. Paperback. $21.95. 0-8230-7635-0.

GRAPHIS MUSIC CDS
edited by B. Martin Pedersen

This wide-ranging international collection from Graphis Publications includes innovative covers, foldouts, inner sleeves, and compact disk surfaces created by graphic designers specializing in cover and packaging design for music CDs. 224 Pages. Over 300 illustrations. Hardcover. $75.95. 0-8230-6470-0.